Measuring and Managing Liquidity Risk

For other titles in the Wiley Finance Series please see
www.wiley.com/finance

Measuring and Managing Liquidity Risk

Antonio Castagna and Francesco Fede

WILEY

A catalogue record for this book is available from the British Library.

ISBN 9781119990246 (hardback) ISBN 9781118652251 (ebk)
ISBN 9781119990666 (ebk)   ISBN 9781119990673 (ebk)

Project managed by Neil Shuttlewood Associates, Gt Yarmouth, Norfolk
Typeset in 10/12pt Times
Printed in Great Britain by CPI Group (UK) Ltd, Croydon, CR0 4YY

AC: To Tatiana, for the patience she almost never lost

FF: To my wife, Gabriella, for her love, patience and support

Contents

Preface

The outbreak of the financial crisis in 2007/2008 brought liquidity risk measurement and management to the attention of practitioners, regulators and, to some degree, academicians.

Up until then, liquidity risk was not considered a serious problem and was almost disregarded by risk control systems within banks and by international and national regulations. Liquidity management and fundraising was seen as routine activity, simply a part of more complex banking activity, deserving little attention or effort.

Although the savvy approach would always be to forecast and devise scenarios under which extreme conditions occur, it was barely conceivable that such a difficult economic environment like the financial crisis of 2007 could ever occur. In the economic and financial environment in which banks used to run their business before 2007, liquidity risk simply did not exist. Moreover, it was never considered a problem that couould possibly extend beyond the limits of organizational issues and the development of basic monitoring tools. The design of procedures and systems were believed to cope with the small effects that banks suffered from liquidity risks.

As a consequence of these general considerations, the theory of liquidity risk was vague and restricted typically to market liquidity risk, which is the risk that assets cannot be sold swiftly in the market at a price close to the theoretical value. Although this is an important aspect of the broader liquidity risk notion, nonetheless it is just a small part of the full story, and in most cases not one strongly impacting banking activity. The only literature available on the aspects of liquidity risk concerning banking activity was mainly written by practitioners working in the industry and by a few academics. A notable example, among a few others, is the book edited by Matz and Peter, *Liquidity Risk Measurement and Management: A Practitioner's Guide to Global Best Practices* [87], which presents an excellent overview of the most relevant issues in liquidity risk management.

We felt there was a gap, though, between the need for improved practices after the events of 2007/2008, and what was proposed in the available research. The above-mentioned book by Matz and Peter was published in 2007 and, of course, could not deal with the increased requirements for risk liquidity practices.

This book tries to cover this gap: it should be seen as an attempt to introduce new tools and methods to liquidity risk measurement and management. We do not dwell on every facet of the subject; in particular, problems that are more related to organization and mechanisms that involve higher levels of management to cope with specific liquidity crises, are only briefly analysed for modifications that could be made to existing best practices in the current financial environment.

The book is organized in three parts. Part I is an overview of the crisis in 2007 and describes how it became globalized from the US economy to the rest of the world and how it altered its form during the subsequent years, up until 2013 (when this book was written). In Part I we also show how the banking business is changing (or will be forced to change) in response to the dramatic events that occurred. These triggered a regulatory overshoot the traits of which are extensively investigated towards the end of Part I (Chapters 4 and 5). One of the most challenging tasks was actually updating chapters in the face of (still) continuously evolving regulation, which represents one of the current main drivers of the liquidity framework. For this reason, this will most likely be the part of the book doomed to becoming outdated the quickest and no longer state of the art. The regulations mentioned and studied in this book are accurate at the time of writing in January 2013. Regulations that have been updated since January can be found at the book's website *http://www.wiley.com/go/liquidityrisk*

Moving from a macroeconomic point of view, we analyse the different types of liquidity risk and how they impact on a bank's business activity, in order to find how best to manage it from a microeconomic point of view, based on analysis of the actual structure of the balance sheet and of a comprehensive framework for pricing, monitoring and managing liquidity risk.

In Part II we start quantitative study of liquidity risk, first by introducing standard tools to monitor it: it is here we show how these tools can be enhanced and extended to cope with a substantially more volatile market context. The guiding principle is to draw approaches and models from the robust and thorough theory developed to evaluate financial contracts and to apply them, with a slight shift of perspective, to the measurement and management of liquidity risk. For this reason we stress the importance of concepts such as "cash flow at risk" and "liquidity at risk" that are not new, but have never really been widely adopted in the banking industry.

Starting with Part II, the reader will soon realize that topics are discussed as if there were a sort of pendulum, constantly swinging from fundamental concepts, hinging most of the time on balance sheet analysis and involving basic math (algebraic summation), to complex modelling with stochastic processes, grounded on rather heavy mathematical approaches. We would like to make it clear we have not really created new models to measure the liquidity risk, although in a few cases we actually do so. We only want to show how to apply already available theoretical frameworks and extend their use in the liquidity risk field. For example, we show how to adapt the option pricing theory approach to liquidity risk measurement and management.

Hopefully, our intent will be clear when the chapters devoted to the modelling of market risk factors and behavioural models are read. In these chapters we used a number of instruments, available in the theoretical toolkit prepared for the valuation of derivative contracts, to solve specific problems related to liquidity risk. We left aside our initial fear and opted, like pioneers in unexplored territory, to take routes that eventually may prove not to be optimal or even wrong, but our aim was to show a different mindset when approaching the liquidity risk problem rather than to provide the best solutions.

We must acknowledge that others have tried to adopt a similar approach; namely, Robert Fiedler [89] and, more recently, Christian Schmaltz [109]. Continuing in their footsteps, we applied a bottom-up method by modelling the main items of a bank's balance sheet. In theory, the bank is then able to simulate the entire balance sheet on a very granular basis, allowing for a rich set of information that can be extracted for liquidity risk purposes.

The theoretical apparatus developed for derivative contract evaluation is even more fruitful because modern liquidity risk does not only refer, as typically in the past, to the quantitative dimension of cash flow imbalances. In fact, a new and sometimes even more important dimension is the cost of liquidity that financial institutions can raise in the market. The dramatic increase in the levels and volatility of funding spreads paid over the risk-free rate is a factor that definitely cannot be disregarded in the pricing of contracts dealt with clients and the more general planning of banking activity. This is why we devoted the third and final part of the book to the analysis of this topic.

We start Part III with definitions of funding costs and counterparty risk and the interrelations between them, which demonstrate that banks are ultimately forced to consider the cost to raise liquidity in the market as a business-related factor that cannot be hedged. We present a new framework to model funding costs keeping in mind the multiplicity of sources and the dynamicity of the activity. We introduce a novel measure of risk implicit in the rollover of maturing liabilities and we show how corresponding economic capital should be allocated to cope with it and how corresponding costs should be included in the pricing of products a bank offers to its clients.

The inclusion of funding costs is much more subtle when dealing with derivative contracts; this is why we dwell in the final chapters of the book on possible approaches to dealing with them and point out how the classical results of option pricing theory are modified when these additional factors are taken into account in the evaluation process.

In conclusion, we would like to thank everyone who helped us in elaborating the ideas presented in the book. The list would be so long and would involve so many colleagues, who have analysed and discussed these topics with us over recent years, that not only would many pages be required to name them all, but we would also run the serious risk of forgetting someone.

However, Francesco would like to thank his employer (Banca IMI) and bosses for creating a conducive and stimulating environment, in which many topics treated in this book have found continuous reference regarding analysis and applicability; many friends and colleagues, within the counterparty risk management desk and financial engineering desk, the Finance & Investments Department and the Capital Market Department of Banca IMI, the risk management desk and treasury desk of Intesa Sanpaolo, who have always been ready to exchange ideas and interesting opinions and contributions about these topics; last but not least, to all colleagues of the market treasury desk, for their friendship, support and constructive example set during their daily activity. Obviously, the book expresses only the views of the authors and does not represent the opinions or models of Francesco's employers (Banca IMI and Iason).

Finally, we want to acknowledge a number of people to whom we owe a special debt of gratitude. In particular, Raffaele Giura, of Banca IMI, who constantly discussed with us many of the issues covered and always gave us insightful and fruitful perspectives to examine in depth. Antonio discussed many of the ideas related to the liquidity of derivative contracts with Fabio Mercurio. Caterina Covacev and Luca Visinelli, of

Iason, contributed massively to refining some of the models presented, to writing the code to test them and to preparing the examples. Finally, Francesco Manenti, of Iason, helped us to estimate and test behavioural models for non-maturing liabilities.

Although the book is a joint work, during its writing we split the tasks so that Francesco mainly dealt with the topics in Part I, whereas Antonio focussed on Parts II and III. We hope the reader will find the text conducive to a better understanding of liquidity risk and perhaps go on to develop and improve the ideas outlined.

Antonio Castagna
Francesco Fede
Milan, January 2013

About the authors

Antonio Castagna is currently partner and co-founder of the consulting company Iason Ltd, focusing on the design of models to price complex derivatives and to measure financial, liquidity and credit risks. Previously he was with Banca IMI Milan, from 1999 to 2006, where he first worked as a market maker of caps/floors and swaptions and then he set up the FX options market-making desk. He started his career in 1997 at IMI Bank Luxembourg, in the Risk Control Department. He graduated in Finance at LUISS University in Rome in 1995. He has written papers on different issues, including credit derivatives, managing exotic options risks and volatility smiles and is also the author of *FX Options and Smile Risk*, Wiley.

Francesco Fede is a graduate of the LUISS University of Rome. He has worked for IMI Bank Luxembourg as financial controller and risk manager since 1996. In 1998 he moved to Banca IMI Milan, where he started his career as short-term interest derivative trader in 2001. Since then, he has covered many tasks in Treasury and ALM activities. Currently he is the head of the Market Treasury desk of Banca IMI. Over the last couple of years he has focused on the pricing of liquidity risk for structured loans and derivative products, and on the impact of liquidity risk on both the trading book and banking book.

Abbreviations and acronyms

ABCP	Asset Backed Commercial Paper
ABS	Asset Backed Security
AFS	Available For Sale
AIG	American International Group
ALM	Asset Liability Management
ASF	Available Stable Funding
bAJD	basic Affine Jump Diffusion
BBA	British Bankers' Association
BCBS	Basel Committee on Banking Supervision
BSL	Balance Sheet Liquidity
c.l.	confidence level
CBC	CounterBalancing Capacity
CC	Central Clearing
CCS	Cross Currency Swap
CD	Certificate of Deposit
CDO	Collateralized Debt Obligation
CDS	Credit Default Swap
CEBS	Committee of European Banking Supervisors
cfAR	cash Flow At Risk
CFP	Contingency Funding Plan
CIR	Cox, Ingersoll and Ross (model)
CM	Clearing Membership
CMBS	Commercial Mortgage Backed Security
CME	Chicago Mercantile Exchange
CP	Commercial Paper
CPR	Constant Prepayment Rate
CRT	Credit Risk Transfer
CSA	Credit Support Annex
CVA	Credit Value Adjustment
DF	Discount Factor
DVA	Debit Value Adjustment
EAD	Exposure At Default
EBF	European Banking Federation

EC	Economic Capital
EEA	European Economic Area
EFC	Expected Funding Cost
EL	Expected Loss
ELoP	Expected Loss on Prepayment
EM	Empirical Model
ENE	Expected Negative Exposure
Eonia	Euro overnight index average
FAS	Financial Accounting Standards
FASB	Financial Accounting Standards Board
FC	Funding Cost
FCAVL	Forward Cumulated AVailable Liquidity
FFT	Fast Fourier Transform
FO	Financial Option
forex, FX	Foreign eXchange
FRA	Forward Rate Agreement
FSA	Financial Services Authority
FSB	Federation of Small Businesses
FSB	Financial Stability Board
FTO	Fine-Tuning Operations
FTP	Fund Transfer Pricing
FVA	Funding Value Adjustment
FX	Foreign eXchange
(G)CDS	Global Credit Default Swap
G-SIFI	Global-Systemically Important Financial Institution
GDP	Gross Domestic Product
HLA	High Liquidity Asset
HQLA	High Quality Liquid Asset
IAS	International Accounting Standards
IASC	International Accounting Standards Committee
IFRS	International Financial Reporting Standards
ILAA	Individual Liquidity Adequacy Assessment
ILAS	Individual Liquidity Adequacy Standard
ILG	Individual Liquidity Guidance
IMF	International Monetary Fund
IRS	Interest Rate Swap
ISP	Intesa SanPaolo
ITA	ITAlian Treasury
LA	Liquidity Adjustment
LB	Liquidity Buffer
LBC	Liquidity Buffer Cost
LCH	London Clearing House
LCR	Liquidity Coverage Ratio
LEA	Liquid Equivalent Adjustment
LGC	Liquidity Generation Capacity
Liffe	London International Financial Futures and Options Exchange

LLR	Lender of Last Resort
LMM	Libor Market Model
LO	Liquidity (Behavioural) Option
LTRO	Long Term Refinancing Operation
LVA	Liquidity Value Adjustment
LVA	Liquidity Value Adjustment
MBS	Mortgage Backed Security
MRO	Main Refinancing Operation
MTA	Minimum Transfer Amount
MTM	Mark To Market
MTN	Medium Term Note
MVAR	Market Value At Risk
NCB	National Central Bank
NCO	Net Cash Outflow
NINJA	No Income No Job (or) Asset
NML	Non-Maturing Liability
NPV	Net Present Value
NSFR	Net Stable Funding Ratio
OAS	Option Adjusted Spread
OBS	Off Balance Sheet
ODE	Ordinary Differential Equation
OIS	Overnight Indexed Swap
OLS	Orthogonal Least Square
OMO	Open Market Operation
OMT	Outright Monetary Transaction
ON	Over Night
OTC	Over The Counter
OTD	Originate To Distribute
P&L	Profit and Loss
PD	Probability of Default
PDCF	Primary Dealer Credit Facility
PDE	Partial Differential Equation
PDF	Probability Density Function
PFE	Potential Future Exposure
PL	Probability of Loss
PSE	Public Sector Entity
PVA	Price Volatility Adjustment
PVECF	Present Value of the sum of Expected Capital Cash Flow
RFV	Recovery of Face Value
RAROC	Risk-Adjusted Return On Capital
RBS	Royal Bank of Scotland
RI	Refinance Incentive
RMBS	Residential Mortgage Backed Security
RMV	Recovery of Market Value
ROE	Return On Equity
RPM	Rational Prepayment Models
RSF	Required Stable Funding

RTGS	Real Time Gross Settlement
SDE	Stochastic Differential Equation
SF	Standing Facility
SF	Stochastic Factor
SIFI	Systemically Important Financial Institution
SIV	Structured Investment Vehicle
SLRP	Supervisory Liquidity Review Process
SMP	Securities Market Programme
SP	Survival Probability
SPV	Special Purpose Vehicle
TA	Total Asset
TAF	Term Auction Facility
TARGET2	Trans-European Automated Real-time Gross-settlement Express Transfer
TARP	Troubled Asset Relief Program
TLA	Targeted Liquidity Assistance
TN	TurNover
TPC	Total Prepayment Cost
TRS	Total Return Swap
TSECCF	Term Structure of Cumulated Expected Cash Flow
TSECF	Term Structure of Expected Cash Flow
TSFCFu	Term Structure of Forward Cumulated Funding
TSFu	Term Structure of available Funding
TSL_e	Term Structure of expected Liquidity
TSLaR	Term Structure of Liquidity at Risk
USG	USaGe metric
VA	Value Added
VaR	Value at Risk
ZC	Zero Coupon

Part I

Liquidity and banking activity

1

Banks as lemons?

1.1 INTRODUCTION

It was a sunny and warm Thursday of midsummer. Some dark clouds in the previous days suggested that sudden showers had been expected to fall in the short term, but no one would have forecast the magnitude of the incoming financial tsunami.

But, citing L. McDonald [87], Wall Street's most sinister troubles occasionally arrive without the thunder of the guns and the clash of mounted cavalry on the trading floor. Some deadly problems come creeping in unannounced and often unnoticed, when financial players unobtrusively arrive at a single conclusion at around the same time. No one can say anything about collective changes: suddenly there is a lightning bolt of fear crackling through the market, and the consequences are there.

That day was August 9, 2007. Some years later, that day be referred to as the dawn of the worst crisis to hit financial markets in the last two decades. It begun with newswires reporting the announcement by some BNP Paribas funds to freeze redemptions, citing difficulties in valuing their assets due to the lack of liquidity in subprime mortgage markets. In a few hours the international money market had been seriously deadlocked: central banks had to inject an enormous and unprecedented amount of liquidity into the system to settle its daily payment obligations (e.g., the special refinancing operation conducted by the ECB with overnight maturity registered a request record for EUR95 billion; on the same day the Fed injected USD24 billion). The day of reckoning had eventually come: the financial market started the long-awaited process of risk

---

Box 1.1. Some dark clouds

On July 24 the major US home loan lender, Countrywide Financial Corp., announced an earnings drop. The market rumoured that almost one in four of all Countrywide's subprime loans were delinquent (10% of those were 90 days delinquent or more). With the ABCP market finally faltering, there was no easy access to cheap, fast money for this shadow bank that was going to be in a deadly situation.

On July 30 German bank IKB warned of losses related to subprime mortgage fail-lout: as a consequence the five-year European iTraxx Crossover index reached a peak of 500 bp and liquidity in the European government bond market declined sharply.

On July 31 American Home Mortgage Investment Corp. announced its inability to fund lending obligations, and it subsequently declared bankruptcy on August 6.

reappreciation, which had been evoked by regulators and supervisors several times in previous months.

What was going to happen?

1.2   THE FIRST WAVE

During the previous years the combination of (i) large financial market liquidity; (ii) increasing risk appetite; (iii) rising leverage in market strategies and derivative products led to an aggressive search for higher yield by investors. This process was suddenly reversed when the number of delinquencies in the US hugely increased from early 2007. The related sharp decline in the credit quality in the subprime mortgage market impacted on the fundamentals of structured credit products. It ignited rising concerns that the delinquency rate could have risen to unprecedented levels and led some rating agencies to downgrade several issues of ABS, backed by pools of subprime mortgages. Moreover, they announced a revision of their methodologies for assigning new ratings.

At this point investors realized that (i) risk assessment and (ii) pricing methods for a large proportion of complex instruments were definitely inadequate. These factors produced great uncertainty about the fundamentals of the ABS market and increased trading frictions. At last, they translated to bid–ask spreads that grew wider and wider up to the point where all the ABS markets dried up.

Why did the announcement of these downgrades and methodology revisions impact so heavily on the market and spread far beyond a risk reappraisal and a simple shock related to the subprime sector?

First, claims on the cash flows generated by subprime loans used to be embedded by the financial industry in a broad array of structured credit products (starting with RMBS, followed by CDOs containing some exposure to these RMBS, and ultimately by CDO squared). This partly explained why indirect exposures to US subprime loans through ABS had been widespread much more than initially forecast by regulators and financial firms.

Box 1.2. The phantom menace

On the May 4 UBS shut down its internal hedge fund, Dillon Read, after suffering about USD 125 million of subprime-related losses. In mid-June two hedge funds run by Bear Stearns and involved in the subprime market experienced serious trouble in fulfilling their margin calls, leading the bank to inject USD 3.2 billion in order to protect its reputation. These were not the first episodes about a possible spill-over from the US mortgage market: on the February 27, 2007 global equity markets dropped on fears about Asian equity markets and growing concerns over further deterioration in the US subprime mortgage sector. The relatively small correction (Dow Jones Euro STOXX −8%, S&P 500 −6%) ended on March 14 when equity markets resumed their upward trend.

Box 1.3. The warning of Cassandra

According to Homer, the princess Cassandra was gifted a prophecy by Apollo; but afterwards the god, offended with her, rendered the gift unavailing by ordaining that her predictions should never be believed. Like the Trojan Cassandra, not listened, the former ECB president Jean-Claude Trichet often warned the financial community about the reassessment of risk.

From the Q&A session of the ECB press conference on March 8, 2007:

Question: "When we were all in Madrid last year and the financial markets were doing their gymnastics then, you stressed that an appropriate assessment of risk was not the worst thing in the world and that perhaps some valuable lessons were being learnt. We have a similar situation now, albeit with different kinds of contours, and I wanted to see if you might be of a similar sentiment today?"

Mr Trichet's answer: "Concerning the recent events that we have observed, it is true that the Governing Council of the ECB widely felt—and I would say that it was very largely a consensus, a consensus that I myself have expressed on a number of occasions as the chairman of the G10 group of central bank governors—that we were perhaps in a phase in global finance where risks in general were not necessarily assessed at their real price. This was materializing in the levels of spreads and risk premia and in a number of other considerations, perhaps including low real interest rates. This was our diagnosis. What we have been observing for a number of days has been a certain reassessment of risks on the upside and across the board and a higher level of volatility. This is a phenomenon that we are following very carefully. It has positive aspects, obviously. It represents a more realistic appreciation of risks in general. It must also of course be monitored very carefully because what is of the essence in our view is that such corrections are orderly and smooth and are not abrupt.

On July 10 Chuck Prince, the former Citigroup's CEO, by referring to Keynes' analogy between bubbles and musical chairs, said: "When the music stops, in terms of liquidity, things will be complicated. But as long as the music is playing, you've got to get up and dance. We're still dancing" (see Brunnermeier [38]).

From the Q&A session of the ECB press conference on August 2, 2007:

Question: "The current phase of market movements that we see, is that something that you would characterise as a smooth reappreciation of risk or is that something that is abrupt and undesirable?"

Mr Trichet's answer: "We are in an episode where prices that were under-assessing an element of risk in a number of markets are normalising. I will not give any other qualification to the situation: it is a process of normalisation. The first quality to be demonstrated in circumstances when we see significant increases in measures of volatility in a large range of markets and asset classes by market participants and investors, and of course by authorities is to keep their composure. That is something important and it would permit the evolution of the market to be as effective as possible in terms of going back to a normal assessment of risks in general."

Second, questioning the methodology to assign ratings to these products implied questioning underlying assumptions about the distribution of returns on a wider variety of ABS products. ABS secured by pools of different assets, such as corporate bonds, bank loans, automobile loans and credit cards, were structured, rated and priced by using a similar methodology. Investors abruptly realized that similar properties could no longer be used for both corporate bonds and structured credit products. Without essential data about rating transition probabilities and market liquidity risk, they could no longer quantify the risk in these structured products with any degree of confidence. Many of these instruments, tailor-made to the risk–reward profile of investors and illiquid by definition, were valued by models. These models no longer worked when input data, such as market prices for ABS indices, were either not available or unreliable. Then the calculation of the fair value for most products became simply impossible.

Other market sectors were already negatively influenced: the issuance volumes of CDOs/CLOs registered a sharp decline. Growing uncertainties toward those products led to widespread refusal by financial investors to maintain their ABCP when they matured. Some ABCP issuers had to roll their debt into issues of only a few days' maturity: as a result, the average maturity of new issued paper significantly lowered. The weekly figures published by the Fed, unknown until then by a large part of market players, became one of the principal market drivers. Going on, this risk reappreciation process hit the refinancing strategies of SPV/SIV: with their usual funding channels dried up, they had to draw on their committed credit lines from their sponsoring banks. In the first half of August two German banks, IKB and Sachsen LB, were unable to honour their liquidity and credit commitments. Given the aggregate large exposures relative to the size of the sponsoring banks' balance sheets, after hectic negotiations, emergency rescues from a number of other financial institutions had to be arranged.

Under the ongoing pressure of the turmoil, financial firms finally began to wonder about the soundness of their liquidity policies. Some of them were targeted by bank runs and heavily hit by the growing credit crunch. As a result a number of small credit institutions failed, others were saved by the public sector (Northern Rock in the UK) or the private sector (Bear Stearns).

More enterprises received capital injections from governments (i.e., Citigroup, Royal Bank of Scotland, Fannie Mae, Freddie Mac, Indie Mac). A lot of them recorded profit warnings and credit losses. Spreads in interbank funding and other credit-related products rose sharply and funding strains were experienced in the secured financing market.

In mid-September 2008 the financial turmoil reached its peak. After pre-announcing its disappointing third-quarter figures, Lehman Brothers, one of the four major US investment banks, was unable to raise capital or find strategic investors: it experienced a destructive run on its liquid assets and was forced to file for creditor protection under Chapter 11 on September 15, 2008. On the same day Merrill Lynch accepted being taken over by Bank of America and, only two days later, the giant insurer AIG was rescued by the US government as it teetered on the edge of collapse due to rising requests for post-collateral payments on derivatives trades after its rating downgrading. Eventually, Morgan Stanley and Goldman Sachs decided to transform themselves from investment banks into commercial bank holding companies to gain advantage from lender-of-last-resort support and the deposit insurance scheme, and to use deposits as a source of funding.

These events ignited concerns about the scale and distribution of counterparty losses, and challenged the widespread view that any large bank too big to fail would need public support. Fear and rumours of further defaults in financial sectors resulted in some banks struggling to obtain funds at any market level.

A dangerous mix of credit problems, wholesale deposit runs and incipient retail deposit runs led to the collapse of some financial institutions on both sides of the Atlantic Ocean (Washington Mutual, Bradford & Bingley, Icelandic banks).

In late September, two large European banks, Dexia and Fortis, with cross-border activities in Benelux and France, came under intense pressure, due to perceptions of low asset quality, liquidity and capital shortages, and needed public and private support. In Germany a major commercial property lender, Hypo RE, had to be saved from the brink of collapse.

At that point the unsecured money market was definitely deadlocked: prime banks were unable to get funds for terms longer than one or two weeks. Eventually, banks with liquid balances preferred to hoard liquidity or to deposit it in central banks, for fear of economic losses related to the counterparty credit risk and uncertainty about (i) the mark-to-market of illiquid assets and (ii) the effective amount of liquidity in their balance sheet. As a result money market spreads climbed higher and higher.

1.3 BANKS AS LEMONS?

To the eyes of investors all banks were going to become "lemons", according to the famous example provided by Akerlof [3] in the 1970s. In this classical paper Akerlof showed how the interaction of quality differences in products and the uncertainty about them may impact on market equilibrium, producing frequent cases of adverse selection and moral hazard.

Adverse selection is related to asymmetric information about the quality of goods, services and products. For instance, if an insurer is unable to classify customers

---

Box 1.4. The growing avalanche

A subprime mortgage is a short-reset loan where the interest rate is not constant during the life of the deal. The rate initially charged is much lower than for a standard mortgage but it is normally reset to a much higher rate, usually after a two/three-year period.

Thanks to this kind of reset the rising of short-term US interest rates from mid-2004 onwards was not immediately translated into higher mortgage repayment burdens, but delayed it until sometime later. Moreover, the high rates of house price inflation recorded during the previous decade fuelled the interest rate for these mortgages for some householders, who borrowed for house purchases with the intention of refinancing or repaying the mortgage before the reset date. Once mortgage interest rates started to rise and house prices began to fall, many borrowers became delinquent on their loans sometimes even before the reset period.

Box 1.5. Some mysterious initials

An asset-backed security is a financial product whose value and income payments are derived from and "backed" (collateralized) by a specific pool of underlying assets. These assets are typically illiquid and unable to be sold individually (such as payments from credit cards, auto loans, residential mortgages, aircraft leases, royalty payments, movie revenues). By the process of securitisation these assets can be sold to investors and the risk related to the underlying product diversified because each security represents only a fraction of the total value of the pool of different assets.

An RMBS (CMBS) is a residential (commercial) mortgage-backed security (i.e., an ABS backed by a pool of residential or commercial mortgages). A CDO is a collateralized debt obligation, while a CLO means a collateralized loan obligation. Last, a CDO squared is a CDO collateralized by another CDO.

The most amazing acronym is surely the NINJA mortgage, where NINJA stands for "no income no job (or) asset" and describes one of many documentation types used by lenders and brokers for those people with hard-to-verify incomes. It also works as an allusion to the fact that for many loans borrowers used to disappear like ninjas. Such mortgages were granted under the premise that background checks were not necessary because house prices could only rise, and a borrower could thus always refinance a loan using the increased value of the house.

---

according to their risk level, he is likely to select more risky customers who will find the initial premium cheaper and will buy more protection than needed: as a result the insurance premium will rise, by excluding the safest customers from the market. Instead, asymmetric information concerning players' behaviours can lead to moral hazard. In this case it arises because an individual does not take the full consequences of his actions, and therefore tends to act less carefully than he otherwise would (after being insured, a customer could be less cautious about locking his car). If the information about products, services or behaviours was available for all market players in the same quantity and quality, they would be priced and exchanged with more contracts at different levels. Both adverse selection and moral hazard can prevent us from reaching Pareto-efficient allocation: departures of the economy state from the complete markets paradigm.

According to Akerlof, in the automotive market, where people buy new automobiles without knowing whether the car they buy will be good or bad ("lemon"), the price for equilibrium is defined by demand and supply for a given average quality. Good cars and lemons must still sell at the same price (the fair price for the average quality of used cars), since it is impossible for a buyer to tell the difference between a good and a bad car, and only sellers have accurate knowledge about the car quality.

With information not uniformly distributed among market participants, the demand for used cars depends most strongly on two variables, the price and the average quality: the latter still depends on the price. As the price falls, the quality perceived by the market will also fall.

Then asymmetrical information can lead good cars to be driven out of the market by lemons and can create worse pathologies in a more continuous case with different grades

> **Box 1.6.** The funding strategy of SIVs through ABCP
>
> The asset-backed commercial paper (ABCP) market lies at the crossroads between the cash money market and structured credit markets. An ABCP programme creates a means of removing assets, which have a risk-weighted capital requirement, from the bank's balance sheet while retaining some economic interest through income generation from the management of their special purpose vehicles (SPVs) which issue ABCP (asset-backed commercial paper) or MTNs (medium-term notes). There are a variety of ABCP structures, depending on the type of collateral, the liability structure and the amount of third-party liquidity/credit enhancement required. On the one hand there are traditional cash flow structures such as ABCP conduit issues with close-to-complete liquidity support, credit enhancement, short-term funding and no marking-to-market of assets. On the other hand there are structured investment vehicles (SIVs) and SIV-lites, which issue paper which depends primarily on the market value of assets for both liquidity and credit enhancement and consequently mark their assets to market.
>
> These vehicles operate a maturity transformation as "virtual" banks, by earning the spread between their long-term assets and short-term liabilities sold to public investors. Unluckily, their liabilities are more volatile than a bank's, because they miss retail deposits, which are stable on longer periods and are less dependent on market conditions. Therefore, their funding strategies rely boldly on being able to continuously roll over their short-term issues when matured. Traditional ABCP conduits are not capitalized as they depend totally on liquidity provision to solve any funding problems, whereas market value structures have their own capital. In case of difficulty, conduits have to turn to their sponsoring banks which are committed to support them with backstop liquidity via credit lines, letters of credit and cash reserve accounts. (For more details, see FRS [14].)

of goods: it ignites such a sequence of events that no markets can exist at all. For instance, the bad drives out the not so bad which drives out the medium which drives out the not so good which drives out the good.

In our case illiquid banks play the role of good cars while insolvent banks are the lemons. When market spreads climbed, the average quality of banks' balance sheets was perceived poorer and poorer: it was impossible for cash-giver banks to distinguish between illiquid and insolvent banks. Central bank intermediation became vital to restoring orderly functioning of the market.

1.4   THE RESPONSE

Even so, despite the delay, the response of central banks to this drastic list of events was impressive, by using several and, in some cases, unprecedented tools to achieve their goals. First of all, in early October they cut interest rates by 50 bp in a coordinated worldwide action. The only inactive central bank, the Bank of Japan, unable to do the same due to the already close-to-zero level of its key rates, obviously welcomed and strongly supported this decision.

Box 1.7. The fall of the Bear

In March 2008 the spread between agency and Treasury bonds started to widen again, leading to a Dutch hedge fund, Carlyle Capital, seizing and partially liquidating its collateralized assets due to unmatched margin calls. One of Carlyle's major creditors was Bear Stearns, which was targeted in the meantime by some rumours related to the Term Securities Lending Facility announced by the Fed on March 11, 2008. This programme allowed investment banks to swap agency and other mortgage-related issues for Treasury bonds, without disclosure about participants. Markets started to speculate that the Fed knew that some investment bank might be in trouble and was going to save it. The easiest target became the smallest, most leveraged investment bank with large mortgage exposure: Bear Stearns.

Moreover, a late acceptance of the proposed novation by Goldman Sachs of some contracts between a hedge fund and Bear Stearns ignited other speculation about the actual soundness of Bear Stearns, which was targeted by an immediate run by its hedge fund clients and other financial counterparties. Its liquidity situation worsened dramatically the next day and it became unable to secure funding on the repo market. You can see in Figure 1.1 how quickly the Bear Stearns liquidity pool had dramatically deteriorated over a few days. Over the weekend the Fed helped broker a deal, through which JPMorgan Chase would acquire the US's fourth largest investment bank for USD236 million, at USD2 per share, ultimately increased to USD10 per share. (For more on these events, see [38].)

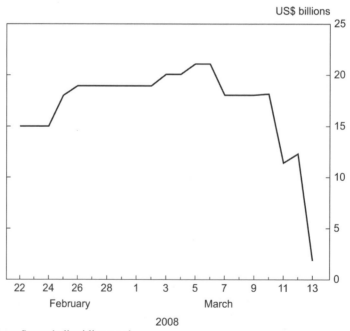

Figure 1.1. Bear Stearn's liquidity pool
Source: Bank of England

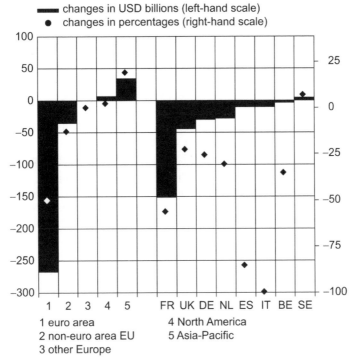

Figure 1.2. US government Money Market Fund variations between May and October 2011.
Source: Security and Exchange Commission and ECB calulations

Under its Troubled Asset Relief Programme the Federal Reserve pledged USD700 billion for the purchase of obligations directly issued by government-sponsored enterprises, such as Fannie Mae and Freddie Mac, or mortgage-backed securities underwritten by them. Eventually, the US government used a portion of this amount to recapitalize all major US banks to prevent any loss of confidence about their financial soundness. The Fed also widened the criteria of collateral eligible under its Primary Dealer Credit Facility and expanded its Term Securities Lending Facility, as well as holding various US dollar auctions in coordination with the other major central banks (Term Auction Facility). The TAF succeeded in mitigating some money market tensions which were going to transmit from the US to the euro money market by means of the foreign exchange swap market and helped to address non-US financial institutions' funding needs in US dollars.

In the UK the Bank of England made available to the banking system GBP200 billion under the Special Liquidity Scheme. It was one of the three parts of the bank rescue package (around GBP500 billion) promoted by the government. The other two were capital injection in the eight major banks, with further provisions if needed, and a temporary bank loans guarantee for up to GBP250 billion, subsequently converted into a new issued bond guarantee. In Switzerland, the government injected CHF6 billion in UBS, and the Swiss National Bank bought troubled assets for USD60 billion.

In Europe the ample liquidity provided by the ECB in its main refinancing operations (MROs), which allowed banks to frontload their reserve requirements during

Box 1.8. The foreign exchange swap market

One of the traditional US dollar funding channels for non US-financial institutions has always been the foreign exchange swap market. This market allows banks not headquartered in the US to cover their US dollar needs without assuming a substantial foreign exchange balance sheet exposure. FX swaps enable banks which have raised funds in one currency to swap those proceeds and their subsequent interest payments in another currency over a finite period: they broaden the availability of funding to cover multiple currency markets.

Under the significant stress produced by the financial turmoil, banks experienced considerable difficulty in attracting liquidity from US providers: therefore, they increased recourse to this liquidity channel. As a result of the positive correlation between foreign exchange swap and euro money market spreads, (i) higher counter-party risk and (ii) the greater importance of liquidity as a valuable asset in turbulent times in the US market led to increased euro money market spreads, ignited by increased swap rates as a result of the unsecured euro interbank market.

The *2008 Financial Stability Review* [15] published the results of an analysis based on a cointegrated VaR framework to model the direction of the transmission of USD, GBP and EUR market tensions. It showed that, in the short term, unexpected tensions are transmitted from USD and GBP to EUR, but not vice versa.

maintenance periods, and in its supplementary long term refinancing operations (LTROs) was no longer enough to alleviate liquidity pressures. The ECB recorded frequent recourses to its marginal lending facility in spite of the abundant liquidity into the system. At the same time, amounts lodged in the deposit facility rose as well, testifying that the redistribution of interbank liquidity had become extremely impaired. Consequently, the participation of banks in ECB tenders and bidding rates submitted by treasurers both increased. The unsecured interbank money market was facing severe dysfunctionality, with no lending available for maturities longer than overnight, and banks increasingly dependent on central bank liquidity.

On October 8 the ECB announced its intention to conduct its MROs through a fixed rate tender procedure with full allotment (a sort of "eat all you want"), and to reduce the money market corridor defined by its standing facility rates from 200 bp to 100 bp, as long as needed. Moreover, on October 15 it further expanded the list of assets eligible as

Box 1.9. The three letters that sustain *govies*

Under the SMP, the ECB can buy in the secondary market public and private debt securities of euro area countries to ensure depth and liquidity in dysfunctional market sectors and to restore the proper functioning of the monetary policy transmission mechanism. SMP interventions are temporary by nature, limited and fully sterilized to avoid effects on the monetary base.

collateral in its refinancing operations and added other longer term tenders to fully meet increasing bank demands for liquidity at three and six-month maturities.

These measures succeeded to halt, at least temporarily, the vicious cycle between liquidity constraints and counterparty credit risk, which was going to produce negative spillover effects of the financial crisis with huge impacts on the real economy. Obviously, they were not able to fix the root causes of the financial issues that have generated the turmoil and need to be addressed by means of new and strong regulation and supervision.

1.5   THE SECOND WAVE

Sadly enough, after almost five years, many of these interventions are still in place, testifying to the difficulty of addressing the main problems of the worst financial crisis since WW2. Concerns related to the financial sector have been replaced by fears of insolvency of European peripheral countries such as Greece, Ireland and Portugal, which had to apply for assistance from the EU/IMF. The contagion eventually spread to the heart of Europe, pushing Spain and Italy to the edge of collapse. Amid rising financial tensions and lack of credible responses by European politicians, only the reactivation of the Securities Market Programme (SMP) by the ECB in early August 2011 temporarily avoided the worst and reduced the adverse feedback loop between the sovereign and financial sectors.

As stressed in the *2011 Financial Stability Review* [16], a combination of weakening macroeconomic growth prospects and the unprecedented loss of confidence in sovereign signatures, ratified by several downgrades, both within and outside the euro area, by major credit rating agencies, had increased risks to euro area financial stability. Contagion effects in larger euro area sovereigns gathered strength amid rising headwinds from the interplay between the vulnerability of public finances and the financial sector. The heightened uncertainty was going to affect views on the backstop potential of governments to support national banking systems. In the meantime, high government refinancing needs created concerns that the public sector may in some cases compete with, and even crowd out, the issuance of debt securities by banks.

Box 1.10. MMF liquidity dries up

In October 2011, total holdings of European paper by the US government's MMF (Money Market Fund) declined by 9% relative to the previous month and by 42% (!!) since May (see Figure 1.2). It is worth stressing that the fall in the supply of such funding was global during the crisis in 2008, while the change over the summer of 2011 was basically a European phenomenon. Within the euro area, the impact of this development focused on a few banking sectors (France, Italy, Spain). For instance, French banks' commercial paper and certificate of deposit holdings declined by USD34 billion between May and August 2011. This reduction in outstanding volumes was joined by a marked shortening of maturities (the average maturity of French CP/CDs decreased from about 80 days to 40 days), making reliance on this source of funding more fragile and volatile.

Box 1.11. The drivers behind the EUR/USD basis

Prior to the financial crisis, many banks used unsecured USD funding as an attractive source of funding. The favourable funding conditions in USD reflected the size of the wholesale USD money market and the fact that unsecured funding was available for longer maturities than in the euro market. Many European banks used to raise more USD funds than needed and swapped back their surplus into EUR. At the time, the cost of swapping EUR into USD, measured by the 3-month EUR/USD basis swap, was close to zero, meaning that the cost of funding in USD was in line with the Libor fixing and that there was no significant imbalances in the demand for USD or EUR from market participants. The so-called basis is the premium or the discount paid by market participants to obtain USD. The premium is calculated as the difference between the USD interest rate implicit in the swap (by assuming the 3-month EURIBOR fixing as the 3-month EUR rate) and the unsecured USD interest rate, normally the Libor fixing.

With the propagation of the financial crisis and the introduction of regulatory changes impacting the US MMF, the EUR/USD basis has been negative since January 2010, underscoring a structural need for European banks to borrow USD via the FX swap market. After the collapse of Lehman Brothers, the USD rate implied in 3-month FX swaps reached a peak of 200 bp above Libor, but in a few months it declined rapidly to levels close to those prevailing before September 2008, thanks to the use of the swap lines between central banks (at the end of 2008, the USD liquidity provided by the ECB to European banks peaked at almost USD300 billion).

In the first part of 2011 any increase in the EUR/USD basis was subdued due to the favourable funding conditions on shorter maturities for European banks, and the building of USD cash buffers on the balance sheets of their US branches or subsidiaries, as recorded by Federal Reserve figures. The re-emergence of financial tensions in the second part of 2011 ignited a sharp increase in basis swaps and called for a reopening of the swap lines as a precautionary measure. Moreover, the shape of the basis swap curve remained upward sloping, mainly reflecting that not only short- term but also medium-term funding was impaired, and suggesting that forward-looking concerns were uppermost relative to immediate funding tensions. This was the opposite of the situation in 2008 when the EUR/USD basis curve inverted. Unlike previous cases, however, the actual use of the swap line established by central banks over the last year appears to be hampered by negative reputational costs (the so-called "stigma"). (On this topic, see also the *2011 Financial Stability Review* [16].)

The first victim of this second wave of the financial crisis was Dexia, which avoided default only by the intervention of the French and Belgian governments in October 2011. With the euro area banking sector engaged in a de-leveraging process the ECB once again had to introduce some "non-conventional" measures to reduce market funding strains. While unsecured medium and long-term funding markets have been closed to a number of European banks, access to collateralized term funding has been warranted for ECB counterparties by the aforementioned full allotment procedure used by the central bank in its main refinancing operations, as well as by its complementary and longer term operations. For the future, the ECB has decided on two three-year refinancing operations with a monthly early repayment option after one year. It also broadened the pool of eligible collateral and lowered the reserve requirements from 2 to 1% on December 8, 2011. In order to increase the collateral available to banks, the ECB has lowered the rating threshold for certain asset-backed securities, and has allowed national central banks, on a temporary basis, to accept some performing credit claims (i.e., for Italy linked to the factoring and leasing business) not eligible at the Eurosystem level.

In order to alleviate further funding vulnerability stemming from the heavy reliance of some large European banks on short-term and highly risk-sensitive US dollar funding, mainly through credit provided by money market funds in the US, which reduced their exposures to European financial institutions in terms of both amounts and maturities since May, on November 30, 2011 the ECB, the Bank of Canada, the Bank of England, the Bank of Japan, the Federal Reserve and the Swiss National Bank agreed to lower the pricing of US dollar liquidity swap arrangements by 50 bp, so that the new allotment rate will be the US dollar OIS rate plus 50 bp instead of 100 bp. As a consequence of this announcement, the 3-month EUR/USD basis dropped by 25 bp in a day.

1.6   CONCLUSION

Analysis of the timing, methods and effectiveness of the interventions of central banks over these years is beyond the scope of this book. Certainly, they tried to address banks' liquidity issues by offering enormous amounts of central bank liquidity to restore the interbank money market and, by doing so, to halt the vicious circle between funding and market liquidity that fuelled liquidity risk.

In order to understand where the root cause of liquidity risk lies, it is therefore useful to analyse in detail the three aforementioned different types of liquidity.

2

A journey into liquidity

2.1 INTRODUCTION

In the previous chapter we stressed how the recent financial crisis was exacerbated by an increased funding liquidity risk that contaminated market liquidity for many structured products. In order to understand how liquidity risk can impact financial stability, we have to look closer at the various types of liquidity and deeply analyse the concept of liquidity itself, still vague and elusive in the literature.

The concept of risk is related to the probability distribution of the underlying random variable, with economic agents having well-defined preferences over the realizations of the random variable of interest. As economic agents would have a preference over liquidity, the probability of not being liquid would suggest the existence of liquidity risk.

To begin with, we need a coherent framework that properly defines and differentiates the financial liquidity types, and describes the transmission channels and spillover directions among them. For each liquidity type the respective liquidity risk will be defined.

We will refer to the work of Nikolaou [96], which provided a unified and consistent approach to financial liquidity and liquidity risk. She moved from the academic literature that treated the different concepts of liquidity in a rather fragmented way (central bank liquidity in the context of monetary policy, market liquidity in asset-pricing models, funding liquidity in the cash management framework) by concentrating, condensing and reinterpreting the linkage between these broad liquidity types.

Box 2.1. How do reserve requirements work?

Commercial bank money is generated through the fractional reserve banking practice, where banks keep only a fraction of their demand deposits in reserves, such as cash and other highly liquid assets, and lend out the remainder, while maintaining the obligation to redeem all these deposits upon demand. The process of fractional reserve banking has the cumulative effect of money creation by commercial banks, as it expands money supply (cash and demand deposits) beyond what it would otherwise be. Because of the prevalence of fractional reserve banking, the broad money supply of most countries is a multiple larger than the amount of base money created by the country's central bank. That multiple (called the money multiplier) is determined by the reserve requirement or other financial ratio requirements imposed by financial regulators.

2.2   CENTRAL BANK LIQUIDITY

By using Williamson's definition (see [114]) liquidity is "the ability of an economic agent to exchange his existing wealth for goods and services or for other assets". It is a concept of flows, exchanged among the agents of the financial system, like central banks, commercial banks and market players. Obviously, the inability of the agent to realize or settle these flows leads to his illiquidity. The liquidity may be seen as the oil greasing the wheels of the financial system, so that they work in a frictionless and costless way.

Central bank liquidity can be defined as (see [96]) "the ability to supply the flow of the monetary base needed to the financial system": the monetary base, or base money or M0, comprises banknotes in circulation and banks' reserves with the central bank. In accordance with the monetary policy stance in terms of the level of key policy rates, this type of liquidity results from managing the central bank's balance sheet.

The main components on the liabilities side are net autonomous factors and reserves. Net autonomous factors consist of transactions that are out of control according to the monetary policy function: for the Eurosystem they are banknotes in circulation, government deposits, net foreign assets and "other net factors". Reserves are cash balances

---

Box 2.2. The monetary corridor

A central bank steers short-term money market rates by signalling its monetary policy stance through its decisions on key interest rates and by managing liquidity conditions in the money market. The central bank acts as a monopoly supplier of the monetary base, needed by the banking system to meet the public demand for currency, to clear interbank balances and to meet the requirements for minimum reserves. For instance, the ECB uses two different types of operation to implement its monetary policy: open market operations (OMOs) and standing facilities (SFs). OMOs include main refinancing operations (MROs), long term refinancing operations (LTROs) and fine-tuning operations (FTOs). Through MROs, the ECB lends funds to its counterparties against adequate collateral on a weekly basis. Currently, this lending takes place in the form of reverse repo transactions or loans collateralized by a pool of assets, conducted at fixed rate (the refi rate) with full allotment allocation.

In recent years, auctions have been conducted for an ex ante unknown allotment at competitive rates, floored by the refi rate. In order to control the level and reduce the volatility of money market interest rates, the ECB also offers two SFs to its counterparties, both available on a daily basis on their own initiative: the marginal lending facility (borrowing of last resort at a penalty rate against eligible collateral for banks) and the deposit facility (lending money to the central bank at a discounted rate). As a result, financial institutions used to activate both facilities only in the absence of other alternatives. In the absence of limits to access these facilities (except for the available collateral in case of marginal lending), the marginal lending rate and the deposit facility rate provide a ceiling and a floor, respectively, for the corridor within which the unsecured overnight rate can fluctuate.

owned by banks and held by the central bank to meet banks' settlement obligations from interbank transactions and to fulfil their reserve requirements.

Both demand for banknotes and reserve requirements create a structural liquidity deficit in the financial system, thereby making it reliant on central bank refinancing through its open market operations (OMOs). Credits deriving from these operations represent the assets side of the central bank's balance sheet. Ideally, the central bank tends to provide liquidity equal to the sum of the autonomous factors plus the reserves, in order to compensate its assets and liabilities, and manages its OMOs so that the very short-term interbank rates remain close to its target policy rate.

Central bank liquidity should not be confused with macroeconomic liquidity. The latter refers to the growth of money, credit and aggregate savings: it represents a broader aggregate and includes the former. A central bank can only influence the latter by defining the former.

Does central bank liquidity risk exist? As a central bank can always dispense all the monetary base needed, it can never be illiquid: therefore, this kind of risk is non-existent. Ideally, a central bank should only become illiquid if there was no demand for domestic currency. In this case the supply of base money from the central bank, even if available, could not materialize, such as occurred in cases of hyperinflation or in an exchange rate crisis. Obviously, the absence of liquidity risk does not mean that a central bank, in its role of liquidity provider, could not incur costs related to the counterparty credit risk linked to collateral value, to the wrong signalling of monetary policy or to the moral hazard generated by emergency liquidity assistance in turbulent periods.

2.3   FUNDING LIQUIDITY

Funding liquidity can be defined as (see [96]) "the ability to settle obligations in central bank money with immediacy".

This definition stresses the crucial role played by central bank money in settling bank transactions: in most developed economies, large-value payment and settlement systems rely on central bank money as the ultimate settlement asset. Therefore, the ability of banks to settle obligations means the ability to satisfy the demand for central bank money. The latter is determined by central banks and is beyond the control of a single bank, which by itself can create only commercial bank money through the fractional reserve banking practice.

The funding liquidity risk[1] is the possibility that over a specific horizon the bank could become unable to settle obligations with immediacy. Ideally and in line with other risks, we should measure this risk by the distribution summarizing the stochastic nature of underlying risk factors. Unfortunately, such distributions cannot be easily estimated because of lack of data.

It is worth highlighting that funding liquidity is essentially a binary concept: a bank can either settle obligations or it cannot, and it is always associated with one particular point in time. On the other hand, funding liquidity risk can take infinitely many values as it is related to the distribution of future outcomes: it is forward looking and measured over a specific horizon.

---

[1] We spend much more time on funding liquidity risk in Chapter 6, where quantitative tools to monitor it will be presented.

Box 2.3. TARGET2 imbalances

A letter written by the Bundesbank's Jens Weidmann to the ECB president, Mario Draghi, in February 2012 stressed the role of so-called TARGET2 imbalances as a destabilizing factor for the financial system. The TARGET2 (Trans-European Automated Real-time Gross-settlement Express Transfer) system allows banks to settle payments between each other through national central banks' accounts. One characteristic of the system is that payments from one bank to another in a different eurozone country are processed through the respective national central banks (NCBs): claims among NCBs resulting from cross-border payments are not necessarily balanced. If payments predominantly flow in one direction, obviously receiving central banks' claims will continue to rise, creating ever-growing imbalances in the TARGET2 system: in recent years the Bundesbank, and to some extent the Banque de France and the Nederlandsche Bank, have recorded significant net claims against central banks in the periphery.

Peripheral countries partly ran very sizable current account deficits, which were financed through borrowing from core countries, mainly through the banking system. These loans were privately funded and, although processed through the TARGET2 system, did not lead to imbalances. As banks in the core economies were no longer willing to extend credit to peripheral banks, NCBs in the periphery stepped in and refinanced peripheral banks. Consequently, they financed the current account deficits of peripheral countries. It is this replacement of privately lent money through central bank funding that led to the rise in net claims of core NCBs against peripheral NCBs. As long as peripheral NCBs are able to replace private funding—the limiting factor is the amount of collateral that can be pledged—there is no additional risk due to TARGET2 imbalances. These imbalances can arise simply by tightening funding conditions for banks that led to stronger reliance on the central bank as a funding source, as experienced dramatically by Greece, Ireland and Portugal over the last two years. By increasing its liquidity provisions to eurozone banks, the Eurosystem also inevitably increased the credit risk it faces, despite the various haircuts applied to the collateral pledged.

Potential losses are distributed among the NCBs regardless of where they materialize: the rise in TARGET2 imbalances has increased the risk for core NCBs only to the extent that without these imbalances the liquidity provision of peripheral banks would have been smaller. However, core NCBs face one specific risk that can be traced back to TARGET2 imbalances, and this refers to the possibility that a country might decide to leave the euro area. In such a scenario, the net claims the remaining NCBs have acquired vis-à-vis that country reflect a genuine risk that would not exist without these imbalances. This could—in the extreme case of a total breakup of the euro area, and assuming that peripheral NCBs could not repay their liabilities—mean that the losses would materialize on the Bundesbank's balance sheet: hence the warning of Jens Weidmann. Hopefully, the pledge of Mario Draghi "to do whatever it takes to preserve the euro" made in London in July 2012 and in September 2012 the consequent announcement of the Outright Monetary Transaction (OMT) program finalized to buy an unlimited amount of Euro government bonds under strict conditionality should have reduced the tail risk about a euro breakup.

Table 2.1. Funding sources of inflows and outflows for SIFI

Source	Inflow	Outflow
Depositors (D)	$DL_{new} + DA_{due} + DAI_{due}$	$DL_{due} + DLI_{due} + DA_{new}$
Interbank market (IB)	$IBL_{new} + IBA_{due} + IBAI_{due}$	$IBL_{due} + IBLI_{due} + IBA_{new}$
Asset market (A)	A_{sold}	A_{bought}
Off-balance-sheet items (OB)	OB_{out}	OB_{in}
Central bank (CB)	$mroCB_{due} + mroCBI_{due} + otherCB_{out}$	$mroCB_{new} + otherCB_{in}$

In order to match its funding gap a bank can use different liquidity sources. It can get liquidity from depositors, who entrust their savings to the banking system. It can use the market as a liquidity source, through assets sale, securitization or loans syndication. Moreover, it can operate on the interbank market, by dealing unsecured or secured deposits. Finally, as is known, a bank can get liquidity directly from the central bank through OMOs by posting eligible collateral. Typically, funding liquidity risk depends on the availability of these four liquidity sources, and the ability to satisfy the budget constraint over the respective period of time.

Let us define the cash flow constraint as:

$$\text{cf}^- \leq \text{cf}^+ + \text{MS}$$

where $\textbf{cf}^-$ is the amount of outflows (negative cash flows), $\textbf{cf}^+$ is the amount of inflows (positive cash flows) and MS is the stock of money.

This constraint has to hold in each currency, but we can ignore currency differences under the hypothesis that funding liquidity can be easily transferred from one currency to another as long as foreign exchange swap markets are properly functioning.

In Table 2.1 we summarize the key components and the main funding sources for inflows and outflows of money for a systemically important financial institution (SIFI). To reduce notation to the minimum the time subindex has been dropped for each factor.

The first source is defined by the behaviour of depositors. A bank receives an inflow when a borrower pays back the amount (DA_{due}) and/or the interests (DAI_{due}) of his loan, or when it receives new deposits (DL_{due}). Outflows can derive from money withdrawn by depositors (DL_{due}), interest paid on deposits (DLI_{due}) or a new loan issuance (DA_{new}). Not all depositors' withdrawals have to be considered, but only those which lead to a change in central bank liquidity balance. In other words, if consumer X pays company Y and both have an account at the same bank, this money transfer gets settled in the bank's own money and does not change its central bank liquidity. Otherwise, if company Y has an account with another bank, the transfer between banks has to be settled in central bank money.

The second source is the interbank market, where banks used to trade unsecured and secured funding. Basically, we are talking about the same kind of inflows and outflows already defined (IBL_{new}, IBA_{due}, $IBAI_{due}$, IBL_{due}, $IBLI_{due}$, IBA_{new}), but to distinguish between an interbank player and private depositor is important because their behaviour is significantly different. The latter is generally very sluggish to react and is not able to monitor a bank's soundness with efficacy, whereas the former is going to adjust his preferences continuously. A further important difference between the private sector and the interbank market is that all money transfers among large banks are always settled in central bank money through a real-time gross settlement system. For this kind of

Box 2.4. Some definitions of funding liquidity

Other definitions of funding liquidity have been made available by practitioners and academics so far.

According to Nikolau [96] and Brunnermeier and Pedersen [40], amongst others, funding liquidity can be viewed as the ability to raise cash at short notice either via asset sales or new borrowing. This kind of definition seems to be more appropriate for counterbalance capacity. Whilst it is the case that a bank can settle all its obligations in a timely fashion if it can raise enough central bank money at short notice, the reverse is not always true as a bank may well be able to settle its obligations as long as its current stock of central bank money is large enough to cover all outflows.

The IMF (2008) defines funding liquidity as "the ability of a solvent institution to make agreed-upon payments in a timely fashion". This reference to solvency has to be carefully analysed because it is important to distinguish between liquidity and solvency, as welfare losses associated with illiquidity arise precisely when solvent institutions become illiquid.

The definition of the Basel Committee of Banking Supervision [99] for funding liquidity is "the ability to fund increases in assets and meet obligations as they come due, without incurring unacceptable losses". The second part is rather related to funding liquidity risk, but it is omits to define what "unacceptable losses" really means.

analysis it does not matter whether interbank deposits are secured or not, therefore repo transactions are included in interbank flows.

Asset sales/purchases are the third source of inflows and outflows of liquidity. We consider both asset sales/purchases from the trading book and from the banking book. Practically, securities held for trading can often be traded on organized exchanges in relatively liquid markets, while assets held to maturity used to be sold and purchased via securitization programmes "over the counter". This activity requires time and effort, and delivers results over a longer period in a less liquid market, especially during stressed times.

These two main market liquidity sources (i.e., the interbank market, where liquidity is being traded among banks, and the asset market, where assets are being traded among financial agents) have to be carefully analysed because of their important role in a bank's funding strategy.

2.4 MARKET LIQUIDITY

Continuing our discussion of liquidity sources let us introduce the third type of liquidity. Market liquidity can be defined as (see [96]) "the ability to trade an asset at short notice, at low cost and with small impact on its price". In a deep, broad and resilient market any

---

Box 2.5. The funding liquidity risk for a leveraged trader

Let us consider the case of a leveraged trader (such as a dealer, a hedge fund or an investment bank) who is used to borrowing liquidity in the short term against the purchased asset as collateral. He is not able to finance the entire market value of the asset, because a margin or haircut against adverse market movements is required by market players for secured transactions. This difference must be ideally financed by the trader's own equity capital. Haircuts are financed in the short term because they have to be adapted on a daily basis, while equity capital and longer term debt financing are more expensive and difficult to obtain when the firm suffers a debt overhang situation. As a consequence, traders avoid carrying much excess capital and are forced to de-leverage their positions by increased margins or haircuts.

Financial institutions that rely on commercial paper or repo instruments to finance their assets have to roll over their debt continuously. A drying up of the commercial paper market is equivalent to margins increasing to 100%, just as if the firm becomes unable to use its assets as a basis for raising liquidity. A similar effect is produced by withdrawals of demand deposits for a commercial bank or by capital redemption from an investment fund.

To sum up we have already identified three forms of funding liquidity risk:

- margin/haircut funding risk
- short-term borrowing rollover risk
- redemption risk

All these risks will be analysed in more depth in the second part of this book.

---

amount of asset can be sold anytime within market hours, quickly, with minimum loss of value and at competitive prices.

A market is deep when a large number of transactions can occur without affecting the price, or when a large number of orders are in the order books of market makers at any time. A market is broad if transaction prices do not diverge significantly from mid-market prices. A market is resilient when market price fluctuations from trades are quickly dissipated and imbalances in order flows are quickly adjusted.

We can refer to market and funding liquidity in the following way: market liquidity is the ability to transfer the entire present value of the asset's cash flows, while funding liquidity is a form of issuing debt, equity, or any other financial product against a cash flow generated by an asset or trading strategy.

Market liquidity risk relates to the inability to trade at a fair price with immediacy. It represents the systemic, non-diversifiable component of liquidity risk. It implies commonalities in liquidity risk across different market sectors, such as bond and equity markets, and requires a specific pricing. From this specific point of view liquidity risk has often been regarded in the asset-pricing literature as the cost/premium that affects the price of an asset in a positive way, by influencing market decisions through optimal portfolio allocation and market practices by reducing transaction costs.

2.5   THE VIRTUOUS CIRCLE

These three liquidity types are strongly linked, so they can easily lead to a virtuous circle by fostering financial stability during normal periods or to a vicious circle by destabilizing markets during turbulent periods.

Under normal conditions the central bank should provide a "neutral" amount of liquidity to the financial system to cover its structural liquidity deficit and balance liquidity demand and supply. Banks should receive central bank liquidity and, through interbank and asset markets, should redistribute it within the financial system to liquidity-needing players, who ask for a liquidity amount to satisfy their liquidity constraint. After this redistribution on an aggregate basis, the central bank should calibrate the new liquidity amount to satisfy liquidity demand, and the virtuous circle starts again.

In this scenario each liquidity type plays a specific role. Central bank liquidity represents provision of the amount of liquidity to balance aggregate demand and supply. Market liquidity warrants the redistribution and recycling of central bank liquidity among financial agents. Funding liquidity defines the efficient allocation of liquidity resources from the liquidity providers to the liquidity users. As each liquidity type is unique in the financial system, the three liquidity types can only play their specific role by relying on the other two working well and the system overall being liquid. This means that the neutral amount of liquidity provided by the central bank can flow unencumbered among financial agents as long as market liquidity effectively recycles it and funding liquidity allocates it within the system in an efficient and effective way. Markets are liquid because there is enough liquidity in the financial system on aggregate (i.e., there is no aggregate liquidity deficit due to the supply from the central bank) and each counterparty asks for liquidity according to their specific funding needs without hoarding additional liquidity provisions. Obviously, funding liquidity depends on the continuous availability of all funding liquidity sources, so a bank is going to be liquid as long as it can get enough liquidity from the interbank market, the asset market or the central bank. These are all preconditions typical of frictionless and efficient markets. In fact, if markets are efficient, banks have recourse to any of the available liquidity options, so the choice will depend only on price considerations.

2.6   THE VICIOUS CIRCLE

The links described until now can be distorted in cases of liquidity tensions and are likely to serve as risk propagation channels, by reverting from a virtuous circle to a vicious spiral in the financial system. Each liquidity type is subject to a specific liquidity risk, which lies in coordination failures among economic agents such as depositors, banks or traders, due to asymmetric information and incomplete markets.

Look at funding liquidity risk, which is likely to be the first source for idiosyncratic and systemic instability. Funding liquidity risk lies at the very heart of banking activity because banks develop their business basically by means of maturity transformation to fund illiquid long-term loans with liquid short-term deposits.

More specifically, banks provide liquidity to the financial system through the intermediation of economic agents. They provide illiquid loans to investors, who are funded with liquid deposits from depositors. In so doing, banks create funding liquidity

---

Box 2.6. Where do bank activity benefits come from?

By properly planning deposit-taking and lending activities, banks are able to create an economy of scale that reduces the amount of costly liquid assets that are required to support loan commitments. Given the existence of some liability guarantees, such as deposit insurance, central bank liquidity availability and targeted liquidity assistance, many papers ([71], amongst others) provide empirical evidence of negative covariance between deposit withdrawals and commitment takedowns, and argue that deposits can be viewed as a natural hedge, up to a certain point, against systematic liquidity risk exposure stemming from issuing loan commitments and lines of credit.

---

for financial and private sectors and promote the efficient allocation of resources in the system.

From a systemic point of view, the tradeoff for this activity is the inherent liquidity risk linked to the asset–liability maturity mismatch. This mismatch can generate instability in the bank's role of liquidity provider on demand to depositors (through deposit accounts) or borrowers (through committed credit lines), if not mitigated by liquid asset buffers. As liquid assets usually yield low returns, banks have to continuously redefine their investment strategy between low-yield liquid assets and high-yield illiquid ones.

The worst output of funding liquidity risk is obviously represented by a bank run, which ultimately leads to the bank's failure. Funding liquidity risk could represent a cause of concern for regulators when it is transmitted to more than one bank, because it, becoming systemic, can increase market liquidity risk to the interbank and the asset market.

Focusing on the interbank market, individual bank failures can shrink the common pool of liquidity which links the financial system and can propagate the liquidity shortage to other banks, leading to a complete meltdown of the system, as occurred with Lehman's default. Such a propagation mechanism is reinforced by the extensive inter-linkages among banks, like the interconnected bank payment systems, balance sheet linkages, or cross-holdings of liabilities across banks represented by interbank loans, credit exposures managed by margin calls, or committed credit lines. In some cases, an informational spillover to the interbank market could lead to generalized bank runs. Such interlinkages represent crisis propagation channels in the presence of incomplete markets and asymmetric information, as explained in the previous chapter. They easily stimulate fears of counterparty credit risk when the absence of a complete set of contingent liabilities (even more crucial for the completion of markets and to provide effective tools for hedging against future liquidity outcomes) combines with information asymmetries about the illiquidity and the insolvency of banks.

According to this framework, insolvent banks may act as merely illiquid ones and decide to free-ride on the common pool of liquidity in the interbank market: they can then engage in risk-prone behaviour by underinvesting in liquid assets and gambling for assistance. Ultimately, this form of moral hazard can lead to adverse selection in lending, with insolvent banks, mistaken as simply illiquid, granting liquidity, instead

Box 2.7. A bank's worst nightmare

A bank run is defined as a situation where depositors decide to liquidate their deposits before the expected maturity of the investment, leading to increased demand for liquidity that the bank is not able to satisfy, due to the fractional reserve banking practice. It can materialize when bad expectations among economic agents lead to self-fulfilling prophecies, such as when depositors believe other depositors will run. When news about the borrower increases uncertainty among depositors, a bank run can occur because it is optimal to pre-empt the withdrawals of others by borrowing first. For instance, late movers may receive less if the run occurs for fundamental reasons (investing in bad projects could reduce the net worth of the bank) or if it occurs for funding liquidity reasons. In this case, early withdrawals force a bank to liquidate long-maturity assets at fire sale prices: it leads to an erosion of the bank's wealth and leaves less for those who withdraw their money late.

In the current financial world deposit insurance has made bank runs less likely (the only recent case was Northern Rock), but modern runs can occur at higher speed than in the past and in different ways. On May 15, 2012 the president of Greece, Karolos Papoulias, announced that he had been warned by the central bank that depositors had just withdrawn EUR1.2 billion in the two previous days, after the announcement of another poll in mid-June. These runs started not with a queue of people lining up to withdraw cash but with clicks of a computer to transfer money abroad or to buy bonds, shares or other assets.

Modern forms of bank runs are represented by not rolling over commercial paper for the issuer of ABCP, pulling out sizable amounts of liquid wealth parked by hedge funds for their prime brokers, by increased margins or additional liquidity buffers on collateralized products for downgraded institutions or by capital redemption requests for an investment fund.

of solvent but illiquid ones; in limited commitment of future cash flows; in liquidity hoarding, because of doubts about their own ability to borrow in the future. Eventually, some banks would be rationed out of the system, and few remaining cash-giver banks could take advantage of their oligopoly position by underproviding interbank lending in order to exploit the others' failure or to increase the cost of funding for liquidity-thirsty banks.

In the case of severe impairment of the interbank channel, market liquidity risk can easily propagate to the asset market as banks may look for liquidity through fire sales, with relevant impacts on asset prices and liquidity. The propagation process runs through the assets side of banks' balance sheets by means of portfolio restructuring which needs to find buyers for distressed assets in order to avoid more expensive project liquidation. In the case of incomplete markets, the supply of liquidity is likely to be inelastic in the short run and financial markets may only have limited capacity to absorb assets sales, with prices likely to fall below their fundamental value. This results in increased volatility of asset prices, a huge reduction in market depth, and distressed pricing, where the asset market clears only at fire sale prices.

2.7 SECOND-ROUND EFFECTS

Unfortunately, up to now we have only summarized the first-round effects of a vicious circle related to a liquidity crisis. The strong linkages existing between market and funding liquidity are likely to produce second-round effects as well, which may deepen market illiquidity and lead to downward liquidity spirals, with outcomes that can easily outweigh in magnitude the original shock.

In the current financial system many assets are marked-to-market and subject to regulations. In this environment, asset price movements produce changes in the net worth of the asset side of the balance sheet and require responses from financial intermediaries who have to adjust the size of their balance sheets according to their leverage targets, thereby effectuating speedy transmission of the feedback effect.

The combination of new lower prices, solvency constraints and capital adequacy ratios defined by regulators, and internally imposed risk limits, can require further asset disposals. Then distressed pricing can become worse due to further frictions in trading: trading regulations, limits to arbitrage and predatory trading could renew the vicious circle and exacerbate the downward spiral.

Moreover, sharp declines in asset prices lead to a loss of value for the collateral received/paid versus derivative portfolio exposure or securities lending activity. Changes in collateral values result in adjusted values for margin calls and haircuts. Under such circumstances, banks are therefore vulnerable to changes in the value and market liquidity of the underlying collateral, because they have to provide additional collateral, in the form of cash or highly liquid securities, at short notice, which affects their funding liquidity risk. The more widely collateralization is used, the more significant this risk becomes, especially as market price movements result in changes in the size of counterparty credit exposure. As required margins and haircuts rise, financial institutions have to sell even more assets because they could need to reduce their leverage ratio, which is supposed to be held constant during the loss spiral.

Box 2.8. The loss spiral

As explained by Brunnermeier and Pedersen [41], the loss spiral is "a decline in the assets' value which erodes the investors' net worth faster than their gross worth and reduces the amount that they can borrow". It depends on the expected leverage ratio of the firm.

Let us suppose that an investor works with a constant leverage ratio of 10. He buys USD100 million worth of assets at a 10% margin: he finances only USD10 million with his own capital and borrows the other USD90 million. Now suppose that the value of the asset declines to USD95 million. The investor has lost USD5 million and has only USD5 million of his own capital remaining because of the mark-to-market. In order to keep his leverage ratio constant at 10, he has to reduce the overall position to USD50 million, which implies selling assets worth USD45 million exactly when the price is low. This sale depresses the price further, inducing more selling and so on. (This example was suggested by Brunnermeier [38])

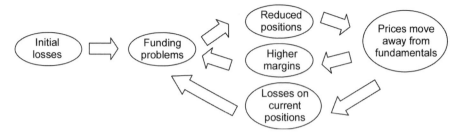

Figure 2.1. The loss spiral and margin spiral
Source: Brunnermeier and Pedersen [41]

The spike in margins and haircuts, related to significant price drops, leads to a general tightening of lending. It is produced by two main mechanisms: moral hazard in monitoring and precautionary hoarding.

Lending is basically intermediated by banks, which have good expertise in monitoring borrowers' investment decisions due to their own sufficiently high stake. Moral hazard arises when the net worth of the stake of intermediaries falls because they may be forced to reduce their monitoring effort, pushing the market to fall back to a scheme of direct lending without proper monitoring.

Precautionary hoarding is required when lenders are afraid that they might suffer from interim shocks and that they will need additional funds for their own projects and trading strategies. The size of this hoarding depends on the likelihood of interim shocks and the availability of external funds. In the second half of 2007, when conduits, SIVs/SPVs and other off-balance-sheet vehicles looked likely to draw on committed credit lines provided by the sponsored banks, each bank's uncertainty about its own funding needs skyrocketed. In the meantime, it became more uncertain whether banks could tap into the interbank market since it was not known to what extent other banks faced similar problems.

A visual representation of the loss spiral is in Figure 2.1.

The new business model of credit, based on risk transfer techniques, has strengthened linkages between market and funding liquidity, leading to more direct contagion channels and faster propagation of second-round effects. Securitization is broadly used by banks to manage their credit and funding liquidity risk, by transferring credit risk off its balance sheet and creating a larger and more disperse pool of assets, which while satisfying various risk appetites has made banks more dependent on market funding, through market structures like special purpose vehicles. Nowadays, banks' incentives and ability to lend are expected to depend on financial market conditions to a larger extent than in the past, when banks were overwhelmingly funded via bank deposits. This intensifies the link between market liquidity and funding liquidity risk and eases the propagation of downward liquidity spirals.

2.8   THE ROLE OF THE CENTRAL BANK, SUPERVISION AND REGULATION

The first and second-round effects of the aforementioned vicious circle can potentially lead to systemic failures within the financial system, with negative effects for taxpayers

---

Box 2.9. Should a central bank provide emergency liquidity through TLA or OMOs?

By TLA we mean targeted liquidity assistance provided to individual institutions through the discount or marginal lending facilities, whereas OMO stands for open market operations, which lend the monetary base to the market as a whole. Both solutions can produce moral hazard, the choice therefore depends on the functioning of the interbank market and the goals of the monetary policy.

OMOs are mainly used in order to implement monetary policy. They are useful when it is necessary to target some market rates, such as during liquidity crunches when high market rates can increase liquidation costs or during generalized liquidity shortages when support is required by the market as a whole. They allow avoiding the stigma associated with borrowing from the discount window, but mainly rely on the well-functioning interbank market to redistribute liquidity effectively into the system. On the contrary, banks are forced to ask for more liquidity than needed on a precautionary basis.

In the case of an inefficient interbank mechanism, TLAs could be a more flexible tool to tackle liquidity deadlocks because, in the form of a discount window, they allow some specific banks to be financed in the fastest and most direct way. In doing so, they avoid the moral hazard linked with OMOs, where distressed banks and "greedy" investors compete for excess funding provided during the crisis, given frictions in the interbank market.

---

and the real economy. The cost to fix ex post systemic liquidity risk with its potential to destabilize the whole financial sector could be dramatic, as was shown to be the case with Lehman's failure, so in such cases emergency interventions and liquidity provisions to halt negative spirals and restore balance appear to be very useful.

In its role of guarantor—not only of financial stability, but of the entire economy—a central bank should be in a position to tackle systemic liquidity risk. Its role is unique among other financial supervisors and regulators, due to the potential size of its balance sheet and its actual immunity to bankruptcy. Acting as an LLR (lender of last resort) a central bank can activate tools to enable market stabilization, by preventing panic-induced collapses of the banking system and reducing the cost of bank runs and forced liquidations in thin markets. The most effective tools are liquidity provision mechanisms via OMOs or TLA.

Unfortunately, when acting as an LLR, a central bank can only focus its intervention on shock amortization and not on shock prevention. It tries to minimize secondary repercussions of financial shocks, such as contagion, spillover or domino effects, by providing temporary injections of central bank liquidity with the purpose of breaking the loop between market and funding liquidity risk, so that downward liquidity spirals would fail to further distress markets. In doing so, however, a central bank has not guaranteed success over the financial crisis: it cannot tackle the root cause of liquidity risk because its very function is hampered by incomplete information.

In fact, the potential benefits are limited by the fact that a central bank cannot distinguish between illiquid and insolvent banks with certainty. This inability can create

Box 2.10. A revision of Bagehot's view

Whether and how a central bank should intervene to tackle systemic liquidity risk is a topics well analysed in the literature (see, for example, [66]). According to [13], "the central bank should be known to be ready to lend without limits to any solvent bank against good collateral and in penalty rates", so that banks do not use them to fund their current operations. Only in the presence of a well-functioning, deregulated, uncollateralized interbank market [74] could central bank intervention be effective in providing emergency liquidity assistance.

A fascinating debate has begun about the "to be known" part, and concerns the dichotomy between constructive ambiguity and pre-committed intervention (see [106]). The latter may act as public insurance against aggregate risk in an incomplete market economy, but at the cost of fuelling expectations of insurance for financial institutions against virtually all types of risk. The former should strengthen market discipline and mitigate the scope for moral hazard, as long as it is coupled with procedures for punishing managers and shareholders for imprudent strategies.

This debate can be overcome by providing liquidity at penalty rates: this would discourage insolvent banks from borrowing continuously, as if they were merely illiquid, and should help to discern illiquid from insolvent banks. In turbulent times, however, recourse from the banking sector to emergency assistance could become significant, and applying penalty rates could increase the liquidity cost for illiquid but solvent banks. Perhaps the most stimulating debate has been focused on the part related to "lend to (only) any solvent bank" is perhaps the most stimulating one. Obviously, lending only to solvent banks would be optimal because it would minimize intermediation costs and reduce moral hazard. Unfortunately, as previously said, screening ex ante between insolvent and illiquid banks is almost impossible such that, with incomplete and costly information, the only way is to lend to any bank at a pooled rate, but this leads to adverse selection and moral hazard in emergency times.

Lending only against good collateral could facilitate the screening of insolvent from illiquid banks, because the probability that an illiquid, but solvent bank lacks enough good collateral is quite small. Unfortunately, the devil is in the details again, because good collateral may not be abundant or available during periods of crisis, when a large part of securities are likely to be hampered by rating agency downgrades. In these cases, accepting only good collateral (namely, with a minimum rating above the threshold used in normal times), transparent to value and easy to liquidate, could ultimately come into conflict with the authorities' responsibility for financial stability.

Accepting a wider range of collateral, as all central banks have done in recent years, is conducive to improving market liquidity conditions, because their willingness to accept certain asset classes as collateral will in turn affect the liquidity or, at least, the marketability of such assets. The counterargument is related to the worst eligible collateral delivery option sold for free to the banking sector, while allowing it to access the market with its better collateral. However, the prevailing view suggests that a central bank should be willing to accept some losses linked to the widening of eligible criteria, in order to address severe interbank market dislocations and minimize the social costs of systemic failures.

bidirectional links from central bank liquidity to funding and to market liquidity, and also hurt the central bank itself. By rescuing insolvent institutions, which do not deserve its assistance, a central bank is implicitly penalizing solvent but illiquid banks, mainly because it is increasing their cost of funding. This could render them potentially unable to borrow or to repay loans, thereby enhancing their funding liquidity risk. During turbulent times, markets could assume the implicit central bank liquidity provision as an insurance or safety net for financial institutions. Misallocation of central bank liquidity can promote excessive risk-taking by banks and create moral hazard, by stimulating risk-prone behaviour by insolvent institutions that can gamble for resurrection with central bank money. Moreover, lending to undeserving institutions could ultimately turn against a central bank's stabilizing role, because the recovery of the financial system could be more uncertain, lengthy and expensive. It can require higher costs of maintaining the financial safety net, in terms of credit risk in the central bank's balance sheet and the ability to achieve its monetary policy objectives.

Central banks have little choice but to undertake a cost tradeoff analysis. On the one hand, a central bank faces the danger of welfare costs due to costly bank runs and forced liquidations; on the other hand, it has to face spiralling costs linked to excessive risk-taking, the ignition of future liquidity crises and increased credit risk in its portfolio. During crises a central bank can only give temporary support to the financial system, until the structural causes of liquidity risk can be dealt with. It provides significant aid, but is definitely not a panacea. As long as other weapons, like more supervision and tougher regulation, are not used to tackle the causes of the crisis, the temporary liquidity injected by a central bank can only break the vicious circle and risk, in the long run, its stabilizing role.

Effective supervision—not only official and centralized, but also in the form of interbank peer-monitoring—can balance information asymmetries because it facilitates the distinction between illiquid and insolvent banks. Obviously, effective implementation of peer-monitoring may be difficult, due to commitment problems by governments. In those cases regulation, in the form of liquidity requirements and a binding contingency plan, may be a useful way to address some issues. Efficient supervision and regulation can also support the development of new financial products that may contribute to reducing incomplete markets. To the extent that liquidity risk is endogenous in the financial system, the quality and the effectiveness of supervision and regulation in the financial system impact both the scope and the efficiency of central bank liquidity.

2.9   CONCLUSIONS

In this chapter we analyzed the complex and dynamic linkages between market liquidity and funding liquidity, which are able to enhance the efficiency of the financial system in normal periods, but can destabilize financial markets in turbulent times. Central banks can only halt temporarily the negative effects of the vicious circle and restore balance, but they are not able to tackle the root causes of systemic liquidity risk, which rest in departure from complete markets and the symmetric information paradigm.

In order to fix these issues, is it of the essence to minimize asymmetric information and moral hazard between financial players through effective monitoring mechanisms of the financial system: supervision and regulation are the fundamental weapons needed to wage war against liquidity crises, by increasing the transparency of liquidity management practices. Nevertheless, fitting the optimal size of supervision and regulation to a financial system is a challenging task, because gathering data for supervision and establishing, implementing and monitoring regulation can be very expensive. In order to promote better transparency and create economies of scale in acquiring information to reduce the cost of monitoring banks, a central bank could consolidate official supervision and regulation by taking them into its own hands. This would make it easier to distinguish illiquid from insolvent agents, to calibrate interventions carefully and therefore to reduce its costs.

3

Too big to fail

3.1 INTRODUCTION

In Chapter 2 we often referred to financial systemic risk and the related meltdown in the case of default by one or more banks considered "too interconnected" to be allowed to fail.

This topic deserves great consideration because it is strictly linked to the issue of moral hazard. As stated previously, without symmetric and complete information on the financial system, moral hazard can arise as insolvent banks may act as merely illiquid ones by underinvesting in liquid assets and gambling for assistance. In the literature many authors have written about the moral hazard and the social cost related to saving insolvent institutions, and made clear they were against any form of support or rescue for them.

We pointed out that in practice it is really difficult for central banks and supervisors to distinguish ex ante between illiquid and insolvent institutions. Nevertheless, we have

---

Box 3.1. Systemic risk

The notion of systemic risk is closely linked to the concept of externality, meaning that each financial player individually manages its own risk but does not consider the impact of its actions on the risk to the system as a whole. As a consequence, the aggregate amount of risk in the financial system can prove excessive and, on account of interdependencies, larger than the sum of the risks of individual banks in isolation. At the same time, once the system has reached a certain degree of fragility, even an apparently small shock–such as the fall of the US subprime mortgage market in 2007—may trigger a disruptive chain of events.

Box 3.2. How does the PDCF work?

The Primary Dealer Credit Facility was introduced by the Fed on March 17, 2008. It is a lending facility, available to all financial institutions listed as primary dealers, and works as a repo, whereby the dealer transfers a security in exchange for funds through the Fed's discount window. The security acts as collateral for the loan, and the Fed charges an interest rate equivalent to its primary credit rate. The creation of the PDCF was the first time in the history of the FED that it had lent directly to investment banks.

already verified what can happen when a systemically important financial institution (SIFI) is allowed to fail: systemic meltdown and financial turmoil are not remote warnings to list in academic papers, they may become the worst and most dramatic side of a financial crisis.

3.2 WHEN GIANTS FALL

Let us consider the largest bankruptcy in history, the fall of Lehman Brothers. It was Monday, September 15, 2008: on that day the financial world realized that anyone, even the US's fourth largest investment bank, could fail if it was unable to counterbalance a liquidity crisis.

Once again, the root causes of the Lehman Brothers crisis lay in the huge exposure to real-estate mortgage and structured product markets, and to an excessive leverage ratio. Over the previous months, only heavy recourse to the Fed's Primary Dealer Credit Facility eased Lehman's liquidity problems, but the bank failed to strengthen its balance sheet by issuing new equity.

Lehman Brothers felt that stepping forward as a single bank to issue enough new shares, without a concerted effort among all banks, would be very expensive, because it would be perceived as a sign of desperation. Lehman's share price started to erode more and more, and the share plunged on September 9, 2008. This was followed by the bank announcing very disappointing third-quarter figures and talks with the state-controlled Korea Development Bank to sell Lehman Brothers suddenly halted. Subsequently, Lehman Brothers had to collateralize by cash some credit lines to fulfil significant margin calls: it experienced a lack of liquid, unencumbered assets to use as eligible collateral.

During a dramatic weekend the president of the Federal Reserve Bank of New York, Timothy Geithner, summoned all major banks' most senior executives to secure Lehman's future. Only two possible suitors were on the table: Bank of America and Barclays. The former decided to buy Merrill Lynch for USD50 billion, the latter refused to take over Lehman without a government guarantee. Eventually, Treasury and Fed officials decided not to offer this guarantee, because Lehman, as well as its customers and counterparties, had enough time to prepare for liquidity shortage: a bailout funded by taxpayers' money would have represented another case rewarding moral hazard. Lehman filed for Chapter 11 bankruptcy in the early morning of September 15, 2008. It was a similar case to that of Bear Stearns: both were investment banks, too interconnected to fail but with a dramatic liquidity shortage. They experienced different ends: the

---

Box 3.3. Closeout risk

During the closeout of exposures against a specific counterparty in its default situation, adverse movements can occur between the value of derivatives and the value of the collateral held. This risk—that prices can change during the period that it takes to close out a position after the default—is often referred to as "closeout risk".

Box 3.4. TARP

TARP stands for Troubled Asset Relief Program and was originally expected to cost USD300 billion for US taxpayers, with authorized expenditures of USD700 billion. Ultimately, it was converted to government capital injection into the US's largest banks. By March 3, 2011, the Congressional Budget Office stated that total disbursements would be USD432 billion and estimated total costs would be USD19 billion. Of the USD245 billion handed to US and foreign banks, over USD169 billion had been paid back at the end of 2011, including USD13.7 billion in dividends, interest and other income.

private sector was able to save Bear Stearns, but no rescuer (public or private) was found for Lehman Brothers.

The negative effects of Lehman's default immediately spread into the global financial markets: every trader was going to evaluate net exposure versus Lehman for both collateralized and unsecured transactions; a lot of collateral had to be sold in the market to minimize counterparty risk. Lehman had in place collateral agreements with many market counterparties: moreover, it was prime broker for many hedge funds.

All players were wondering about the effects of Lehman's "jump to default" on their own books and were trying to hedge the incoming closeout risk. Only the proper functioning of SwapClear, the clearing house for derivative products, whose members included Lehman among others, avoided further destabilizing effects on the financial system. Nevertheless, the Dow Jones index went into a savage downward, dropping 500 bp on the day: everyone was on edge, braced for a new shock, and there was not long to wait!

The day after, it was the turn of the world's biggest insurance corporation, American International Group, to drop sharply (more than 60%). AIG was one of the major players in the CDS market and was exposed to billions of US dollars against the failure of Lehman. Now the unthinkable had happened and AIG simply did not have the cash to make the payouts promised. Moreover, it had invested its insuring profits heavily in the CDO market, which was going to collapse with mass defaults by mortgage holders. Rating agencies immediately downgraded it, which required AIG to post other collateral with its trading counterparties. Facing a deadly liquidity shortage, AIG was on the brink of bankruptcy as well. But this time the authorities realized that AIG was too interconnected in the credit derivative business to allow it to fail: the Fed immediately announced the creation of a secured credit facility of USD85 billion, in exchange for an 80% equity stake. October and November figures called for another USD77 billion.

The huge recourse to taxpayers' money saved AIG, but over the following months everyone was wondering about the opportunity to save Lehman in order to avoid the consequent meltdown: How much did the Lehman failure cost the US government in terms of massive additional bailout funds for AIG and other financial sectors? If Lehman was saved, would the cost to taxpayers have been lower?

3.3   A HARD LESSON

However, in spite of the actions of the Fed and the US Treasury, the financial situation was going to be worse every passing day. Mass uncertainty and a fall in confidence, with no foreseeable solutions except government intervention, were hampering market sentiment. On September 23, 2008, Ben Bernanke, chairman of the Fed, testified before the Joint Economic Committee of the US Congress. He put forward a clear representation of the crisis and strongly supported the request of the Secretary of the Treasury, Hank Paulson, to use USD700 billion of taxpayers' money to buy toxic assets from the banks (the so-called TARP).

First of all, he came up with a list of the theoretical options available to a financial firm to address its difficulties: through private sector arrangements (e.g., by raising new equity capital), or by negotiations leading to a merger or acquisition, or by an orderly winddown. In his opinion (see [20]), "Government assistance should be given with the greatest of reluctance and only when the stability of the financial system, and, consequently, the health of the broader economy, is at risk." This was the case with Fannie Mae and Freddie Mac, for which capital raises of sufficient size appeared infeasible and the size and government-sponsored status of the two companies had precluded a merger with or an acquisition by another company.

He then analysed the course of decisions that led to a different kind of output for the AIG and Lehman cases. In his words (see [20]), "... The Federal Reserve and the Treasury attempted to identify private-sector solutions for AIG and Lehman Brothers, but none was forthcoming. In the case of AIG, the Federal Reserve, with the support of

---

Box 3.5. White lie or miscalculation?

The statement by Ben Bernanke about Lehman at that time puzzled many observers. While correct in principle, it was clear that a bank like Lehman was too interconnected to think that it would have failed without significant effects for financial stability and the economy. Moreover, this position was not in line with the conduct adopted for Bear Stearns only six months before. Was the Princeton professor, who studied the Great Depression in detail, really not able to forecast what would have produced a default like that?

The truth was revealed by Ben Bernanke himself two years later. He regretted not being more straightforward on Lehman and supporting, in doing so, the myth that the Fed and the Treasury did have a way of saving Lehman. The authorities had no means of saving Lehman because of inadequate collateral: they decided at the time against saying Lehman was unsalvageable because it may have risked further panic in financial markets, already under tremendous stress and with other financial institutions under threat of a run or panic. He revealed (see [83]): "Lehman was not allowed to fail in the sense that there was some choice being made. There was no mechanism, there was no option, there was no set of rules, there was no funding to allow us to address that situation ... It was the judgement made by the leadership of the New York Fed and the people who were charged with reviewing the books of Lehman that they were far short of what was needed to get cash to meet the run." Better late than never ...

the Treasury, provided an emergency credit line to facilitate an orderly resolution. The Federal Reserve took this action because it judged that, in light of the prevailing market conditions and the size and composition of AIG's obligations, a disorderly failure of AIG would have severely threatened global financial stability and, consequently, the performance of the U.S. economy. To mitigate concerns that this action would exacerbate moral hazard and encourage inappropriate risk-taking in the future, the Federal Reserve ensured that the terms of the credit extended to AIG imposed significant costs and constraints on the firm's owners, managers, and creditors."

The outcome for Lehman was different (see [20]): "the Federal Reserve and the Treasury declined to commit public funds to support the institution. The failure of Lehman posed risks. But the troubles at Lehman had been well known for some time, and investors clearly recognized—as evidenced, for example, by the high cost of insuring Lehman's debt in the market for credit default swaps—that the failure of the firm was a significant possibility. Thus, we judged that investors and counterparties had had time to take precautionary measures . . . ."

Ben Bernanke recognized that, while perhaps manageable in itself, Lehman's default, combined with the unexpectedly rapid collapse of AIG, exacerbated the extraordinarily turbulent conditions in the global financial market. They led to a sharp decline in equity prices, a spike in the cost of short-term credit, where available, and a lack of liquidity in many markets. Losses at a large money market mutual fund sparked extensive withdrawals from a number of such funds. To avoid the broad repercussions of a run on US money market funds, the US Treasury set aside USD80 billion to guarantee brokers' money market funds. Prices paid for CDSs on financial names climbed, as each bank tried to protect itself against counterparty credit risk. Financial non-asset-backed commercial paper experienced a sharp decline, which led to the introduction of the Commercial Paper Funding Facility by the FED.

Unfortunately, these actions were not enough to stabilize markets and to halt the incumbent meltdown. Congress was asked to vote on state aid for the banking system in order to avoid the catastrophe. At one point during the audience, Hank Paulson, frustrated at the lawmakers themselves for asking why, in essence, taxpayers should be hit up for cash to cover Wall Street's mistakes, answered (see [73]): "When you ask about taxpayers being put on the hook, guess what? They're already on the hook." Ben Bernanke gave dark predictions about what would happen if the market were left to its own devices and how hard times would spread farther across the country. He said (see [73]): "The financial markets are in quite fragile condition and I think absent a plan they will get worse. I believe if the credit markets are not functioning, that jobs will be lost, that our credit rate will rise, more houses will be foreclosed upon, GDP will contract, that the economy will just not be able to recover in a normal, healthy way."

"We have a serious 'too big to fail' problem in this economy," he concluded. "If the crisis has a single lesson, it is that the too-big-to-fail problem must be solved . . . A promise not to intervene in and of itself will not solve the problem."

3.4 CLOSER SUPERVISION

The large-ripple effects of Lehman's default affected financial stability for a long time: many months were needed for authorities to address effectively the open issues and to fix

---

Box 3.6. The CDS spiral

Rumours or negative news about the soundness of a specific financial firm can easily fuel a run to hedge the credit risk related to those counterparties that are supposed to get significant exposure to the troubled firm and to be significantly affected by its default. Banks' concerns about counterparty risk lead them to buying protection via CDSs, producing generalized widening of CDS spreads. This can lead to some rating downgrades by rating agencies, which hurt banks' cash flow and liquidity situation.

---

the situation. The vicious circle was only broken when the US government decided to convert TARP into a binding capital injection for all major US banks. By so doing, the dilemma between illiquid and insolvent institutions was ultimately resolved, because no longer could anyone doubt the solvency of the banking system after this recapitalization.

Since then, no other large bank has been allowed to fail in order to prevent relevant spillover effects to the real economy. However, it was clear that mistakes made in the past should not be repeated in the future. For all the disagreements among legislators, regulators, technicians, policy officials and the public over the right set of financial reform measures, on one point there was near unanimity: no one wanted another TARP, not those who thought TARP was the best of the bad set of options available in 2008, certainly not those who opposed it, not American citizens many of whom saw the injection of billions of dollars of government capital into financial firms as more a bailout of large banks than an imperative to stabilize the financial system, nor even most of the large financial firms that were obliged to receive government aid and tried to pay it back as soon as possible.

The main lesson learnt about Lehman is not that financial institutions that are too interconnected do not have to fail, but that they require more supervision, in order to tackle the root causes of the problems that can push them to the verge of collapse. Before this crisis a systemic bank had many incentives to become larger and more interconnected, because it could have maximized the bailout probability ("hang on to others and take positions that drag others down when you are in trouble"). In a boom, a SIFI may play a role in the buildup of leverage and wider maturity mismatches, while at the same time fostering recourse to complex and opaque forms of financial innovation. This mechanism is reversed during a downswing, when a SIFI has a disproportionate effect on the deleveraging process. The intensity of deleveraging, liquidity hoarding and asset fire sales is proportional to the size and interconnectedness of the balance sheet of a SIFI. Furthermore, the economic losses and the deterioration of confidence triggered by the distress of a SIFI are likely to generate ripple effects that dwarf those stemming from a non-systemic institution.

A too-big-to-fail firm produces two different types of negative externalities (see Brunnermeier [39]). First, its own maturity mismatch easily affects the worth of the balance sheet of other players, because fire sales needed to adjust its liquidity situation are likely to reduce the assets value of other counterparties. Second, it is likely to take on an opaque connected position whose counterparty risk adversely affects other players. The latter, often known as "network externality", can be effectively tackled by the introduction of clearing house arrangements, which would allow netting among opposite exposures and would reduce counterparty credit risk. These measures could be powered by imposing higher capital charges on OTC contracts not centralized to a clearing house. In this way the CDS spiral, ignited by the failure of Lehman, should be avoided in the future.

It is worth pointing out that centralizing the larger part of derivative transactions in one or more clearing houses is an effective measure for reducing counterparty risk, but it simply substitutes this kind of risk with the liquidity risk related to higher initial and additional margins required by clearing houses to cover the default of major counterparties for exposures. It seems that the priority for regulators now is the reduction of counterparty risk, as if liquidity risk can always be coped with by means of liquidity provisions or, as a last resort, by central bank liquidity. As already explained, central bank liquidity can only be supposed to be always available during crisis times after having posted eligible collateral: it is not unlikely in the near future that there may be a shortage of collateral to enhance systemic liquidity provisions. In this case, the only way to pump central bank liquidity into the system is to reduce eligibility criteria, with the consequence that some components of counterparty risk could ultimately affect the soundness of a central bank's balance sheet.

The so-called fire sale/maturity mismatch externality can be managed only by regulation, by imposing stricter liquidity ratios on a SIFI. Stricter capital ratios or tailor-made leverage ratios for a SIFI are useful tools to cover all the dimensions of a financial crisis only if they are combined with effective liquidity ratios. Indeed, capital or leverage ratios are not able to capture the strong reliance on shorter term borrowing though repos and CP. In that case more capital can only reduce the negative effects of bad management, but it may not prevent future crises.

3.5   G-SIFI REGULATIONS

One of the first responses from regulators was the important package of reforms in capital regulation known as Basel III. The Basel III requirements for better quality of capital, improved risk weightings, higher minimum capital ratios, liquidity and leverage ratios, and a capital conservation buffer comprise a key component of the post-crisis reform agenda. Although a few features of Basel III reflect macroprudential concerns, in the main it is a microprudential exercise: thus, a macroprudential perspective on capital requirements is required to complement the microprudential orientation of Basel III.

There would be very large negative externalities, as stated before, associated with the disorderly failure of any SIFI, distinct from the costs incurred by the firm and its stakeholders. According to Daniel Tarullo, governor of the Fed's board (see [110]): "The failure of a SIFI, especially in a period of stress, significantly increases the chances that other financial firms will fail, for two reasons. First, direct counterparty impacts can lead to a classic domino effect. Second, because losses in a tail event are much more likely to be correlated for firms deeply engaged in trading, structured products, and other capital market instruments, all such firms are vulnerable to accelerating losses as troubled firms sell their assets into a declining market. A SIFI has no incentive to carry enough capital to reduce the chances of such systemic losses. The micro-prudential approach of Basel III does not force them to do so. The rationale for enhanced capital requirements for SIFI is to take these costs into account, make SIFI less prone to failure, and thereby to make the financial system safer. An ancillary rationale is that additional capital requirements could help offset any funding advantage derived from the perceived status of such institutions as too-big-too-fail."

On November 4, 2011, the Financial Stability Board took the first step toward stricter regulation for G-SIFIs (global systemically important financial institutions), by giving the first list of 29 globalized banks that are required to have loss absorption capacity tailored to the impact of their default, rising from 1 to 2.5% of risk-weighted assets (with an empty bucket of 3.5%, to discourage further systemicness), to be met with common equity by end-2012. This list will be updated annually and published by the FSB each November. In the communiqué (see [30]) the FSB and BCBS stated they had assessed the macroeconomic impact of higher loss absorbency requirements for G-SIFIs: "the enduring global economic benefits of greater resilience of these institutions far exceed the modest temporary decline of GDP over the implementation horizon."

SIFIs are defined as "financial institutions whose distress or disorderly failure, because of their size, complexity and systemic interconnectedness, would cause significant disruption to the wider financial system and economic activity" (see [30]). It is crucial to gauge the systemic relevance of a financial institution on the basis of a combination of several factors, instead of some specific ones. The size, either in absolute or in relative terms, can be reflected by a dominant position in a specific market or product or service. Interconnectedness stands for the linkage with the rest of the system, mostly via interbank lending or a special position as counterparty in key markets, as critical participant in various payment systems and as provider of major functions related to the risk management of market infrastructures. Another factor to gauge with care is substitutability (i.e., the extent to which other components of the system can provide the same service in the event of a failure).

These points have to be evaluated in combination of other relevant characteristics of the firm, as the institution's specific risk profile (leverage, liquidity, maturity mismatches and concentration of asset/liabilities) and its organisational and legal structure. The assessment of systemic importance is obviously a dynamic, time-varying and forward-looking process, depending, inter alia, on the particular conditions of financial markets. The ultimate aim of the classification should be to achieve a continuous or at least a finely granular ranking, as opposed to a simple division of firms into either systemically relevant or not, that can easily lead to some arbitrage practices for firms that can switch from one category to the other according to some quantitative ratio or indicator.

They recognize that addressing the too-big-to-fail problem requires a multi-pronged and integrated set of policies. In addition to capital requirements, the policy measures comprise:

- a new international standard, as a point of reference for reform of national resolution regimes, setting out the responsibilities, instruments and powers that all national resolution regimes should have to enable authorities to resolve failing financial firms in an orderly manner and without exposing the taxpayer to the risk of loss (the so-called "effective resolution regime");
- requirements for resolvability assessments and for recovery and resolution planning for G-SIFIs, and for the development of institution-specific cross-border cooperation

agreements so that home and host authorities of G-SIFIs are better equipped for dealing with crises and have clarity on how to cooperate in a crisis;
● more intensive and effective supervision of all SIFIs, including through stronger supervisory mandates, resources and powers, and higher supervisory expectations for risk management functions, data aggregation capabilities, risk governance and internal controls.

About the last point it is crucial not to scatter possible synergies between supervision and monetary policy. The systemic regulatory authority at the national level should be the national central bank or an institution closely associated to it. The UK example, with competencies shared between the FSA and the Bank of England, could not optimize the effectiveness of supervision because of lack of a continuous information flow between bank supervision and the central bank. For instance, having direct access to bank supervision information is essential to making a speedy bailout versus no bailout decision, to use the "lender of last resort" functions in a timely manner.

3.6   THE NEXT STEPS

Widespread discussion is well under way concerning possible rules to reduce the risk of failure of a SIFI or to mitigate the consequences of such failure for the financial system as a whole. Proposals as a result of the current debate can be classified in two main categories: (i) ex ante measures aimed at reducing the probability and impact of a SIFI's default; (ii) ex post measures aimed at ensuring that the failure of a financial institution can be solved in an orderly fashion. In the first group we can list the regulations for G-SIFIs defined by the FSB and the so-called "Volcker rule". This proposal aims to limit proprietary trading and investment in hedge funds or private equity funds, as well as the excessive growth of leverage of the largest financial institutions relative to the financial system as a whole.

The new challenge now is to define effective ex post measures able to decrease the expected burden on taxpayers in case of a SIFI crisis. Authorities have to be endowed with appropriate mechanisms to resolve the failure of a SIFI in an orderly and prompt manner, with the cost of default or restructuring falling on equity holders and bondholders without "socialization" of losses. The major step is the development of credible plans for recovery and resolution, often known as "living wills" [29]. Recovery or going concern plans include contingency funding and derisking plans and should be prepared and periodically updated by a SIFI and reviewed by competent authorities. Resolution or gone concern plans should identify the actions to be taken once the going concern plans have proven insufficient without taking into account the possibility of public support.

In the 2011 consultation paper issued by the FSB [28] the following resolution tools were proposed:

● Sale of the business:
The authorities would be able to effect the sale of a financial institution or all or part of its assets and liabilities to one or more purchasers on commercial terms, without requiring the consent of the shareholders or complying with procedural requirements that would otherwise apply.

Box 3.7. The Liikanen report

In October 2012 the High-level Expert Group, chaired by governor of the Bank of Finland Erkki Liikanen, recommended (see [84]) a set of measures to augment and complement the set of regulatory reforms already enacted or proposed by the EU, the Basel Committee and national governments.

First, proprietary trading and other significant trading activities should be assigned to a separate legal entity if the activities to be separated amount to a significant share of a bank's business. This would ensure that trading activities beyond the threshold are carried out on a standalone basis and separate from the deposit bank. As a consequence, deposits, and the explicit and implicit guarantee they carry, would no longer directly support risky trading activities.

Second, the Group emphasizes the need for banks to draw up and maintain effective and realistic recovery and resolution plans, as proposed in the Commission's Bank Recovery and Resolution Directive.

Third, the Group strongly supports the use of designated bailin instruments. Banks should build up a sufficient large layer of bailinable debt that should be clearly defined, so that its position within the hierarchy of debt commitments in a bank's balance sheet is clear and investors understand the eventual treatment in case of resolution. Such debt should be held outside the banking system!

Fourth, the Group proposes to apply more robust risk weights in the determination of minimum capital standards and more consistent treatment of risk in internal models.

- A bridge bank:
  The authorities would be able to transfer all or part of a credit institution to a bridge bank. This would be a publicly owned institution and the ultimate objective would be to facilitate the sale of the bridge bank. The operations of the bridge bank should be temporary and should be terminated within one year, although this may be extended by up to one year.
- Asset separation:
  The authorities would able to transfer certain assets of a SIFI to an asset management vehicle for the purpose of facilitating the use or ensuring the effectiveness of another resolution tool. In order to address concerns about moral hazard associated with the use of this tool that might otherwise arise, it should only be used in conjunction with another resolution tool. Then, the selected assets should be transferred to an asset management vehicle for fair consideration. Lastly, the resolution authority should appoint asset managers to manage the assets with the objective of maximizing their value through eventual sale.
- Debt writedown:
  The EC is considering a mechanism to write down the claims of some or all of the unsecured creditors of a failing institution and, possibly, to convert debt claims to equity, as a valuable additional resolution tool that would allow authorities greater flexibility. The paper makes it clear that this relates to possible future legislative changes which would be subject to full assessment and appropriate transition

---

Box 8.8. How to implement the debt writedown tool?

The consultation paper describes two different approaches to how a debt writedown tool might be implemented. The comprehensive approach provides statutory power to write down by a discretionary amount or convert all debt into equity to return a bank to solvency. It would only apply to new issued debt and this feature should be contractually recognized within bond documentation in the future.

The paper notes that some exclusions might be necessary, such as swap, repo and derivatives counterparties and other trade creditors; short-term debt (defined by a specified maximum maturity); retail and wholesale deposits and secured debt (i.e., covered bonds). Without dwelling on the matter, we note that there could be several technical problems with this. For example, How would tapped bonds be treated? Would this not encourage banks to fund themselves with short maturities to avoid having to issue debt with writedown language? Is there not a risk of subverting the normal ranking of bank bonds?

The targeted approach requires institutions to have a fixed volume of bailin debt in issue which would be written down or converted via a statutory trigger. This would need to include a contractual term that would specify that the relevant resolution authority could use statutory power to write down debt when an institution meets the trigger conditions for entry into resolution. This could include a fixed minimum for all institutions (e.g., as a percentage of total liabilities).

---

provisions and periods to avoid market instability or unintended consequences. It also notes that it is not envisaged to apply the measures adopted to debt currently in issue: wisely, this avoids automatically considering current unsecured debt as a new kind of subordinated debt.

The fourth resolution tool aims to address the associated moral hazard to the notion of "too big or too interconnected to fail". It arises from the general acknowledgment that governments and supervisory authorities would not let an ailing SIFI fail, given the significant damage to the financial system. In turn, this expectation of central bank or government support translates into a funding advantage compared with non-systemic banks.

When debtholders do not have to consider the risk of default on their investment, they will naturally tend to require a lower rate of return on the debt issued by systemic institutions. This lack of market discipline is by itself conducive to risk-taking: endowed with an implicit subsidy on its cost of funding, it is economically convenient for a SIFI to engage riskier strategies, expanding its balance sheets without appropriate price penalties.

To sum up, SIFIs benefit from double distortion to fair competition. In fact, the ex post subsidy embodied in implicit or explicit bailout guarantees translates into an ex ante funding advantage, which compounds the incentives to excessive risk-taking driven by pervasive moral hazard.

3.7 CONCLUSION

The scale of the potential fallout from the failure of a SIFI has been unveiled by the current financial crisis. In order to address, or mitigate, their potential contribution to financial instability, an overarching approach is strongly required of international policymakers and authorities. From a microprudential perspective, they are developing a strengthened regulatory and supervisory regime in order to reduce the risk contribution of the failure of a SIFI and to increase the overall resilience of the financial system. The collective behaviour of financial institutions and their interconnectedness stress the importance of recognizing the public aspect of financial stability, and underpin the recent emphasis on a joint micro and macroprudential approach to regulation and supervision.

The requirements defined by the FSB for G-SIFIs represent only the first steps to implement effective supervision and regulation to avoid new financial crises. As many banks are globalized it is very difficult for any national authority to perform these tasks successfully: for the eurozone it is strongly advised to fill as soon as possible one of the many holes in the single currency's original design. Since the euro's creation, integration of the finance industry has been rapid, with banks sprawling across national borders. The obvious answer is to move the supervision and eventual support, if required, for banks (or at least for big ones) away from national regulators to European ones.

The first and easier step was taken by the EC in the second half of 2012, placing the ECB in charge of the supervision of all European banks by the end of 2013. At a minimum there should be a eurozone-wide system of deposit insurance (to prevent loss of confidence that ignites bank runs) and oversight, with collective resources for the recapitalization of endangered institutions and regional rules for the resolution of truly

---

Box 3.9. The ECB's stance on bank rescue

On April 26, 2012, the president of the ECB, Mario Draghi, called on authorities to set up a body to manage bank rescues in the eurozone, marking the central bank's strongest intervention yet in the debate on whether the costs of bailing out troubled banks should be shared. He said: "The case for strengthening banking supervision and resolution at the euro area level has become much clearer [as a result of the crisis]. Work on this would be most helpful at the current juncture," he added.

The bank's vice president, Vítor Constâncio, laid out the priorities. "The sequence now is to go as much as possible for a pan-European resolution regime that is harmonized ... Also for the biggest systemically relevant banks, there are around 36 big banks, we really need a resolution fund, because that is the only way of overcoming the very thorny question of burden sharing in a crisis," he said.

He also urged the eurozone to copy a body that the US government has created to guarantee deposits and wind down failed banks. "What we need is really a solution that would be similar to what in the US is the Federal Deposit Insurance Corporation ... The FDIC resolved, liquidated and restructured more than 400 banks since the crisis began, some of them sizable in European terms," he suggested.

failed banks. With a European rescue fund to recapitalize weak banks, and a common system of deposit insurance, politicians would no longer be able to force their banks to support national firms or buy their government bonds: banks would no longer be Italian, Spanish or German, but increasingly European. It should be the ultimate in European financial integration.

4

The new framework

4.1 INTRODUCTION

The financial crisis which started in mid-2007 took financial institutions and supervisors by surprise because it followed a long period of time characterized by ample liquidity, compressed spreads and low volatility. The wave of deregulation, coupled by increasing globalization and the development of increasingly complex derivatives products, led to risk-prone behaviours and weakened the resilience of the financial system to the shock that originated in the core business of the banking system, the asset–liability maturities' mismatch.

Since the most relevant shocks to financial markets over the previous years had been produced by excessive exposures to market factors or counterparty risk, the Basel II framework aimed at addressing mainly these issues rather than focusing on liquidity risk. As a consequence, this kind of risk was widely downplayed or ignored by academics and practitioners, while the backdrop of financial innovation quickly made both current banks' liquidity risk management practices and supervisory standards irrelevant.

The impact on global liquidity recorded during the crisis was largely affected by two main trends: increased recourse by capital markets to funding and augmented reliance on short-term maturity funding instruments. They were reinforced by the concurrent buildup of many forms of contingent liquidity claims (e.g., those linked to off-balance-sheet vehicles) and increasingly frequent margin requirements that were rating related (e.g., from derivatives transactions).

The financial crisis showed how quickly a bank could be affected by liquidity tensions if it was not well equipped with sound liquidity practices: in these cases the capital requirements defined by Basel II were little more than useless at preventing a liquidity crisis, despite the fact that well-capitalized banks should be facilitated, *ceteris paribus*, to raise funds on the interbank or capital markets. Indeed, capital ratios aim at warranting the solvency of banks, but they are not able to prevent their illiquidity.

In addition to the regulatory framework aimed at addressing the supervision and resolution of SIFIs, regulators have developed in recent years an international liquidity risk framework to improve banks' resilience to liquidity shocks led by market-related or idiosyncratic scenarios, and at the same time increase market confidence in banks' liquidity positions. Nevertheless, in some cases regulatory and supervisory regimes continue to be nationally based and substantially differentiated, pointing up the significant differences that do not allow a level playing field and, in some circumstances, could produce regulatory arbitrages, as well as reducing the effectiveness of supervisory actions.

4.2 SOME BASIC LIQUIDITY RISK MEASURES

Since 1992, according to the overall supervisory approach, the BCBS (Basel Committee on Banking Supervision) have made efforts to define a framework for measuring and managing liquidity, but it failed to deliver methodologies or incentives for the bank industry to develop or improve consistent and sound liquidity management practices. In its first document issued on 1992 it only suggested that supervisors differentiate their approaches to large international banks and domestic ones, while listing some methodologies based alternatively on maturity ladder or scenario analysis in order to implement effective liquidity management. Eight years later, it simply provided some definitions of liquidity risk and illustrated some developments in liquidity management and supervision, but progress on this topic was slow and inadequate to manage increasing financial innovation. In 2006 the financial industry still continued to adopt significantly differentiated risk management practices for facing liquidity risk and supervisors also persisted in adopting divergent and heterogeneous models in order to assess the liquidity profiles of financial institutions.

The financial turmoil which began in 2007 showed how the banking sector was clearly not properly equipped to manage liquidity shocks: the models adopted by banks to predict liquidity crises were demonstrated to be ineffective; contingent liquidity plans were not always successful in avoiding liquidity tensions and failed to consider extreme market events, which actually occurred; moreover, the models used by supervisors were demonstrated to be excessively optimistic. Until then, managing and measuring liquidity risk was rarely considered to be one of the top priorities by the majority of financial institutions. The financial community and the available literature did not even agree on the proper measurement of liquidity: therefore, a widely adopted integrated measurement tool capable of covering all the dimensions of liquidity risk was mere Utopia.

Among the liquidity risk metrics in use, some had adopted analytical approaches, such as VaR, which are focused on assessing potential effects on profitability, while others had developed liquidity risk models and measures aimed at accessing cash flow projections of assets and liabilities, or the inability to conduct business as a going concern as a result of a reduction of unencumbered liquid assets and of the capacity to attract additional funding. The different approaches to measuring liquidity risk were based on stock ratios, cash flow analysis, and a maturity mismatch framework.

Stock-based approaches consider liquidity as a stock and are used to compare and classify all balance-sheet items according to their "monetization", in order to define the bank's ability to reimburse its payment obligations.

An example is represented by the long-term funding ratio, which is based on the cash flow profile arising from on and off-balance-sheet items, and indicates the share of assets that have a specific maturity or longer, funded through liabilities of the same maturity.

Another stock approach is provided by the cash capital position [86], which aims at keeping an asset/liability structure fairly balanced under the profile of "monetization": illiquid assets funded by stable liabilities and marketable assets funded by volatile liabilities, as shown by the stylized reclassification of a simplified balance sheet in Table 4.1.

According to Moody's approach, which initially aimed at estimating the ability of a bank to continue its going concern activity on a fully collateralized basis, assuming that

Table 4.1. Reclassified balance sheet to show the cash capital position in a stock-based approach

	Assets	*Liabilities*	
Liquid assets	Cash	Non-core deposits	Volatile liabilities
	Collateral value of unencumbered assets	Short-term funding (CP, euro CP, short-term bank facilities, etc.)	
	Reverse repos	Repos	
	Total liquid assets	*Total volatile liabilities*	
		Core deposits	Stable liabilities
Illiquid assets	Illiquid assets	Medium/long-term funding	
	Haircuts	Equity	
	Total on balance sheet		
	Contingent outflows	Contingent funding capacity	

access to unsecured funding is likely to be lost after some severe short-term rating's downgrading, the cash capital position is represented by the difference between the collateral value of unencumbered assets and the sum of the volume of short-term funding and the non-core part of non-interbank deposits.

The above simplified reclassification of the balance sheet also shows us the reverse of this measure by focusing on the less liquid part of the balance sheet (i.e., the difference between the sum of core deposits, medium and long-term funding, capital and the sum of illiquid assets and the haircuts applied to liquid assets), where "contingent outflows" and "contingent funding capacity" represent the only flow component that can increase or reduce the measure according to its sign.

The main drawback of this measure derives from classifying balance sheet items as liquid and illiquid, without asking when exactly some positions can be liquidated or become due. This binary approach, which is a feature of all stock-based approaches, is obviously unsatisfactory as it is unable to properly qualify the variety of liquidity degree. Furthermore, stock-based approaches are not forward looking.

Cash flow–based approaches aim at keeping the bank's ability to meet its payment obligations by calculating and limiting maturity transformation risk in some way, based on the measurement of liquidity-at-risk figures. The main risk management tool is represented by the maturity ladder that is used to compare cash inflows and outflows on a daily basis as well as over a series of specified time periods (e.g., daily tenors up to 1 month and monthly buckets thereafter).

Cash flows are related to all assets, liabilities and off-balance-sheet items. In its simplest structure such analysis is not supported by any explicit assumption on the future behaviour of cash flows (new-business scenario or stressed scenario): consequently, on the basis of the grid that shows the "cash flow mismatch" or the "liquidity gap" for each time bucket, a calculation of the cumulative net excess or shortfall over the time frame (T) for liquidity assessment is easily performed:

$$\mathrm{CFR}(T) = \sum_{i=1}^{N} \mathrm{NFR}(t_i)$$

Box 4.1. The main rules

The main liquidity adequacy rules are provided by BIPRU 12.2.1 and 12.2.3 (see [9]). According to the former: "A firm must at all times maintain liquidity resources which are adequate, both as to amount and quality to ensure that there is no significant risk that its liabilities cannot be met as they fall due." The latter requires that "A firm must ensure that it maintains at all times liquidity resources sufficient to withstand a range of severe stress events which could impair its ability to meet its liabilities."

---

where $\mathrm{CFR}(T)$ is the cumulative funding requirement over the chosen time horizon ending in T, and $\mathrm{NFR}(t_i)$ is the net funding requirement at time t_i, with $t_N = T$.

The granularity of time horizons must be carefully considered. An extremely detailed breakdown provides some valuable information, but can also generate a certain amount of confusion in interpretation, especially if in a very dynamic environment where cash flows expected in 2 or 3 weeks can substantially change.

The optimal level of granularity should be chosen in accordance with the experience of the user (more granular for treasurers, less for management). Finally, the maturity ladder can assume a multiplicity of structures and cash flow composition according to the different objectives, time horizons and business units involved, with the main purpose represented by simulating the path of short-term treasury liquidity gaps, based on neutral assumptions on balance sheet items' future growth.

The maturity mismatch framework is a hybrid approach that combines elements of cash flow matching and of the liquid assets approach. As every financial institution is exposed to unexpected cash inflows and outflows, which may occur at any time in the future because of unusual deviations in the timing or magnitude, so requiring a considerably larger quantity of cash than initially forecast for business, it tries to match expected cash flows and unexpected outflows in each time bucket against a mix of contractual cash inflows, plus additional inflows that can be generated through assets sale or secured borrowing.

Therefore, unencumbered liquid assets have to be positioned in the shortest time buckets, while less liquid assets are mapped in later time buckets. In this framework, a bank is expected to hold an adequate cushion of unencumbered assets or, more generally, to develop an appropriate counterbalancing capacity in order to reduce net cumulative outflows.

The maturity ladder and, more generally, the term structure of liquidity will be analysed in detail in Chapter 6. In Chapters 7 and 8 we will study how to monitor and manage maturity mismatch by means of an adequate liquidity buffer.

4.3 THE FIRST MOVER

The UK regulator was the first to react to the 2007 financial crisis by developing a binding framework to measure and manage the liquidity risk of all financial entities active in the UK. The bank run that hit Northern Rock and the liquidity crisis experienced by the RBS stressed the urgency to develop some stricter rules in order to safeguard the stability of the UK banking system and to reassure the world's investors about the soundness of London's financial sector, which represents one of the core assets of the British economy.

Over 2009 the UK Financial Service Authority (FSA) issued some binding liquidity proposals that contemplate a major overhaul of the previous regime for all FSA-regulated firms subject to the FSA's BIPRU (*Prudential Sourcebook for Banks, Building Societies and Investment Firms*), UK branches of the EEA (European Economic Area) and third-country banks: liquidity regulation and supervision should have been recognized as of equal importance to capital regulation.

Each entity covered has to assess its liquidity self-sufficiency through a systems and control questionnaire that monitors the Individual Liquidity Adequacy Standard (ILAS). Basically, the bank runs a periodic assessment of its own liquidity risk measurement system by providing for figures required as a result of a stress-testing and contingency-funding plan. This assessment concerns both the risk management framework (in terms of risk appetite, systems and controls, stress analysis under multiple firm-driven scenarios and the reverse stress-testing, contingency funding plan) and liquidity adequacy (in terms of quantification of a liquid assets buffer that has to be an effective liquidity cushion under three prescribed stress tests driven by ten different risk factors), which has to be covered appropriately in all aspects.

The FSA, according to its Supervisory Liquidity Review Process (SLRP), reviews the Individual Liquidity Adequacy Assessment (ILAA) of the firm in terms of backstop purposes (the percentage of the ILAA stress scenario that the firm can currently meet and the percentage of an individualized scenario, within benchmark ranges, that the firm can currently meet) and gives individual liquidity guidance (ILG) to manage a tightening glide path, by increasing the percentage of individualized stress scenarios that need to be met over time and by recalibrating the standard stress scenario.

The ILG letter defines the prudent funding profile required of the firm, by providing short-term net type A wholesale gap limits (unsecured and secured) and the structural funding ratio. Eventually, this is followed up by checks. The figures are collected by the seven main reports described in Table 4.2.

The assessment has to be performed under some severe stress scenarios, which produce both idiosyncratic and market-wide impacts. Under idiosyncratic stress, during the first two weeks of stress, it is supposed there is

1. An inability to roll over wholesale funding that is unsecured from credit-sensitive depositors or not secured on the most liquid securities (with a sustained leakage of funding lasting out to three months).
2. A sizeable retail outflow (with a sustained outflow out to three months).
3. A reduction in the amount of intraday credit provided to a customer by its settlement bank.
4. An increase in payments withheld from a direct participant by its counterparties.
5. An increase in the need for all firms (both direct and indirect participants) to make payments.
6. The closure of FX markets (it is worth noting that the FSA at the moment is the only regulator that requires such an abrupt dislocation of the FX market to be assumed!).

Table 4.2. The seven reports that UK banks must produce to comply with the FSA's liquidity regulation

Report	Description
FSA047: daily flows	Collects daily contractual cash flows out to 3 months
FSA048: enhanced mismatch report	Collects contractual cash flows across the full maturity spectrum
FSA050: liquidity buffer qualifying securities	Captures firms' largest liquid asset holdings
FSA051: funding concentration	Captures firms' funding from wholesale and repo counterparties
FSA052: pricing data	Average transaction prices and transacted volumes for wholesale liabilities
FSA053: retail, SME and large enterprise funding	Firms' retail, SME and corporate funding profiles
FSA054: currency analysis	Analysis of foreign exchange exposures

7. The repayment of all intragroup deposits at maturity without rolling over, and the treatment of intragroup loans as evergreen (in so doing, the mismatch to be managed by the central treasury becomes very challenging!).
8. A severe downgrade of long-term rating, with a proportional impact on all other downgrade triggers.

Under the market-wide stressed scenario the firm has to face

1. Rising uncertainty about the accuracy of the valuation of its assets and those of its counterparties.
2. The inability to realize or only at excessive cost some particular classes of assets.
3. Risk aversion among participants in the markets on which the firm relies for funding.
4. Uncertainty over whether many firms will be able to meet liabilities as they fall due.

ILAA should not be considered just a list of documents required to be compliant with regulation: the ultimate goal is to show how firms can manage the liquidity risk. It is a firm-specific process with both quantitative and qualitative information continuously revised and updated. The FSA framework is a very tough regime and for that reason not easily accepted by practitioners, but so far it has been successful at addressing the liquidity problems experienced by the UK's financial sector as a result of the 2007–08 crisis.

One of the main criticisms relates to the lack of coordination with other regulators, with some requirements not fully consistent with the Basel III liquidity framework. One classic example is represented by the asset classes eligible as liquidity buffer: according to Basel III, corporate and covered bonds, with some specific limitations, are included, whereas the FSA does not admit them. In these cases regulated entities of the EEA with UK branches in whole-firm modification mode, with ILAA waived, could be compliant

Box 4.2. "Dear Treasurer"

In a letter sent to all treasurers [11], the FSA highlighted the importance of consistent fund transfer pricing (FTP) practices as part of the preparation for ILAA. It required "an evidential provision for firms accurately to quantify the liquidity costs, benefits and risks in relation to all significant business activities— whether or not they are accounted for on-balance sheet—and to incorporate them in their (i) product pricing; (ii) performance measurement; and (iii) approval process for new products. The quantification of costs, benefits and risks should include consideration of how liquidity would be affected under stressed conditions ... Firms should ensure that the costs, benefits and risks identified are explicitly and clearly attributed to business lines and are understood by business line management."

FTP thus becomes a regulatory requirement and an important tool in the management of firms' balance sheet structure, and in the measurement of risk-adjusted profitability and liquidity and ALM risk. Failure to apply appropriate FTP processes can lead to misaligning the risk-taking incentives of individual business lines and misallocating finite liquidity resource and capital within the firm as a whole.

This can manifest itself in the conduct of loss-making business or in business where rewards are not commensurate with the risk taken, and thereby ultimately undermines sustainable business models. Some answers provided by firms surveyed are publicly criticized because of reference to the weighted average cost of funding either already on the balance sheet or projected in an annual budget process: according to the FSA this framework lacks sufficient flexibility to incentivize or discourage business behaviour and appropriately charge for the duration of risk.

Examples are represented by some cases in 2007 with the buildup of large inventory positions in certain asset classes, where returns were not commensurate with the risk taken, and in the onset of volatile conditions where marginal costs rose sharply and the FTP regime did not appropriately reflect the market conditions for business lines. By criticizing the use of the projected weighted average cost of funding in other cases as reference to the marginal cost of funding, the FSA ultimately seems to support the "matched funding" principle and the marginal cost of funding as the most appropriate references for an effective FTP framework.

with their home country regulation (Basel III) but not with FSA rules, though they are required to submit periodically the above-described reports to the FSA as well in order to warrant the activity of their branches in the UK.

4.4 BASEL III: THE NEW FRAMEWORK FOR LIQUIDITY RISK MEASUREMENT AND MONITORING

While the FSA was reviewing and introducing its new binding liquidity regime, Europe was some steps behind due to the heterogeneous mix of requirements and rules defined

Box 4.3. The BCBS' principles

The BCBS' principles seek to promote a true culture of sound management and supervision practices for liquidity risk, based on a specific liquidity risk tolerance defined by top management according to their business strategy, and an articulate framework for risk management, product pricing and performance measurement to warrant full consistency between risk-taking incentives for business lines and related liquidity risk exposures for the bank as a whole.

They outline the role played by a "cushion" of unencumbered, high-liquidity assets to withstand a range of stress events that can affect the bank's liquidity position on the very short term and even on an intraday basis. They suggest a funding strategy that provides effective diversification in the sources and tenors of funding. Also, the funding strategy and contingency plans are to be adjusted timely and properly according to stress tests performed on a regular basis, for a variety of firm-specific and market-wide stress scenarios (both individually and in combination!) to identify sources of potential liquidity strain, and to ensure that current exposures remain in accordance with a bank's established liquidity risk tolerance.

by local regulators. With regard to the level of application, some countries applied the same supervisory requirements to all entities covered independently of their size and category, whereas in other jurisdictions different rules were implemented for different types of banks (e.g., the supervisory framework admitted a more sophisticated approach for certain banks, with more flexibility to use internal modelling methods), while a more prescriptive approach was basically defined for smaller banks.

Across jurisdictions, there were diverse approaches to liquidity supervision within some countries: the "proportional approach" was widely diffused, with an increasing intensity of supervision for larger and more systematically important firms, in proportion to the assumed increase in risk.

Following the BCBS' principles issued in September 2008 about the management and supervision of liquidity risk, in December 2010 the Basel Committee issued a document titled *International Framework for Liquidity Risk Measurement, Standards and Monitoring* [100] with the goal of promoting a more resilient banking sector to absorb shocks arising from liquidity stress, thus reducing the risk of spillover from the financial sector to the real economy, as has occurred since 2007. This document was later amended (January 2013) with the publication of the document *Basel III: The Liquidity Coverage Ratio and Liquidity Risk Monitoring Tools* (see [103]).

In order to translate these principles in some technical measures, this document proposes specific liquidity tests that, although similar in many respects to tests historically applied by banks and regulators for management and supervisory purposes, going forward will be required by regulation to improve a bank's liquidity management and to promote the short-term resilience of a bank's liquidity profile. The so-called "liquidity proposal" provided by the Basel Committee is based on three key elements:

Box 4.4. The importance of being unencumbered

Both the liquidity proposals of the Basel Committee and the *Guidelines on Liquidity Buffers* provided by the CEBS stress that all assets, used as a liquidity buffer to be converted into cash at any time to fill funding gaps between cash inflows and outflows during stressed periods, must be unencumbered. "Unencumbered" means not pledged (either explicitly or implicitly) to secure, collateralize or credit-enhance any transaction. However, assets received in reverse repo and securities financing transactions—which are held at the bank, have not been rehypothecated, and are legally and contractually available for the bank's use—can be considered as stock. In addition, assets which qualify as the stock of high-quality liquid assets that have been pledged to the central bank or a public sector entity (PSI), but are not used, may be included as stock.

The stock of liquid assets should not be commingled with or used as hedges on trading positions, be designated as collateral, be designated as credit enhancements in structured transactions or be designated to cover operational costs (such as rents and salaries), but should be managed with the clear and sole intent for use as a source of contingent funds.

Last but not least, this stock should be under the control of the specific function charged with managing the liquidity risk of the bank (typically the treasurer). A bank should periodically monetize a proportion of the assets in the stock through repo or outright sale to the market in order to test its access to the market, the effectiveness of its processes for monetization and the usability of the assets, as well as to minimizing the risk of negative signalling during a period of stress.

- a liquidity coverage ratio (LCR), designed to ensure that a bank maintains an adequate level of unencumbered, high-quality assets that can be converted into cash to meet its liquidity needs for a 30-day time horizon under an acute liquidity stress scenario specified by supervisors;
- a net stable funding ratio (NSFR), designed to promote more medium and long-term funding of the assets and activities of banks over a 1-year time horizon in order to tackle banks' longer term structural liquidity mismatches;
- a set of common metrics—often referred to as monitoring tools—that the Basel Committee indicates should be considered the minimum types of information that banks should report to supervisors, as applicable, and supervisors should use in monitoring the liquidity risk profiles of supervised entities.

Compliance with the two ratios and monitoring tools will be mandatory for all international active banks. Nevertheless, it is expected that they will be used for other banks and for any subset of subsidiaries of internationally active banks identified by supervisors.

4.4.1 The liquidity coverage ratio

The LCR is defined as the ratio of a bank's stock of high-quality liquid assets divided by a measure of its net cash outflows over a 30-day time period. The standard requires that the ratio be no lower than 100%. Both the numerator and denominator are defined in a way intended to ensure that sufficient liquid assets are available to meet any unexpected cash flow gaps throughout a 30-day period following an acute liquidity stress scenario that entails

- a significant downgrade (three-notch) in the bank's public rating;
- runoff of a proportion of retail deposits;
- a loss of unsecured wholesale funding capacity and reductions of potential sources of secured funding on a term basis;
- loss of secured, short-term financing transactions for all but high-quality liquid assets;
- increases in market volatilities that impact the quality of collateral or potential future exposures of derivative positions and thus require larger collateral haircuts or additional collateral;
- unscheduled draws on all the bank's committed but unused credit and liquidity facilities;
- the need for the bank to fund balance sheet growth arising from non-contractual obligations honoured in the interest of mitigating reputational risk.

High-quality liquid assets for purposes of the numerator are intended to meet four fundamental characteristics (low credit and market risk, ease and certainty of valuation, low correlation with risky assets, and listed on a developed and recognized exchange market) and four market-related characteristics (active and sizeable market, presence of committed market makers, low market concentration, "flight to quality" considerations).

According to the first draft of the Basel Committee's document [101] the only assets to meet these characteristics were cash; central bank reserves (to the extent that they can be drawn down in times of stress); marketable securities representing claims on or claims guaranteed by sovereigns, central banks, non-central government public sector entities, the BIS, the IMF, the EC, and certain multilateral development banks which meet specified criteria; and, last, government or central bank debt issued in domestic currencies by the country in which the liquidity risk is being taken or the bank's home country.

There are few conditions on sovereign debt that can be used as part of the pool of Level 1 assets: a bank can hold any sovereign bond issued in domestic currency in its home country, as well as any sovereign debt in foreign currency, so long as it matches the currency needs of the bank in that country.

However, it can also stock up on the debt of any other country that is assigned a 0% risk weight under the Basel II standardized approach. Under the increasing pressure ignited by the ongoing eurozone sovereign debt crisis, this requirement is now under scrutiny to be fine-tuned to include a rating component. Obviously, this plan has received a frosty reception from some market participants, already worried about the role that rating agencies should play. Moreover, introducing some kind of liquidity rating approach to the use of sovereign bonds and other assets as a liquidity buffer could be dangerously procyclical because it forces banks to replace assets that are no longer deemed eligible for this purpose. By selling them into the market, this would amplify stress effects and make it even more difficult for issuers to sell their debt at a time when they are already likely to be under pressure from the markets. Luckily, the last version of the document issued in January 2013 [103] did not introduce any significant modification about this topic, by de facto rejecting all proposals that were credit rating oriented.

After gathering data on the liquidity of corporate and covered bonds, the Basel Committee indicated that banks are allowed to consider as a liquidity buffer (so-called Level 2A) a portion of lower rated sovereign, central bank and PSE bonds, qualifying for a 20% risk weighting and high-quality covered bonds, with a minimum credit rating equal to AA−, subject however to some haircuts. An 85% factor has to be applied and multiplied against its total amount.

The reference to a minimum rating of AA− for eligibility as a liquidity buffer, instead of some link to the assets' marketability, is questionable for the same reasons mentioned above about the dependence on rating agencies and the procyclical impacts of their decisions. An alternative to the rating could be represented by some combination of the following parameters to map the assets' marketability: daily traded volumes, bid/offer spreads, outstanding amounts, sizes of deals, active public market and repo haircuts.

In any case all financial bonds are correctly excluded to avoid evident "wrong-way risk": more questionable was the exclusion of equities quoted in most worldwide liquid indices, which have remained very liquid even in the most acute times of stress following Lehman's default. Daily traded volumes over recent years for the most liquid and less volatile stocks with low correlation to the financial sector strongly supports the call for their inclusion in Level 2 of the liquidity buffer.

Eventually, the recent draft issued by the BCBS in January 2013 has introduced some attempts aiming to prevent some potential shortage of liquidity buffers with detrimental effects on lending activity. Under mounting pressure from the financial community, who strongly suggested expanding in some ways the list of eligible asset classes for the liquidity buffer, the BCBS introduced Level 2B assets, composed of RMBS, corporate bonds and commercial paper, common equity shares, which satisfy certain specific conditions.

RMBS must: be rated AA at least; not be issued by, or the underlying assets not originated by, the bank itself; be "full recourse" in nature (i.e., in the case of foreclosure, the mortgage owner remains liable for any shortfall in sales proceeds from the property); must comply with risk retention requirements; must respect an average LTV (Loan To Value) at issuance of the underlying mortgage pool not exceeding 80%; must have recorded a maximum decline in price less than 20%, or an increase in the haircut over a 30-day period not exceeding 20 percentage points (they ultimately will be subject to a 25% haircut). Due to the sovereign caps in effect on the rating for many European jurisdictions, the minimum AA rating resulted in only UK and Dutch RMBS bonds being actually eligible.

The document seems to imply that just a single rating by an agency may be required and central bank repo eligibility may not be necessary, since there is no mention of it: if this is the case, then some Italian RMBS may be eligible as well, for example. However, we doubt that ultimately just one rating will be required for RMBS: this is because almost all of the recent regulations (including CB eligibility criteria) have moved towards requiring two ratings. Specifying LTV levels as a proxy to determine high credit quality is questionable, because LTV is only one of the many drivers behind a borrower's default. Even a well-performing sector across Europe like that of the Netherlands is not able to match the current average original LTV requirement (currently its level is equal to 95.3%). Hence, with this rule, currently only UK RMBS bonds will benefit from inclusion in the LCR.

Corporate bonds and commercial paper will be subject to a 50% haircut. They do not have to be issued by a financial institution, must have a minimum rating of BBB− and match the same rule defined for RMBS about the proven record of being a reliable source of liquidity in the markets.

Equities will be subject to a 50% haircut: they do not have to be issued by financial institutions, must be exchange-traded and centrally cleared; and must be a constituent of the major stock index in the jurisdiction where liquidity risk is being taken. They must have recorded a maximum decline in price less than 40%, or an increase in the haircut over a 30-day period not exceeding 40 percentage points, in order to represent a reliable liquidity source.

In the final analysis, equities have been accepted by the BCBS as a reliable liquidity source, but the haircut and the limit related to the liquidity risk centre are likely to reduce the potential benefits of this inclusion. First, a 50% haircut is too onerous and certainly higher than haircuts commonly found in tri-party funding programs or through stock lending activity; second, the limitation to equities only, which make up the index of the jurisdiction where the liquidity risk lies, will bring about Balkanization of this funding source, similar to the differentiation already defined for government bonds linked to the liquidity centre in order to be accepted without matching risk-weighted criteria.

Moreover, in order to mitigate the cliff effects that could arise if an eligible liquid asset became ineligible (i.e., due to a rating downgrade), a bank is permitted to keep such assets in its stock of liquid assets for an additional 30 calendar days: this would provide the bank additional time to adjust its stock as needed or replace the asset. Another mitigating rule is represented by the provision, assigned by local jurisdictions, to allow banks to apply local rating scales to Level 2 assets, meaning that bonds, which would have been affected by sovereign ceilings, may be considered eligible when there is insufficient supply of eligible assets.

High-quality liquid assets are classified in two different classes (Level 1 and Level 2, with two sublevels: 2A and 2B) on the basis of their liquidability. The proposal fixes a cap for assets included in the Level 2 class: they can only comprise 40% of the pool of high-quality liquid assets. Within Level 2 assets, so-called Level 2B assets should comprise no more than 15% of the total stock of high-quality liquid assets (HQLA). To avoid any arbitrage it is therefore necessary:

$$LA = L1 + L2A + L2B$$
$$-\max[(AdjL2A + AdjL2B) - 2/3 \times AdjL1; AdjL2B - 15/85 \times (AdjL1 + AdjL2A)]$$

where

- LA is the amount of liquid assets;
- $L1$, $L2A$ and $L2B$ are, respectively, the amount of Level 1, Level 2A and Level 2B assets;
- $AdjL1A$ (adjusted Level 1 assets) is the amount of Level 1 assets that would result if all short-term secured funding involving the exchange of any Level 1 assets for any non-Level 1 assets were unwound;
- $AdjL2A$ (adjusted Level 2 assets) is the amount of Level 2 assets that would result if all

short-term secured funding involving the exchange of any Level 2 assets for any non-Level 2 assets were unwound.
- *adjL2B* (adjusted Level 2B assets) is the amount of Level 2B assets that would result if all short-term secured funding involving the exchange of any Level 2B assets for any non Level 2 assets were unwound.

Factors of 100 and 85% are defined, respectively, for Level 1 and Level 2 assets.

Net cash outflows are defined as "cumulative expected cash outflows minus cumulative expected inflows arising in the specified stress scenario in the time period under consideration." The liquidity proposal includes very detailed provisions with respect to cash outflows and inflows. The approach is to identify a cash source and then apply a runoff factor to the proportion of this cash source that is expected to be paid out or received in the relevant period. Then, total expected cash outflows are calculated by multiplying the outstanding balances of various categories or types of liabilities and off-balance-sheet commitments by the rates at which they are expected to run off or be drawn down.

Runoff rates are calibrated according to expected stability factors such as government protection, public guarantee schemes, duration of client relationships with the bank, purpose of the account (e.g., transactional or savings account). Accordingly, total expected cash inflows are calculated by multiplying the outstanding balances of various categories of contractual receivables by the rates at which they are expected to flow in under the scenario, up to an aggregate cap of 75% of total expected cash outflows. This means that at least 25% of cash outflows are to be covered by holding a stock of high-quality liquid assets.

The most significant changes introduced by the January 2013 version affecting the modelled liquidity shock are:

- outflow of insured retail deposits reduced by 2% (from 5 to 3%);
- outflow of insured non-retail, non-bank deposits reduced by 20% (from 40 to 20%);
- outflow of uninsured non-retail, non-bank deposits reduced by 35% (from 75 to 40%);
- drawdown rate on unused portion of committed liquidity facilities to non-financial corporates, sovereigns, CBs and PSEs reduced by 70% (from 100 to 30%);
- outflow of interbank liquidity facilities reduced by 60% (from 100 to 40%).

In Tables 4.3 and 4.4 we detail the runoff factors required for any kind of cash outflow. In Table 4.5 we detail the runoff factors required for any kind of cash inflow.

It is evident that the introduction of a binding LCR has to be fine-tuned with the status of the economic cycle and the evolution of the European crisis, because banks are called to increase their liquidity buffer with uncorrelated assets (low risk and return with negative impacts on profitability figures) and lengthen the term of funding well beyond 30 days (without restoring confidence it is really challenging for European banks to attract stable funding on longer maturities), by scaling back liquidity shock–sensitive assets. The close link between sovereign debt and the banking system has to be previously broken and definitely addressed in order to avoid spillover effects on buffer composition and on market liquidity under stressed conditions.

On the basis of these considerations and on the data collected during the monitoring period already covered, the BCBS decided to delay full implementation of the LCR,

Table 4.3. First group of runoff factors in the LCR

Funding from	Typology	Runoff factor (%)
Retail demand and term deposits (less than 30 days maturity)	Stable deposits (with deposit insurance scheme)	3
	Stable deposits	5
	Less stable deposits	10
Small-business customers demand and term deposits (less than 30 days maturity)	Stable deposits	5
	Less stable deposits	10
Operational deposits generated by clearing, custody and cash management	Portion covered by deposit insurance	5
	The other portion	25
Cooperative banks in an institutional network	Qualifying deposits with the centralized institution	25
Non-financial corporates, sovereigns, central banks and PSE		40
	If the amount is fully covered by a deposit insurance scheme	20
Other legal entity customers		100
Term deposits with residual maturity >30 days		0
Secured funding transactions backed by	Level 1 assets, with any counterparty	0
	Level 2A assets, with any counterparty	15
	Non Level 1 or Level 2A assets, with domestic sovereigns, multilateral development banks, or domestic PSE	25
	RMBS included in Level 2B	25
	Other Level 2B assets	50
All other secured funding transactions		100

previously scheduled for January 2015. The LCR will therefore be introduced as originally planned in January 2015, but the minimum requirement will be set only at 60% (!) and rise in equal annual steps to reach 100% in January 2019. This phase-in approach should ensure that introduction of the LCR will not produce any material disruption to the orderly strengthening of banking systems or the ongoing financing of economic activity.

Table 4.4. Second group of runoff factors in the LCR

Other components	Customer or typology	Runoff factor
Liabilities related to derivative collateral calls for a three-notch downgrade		100% of collateral required
Market valuation changes on derivative transactions	Lookback approach	Largest absolute net 30-day collateral flows realized during the preceding 24 months
Valuation changes on non Level 1 posted collateral securing derivatives		20%
Excess collateral that could contractually be called back at any time		100%
Liquidity needs related to collateral contractually due from the reporting bank on derivative transactions		100%
Increased liquidity needs related to derivatives, which allow collateral substitution to non-HQLA		100%
Liabilities from maturing ABCP, SIVs, conduits, etc.		100% of maturing amounts and 100% of returnable assets
ABS (including covered bonds)		100% of maturing amounts
Currently undrawn portion of committed credit and liquidity facilities to:	Retail and small-business clients	5% of outstanding credit and liquidity lines
Credit facilities to:	Non-financial corporates, sovereigns, central banks, PSEs	10% of outstanding credit lines
Liquidity facilities to:	Non-financial corporates, sovereigns, central banks, PSEs	30% of outstanding liquidity lines
Credit and liquidity facilities to:	Banks subject to prudential supervision	40%
Credit facilities to:	Other financial institutions	40%
Liquidity facilities to:	Other financial institutions	100%
Credit and liquidity facilities to:	Other legal entity customers	100% of outstanding lines

(*continued*)

Table 4.4 (*cont.*)

Other components	Customer or typology	Runoff factor
Other contingent funding liabilities	Guarantees, letters of credit, etc.	National discretion
	Trade finance	0–5%
	Customer short positions	50%
Any additional contractual outflow		100%
Net derivative payables		100%
Any other contractual cash outflow		100%

Table 4.5. Runoff factors in the LCR for cash inflows

Cash inflows from	Runoff factors
Level 1 assets	0%
Level 2A assets	15%
Eligible RMBS	25%
Other Level 2B assets	50%
Margin lending backed by all other collateral	50%
All other assets	100%
Operational deposits held at other financial institutions	0%
Deposits held at centralized institution of a network of cooperative banks	0% of qualifying deposits
Amounts receivable from retail counterparties	50%
Amounts receivable from non-financial wholesale counterparties, from transactions other than those listed in the inflow categories above	50%
Amounts receivable from financial institutions, from transactions other than those listed in the inflow categories above	100%
Net derivative receivables	100%
Other contractual cash inflows	Treatment determined by supervisors in each jurisdiction

4.5   INSIDE THE LIQUIDITY COVERAGE RATIO

The LCR represents a hybrid combination of the stock-based approach and the maturity mismatch approach, aiming to identify a firm's counterbalancing capacity to react to a liquidity shock in the short term. It aims at building a sort of water tank to be used when liquidity needs increase unexpectedly [104], as represented in Figure 4.1, which was provided by the FSA's introductory presentation to liquidity risk (see [8]).

This technical measure is the answer to CEBS Recommendation 16 in [6], which requires that: "liquidity buffers, composed of cash and other highly liquid unencumbered assets, should be sufficient to enable an institution to weather liquidity stress during its defined 'survival period' without requiring adjustments to its business model." The liquidity buffer should be composed mainly of cash and most reliable liquid uncorrelated assets which banks can monetize on markets by true sales or repos regardless of their own condition without accepting large fire sale discounts. It is recommended to avoid holding a large concentration of single securities and currencies and there be no legal, regulatory or operational impediments to use them. In order to reduce the potential stigma effect banks should be active on a regular basis in each market in which they are holding assets for liquidity purposes and on platforms used to raise funds promptly in emergency cases.

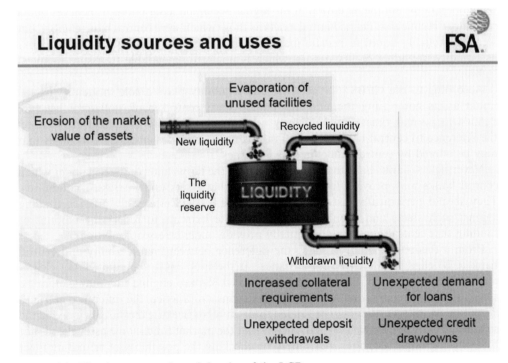

Figure 4.1. Visual representation of the aim of the LCR
Source: FSA's introductory presentation to liquidity risk [8]

The low correlation between a liquid asset and a holder is obviously of the utmost importance to assure the effectiveness of the liquidity buffer. The first version of the international framework for managing liquidity risk was issued after Lehman's collapse when government bonds had represented an actual "cushion" against the shock and recorded an impressive "flight to quality".

Unfortunately, over the last couple of years European peripheral government bonds have become one of the key issues for the euro crisis and for the soundness of banks' balance sheets, because of the large number of these securities held for trading and liquidity purposes. On February 10, 2011, the president of Banque De France, Christian Noyer, said: "We know by experience now, after the sovereign debt crisis, that the government debt securities market is not necessarily at all moments the most liquid and the safest, so that this concentration may be very risky."

Up to the present, Spanish and Italian bonds have been traded and funded by repos with good liquidity even in the most acute phases of the stress: therefore, the requirement for their marketability has always been respected. It was different for Portuguese and Greek bonds, which lacked liquidity after the two governments applied for IMF and EC funds. The monetization of these securities, for certain periods of time, has only been assured by ECB refinancing.

This example highlights the importance of properly analysing the link between an asset's monetization and its eligibility for central bank refinancing. For instance, the position of the FSA, strongly endorsed by the Bank of England, is that the buffer should focus on high-quality government bonds. According to the Bank of England it is particularly important that no automatic link be drawn between eligibility in central bank operations and the definition of the regulatory liquid asset buffer. It believes that a regulatory regime that defined liquid assets as those which were central bank eligible, but were not reliably liquid in private markets, would imply a reliance on central banks as liquidity providers or first resort, which is not recommendable to assure financial stability.

According to the CEBS [6], "central bank eligibility plays a role in identifying the liquid assets composing the liquidity buffer, since central bank collateral lists are defined in normal times predominantly around marketability criteria. Furthermore, the reference to central bank eligibility in this paper excludes emergency facilities that may be offered by central banks in stressed times."

Nevertheless, banks have to clearly understand the terms and conditions under which central banks may provide funding against eligible assets under stressed conditions. They should periodically test whether central banks will effectively provide funding against such assets and should apply appropriate haircuts to reflect the amount of funding that central banks might actually provide under stressed conditions.

From a theoretical point of view, the difference between marketability and central bank (CB) eligibility is clear: for instance, at the moment some equities are clearly marketable but not CB eligible, whereas some ABSs are eligible but they cannot be sold easily on the market under stressed conditions. In practice, the difference becomes narrower. Many securities may be funded through repos because they are included in the so-called "ECB eligible basket": this means that the market funds some asset classes not by analysing single securities, but simply by checking the possibility of refunding them by means of the CB if needed. In this case, ECB eligibility is a quality check stamp that helps to increase market demand for an asset (if banks believe that they will be able to generate liquidity from the CB and as the CB acts in some ways like a significant additional market participant) and allows refinancing of the security through the repo market; but this market behaviour is based on the mistaken belief that ECB eligibility means automatic marketability (because some CBs use marketability as the key criterion for determining their own eligibility list), with some dangerous procyclical impacts in case the ECB decides to no longer accept some securities as eligible collateral.

It is important for banks to demonstrate adequate diversification in the total composition of the buffer so as to guarantee to supervisors that they are not relying too heavily on access to central bank facilities as their main source of liquidity. On the other hand, regular participation in open market operations should not, *per se*, be interpreted as close dependence on central banks: as shown in Chapter 2, without CB liquidity banks would not be able to make their payment obligations at all.

The liquidity buffer represents the excess liquidity available outright to be used in liquidity stress situations within a given short-term period. Its size should be determined according to the funding gap under stressed conditions over some defined time horizon (the "survival period"), which represents just the time period during which any institution can continue operating without needing to generate additional funds and still meet all its payments due under the stress scenarios assumed: this topic, as well as the relation between the liquidity buffer and counterbalancing capacity, will be analysed in detail in the second part of the book. Both the liquidity buffer and survival periods should not represent exhaustive tools to manage liquidity risk: they should not supersede or replace other measures taken to manage the net funding gap and funding sources, as the institution's focus should be on surviving well beyond the stress period.

In order to define the severity of stress and the time horizon, the Basel Committee has defined another two dimensions of the analysis: a period of one month as the time horizon, by accepting the suggestion of the CEBS ("A survival period of at least one month should be applied to determine the overall size of the liquidity buffer under the chosen stress scenarios. Within this period, a shorter time horizon of at least one week should be also considered to reflect the need for a higher degree of confidence over the very short term," according to Guideline 3 on liquidity buffers [6]) and the characteristics of the assets to be eligible as a liquidity buffer.

Runoff factors are the drivers defined to implement the stress scenario for balance sheet items. In a very simplified approach they allow a static simulation to be run over assets and liabilities items in order to provide, as output, a synthetic ratio that combines features of both the stock-based and cash flow–based approaches. Fortunately, some questionable provisions of the previous version of the document have been properly amended in the recent draft [86]: for instance, the assumptions about the drawdown of credit and liquidity lines have been modulated according to the different types of borrowers and some severe percentages have been scaled back.

However, uncommitted lines should not be assumed to be drawn down as a matter of fact, but subject to an evaluation of the related reputational risk. As for secured lending (e.g., reverse repos), the approach still appears too binary: for high-quality liquid assets the haircuts are small, for other assets it is supposed there is no rollover at all. They are either fully liquid and part of the liquidity buffer or completely illiquid (in which case there are no cash inflows). This is at odds with actual experience, where things are not black and white, but often grey. In some cases the asymmetrical treatment of items is questionable: an owned liquidity line should not be denied and given the same drawdown assumption as a sold liquidity line.

Last but not least, inflows accepted for the LCR calculation have to be "contractual" for Italian banks (i.e., with a specific maturity agreed in the contract): therefore, so-called "sight assets", or assets on demand, are excluded from the calculation of inflows in the LCR as they do not have a defined contractual maturity. This obviously penalizes some jurisdictions, like the Italian one, where sight assets are the traditional instrument used by banks to finance their corporate customers. Actually, sight assets are not different from loans with a contractual maturity of less than 30 days and the probability that both are actually repaid is virtually the same, since the right to request payment with such terms contractually defined applies to the first ones as well.

4.6   THE OTHER METRICS

The net stable funding ratio is defined as the ratio of the bank's "available amount of stable funding" divided by its "required amount of stable funding". The standard requires that the ratio be no lower than 100%. It is designed to ensure that investment banking inventories, off-balance-sheet exposures, securitization pipelines and other assets and activities are funded with at least a minimum amount of stable liabilities in relation to their liquidity risk profiles, in order to limit overreliance on short-term wholesale funding during times of buoyant market liquidity.

The ultimate goal is to reduce the aggressive maturity transformation of the banking sector by creating an incentive to have a matched funding of assets at a higher level than in the past: this longer term structural liquidity ratio is therefore intended to deal with longer term structural liquidity mismatches by establishing a minimum acceptable amount of stable funding based on the liquidity characteristics of a firm's assets and activities over a one-year horizon. Ultimately, it represents a cap on liabilities/assets turnover.

Generally, the numerator in the ratio is calculated by applying to designated items on the right-hand side of the balance sheet (the liabilities side) an ASF (available stable funding) factor, ranging from 100% to 0% depending on the particular equity or liability component, with the factor reflecting the stability of funding. Similarly, the denominator in the ratio is calculated by applying to each asset on the left-hand side of the balance sheet (the assets side) and certain off-balance-sheet commitments a specified required stable funding (RSF) factor, reflecting the amount of the particular item that supervisors believe should be supported with stable funding. More specifically, with respect to the numerator in the ratio:

- available stable funding is defined as the total amount of a bank's capital (Tier 1 and 2 capital after deductions), plus preferred stock with a maturity of one year or more, plus liabilities with effective maturities of one year or more, plus that portion of stable non-maturity deposits and/or term deposits with maturities of less than one year which would be expected to stay with the bank for an extended period in an idiosyncratic stress event;
- ASF factors range from 100% to 0%, with more stable funding sources having higher ASF factors and, accordingly, contributing more to meeting the minimum 100% requirement. For example, Tier 1 and 2 capital are assigned 100% factors, stable

retail deposits 85%, less stable retail deposits 70%, certain wholesale funding and deposits from non-financial corporate customers 50%, and other liabilities and equity categories 0%.

With respect to the denominator in the ratio:

- the required amount of stable funding is calculated as the sum of the value of assets held, after converting certain off-balance-sheet exposures to asset equivalents, multiplied by a specified RSF factor;
- RSF factors range from 0% to 100%, with less stable funding sources having lower RSF factors and, accordingly, contributing more to meeting the minimum 100% requirement. For example, cash and money market instruments are assigned a 0% factor, unencumbered marketable securities with maturities of one year or more and representing claims on sovereigns a 5% factor, unencumbered AA corporate bonds with maturity of one year or more 20%, gold 50%, loans to retail clients having a maturity of less than one year 85%, and all other assets 100%.

The introduction of a binding NSFR is likely to produce significant impacts on the real economy, because the ratio represents an actual limit to the maturity transformation performed by banks. They are requested to work according to the "matched funding" criterion, which is likely to lead to a general review of current liquidity pricing policies, with loans more expensive for corporate and private customers. Moreover, it tends to discourage securitization activities, through which banks transform their illiquid assets into more liquid instruments.

As the ABSs resulting from the securitization process are likely to be non-marketable instruments, all holdings of these ABSs with a weighted average life exceeding one year are 100% accounted for in the determination of required stable funding and must be watched with medium/long-term funding. From the perspective of a bank willing to grant medium/long-term credit to its customers in the form of mortgages, credit card loans, personal loans, etc. the NSFR states that loans with maturities exceeding one year must be funded with medium/long-term funding up to percentages that depend on loan credit quality and are completely independent of the possibility of being securitized. As a result, lending banks cannot draw any benefits in terms of treasury from securitizations.

The BCBS agreed that the NSFR will move to a minimum standard by January 1, 2018, in order to avoid any unintended consequences on the functioning of the funding market. Similarly, as pointed out earlier about the LCR, it will be very challenging for the financial sector to support the real economy without the normal functioning of capital markets, whereas banks are focused on lengthening the longer term of funding and reducing maturity mismatch by scaling back activities vulnerable to stress tests. The EBA, based on reporting required by regulation, will evaluate how a stable funding requirement should be designed. On the basis on this evaluation, the Commission should report to the Council and the European Parliament together with any appropriate proposals in order to introduce such a requirement by 2018. Although the last version of the BCBS document about liquidity ratios confirmed January 1, 2018 as the start date for the NSFR, the phase-in period defined for the LCR obviously suggests that a similar approach could be introduced in the near future for the NSFR as well.

Last but not least, the liquidity proposal outlines four monitoring tools, or metrics, to accompany the two ratios with the intention of providing "the cornerstone of information which aids supervisors in assessing the liquidity risk of a bank.". The metrics aim to address contractual maturity mismatch, concentration of funding, available unencumbered assets and market-related monitoring tools.

Contractual maturity mismatch collects all contractual cash and security inflows and outflows, from all on and off-balance-sheet items, which have been mapped to define time bands based on their respective maturities. The precise time buckets are to be defined by national supervisors.

Concentration of funding is measured by the following data: the ratio of funding liabilities sourced from each significant counterparty to the "balance sheet total" (total liabilities plus shareholders' equity), the ratio of funding liabilities sourced from each significant product/instrument to the bank's balance sheet total, as well as a list of asset and liability amounts by each significant currency. Each metric should be reported separately for time horizons.

Box 4.5. What does "significant" stand for in the preceding paragraph?

A "significant counterparty is defined as a single counterparty or group of affected or affiliated counterparties accounting in aggregate for more than 1% of a bank's total liabilities. Similarly, a "significant instrument/product" is defined as a single instrument/product or group of similar instruments/products which in aggregate amount to more than 1% of the bank's total liabilities, and a "significant currency" is defined as liabilities denominated in a single currency, which in aggregate amount to more than 1% of the bank's total liabilities.

Diversifying the number of counterparty names is a very common strategy, but it is not always effective, because wholesale fund providers are often cynical arbiters of credit quality. They may take some days longer than others before refusing to extend credit, but the end result is the same: during a liquidity crisis it hardly represents a stable funding source.

A far cleverer approach is to diversify the type of counterparty, instead of the name. Actually, all institutional fund givers set their own counterparty limits restricting the amount they can provide to any single borrower, no matter the form of the borrowing.

Some concentration in counterparty type does not always represent a negative factor: let us think about retail deposits, which are actually stickier than other types. This is a case of concentration that almost certainly reduces risk. Diversification by counterparty type should focus on assuring that, among the most volatile funding sources, there is no significant concentration for a single counterparty, for a group of similar counterparties or for single markets.

As already noted, since retail deposits tend to be more stable even during crises while wholesale funding tends to be more volatile and to dry up more quickly, it is crucial to analyse the degree of diversification of the funding. Oddly, although the connection between diversification and liquidity risk is well known, in the past many firms have failed to grasp how the relationship can contribute to liquidity shortage.

Northern Rock is a good example: it maintained a low level of diversification from the perspective of both assets (business segment specialization) and liabilities (retail deposit base) and, on the verge of collapse, was saved by the Bank of England in August 2007. Ironically, only two months before, it had stated that calculations of capital requirements showed an excess of capital, allowing the bank to initiate a capital repatriation program: when performing these calculations, the bank obviously failed to take into account all factors that could affect its liquidity position even in the very short term, like the dangerous concentration of its balance sheet.

The aim of the two other tools is only informational. Available unencumbered assets are defined as "unencumbered assets that are marketable as collateral in secondary markets and/or eligible for central banks' standing facilities." For an asset to be counted in this metric, the bank must have already put in place operational procedures needed to monetize it. Market-related monitoring tools are early-warning indicators of potential liquidity difficulties at banks. They include market-wide information, financial sector–related and bank-specific data.

Although monitoring tools used to be downplayed by academics and practitioners who prefer to focus on ratios, stress scenarios and contingency funding plans, they are of the utmost importance in filling the gap of information asymmetries between financial actors and regulators. By gathering exhaustive and granular data from covered entities, regulators can remove one structural issue that represents one of the root causes of liquidity risk—asymmetric information—which does prevent distinguishing between illiquid and insolvent banks and blurs interbank peer-monitoring among financial players.

4.7 INTRADAY LIQUIDITY RISK

For the largest banks, deeply involved in settlement and payment systems, another crucial risk to monitor is represented by intraday liquidity risk. It is related to intraday liquidity, which can be defined as [101] "funds which can be accessed during the business day, usually to enable financial institutions to make payments in real-time."

This topic has received little attention by regulators until recently. It was only in July 2012 that it gained momentum with the consultative document *Monitoring Indicators for Intraday Liquidity Management* issued by the BCBS.

Surprisingly, this document lacks a clear definition of intraday liquidity risk and focuses only on intraday liquidity management (i.e., the measurement and mitigation of this risk in order to ensure the reasonable continuation of payment flows and the smooth functioning of payment and settlement systems).

Intraday liquidity risk is related to cases in which banks are not able to actively manage their intraday liquidity positions to meet payment and settlement obligations on a timely basis under both normal and stressed conditions: for direct participants to payment systems, because outgoing payment flows can precede compensating incoming payment flows and sources, including collateral transformation, overdrafts and extraordinary sources; for indirect participants, because the correspondent bank can be under liquidity or operational stress. Such relevant elements as intraday liquidity profiles can therefore differ between banks depending on whether they access payment and settlement systems directly or indirectly, or whether or not they provide correspondent banking services and intraday credit facilities to other banks.

Box 4.6. BCBS Principle 8

The BCBS refers to intraday liquidity risk in [99], Principle 8, which suggests, *inter alia*, that a bank

- should have the capacity to measure expected daily gross liquidity inflows and outflows, anticipate the intraday timing of these flows where possible and forecast the range of potential net funding shortfalls that might arise at different points during the day;
- have the capacity to monitor intraday liquidity positions against expected activities and available resources (balances, remaining intraday credit facility and available collateral);
- arrange to acquire sufficient intraday funding to meet its intraday objectives;
- have the ability to manage and mobilize collateral as necessary to obtain intraday funds;
- have a robust capability to manage the timing of its liquidity outflows in line with its intraday objectives.

In its consultative document [101], the BCBS seeks feedback from the financial industry about some indicators designed to enable banking supervisors to monitor a bank's intraday liquidity risk management and to gain (i) a better understanding of payment and settlement behaviour and (ii) the management of intraday liquidity risk by banks.

It has been stressed [102] that the proposed indicators are for monitoring purposes only and do not represent the introduction of new standards around intraday liquidity management. Nevertheless, there is a concern that these requirements could represent the first step toward defining new binding indicators, with potential overlapping with the LCR. Bank data demonstrating insufficient liquidity over specific time intervals, or operation very close to the bone with its daily liquidity flows, will be scrutinized by supervisors: this could drive banks to slow the pace of scheduled payments so that their results appear stronger on both absolute and relative bases, with an increase in systemic risk. Moreover, if banks decide to withhold scheduled payments, gridlock across and between multiple payments systems may ensue. This scenario could become procyclical during periods of systemic stress, when many correspondent banks increase prefunding requirements. It is crucial that the final release gives greater prominence and clarifies beyond any doubt that these indicators are simple monitoring tools.

Some concern is related to the monitoring and reporting requirements for indirect payment system participants. First, many banks are direct participants in some systems and indirect participants in others, with needs to aggregate data for different purposes. Second, indirect participants lose control of their payments once they submit instructions to the correspondent bank, because payments are made at the correspondent bank's discretion: this inability to control when payments are actually made or to receive in many cases intraday liquidity data could obviously affect the reporting of indirect participants. Finally, for all banks collecting intraday liquidity data will represent a very challenging task, with significant issues of capacity in gathering and storing thousands upon thousands of data points every month for all used payment systems across all legal entities, all significant overseas branches and all currencies [103].

Box 4.7. The proposed set of indicators for intraday liquidity risk

The list of indicators proposed by the BCBS [101] is:

- Daily maximum liquidity requirement: this is the bank's largest negative net cumulative position (difference between the value of payments received and the value of payments made at any point in the day) calculated on actual settlement times during the day. The actual use of liquidity instead of what is required to fulfil payment obligations in a timely manner is counterintuitive, because in several systems payments are released earlier than required to ensure smooth flows: measuring actual use could discourage such beneficial timing decisions and increase payments hoarding. Moreover, because payments are a zero-sum game, at the same time there will be at least one bank in a positive position and one in a negative situation. This requires good management and continuous judgement to properly address not only the activity of a single bank but also to avoid gridlock in the system and operational risk for the banking system.
- Available intraday liquidity: this is the amount of intraday liquidity available at the start of each business day and the lowest amount of available intraday liquidity by value on a daily basis throughout the reporting period. All forms of liquidity buffers and reserves potentially represent intraday liquidity and should be considered, because the stress scenarios analysed by this consultative document are exactly those for which the LCR buffer is held.
- Total payments: these are the total value of the gross daily payments made and received in payment and settlement systems.
- Time-specific and other critical obligations: these are obligations which must be settled at a specific time within the day or have an expected intraday settlement deadline. Unfortunately, for a large bank cutoff times are actually scheduled at least at every hour during the day. Banks should report the volume and value of obligations and the same figures for obligations missed during the report period.
- Value of customer payments made on behalf of financial institution customers: this is the gross value of daily payments made on behalf of all financial institution customers, with the value for the largest five financial institution customers given in greater detail.
- Intraday credit lines extended to financial institution customers: this is the total sum of intraday credit lines extended to all financial institution customers, with the value of secured and unsecured credit as well as of committed and uncommitted lines for the largest five financial institution customers given in greater detail.
- Timing of intraday payments: this is the average time of a bank's daily payment settlements over a reporting period.
- Intraday throughput: this is the proportion, by value, of a bank's outgoing payments that settle by specific times during the day (i.e., 9.00 AM, 10.00 AM, etc.)

Banks would be obliged to report these indicators once a month, along with the average level, the highest and lowest value for each indicator, under normal times and four stress scenarios (own financial stress, counterparty stress, customer stress, market-wide credit or liquidity stress). In addition, they have to report the 5th percentile value for available intraday liquidity, and the 95th percentile value for the other six quantitative indicators.

4.8 BEYOND THE RATIOS

The aim of the regulator was clearly to define some effective measures to be implemented by all covered entities, from the more complex financial group to the smallest bank. This represents a kind of simplified standard approach that gives the international financial industry a common "level playing field" on liquidity risk.

One of the most obvious criticisms of these measures is related to this one-size-fits-all approach. These ratios are calculated with predefined standard aggregations and stress assumptions, but these assumptions should differ across banks according to their different sizes and business models, such that the operating processes prevailing in different countries are also considered.

The "one-size-fits-all" assumption sets for both ratios cannot properly fit the differences in the funding processes of different economies: for instance, within the eurozone, households' savings are different in amounts and structures, notably due to tax incentives (e.g., the Netherlands, France); corporate behaviour regarding deposits is not standardized and strongly depends on all outstanding relations with the bank (e.g., Italy).

To the extent that funding requirements would not be consistent with what funding providers (i.e., households at the end of the day) can deliver in balance or terms, or with the required rates to attract those funds compared with the acceptable rates for funding needs (i.e., households, corporates and governments), the impacts would be detrimental to the economy as a whole. These effects would be more significant on the European economy, as it is bank-intermediated much more than the US economy in the funding process.

Both ratios treat assets and liabilities in many cases in an asymmetric way: inflows and liabilities are always subject to time decay, whereas in some cases outflows and assets are required to be mapped as constant maturity products. This leads banks to overfund the actual need of the investment and to reinvest liquidity excess in shorter term or in highly liquid assets.

Focussing on the LCR, one of the most widespread criticisms across the financial community relates to the use of liquidity buffers during phases of stress. Since the prudential stressed scenario defined by runoff factors, as above explained, represents de facto a situation with already severe liquidity strains, common sense would suggest that buffers, or at least some of them, should be used in cases of crisis, acting as anticyclical factors that can be replenished as soon as market conditions allow. Disallowing this would mean no longer discussing liquidity buffers, but some form of unavailable collateral instead, pledged to cover unspecified risks that could occur after the likely liquidity crisis of the bank.

Obviously, regulators have to face a challenging tradeoff between easing the tough requirement of LCR above 100% in any state of the world and risking allowing banks to use and evaporate the main line of defence against liquidity shocks before the crisis moves toward the most acute phase of stress. The January 2013 draft addresses this issue in a general way, by stating that "during a period of financial stress, however, banks may use their stock of HQLA, thereby falling below 100%, as maintaining the LCR at 100% under such circumstances could produce undue negative effects on the bank and other market participants. Supervisors will subsequently assess this situation and will adjust their response flexibly according to the circumstances". While stressing the opportunity of accounting not only for the prevailing macrofinancial conditions, but also the forward-looking assessments of macroeconomic and financial conditions, the BCBS provides a list of potential factors that supervisors should consider in their assessment in order to avoid some procyclical effects:

- the reason the LCR fell below 100% (i.e., using the stock of HQLA, an inability to roll over secured funding or large unexpected draws on contingent obligations, general conditions of credit and funding markets);
- the extent to which the reported decline in the LCR is due to firm-specific or market-related shock;
- a bank's overall health and risk profile;
- the magnitude, duration and frequency of the reported decline in HQLA;
- the potential for contagion of the financial system and additional restricted flow of credit or reduced market liquidity due to actions to maintain an LCR at 100%;
- the availability of other sources of contingent funding such as CB funding.

The observation period of the LCR is clearly standardized, but for a bank involved in correspondent banking, clearing and settlement activities, even a 30-day timeline could be too long. As for the application, ongoing monitoring is required and reported at least monthly, with any delay less than 2 weeks. Even if a higher reporting frequency is required during stressful times, non-continuous monitoring could turn out to be suboptimal because it could easily be behind the curve. Both ratios look at the liquidity gap over some predefined time horizons: no information is provided about liquidity exposures over other periods of time.

Let us turn to the role played by capital in both ratios: it is eligible for the NSFR as a stable funding source, whereas it is taken into account for the LCR only to the extent it is invested in eligible liquid assets. The basic idea put forward by the Basel Committee is that banks should first raise some amount of new capital, and then invest it to build a liquid asset buffer that is compliant with liquidity requirements.

On the question of derivatives, the BCBS requires consideration be given to the largest absolute net (based on both realized outflows and inflows) 30-day collateral flow realized during the preceding 24 months as an outflow for the LCR. This requirement should aim to capture banks' potential and substantial liquidity risk exposure to changes in mark-to-market evaluation of derivatives transactions, under collateral agreements, that can lead to additional collateral posting in case of adverse market movements. Unfortunately, it would have been better to adopt an approach based on the actual exposure of the derivative portfolio to market parameters, instead of measuring this potential outflow on the basis of a lookback approach. Indeed, the current requirement, although very easily implemented by all covered entities, could fail to capture the actual liquidity risk in case of increased market risk exposures compared with those of the past.

The need to increase the size of the liquid asset buffer (for the LCR) and to raise medium/long-term liquidity (for the NSFR) is likely to impact financial markets. So, the decision to fix different timelines for the ratios is welcome: an observation period until 2015 for the LCR and 2018 for the NSFR. Nevertheless, the ratios' requirements are likely to generate some distorting effects on bond markets, as already seen in recent years with the increasing demand for government bonds. In fact, additional shifts in demand towards assets eligible for inclusion in the liquidity buffer are to be expected.

Last but not least, let us look at things from the treasurer's perspective. The already dying interbank deposit market is likely to be over or, at least, drastically reshaped. Both the LCR and NSFR are based on stress assumptions that no maturing interbank liabilities will be rolled over and no new interbank funding will be available. This means that banks can only rely on outstanding interbank funding to the extent that they possess a contractually formalised right to avoid repayment for more than 30 days (LCR) or for more than one year (NSFR).

4.9   CONCLUSION

Over the last five years policymakers have tried to develop and reinforce some effective measures and tools to monitor and manage liquidity risk by enhancing supervision and regulation. G-SIFI supervision and the Basel III requirements in terms of liquidity ratios represent only the first step toward defining a comprehensive framework for handling the negative externalities derived from banks' liquidity risk management and improve the resilience of the financial sector to severe shocks. While the UK and the USA seem at the moment to be in better shape to face the new challenges from financial innovation in order to preserve financial stability, Europe has still a lot of homework to do. The banking supervision assigned to the ECB is only the first step to addressing certain relevant issues that threaten to undermine the future path of European construction. Other measures (such as a eurozone-wide system of deposit insurance and a European resolution scheme and rescue fund) need to be quickly implemented in order to break the vicious circle between the debt government crisis and the banking system. These are prerequisites to restoring confidence in the banking system and to allowing effective regulation. Unless confidence in the banks is restored, every measure defined by regulation is likely not to achieve its goals.

The new liquidity framework defined by Basel III is an important "piece of the puzzle" to building sound and consistent liquidity practices updated by financial innovation and the continuous development of the financial sector. It is a simple one-size-fits-all approach valid for the whole international financial system, and aims to represent a basic level playing field. It is likely to play the same role as the Basel I framework (i.e., waiting for the future development of the industry in order to admit internal and more evolved models). Even before actual introduction (the LCR is scheduled for 2015 and the NSFR by 2018) some measures already require some fine-tuning, primary among which is a wider list of eligible assets for inclusion in a liquidity buffer in order to reduce significant recourse to government bonds to build a liquidity cushion. However, the new liquidity standard is expected to be the object of continuous fine-tuning so as not to cause any unintended consequences such as pricing or market distortions, and to be properly scheduled in order to avoid procyclical effects on the economic cycle.

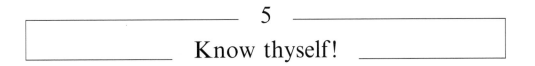

5

Know thyself!

5.1 INTRODUCTION

When the ancient Greeks went into the forecourt of the temple of Apollo at Delphi they would read the aphorism "Know thyself" inscribed on the wall. This maxim likely derives from an Egyptian proverb, which called on initiates to prove their worth so that they could acquire higher knowledge ("Man, know thyself ... and thou shalt know the gods").

In the dialogue *Philebus*, Plato argues that gaining more knowledge of ourselves would lead us to a greater understanding of the nature of human beings. Gods and human beings are beyond the scope of this analysis but, focusing on the financial sector, it is obvious that knowing our own financial institution better is a prerequisite to being better equipped to cope with the liquidity risk associated with it.

As argued in the previous chapter, the main contribution provided by the new international regulatory framework on liquidity risk is not the two binding ratios, which are a simple combination and evolution of existing liquidity measures already used by the industry, but the comprehensive development of sound management and supervision practices about liquidity risk. This moves away from the definition of specific liquidity risk tolerance, defined by top management according to their business strategy, and calls for an articulate system of risk management, product pricing, performance measurement to warrant full consistency between risk-taking incentives for business lines and the related liquidity risk exposures for the bank as a whole.

In this framework early-warning signals, what-if analyses and internal stress test scenarios are crucial and have to be tailor-made on the basis of the risks of the business model: each bank is therefore called to analyse in detail its own business in order to identify and to face as properly as possible the worst (or a combination of) liquidity stressed scenarios and survive them by making the impact on ongoing business as small as possible.

5.2 SOME CHANGES ON THE LIABILITIES SIDE

It has already been pointed out, liquidity risk lies at the heart of traditional banking activity where banks do their business by performing maturity transformation to fund less liquid long-term assets with more liquid short-term liabilities. By doing their traditional financial intermediation, commercial banks play a pivotal role in the real economy and mitigate some negative effects related to several market failures, such as incomplete markets or asymmetric information. They facilitate payments and the smooth transfer of goods and services. They match savers who may lack detailed knowledge of borrowers and who usually want to be able to withdraw their money at short notice with borrowers who often wish to repay their loans over a longer term

horizon, according to the returns of their investment projects. This maturity transformation is essentially addressed to allow capital to be invested in a productive way in order
to support economic growth.

The key factor to success with this activity is to manage carefully the liabilities side of
the balance sheet, according to the different degree of monetization of the assets: the less
liquid the asset side of the balance sheet, the more stable the funding sources have to be,
such as savings or retail deposits, or medium/long-term wholesale funding. A stable
funding source is a prerequisite to carrying out maturity transformation over time,
because it has to be rolled out in the short term in order to fund the less liquid and
longer term asset that has an economic positive return.

Unfortunately, in the financial world nothing remains the same for very long: business
models based on very liquid funding sources, such as the unsecured money market in the
last two decades, did not perform as expected in the 2000s financial environment [37]. In
the 1980s and early 1990s commercial banks played a central role in financial systems,
acting as a redistribution function of liquidity, because they had a quasi-monopoly on
the collection of deposits. The US fund industry was still developing, in Europe and
Japan money market funds did not yet exist, and households were left with no choice but
to hold their balances with commercial banks. With high segmentation between the
traditional peer-to-peer interbank market and other financial segments, the resources
collected by financial institutions and pension funds did not necessarily find their way
onto the broader capital market. Moreover, security issuance as a funding instrument
was less important and asset-backed repos were used only anecdotally in the interbank
market by trading desks to cover their short exposure, but not for liquidity management
purposes. This was a typical bank-centric financial system, where commercial banks
collected money from other players such as central banks, private customers andfirms.

In the second part of the 1990s the bank-centric system was quickly over. The
disintermediation of the money market led to substantial changes in commercial banks'
liability mixes: security issuances and securitized funding had to compensate the
reduction of interbank unsecured liabilities and of sight/term customer deposits.

Three main factors had significantly altered the distribution of liquidity in the
interbank market and its very functioning: the mainstreaming of the fund management
industry, the advent of repo operations and the entry of new players like pension funds
and insurance companies. Money funds and pension funds are now collectors of private
savings in competition with the banking system: in many cases they had replaced banks
in their function of collecting money from the private sector, by de facto reducing the
total liquidity pool of the interbank unsecured money market.

As a consequence, banks had to deeply reorganize their funding channels. As
customer savings shifted towards the fund management industry, banks started to
borrow from money market funds in the wholesale market using different instruments
(CD/CP issuance and repo operations among others). Obviously, this substitution was
not painless for them, because they replaced stable funding with more volatile sources.
Over time this kind of funding gradually overtook the traditional funding model of
deposits from rich banks using long cash positions to place funds with interbank
counterparties.

The significant reduction in the percentage of interbank unsecured funding recorded
over the last decade pushed banks to optimize monetization of the asset side of their
balance sheets, starting from the more liquid securities with an active repo market. For

instance, data from the French Banking Commission, collected in 2006 (i.e., before the start of the financial crisis that deadlocked the unsecured money market), already recorded a significant shift in the composition of banks' liabilities: the share of French interbank liabilities was equal to 22% in 2006 down from 39% in 1990. Nowadays, market-related funding of banks is essentially securitized or security related, with a negligible contribution from the unsecured interbank channel: this has obviously increased market funding liquidity embedded within the bank's balance sheet.

This relative decline in interbank transactions versus other liabilities was accompanied by a gradual shift of the traded volume towards the very short term. This phenomenon was strictly related to two different factors.

First, back-office and trading system automation allowed a greater number of transactions to be carried out per day so that the material burden of rolling over many ON and TN operations ceased to be an issue. This led to impressive activity on the very short-term tenors of the repo market, which allow banks to roll over their position on a daily basis with lower costs, not by reducing the risk premium embedded in the interest rate term structure, but by increasing the dependence on market liquidity.

Second, the increased importance of regulatory capital adequacy constraints dramatically shortened the potential horizon of unsecured interbank operations, such as treasurers witness at every end of quarter. Since treasurers reduced the term of their interbank loans, while still being willing to borrow unsuccessfully at longer term maturity, they set in motion a self-fulfilling mechanism that gradually hollowed tenors beyond 1 month, making it almost impossible to raise significant amounts for longer terms.

Figures 5.1 to 5.4 show some aggregate data from the ECB's 2012 *Euro Money Market Survey* (see [18]), conducted on 105 active banks in the euro money market: average daily volumes on both the unsecured lending and borrowing sides are lowering year by year versus substantial constant figures for secured funding, with a strong concentration of unsecured transactions on overnight tenor.

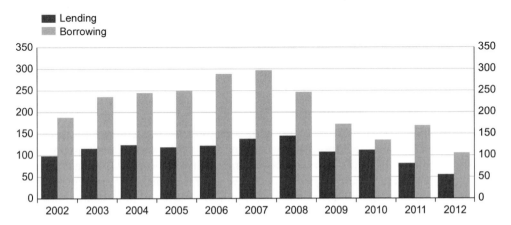

Figure 5.1. Average daily turnover in unsecured lending and borrowing (index cash lending volume in 2002 = 100)
Source: ECB's *Euro Money Market Survey* (2012) [18]

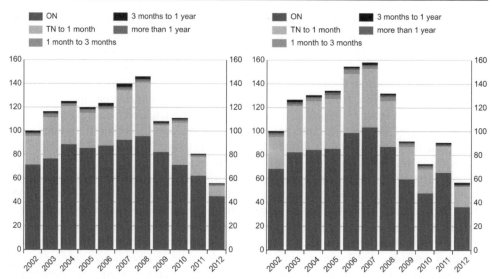

Figure 5.2. Maturity breakdown for average daily turnover in unsecured lending (left-hand side) and borrowing (right-hand side) (index cash lending volume in 2002 = 100)
Source: ECB's *Euro Money Market Survey* (2012) [18]

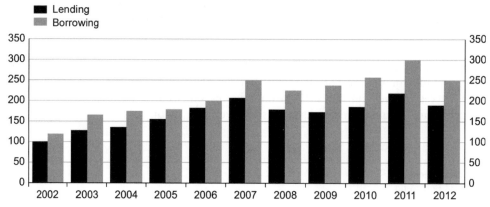

Figure 5.3. Average daily turnover in secured lending and borrowing (index cash lending volume in 2002 = 100)
Source: ECB's *Euro Money Market Survey* (2012) [18]

To sum up, the current state of the money market is characterized by three key features: (a) interbank operations in the narrow sense (peer-to-peer) now represent a much smaller share of banks' market-related funding than in the past; (b) banks' market funding is now more reliant on banks' access to several segments of the repo market, securitized funding, or on how they raise funds by means of non-banking entities (money market funds, insurance companies and pension funds through repos or CD/ CP subscriptions), which have become actual significant lenders in the money market; and, last but not least, for the consequences on the derivative products, (c) Libor/ Euribor quotations now represent only a remote proxy of their overall funding costs.

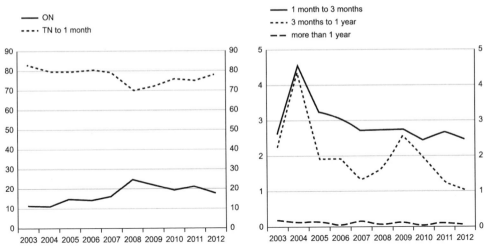

Figure 5.4. Maturity breakdown for average daily turnover in secured lending and borrowing
Source: ECB's *Euro Money Market Survey* (2012) [18]

5.3 THE ROLE OF LEVERAGE

Use of the repo market as the main source to fund the marketable asset side of the balance sheet has produced an interesting effect on how banks adjust the ratio known as "leverage" (i.e., the ratio of total assets to equity or net worth in response to any variation in the value of their balance sheet assets [1]).

As liabilities are more volatile than assets, commercial banks used to increase their liabilities more than they increased their assets during booms; they do the reverse during downturns. Thus, the overall book leverage of commercial banks, calculated as the value of the total assets divided by the value of total equity (where equity is calculated as assets minus liabilities) tends to rise during booms and to fall during downturns, showing a procyclical pattern.

It is interesting to note that for commercial banks a large proportion of assets are represented by loans carried in the financial accounts at book value rather than being adjusted for the fluctuations in value that arise from changes in market and credit risk over the cycle. This feature is not replicated in the financial account of security brokers and dealers, or that of investment banks generally, whose assets are securities, receivables or claims that are either marketable or very short term in nature: thus, the discrepancy between book and market values is smaller for investment banks than for commercial ones.

As shown in [2] there is a strongly positive relationship between leverage and the total assets of investment banks. This result can be reached only if investment banks actively respond to a rise in asset value by expanding their balance sheets because, *ceteris paribus*, a rise in the value of total assets would boost equity as a proportion of total assets, leading instead to a decline in leverage. The instrument used by investment banks to expand their balance sheets is collateralized borrowing or, more precisely, repos: they allow securities on the asset side of the balance sheet to be funded at a higher market value, by increasing the funding amount to be invested in other assets with respect to the initial purchase value.

Box 5.1. The Libor review: mission impossible?

Both Libor and Euribor are benchmark rates widely used as reference indexes in international money markets and for derivative products [76]. The former is published by the British Bankers' Association (BBA) for a given number of currencies, the latter by the European Banking Federation (EBF) for the euro. They are set by assessments of the interbank market made by a number of banks, which contribute rate submissions each business day as panel members selected by the BBA and EBF.

These submissions do not represent averages of the relevant banks' transacted rates on a given day (as occurred for Eonia); rather, both indexes require contributing banks to exercise their subjective judgement in evaluating the rates at which money may be available in the interbank market in determining their submissions.

The nature of the judgement required differs for the two rates: Libor is defined by the BBA as "the rate at which an individual contributor panel bank could borrow funds, were it to do so by asking for and then accepting interbank offers in reasonable market size just prior to 11:00 London time"; Euribor is defined as "the rate at which euro interbank term deposits are being offered within the EMU zone by one prime bank to another at 11:00 AM Brussels time" [10]. Hence, banks quoting Libor submissions are passing on information about themselves, while for Euribor they are called to forecast the funding level of a theoretical prime bank.

Over the last five years the persistent and severe discontinuation of deposit trading eroded the incentives or the ability for market participants to price fixings correctly hence implying the indexes were doomed to lose their physical anchor to the underlying market and become more notional references. In such cases, as a large number of rates applied to retail and corporate customers are indexed on these fixings, any mispricing would automatically be translated in rates applied to the real economy. Moreover, derivatives cash-settled on these fixings (like Liffe Euribor or CME eurodollar futures) could be subject to disanchored evolution, with an arbitrage relationship that no longer works: the effects of these "virtual" rates, detached from reality, could be dramatic for trillions of derivative products written on such references.

The financial crisis eventually put under scrutiny the effectiveness of such references for a dying interbank market, but the *coup de grâce* for this instable construction was struck by widespread suspicions that Libor/Euribor rates were being rigged, initially driven by greed and later used to downplay the intensity of funding stress on the banking system, and by a lot of evidence showing attempts to game the benchmark by the contributing banks.

The fixing system was definitely broken and had to be refixed. The Wheatley Review in September 2012 suggested reducing Libor fixings to only five currencies (GBP, EUR, JPY, CHF and USD), with minor tenors scrapped and quotations not only always verifiable, but also reflective of actual transactions and real-life bank borrowing costs [43]. This approach aims at phasing out the Libor system without generating any significant market disruption related to the switch to a new benchmark, but obviously it is not able to address the main problem: if the interbank money market dries up again or simply does not restart at a size that is significant there is no means to verify the quality of the quotations.

Sooner or later market participants will be forced to find some new benchmark to succeed Libor/Euribor. One candidate is the OIS rate, quoted on the same tenors required for Libor/Euribor: the reference rate for OIS is the only unsecured money market index calculated on actual transactions (i.e., the ON index which is based on Eonia, Fed Fund Effective Rate, Sonia, etc.). This feature supports the call for OIS rates as natural successors to Libor/Euribor. Daily fixings for Eonia swaps are already provided in the eurozone by the same contributing panel of Euribor, and the OIS market in the short term is very liquid, with operative prices and sizes always available and verifiable.

OIS rates already meet four of the five criteria required to be accepted as a Libor replacement by the Wheatley Review: to be resilient to stress and illiquidity, to have a liquid underlying market across multiple currencies, to avoid too much complexity, to have a measurable history to allow past comparison for pricing and risk models [95]. Only coverage of all maturities is missing, because liquidity is often inadequate for longer maturities of minor currencies.

Starting to use this rate as a new reference benchmark for OTC derivatives surely would help to improve market liquidity, combined with the circumstance that the OIS market is already growing on longer maturities because OIS rates have now become the standard for collateralized derivatives discounting. The main objection is that OIS rates may represent a fair proxy only for pure interest rate exposures, they do not reflect actual bank funding costs. This may be well and good, but since many banks currently are no longer able to fund themselves at Libor/Euribor flat, where is the great difference between calculating actual funding costs as spreads over Libor/Euribor or over OIS?

Investment banks acts procyclically, by increasing their liabilities by more than their assets have risen during booms and by doing the reverse during downturns. Investment banks' actions are driven by the risk models and economic capital measures adopted. In particular, banks will adjust assets and liabilities to ensure their total equity is proportional to the total value at risk (VaR) of their assets. For a given amount of equity, a lower VaR allows banks to expand their balance sheets: since this measure or risk is by definition countercyclical, lower during booms and higher during busts, the bank's efforts to control risk will likely lead to procyclical leverage.

Let us consider a boom scenario in which the assets held by financial players with procyclical leverage increase in price. This price increase will boost the equity as a proportion of total assets, with leverage falling. Because institutions have procyclical leverage, they will respond to this erosion by raising leverage upward. The easier way is to borrow more, then use these proceeds to buy more of the assets they already hold: this behaviour clearly reverses the normal demand response. Increased demand for assets leads to upward pressure on its prices, with potential circular feedback effects.

During downturns, the mechanism works in reverse: the net worth of institutions will fall faster than the rate at which the value of their assets decreases, by increasing de facto their leverage. Hence, they will attempt to reduce leverage quite drastically in some cases, as happened in 2008: they will try to sell some assets, then use the proceeds to pay down debt. Thus, a fall in the price of the assets can lead to an increase in the supply of the assets, overturning the normal supply response to a drop in asset price. This greater supply will exercise downward pressure on asset prices, by fuelling a negative feedback effect.

The massive recourse to collateralized lending and borrowing by financial institutions, especially by investment banks, as the main tool to manage their procyclical leverage, allows the balance sheet to expand and contract by amplifying, rather than counter-acting, the credit cycle, and can distort in a number of ways the effects of the traditional measures of monetary policy based on money stock. A deeper analysis of the evolution of the stock of overall collateralized borrowing during the different phases of the economic cycle is therefore strongly suggested not only for financial players in order to better monitor the functioning of the money market and to capture the role played by the adjustment of institutions' balance sheets and the overall supply of liquidity, but also for policymakers in order to fine-tune the size and timing of their monetary measures.

5.4   THE ORIGINATE-TO-DISTRIBUTE BUSINESS MODEL

Over the last decade, the greatest change to impact the asset side of banks' balance sheets has undoubtedly been the development of credit risk transfer (CRT) techniques, often known as securitization. These techniques were developed in the US but quickly spread throughout the world thanks to the interaction between deregulation (which eliminates barriers between investment and commercial banking by fostering com-petition within the financial system), development in technology (via dramatic improve-ments in the storage, processing and pricing of financial data) and financial innovation (which makes markets more complete by satisfying more complex financing needs and more frequent requests for structured riskier investments with higher returns). Secur-itization can be defined as the process whereby individual bank loans or other formerly illiquid assets are bundled together into tradable securities that are sold within the secondary market to economic agents that have additional capacity to bear the risk of associated assets.

Over recent years, securitization activity has definitely changed the monitoring role played by banks, reducing their fundamental function of liquidity transformation. For instance, even if a project was illiquid, through securitization the underlying loan could still be sold to the market, providing banks with additional sources of financing and with the possibility to transfer the underlying credit risk. This reduced for banks the costly economic capital needed as a buffer against their risky lending activities, allowing them to reinvest freed-up resources into the economy. Moreover, the prices of ABSs are expected to transmit extra information to the market, with positive results for its efficiency.

As a result, banks have maintained a major role as originators of credit, while progressively losing importance in their function as primary holders of illiquid assets and weakening the impact of their maturity transformation: this has produced a funda-mental shift in the business of banking from the traditional originate-to-hold strategies to the so-called originate-to-distribute (OTD) models, by which banks used to originate loans and then repackage the cash flows generated by these loans into ABSs, often via so-called SPVs/SIVs, and sell on the securities to investors or finance them through the ABCP issued by conduits.

As argued in [112], the OTD model had undoubtedly produced some advantages for the economy as a whole, because banks are actually able to transfer part of the credit risk in their loan portfolio and enhance the liquidity of their assets: this monetization of previous illiquid assets represents an additional source of funding to expand lending. In so doing, banks can maintain a given level of credit supply with a lower volume of capital, or a higher leverage ratio, by reducing the cost of financing for borrowers. Moreover, economic efficiency has been improved, with capital available to productive sectors that would otherwise have no access to; by increasing the liquidity of credit markets; by lowering the credit risk premium; by offering investors greater flexibility in terms of the supply of assets and hedging opportunities.

Unfortunately, a key condition for such a business model to work is that liquidity is permanently available at market prices for each participant in the process. In fact, the funding strategy of the SPV/SIV is based on short-term ABCP issuance through conduits, with the continuous rollover of funding over time.

The events of 2007 demonstrated that this hypothesis is not always verified in the current financial market, with significant drawbacks for the OTD model. Moreover, removing assets from balance sheets does not imply that banks are no longer exposed to the risks associated with them. First, other significant risks, such as reputational or pipeline risk, continue to threaten bank activity. Second, conduits and SPVs perform maturity transformation by financing long-term illiquid assets with short-term volatile liabilities, in much the same way as banks do, but they are far less well equipped than them to cope with credit deterioration and liquidity strains.

In fact, often these vehicles do not have capital requirements to fulfil, because they are not supervised by any authorities; furthermore, before the crisis banks had to set aside capital to support liquidity commitments to vehicles, but such commitments were treated as senior exposures, with lower capital requirements for shorter maturities and the consequent incentive to regulatory arbitrage. As stressed in the first chapter, so-called "constructive obligation" (i.e., the gap between the legal commitments of banks through liquidity support and credit enhancement and the actual level of implicit support they felt obliged to take in order to protect their reputation), emerged dramatically during the crisis when banking originators, who usually retain exposure to the first defaults on loans sold, recorded profit reduction and growing the balance sheet, lowering the amount of excess capital and liquidity available to back new lending, as they were forced to satisfy vehicles' calls for liquidity support.

The market efficiency of CRT techniques was undermined by the less accurate credit scrutinizing activity performed by originators as "delegated monitors" of their borrowers, since they were expected to transfer their credit risk to other investors. Moreover, even if rating agencies were fully transparent about their methodology, they carried an enormous conflict of interest resulting from the fact they are paid by issuers for providing a service to investors. Last but not least, most investors of ABS products were not fully aware that the rating assigned by agencies did not include liquidity risk, despite this being one of the principal risks to which holders of these products were exposed.

For corporate debt, there is supposed to exist a steady and consistent relationship between the rating, in terms of mean expected loss, and the variance of losses or defaults in a cyclical downturn, but CRT techniques broke this relationship and created securities with low expected loss but high variance of loss in the cycle: therefore, the rating no longer meant the same for both a corporate bond and an ABS product, because the latter has a higher volatility of loss than the former. In general, a firm is more resilient than a vehicle to economic shocks, because it is able to adjust its balance sheet to the new market conditions in a proper and timely manner.

In fact, ratings for structured products refer to the performance of a static pool instead of a dynamic corporation, rely more on quantitative models while corporate debt ratings also rely on analyst judgment, and are heavily based on a forecast of economic conditions.

Even if the recent financial crisis pushed banks and regulators to rethink the whole securitization process for unexpected effects on business sustainability and financial stability, the significant contribution made by securitization to liquefy the less liquid part of the asset side of the balance sheet for funding purposes should not be underestimated: hence, the main goal of these techniques is likely to be enhanced refinancing of these assets instead of the capital optimisation sought in the past.

5.5   THE LIQUIDITY FRAMEWORK

The most peculiar feature of liquidity risk, compared with other types of risks, is its strong interdependence with other risks that can affect bank's balance sheets. After having explored the funding and market component of liquidity risk in Chapter 2, it is of the outmost importance to analyse the factors that make up liquidity risk, which can

---

Box 5.2. Securitization and the bank lending channel

Securitization has probably reduced the relevance of the bank lending channel of monetary policy transmission compared with the past when banks were less integrated in groups and less able to liquidate loans into secondary markets. According to [5], securitization has altered the bank characteristics traditionally used to identify shifts in loan supply.

The size indicator is now less significant because securitization activity can considerably reduce the amount of loans on banks' balance sheets. In response to monetary tightening, the credit channel works if the reduction in supplied loans is not counterbalanced by greater access by firms to capital markets (i.e., when bonds and loans are imperfect substitutes). But, through securitization, banks may obtain additional liquidity independently of their securities holdings and the standard liquidity indicator may be less informative than in the past. In this way, securitization strengthens bank capacity to supply new loans to households and firms for a given amount of funding. However, this capacity should not to taken for granted because it changes over time and is dependent on business cycle conditions as well as on a bank's risk situation.

By reducing capital requirements securitization also makes the standard capital-to-asset ratio a poor approximation of the relevant capital constraints faced by originators in this regard and allows for a positive net effect on loan supply. More broadly, securitization provides banks with additional flexibility to face changes in market conditions associated with monetary policy movements.

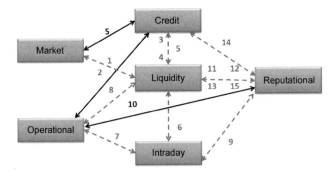

Figure 5.5. The web of risks. Dotted lines are links with intraday and liquidity risks
Source: Adapted from a graph of Vento and La Ganga [112]

rather be triggered or exacerbated by other financial and operating risks within the banking business.

These interrelationships define a sort of web of risks (some are shown in Figure 5.5), which have to be constantly monitored and updated by risk managers and treasurers in order to manage liquidity risk properly.

For example, strong links exist with both market and credit risk: adverse market conditions tend to create uncertainty about the value of assets in the liquidity management framework (1); margin calls on derivatives products implied by negative market developments also have repercussions on liquidity risk (2); credit risk often arises from a liquidity shortage when scheduled repayments fall due (3); credit worries can often require additional margins under collateral agreements with negative impacts on funding risk (4); and a rating downgrade below a specified notch can preclude access of a bank to the wholesale market (5). Interest rate and credit quality–related option risk can produce material effects on liquidity (e.g., when prevailing rates are low, loan prepayments and investment calls accelerate cash flows). On the other hand, cash flow projections may prove too high if prevailing rates rise.

Another significant block of interactions is provided by links among liquidity risk, operational risk and intraday risk. As far as intraday liquidity risk is concerned, severe disruptions in significant payment systems could affect money market conditions and increase liquidity risk (6); in addition, some operational risk can lead to a delay of other less essential payments, and might also push other institutions to delay their own settlements (7); and when there is significant disruption, operational risk can ignite liquidity risk because many banks could be forced to manage increased uncertainty about their intraday funding needs (8).

Last but not least, reputational risk can be one of the causes undermining confidence in a bank, and can easily generate liquidity and intraday risk (9), sometimes also linked to some operational problems (10). A bank's reputation for operating in a safe and sound manner is essential to attracting funds at a reasonable cost, as well as for retaining funds during crises (11). On the other hand, negative public opinion may push retail depositors, other funds providers and investors (12) to ask for greater compensation, such as higher rates (market liquidity risk) or collateral (funding liquidity risk), or conducting any other business with it: reputational risk is obviously more of an issue for banks that depend on unsecured, wholesale funding and for banks that sell or securitize loans (13). Reputational risk is likely to translate into augmented own credit risk, with a potential negative outlook and rating downgrades (14), or simply magnify the usual flowback of a bank's own issues from the secondary market (15).

Once identified all risks related to the bank model, specific metrics and limits for each type of risk have to be defined by top management in order to address the business strategy in the most efficient way. For liquidity risk this limit is commonly known as "liquidity risk tolerance" and has to be fixed directly by top management according to their risk appetite. It is important to define a measure so that it is easy to understand for people who are not practitioners, like a "survival horizon" for the short term and a "maximum cumulative mismatch" for the long term. It is also crucial that senior management are directly involved in developing policies and practices to manage liquidity risk in accordance with the defined risk tolerance, in order to avoid risk-prone behaviours led by budget figures that are not consistent with some assigned limits.

As suggested by the BCBS' *Principles for Sound Liquidity Risk Management and Supervision* [99], "senior management should continuously review information on the bank's liquidity developments and report to the board of directors on a regular basis. A bank's board of directors should review and approve strategy, policies and practices related to the management of liquidity at least annually and ensure that senior management manages liquidity risk effectively." Top management being well aware of the liquidity risk generated by business activity is therefore one of the key drivers to ensure the governance and management of liquidity risk based on sound practices.

An effective liquidity framework (as stylized in Figure 5.6) needs intrinsic consistency among risk appetite level, performance measurement system and pricing process. In fact, the risk tolerance threshold can be used as input data to define the budget figures of all business units and the liquidity funding plan for the treasury department. In order to translate the risk appetite level into measures and processes that properly address business strategies, the role played by liquidity risk metrics is crucial. The term "metric" is used for a measure that facilitates quantification of some particular characteristic of a bank's liquidity position or risk.

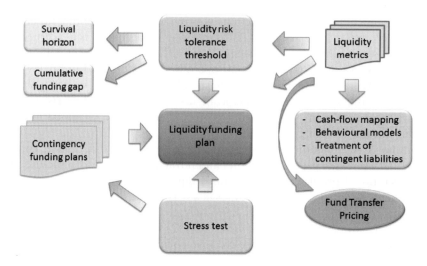

Figure 5.6. The liquidity framework

Different approaches to cash flow mapping, behaviour models, treatment of contingent liabilities, to name but a few, have relevant impacts not only on risk measurement, but also on pricing and the commercial strategies of some products. For instance, if deposits from medium and large corporate firms are considered less stable than those from retail customers, banks are likely to have more interest to attract and pay more than the latter, because they generate more value for liquidity metrics. Moreover, liquidity metrics, in their role as interpreter of the liquidity risk appetite in practical measures to address the bank's business, represent prerequisites to definition of a liquidity funding plan.

A liquidity funding plan aims at defining the funding strategy, in terms of timing, mix of instruments and funding channels, to support expected and ongoing business over at least one year, taking into account budget figures, funding expiring after a given period of time and expected market conditions, with the goal of optimizing the cost of funding on the entire term structure. Implementation of a liquidity funding plan has to be continuously monitored and timely adjusted, since liquidity is not always available and its lack can compromise strategic targets. A liquidity funding plan always has to be supported by specific contingency funding plans that should allow, under some acute stress scenarios tailor made for actual bank business (including the combination of idiosyncratic and market-related shocks), management of a potential liquidity crisis, without implementing procedures and/or employing instruments that, due to their intensity or manner of use, do not qualify as ordinary administration.

In order to properly address the activities that impact on the overall liquidity profile, each bank has to define an accurate system of fund transfer pricing (FTP), which allocates the relevant costs and benefits, both direct and indirect, related to liquidity risk to all business units. With such a system, business decisions are always forced to factor the liquidity component into the pricing, and the cost (benefit) of liquidity can be transferred ideally to business lines even at the trade level.

The FTP system is the transmission chain that communicates to all desks changes in the risk-tolerance threshold or in market funding spreads: it represents one of the key factors to building a consistent risk-adjusted performance measurement system. The FTP system should always be linked to the market and be representative of the real funding capacity of the firm: it is closely linked to liquidity metrics and a liquidity funding plan. One of the key features for a successful FTP system to achieve individual and aggregate targets is its "fairness": rules have to be clear, well understood from the top to the bottom of the firm and clearly defined in formalized procedures, in order (i) to protect business lines from risks they are unable to control and manage; and (ii) to stop them from arbitraging the system. The mechanism should be designed to ensure that end users can understand the output and know how to use it in order to facilitate decisions that will ultimately impact the financial situation of the firm. Internal prices should percolate down to decision makers at the transaction level in order to ensure maximum impact. A constant dialogue between business lines and the functions responsible for calculation and application of the FTP system is strongly suggested. Business lines should understand the rationality of internal prices and the treasury needs to understand the rationale and funding implications of the transacted deal.

Ideally, the FTP system should be kept as simple as possible, with a strict distinction required between the function that fixes the rules to determine FTP daily values and the function (typically the treasury) that applies them. In order to work properly even under

Box 5.3. CP 36

In March 2010 the Confederation of European Banking Supervisors (CEBS) issued *Guidelines on Liquidity Cost Benefit Allocation* (CP 36) [7], in accordance with Recommendation 2 provided by the CEBS to the EC on liquidity risk management (CEBS 2008 147): "Institutions should have in place an adequate internal mechanism—supported where appropriate by a transfer pricing mechanism—which provides appropriate incentives regarding the contribution to liquidity risk of the different business activities. This mechanism should incorporate all costs of liquidity (from short to long-term, including contingent risk)."

The guidelines should help institutions to link their strategic direction with liquidity resource allocation. Using internal pricing mechanisms allows institutions to improve their process for pricing products, measuring performance, assessing new products and enhancing the tool for asset/liability management. This should be applicable to all significant business activities, both on and off balance sheet. It also serves to align the risk-taking incentives of individual business lines with the liquidity risk exposures that their activities create for the institution as a whole.

Some interesting points are provided by Guideline 2: the prices should be used for internal pricing of liquidity, performance measurement and the appraisal of new products or business for all significant activities, both on and off balance sheet: hence, discrepancies between pricing and performance measurement are not welcome. If management wish to incentivize certain behaviours, this should be subject to a separate approval and reporting process: therefore, exceptions have to be authorized and, consequently, monitored and evaluated in a different way.

The objectivity of internal prices should be maintained for the correct pricing and reporting of liquidity. Concerning to the treasury, "the area or responsible function ultimately charged with implementing the internal prices should be service-oriented and not have a profit target for this specific role. Equally, for larger institutions, personnel working within the area should not be set profit targets for this activity" [7]. Therefore, the treasury is not a profit centre for this activity, otherwise it could adjust prices according to its target, but in the meantime it cannot be a cost centre as well, which means the costs of each exception authorised by management do not have to be borne by the treasury.

Last but not least, Guideline 25 states: "The internal prices used should reflect the marginal cost of funding. The price should reflect the marginal cost over a homogenous product group as an average, but it should also reflect current costs. Funding already acquired (tapped) should already be taken into account in the prices of products sold (or being sold). In order to achieve a reliable marginal funding cost, an institution should be able to adjust transfer prices according to current demand for new funding, mainly, when calculating the contingent liquidity cost price. As the required size of the liquidity buffer (and its cost) changes with any new product sold, as well as any new funding tapped, an institution should ideally be able to recalculate the transfer price according to its expected balance sheet term structure (dynamic price setting)" [7].

stressed conditions and very volatile phases it is strongly suggested to define some mechanisms to reduce excessive volatility of quotations in the very short term to avoid some drawbacks in customer relations, and to override values in order to address some strategic activities. In these cases modifications should always be consistent with the overall risk tolerance threshold and liquidity metrics, and adequately tracked by the performance measurement system.

5.6   STRESS-TESTING AND CONTINGENCY FUNDING PLAN

As previously stated, the liquidity risk appetite is analytically defined by the "risk tolerance threshold" that is applied to some specific measures (liquidity ratios, cumulative funding gaps and survival horizons): it represents the maximum level of risk that the bank is willing to accept. The quantification of risk tolerance presupposes that (i) a probability space can be defined that spans all material realizations of a stochastic variable; (ii) a probability distribution can be reasonably well approximated over the probability space. Thus, given a probability distribution of shocks that can generate liquidity risk, each bank could decide on the risk-bearing capacity that it wants to hold, in terms of the cumulative probability distribution of shocks it wants to survive (normally 99.9% since we are talking about the survival of a firm).

Unfortunately, the number of observable liquidity shocks and their institution-specific nature, depending on the actual structure of the balance sheet, would attach high uncertainty to the definition of the probability space and the approximation of the probability distribution. Tail risks are likely to arise and have to be properly captured by specific stress tests as part of liquidity risk management.

Shocks are usually defined as certain specific scenarios that can be applied to a bank's cash flow distribution in order to perform stress tests. The scenarios are based on certain risk factors that, accurately modified, produce new values for expected cash flows mapped on the maturity ladder: both idiosyncratic and market-related scenarios have to be tailor made to fit the firm's business model, since they are mainly risk management tools—not simple regulatory requirements. This means that it is not enough to simply mimic severe past liquidity shocks but it is necessary to get scenario reviews focused on the changing nature of banks' liquidity risk exposure (e.g., taking into account new products, new markets, new funding sources or changes in counterparty behaviour).

Moreover, it is of the utmost importance to use combined market-related (systemic crisis) and idiosyncratic (own name crisis) stress scenarios since focusing on isolated risk factors implicitly assumes in too optimistic a way that (i) these risks are independent of each other; (ii) they have very low probability; and (iii) their combined probability is therefore negligible.

The risk factors used by banks for the idiosyncratic scenario often comprise rating downgrades, reduced access to wholesale funding (both secured and unsecured), reduction in the credit lines available and counterparty limits, increased haircuts and collateral calls, utilization of credit commitments, inability to draw down precommitted lines, currency redenomination risk and increase in demand for financial funding by entities within the group.

A list of market-related events can include a particular geographical context (central European liquidity crisis, global markets, emerging markets, local money market or retail deposit markets), the cause of the stress (subprime crisis, government crisis or unexpected change in monetary policy, sudden and deep recession, default of a primary market counterparty), the closure of key funding markets (senior and covered bond markets, unsecured and secured interbank markets, securitization market, disruption in CP and CD segments, dislocation in the forex swap market), a set of negative economic indicators (rise in bond yields, drop in stock prices, widening in credit spreads) and the perceived severity of stress. The correlation between some risk factors is easier to calibrate (i.e., causes linked to a particular context or financial indicators) and sometimes the task is more challenging. However, it is crucial not to consider these cases on a standalone basis, because liquidity tensions are often driven by different factors that work together and feed on each other.

From the computational point of view each bank should be able to run periodic simulations to manage stress-testing on certain specific and combined forecast scenarios (i.e., closure of forex market, severe retail outflow, etc.). The simulation engine should allow what-if scenarios to be run and calculate expected cash flows impacted by certain risk factors (new prepayments, new default probabilities, new rollover, new balance sheet growth, new haircuts, new market risk parameters, etc.): for every new simulation item a specific behaviour hypothesis should be defined so that they can be reused in a combined scenario.

For the largest banks, deeply involved in settlement and payment systems, it is crucial to monitor intraday liquidity risk as well. Intraday liquidity can be defined as "funds which can be accessed during the business day, usually to enable financial institutions to make payments in real-time" [101]. Intraday liquidity risk is therefore related to cases in which banks are not able to actively manage their intraday liquidity positions to meet payment and settlement obligations on a timely basis under both normal and stressed conditions, and thus contribute to the smooth functioning of payment and settlement systems. The elements relevant to intraday liquidity profiles can differ between banks depending on whether they access payment and settlement systems directly or indirectly, or whether or not they provide correspondent banking services and intraday credit facilities to other banks.

A continuous and updated stress test analysis is a prerequisite to implementing an effective contingency funding plan (CFP). This consists of defining and setting an infrastructure, in terms of actions and processes aimed at safeguarding the bank's asset value and guaranteeing the continuity of operations under certain conditions of extreme liquidity emergency. Its main goal is to keep the business franchise and to preserve customer relationships. It ensures (i) identification of early-warning signals and their ongoing monitoring; (ii) definition of procedures to be implemented in situations of liquidity stress; (iii) immediate lines of action; and (iv) intervention measures for the resolution of emergencies.

As already stated, the dangers of liquidity risk lie in its potential to be very severe despite its low probability: it can easily lead to serious disruption of a bank because the contingent liquidity risk is related to the situation of not having sufficient funds to meet sudden and unexpected short-term obligations. Rising uncertainty can affect both funding needs and sources. For instance, among the unforeseen increases in funding required are unexpected loan demand, unexpected credit drawdown, other commitment draws and some requirements for increased collateral pledging. Moreover, unforeseen decreases in the funding available can comprise unexpected deposit withdrawals, the evaporation of unused funding capacity and erosion of the market value of unencumbered, marketable assets.

The combination of early-warning procedures and advance preparation for liquidity perils that are very serious, despite their low probability, must fit together with the bank's liquidity management and stress-testing analysis. Funding crises almost always progress in stages: being prepared to enhance liquidity provisions quickly at the first sign of increased need is one of the most important best practices for liquidity risk management. It has to be pointed out that some remedies available to treasurers in the early stages of a funding difficulty may disappear if trouble progresses to a more severe stage, such as when new unsecured funding can only be raised in case of a minor funding problem, or when new secured borrowing is at an intermediate stage, or when the only recourse is CB refinancing as the crisis deepens.

Moreover, market access should not be overestimated even in the first phases of a funding problem, because wholesale counterparties, who are used to providing large amounts of funds, are very sensitive to rumours or bad news and tend to disappear at the first sign of idiosyncratic shock. In that case the bank can experience unavailability of new funding, no matter how much it is ready to pay: it is not a simple matter of cost, but of market capacity to absorb the new demand for funds when some channels are closed due to a single-name problem. Because new secured funding depends on collateral availability the key factor in the short term is once again to have a well-dimensioned pool of unencumbered highly liquid securities.

The CFP is a combination of measures defined by common sense: it has to be seen as a menu with many choices—not as a list of instructions. Several plans have to be developed for funding in multiple currencies: when markets are stressed or when the bank's rating is under pressure, it may be very difficult to transfer funds between currencies. Different kinds of crises obviously require different kinds of preparation. A CFP should be a "living plan" that needs to be periodically updated, in order to rely only on the actual funding strategies available in certain market situations. Advanced planning, though ambitious and challenging in its goal to face the unknown, is still invaluable at times when scenarios could be shown to be wrong and priorities could be quickly modified. Some rules of common sense should not be underestimated: for instance, previous positive experiences should not take precedence over contingency planning. As already stated, relying on market access can be logical only under normal or mildly disturbed funding conditions, even though some feedbacks provided by the financial industry to a BSC survey [65] surprisingly recorded huge confidence in interbank market functioning (see Figure 5.7). The ultimate goal is to buy time in a period of crisis: it can make the difference between survival and bankruptcy.

The CFP is a tool to manage outside firms' perceptions by minimizing reputational risk and ensuring goingconcern activity. Its scope is to limit excessive funding costs, to mitigate and control crisis contagion and escalation within the group, by preserving the business franchise. It is defined to answering the following basic calls: When? What for? How? Actually, a CFP must be activated whenever the liquidity position is threatened by market-related or firm-specific events. It has to meet current and future financial obligations at all times, in all currencies, and for all group companies, by addressing questions about consolidated and unconsolidated CFP elements; to sum up, it provides a guideline for all players within the firm in the event of a liquidity crisis by providing a clear escalation plan.

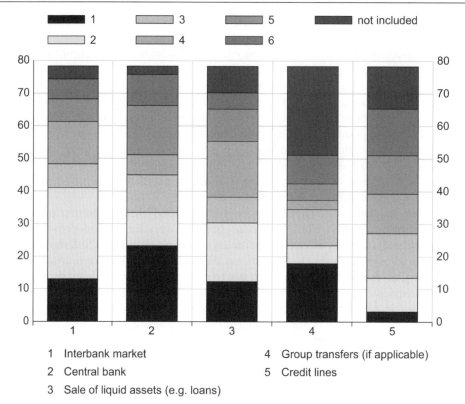

Figure 5.7. Idiosyncratic liquidity stress scenarios in funding sources. Distribution of importance (1 = most important to 6 = least important) of individual funding sources in the 78 idiosyncratic scenarios that were described by 67 banks (some banks run more than one idiosyncratic scenario) *Source*: BSC Survey [65]

One of the key elements of a good CFP is to clearly identify who will make decisions about internal and external communications. A liquidity crisis is often related to a crisis in the firm's confidence, which can be easily further eroded by unclear or inconsistent communications. Prompt and proactive communications with major depositors, lenders and regulators have to be quickly activated. During a liquidity crisis a bank is likely to counter rumours, allay concerns of lenders, avoid unwanted regulatory attention: when material negative information about its situation becomes public, the bank should be prepared to immediately announce corrective actions that are being taken. This behaviour could help to mitigate market fears and demonstrate that top management are focused on problems as they arise.

The sources of funding and strains are, of course, strongly dependent on tension typology: among the strains most likely experienced are runs on many, if not all, irrevocable commitment lines on the asset side and evaporation of interbank and wholesale funding combined with a significant reduction in the core deposits of savings on the liability side. The activation of some potential liquidity sources is related to the severity and duration of liquidity: on the asset side the first line of defence (see Figure 5.8) is clearly provided by the liquidity buffer (i.e., unencumbered financial investments

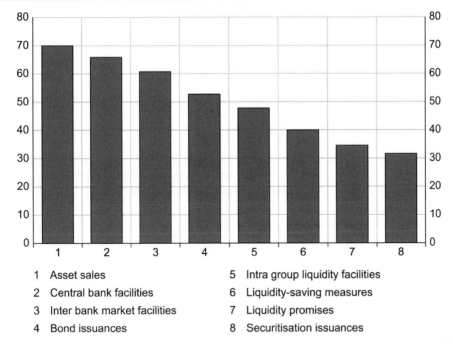

Figure 5.8. Sources of liquidity in CFPs. Which of these measures are included in your CFP?
Source: BSC Survey [65]

to monetize, followed by the squaring of trading positions and asset disposal). With more time, asset securitizations can be implemented in order to raise funds from the market or central bank through collateralized borrowing. Recourse to "the three S's" (i.e., syndication, sales and securitization) should not be overestimated because, in order to be effective, it has to be activated at the very first stage of the problem. Moreover, selling or transfer assets could lead to an increase in the average risk of the remaining assets, because the highest quality assets are likely to be sold. On the liability side there are tools like the issuance of covered bonds or debt bonds that can be used in the retail market or wholesale channels if still available; recourse to some form of wholesale funding (CD/CP) or secured funding, as already pointed out, depends on features of the incoming crisis.

The CFP system of early-warning indicators is designed to provide a monitoring tool able to intercept the first signs of incoming liquidity tension or crisis. These indications are crucial because, in crisis situations, there could be very limited time to find the right processes to determine the severity and likely duration of the crisis, and to ascertain adequate funding needs and sources.

The values of early-warning indicators (both quantitative and qualitative) are often combined in order to identify several potential states of the crisis: they aim at defining the importance of the trigger, from the lowest level identified as "ongoing" (business as usual) to the highest one of "alarm", which leads to activation of the CFP, because of a name-specific crisis or a stressed liquidity position. Other intermediate levels include "attention", still defined as business as usual but with some captured stress (market or

---

Box 5.4. The CEBS quantitative information set [98]

Short-term resilience (liquidity coverage ratio) to maturity mismatch and contingent liabilities takes the following into account:

- Liquidity buffer
  —Size
  —Composition (asset type, duration, currency)
  —Contextual information (stress scenario, time horizon)
  —Stress scenario (idiosyncratic, market related, combined)
  —Time horizon (acute stress: 1 or 2 weeks; persistent stress: from 1 to 3 months)
  —Stress indicators (bank specific, such as share price, financial index, CDS, senior unsecured and covered ASW spread, CDs and CP debt spread, ordinary savings interest rate, ECB financing quote)
- Counterbalancing capacity
  —Asset liquidability
  —Contingent funding sources
- Longer term resilience (balance sheet structure modification)
  —Net stable funding ratio
    * Ratio components (retail and wholesale funding, equity, illiquid assets, contingent liabilities, haircuts)
  —Diversification of funding structure
    * Wholesale funding ratio
    * Funding counterparty concentration indicator
  —Asset time to liquidability (securitization, sale)
- Maturity ladder
  —Contractual data and behaviour assumptions (rollover and reputational risk)
  —Liquidity gap for time band
  —Cumulative liquidity gap
- Currency liquidity mismatch
- CB refinancing dependency
  —Current percentage of CB funding versus average percentage
  —Current percentage versus country percentage
  —Current percentage versus total percentage
- Illiquid assets:
  —Non-marketable assets
  —Non-maturing relatively non-marketable assets
  —Haircuts to liquid assets
  —Contingent liabilities (committed lines, financial guarantees)
  —Derivatives (cash flows, margin calls, contingent liabilities related to securitization, due to performance or rating triggers or buybacks)

---

own name) and "alert", which should intercept the first signs of a market-generalized crisis. During the "attention" phase the objective should be not only to limit potential escalation but to prepare for it as well; the "alert" phase calls for excessive funding costs to be avoided and sufficient funding ensured, with some slowdown of growth plans.

Early-warning indicators related to a firm-specific crisis are often variables constantly monitored by the bank in its daily activity, such as the trend of the spread (difference between the funding cost paid by the firm and the one paid by peers) paid for unsecured deposits, borrowed funding or asset securitisation, or retail deposit withdrawals. Alerts from wholesale funding can be provided by reducing the tenors potential lenders are willing to impose, or by requests for collateral or for smaller transaction sizes from lenders previously willing to provide unsecured funding or larger transaction amounts (did they fill the credit line or cut it?).

Other dangerous factors include a significant drop in stock prices (research has shown that in many cases idiosyncratic liquidity stress was preceded by a decline in the share price of the institution, particularly when it diverged from the general index for comparable financial firms, as occurred for Lehman); negative outlook or rating downgrade, especially if unexpected; increase in the use of committed lines from customers; market pressures to buy back its own obligations in the secondary market. Any violation of the liquidity risk limit or cases in which multiple measures of liquidity risk are approaching limits are obviously causes of concern.

Another stress indicator can be found in the credit spreads on the various debt products issued by an institution. The delta in CDS spreads and in bond yield spreads versus the yield on government debt (Treasuries) with the same maturity, or versus the swap yield on the same tenor, should normally provide the same indications, but they could diverge due to market liquidity. They may be used together or alternatively. Subordinated debt will be more sensitive than senior debt, but both may be used as indicators. As with equity prices, a comparison should be made with peers, based on a relevant index for the peer group (i.e., 5Y iTraxx financial senior).

Early-warning indicators for market-related shocks are often linked to some market quotations or figures, such as the weekly rollover of new issuances of CP/CD, or the spread between the 5Y ITraxx financial senior and government yield, or the spread between European core government bond yield and peripheral bond yield, in order to capture flight to quality in capital markets. Widening of the spread among repo rates for different asset classes can represent evidence of tensions or disruption for some market segments, as well as a huge gap between the unsecured ON rate and the refi rate fixed by the ECB. These quotations must always be monitored in combination with other measures that give some clue to the liquidity excess available on the market, such as the sum of "daily deposit facility" − "daily marginal lending" + "daily current account amounts" in the current environment under a full allotment regime defined by the ECB, or the allotted amount versus the benchmark for MRO in cases of competitive tenders. The spread between the 3-month Euribor versus the 3-month US Libor is a useful tool to monitor tension on the forex swap market, because this measure reacts very quickly to liquidity tensions driven by USD shortage for the whole market or some specific segments (i.e., European banks over the last two years).

5.7 THE CEBS IDENTITY CARD

Although financial institutions are different for business models and activities, some common features can always be identified as crucial for liquidity risk monitoring and measurement. In 2009 the CEBS (now EBA) proposed the so-called "liquidity identity card" (hereafter "liquidity ID", [98]), with the aim at enabling supervisors to gain a common understanding of the liquidity risk and resilience of a group and its entities (subsidiaries and branches) in both the short and longer term, given the specificities of the group's business and its risk tolerance. It represents up to now the most detailed public attempt to gather data in order to fill the information gap between financial players and regulators.

The liquidity ID provides qualitative and quantitative information on liquidity risk and liquidity risk management that can be used not only by regulators, but also by firms themselves to fully understand their overall liquidity risk profile. It is composed of two parts: the first part provides a common set of information (core ID), general and qualitative information regarding the liquidity strategy, cash pooling, the liquidity support provided by the parent company to all entities of the group in normal times, stress test scenarios, the liquidity buffer, the funding concentration, the liquidity policy, the obstacles to liquidity transfers and the CFP; the second part provides quantitative information concerning the liquidity buffer, the long-term funding ratio, diversification of the funding structure and the domestic quantitative ratio.

The most interesting part of the document is perhaps the so-called "additional à la carte information", which deals with market indicators, a synthetic maturity ladder, a core funding ratio and examples of additional metrics for specific vulnerabilities, listed in the appendix (Section 5.9).

For this purpose illiquid assets are defined as:

- Haircuts to liquid assets (if available): the sum of all haircuts, whether derived from central bank policies or from internal policies, applied to the liquid, marketable, and CB-eligible assets that are taken into account when computing liquidity buffers.
- Contingent liabilities, including the maximum off-balance-sheet credit risk exposure according to IFRS 7 as included in paragraph 36(a): "the amount by class of instruments that best represents the entity's maximum exposure to credit risk at the end of the reporting period without taking account of any collateral held or any other credit enhancements (such as netting agreements that do not qualify for offset under IAS 32)." This definition includes the amount of undrawn loan commitments that are irrevocable over the life of the facility or are revocable only in response to a material adverse change. If the issuer cannot settle the loan commitment net in cash or another financial instrument, the maximum credit exposure is the full amount of the commitment. It also includes financial guarantees. In this case, maximum exposure to credit risk is the maximum amount the entity would have to pay if the guarantee is called on.
- For derivative contracts, the maximum credit risk exposure under IFRS 7 includes only the on-balance-sheet carrying fair value amount of the contract (if the resulting asset from derivatives is measured at fair value). In the context of Part II, an additional best estimate proxy amount of market risk related to potential off-balance-sheet liabilities may be agreed. This may also be the case for contingent liabilities related to securitization (e.g., due to performance triggers or buybacks) and any non-contractual reputation-related liability.

Retail funding includes SMEs with less sophisticated treasuries, and represents the most behaviourally stable component of funding as a whole. Wholesale funding is funding provided by professional credit risk–sensitive counterparties. It should include at least the following items:

- issued debt securities, both unsecured and secured (e.g., covered bonds);
- deposits and secured funding (e.g., repos) from credit institutions, other financial institutions and governments;
- secured and unsecured funding from central banks;
- deposits and secured funding from professional money market players with a professional treasury function, such as institutional investors and large corporations.

In the appendix (Section 5.9) we show the identity card as proposed by the CEBS in the annex of the aforementioned document.

5.8 CONCLUSIONS

This chapter terminates the first part of this book, whose goal was to show how liquidity risk may affect the business of a financial institution. Starting from a brief description of the causes that led to the crisis which has afflicted the financial industry over the last five years we have identified and analysed the three types of liquidity risk (and dangerous combinations of them).

From a macroeconomic point of view, focused on the attempts of regulators to address and monitor liquidity risk on the business of a bank, we moved to a micro-economic analysis with the aim of developing a comprehensive framework of sound management and supervision practices about liquidity risk, whose building blocks are represented by an articulate system of risk management, treasury tools, product pricing and performance measurement to warrant full consistency between liquidity risk-taking activities and the risk tolerance threshold defined for the firm.

It is now time to move from principles to the analysis of the tools used to manage liquidity risk effectively currently at the disposal of risk managers and treasurers.

5.9   APPENDIX: THE CEBS IDENTITY CARD ANNEX (CEBS [98])

1. Intragroup exposures	Refers to	Vulnerabilities
Intrabank Intragroup	Liability side/cash outflow	Intragroup/bank drawings: • Unsecured • Secured (collateral adequacy)
Centralized management Non-centralized	Asset side/cash inflow	• Branches' exposure to foreign head office • Funding concentration from consolidated entity/subsidiary • Market access • Subsidiaries' exposure to other group members • Collateral value of secured exposures • Regulatory ring-fencing by home or host supervisor
	Gap position	Net exposure

2. Foreign currencies	Refers to	Vulnerabilities
	Liability side/cash outflow	Convertibility, currency swap market functioning, general/idiosyncratic
	Asset side/cash inflow	Asset currency denomination
	Gap position	Currency mismatch

3. Payment and settlement	Refers to	Vulnerabilities
RTGS systems	Liability side/cash outflow	• Unencumbered collateral position at CB • Credit line usage of correspondent bank • Undefined limits
Other	Asset side/cash inflow	• Unexpected encumbrance of assets
Correspondent banking	Gap position	• Net scheduled unencumbered collateral position

Metrics: Amount of failed trades on average, maximum collateral usage for each payment (settlement) system (peak position of encumbered collateral during period x).

4. Clearing and settlement business	Refers to	Vulnerabilities
Central clearing (CC)	Liability side/cash outflow	• Margin requirements • Clearing fund commitments • Withdrawal of institutional clients' deposits and collateral • CM responsibility to CC for customers' short positions
Clearing membership (CM)	Asset side/cash inflow	• Market value/market liquidity of collateral • Adequacy of haircuts
	Gap position	Mismatch between liquid collateral/deposits received and (potential) customers' liabilities from trading positions

Metrics: Correlated client deposit concentration (e.g., from hedge funds) as percentage of total deposit/liabilities.

5. Secured funding	Refers to	Vulnerabilities
Repo business	Liability side/cash outflow	Contingent liabilities • Margin/collateral calls • Market liquidity • Credit/liquidity facilities
Securities lending/borrowing	Asset side/cash inflow	• (Un)encumbrance planning/scheduling • Transparency of market values • Liquidity of securities
Securitization	Gap position	Net position to deliver securities Operational settlement risk Fast increasing mismatch due to stressed funding of ABSs, ABCP

6. Central bank relations	Refers to	Vulnerabilities
G10 central banks	Liability side/cash outflow	Rollover dependency of central bank standard facilities: • Tender-based assignments, no guarantee to full assignment • Temporary longer term refinancing operations • Stigma/reputational risk with regard to emergency (ON) refinancing operations

6. Central bank relations	Refers to	Vulnerabilities	(cont.)
Other central banks	Asset side/cash inflow	Adequacy of eligible collateral: • Various eligibility criteria by different CB • Denomination in eligible currencies • CB, (G)CDS location, geographical location, transferability • Variations in haircuts and range of eligible collateral • Temporary extended range of collateral, securities swap arrangements, etc. • Potential cliff effect at end of special crisis rules • Market valuation of eligible collateral • Encumbrance due to RTGS payment and settlement systems	
	Gap position	CB refinancing dependence related to maturity mismatch	

7. Derivatives	Refers to	Vulnerabilities	
Futures/forward/swaps/options	Liability side/cash outflow	• Futures/options: variation margin • Forward/Swaps: cash margin/collateral requirements • CDS: downgrade trigger-related collateral requirements • TRS: term structure vulnerability • Misstated liquidity characteristics of call features embedded in structured investment products (auto-callable certificates)	
Credit derivatives	Asset side/cash inflow	Inverse correlation between asset derivative complexity and its liquidity • Volatile MTM asset value • Documentation risk related to settlement issues	
Margin and collateral requirements	Gap position	• Liquidity gap due to TRS term structure • Net margin requirements due to uncovered liquidity hedge from a basically VaR-neutral hedged position based on exchange-traded and OTC derivatives • Negative basis transactions	

Metrics: Downgrade triggers levels with regard to collateral agreements (CSA); liquidity gap due to TRS term structure mismatches or negative basis transactions.

8. Liquid assets, collateral	Refers to	Vulnerabilities
Liquidity of assets	Liability side/cash outflow	• Adequacy of collateral movements scheduling • Shortage in securities borrowing market for return delivery of securities borrowed
Collateral management	Asset side/cash inflow	• Adequacy of a liquidity buffer for short-term purposes (1 month) with marketable and eligible assets relative to a pool of marketable assets for counterbalancing purposes on a longer term • Appropriateness of the ratio between "CB eligible/highly marketable assets" and "CB eligible but less marketable assets" Unencumbered marketable assets: • Time to convert to cash • Market liquidity and price volatility for outright sale • Market and bank-specific related haircut variability or access impediments • Transferability issues (local impediments such as regulatory ring-fencing, tax issues, operational infrastructure) • Adequate collateral management/scheduling of collateral movements and projected period of encumbrance • Appropriate currency denomination/related currency conversion hurdles
	Gap position	• Net availability of scheduled unencumbered eligible assets/collateral • Net availability of scheduled unencumbered highly liquid and marketable assets/collateral • Net availability of scheduled less liquid unencumbered marketable assets/collateral

Metrics: Distinction in the portfolio of pledgeable (CB and industry criteria) and repoable assets in the market during stress; relative size of haircuts applied; resilience to haircut fluctuations.

9. Saving business	Refers to	Vulnerabilities
Specialized "direct" banking entities and specialised ordinary savings	Liability side/cash outflow	Correlated rapid withdrawal related to: ● Entity's, group's or industry's reputation/capital adequacy ● Relative extent of deposit insurance Decay of deposits due to: ● Competitiveness of interest rates ● Level of interest rates
	Asset side/cash inflow	● Non-diversified assets ● Marketability, eligibility ● Intragroup exposures (savings-orientated banks are dependent on intragroup assets)
	Gap position	● Fixed term: contractual maturity, early redemption due to penalty clauses ● Open term: core duration according to stochastics

Metrics: Distinction between insured and non-insured savings. In cash flow projections, higher retention (or rollover) rates may be assumed for insured savings. Lower retention/rollover rates should be applied to savings attracted via Internet direct banking formulas, if clients ties can be assumed to be loose. Cash flow projections for stressed scenarios may be insufficient if based only on stochastic approaches.

10. Residential mortgage business	Refers to	Vulnerabilities
Secondary home market residential mortgages	Liability side/cash outflow	● Growth of funding vulnerability ● Required rather long effective funding duration (no securitization) ● Core retail deposits stochastics, correlated reputation-related withdrawals during stress ● High credit risk–related wholesale funding sensitivity during downturn ● Unsecured: idiosyncratic credit risk and general wholesale/interbank market liquidity linked risk of impeded market access and withdrawals ● Secured: general market and counterparty credit risk linked to risk of hampered market access

10. *Residential mortgage* business	*Refers to*	*Vulnerabilities*	*(cont.)*
		• Issued unsecured debt, securitizations • Covered bond • Rollover on adequate terms related to relative price of short/long-term funding (yield curve related risk) • Credit spread long-term funding • Originator and/or sponsor–related contingent liabilities due to recourse, performance triggers, collateral calls, and other committed credit enhancement/liquidity facilities to securitizations and conduits/SPVs	
New home/building mortgages	Asset side/cash inflow	• Illiquidity of assets • Wholesale market-related securitization risks • Liquidity of ABSs, ABCP markets, resecuritizations • Credit-related payments delays • Asset value if not diversified and if dependent on collateral funding • Home price/credit-related asset prices • Foreclosures: fire sale home prices	
Mortgage offers	Gap position	• Inherent large contractual maturity mismatch: often relatively weak cash capital position • Stochastic general market stress-sensitive securitisation related to effective asset duration, combined with interest-driven early redemption stochastics	

11. *Large corporate/* *government*	*Refers to*	*Vulnerabilities*
Large corporate loans/ deposits	Liability side/cash outflow	• On-demand and short-term wholesale funding: professional money market behaviour stochastics: credit risk/reputation-linked risk of rapid withdrawals • Fixed term deposits, longer term roll-over risk stochastics dependent on concentration • High credit risk sensitivity • Correlated/concentrated early withdrawals with penalty during bank-specific stress • Secured funding • Repo market access impediments, market stress related and/or idiosyncratic • Dependent on asset value • Credit lines, underwriting, standby facilities • Contractual/irrevocable • Inclusive project finance related • Non-contractual reputation-linked risk • Corporates: business cycle related to usage of credit lines • Upward phase: investment related • Downturn: increasing stock and loss financing
Money market (funds) professional-related business	Asset side/cash inflow	Large corporate loans specifics: • Part of core business with substantial pressure to rollover (reputation sensitive) • Loans: net cash (in)flows according to maturity schedule after LC client related to loan rollover/reinvestment stochastics • Unstable during stress
Government, except small local	Gap position	LC loan/deposit gap specifics: • Net cash flows after loan and deposit rollover • Money market fund related to ABCP funding business: potential gap driven by securitization stochastics and backup facilities

Metrics: Concentration of short-term wholesale funding; secured borrowing capacity; ratio of unencumbered liquid assets to uninsured retail deposits and wholesale funding; relative size of haircuts applied to secured funding; amount of undrawn irrevocable commitments of contingent wholesale funding; geographical concentration of funding

12. Commercial mortgages	*Refers to*	*Vulnerabilities*
Project finance	Liability side/cash outflow	Wholesale funding: • On-demand and short-term wholesale funding: professional money market behaviour stochastics: credit risk/reputation-linked risk of rapid withdrawals • Fixed term deposits • Longer term rollover risk stochastics dependent on concentration • High credit risk sensitivity • Correlated/concentrated early withdrawals with penalty during bank-specific stress
	Asset side/cash inflow	• Illiquid, long-term assets • Liquidity of securitization in pipeline • Credit lines • Contractual committed, irrevocable • Inclusive of project finance covenants sensitivity • Non-contractual, reputation related
	Gap position	Inherent large maturity mismatch

13. Interbank wholesale business	*Refers to*	*Vulnerabilities*
Interbank loans/deposits	Liability side/cash outflow	• Idiosyncratic runoff • On-demand and short-term wholesale funding: professional money market behaviour stochastics: credit risk/reputation-linked risk of rapid withdrawals • Impeded access to secured lending due to repo-related counterparty credit risk • Money and capital market liquidity related to decay and shortening of funding terms due to systemic liquidity hoarding, money market shortages or systemic transparency issues

13. *Interbank wholesale* business	*Refers to*	*Vulnerabilities*	(*cont.*)
		• Fixed term: early withdrawal possibility • Credit lines/guarantees/margin/collateral requirements • Contractual/irrevocable • Contingent liabilities • Downgrade triggers related • Non-contractual: less applicable to pure interbank	
Correspondent banking	Asset side/cash inflow	Assumed 100% liquidity value of amounts on demand and instalments to receive	
	Gap position	According to runoff scenario during stress	

14. *Wholesale securitization* business	*Refers to*	*Vulnerabilities*
Securitization	Liability side/cash outflow	Conduit, SPV, securitization-related contingent liabilities: • Originator-related performance triggers, buybacks • Sponsor-related credit enhancements (e.g., CSA-based collateral requirements related to downgrade, SPV/conduit, CDS) • Sponsor and/or liquidity provider: correlated/concentrated drawings on general market and idiosyncratic (SPV) related to liquidity facilities • Non-contractual reputation-related buybacks (SPVs, SIVs), ABCP support • Inadequate limit structure to relevant contingent liabilities • Treasury inadequately informed about the nature of structured products On balance sheet: • Pipeline funding rollover • Deposit withdrawals by SPVs/conduits • Funding requirements of buybacks and ABCP support

14. *Wholesale securitization* business	*Refers to*	*Vulnerabilities*	*(cont.)*
Resecuritization	Asset side/cash inflow	• Warehousing: securitization related to liquidity horizon of pipeline assets during protracted market stress • Liquidity of assets bought back from SPVs • Liquidity of bought/supported ABCP from SPVs/conduits	
Structured products	Gap position	Potential high maturity mismatch due to market-driven liquidity squeeze caused by shortening of available funding and illiquidity of bought-back assets	

15. *Wholesale prime* brokerage business	*Refers to*	*Vulnerabilities*
Hedge funds	Liability side/cash outflow	Idiosyncratic stress: • Concentrated deposit withdrawals during idiosyncratic stress • Loss of funding possibility by rehypothecation of received collateral due to withdrawal of accounts Market stress: • Impediments to securities borrowed needed to cover liabilities related to repo and securities lending/borrowing business
Clearing member of exchange-related professional market makers in securities and derivatives	Asset side/cash inflow	Market stress: • Liquid/illiquid ratio of collateral by hedge funds • Extremely illiquid collateral, low frequent valuation for hedge of hedge funds • Risk of shortfall of deposits and liquid collateral for market makers
	Gap position	Potential high mismatch due to withdrawal of deposits and collateral due to cancelled accounts

16. Retail-linked wholesale business	Refers to	Vulnerabilities
Fiduciary funds	Liability side/cash outflow	• Stress: on-demand and short-term wholesale funding, professional money market behaviour stochastics, liquidity/credit risk/reputation-linked risk of rapid withdrawals • Fixed term deposits • Longer term rollover risk stochastics dependent on concentration • High credit risk sensitivity • Correlated/concentrated early withdrawals with penalty during bank-specific stress
Trust funds	Asset side/cash inflow Gap position	

17. Trade finance	Refers to	Vulnerabilities
Letter of credit	Liability side/cash outflow	• Stable projected cash flows • Possible funding of irregular (pre)finance • Drawing on letters of credit
Exchange bills	Asset side/cash inflow	• Liquidity value of exchange bills • Interbank claims
Documentary credit	Gap position	

18. Custody services	Refers to	Vulnerabilities
G(CDS)	Liability side/cash outflow	If contractually allowed: vulnerabilities of rehypothecation, repo transactions, and securities lending/borrowing
	Asset side/cash inflow	If allowed to use customers' assets: (un)encumbrance planning
	Gap position	Possible mismatch in specific securities needed and availability in the securities borrowing/lending market

Part II
Tools to manage liquidity risk

6

Monitoring liquidity

6.1 A TAXONOMY OF CASH FLOWS

The identification and taxonomy of the cash flows that can occur during the business activity of a financial institution is crucial to building effective tools to monitor and manage liquidity risk.

Many classifications have been proposed (see, amongst others, [86]; a good review is [107]). The taxonomy we suggest, not too different from the others just mentioned, focuses on two main dimensions: time and amount; it is sketched in Figure 6.1. Like any other classification, this one also depends on the reference point of view. More specifically, in our case, we classify cash flows by considering them from a certain point in time; for example, cash flows may fall in one of the categories we will present below when we look at them from, say, today's point of view of. They can also change category when we shift the point of view in some other date in the future.

The first dimension to look at, when trying to classify future cash flows, is time: cash flows may occur at future instants that are known with certainty at the reference time (e.g., today), or they may manifest themselves at some random instants in the future. In the first case we say that, according to the time of their appearance, they are deterministic. In the second case we define them as stochastic (again, according to time).

The second dimension to consider is the amount: cash flows may occur in an amount that is known with certainty at the reference time, or alternatively their amount cannot be fully determined.For the amount, the main distinction will be between deterministic cash flows, if they fall in the first case, or stochastic cash flows, if they belong to the second case. Classification according to the amount, though, can be further broken down such that subcategories can be identified.

Moreover, when the amount is deterministic, cash flows can be labelled simply as fixed as a result of being set in such a way by the terms of a contract.

When the amount is stochastic, it is possible to recognize four possible subcategories labelled as follows: credit related when amount uncertainty can be due to credit events, such as the default of one or more of the bank's clients; indexed/contingent, when the amount of cash flows depends on market variables, such as Libor fixings; behavioural, when cash flows are dependent on decisions made by the bank's clients or counterparties: these decisions can only be loosely predicted according to some rational behaviour based on market variables and sometimes they are based on information the bank does not have; and, finally, the fourth subcategory is termed new business: in which cash flows originated by new contracts that are dealt in the future and more or less planned by the bank, so that their amount is stochastic.

Based on the classification we have introduced, we can provide some examples of cash flows, with the corresponding category they belong to, according to the time/amount criterion. The examples are also shown in Figure 6.1.

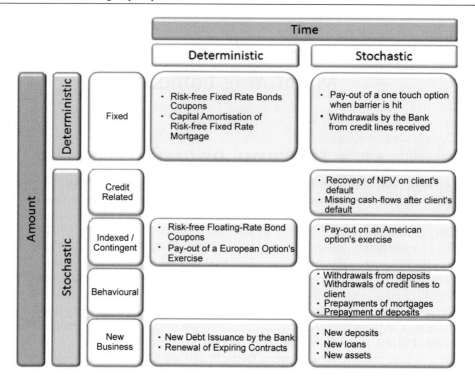

Figure 6.1. Taxonomy of the cash flows

Let us begin with deterministic amount/deterministic time cash flows: they are typically related to financial contracts, such as fixed rate bonds or fixed rate mortgages or loans. These cash flows are produced by payments of periodic interests (e.g., every six months) and periodic repayment of the capital instalments if the asset is amortizing. It should be noted that not only bonds or loans held in the assets of the bank generate these kinds of cash flows, but also bonds issued and loans received by the bank held in its liabilities. Moreover, when considering assets, that cash flows belong to the fixed amount/deterministic time category can only be ensured if the obligor, or the bond's issuer, is risk free, so that credit events cannot affect the cash flow schedule provided for in the contract.

Deterministic amount cash flows can also occur at stochastic times, either because the contract can provide for a given sum to be paid or received by the bank, or because the amount depends on a choice made by the bank. An example of the first kind of cash flow can be represented by the payout of one-touch options: in fact, the buyer of this type of option receives a given amount of money when the underlying asset breaches some barrier level, from below or from above. The time is unknown from the reference instant, but the amount can easily be deducted from the contract's terms. An example of cash flows that depend on the bank's decisions can be represented by the positive cash flows originated by the withdrawals of credit lines received by the bank. In this case, the amount can safely be assumed to be some level between 0 and the limit of the credit line chosen by the bank depending on its needs, but it can occur at any time until the expiry of the contract, since liquidity needs may arise at some stochastic time.

Shifting the analysis to the stochastic amount category, we first identify credit-related cash flows that are due to the default of one or more clients, so that once the default time is fixed, their amount can be implied. The default time is obviously not known at the reference time, so that the time when these cash flows occur is stochastic. An example can be represented by the missing cash flows, after the default, of the contract stream of fixed interests and of capital repayment of the loan. A missing cash flow may be considered a negative cash flow that alters a given cash flow schedule: if a loan, for example, is fixed rate amortizing, then we have a modified cash flow schedule on the contract interest rate and capital repayment times. Moreover, the recovery value after default can be inserted in this category of cash flows.

Stochastic amount cash flows we can also be indexed/contingent (i.e., linked to market variables). Examples of such cash flows are, amongst others, floating rate coupons that are linked to market fixings (e.g., Libor) and the payout of European options, which also depend on the level of the underlying asset at the expiry of the contract. In these the time of the occurrence of cash flows is known (the coupon payment, the exercise date), but there may also be indexed/contingent cash flows that can manifest at stochastic times. Examples are the payout of American options, both when the bank is long or short them, because the exercise time is stochastic and depends on future market conditions that determine the optimality of early exercise. Again, here we have to stress that we are referring to contracts whose counterparty to the bank is default risk free.

Anther type of stochastic amount cash flow is behavioural; for example, when a bank's clients decide to prepay the outstanding amount of their loans or mortgages. In this case the bank may compute the prepaid amount received on prepayment: the prepayment time cannot be predicted with certainty by the bank, so that the time when the cash flows occur is stochastic in this case. Missing cash flows with respect to the contract schedule can be determined once prepayment occurs. If the prepaid mortgage, as before, is fixed rate amortizing, then we have a modified cash flow schedule on the contract interest rate and capital repayment times.

Other behavioural cash flows, befalling at stochastic times, are those originated by credit lines that are open to clients: withdrawals may occur at any time until the expiry of the contract and in an uncertain amount, although within the limits of the line. Withdrawals from sight or saving deposits belong to this category too.

Finally, we have stochastic amount cash flows related to the replacement of expiring contracts and to new business activity. For example, the bank may plan to deal new loans to replace exactly the amount of loans expiring in the next two years, and this will produce a stochastic amount of cash flows since it is unsure whether new clients will want or need to close such contracts. Old contracts expire at a known maturity so that cash flows linked to their replacement are known as well. Moreover, the new issuance of bonds by the bank can be well defined under a time perspective, but the amount may not be completely in line with the plans.

By the same reasoning, the evolution of completely new contracts may not follow the pattern predicted in business development documents, so that related cash flows are both amount and time stochastic. For example, new retail deposits, new mortgages and new assets in general may be only partially predicted. In general, cash flows due to new business, or to the rollover of existing business, are quite difficult to model and to manage.

6.2 LIQUIDITY OPTIONS

Some of the categories of cash flows described above are connected with the exercise of so-called liquidity options. These kinds of options are conceptually no different from other options, yet the decision to exercise them depends on their particular nature.

More specifically, a liquidity option can be defined as the right of a holder to receive cash from, or to give cash to, the bank at predefined times and terms. Exercising a liquidity option does not directly entail a profit or a loss in financial terms, rather it is as a result of a need for or a surplus of liquidity of the holder. This does not necessarily exclude linking the exercising of a liquidity option to financial effects; on the contrary, such a link is sometimes quite strong: this is clear from the examples of liquidity options we provide below.

Comparing these options with standard options usually traded in financial markets, the major difference is that the latter are exercised when there is a profit, independently of the cash flows following exercise, although typically they are positive. For example, a European option on a stock is a financial option that is exercised at expiry if the strike price of the underlying asset is lower than the market price. The profit can immediately be monetized by selling the stock in the market so that the holder receives a positive net cash flow equal to the difference between the strike price (paid) and the sell price (received). Alternatively, options may be exercised and the stock not immediately sold in the market, so that only a negative cash flow occurs: this is because the holder wants to keep the stock in her portfolio, for example, and it is more convenient to buy it at the strike price instead of the prevailing market price. The convenience to exercise is then independent of the cash flows after exercise.

On the other hand, a liquidity option is exercised because of the cash flows produced after exercise, even if it is sometimes not convenient to exercise it from a financial perspective. For example, consider the liquidity option that a bank sells to a customer when the bank opens a committed credit line: the obligor has the right to withdraw whatever amount up to the notional of the line whenever she wants under specified market conditions, typically a floating rate (say, 3-month Libor) plus a spread, that for the moment we consider determined only by the obligor's default risk. The option to withdraw can be exercised when it also makes sense under a financial perspective; for example, if the spread widened due to worsening of the obligor's credit standing: in this case funds can be received under the contract's conditions (which are kept fixed until expiry) and hence there is a clear saving of costs in terms of fewer paid interests on the line's usage rather than opening a new line. On the other hand, the line can be used even if the credit spread shrinks, so that it would be cheaper for the obligor to get new funds in the market with a new loan, but for reasons other than financial convenience it chooses to withdraw the needed amounts from the credit line.

Another example of a liquidity option is given by sight and saving deposits: the bank's clients can typically withdraw all or part of the deposited amount with no or short notice. The withdrawal might be due to the possibility to invest in assets with higher yields more than compensating for higher risks, or it might be due to the need of liquidity for transaction purposes. So, even in this case there may exist some financial rationale behind exercising a liquidity option, but it can also be triggered by many other different reasons that are hardly predictable, or can be forecast on a statistical basis.

Exercising a liquidity option can also work the other way round: the bank's client has the right to repay the funds before the contract ends. Although the bank would benefit in this case from the greater amount of liquidity available, economic effects are usually negative and thus cause a loss. An example is given by the prepayment of fixed rate mortgages or loans: they can be paid back before the expiry for exogenous reasons, often linked to events in the life of the client such as divorces or retirements; more often prepayment is triggered by a financial incentive to close the contract and reopen it under current market conditions if the interest rate falls. In the first case the bank would not suffer any loss if market rates rose or stayed constant, on the contrary it could even reinvest at better market conditions those funds received earlier than expected. In the second case, prepayment would cause a loss since replacement of the mortgage or closure of the the loan before maturity would be at rates lower than those provided for by old contracts.

In the end, although liquidity options can be triggered by factors other than financial convenience, the effect on the bank can be considered twofold:

1. A liquidity impact on the balance sheet, given by the amount withdrawn or repaid.
2. A (positive or negative) financial impact, given by the difference between the contract's interest rates and credit spread and the market level of the same variables at the time the liquidity option is exercised, applied on the withdrawn or repaid amount.

Sometimes the second impact is quite small, as, for example, when a client closes a savings account: the bank's financial loss is given in this case by the missing margin between the contract deposit rate and the rate it earns on the reinvestment of received amounts (usually considered risk-free assets), or by the cost to replace the deposit with a new one that yields a higher rate. The liquidity impact, on the other hand, can be quite substantial if the deposit has a big notional.

While the financial effects of liquidity options can be directly, although partially, hedged by a mixture of standard and statistical techniques, the liquidity impact can only be managed by the tools that we analyse in the following. These tools, loosely speaking, involve either cash reserves or a constrained allocation of the assets in liquid assets or easy access to credit lines (i.e., a long position in liquidity options for the bank). All of these imply costs that have to be properly accounted for when pricing contracts to deal with clients, so that models to price long and short liquidity options have also to be designed. Since, as shown above, liquidity options also produce financial profits or losses when exercised, so that they can also be seen under some respects as financial options, models must jointly consider liquidity and financial aspects.

6.3   LIQUIDITY RISK

Risk is always related to uncertainty about the future: this may turn out to be more favourable than initially expected or, on the contrary, more adverse than forecast. Although positive and negative outcomes should be balanced, in practice it is the adverse unexpected states of the world that is of interest. Bearing this in mind, a very general definition of liquidity risk for a financial institution is the following.

Definition 6.3.1 (Liquidity risk). *The event that in the future the bank receives smaller than expected amounts of cash flows to meet its payment obligations.*

We have already analysed the different kinds of liquidity concepts and related risks in Chapter 2. Definition 6.3.1 encompasses both funding liquidity risk and market liquidity risk. In fact, if a bank is not able to fund its future payment obligations because it is receiving less funds than expected from clients, from the sale of assets, from the interbank market or from the central bank, this risk may produce an insolvency situation if the bank is absolutely unable to settle its obligations, even by resorting to very costly alternatives. Market liquidity risk according to the definition above is the result of the inability to sell assets, such as bonds, at fair price and with immediacy, and leads to a situation in which the bank receives smaller than expected amounts of positive cash flows.

The risk dimension considered in Definition 6.3.1 refers to the quantity of flows, so we call this quantitative liquidity risk. Nonetheless, we claim that another risk dimension for liquidity should be considered: the cost of liquidity, or cost of funding, and the related risk can be defined as follows.

Definition 6.3.2 (Funding cost risk). *The event that in the future the bank has to pay greater than expected cost (spread) above the risk-free rate to receive funds from sources of liquidity that are available.*

This can be defined as cost of liquidity risk or cost of funding risk. Not too much attention has been paid to the modelling of funding cost risk, although in the past it was always recognized as such but deemed to have little impact on banking activity. The reason for this is quite simple to understand if one looks at Figure 6.2, which shows the rolling series of the CDS Itraxx Financial spread. We use this as a proxy for funding spread over the risk-free curve for top European banks on a 5-year maturity. As is manifest, the spread was almost constant and low until 2007 (the outbreak of the subprime crises in the US). This means that banks were considered virtually default risk free and funding costs, meant as the spread over the risk-free curve, had a very limited effect on the profitability of banks.

Moreover, it should be stressed that in such a constant low-spread environment, the rollover of the bank's liabilities that expire entails negligible risk in terms of unexpected spread levels. This combined with abundant liquidity such that the quantity of funding available was in practice without relevant limits, banks were able to decide how to finance their assets as they preferred: the rollover of maturity was an almost risk-free activity. For these reasons, trying to predict funding costs was a futile exercise and their inclusion in the pricing of contracts was straightforward.

Since the middle of 2007, financial institutions have no longer been able to always raise funds at low spreads: the volatility of spreads even over interbank market rates (e.g., Libor) dramatically increased, and the amount of funding available in the capital market declined, at least for the banking sector. As a consequence of these two reasons, the funding policy of banks is now subject to constraints so as to abate the average funding cost, reduce rollover risk (regarding both the quantitative and risk dimension) and hence make credit intermediation activity still a profitable business.

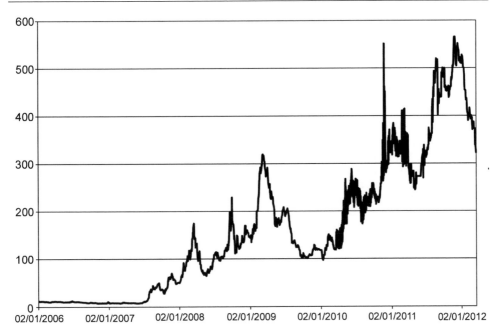

Figure 6.2. CDS Itraxx Financial rolling series from September 2004 to September 2011
Source: Market quotes from major brokers

The conclusion we can draw from this is that modern liquidity risk management must consider both the quantitative dimension and the cost dimension as equally important and robust modelling must be developed for the two dimensions. We can synthesize both dimensions of liquidity risk in the following comprehensive definition.

Definition 6.3.3 (Liquidity risk). *The amount of economic losses due to the fact that on a given date the algebraic sum of positive and negative cash flows and of existing cash available at that date, is different from some (desired) expected level.*

This definition includes a manifestation of liquidity risk as:

1. Inability to raise enough funds to meet payment obligations, so that the bank is forced to sell its assets, thus causing costs related to the non-fair level at which they are sold or to suboptimal asset allocation. The complete inability to raise funds would eventually produce an insolvency state for the bank. These costs refer to the quantitative dimension of liquidity risk.
2. Ability to raise funds only at costs above those expected. These costs refer to the cost dimension of liquidity risk.
3. Ability to invest excess liquidity only at rates below those expected. We are in the opposite situation to point 2, and it is a rarer risk for a bank since business activity usually hinges on assets with longer durations than liabilities. These (opportunity) costs also refer to the cost dimension of liquidity risk.

6.4 QUANTITATIVE LIQUIDITY RISK MEASURES

We introduce a set of measures to monitor and manage quantitative liquidity risk.[1] These measures aim at monitoring the net cash flows that a bank might expect to receive or pay in the future and ensure that it stays solvent. Cash flows, however, classified according to the taxonomy above are produced by two classes of factors.

Definition 6.4.1 (Causes of liquidity). *All factors referring to existing and forecast future contracts originated by the ordinary business activity of a financial institution can be considered as the causes of liquidity risk. Cash flows generated by the causes of liquidity can be both positive and negative.*

The other class of factors is given by Definition 6.4.2.

Definition 6.4.2 (Sources of liquidity). *All factors capable of generating positive cash flows to manage and hedge liquidity risk and can be disposed of promptly by the bank determine the liquidity generation capacity (defined in the following) of the financial institution.*

First we set the notation. Let us indicate with $cf_e^+(t_0, t_i) = \mathbf{E}[cf^+(t_0, t_i)]$ the sum of expected positive cash flows occurring at time t_i from the reference time t_0. Similarly, we indicate by $cf_e^-(t_0, t_i) = \mathbf{E}[cf^-(t_0, t_i)]$ the sum of expected negative cash flows occurring on the same date.

We analysed above the different categories of cash flows and saw that many are stochastic in terms of the amount or time of occurrence or both. This is the reason we have stressed the fact that the sum of cash flows, either positive or negative, is just expected. On the other hand, if cash flows are expected, this also means that their distribution at each time should be determined so as to recover measures other than the expected (average) amount, to increase the effectiveness of liquidity management. We will come back to this later on, but for the moment we can formally define the positive and negative cash flows for the set of contracts and/or securities $\{d_1, d_2, \ldots, d_N\}$ as:

$$cf_e^+(t_0, t_i) = \mathbf{E}\left[\sum_{j=1}^{N} cf^+(t_0, t_i; d_j)\right] \tag{6.1}$$

and similarly

$$cf_e^-(t_0, t_i) = \mathbf{E}\left[\sum_{j=1}^{N} cf^-(t_0, t_i; d_j)\right] \tag{6.2}$$

Assume we are at the reference time t_0: we define by $CF(t_0, t_j)$ the cumulative amount of all cash flows starting from date t_a up to time t_b:

$$CF(t_0, t_a, t_b) = \sum_{i=a}^{b}(cf_e^+(t_0, t_i) + cf_e^-(t_0, t_i)) \tag{6.3}$$

Expected cash flows and cumulated cash flows allow us to construct the basic tools for liquidity monitoring and management: the term structure of expected cash flows.

---

[1] In this section we elaborate on the main ideas presented in [86, Chapter 8] and [85, Chapter 15].

6.4.1   The term structure of expected cash flows and the term structure of expected cumulated cash flows

The term structure of expected cash flows (TSECF) can be defined as the collection, ordered by date, of positive and expected cash flows, up to expiry referring to the contract with the longest maturity, say t_b:

$$\text{TSECF}(t_0, t_b) = \{\text{cf}_e^+(t_0, t_0), \text{cf}_e^-(t_0, t_0), \text{cf}_e^+(t_0, t_1), \text{cf}_e^-(t_0, t_1), \ldots, \text{cf}_e^+(t_0, t_b), \text{cf}_e^-(t_0, t_b)\}$$

$$(6.4)$$

At the end of the TSECF, with an indefinite expiry corresponding to the end of business activity, there is reimbursement of the equity to stockholders. TSECF is often referred to as the maturity ladder: we reserve this name for the initial part, up to one-year maturity, of the TSECF. It is also standard practice to identify short-term liquidity, up to one year, and structural liquidity, beyond one year.

The term structure of cumulated expected cash flows (TSECCF) is similar to the TSECF: it is the collection of expected cumulated cash flows, starting at t_0 and ending at t_b, ordered by date:

$$\text{TSECCF}(t_0, t_b) = \{\text{CF}(t_0, t_0, t_1), \text{CF}(t_0, t_0, t_2), \ldots, \text{CF}(t_0, t_0, t_b)\} \qquad (6.5)$$

The TSECCF is useful because banks are interested not only in monitoring the net balance of cash flows on a given date, but also how the past dynamic evolution of net cash flows affects its total cash position on that date. If on a given date the balance of inflows and outflows is net negative, this position can be netted out with a positive cash position originated by past inflows. Obviously the reverse can also be true and the bank can use a net positive inflow on a given date to cover a short cash position deriving from past outflows, although in this case it should be noted that short cash positions must be financed in any case, typically with new liabilities (see below), so that positive inflows are used to pay back these debts.

Conceptually, building the TSECF and TSECCF is quite simple and can be shown with an example.

Example 6.4.1. *Consider a bank with a simplified balance sheet like the one in Figure 6.3. The assets comprise investments in bonds and loans; they are financed with deposits, bonds and equity. Assume that the assets bear no default risk and no liquidity options are embedded within deposits. The first step to build the TSECF is to order the assets and the liabilities according to their maturity, disregarding which kind of contract they are. This is shown in Table 6.1.*

When assets expire positive cash flows are received by the bank, whereas when liabilities expire negative cash flows must be paid by the bank. The amount of the cash flows is simply the notional of each contract in the assets and liabilities and, under the assumptions we are working with, these amounts are deterministic both under a time and amount perspective. Collecting them and ordering them by date, we obtain the TSECF in Figure 6.4.

Cash flows in themselves are not enough to monitor the liquidity of a bank, since what matters in the end is the cash available up to a given time, which is given by the cumulated cash flows. At each date, cash flows from the initial date t_0 up to each date t_i are cumulated according to formula (6.3) and entered in the TSECCF: the result is also shown in Figure 6.4.

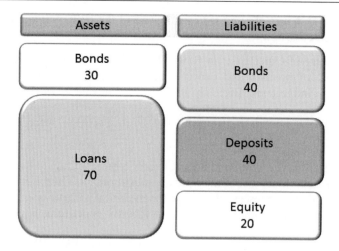

Figure 6.3. Balance sheet of a bank with types of assets and liabilities and their quantities.

Table 6.1. Assets and liabilities reclassified according to maturity

Expiry	Assets	Liabilities
1	20	
2		10
5	50	
7		70
10	30	
>10		20
	100	100

This overly simplified example can be made a bit more realistic if we also consider the interest payments that assets and liabilities yield. Assume a yearly period for coupon payments and an average yield common to all contracts expiring on a given date: the interest yielded by each contract is shown in Table 6.2.

When interest payments are added, the TSECF is built as in Table 6.3, where there is also the TSECCF. In Figure 6.5 the TSECF is represented for each date, decomposed in positive and negative cash flows, and in the bottom diagram cumulated cash flows are also shown.

In Example 6.4.1 shows a very simple balance sheet producing a very simple TSECF and related TSECCF. In a real balance sheet the number and type of contracts entering into the analysis is much greater and is not just limited to those existent at the reference time, but also all new activities that can be reasonably expected to be operated and in most of cases belonging to the category of new business of Figure 6.1.

In greater detail, the cash flows of the TSECF are those produced by all the causes of cash flows, as defined above. This means that the TSECF

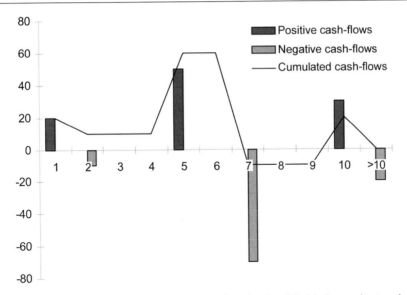

Figure 6.4. Term structure of expected cash flows for the simplified balance sheet reclassified in Table 6.1

Table 6.2. Interest yield of the assets and liabilities of the simplified balance sheet reclassified in Table 6.1

	Interest yield	
Expiry	*Assets* (%)	*Liabilities* (%)
1	5.00%	
2		4.00%
5	6.00%	
7		4.50%
10	6.50%	
>10		

- includes the cash flows from all existing contracts that comprise the assets and liabilities: in many cases cash flows are stochastic because they can be linked to market indices, such as Libor or Euribor fixings (interest rate models are needed to compute expected cash flows);
- cash flows are adjusted to consider credit risks: credit models have to be used to take into account defaults on an aggregated basis by also considering the correlation existing amongst the bank's counterparties;
- cash flows are adjusted to account for liquidity options: behavioural models are used for typical banking products such as sight deposits, credit line usage and prepayment of mortgages;

Table 6.3. The term structure of cash flows and of cumulated cash flows

	cf^+		cf^-		
	Notional	Interest	Notional	Interest	TSECCF
1	20	5.95	0	−3.55	22.40
2	0	4.95	−10	−3.55	13.80
3	0	4.95	0	−3.15	15.60
4	0	4.95	0	−3.15	17.40
5	50	4.95	0	−3.15	69.20
6	0	1.95	0	−3.15	68.00
7	0	1.95	−70	−3.15	−3.20
8	0	1.69	0	0	−1.51
9	0	1.69	0	0	0.18
10	30	1.69	0	0	31.87
>10	0	0	−20	0	11.87

- cash flows originated by new business increasing the assets should be included: they are typically stochastic in both the amount and time dimensions, so they are treated by means of models that consider all related risks;
- the rollover of maturing liabilities, by similar or different contracts, and new bond issuances (which could also be included in the new business category) to fund the increase in assets, have to be taken into account. The risks related to the stochastic nature of these flows have to be properly measured as well resulting in a need to set up proper liquidity buffers and we will dwell on that in Chapter 7.

The TSECF, and hence the TSECCF, do not include the flows produced by the sources of cash flows, which we analyse below. The sources of cash flows are tools to manage the liquidity risk originated by the causes of cash flows.

The task of the Treasury Department is to monitor the TSECF and the TSECCF. The perfect condition is reached if the TSECCF is positive at all times. This means that positive cash flows are able to cover negative cash flows, both of which are generated by usual business activity. Although this is the ideal situation it cannot be verified for two reasons:

1. Many of the cash flows belong to categories that are stochastic in the amount and/or the time dimension, such that the TSECF always forecasts just the expected value of a distribution of flows. As a result the TSECCF contains only expected values as well: if it is positive on average most of the time, the distribution of cumulated cash flows at a given time can also actually envisage negative outcomes with an assigned probability.
2. The temporal distribution of the maturities of the assets and the liabilities could produce periods of negative cumulated cash flows. These periods may be accepted if they are short and can be managed effectively with the tools we introduce below.

When the TSECCF shows negative values, on an expected basis, this means that the bank may become insolvent and eventually go bankrupt. This is why the treasurer's main task is to ensure that the future TSECCF is always positive. But since we have seen

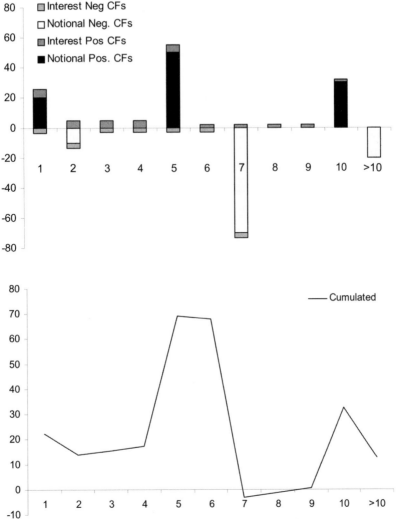

Figure 6.5. Term structure of expected cash flows for the simplified balance sheet reclassified in Table 6.1 including interest payments (top) and term structure of expected cumulated cash flows (bottom)

that this ideal situation cannot always be fulfilled, we need to discover which tools can be used to cope with the case when the TSECCF has negative values.

6.4.2   Liquidity generation capacity

Liquidity generation capacity (LGC) is the main tool a bank can use to handle the negative entries of the TSECCF. It can be defined as follows.

Definition 6.4.3 (Liquidity generation capacity). *The ability of a bank to generate positive cash flows, beyond contractual ones, from the sources of liquidity available in the balance sheet and off the balance sheet at a given date.*

The LGC manifests itself in two ways:

1. Balance sheet expansion with secured or unsecured funding.
2. Balance sheet shrinkage by selling assets.

Balance sheet expansion can be achieved via

- borrowing through an increase of deposits, typically in the interbank market (retail or wholesale unsecured funding);
- withdrawal of credit lines the financial institution has been granted by other financial counterparties (wholesale unsecured funding);
- issuance of new bonds (wholesale and retail unsecured funding).

It is worth noting that new debt is not the same as that planned to roll over existing contracts or to fund new business: in this case the related cash flows would be included in the TSECF and in the TSECCF, as seen above.

Balance sheet shrinkage is operated by selling assets, starting from more liquid ones such as Treasury bonds, corporate bonds and stocks: they are traded in the market actively and can be sold within a relatively short period. Reduction may also include the sale of less liquid assets, such as loans or even buildings owned by the bank, within a more extended time horizon.

Repo transactions can also be considered separately from the other cases and labelled as "balance sheet neutral".

The bank may prefer to consider only liquidity that can be generated without relying on external factors, such as clients or other institutional counterparties. It is easy to recognize that LGC related to balance sheet expansion is dependent on these external factors, whereas balance sheet reduction, or "balance sheet neutral" repo transactions, are not. So it is possible to present an alternative distinction within LGC; namely, we can identify

- balance sheet liquidity (BSL), or liquidity that can be generated by the assets existing in the balance sheet. BSL is tightly linked to balance sheet reduction LGC and it is also the ground on which to build liquidity buffers, which we will analyse in Chapter 7;
- remaining liquidity, originated by the other possible ways mentioned above, which relates to balance sheet expansion.

A similar classification within LGC is based on the link between the generation of liquidity and the assets in the balance sheet, so that we have:

- Security-linked liquidity including
  - secured withdrawals of credit lines received from other financial institutions;
  - secured debt issuance;
  - selling of assets and repo.
- Security-unlinked liquidity including
  - unsecured borrowing from new clients through new deposits;
  - withdrawals of credit lines received from other financial institutions;
  - unsecured bond issuance;

It is immediate clear that security-linked liquidity is little more than BSL liquidity, or the liquidity obtained by balance sheet reduction.

To sum up, we can identify three types of sources of liquidity that can be included in the classifications above:

1. Selling of assets, AS.
2. Secured funding using assets as collateral and via repo transactions, RP.
3. Unsecured funding via withdrawals of committed credit lines available from other financial institutions and via deposit transactions in the interbank market, USF.

The first two sources generate security-linked BSL by reducing the balance sheet or keeping it constant. The third source generates security-unlinked non-BSL by expanding the balance sheet. It is worth stressing that the unsecured funding of point 3 is not the same as the unsecured funding we inserted in the TSECF and TSECCF, but is mainly related to the rollover of existing liabilities or the issuance of new debt to finance business expansion. In fact, while in the latter case we referred to existing and planned activity funding usual banking activity, the operations involved in LGC refer to shorter term exceptional unsecured funding, in most cases unrelated to a bank's bond issuance and other forms of fundraising.

We can now define the term structure of LGC as the collection, at reference time t_0, of liquidity that can be generated at a given time t_i, by the sources of liquidity, up to a terminal time t_b:

$$\text{TSLGC}(t_0, t_b) = \{\text{AS}(t_0, t_1), \text{RP}(t_0, t_1), \text{USF}(t_0, t_1), \dots, \text{AS}(t_0, t_b), \text{RP}(t_0, t_b), \text{USF}(t_0, t_b)\} \tag{6.6}$$

where $\text{AS}(t_0, t_i)$ is the liquidity that can be generated by the sale of assets at time t_i, computed at the reference time t_0; $\text{RP}(t_0, t_i)$ and $\text{USF}(t_0, t_1)$ are defined similarly.

Analogously, the term structure of cumulated LGC is the collection, at the reference time t_0, of the cumulated liquidity that can be generated at a given time t_i, by the sources of liquidity, up to a terminal time t_b:

$$\text{TSCLGC}(t_0, t_b) = \left\{ \sum_{i=0}^{1} \text{TSLGC}(t_0, t_i), \sum_{i=0}^{2} \text{TSLGC}(t_0, t_i), \dots, \sum_{i=0}^{b} \text{TSLGC}(t_0, t_i) \right\} \tag{6.7}$$

Remark 6.4.1. *The quantities entering in the TSLGC and hence the TSCLGC are expected values, since they all depend on stochastic variables such as the price of assets and the haircut applied to repo transactions. Moreover, the stochasticity of the amount of unsecured funding that it is possible to raise in the market could and should be considered.*

The sources of liquidity contributing to the TSLGC belong either to the banking or the trading book. In the banking book the sources of liquidity are all the bonds available for sale[2] (AFS) and other assets that can be sold and/or repoed relatively easily: they are referred to collectively as eligible assets. In all cases these assets are unencumbered; that is, they are not already pledged to other forms of secured funding such as the ones we present just below. To determine at a given date t_i the liquidity that can be generated by these sources, one needs:

---

[2] The term "available for sale" in our context is not related to the same definition used for accountancy purposes. We simply refer to assets that can be sold because they are unencumbered, as explained in the following.

- AFS bonds: the expected future value of each bond, considering the volatility of interest rates and credit spreads, and of the probability of default. Moreover, the possibility that the bonds may become more illiquid, thus increasing bid–ask spreads and lowering the selling price, has to be considered in the analysis.
- For other assets the selling period and the expected selling price have to be properly taken into account.

As mentioned above, assets in the banking book can be also repoed; that is, the bank can sell them via a repo transaction and buy them back at expiry of the contract. The repo can be seen as a collateralized loan that the bank may receive: as such it can be safely assumed that liquidity can be obtained more easily than unsecured funding, since the credit risk of the bank is considerably abated. For the same reason the funding cost, meant as the spread over the risk-free rate, is also dramatically reduced for the bank.

Besides the factors that affect liquidity that AFS bonds can generate, there is another factor determining the actual liquidity that can be obtained by a repo or a collateralized loan transaction: the haircut, or the cut in the market value of the bond indicating how much the counterparty is willing to lend to the bank, given an amount of bonds transferred as collateral. The haircut will depend on the volatility of the price of the collateral bond and on the probability of default of the issuer of the bond.

Haircuts have to be modelled not only for unencumbered assets to assert their liquidity potential, but also for encumbered assets, involved in collateralized loans, to forecast possible margin calls and reintegration of the collateral when their prices decline by an appreciable amount.

Finally, received committed credit lines, which are not exactly in the balance sheet until they are used (in which case they become liabilities) have to be included in the TSLGC and their amount and future actual existence taken into account. In fact, although it is also quite reasonable to receive committed credit lines from other financial institutions after the expiry of the lines currently received, their amount could be constrained by possible systemic liquidity issues. Moreover, the costs in terms of funding spreads and other fees to be paid have to be considered as well.

If we move to the trading book, we can identify bonds and other assets similar to those included in the banking book as sources of liquidity. Amongst the other assets that can be used to generate liquidity we may add stocks and also some structured products, such as eligible ABSs or even more complex structures.[3] These assets, provided they are unencumbered, can be sold or they can be pledged in collateralized loans or repoed. In these cases the same considerations we have made above can be repeated here and the same factors have to be included in the assessment of the liquidity potential to include in the TSLGC.

Unsecured funding on the interbank market via deposit transactions, usually up to one-year expiry, are part of the banking book for accounting reasons. Also here, the possibility to resort to this source of liquidity should be carefully weighted by the possibility to experience systemic liquidity crises (e.g., as in 2008) that strongly limit the availability of funds via this channel. The other important factor is the costs related to the funding spread.

---

[3] The liquidity of structured products can be strongly dependent on the more general economic environment. For example, it used to be quite easy to pledge ABSs as collateral before 2007, but after the subprime crisis in the US banks were no longer willing to accept them as collateral.

Building the TSLGC can be very difficult, since the assumptions made for a given period affect other periods. For example, if the bank wants to compute the liquidity-generating capacity provided by a given bond held in the assets, assuming it is pledged as collateral for a loan starting in t_1 and expiring in t_2 to cover negative cumulated cash flows occurring during the same period, then the same bond has to be excluded for the same period and other overlapping periods from the TSLGC. This means that the process to build the actual TSLGC should be carried out in a greater number of steps.

It should also be stressed that the TSLGC is intertwined with the TSECF (and thus the TSECCF): there are feedback effects when defining the TSLGC that affect expected cash flows. which makes the building process a recursive procedure to be repeated until an equilibrium point is reached. For example, if we still consider that the TSLGC for a given period can be fed by a bond that can be pledged as collateral or repoed, then the cash flows of this bond should be excluded from the TSECF for the period of the loan or repo contract.[4] Missing cash-flows for the corresponding period worsen the cash flow term structure (although marginally), but this means that they must also be included in the analysis.

In the end, most of the problems in building the TSLGC are caused by unencumbered assets (most of which are what we earlier referred to as AFS bonds), both because the bank must keep track of how many are either sold or repoed out, and because the liquidity amount that can be extracted from these assets depends on several risk factors. It is useful then to introduce a tool that helps monitoring this part of the LGC more thoroughly: it is the term structure of available assets (TSAA) and will be described in the next section.

6.4.3 The term structure of available assets

In the previous section we stressed that BSL is originated by selling assets and/or by the repo transactions made on them. When building the TSLGC, it is important to ascertain whether BSL is the result of setting assets or carrying out repo transactions, since both operations have different consequences in terms of liquidity.

When an asset, such as a bond, is purchased by a bank a corresponding outflow equal to the (dirty) price is recorded in the cash position of the bank. During the life of the bond coupon flows are received by the bank and finally, at expiry, the face value of the bond is reimbursed by the issuer. All these cash flows should be considered contract related, so that they are included in the TSECF and the TSECCF. The likelihood of the issuer defaulting should also be taken into account.

The TSAA is affected by purchases, since it records increases in the security for the amount bought. When the asset expires, the TSAA records a reduction to zero of its availability, since it no longer exists. During the life of the asset, the availability is affected by total or partial selling of the position, and by repo transactions.

The TSAA is also affected by other kinds of transactions that can be loosely likened to repo agreements, but have different impacts. Namely, we also have to analyse buy/sellback (and sell/buyback) transactions and security lending (and borrowing). What

---

[4] At the end of the loan or repo, cash flows generated by the bond are usually given back to the borrower by the counterparty, although the contract may sometimes provide for different solutions.

matters in terms of availability for liquidity purposes is the possession of the asset rather than its ownership. We summarize all possible cases in the following:

- Repo transactions: at the start of the agreement the bank receives cash for an amount equal to the price of the asset reduced by the haircut; at the same time it delivers the asset to the counterparty. Although the asset is still owned by the bank, its possession passes to the counterparty, so that the bank no longer has availability of the security. This will become encumbered and cannot either be sold or used as collateral until the end of the repo agreement, when it is returned. Payments by the asset during the repo agreement belong to the bank since it is the owner, so that the TSECF and in the TSECCF are not affected in any way. The TSAA of the asset is reduced by an amount equal to the notional of the repo agreement, whereas the cash flow received by the bank at the start and the negative cash flow at the end are both entered in the TSLGC. Repo transactions produce a liability in the balance sheet, since they can be seen as collateralized debts of the bank.
- Reverse repo transactions: at the start of the agreement the bank pays cash for an amount equal to the price of the asset reduced by the haircut and receives the asset. The asset is owned by the counterparty, but it is now in the possession of the bank, so that it can be used as collateral by the bank for other transactions until the end of the repo agreement, when the obligation that it is to be returned to the counteparty has to be honoured by the bank. The payments by the asset during the repo agreement belong to the counterparty, so that they do not enter the TSECF or the TSECCF, but we include the cash flow paid by the bank at the start and the cash flow received at the end as contract, but only once. The TSAA of the asset is increased by an amount equal to the notional of the repo agreement. The TSLGC is not affected but the asset can be repoed until the end, so that it can be altered until this date. Reverse repo transactions are treated as assets in the balance sheet, since they can be seen as collataralized loans to the counterparty.
- Sell/buyback transactions: similar to repo transactions in terms of the exchange of cash and of the asset, with the difference that ownership passes to the buyer (the counterparty) at the start of the contract together with the possession. All payments received for the asset before the buyback belong to the counterparty.[5] The cash flows between the start and end of the contract will be taken from the TSECF and the TSECCF. The TSAA of the asset decreases by an amount equal to the notional of the sell/buyback contract. The TSLGC is affected in the same way as in the repo agreement, since sell/buyback transactions are a way to generate BSL. Sell/buyback transactions represent a commitment for the bank at the end of the contract.
- Buy/sellback transactions: similar to reverse repo transactions in terms of the exchange of cash and of the asset, with the difference that ownership passes to the buyer (the bank) at the start of the agreement together with the possession. This implies that the payments received for the asset before the sellback belong to the bank, so that they enter the TSECF and the TSECCF, along with the cash flows at the start and end that relate to the purchase and sale, since they are contract flows. The TSAA

---

[5] This was generally true until an annex was incorporated in the standard GMRA (the master agreement signed by banks for all repo-like transactions). Currently sell/buyback (and buy/sellback that we will address in the following point) are treated very similarly to a repo agreement, so that all payments are returned to the seller, although only at the end of the contract and not on each payment date as in the repo case. In this case the effects on the different term structures are similar to those we have shown for repo (and reverse repo for buy/sellback) transactions.

of the asset is increased by an amount equal to the notional of the buy/sellback agreement. The TSLGC is not affected but the asset can be repoed until the end, so that it can be altered until this date. Buy/sellback transactions represent an asset for the period of the contract.

- Security lending: similar to sell/buyback transactions in terms of exchange of the asset, but no cash is paid by the counterparty to the bank (except a periodic fee as service remuneration). Only possession passes to the counterparty, so that the payments received for the asset before the end of the contract belong to the bank and they enter the TSECF and the TSECCF, as does the interest paid by the countertparty at expiry when returning the asset to the bank. The TSAA of the asset decreases by an amount equal to the notional of the lending, since the bank cannot use it as collateral or sell it. The TSLGC is not affected and the asset cannot produce any liquidity until the end of the contract. Security lending represents an asset of the bank for the period of the contract.
- Security borrowing: similar to buy/sellback transactions in terms of exchange of the asset, but no cash is paid by the bank to the counterparty (except a periodic fee as service remuneration). Possession passes to the bank, so that the payments received for the asset before the end of the contract belong to the counterparty. The TSECF and the TSECCF are not affected apart from the interest paid by the bank at expiry of the borrowing. The TSAA of the asset increases by an amount equal to the notional of the borrowing, since the bank can use it as collateral provided it returns it to the counterparty at expiry. The TSLGC is not affected but the asset can produce liquidity until the end of the contract. Security borrowing represents a liability of the bank.

Other assets, such as stocks, do not have a specific expiry date. In this case contract cash flows entering the TSECF and the TSECCF are just the initial outflow representing the price paid to purchase the asset and the periodic dividend received. Moreover, non-maturing assets can be the underlying of repo transactions, buy/sellback (sell/buyback) contracts and security lending (and borrowing): the analysis is the same as above.

In Table 6.4 we recapitulate the results for all types of contracts that can be written on assets. It is worth noting that TSLGC is always affected either because the contract is dealt to generate BSL or because LGC is potentially increased over its lifetime. The only contract that does not increase the TSLGC is security lending, which actually decreases LGC related to BSL.

The TSAA can now be built keeping these results in mind, since for a given asset it is defined as the collection, for each date from an initial time t_0 to a terminal date t_b, of the quantity in possession of the bank, regardless of its ownership. In fact, the main purpose of the TSAA is to indicate how much of the asset can be used to extract liquidity and thus its contribution to global LGC. In more formal terms, for an asset A_1 we have:

$$\text{TSAA}^{A_1}(t_0, t_b) = \{A_1^P(t_0), A_1^P(t_1), \ldots, A_1^P(t_b)\} \tag{6.8}$$

where $A_1^P(t_i)$ is the quantity of the asset in possession of the bank at time t_i. On an aggregated basis, regarding a set of M securities in possession of the bank, the total TSAA including all the assets is:

$$\text{TSAA}(t_0, t_b) = \left\{ \sum_{m=1}^{M} A_m^P(t_0), \sum_{m=1}^{M} A_m^P(t_1), \ldots, \sum_{m=1}^{M} A_m^P(t_b) \right\} \tag{6.9}$$

Table 6.4. Types of contracts involving assets and effects on the TSECF/TSECCF, TSAA and TSLGC.

Type	Ownership	Possession	TSECF/ TSECCF	TSAA	TSLGC
			Changes to		
Buy	Bank	Bank	Yes	Yes	No/Possible
Sell	Counterparty	Counterparty	Yes	Yes	Yes
Repo	Bank	Counterparty	No	Yes	Yes
Reverse repo	Counterparty	Bank	Yes	Yes	No/Possible
Sell/buyback	Counterparty	Counterparty	Yes	Yes	Yes
Buy/sellback	Bank	Bank	Yes	Yes	No/Possible
Security lending	Bank	Counterparty	Yes	Yes	No
Security borrowing	Counterparty	Bank	Yes	Yes	No/Possible

The TSAA only shows how many single securities, or all of them, are available for inclusion in LGC. Obviously, this does not imply that the notional amount can be fully converted into liquidity. According to the type of operation (selling or repo) the price and/or the haircut are factors that need to be considered to determine the actual amount of liquidity that can be generated. Hence, we need proper models that allow the bank to forecast expected (or stressed) values for the price and the haircut, both at the single and aggregated assets level: such models will be introduced in Chapter 7 when we discuss the liquidity potential of a buffer comprising bonds.

In Example 6.4.2 we show how the interrelations amongst the different term structures operate in practice.

Example 6.4.2. *The bank buys a bond at time 0 for a notional amount of 1,000,000 at a price of 98.50; the payment is settled after 3 days, when the bond's possession also passes to the bank. In Table 6.5 we show what happens to the term structures. The bond pays a semiannual coupon of 10% p.a. and it expires in 2 years.*

The TSECF records an outflow equal to the notional amount of the bond times the price (we assume the bank buys the bond upon a coupon payment, so that the dirty price and the clean price are the same) occurring on the settlement date, 3 days after the reference time 0 (or 0.01 years). The TSAA records an increase of the quantity available to the bank of the bond until its expiry, when it is reset to zero. The TSLGC is unaffected. The last two columns show the price and the haircut. They are expected values and for the moment we consider them as given, although they can be the output of some model or just assumptions of the bank.

Assume now the bank decides to sell a quantity of the bond equal to a notional of 500,000 after 9 months (or 0.75 years). We know that this trade can be dealt to generate liquidity, so that the TSCLGC records an inflow equal to the amount times the price, including the accrued interests ($500,000 \times (99.90/100 + 10\% \times 0.25) = 512,000$) as well. The TSECF and the TSECCF are modified so as to show the reduced amounts of interest and capital received on the scheduled dates. The TSAA records a cut in the available amount for 500,000 until expiry of the bond, when it drops to zero. Table 6.6 shows the results.

Table 6.5. Purchase of a bond: effects on term structures

Time	Operation	TSECF	TSECCF	TSAA	TSCLGC	Price	Haircut (%)
0	Buy					99.85	15
0.01	Settlement	−985,000	−985,000	1,000,000		99.85	15
0.25				1,000,000		99.85	15
0.5	Coupon	50,000	−935,000	1,000,000		99.85	15
0.75				1,000,000		99.90	15
1	Coupon	50,000	−885,000	1,000,000		99.90	15
1.25				1,000,000		99.90	15
1.5	Coupon	50,000	−835,000	1,000,000		99.95	15
1.75				1,000,000		99.95	15
2	Coupon + Reimbursement	1,050,000	215,000	—		100.00	15

Table 6.6. Selling of a bond: effects on term structures

Time	Operation	TSECF	TSECCF	TSAA	TSCLGC	Price	Haircut (%)
0	Buy					99.85	15
0.01	Settlement	−985,000	−985,000	1,000,000		99.85	15
0.25						99.85	15
0.5	Coupon	50,000	−935,000			99.85	15
0.75	Sell			500,000	512,000	99.90	15
1	Coupon	25,000	−910,000		512,000	99.90	15
1.25					512,000	99.90	15
1.5	Coupon	25,000	−885,000		512,250	99.95	15
1.75		—			512,250	99.95	15
2	Coupon + Reimbursement	525,000	−360,000	—	512,500	100.00	15

Let us now analyse the effects of repo and reverse repo transactions on term structures. Assume the bank repoes the bond after 3 months (0.25 years) for a notional amount equal to 500,000 and a period of 6 months. Given the price and the haircut of the bond, and keeping accrued interest in mind, the amount of cash received by the bank is:

$$500,000 \times (99.85\% + 10\% \times 0.25) \times (1 - 15\%) = 424,469$$

In Table 6.7 the TSCLGC indicates an increase of liquidity, whereas the TSAA indicates that the available quantity of the bond dropped to 500,000.

The bank pays 9% as interest on this repo transaction, so that the terminal price paid when getting the bond back is:

$$424,469 \times (1 + 9\% \times 0.5) = 443,569.84$$

The difference 443,569.84 − 424,469 = 19,101.09 should be considered as a contract cash flow so that it enters the TSECF on the date at the end of the repo. The TSCLGC drops to zero and the TSAA returns the available amount back to 1,000,000.

Table 6.7. Repo and reverse repo of a bond: effects on term structures

Time	Operation	TSECF	TSECCF	TSAA	TSCLGC	Price	Haircut (%)
0	Buy					99.85	15
0.01	Settlement	−985,000	−985,000	1,000,000		99.85	15
0.25	Repo		−985,000	500,000	424,469	99.85	15
0.5	Coupon	50,000	−935,000	500,000	424,469	99.85	15
0.75	End repo	−19,101	−954,101	1,000,000	—	99.90	15
1	Coupon	50,000	−904,101	1,000,000		99.90	15
1.25	Reverse repo	−424,681	−1,328,782	1,500,000		99.90	15
1.5	Coupon	50,000	−1,278,676	1,500,000		99.95	15
1.75	End reverse repo	471,396	−807,386	1,500,000		99.95	15
2	Coupon + Reimbursement	1,050,000	195,899	—		100.00	15

After 1 year and 3 months (1.25 years) the bank deals a 6-month reverse repo on this bond for a notional of 500,000. The price it pays to deliver the bond at inception is

$$500,000 \times (99.90\% + 10\% \times 0.25) \times (1 - 15\%) = -424,681$$

This amount enters the TSECF and alters the TSECCF as a consequence; what is more, the TSAA increases up to 1,500,000 since the bond is in possession of the bank. All this is shown in Table 6.7. The TSCLGC is left unchanged.

At the end of the reverse repo contract, assuming the interest rate paid by the counterparty is 11%, the inflow received by the bank is:

$$424,681 \times (1 + 11\% \times 0.5) = 471,396$$

which should be considered fully as a contract cash flow, thus entering the TSECF; the bond is returned to the counterparty and consequently the TSAA is set back to 1,000,000 as shown in Table 6.7.

When the bank operates buy/sellback (or sell/buyback) operations, the effects are different. Assume that after 3 months (0.25 years) the bank buys 400,000 bonds and sells it back after 6 months at the forward price. At the start of the contract the bank pays:

$$400,000 \times (99.85\% + 10\% \times 0.25) = 409,400$$

This sum enters the TSECF and the quantity of the bond available increases to 1,400,000 in the TSAA. The TSCLGC is not modified by this operation. During the lifetime of the contract the bank is the legal owner of the bond and receives all the payments as well.

At the end of the contract (0.75 years) the bank sells the bond back at the contract price, typically the forward price prevailing at the inception of the contract (which we assume equal to the predicted price 99.90). The sum it receives also includes accrued interest:[6]

$$400,000 \times (99.90\% + 10\% \times 0.25) = 409,600$$

---

[6] We assume the bank closed a buy/sellback transaction that was not following more recent conventions, whereby the effects would be the same as in the repo case as far as the TSECF is concerned. The effects on the TSAA would remain the same as those we describe here.

Table 6.8. Buy/sellback and sell/buyback of a bond: effects on term structures

Time	Operation	TSECF	TSECCF	TSAA	TSCLGC	Price	Haircut (%)
0	Buy					99.85	15
0.01	Settlement	−985,000	−985,000	1,000,000		99.85	15
0.25	Buy	−409,400	−1,394,400	1,400,000		99.85	15
0.5	Coupon	70,000	−1,324,400	1,400,000		99.85	15
0.75	Sellback	409,600	−914,800	1,000,000		99.90	15
1	Coupon	50,000	−864,800	1,000,000		99.90	15
1.25	Sell		−864,800	700,000	307,200	99.90	15
1.5	Coupon	35,000	−829,800	700,000	307,200	99.95	15
1.75	Buyback		−829,800	1,000,000	−314,726	99.95	15
2	Coupon + Reimbursement	1,050,000	220,200	—		100.00	15

This sum also enters the TSECF, while the TSAA shows a reduction of the available quantity back to 1,000,000. All this is shown in Table 6.8.

In Table 6.8 we also show the effects of a sell/buyback of the bond starting after 1 year and 3 months (1.25 years) and terminating after 6 months (1.75 years). The price received by the bank is:

$$300,000 \times (99.90\% + 10\% \times 0.25) = 307,200$$

which is included in the TSCLGC since the operation can be seen as a way to extract BSL from the available assets; the TSAA indicates a reduction of the available quantity down to 700,000. At the end of the contract the bank buys the bond back and pays:

$$300,000 \times (99.95\% + 10\% \times 0.25) = 314,726$$

which is included in the TSCLGC. The TSAA increases back to 1,000,000. The coupon paid during the life of the contract is proportional to the available quantity of 700,000.

We now show what happens to the different term structures when a security lending and borrowing is operated by the bank. Let us start with a case in which the bank lends 500,000 of the bond after 3 months for a period of 6 months. The TSECF does not record any cash flow at the inception of the contract, whereas the TSAA shows a reduction of the available quantity of 500,000. After 6 months the bond is returned to the bank (the TSAA increase) and the bank receives a fee for the lending, which we assume equal to 3% p.a.:

$$500,000 \times (3\% \times 0.5) = 7,500$$

The coupon paid during the lifetime of the contract are possessed by the legal owner (i.e., the bank). This can be observed in Table 6.9.

The bank borrows a quantity of 300,000 of the same bond at 1.25 years for a period of 6 months. The TSAA is only affected at the start and end of the contract. The TSECF only records the borrowing fee paid by the bank:

$$300,000 \times (3\% \times 0.5) = 4,500$$

Table 6.9. Lending and borrowing of a bond: effects on term structures

Time	Operation	TSECF	TSECCF	TSAA	TSCLGC	Price	Haircut (%)
0	Buy					99.85	15
0.01	Settlement	−985,000	−985,000	1,000,000		99.85	15
0.25	Start lending		−985,000	500,000		99.85	15
0.5	Coupon	50,000	−935,000	500,000		99.85	15
0.75	End lending	7,500	−927,500	1,000,000		99.90	15
1	Coupon	50,000	−877,500	1,000,000		99.90	15
1.25	Start borrowing		−877,500	1,000,000		99.90	15
1.5	Coupon	50,000	−827,500	1,000,000		99.95	15
1.75	End borrowing	−4,500	−832,000	1,000,000		99.95	15
2	Coupon + Reimbursement	1,050,000	218,000	—		100.00	15

6.5 THE TERM STRUCTURE OF EXPECTED LIQUIDITY

The term structure of expected liquidity (TSL_e) is basically a combination of the TSECCF and the TSLGC. Formally, it can be written as:

$$TSL_e(t_0, t_b) = \{TSECCF(t_0, t_0), TSECFF(t_0, t_1) + TSCLGC(t_0, t_1),$$
$$TSECCF(t_0, t_2) + TSCLGC(t_0, t_2), \ldots,$$
$$TSECCF(t_0, t_b) + TSCLGC(t_0, t_b)\} \tag{6.10}$$

where we have included the term $TSECCF(t_0, t_0)$: although it may seem strange, it is simply the cash existing at the initial time in the balance sheet, so that:

$$TSECCF(t_0, t_0) = Cash(t_0)$$

The TSL_e is in practice a measure to check whether the financial institution is able to cover negative cumulated cash flows at any time in the future, calculated at the reference date t_0.

If the Treasury Department aims at preserving a positive sign for the TSECCF for all maturities, and this cannot always be guaranteed, as soon as we add it to our analysis of the TSCLGC we end up with a total picture for projected expected liquidity and the means the financial institution has at its disposal to cover negative cumulated cash flows (i.e., the TSL). The TSL must always be positive if the financial institution has to be solvent all the time. The TSL_e includes all possible expected cash flows generated by ordinary business activity, new business, the liquidity policy operated and the measures taken to cope with negative cumulated cash flows. If in the end it is impossible to exclude negative expected cumulated cash flows, then it is also impossible to prevent the financial institution from becoming insolvent.

Example 6.5.1. *Let us revert back to Example 6.4.1 and expand it to take account of the TSAA and the TSCLGC with the objective of finally building a TSL_e. The main results are shown in Table 6.10.*

Table 6.10. The term structure of expected liquidity and its building blocks

Years	TSECF	TSECCF	TSCLGC	TSL_e	TSAA	Price
0	0	0	0	0	30	97.00
1	22.4	22.4	0	22.4	30	97.20
2	−8.6	13.8	0	13.8	30	97.45
3	1.8	15.6	0	15.6	30	97.60
4	1.8	17.4	0	17.4	30	98.00
5	51.8	69.2	0	69.2	30	98.20
6	−1.2	68	0	68	30	98.60
7	−71.2	−3.2	3.96	0.76	26	99.00
8	1.69	−1.51	3.96	2.45	26	99.50
9	1.69	0.18	3.96	4.14	26	99.75
10	27.69	27.87	3.96	31.83	—	
100.00						
>10	−20	7.87	0	7.8		

First, we start with the TSECF and the TSECCF of Table 6.3 of Example 6.4.1: the TSECCF is negative between the 7th and 8th year. This negative cumulated cash flow must be covered and in the balance sheet there is a bond that can be sold to create (BSL) liquidity. In fact, in Table 6.10 the TSAA includes an amount for the bond equal to 30 until the 6th year, then in the 7th year an amount of 4 is sold at the (expected) price of 99.00, so as to generate a liquidity of 3.96, which is included in the TSCLGC thereafter.

It should be noted that selling the bonds affects the TSECF, and hence the TSECCF, in the two ways shown in the previous section: there are fewer inflows for interest paid by the bond and the final reimbursement is lower as well. In this example the change in the TSECF does not produce other negative cumulated cash flows, so the LGC can be limited to selling the bond.

The TSL_e is the sum of the TSECCF and the TSCLGC at each period as shown in Table 6.10: it is always greater than or equal to zero, so the bank is in (expected) liquidity equilibrium. Figure 6.6 shows how the TSECCF, the TSCLGC and the TSL_e have evolved: the first and the last term structure clash on the same line until the seventh year, when the TSECCF becomes negative and it has to be counterbalanced by the TSCLGC.

6.6 CASH FLOWS AT RISK AND THE TERM STRUCTURE OF LIQUIDITY AT RISK

Section 6.1 discussed a taxonomy of cash flows according to the time and amount of their occurrence, most cash flows are stochastic in either or both dimensions. This is the reason we introduced the term structure of expected cash flows, cumulated cash flows and expected liquidity generation capacity: they flow into the term structure of expected liquidity which represents the main monitoring tool of a Treasury Department.

Nonetheless, the fact that cash flows are stochastic suggests that not only one synthetic metric of the distribution (i.e., the expected value) should be taken into account, but also some other measure related to its volatility. In this way it is possible

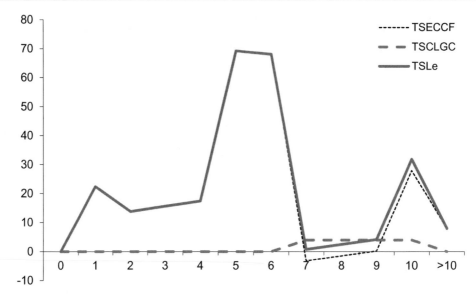

Figure 6.6. Term structure of expected cumulated cash flows, of cumulated liquidity generation capacity and of expected liquidity

to build the same term structure we analysed above from a different perspective showing the extreme values that both positive and negative cash flows may assume during the time of their occurrence.

In order to achieve this result, we need to link the single cash flows originated by contracts on and off the balance sheet to risk factors related to market, credit and behavioural variables. A number of approaches are described in Chapters 8 and 9. Here we show the general principles to build term structures that we define as unexpected with respect to the expected ones we looked at earlier.

The first concept to introduce is the positive cash-flow-at-risk, defined as

$$\text{cfaR}_\alpha^+(t_0, t_i) = \text{cf}_\alpha^+(t_0, t_i; \mathbf{x}) - \mathbf{E}[\text{cf}(t_0, t_i; \mathbf{x})] = \text{cf}_\alpha^+(t_0, t_i; \mathbf{x}) - \text{cf}_e(t_0, t_i; \mathbf{x})$$

On a given date t_i, determined by the reference date t_0, the maximum positive cash flow, computed at a given confidence level α ($\text{cf}_\alpha^+(t_0, t_i; \mathbf{x})$), is reduced by an amount equal to the expected amount of the (sum of positive and negative) cash flows on the same date ($\text{cf}_e(t_0, t_i; \mathbf{x})$). It is worthy of note that we have added a dependency of the cash flows on $\mathbf{x}$: this is an array $\mathbf{x} = [x_1, x_2, \ldots, x_R]$ of R risk factors, which include market, credit and behavioural variables.

Analogously, a negative cash-flow-at-risk is defined as:

$$\text{cfaR}_{1-\alpha}^-(t_0, t_i) = \text{cf}_{1-\alpha}^-(t_0, t_i; \mathbf{x}) - \mathbf{E}[\text{cf}(t_0, t_i; \mathbf{x})] = \text{cf}_{1-\alpha}^-(t_0, t_i; \mathbf{x}) - \text{cf}_e(t_0, t_i; \mathbf{x})$$

where in this case on a given date t_i, determined by the reference date t_0, the minimum negative cash flow, computed at a given confidence level α ($\text{cf}_\alpha^+(t_0, t_i; \mathbf{x})$), is netted with the expected cash flow occurring on the same date ($\text{cf}_e(t_0, t_i; \mathbf{x})$).

Note that the distribution of cash flows ranges from the smallest, possibly but not necessarily, negative ones to the largest, possibly but not necessarily, positive ones. Given a confidence level of α, on the right-hand side of the distribution all cash flows bigger than $\mathrm{cf}_\alpha^+(t_0, t_i; \mathbf{x})$, whose total probability of occurrence is $1 - \alpha$, are neglected. In the same way, on the left-hand side of the distribution all cash flows smaller than $\mathrm{cf}_{1-\alpha}^-(t_0, t_i; \mathbf{x})$, whose total probability of occurrence is still $1 - \alpha$, are not taken into account.

Once we have defined the cfaR, it is straightforward to introduce the term structure of unexpected positive cash flows, given a confidence level of α. This is the collection of positive cfaR for all the dates included between the start and the end of the observation period:

$$\mathrm{TSCF}_\alpha^+(t_0, t_b) = \{\mathrm{cfaR}_\alpha^+(t_0, t_0), \mathrm{cfaR}_\alpha^+(t_0, t_1), \ldots, \mathrm{cfaR}_\alpha^+(t_0, t_b) \tag{6.11}$$

Similarly, the term structure of unexpected negative cash flows, given a confidence level of $1 - \alpha$, is:

$$\mathrm{TSCF}_{1-\alpha}^-(t_0, t_b) = \{\mathrm{cfaR}_{1-\alpha}^-(t_0, t_0), \mathrm{cfaR}_{1-\alpha}^-(t_0, t_1), \ldots, \mathrm{cfaR}_{1-\alpha}^-(t_0, t_b) \tag{6.12}$$

The TSCF_α^+ and $\mathrm{TSCF}_{1-\alpha}^-$ can be described as the upper and lower bound of the term structure of cash flows, centred around the expected level that is given by the TSECF. It does not make much sense to build a cumulated TSCF_α^+ and $\mathrm{TSCF}_{1-\alpha}^-$, since they will rapidly diverge upward or downward at unreasonable levels without providing accurate information for liquidity risk management. It is much more useful to build a term structure of unexpected liquidity that includes both the term structure of cash flows and liquidity generation capacity jointly computed at some confidence level α. We will dwell on that below; but first we give an example of TSCF_α^+ and $\mathrm{TSCF}_{1-\alpha}^-$.

Example 6.6.1. *We present a simplified TSCF and TSECF for a set of fixed and floating cash flows for a period covering 14 days. The notional amount for each date and for each type of index is shown in Table 6.11. For example, on the first day a contract of 1,000,000 produces an outflow indexed to 1-month Libor: it could be a bond the bank issued. There*

Table 6.11. Notional amount indexed to different Libor fixings and fixed cash flows, for cash flows occurring in a period of 20 days

Date	1M amount	3M amount	6M amount	1Y amount	1M strike	3M strike	6M strike	1Y strike	Fixed rate amount
1	−1,000,000								
2									
3									
4	2,000,000		−500,000						—
5									
6	1,500,000	−5,000,000	2,500,000	2,000,000					−250,000
7	100,000	200,000	−500,000	1,000					
8	1,500,000	−5,000,000	3,000,000	−1,000,000					
9	2,500,000	−5,000,000	2,500,000	2,000,000					
10	2,000,000	3,000,000	2,500,000	500,000					25,000
11									
12	1,500,000	−5,000,000	2,500,000	2,000,000					
13									
14	2,000,000	3,000,000	2,500,000	500,000					25,000

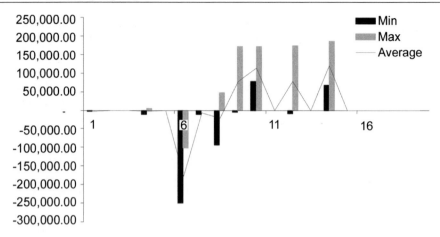

Figure 6.7. Maximum, minimum (at the $\alpha = 99\%$ c.l.) and expected (average) cash flows for a period of 20 days.

are also some dates when cash flows are not indexed to a floating rate, such as Libor, but have a fixed rate.

We simulate 10,000 scenarios with a stochastic model for the evolution of the interest rate: the Cox, Ingersoll and Ross model (CIR, [54]), which will be analysed in greater details in Chapter 8.[7] Each simulation allows different fixing levels for each date to be computed, then correspondingly we can determine the TSCF. For each date we will have 10,000 possible cash flows that are ordered from the lowest to the highest. We choose a confidence level $\alpha = 99\%$, which lets us identify the minimum cash flow as the 100th and the maximum cash flow as the 9,900th in the ordered set of cash flows for the 14 days. Moreover, we compute the expected level on each date, which is simply the average of the 10,000 possible cash flows. The result is shown in Figure 6.7. It is worthy of note that the minimum cash flow is not necessarily an outflow (i.e., a negative number).

To ascertain the impact of possible derivative features on the TSCF, we now introduce some caps at different strike levels for the last two dates (as shown in Table 6.12). In this case, if the index rate to which the cash flows are linked fixes higher than the cap's strike level the level is always considered equal to the strike.

The results are shown in Figure 6.8: they are derived in the same way as above but they take the caps into account as well. Compared with the results in Figure 6.7, it is easy to see that caps have the effect of lowering the maximum cash flow and reducing the expected (average) level as well. The effects are not unequivocally predictable, they depend on the strike level, the notional amount and the buying or selling of the optionality. In any case a simulation is needed to verify the distribution of cash flows for a given period.

As anticipated before setting out Example 6.6.1, it makes little sense to construct a TSL-at-risk simply as the sum of the TSCCF and the TSCLGC computed separately at a given confidence level. In fact, if we try to build a maximum or a minimum TSCCF by

---

[7] For those interested in the details of the simulation, we used the following CIR parameters: $r_0 = 2\%$, $\kappa = 0.5\%$, $\theta = 4.5\%$ and $\sigma = 7.90\%$. We do not consider any spread between the fixing (Libor) rates and the risk-free rate. The notation is the same as that introduced in Chapter 8.

Table 6.12. Notional amount indexed to different Libor fixings and fixed cash flows, for cash flows occurring in a period of 14 days, with some cash flows capped

Date	1M amount	3M amount	6M amount	1Y amount	1M strike	3M strike	6M strike	1Y strike	Fixed rate amount
1	−1,000,000								
2									
3									
4	2,000,000		−500,000						—
5									
6	1,500,000	−5,000,000	2,500,000	2,000,000					−250,000
7	100,000	200,000	−500,000	1,000					
8	1,500,000	−5,000,000	3,000,000	−1,000,000					
9	2,500,000	−5,000,000	2,500,000	2,000,000					
10	2,000,000	3,000,000	2,500,000	500,000					25,000
11									
12	1,500,000	−5,000,000	2,500,000	2,000,000	4.00%	4.50%	5.00%	5.50%	
13									
14	2,000,000	3,000,000	2,500,000	500,000	4.50%	4.75%	5.00%	5.25%	25,000

summing the items that comprise the $TSCF_\alpha$ or the $TSCF_{1-\alpha}$, we would end up with extreme term structures that would look rather unlikely in practice, unless some dramatic event really happens. This is explained by the fact that negative cash flows, although calculated at their minimum at the chosen confidence level, are actually netted by the LGC that is forecast at its maximum at the same confidence level. So, negative cash flows do not really cumulate at extreme values, when considered at the all-encompassing balance sheet level. While it is possible from a mathematical point of

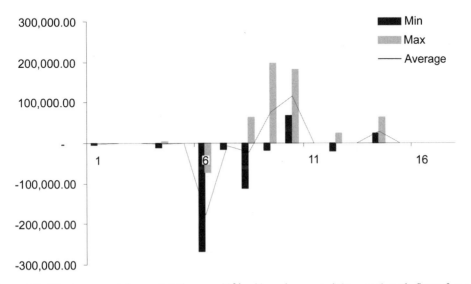

Figure 6.8. Maximum, minimum (at the $\alpha = 99\%$ c.l.) and expected (average) cash flows for a period of 20 days, with some cash flows capped.

view, and meaningful from a risk management point of view, to build the TSECCF and the expected TSCLGC separately and then sum them together in the TSL_e, it is mathematically wrong and managerially misleading to sum two term structures computed separately at extreme levels.

From these considerations, we need to calculate at an aggregated level the net cash flows included in both the TSCF and the TSLGC. To this end we can use the following procedure.

Procedure 6.6.1. *The steps to compute aggregated cash flows and their maxima and minima are:*

1. *Simulate a number N of possible paths for all the R risk factors of the array $\mathbf{x} = [x_1, x_2, \ldots, x_R]$; each path contains M steps referring to as many calendar dates.*
2. *For each scenario $n \in \{1, \ldots, N\}$, the cash flows included in the TSCF and the TSLGC are algebraically summed for each of M steps: we obtain a matrix $N \times M$ of aggregated cash flows:*

$$\text{cf}(t_0, t_m; n) = \sum_{j=1}^{D} \text{cf}(t_0, t_m; d_j, n)$$

   where $\{d_1, d_2, \ldots, d_D\}$ are all the contracts and/or securities generating cash flows at date t_m, included in the TSCF and the TSLGC, under scenario n.
3. *At each step $m \in \{1, \ldots, M\}$, the maximum and minimum cash flows, at a confidence level of α and $1 - \alpha$, respectively, are identified. We denote them as $\text{cf}_\alpha(t_0, t_m)$ and $\text{cf}_{1-\alpha}(t_0, t_m)$, respectively.*

Let us now define the TSL at the maximum and minimum extremes. In fact, the TSL with maximum cash flows at confidence level α is simply the collection of maximum cash flows derived using Procedure 6.6.1:

$$\text{TSL}_\alpha(t_0, t_b) = \{\text{cf}_\alpha(t_0, t_1), \ldots, \text{cf}_\alpha(t_0, t_b)\} \tag{6.13}$$

with the initial condition that $\text{TSL}_\alpha(t_0, t_0) = \text{Cash}(t_0)$. Similarly, the TSL with minimum cash flows at confidence level $1 - \alpha$ is:

$$\text{TSL}_{1-\alpha}(t_0, t_b) = \{\text{cf}_{1-\alpha}(t_0, t_1), \ldots, \text{cf}_{1-\alpha}(t_0, t_b)\} \tag{6.14}$$

The two term structures of liquidity that we have just defined, together with the term structure of expected liquidity TSL_e, allow us to define a term structure of liquidity-at-risk (TSLaR): this is a collection of unexpected cash flows at each date in a given period $[t_0, t_b]$, calculated as the difference between the minimum and the average level of cash flows. Although it is possible to compute the TSLaR for both the unexpected maximum and minimum levels, for risk management purposes it is more sensible to refer to the minimum unexpected levels, since unexpected inflows should not bring about problems. Then we formally define the TSLaR, at a confidence level of $1 - \alpha$, as:

$$\text{TSLaR}_{1-\alpha}(t_0, t_b) = \{\text{cf}_{1-\alpha}(t_0, t_1) - \text{TSECCF}(t_0, t_1) - \text{TSCLGC}(t_0, t_1),$$

$$\ldots, \text{cf}_{1-\alpha}(t_0, t_b) - \text{TSECCF}(t_0, t_b) - \text{TSCLGC}(t_0, t_b)\} \tag{6.15}$$

It is easy to check, by inspecting formulae (6.15) and (6.10), that each element of the

$TSLaR_{1-\alpha}$ is the difference between corresponding elements of the $TSL_{1-\alpha}$ and the TSL_e.

We have already mentioned that the curves presented in this section have to be computed by simulating the risk factors affecting all the cash flows at a balance sheet level. Stochastic models describing the evolution of risk factors are presented in the following chapters. Although their use is generally restricted to simulation engines to generate the TSL_e and the $TSL_{1-\alpha}$, they can be used at a less general level to:

- calculate single metrics of interest, such as the TSAA of a single bond or of a portfolio of bonds, the TSLGC of the liquidity buffer (i.e., the fraction of LGC that relates to BSL);
- compute specific measure for one or more securities, such as haircuts and adjustments due to a lack of liquidity in their dealing in the market;
- measure single phenomena such as prepayments, usage of credit lines or the evolution of non-maturing liabilities (e.g., sight deposits);
- price the liquidity risk embedded in banking and trading book products.

When used independently the information derived by the models is useful for pricing and risk management, with the caveat that we are getting away from the more general picture where correlation effects play a big role. Thus, results obtained in this way should never form the basis for aggregation into a comprehensive measure of liquidity risk.

In the following chapters we present models that allow the bank to simulate the cash flows of the main items on its balance sheet and to build all the metrics we have described. But before doing so, we have to spend more time considering the liquidity buffer and term structure of funding liquidity and the interrelations existing between them when the bank plans an equilibrium liquidity policy.

7

Liquidity buffer and
term structure of funding

7.1 INTRODUCTION

In this chapter we investigate how the liquidity buffer (LB from now on) comes about in the running of the business of a financial institution. In greater detail, we will study:

- when the need to set up a LB arises;
- how the LB is financed;
- how LB costs are charged to banking products.

Hopefully we will clarify some concepts that eventually will assist in the liquidity management and the assignment of costs and/or benefits to the different departments within a financial institution.

7.2 LIQUIDITY BUFFER AND COUNTERBALANCING CAPACITY

It is worth defining the LB and its relationship with counterbalancing capacity (CBC), which is a concept normally used in liquidity management practice, although we have not yet introduced it in our analysis. We should stress the fact that there is not a single definition for both and banks often adopt different criteria to define them.

   In general, it is possible to define CBC such as to embed it in the LB as well, hence making it a part of the LB.

Definition 7.2.1 (counterbalancing capacity). *CBC is a set of strategies by which a bank can cope with liquidity needs by assuming the maximum possible liquidity generation capacity (LGC).*

   CBC identifies all the possible strategies to generate positive cash flows to make cumulated cash flows, up to given future date, always greater than or at least equal to zero. Positive cash flows can be generated by contractual redemptions and/or interest payments to the bank: these cash flows are not considered by CBC. In our analysis we link CBC to the concept of LGC we saw in Chapter 6 in the sense that it is the most effective configuration the latter can assume in terms of liquidity potential. In practice and in most of literature the concept of CBC clashes with our LGC: the distinction we made could prove useful but it is not essential and as long as there is agreement on the terms adopted, we can safely interchange them.

   We give the description of CBC provided by the EBA in the *Guidelines on Liquidity Buffers & Survival Periods* [6] since it may help in bringing about a common definition:

... the counterbalancing capacity should be a plan to hold, or have access to, excess liquidity over and above a business-as-usual scenario over the short, medium and long-term time horizons in response to stress scenarios, as well as a plan for further liquidity generation capabilities, whether through tapping additional funding sources, making adjustments to the business, or through other more fundamental measures. The latter element should be addressed through the establishment of contingency funding plans. Counterbalancing capacity, therefore, includes but is much broader than the liquidity buffer.

The liquidity buffer has no precise definition and banks use different notions for it (sometimes the LB is often assimilated into the BSL, but actually the latter mainly coincides with the former as made clear from our definitions in Chapter 6). Since no unique definition exists in practice, we can resort to the definitions contained in the above-mentioned *Guidelines on Liquidity Buffers & Survival Periods* [6], and define the LB as given in Definition 7.2.2.

Definition 7.2.2 (liquidity buffer). *The available liquidity covering the additional need for liquidity that may arise over a defined short period of time under stress conditions.*

Moreover, again according to the EBA, the LB should be the short end of CBC, and excess liquidity available outright should be used in liquidity stress situations within a given short-term period, excluding the need to take any extraordinary measures.

There are three features that characterize the LB:

1. The *size* of the buffer, which is determined from the funding gap that arises under stressed conditions. To determine the size we need a framework to design stressed scenarios that would cause the gap.
2. The specified time horizon (or *survival period*) considered: funding gaps falling within this period are covered by the buffer. The survival period is only "the period during which an institution can continue operating without needing to generate additional funds and still meet all its payments due under the assumed stress scenarios" [6].
3. *Composition* of the buffer: not only cash, but also highly liquid unencumbered assets can be constituents of the LB.

The main purpose of the LB is to enable a financial institution to get through liquidity stress during a defined survival period, without changing the business model. In what follows we focus on the LB, because we think it is the most important part of CBC for two reasons: (i) it is essential to guarantee the survival of the bank during liquidity stress, and (ii) it is less dependent on strong changes in business-as-usual activity in the medium to long run, which may turn out to be difficult to identify and subject to a high degree of subjectivity.

Definition of the LB and its relationship with the CBC is important but does not provide practitioners with operative rules determining how big the LB should be, when it should be constituted, the cost to the bank of keeping a buffer within the balance sheet, if and how this cost—if any—should be charged to other assets (or liabilities) and, finally, how the composition of the buffer, in terms of cash and other assets included within it, affects its LGC. In the following sections we investigate all these issues.

7.3 THE FIRST CAUSE OF THE NEED FOR A LIQUIDITY BUFFER: MATURITY MISMATCH

First of all, we need to ascertain the occasions when banking activity generates the need to build a LB.

Proposition 7.3.1. *The need for a liquidity buffer is brought about by an investment in an asset whose maturity is longer than the liability used to finance it.*

Proposition 7.3.2. *The investment in an asset that requires a liquidity buffer determines the term structure of the liquidity available to the bank for investments in other assets as well, according to the following factors:*

- *the expiry of the asset the bank wants to invest;*
- *the expiry of the source of liquidity, and hence the number of rollovers needed, to finance the purchase of the asset;*
- *the size of the funding gap on rollover dates under stressed scenarios.*

To prove the propositions, we think the best approach is to analyse the operations of a simplified and stylized bank, from the start of its operations.

Assume the bank starts at $T_0 = 0$ with an equity equal to E, which is deposited in a bank account D_1 yielding no interest; at the same time it issues a (zero-coupon) bond whose present value is K and whose expiry is at $T_1 = 1$: the funds raised are deposited in a bank account D_2. For simplicity we assume that is no credit risk in the economy and that the interest rate paid in one period is r for all securities. The balance sheet of the bank at time 0 is the following:

Assets	Liabilities
$D_1 = E$	$L(1) = K$
$D_2 = K$	
	E

Up to this point there is no need to build a LB: we can devise any stressed scenario, but the bank is perfectly capable to cope with any of it, since its assets are fully liquid, being cash.

Assume now that the bank wants to invest the funds raised to run its major activity: lending money, which is often performed by exploiting one of the expertises of the banking industry (i.e., by maturity transformation). This means that the assets typically have a maturity longer than the liabilities. Let A_3 (the asset the bank wants to invest money in) be a loan expiring at $T_3 = 3$. We also assume that equity is not used to finance investments but is just invested in liquidity to cover unexpected losses.

If this is the case, the bank has to decide how much of the funds raised via the bond issuance can be lent, keeping in mind the bond expiry at $T_1 = 1$, so that it has to roll over with an equivalent bond at times $T_1 = 1$ and $T_2 = 2$. If abundant liquidity is available in the market on rollover dates and the bank has no specific problems in the running of its activities, it can be fairly expected that the rollover can easily be operated.

The bank can also design a stressed scenario in which the rollover is difficult for reasons that could be linked to the market (systemic) or to the bank itself (idiosyncratic).

Assume in a stressed scenario the bank is not able to roll over a percentage $x\%$ of the maturing debt at times 1 and 2. We can think of this percentage as the maximum funding gap that can occur at a given confidence level (say, 99%), similarly to the treatment of the losses suffered for credit or market events on the contracts the bank has in its portfolios.[1]

At time 0 the available liquidity $\text{AVL}(0,3)$ for the investments can be computed as:

$$\text{AVL}(0,3) = K \times (1 - x\%)^2 \tag{7.1}$$

Equation (7.1) states that at each rollover date (there are two of them) the bond's quantity is deducted by $x\%$: this means that the amount of assets expiring at $T_3 = 3$ that can be funded with debt of shorter duration, is only $\text{AVL}(0,3)$ and not K. The difference between the amount raised at 0 via the bond issuance and the $\text{AVL}(0,3)$ is the total liquidity buffer $\text{LB}(0) = K - \text{AVL}(0,3)$.

The LB at time $T_0 = 0$ can also be seen as the sum of the two funding gaps $\text{FG}(1) = x\%K$ and $\text{FG}(2) = x\%K(1 - x\%)$ that may occur under stressed scenarios on rollover dates. It is straightforward to check that:

$$\text{LB}(0) = \text{FG}(1) + \text{FG}(2) = x\%K + x\%K(1 - x\%) = K - \text{AVL}(0,3)$$

We can immediately see that the LB, although determined at the start of the activity, can be used in the case of necessity only on the two rollover dates. For all the other dates between time 0 and the second rollover date 2, the LB can be invested, under the constraint that it "exists" in its full liquid form in the amount required when the stressed condition may hurt bank activity.

In our case the available liquidity that can be invested to buy an asset expiring at time 3 is $\text{AVL}(0,3)$; the remaining liquidity needed to build the LB can be invested for an amount $x\%K$ in an asset A_1 (say, another loan) maturing at time 1, and for an amount $x\%K(1 - x\%)$ in an asset A_2, similar to A_1, maturing at time 2. The liquidity generated by asset A_1 at its expiry is the amount of the LB in its liquid form that is needed to cope with a stressed scenario on the first rollover date. Analogously the liquidity generated by asset A_2 at its expiry is the liquid LB needed to cover the possible funding gap on the second rollover date.

Stressed scenarios and hence the needed liquidity buffer, jointly with the investment in the asset expiring at time $T_3 = 3$, determine the term structure of (available) funding TSFu, defined as:

$$\text{TSFu}(t_0, t_b) = \{\text{AVL}(t_0, t_1), \text{AVL}(t_0, t_2), \ldots, \text{AVL}(t_0, t_b)\} \tag{7.2}$$

In the specific case we are examining, $\text{TSFu}(0,3)$ can be summarized as follows:

TSFu	Amount
$\text{AVL}(0,1)$	$x\%K = \text{FG}(1)$
$\text{AVL}(0,2)$	$x\%K(1 - x\%) = \text{FG}(2)$
$\text{AVL}(0,3)$	$K(1 - x\%)^2$
Total	K

[1] This means the bank accepts a 1% probability of failing under more stressed liquidity conditions, which eventually may produce bankruptcy because an insufficient liquidity "hedge" has been set up.

The total is clearly the amount raised by the issuance of bond L. The TSFu is a byproduct of the size of the total LB and is a function of the liquidity gap that can occur on rollover dates (in our modelling, this is the percentage $x\%$ of the amount of the bond to be rolled over).

The liquidity available is invested in the three assets, so that at time 0 the balance sheet now reads:

Assets	Liabilities
$D_1 = E$	$L(1) = K$
$A_1 = \text{AVL}(0,1)$	
$A_2 = \text{AVL}(0,2)$	
$A_3 = \text{AVL}(0,3)$	
	E

As is immediately apparent, we are trying to build a liquidity buffer in a consistent and sound fashion, strictly linked to the funding of the assets. As such, the LB(0) is build at time 0 to cover funding gaps that may arise in the medium to long term at times 1 and 2, (the periods are likely measured in years in this case). This may appear in stark contrast to Definition 7.2.2, where stressed conditions that need to be covered by the buffer refer to short-term horizons (say, one or two months).

The problem is that, although the LB should be able to cover stressed market condition in the short term, its building and size should be simultaneous with its origination and thus related to a long-term view. What lies behind the need for the LB is the duration mismatch between liabilities and assets, produced by investment of the funds raised. The LB, given the stressed scenarios and the type of the mismatch, can be determined right from the start of the investment. Even if stressed conditions are referred to times far in the future and not to the short term, the approach we outlined is the soundest and most consistent way of setting up a LB to grant financial and liquidity equilibrium in the long term.

The LB can be invested in a risk-free deposit up to the time it is needed to cover potential gaps, or it can be invested in other assets according to the available liquidity schedule we have shown above. In the risk-free economy we are working in at the moment, the two alternatives can be equivalent. The need to have the LB fully liquid in the due amount on rollover dates strictly defines the amount that can be invested in other assets with expiry at times T_1 and T_2. We will see in the following sections what happens when default risk is introduced.

To check whether the LB build at 0 is effective enough to cover future liquidity gaps, we assume that on both rollover dates the stressed scenarios actually happen. Let us see how the activity evolves at time 1: the maturing bond L has to be reimbursed and this can only be done if the bank rolls over the debt for an equivalent amount K. Since the stressed scenario occurs, the actual amount that can be rolled over is only $K \times (1 - x\%)$; the remaining liquidity necessary to fully pay back the maturing bond, $x\% \times K$, is provided by the LB whose liquidity is increased by the maturing asset A_1, which is thus correspondingly abated. The total cash variation ΔCash is, keeping in mind the interest the bank pays on the maturing debt and that it receives on the assets and on the LB(0) (invested between time 0 and 1):[2]

$$\Delta \text{Cash} = -K$$

$$- rK$$

$$+ rA_3 = r\text{AVL}(0,3)$$

$$+ r(A_1 + A_2) = r\text{LB}(0) = r[K - \text{AVL}(0,3)]$$

$$+ K(1 - x\%)$$

$$+ x\%K = -\Delta \text{LB}(1)$$

$$= 0$$

where $\Delta \text{LB}(1)$ is variation of the liquidity buffer at time $T_1 = 1$. The remaining LB is left invested in asset A_2, and the balance sheet is:

Assets	Liabilities
$D_1 = E$ $A_2 = \text{AVL}(0,2)$ $A_3 = \text{AVL}(0,3)$	$L(2) = K(1 - x\%)$
	E

On the rollover date T_2 the bank faces the same stressed scenario, so that it has to reimburse the bond $L(2) = K(1 - x\%)$, but the funds it can raise are only $L(3) = K(1 - x\%)^2$. The difference $K(1 - x\%) - K(1 - x\%)^2$ has to be drawn from the buffer LB(1) that remains, whose liquidity is produced by the expiring investment in $A_2 = \text{AVL}(0,2) = K(1 - x\%) - K(1 - x\%)^2$. Keeping in mind the interest paid and received, variation of the cash available to the bank is:

$$\Delta \text{Cash} = -K(1 - x\%)$$

$$- rK(1 - x\%)$$

$$+ rA_3 = r\text{AVL}(0,3)$$

$$+ rA_2 = r\text{LB}(1) = r[K(1 - x\%) - \text{AVL}(0,3)]$$

$$+ K(1 - x\%)^2$$

$$+ K(1 - x\%) - K(1 - x\%)^2 = -\Delta \text{LB}(2)$$

$$= 0$$

---

[2] Note that we are simply showing the total cash flows that originated on the first rollover date; we are not presenting a formula predicting future cash flows.

The balance sheet at time $T_2 = 2$ is:

Assets	Liabilities
$D_1 = E$ $A_3 = \mathrm{AVL}(0,3)$	$L(3) = K(1 - x\%)^2$
	E

The LB is completely depleted and no longer invested in any asset: this is because it is no longer needed. In fact, at time $T_3 = 3$ the bond $L(3)$ must be reimbursed, requiring a liquidity equal to $K(1 - x\%)^2$ that is covered by the expiry of asset A_3, implying an equal inflow of $\mathrm{AVL}(0,3) = K(1 - x\%)^2$. Keeping in mind the interest paid and received, total cash flow variation is:

$$\Delta\text{Cash} = -K(1 - x\%)^2$$
$$- rK(1 - x\%)^2$$
$$+ rA_3 = r\mathrm{AVL}(0,3)$$
$$+ K(1 - x\%)^2 = -\Delta A_3(3)$$
$$= 0$$

where $\Delta A_3(3)$ is the variation of asset A_3 at time $T_3 = 3$, generating cash for an amount $-\Delta A_3$. The balance sheet is:

Assets	Liabilities
$D_1 = E$ $A_3 = 0$	$L(3) = 0$
	E

It is straightforward to check that such a strategy to set up the LB fully covers all possible stress scenarios. Moreover, given the economy we have assumed without credit risk, the total P&L at the end of each period is nil and the LB does not imply any cost that has to be charged over the assets or the liabilities.

7.3.1 Some or all stressed scenarios do not occur

We extend our analysis to the cases when some or all stressed scenarios do not occur. We can prove the following.

Proposition 7.3.3. *In an economy with no credit risk, and no funding spread paid by the bank over the risk-free rate, the liquidity buffer does not generate any P&L, either if it is used at any predicted time or if it is not used because the stressed scenario does not manifest (or it manifests in a less disruptive fashion than assumed). Thus there are no costs to be charged (or benefits to be assigned) to assets or liabilities.*

Furthermore, we can also verify Proposition 7.3.4.

Proposition 7.3.4. *The LB can be set up at the beginning of the investment in an asset, given the assumptions the bank makes about stressed conditions on rollover dates. More-over, the LB can be reinvested in assets earning the interest rate r (say, loans) as long as these assets mature on the rollover dates or just before them, but* never *after them.*

An immediate consequence is given in Proposition 7.3.5.

Proposition 7.3.5. *The setting of a LB, given the assumptions about stressed conditions on rollover dates, also determines the constraints on the maturity transformation rule that a bank can adopt.*

If stressed scenarios do not occur, then a profit is produced equal to the interest earned on the investment of the LB in single periods. This profit exactly compensates the greater amount of interest paid by the bank on the issued debt. To clarify this point, assume that at $T_1 = 1$ there is no stressed market or bank-specific condition such that the matured bond can be rolled over for the entire amount. In this case the LB does not have to be utilized and its amount at time $T_1 = 1$ is the same as at time $T_0 = 0$. The liquidity generated by the expiry of asset A_1 is invested in asset A_2, whose quantity on the balance sheet is increased. The total variation of the cash is:

$$\Delta\text{cash} = -K$$
$$- rK$$
$$+ rA_3 = r\text{AVL}(0, 3)$$
$$+ r(A_1 + A_2) = r\text{LB}(0) = r[K - \text{AVL}(0, 3)]$$
$$+ K$$
$$+ A_1 = \text{AVL}(0, 1)$$
$$- \Delta A_2(2) = -\text{AVL}(0, 1)$$
$$= 0$$

where $\Delta A_2(2)$ is the cash needed to make the investment in A_2 equal to the liquidity generated by the expiry of asset A_1. The balance sheet is now:

Assets	Liabilities
$D_1 = E$	$L(2) = K$
$A_2 = \text{AVL}(0, 1) + \text{AVL}(0, 2)$	
$A_3 = \text{AVL}(0, 3)$	
	E

No P&L is generated and the total cash flow is nil. At time $T_2 = 2$ a stressed scenario manifests itself, so the debt can be rolled over only for a fraction of its amount which is equal to $(1 - x\%)$; in this case the liquidity buffer is utilized for an amount

$x\%K = \text{AVL}(0,1)$. The remaining liquidity can be invested in asset A_3, whose quantity is correspondingly increased, and we have the following total cash flows:

$$\Delta\text{Cash} = -K$$
$$-rK$$
$$+rA_3 = r\text{AVL}(0,3)$$
$$+r(A_1 + A_2) = r\text{LB}(1) = r[K - \text{AVL}(0,3)]$$
$$+K(1-x\%)$$
$$+x\%K = -\Delta\text{LB}(2)$$
$$-\Delta A_3 = -\text{AVL}(0,2)$$
$$= 0$$

and the new balance sheet is:

Assets	Liabilities
$D_1 = E$ $A_3 = \text{AVL}(0,2) + \text{AVL}(0,3)$	$L(3) = K(1-x\%)$
	E

Note the perfect balance between the cash flows and the P&L, which are both still 0. This balanced condition is preserved through to the last period, when we get as total cash flows:

$$\Delta\text{Cash} = -K(1-x\%)$$
$$-rK(1-x\%)$$
$$+rA_3 = r[\text{AVL}(0,2) + \text{AVL}(0,3)]$$
$$+r\text{LB}(2) = r[K - \text{AVL}(0) - x\%K]$$
$$+A_3 = \text{AVL}(0,2) + \text{AVL}(0,3) = K(1-x\%)$$
$$-K(1-x\%)$$
$$= 0$$

The liquidity needed to reimburse bond $L(3)$ is generated by asset A_3 expiring on the same date. The final balance sheet is:

Assets	Liabilities
$D_1 = E$ $A_3 = 0$	$L(3) = 0$
	E

with no P&L generated.

In the analysis just presented, the amount of asset A_3 that can be funded by shorter liabilities is determined once funding gaps have been determined for rollover dates. This does not mean that the LB implied by the devised stressed scenarios is the only factor affecting the maturity transformation policy: the constraints set by the liquidity buffer can be tightened by other factors other than the funding gap.

7.3.2 The cost of the liquidity buffer for maturity mismatch

Proposition 7.3.6. *In an economy where economic agents (including the bank) can go bankrupt and the bank pays a funding spread over the risk-free rate to remunerate its credit risk, the cost of the liquidity buffer is different from zero and depends on: (i) the level of the funding spread over the risk-free rate paid by the bank, (ii) the bank's preference to invest the buffer in liquid assets traded in the market and (iii) the length of the survival period chosen by the bank.*

To prove Proposition 7.3.6, assume that the economy in which the bank operates also embeds default risk: this means that there are economic agents, including the bank, that may go bankrupt. As a consequence, when borrowing money, defaultable agents have to pay a premium over the risk-free rate to compensate the lender for the default risk it bears. From the borrower perspective, this premium is the funding spread and it is a cost it has to consider when evaluating projects within its business activity; from the borrower perspective, it is remuneration for expected future losses due to the default of the borrower.[3]

In such an economy, the bank pays a funding spread s^B and can invest in assets subject to default risk, requiring a credit spread s^A to match expected future losses. Nevertheless, the expected return on a defaultable asset is actually the risk-free rate in every case. In fact, the credit spread is set so that on maturity of the asset the expected return is the risk-free rate. For example, assuming asset A expires in a single period, we have that:

$$A(1+r) = \mathbf{E}[A \times (1+r+s^A)]$$
$$= A \times (1+r+s^A) \times (1-\mathrm{PD}) + A \times R \times \mathrm{PD}$$
$$= A \times (1+r) - A \times [(1+r) - R] \times \mathrm{PD} + A \times s^A \times (1-\mathrm{PD})$$

So, the starting value A, accrued at the risk-free interest rate, has to be equal to the initial value compounded at the risk-free rate plus the credit spread, weighted by the probability the counterparty survives $(1 - \mathrm{PD})$ or, alternatively, it is the recovery value $A \times R$, weighted by the probability the counterparty defaults (PD), as shown in the second line. The third line rewrites the expression as the sum of the risk-free asset minus the expected loss ($\mathrm{L_{GD}} = [(1+r) - R]$ is the loss given default, expressed as a fraction of the face value A), plus the credit spread weighted by the survival probability.

The fair credit spread can be derived by solving the above equation, and is:

$$s^A = \frac{[(1+r) - R] \times \mathrm{PD}}{1 - \mathrm{PD}} = \frac{\mathrm{L_{GD}} \times \mathrm{PD}}{1 - \mathrm{PD}} \tag{7.3}$$

---

[3] See Chapter 10 for a discussion on the interrelations between credit, funding and liquidity.

So the spread is just the loss suffered upon the counterparty's default, weighted by the probability of default (i.e., the expected loss), divided by the survival probability. We can assume that the credit spread is set in such a way that each asset in which the bank invests its funds earns the risk-free rate, on an expected basis, even if its contract rate may be higher.

Let us investigate what happens to the management of the LB in such an environment. We reprise the example we presented in Section 7.3: at the start of activity at $T_0 = 0$ nothing changes in terms of the AVL invested in assets A_1, A_2 and A_3, each one earning the expected risk-free rate r. The LB is built accordingly and the available liquidity at times T_1 and T_2 is invested in assets earning the (expected) risk-free rate r as well. Let us see which is the total cash flow in $T_1 = 1$:

$$\Delta \text{Cash} = -K$$
$$-(r + s^B)K$$
$$+ rA_3 = r\text{AVL}(0, 3)$$
$$+ r(A_1 + A_2) = r\text{LB}(0) = r[K - \text{AVL}(0, 3)]$$
$$+ K(1 - x\%)$$
$$+ x\% K$$
$$= -s^B K$$

The liquidity gap is covered by the liquid amount of the buffer produced by the expiry of asset A_1. The balance sheet is:

Assets	Liabilities
$D_1 = E - s^B K$	$L(2) = K(1 - x\%)$
$A_2 = \text{AVL}(0, 2)$	
$A_3 = \text{AVL}(0, 3)$	
	E
	$P\&L = -s^B K$

The balance sheet shows the bank suffered a loss at the end of the first period equal to the funding spread (i.e., the spread above the risk-free rate) it has to pay to fund its activity. The loss has been covered by abating the amount of equity deposited in account D_1. This is absolutely normal, since we have assumed that the bank invested the funds raised in assets A_1, A_2, A_3 earning the (expected) risk-free rate. The loss is due to the fact that the bank did not charge the funding spread it has to pay on asset A_3. Note that this loss has nothing to do with the liquidity buffer used to cope with funding gaps.

A bank usually has strong bargaining power with some counterparties, typically retail customers, and is able to transfer all the costs related to banking activity on an asset bought from them. For example, if asset A_3 is a mortgage closed with a retail customer, the bank can charge a spread s^A, over the risk-free rate, to compensate the credit risk of the counterparty and a supplementary spread s^B to cover its funding costs. So the asset would earn (following the same reasoning as above) an expected return equal to the risk-free rate plus the bank's funding spread:[4]

$$E[A_3(1 + r + s^A + s^B)] = A_3(1 + r + s^B)$$

Let us now assume that at time 0 the bank actually closed a mortgage contract charging the funding spread in the contract rate. Assume also that the LB is invested in A_1 and A_2 which are liquid (almost) risk-free bonds, such as a government bond: on these investments the bank does not have the bargaining power to charge all its costs and must accept the yield set by the market, which we suppose to include remuneration for the credit risk only, so that the expected return is the risk-free rate. Under these assumptions, the total cash flow is:

$$
\begin{aligned}
\Delta \text{Cash} = &- K \\
&- (r + s^B)K \\
&+ (r + s^B)A_3 = (r + s^B)\text{AVL}(0,3) \\
&+ r(A_1 + A_2) = r\text{LB}(0) = r[K - \text{AVL}(0,3)] \\
&+ K(1 - x\%) \\
&+ x\% K \\
&= -s^B[K - \text{AVL}(0,3)] = -s^B\text{LB}(0)
\end{aligned}
$$

and the balance sheet is:

Assets	Liabilities
$D_1 = E - s^B\text{LB}(0)$ $A_2 = \text{AVL}(0,2)$ $A_3 = \text{AVL}(0,3)$	$L(2) = K(1 - x\%)$
	E $P\&L = -s^B\text{LB}(0)$

The loss is now reduced to $-s^B\text{LB}(0)$ from $-s^B K$ and it is due only to the fact that the bank invested the amount of the liquidity buffer into liquid assets, whose yield had to be accepted as set by the market when they were bought. This loss can be considered a component of the cost of holding the liquidity buffer and consequently has to be charged on the assets that caused a need for the liquidity buffer, in our case asset A_3.

Although the constraints relating to the expiry of the investment of the LB have to be satisfied, the bank does not have to necessarily invest the entire amount LB(0) in liquid securities traded in the market for all the following periods. From Definition 7.2.2 the liquidity buffer needs to cover funding gaps within a short *survival* period, usually taken equal to one month. So, if the period up to the first rollover date is, say, one year, the

---

[4] There is the assumption here that the spread s^A is set in such a way that it also compensates for the loss on the spread s^B in case of default by the counterparty. Equation (7.3) can easily be modified to include this effect as:

$$s^A = \frac{[(1 + r + s^B) - R] \times \text{PD}}{1 - \text{PD}}.$$

bank may invest the buffer amount in assets traded with retail customers for 11 months, so that it can charge funding costs as well; then it can invest in liquid securities the amount needed to cover the funding gap of the first rollover date just 1 month before $T_1 = 1$. Similarly, the amount needed for the funding gap on the second rollover date can be invested in assets bought from retail customers up to the start of the survival period before T_2.

We can also reasonably assume that, given the risk aversion of the bank, a fraction β is invested in liquid marketable securities in any case, and only a fraction $1 - \beta$ is invested in less liquid assets dealt with retail customers. Parameter β can be considered a preference for liquid investment.

Given these assumptions, we first need to determine the new TSFu and the assets in which the available liquidity can be invested. Let us introduce two more assets, A_1^ℓ and A_2^ℓ, representing liquid securities actively traded in the market and maturing, respectively, at times $T_1 = 1$ and $T_2 = 2$. Moreover, let τ_{sv} be the survival period chosen by the bank, and let $T_1^- = T_1 - \tau_{sv}$ and $T_2^- = T_2 - \tau_{sv}$ be the times before the rollover dates given the length of the survival period. The TSFu is:

TSFu	Amount	Asset
$\mathrm{AVL}(0, 1^-)$	$(1 - \beta)x\%K$	A_1
$\mathrm{AVL}(1^-, 1)$	$(1 - \beta)x\%K$	A_1^ℓ
$\mathrm{AVL}(0, 1)$	$\beta x\%K = \beta\mathrm{FG}(1)$	A_1^ℓ
$\mathrm{AVL}(0, 2^-)$	$(1 - \beta)x\%K(1 - x\%)$	A_2
$\mathrm{AVL}(2^-, 2)$	$(1 - \beta)x\%K(1 - x\%)$	A_2^ℓ
$\mathrm{AVL}(0, 2)$	$\beta x\%K(1 - x\%) = \beta\mathrm{FG}(2)$	A_2^ℓ
$\mathrm{AVL}(0, 3)$	$K(1 - x\%)^2$	A_3

where, with a slight abuse of notation, we indicate $1^- = T_1^-$ and similarly for the other rollover dates. It is worthy of note that, during the period between 0 and the start of the survival period $[0, 1^-]$, the amount $A_1 + A_2 = (1 - \beta)\mathrm{LB}(0)$ is invested in less liquid assets; on the other hand, over the entire first period $[0, 1]$, the amount $A_1^\ell + A_2^\ell = \beta\mathrm{LB}(0)$ is invested in liquid securities traded in the market; during the first survival period $[1^-, 1]$, $A_1^\ell + A_2^\ell + A_2 = \mathrm{LB}(0) - (1 - \beta)\mathrm{FG}(1)$.

The balance sheet at time 0 is then modified as follows:

Assets	Liabilities
$D_1 = E$	$L(0) = K$
$A_1 = \mathrm{AVL}(0, 1^-)$	
$A_1^\ell = \mathrm{AVL}(0, 1)$	
$A_2 = \mathrm{AVL}(0, 2^-)$	
$A_2^\ell = \mathrm{AVL}(0, 2)$	
$A_3 = \mathrm{AVL}(0, 3)$	
	E

The cost of the liquidity buffer is getting more complicated to compute, but it is not a difficult task. In fact, assuming for simplicity's sake[5] that the credit risk of all marketable assets is the same and compensated by a spread s^Y, whereas the credit spread for all other assets is s^A, the LB earns the following return in the first period before the rollover date T_1:

$$\mathcal{R}(1) = \mathbf{E}[(A_1 + A_2)(r + s^A + s^B)(T_1^- - T_0) + (A_1^\ell + A_2^\ell)(r + s^Y)(T_1^- - T_0)$$
$$+ A_1^\ell(r + s^Y)(T_1 - T_1^-) + (A_2(r + s^A + s^B) + A_2^\ell(r + s^Y))(T_1 - T_1^-)]$$
$$= \mathrm{LB}(0)[r + (1 - \beta)s^B](T_1 - T_0) - \mathrm{FG}(1)(1 - \beta)s^B(T_1 - T_1^-) \qquad (7.4)$$

It is worth pointing out the constituent parts of equation (7.4):

- The first line of the equation indicates the fraction $(1 - \beta)$ invested in the less liquid assets A_1 and A_2 earning the risk-free rate plus the credit and the bank's funding spread, for a period between time T_0 and the time of the start of the first survival period T_1^-. The complementary fraction β is invested in the same period in marketable securities $A_1^\ell + A_2^\ell$ earning the risk-free rate plus the credit spread.
- In the second line, for the remaining period $T_1 - T_1^-$ (i.e., the first survival period), an amount equal to the funding gap $\mathrm{FG}(1)$ is invested in liquid asset A_1^ℓ, earning the risk-free rate plus the credit spread; the remaining part of the liquidity buffer $\mathrm{LB}(0)$ is invested in illiquid asset A_2 (whose return includes the bank's funding spread) and liquid asset A_2^ℓ (with a return equal to the risk-free rate plus the credit spread).
- The third line shows the return from the buffer by computing the expectations and by rearranging terms in a more convenient and clear fashion. Basically, the return from the LB is equal, over the entire $[T_0, T_1]$, to the risk-free rate for the full amount, plus the bank's funding spread for the fraction $1 - \beta$. This is given by the first part of the third line, which does not consider the fact that, during the survival period $[T_1^-, T_1]$, a share of the LB equal to the funding gap on the first rollover date, $\mathrm{FG}(1)$, is diverted to investment in liquid assets, so that the return equal to the bank's funding spread on this amount has to be deducted from the total return: this is given by the second part of the third line.

To lighten the notation, we can denote the entire first period by $\tau(1) = T_1 - T_0$, and the survival period by $\tau_{sv}(1) = T_1 - T_1^-$. Equation (7.4) can then be rewritten as:

$$\mathcal{R}(1) = \mathrm{LB}(0)[r + (1 - \beta)s^B]\tau(1) - \mathrm{FG}(1)(1 - \beta)s^B\tau_{sv}(1) \qquad (7.5)$$

It is easy to prove that the return from the LB for the second period is:

$$\mathcal{R}(2) = \mathrm{LB}(1)[r + (1 - \beta)s^B]\tau(2) - \mathrm{FG}(2)(1 - \beta)s^B\tau_{sv}(2) \qquad (7.6)$$

In the case we are examining $\tau(1)$ and $\tau(2)$ are equal to 1, so we can further lighten the notation in what follows.

---

[5] The assumption can easily be relaxed although it would make the notation much heavier, without adding deeper insight to the analysis.

When we take into account the investment policy of the buffer outlined above and use (7.5) to determine the total cash flow for the first period, we get:

$$\Delta \text{Cash} = -K$$

$$-(r+s^B)K$$

$$+(r+s^B)A_3 = (r+s^B)\text{AVL}(0,3)$$

$$+\text{LB}(0)[r+(1-\beta)s^B] - \text{FG}(1)(1-\beta)s^B\tau_{sv}(1)$$

$$+K(1-x\%)$$

$$+x\%K = \text{AVL}(0,1) + \text{AVL}(1^-,1) = -\Delta \text{LB}(1)$$

$$= -[\beta s^B \text{LB}(0) + \text{FG}(1)(1-\beta)s^B\tau_{sv}(1)]$$

where the liquidity necessary to cover the funding gap, $x\%K$, is generated by the expiring asset A_1^ℓ, which is the part of the buffer assigned to the first rollover date. The balance sheet is:

Assets	Liabilities
$D_1 = E - [\beta s^B \text{LB}(0) + \text{FG}(1)(1$ $-\beta)s^B\tau_{sv}(1)]$ $A_2 = \text{AVL}(0,2^-)$ $A_2^\ell = \text{AVL}(0,2)$ $A_3 = \text{AVL}(0,3)$	$L(2) = K(1-x\%)$
	E $P\&L = -[\beta s^B \text{LB}(0) + \text{FG}(1)(1-$ $\beta)s^B\tau_{sv}(1)]$

The cost of the LB for the first period is now:

$$\text{LBC}(1) = \beta s^B \text{LB}(0) + \text{FG}(1)(1-\beta)s^B\tau_{sv}(1)$$

It easy to check whether the bank has no preference for liquid investment of the buffer (i.e., $\beta = 0$) and then the cost of the buffer reduces to the funding spread applied to the amount of the funding gap $\text{FG}(1)$ paid for the survival period: $\text{FG}(1)s^B\tau_{sv}(1)$. On the other hand, when the preference for liquid investment is complete (i.e., $\beta = 1$) then the cost of the liquidity buffer is $s^B\text{LB}(0)$, which is the level we first derived above before introducing the possibility of investing in less liquid assets before the survival period starts.

To have zero total cash flow and P&L for the first period, the bank needs to charge the cost to keep the liquidity buffer on the yield of the asset it buys from retail customers. It is clear this cost can be made small by reducing the preference for liquid securities and/or by reducing the survival period, although it is rather uncommon to set the latter shorter than one month. Anyway, if for the first period the yield requested on asset A_3 is

$(r + s^A + s^B + \text{LBC}(1)/A_3)$ (implying an expected return of $(r + s^B + \text{LBC}(1)/A_3)$), then we can restore an equilibrium condition with no cash imbalances or losses.

$$\Delta\text{Cash} = -K$$
$$-(r + s^B)K$$
$$+ (r + s^B + \text{LBC}(1)/A_3)A_3 = (r + s^B + \text{LBC}(1)/A_3)\text{AVL}(0,3)$$
$$+ \text{LB}(0)[r + (1-\beta)s^B] - \text{FG}(1)(1-\beta)s^B\tau_{ls}(1)$$
$$+ K(1 - x\%)$$
$$+ x\%K = \text{AVL}(0,1) + \text{AVL}(1^-,1) = -\Delta\text{LB}(1)$$
$$= 0$$

and the balance sheet is:

Assets	Liabilities
$D_1 = E$	$L(2) = K(1 - x\%)$
$A_2 = \text{AVL}(0, 2^-)$	
$A_2^\ell = \text{AVL}(0, 2)$	
$A_3 = \text{AVL}(0, 3)$	
	E
	$P\&L = 0$

For subsequent periods, using an analysis identical to that just presented, the LB cost can be shown to be $\text{LBC}(2) = \beta s^B \text{LB}(1) + \text{FG}(2)(1 - \beta)s^B \tau_{sv}(2)$ and $\text{LBC}(3) = 0$. We can immediately see that the LBC for the last period is always nil, since the rollover of the debt stops and no LB needs to be kept. All the costs related to the buffer have to be charged on the yield of asset A_3 at the appropriate times, in our case 1 and 2. We will see later on how to adjust the yield to include the liquidity buffer in a more standardized way.

7.3.3 Liquidity buffer costs when stressed scenarios do not occur

Proposition 7.3.7. *In the presence of funding costs, when assumed stressed conditions do not occur, oversizing of the liquidity buffer does not produce unexpected costs if the bank either: (i) reinvests the unnecessary portion of the buffer in assets on which it can charge the actual costs of the buffer (which are different from those forecast at time T_0 under stressed conditions), or (ii) shrinks the balance sheet simultaneously reducing the amount of issued debt and of the liquidity buffer, just as if stressed conditions actually manifested themselves.*

As we did for the case of an economy where default risk does not exist, we now study what happens if the buffer has not been utilized because a stressed scenario either did not occur or manifested itself in a weaker form. Assume, for example, that at time $T_1 = 1$ the rollover of the debt could be performed without any problem, so that the expected utilization of the LB for an amount $K \times (1 - x\%)$ was not necessary. In this case there are three different rules the bank may follow:[6]

1. The first rule is that the buffer is left unchanged if it is not utilized.

    ○   *At time $T_1 = 1$:* The debt can be rolled over for the entire amount, so that the new liability of the bank is K; the buffer is left unchanged, so we have $LB^*(1) = LB(0)$. The actual buffer at time 1, $LB^*(1)$, is different from the level of buffer $LB(1)$ deduced by the amount needed to cover the funding gap of the stressed scenario. Total cash flow is still zero, although in this case there is no need to use the buffer; the P&L is zero as well, as can easily be checked. In the period $[T_1, T_2]$, $LB^*(1)$ is invested in assets A_2 and A_2^ℓ, which clearly will be held in an amount greater than forecast at time T_0. The actual funding gap at time T_2 will be equal to the forecast funding gap at time T_1: $FG^*(2) = FG(1)$, which is also clearly different from the one predicted at time T_0. The liquidity needed to buy an extra amount of these assets is provided by the expiry of asset A_1^ℓ. The return on the buffer will be:

    $$\mathcal{R}(2) = LB^*(1)[r + (1 - \beta)s^B] - FG^*(2)(1 - \beta)s^B \tau_{sv}(2)$$

    ○   *At time $T_2 = 2$* The LB and the rollover of the debt produces the same cash flows as those predicted at time T_0 for the stress scenario at time $T_1 = 1$. Stressed conditions regarding the rollover occur this time, so the buffer will be reduced accordingly (i.e., $LB^*(2) = (K(1 - x\%) - AVL(0, 3)))$. If the bank charged the $LBC(2)$ (computed on $LB(2)$) on the yield for the second period of the asset, we have total cash flow now as:

    $\Delta Cash = -K$

    $\quad - (r + s^B)K$

    $\quad + (r + s^B + LBC(2)/A_3)A_3 = (r + s^B + LBC(2)/A_3)AVL(0, 3)$

    $\quad + LB^*(1)[r + (1 - \beta)s^B] - FG(2)(1 - \beta)s^B \tau_{ls}(2)$

    $\quad + K(1 - x\%)$

    $\quad + x\%K = AVL(0, 1) + AVL(1^-, 1) = -\Delta LB^*(1)$

    $\quad + AVL(0, 2) + AVL(2^-, 2) = -\Delta A_2$

    $\quad - AVL(0, 2) - AVL(2^-, 2) = -\Delta A_3$

    $\quad = -LBC^*(2) + LBC(2)$

    The funding gap is covered by a fraction of the maturing asset A_2^ℓ in which the $LB^*(1)$ was invested, the remaining part is used to increase the amount of the investment in asset A_3. Since there is no longer a need for a liquidity buffer, the amount left can be entirely used to buy an illiquid asset for an investment in the period $[T_2, T_3]$. Now,

---

[6] In what follows we indicate the actual size of the buffer or the actual amount of buffer costs by an asterisk "*", whereas the same quantities without any sign indicate the value predicted at time T_0 should a stressed scenario occur.

$$\text{LBC}^*(2) = \beta s^B \text{LB}^*(1) + \text{FG}^*(2)(1-\beta)s^B \tau_{sv}(2)$$
$$= \beta s^B \text{LB}(0) + \text{FG}(1)(1-\beta)s^B \tau_{sv}(2),$$

whereas

$$\text{LBC}(2) = \beta s^B \text{LB}(1) + \text{FG}(2)(1-\beta)s^B \tau_{sv}(2).$$

Since the expected levels of LB at the beginning of the activity at $T_0 = 0$ implied that $\text{LB}(0) > \text{LB}(1)$, which means that $\text{LB}^*(1) > \text{LB}(1)$ and $\text{FG}^*(2) > \text{FG}(2)$ we have that:

$$-\text{LBC}^*(2) + \text{LBC}(2) < 0$$

so that total cash flow is negative. On the other hand, the balance sheet is:

Assets	Liabilities
$D_1 = E - \text{LBC}^*(2) + \text{LBC}(2)$ $A_3 = \text{AVL}(0,3) + \text{AVL}(0,2)$ $+\text{AVL}(2^-,2)$	$L(3) = K(1-x\%)$
	E $P\&L = -\text{LBC}^*(2) + \text{LBC}(2)$

with $P\&L < 0$, so that a loss is recorded.

○ *At time $T_3 = 3$:* The debt is fully repaid with funds coming from the maturity of asset A_3. Total cash flow is:

$$\begin{aligned}
\Delta\text{Cash} = &-K(1-x\%) \\
&-(r+s^B)K(1-x\%) \\
&+(r+s^B)A_3 = (r+s^B)[\text{AVL}(0,3) + \text{AVL}(0,2) + \text{AVL}(2^-,2)] \\
&+\text{AVL}(0,3) + \text{AVL}(0,2) + \text{AVL}(2^-,2) = -\Delta A_3 \\
&+[K(1-x\%) - \text{AVL}(0,3)] \\
=&\ 0
\end{aligned}$$

So we have zero cash flow and zero P&L. The only P&L arises from the second period and is negative as shown above. In fact, the balance sheet also shows a negative P&L:

Assets	Liabilities
$D_1 = E - \text{LBC}^*(2) + \text{LBC}(2)$ $A_3 = 0$	$L(3) = 0$
	E $P\&L = -\text{LBC}^*(2) + \text{LBC}(2)$

To conclude, in the presence of funding costs for the bank, oversizing of the liquidity buffer for the periods it is needed causes a cost. This conclusion is different from when no funding spread is paid by the bank on its liabilities.

2. The second rule is that the buffer is abated to compensate for oversizing. The amount by which the buffer should be reduced has to be properly computed. Any excess buffer is used to increase the position in assets similar to A_3. Without too great a loss of generality, we assume that the bank increases the amount of investment in A_3.

o   *At time $T_1 = 1$:* The reduction of the LB can be shown to be equal to $Kx\%(1 - x\%)$, so as to make the buffer adequate for a stressed scenario occurring at time T_2 applied to an amount of debt that is not that predicted after a stressed scenario in T_1, but the full amount K instead. The difference between the actual and predicted buffer is $\mathrm{LB}^*(1) - \mathrm{LB}(1) = x^2\%K$: this higher amount has to be invested, according to the bank's liquidity preferences, in assets A_2 and A_2^ℓ. The funding gap $\mathrm{FG}^*(2)$ will also be higher than the predicted $\mathrm{FG}(2)$. Total cash flow is:

$$\Delta\mathrm{Cash} = -K$$
$$- (r + s^B)K$$
$$+ (r + s^B + \mathrm{LBC}(1)/A_3)A_3 = (r + s^B + \mathrm{LBC}(1)/A_3)\mathrm{AVL}(0,3)$$
$$+ \mathrm{LB}(0)[r + (1 - \beta)s^B] - \mathrm{FG}(1)(1 - \beta)s^B\tau_{ls}(1)$$
$$+ K$$
$$+ Kx\%(1 - x\%) = -\Delta\mathrm{LB}(1)$$
$$- Kx^2\%(1 - \beta) = -\Delta A_2$$
$$+ Kx^2\%\beta = -\Delta A_2^\ell$$
$$- Kx\%(1 - x\%) = -\Delta A_3$$
$$= 0$$

The line before the last one shows that the increase of the position in asset A_3 generates a negative cash flow that is covered by a decrease of the LB. The remaining LB, higher than that predicted at time T_0, increases available liquidity and is invested according to the bank's policy. The cost of the LB for the first period, $\mathrm{LBC}(1)$, is defined as above and is the one computed at time T_0. The balance sheet is:

Assets	Liabilities
$D_1 = E$	$L(2) = K$
$A_2 = \mathrm{AVL}(0, 2^-) + Kx^2\%(1 - \beta)$	
$A_2^\ell = \mathrm{AVL}(0, 2) + Kx^2\%\beta$	
$A_3 = \mathrm{AVL}(0, 3) + Kx\%(1 - x\%)$	
	E
	$P\&L = 0$

which shows zero P&L and a buffer $LB^*(1) = x\%K$ that is different from $LB(1)$, the level supposed if the stressed scenario at 1 happened.

- *At time $T_2 = 2$*: Stressed conditions regarding the rollover occur this time, so the buffer will be reduced accordingly (i.e., $LB^*(2) = Kx\% - Kx\% = 0$). At time T_0 the bank charged $LBC(2) = \beta s^B LB(1) + FG(2)(1-\beta)s^B \tau_{sv}(2)$ on the yield of the asset for the second period, but the actual cost for the buffer is $LBC^*(2) = \beta s^B LB^*(1) + FG^*(2)(1-\beta)s^B \tau_{sv}(2)$. Since it is easy to show that $LB^*(1) = x\%K > LB(1) = x\%(K(1-x\%)$ and hence $FG^*(2) > FG(2)$ (the actual buffer is greater than predicted), we have a negative total and the balance sheet would show a loss equal to $q = LBC^*(2) - LBC(2)$. If this additional cost, not forecast at time T_0, is charged on the increase of the amount of asset A_3, we have the following total cash flow

$$\Delta \text{Cash} = -K$$

$$-(r+s^B)K$$

$$+(r+s^B + LBC(2)/A_3)AVL(0,3) + (r+s^B + q/\Delta A)Kx\%(1-x\%)$$

$$+LB(1)[r + (1-\beta)s^B] - FG(2)(1-\beta)s^B \tau_{ls}(2)$$

$$+K(1-x\%)$$

$$-x\%K = -\Delta A_2^{\ell}$$

$$= 0$$

The balance sheet is:

Assets	Liabilities
$D_1 = E$	$L(3) = K(1-x\%)$
$A_3 = AVL(0,3) + Kx\%(1-x\%)$	
	E
	$P\&L = 0$

so we still have zero total cash-flow and zero P&L.

Remark 7.3.1. *The assumption that the bank is able to charge the extra cost originated by the oversized buffer on the yield of asset A_3 should not be considered too restrictive. If A_3 is an asset such as a mortgage or a loan, the bank has enough bargaining power to increase the contract rate of new deals so as to include the extra costs.*

- *At time $T_3 = 3$*: The debt is fully repaid with funds coming from the maturity of the asset $A_3 = AVL(0,3) + Kx\%(1-x\%) = K(1-x\%)$. Total cash flow is:

$$\Delta \text{Cash} = - K(1 - x\%)$$
$$- (r + s^B)K(1 - x\%)$$
$$+ (r + s^B)(\text{AVL}(0, 3) + Kx\%(1 - x\%))$$
$$+ \text{AVL}(0, 3) + Kx\%(1 - x\%) = -\Delta A_3$$
$$= 0$$

The balance sheet shows zero P&L as well:

Assets	Liabilities
$D_1 = E$	$L(3) = 0$
$A_3 = 0$	
	E
	$P\&L = 0$

So this rule does not produce negative or positive cash flows, as long as the excess buffer is used to buy new assets on which the bank is able to charge (besides the debtor's credit spread) its funding costs and the extra cost (q) due to the actual amount of the buffer larger than that predicted.

3. The third rule is to reduce the amount of the buffer *and* at the same time reduce the amount of rolled-over debt just as if the stressed scenario actually occurred. The difference between this rule and the second one is that in this case the bank is actually reducing the balance sheet (both assets and liabilities) in much the same way as when a stressed scenario produces its effects, whereas in the second rule only the buffer was reduced, but the amount of debt was rolled over entirely since the market was regularly providing liquidity to the bank.

It is easy to check that, by following this rule, the bank has exactly the same total cash flow and P&L at the end of every period as if the stressed scenarios actually occurred. So the equilibrium conditions are preserved without any additional effort by the bank.

The analysis above, proving Proposition 7.3.7, provides the bank with guidance on the safest policy to implement in the management of the LB. In fact, depending on the bank's power to charge on the price of assets bought from retail customers the additional costs for the buffer as well, rule 2 or 3 can be followed so as to ensure that no P&L is generated when stressed conditions do not manifest themselves. On the other hand, rule 1 is clearly not able to prevent unexpected losses when the LB is oversized.

7.3.4 A more general formula for liquidity buffer costs

In a more general fashion, for a given liability used to fund the purchase of asset A, let the number of needed rollovers be nr with each rollover occurring on dates T_{r_j}, with $j = 1, \ldots, nr$. Let $\tau(T_{r_j}) = T_{r_j} - T_{r_{j-1}}$ be the period between two rollover dates, with the convention that $\tau(T_{r_0}) = T_{r_1} - T_0$, with T_0 equal to the reference date. Moreover, let $\tau_{sv}(T_{r_j})$ be the survival period set by the bank before the rollover at time T_{r_j}, starting at time $T_{r_j}^-$ (usually $\tau_{sv}(T_{r_j}) = T_{r_j} - T_{r_j}^- = 1$ month).

Total buffer is simply the sum of the funding gaps' nr rollover dates:

$$\mathrm{LB}^A(0) = \sum_{j=1}^{nr} \mathrm{FG}(T_{r_j}) \tag{7.7}$$

Let $P^D(0, T)$ be the discount factor from time 0 to time T.[7] The total cost of the liquidity buffer for the purchase of asset A is the present value of the sum of the LBC for single periods:

$$\mathrm{LBC}^A(0) = \sum_{j=1}^{nr} P^D(0, T_{r_j}) \mathrm{LBC}(T_{r_j})$$

$$= \sum_{j=1}^{nr} P^D(0, T_{r_j}) \left[\beta s^B \mathrm{LB}(T_{r_{j-1}}) \tau(T_{r_j}) + \mathrm{FG}(T_{r_j})(1 - \beta) s^B \tau_{sv}(T_{r_j}) \right] \tag{7.8}$$

Total liquidity buffer costs depend on:

1. The size of the FG at each rollover date: the size of the funding gap depends, in turn, on the stressed scenario assumed.
2. The number of rollovers nr: they are determined once the maturity of the bought asset and of the liability used to fund it are determined.
3. The bank's preference to invest all the LB in liquid assets traded actively in the market.
4. The funding spread s^B over the risk-free rate paid by the bank.

Remark 7.3.2. *Although the analysis above and in the previous sections provides an in-depth insight into how to set up a liquidity buffer and how to compute and attribute related costs to the asset that generated its need, we should keep in mind that we are depicting a stylized economy. In a real-economy environment we have to account for additional sources of uncertainty that will alter, but not modify, the main results presented.*

Looking at this in greater detail, the stochasticity of the interest rates and of the funding spread add an additional degree of riskiness that has to be properly measured and included in the calculation of the costs related to the LB.

Equation (7.8) can be made even more general by considering the fact that the bank might wish to split the fraction β of the liquidity buffer between liquid securities and cash. Let β_s be the part of fraction β strictly allocated to liquid assets; furthermore let β_c be the remaining part of β kept as cash. So $\beta = \beta_s + \beta_c$. The second term in (7.8) is modified to account for the fact that the bank loses the funding spread on the fraction of the LB it diverts to liquid securities, which is now β_s; on the other hand, the bank also loses the risk-free interest rate on the fraction it keeps as cash that is absolutely

---

[7] In the present setting, since the risk-free rate is constant, $P^D(0, T) = e^{-r^* \times T}$, where $r^* = \ln(1 + r)$.

unproductive of any yield. In conclusion, equation (7.8) reads:

$$\text{LBC}^A(0) = \sum_{j=1}^{nr} P^D(0, T_{r_j})\text{LBC}(T_{r_j})$$

$$= \sum_{j=1}^{nr} P^D(0, T_{r_j}) \left[\beta s^B \text{LB}(T_{r_{j-1}})\tau(T_{r_j}) + \text{FG}(T_{r_j})[(1 - \beta_s)s^B \right.$$

$$\left. + \beta_c(r + s^B)]\tau_{sv}(T_{r_j}) \right] \qquad (7.9)$$

When period $\tau(T_{r_j})$ is longer than one year, the spread s^B cannot be used as indicated in formula (7.9). Typically, the spread will be applied to subperiods of one-year maximum length: let H be the number of these subperiods included in $\tau(T_{r_j})$, so that $\tau_h(T_{r_j}) = T_{(h-1)_{r_j}} - T_{h_{r_j}}$, for $h = 0, \ldots, H$, $T_{0_{r_j}} = T_{r_{j-1}}$ and $T_{H_{r_j}} = T_{r_j}$. Formula (7.9) modifies as:

$$\text{LBC}^A(0) = \sum_{j=1}^{nr} P^D(0, T_{r_j})\text{LBC}(T_{r_j})$$

$$= \sum_{j=1}^{nr} P^D(0, T_{r_j}) \left[\beta s^B \text{LB}(T_{r_{j-1}}) \sum_{h=1}^{H} \frac{1}{P^D(T_{h_{r_j}}, T_{H_{r_j}})} \tau_h(T_{r_j}) \right.$$

$$\left. + \text{FG}(T_{r_j})[(1 - \beta_s)s^B + \beta_c(r + s^B)]\tau_{sv}(T_{r_j}) \right] \qquad (7.10)$$

where we assumed that $\tau_{sv}(T_{r_j})$ is always shorter or equal to one year in every case, so that s^B simply compounded can be applied with no problems.

In the next example we will show how to put all the concepts and the formulae we have introduced so far into practice.

Example 7.3.1. *Assume a bank has one liability in its balance sheet for an amount of 100; the liability has a typical duration of four years and bears a rollover risk of $x\% = 30\%$ on expiry. The bank wants to invest in an asset expiring in 10 years; clearly there is a duration mismatch since two rollovers of the liability (at years 4 and 8) are needed to fund the purchase of the asset until its maturity. So the bank must first consider the available liquidity it can invest up to 10 years and as a consequence it will also determine the investments in illiquid and liquid assets expiring before the start of the two survival periods that include the rollover dates, and in liquid assets during the two survival periods.*

The amount available for an illiquid asset expiring in 10 years is (recalling what we have shown above) $100 \times (1 - 30\%)^2 = 49$. Assuming the bank has a preference for liquid investment parameter $\beta = 20\%$, the funds invested in illiquid and liquid assets up to the start of the two survival periods (i.e., up to 4^- and 5^-, adopting the notation used before) can easily be derived (see Table 7.1). For the maturity up to the start of the first survival period, 4^-, the amount to be invested in illiquid assets is 24 and in liquid assets it is 6; the sum of 30 is the $\text{FG}(4) = 100 \times (1 - 30\%)$. During the survival period $[4^-, 4]$ the full amount of 30 equal to the first funding gap is invested in liquid assets (as shown in Table 7.2).

Table 7.1. Term structure of liquidity to be invested in illiquid (AVL_{NL}) and liquid (AVL_L) assets for the investment in an asset expiring in 10 years with a liability that has a 4-year duration

Maturity	AVL_{NL}	AVL_L
1^-		
2^-		
3^-		
4^-	24.00	6.00
5^-		
6^-		
7^-		
8^-	16.80	4.20
9^-		
10^-	49.00	

Table 7.2. Term structure of liquidity to be invested in liquid (AVL_L) assets during survival periods, for the investment in an asset expiring in 10 years with a liability that has a 4-year duration

Maturity	AVL_L
$1^-, 1$	
$2^-, 2$	
$3^-, 3$	
$4^-, 4$	30.00
$5^-, 5$	
$6^-, 6$	
$7^-, 7$	
$8^-, 8$	21.00
$9^-, 9$	
$10^-, 10$	

Now, let us assume that the risk-free interest rate is constant and equal to $r = 3\%$ p.a. further that the bank funding spread is constant at $s^B = 2\%$ p.a. To compute total LBC we use formula (7.10): the information we need on the amount of the liquidity buffer for each period and the amount of the funding gap on the rollover dates, is shown in Table 7.3. The discount factors are shown in Table 7.4.

Assuming that $\beta_s = 20\%$, so that $\beta_c = 0\%$, and that the survival periods are both equal to one month, formula (7.10) yields:

$$LBC^A(0) = 1.09256$$

This is the final result, which is the sum of:

$$\sum_{j=1}^{2} P^D(0, T_{r_j}) \beta s^B LB(T_{r_{j-1}}) \sum_{h=1}^{4} \frac{1}{P^D(T_{h_{r_j}}, T_{H_{r_j}})} \tau_h(T_{r_j})$$

$$= 20\% \times 2\% \times (0.88849 \times 51 \times 4.183627 + 0.78941 \times 21 \times 4.183627) = 1.03570$$

and

Table 7.3. Amount of the liquidity buffer and the funding gap for the investment in an asset expiring in 10 years with a liability that has a 4-year duration

Maturity	LB	FG
1^-	51.00	
2^-	51.00	
3^-	51.00	
4^-	51.00	30.00
5^-	21.00	
6^-	21.00	
7^-	21.00	
8^-	21.00	21.00
9^-		
10^-		

Table 7.4. Discount factors for maturities from one to 10 years, assuming a constant 3% annual risk-free rate

Maturity	$P^D(0, T)$
1	0.97087
2	0.94260
3	0.91514
4	0.88849
5	0.86261
6	0.83748
7	0.81309
8	0.78941
9	0.76642
10	0.74409

$$\sum_{j=1}^{2} P^D(0, T_{r_j}) \mathrm{FG}(T_{r_j})[(1 - \beta_s)s^B + \beta_c(r + s^B)]\tau_{sv}(T_{r_j})$$

$$= (0.88849 \times 30 + 0.78941 \times 21) \times \tfrac{30}{365} \times 20\% \times 2\% = 0.05671$$

If $\beta_s = 15\%$, so that $\beta_c = 5\%$, then the second part of the formula would be:

$$\sum_{j=1}^{nr} P^D(0, T_{r_j}) \mathrm{FG}(T_{r_j})[(1 - \beta_s)s^B + \beta_c(r + s^B)]\tau_{sv}(T_{r_j})$$

$$= (0.88849 \times 30 + 0.78941 \times 21) \times \frac{30}{365} \times (15\% \times 2\% + 5\% \times (3\% + 2\%)) = 0.06929$$

and total liquidity buffer cost would be:

$$\mathrm{LBC}^A(0) = 1.10499$$

Table 7.5. Risk-free, spread and bank total discount factors for maturities from one to 10 years

Maturity	$P^D(0, T)$	$P^s(0, T)$	$P^B(0, T)$
1	0.970874	0.980952	0.952381
2	0.942596	0.962268	0.907029
3	0.915142	0.943939	0.863838
4	0.888487	0.925959	0.822702
5	0.862609	0.908322	0.783526
6	0.837484	0.89102	0.746215
7	0.813092	0.874048	0.710681
8	0.789409	0.8574	0.676839
9	0.766417	0.841068	0.644609
10	0.744094	0.825048	0.613913

Example 7.3.2. *We assume that the asset expiring in 10 years in Example 7.3.1 is a loan to a counterparty: the capital is paid back at expiry whereas on a yearly basis the counterparty pays interest. To focus on the LBC, we assume the counterparty is default risk free.*

Given the data we used in Example 7.3.1, the bank first derives the risk-free $P^D(0, T)$ and the funding spread $P^s(0, T)$ discount factors, so that the total discount factors including the bank's funding spread are $P^B(0, T) = P^D(0, T)P^s(0, T)$. These are easily found in our simplified example: let $r^* = \ln(1 + r)$ and $s^* = -\ln(1 + r + s) - r^*$; then $P^D(0, T) = e^{-r^* T}$, $P^s(0, T) = e^{-s^* T}$ and $P^B(0, T) = P^D(0, T)P^s(0, T)$. The values are shown in Table 7.5.

To find the fair yearly rate c that the counterparty has to pay, the bank uses the following relation:

$$A = \sum_{i=1}^{10} c A P^B(0, T_i) + A P^B(0, T_{10}) - LBC^A(0)$$

From Example 7.3.1 we know that A = 49 and $LBC^A(0) = 1.09256$ (when $\beta_s = 20\%$). So we get:

$$c = \frac{49 - 49 \times 0.61391 + 1.09256}{7.72173} = 5.29\%$$

If liquidity buffer costs were nil, the fair rate would be 5.00% (i.e., just the risk-free rate plus the funding spread), as it is easy to check by setting $LBC^A(0) = 0$ in the formula above.

7.4 FUNDING ASSETS WITH SEVERAL LIABILITIES

Usual banking activity is run by funding the purchase of assets with a wide range of liabilities, different both in type and maturity. We generalize the results of the previous section by assuming that two liabilities (e.g., two bonds) with different maturities are issued. We also assume that there are two different funding gaps related to each of the two liabilities, depending on one being sold to retail customers and the other to professional investors.

Assume that the bank wants to finance an asset with maturity at $T_3 = 3$ by two bonds L_1 and L_2, the first maturing at $T_1 = 1$ and the other maturing at $T_2 = 2$; both bonds are issued for amounts, respectively, equal to K_1 and K_2. Assume that the funding gap at time 1 for bond L_1 is for $x_1\%$ of the amount to roll over, whereas for bond L_2 it is for $x_2\%$. The available liquidity at time 0 from bond L_1 is:

$$AVL_1(0,3) = K_1 \times (1 - x_1\%)^2$$

since two rollovers are needed at 1 and 2. From bond L_2 the available liquidity is:

$$AVL_2(0,3) = K_2 \times (1 - x_2\%)$$

because only one rollover is necessary at 2. Total liquidity that can be invested is:

$$AVL_T(0,3) = AVL_1(0,3) + AVL_2(0,3)$$

and it is used by asset A with maturity $T_3 = 3$, so that $A = AVL_T(0,3)$. The LB at time 0 is:

$$LB(0) = K_1 + K_2 - AVL_T(0,3)$$

The LB can be seen as the sum of two separate liquidity buffers, each covering its reference bond's funding gap in a stressed scenario. Computing the cost of the LB is straightforward, once the TSFu has been defined along the lines adopted in Section 7.3.2 in the case of a single liability, since it is little more than the sum of the costs of the two buffers considered separately:

$$LBC_T^A(0) = LBC_1^A(0) + LBC_2^A(0)$$

More generally, if the purchase of asset A is financed with N liabilities, of which $M \leq N$ has a maturity shorter than the asset, then total LB is:

$$LB_T^A(0) = \sum_{i=1}^{M} LB_i^A(0) \tag{7.11}$$

and the total cost of the liquidity buffer is:

$$LBC_T^A(0) = \sum_{i=1}^{M} LBC_i^A(0) \tag{7.12}$$

where LB_i^A and LBC_i^A are, respectively, defined in equations (7.7) and (7.9) (or (7.10)).

7.5   ACTUAL SCENARIOS SEVERER THAN PREDICTED

As already pointed out, stressed scenarios are designed to account for the severest liquidity conditions the bank may face at any given level of confidence (say, 99%). All scenarios producing even heavier difficulties but with a probability of occurrence below 1% ($= 100 - 99\%$) are not considered, but in practice they are accepted as an intrinsic risk related to banking activity that cannot be ruled out.

The fact that unlikely scenarios can actually occur should in theory bankrupt the bank. Nevertheless, since liquidity stress does not imply immediate default, some strategies can be implemented although they cannot be defined within "equilibrium" liquidity policies and can be seen as an action of last resort to try and save the bank from default.

There are two strategies that can be identified for such severe scenarios.

1. Immediately use all the available LB, even if allotted to future stressed scenarios, for the part invested in assets that are liquid and readily tradeable in the market.[8] If this strategy is successful, the bank has to reintegrate the buffer for ensuing rollover dates.
2. When no liquid assets are in the balance sheet and when the market still provides short-term liquidity to the bank, finance the greater-than-expected funding gap with short-term debt. This strategy can also be implemented after the one above has been activated but cannot be repeated given balance sheet constraints.

    More specifically, let L_1 be a liability expiring in $T_1 = 1$ used to finance asset A_3 maturing at $T_3 = 3$. There are two rollover dates and a LB is built accordingly. On the first rollover date the funding gap $FG^*(1)$ exceeds the forecast stressed scenario and is even bigger than the entire LB available, so that $FG^*(1) > LB(0)$.

    The bank may have invested the buffer in readily tradeable assets for the fraction β, so that this fraction can be used to cover any abnormal funding gap. Let us indicate by $y\% K = FG^*(1) - FG(0) - \beta LB(1)$ the amount of the funding gap exceeding that assumed in the stressed scenario minus the fraction β invested in the marketable assets of the residual buffer still available at time 1. Assume also that the bank can issue a short-term liability L_2 maturing at $T_3 = 3$. Moreover, this liability needs to be rolled over twice, since its duration is single period, and the stressed scenario predicts a funding gap of $z\%$ for each rollover date.

In the table below we show variations of the liabilities and of the assets, including the liquidity buffer. At time T_2 the liquidity buffer built at time T_0 is not enough to cover an abnormal stressed scenario, so that short-term funding is used to cover the funding gap by issuing new debt L_2. Furthermore, this debt has to be rolled over at T_3, so a liquidity buffer $LB(1)$ is formed based on the assumption that $z\%$ in a stressed scenario cannot be financed. Actually. we suppose that this stressed scenario happens at T_3, so that the buffer is used to cover the funding gap. Finally, at T_4 the short-term debt L_2 is paid back with proceeds from asset A_4.

Time	0	T_1	T_2	T_3	T_4
Liabilities					
	$L_1 = K$		$L_1 = K(1 - x\% - y\%)$		
			$L_2 = y\%K + y\%Kz\%$	$L_3 = y\%K$	0
Assets					
		$A_4 = (1 - x\%)K$			0
LB					
		$LB(0) = x\%K$	0	0	0
			$LB(1) = y\%Kz\%$		

---

[8] Recall that this part of the LB is determined by the preference parameter for liquid investments β we introduced above.

In the table below we show the cash flows at each time associated with variations of the liabilities, of the assets and of the liquidity buffer.

Time	0	T_1	T_2	T_3	T_4
Inflows	$L_1 = K$		$L_1 = K(1 - x\% - y\%)$		
			$LB(0) = x\%K$	$LB(1) = y\%Kz\%$	
			$L_2 = y\%K + y\%Kz\%$	$L_3 = y\%K$	$A_4 = (1 - x\%)K$
Outflows		$A_4 = (1 - x\%)K$	$L_1 = K(1 - x\% - y\%)$	$L_2 = y\%K + y\%Kz\%$	$L_3 = y\%K$
					$L_1 = K(1 - x\% - y\%)$
Net		$LB(0) = x\%K$	$LB(1) = y\%Kz\%$	0	0

The problem with the second approach the bank can follow in an abnormal stressed scenario is that it clearly suffers from the fact that short-term financing covering funding gaps also may not be fully protected by the liquidity buffer, since other abnormal scenarios may happen. So this approach should be seen as an extreme measure to avoid bankruptcy when scenarios manifest themselves with a severity beyond the chosen confidence level (e.g., 99%), but they should not be used as sound practices to establish funding and liquidity buffer policies.

7.6 THE TERM STRUCTURE OF AVAILABLE FUNDING AND THE LIQUIDITY BUFFER

Having analysed how the liquidity buffer is generated by the maturity mismatch, how its amount is determined and what are the associated costs, we will now focus on how it is possible to build a generic term structure of available funding, considering both the liquidity that can be invested in illiquid and liquid assets. We also assume a situation somewhat nearer to reality than the stylized one sketched in the previous sections.

More specifically, we suppose that the bank funds its activities by means of a fairly wide range of funding sources, each one characterized by its own typical duration and funding spread. All funding sources contribute to the financing of activities indistinctly and proportionally to the weight of each of them. If we accept this assumption, keeping in mind predicted funding gaps, then the TSFu is readily derived.

Let the number of funding sources be M and let T_{1_m} be the expiry of each funding source for $m = 1, \ldots, M$. We assume that each source has a typical duration that is the same in the future as well, when the liability will be rolled over by the bank; this means that the typical duration for each source is τ_m. Assume we want to build the TSFu between time T_0 and time T_b (i.e., TSFu(T_0, T_b)). For simplicity's sake, we assume that each funding source starts at time T_0, meaning that all corresponding liabilities are sold at time T_0; we also assume that the typical duration of each funding source is contained an integer number of times in the period $[T_0, T_b]$ (e.g., 3 times, but not 3.7 times): this assumption is easily relaxed and the approach we are sketching here can be extended to more general cases when some or all liabilities do not start at T_0.

Under the assumptions above, the number of rollovers for the m-th funding source is:

$$N_m = \frac{T_b - T_0}{\tau_m} - 1$$

We can determine the TSFu for this funding source at the end of the horizon we are considering, which is T_b, given that the initial amount of the corresponding liability at time T_0 is $L_m = L(T_0, T_{1_m})$, where T_{1_m} is the expiry of the m-th funding source, corresponding to the first rollover date. The available liquidity is computed in the same way as done in Section 7.3: indicating by $x_m\%$ the percentage of the amount that the bank is not able to roll over on each of N_m rollover dates. In this way, we get the available liquidity for investments in illiquid assets up to time T_b:

$$\text{AVL}_{NL}(T_0, T_b) = L_m(1 - x_m\%)^{N_m}$$

which is the initial amount of funds L_m raised at time T_0 by source m, including the deduction of $x_m\%$ on each rollover date for N_m number of times. The difference between this quantity and the initial amount L_m contributes to the liquidity buffer.[9]

We also know, from the analysis above, that the liquidity buffer can be reinvested in liquid and illiquid assets, according to proportions indicated by the bank's preference parameter β to invest in liquid securities. Let us examine how the LB is invested for the m-th funding source: first consider $\text{AVL}_{NL}(T_0, T_{1_m}^-)$, the quantity of LB that can be invested in non-liquid assets (such as loans), up to the time $T_{1_m}^-$ when the survival period including the first rollover starts: this is basically an amount equal to the funding gap for the first rollover, taking into account the parameter for the preference of liquid assets β, so $(1 - \beta)$ is invested in illiquid assets: $\text{AVL}_{NL}(T_0, T_{1_m}^-) = (1 - \beta)\text{FG}_m(T_{1_m}^-)$.

The formula can be generalized in a straightforward way to the N_m rollovers of the m-th funding source, so as to obtain the available liquidity for investments in illiquid assets from time T_0 to the beginning of the survival periods for the N_m rollover date, $T_{n_m}^-$, for $n_m = 1, \ldots, N_m$:

$$\text{AVL}_{NL}(T_0, T_{n_m}^-) = (1 - \beta)\text{FG}_m(T_{n_m})$$

For the same periods, a complementary fraction β is invested in liquid assets, so that the corresponding available liquidity is:

$$\text{AVL}_L(T_0, T_{n_m}^-) = \beta\text{FG}_m(T_{n_m})$$

Finally, during the survival periods τ_{n_m}, referring to the n-th rollover of the m-th funding source, the available liquidity must be invested in liquid assets for an amount equal to the predicted funding gap $\text{FG}_m(T_{n_m})$, so that we have (recalling that $\tau_{sv}(T_{n_m}) = T_{n_m} - T_{n_m}^-$):

$$\text{AVL}_L(T_{n_m}^-, T_{n_m}) = \text{FG}_m(T_{n_m})$$

---

[9] In Chapter 9 we will introduce a behavioural model that allows the future probability distribution of deposit volumes to be determined. It is then possible to exploit the distribution to set the implied $x_m\%$ after a suitable confidence level is chosen (say, the lowest level of volumes at the 99% c.l.).

Collecting all results and summing over M funding sources, we have that the TSFu is:

$$\text{TSFu}(T_0, T_b) = \left\{ \sum_{m=1}^{M} \text{AVL}_{NL}(T_0, T_{1_m}^-), \sum_{m=1}^{M} \text{AVL}_L(T_0, T_{1_m}^-), \sum_{m=1}^{M} \text{AVL}_L(T_{1_m}^-, T_{1_m}), \dots, \right.$$

$$\left. \sum_{m=1}^{M} \text{AVL}_{NL}(T_0, T_{N_m}^-), \sum_{m=1}^{M} \text{AVL}_L(T_0, T_{N_m}^-), \sum_{m=1}^{M} \text{AVL}_L(T_{N_m}^-, T_{N_m}) \right\}$$

$$(7.13)$$

In Example 7.6.1 we show how to build the TSFu in practice.

Example 7.6.1. *In this example we show how to build a complete TSFu for a given time horizon. Assume we have three funding sources ($M = 3$) and that the horizon is between times $T_a = 0$ and $T_b = 10$. The three sources have the typical durations shown in Table 7.6, where the number N_m of rollovers, the funding gap percentage $x_m\%$ (for $m = 1, 2, 4$) and the initial amount in 0 are also indicated.*

Table 7.6. Input data for the three funding sources.

Source	Duration (years)	No. of rollovers	Funding gap (%)	Amount
1	1	9	20	100
2	4	2	40	150
3	7	1	70	90

We assume that the preference parameter to invest in liquid assets is $\beta = 20\%$.

For the first liability, the number of rollovers is 9, so that the available liquidity after the last rollover, until the end of the chosen horizon of 10 years, is $AVL_{NL}(0, 10) = 100(1 - 20\%)^9 = 13.42$. Similarly we have that $AVL_{NL}(0, 10) = 150(1 - 40\%)^2 = 54$ and $AVL_{NL}(0, 10) = 90(1 - 70\%)^2 = 27$.

The liquidity buffer for each source can be reinvested in illiquid assets for a fraction $1 - \beta = 80\%$ until the first rollover date. So, for example, for the first source and the first rollover date at time 1, we have $AVL_{NL}(0, 1^-) = (1 - \beta)FG_1(1) = 80\% \times 20\% \times 100 = 16$, for the second source the available liquidity given by the LB to be invested in non-liquid assets is $AVL_{NL}(0, 4^-) = (1 - \beta)FG_2(4) = 80\% \times 40\% \times 150 = 48$ and for the third source $AVL_{NL}(0, 7^-) = (1 - \beta)FG_3(7) = 80\% \times 70\% \times 90 = 50.40$.

The amount that has to be invested in liquid assets from the LB generated by the funding source 1 is $AVL_L(0, 1^-) = \beta FG_1(1) = 20\% \times 20\% \times 100 = 4$, for the LB generated by funding source 2 we have $AVL_{NL}(0, 4^-) = \beta FG_2(4) = 20\% \times 40\% \times 150 = 12$ and for funding source 3 we have $AVL_{NL}(0, 7^-) = \beta FG_3(7) = 20\% \times 70\% \times 90 = 12.60$.

Finally, during the survival period relating to each rollover date, an amount equal to the funding gap for that date has to be invested in liquid assets. For example, for the first rollover date of the first funding source $AVL_L(1^-, 1) = FG_1(1) = 20\% \times 100 = 20$, for the second funding source $AVL_L(4^-, 4) = FG_2(4) = 40\% \times 150 = 60$ and for the third funding source $AVL_{NL}(7^-, 7) = FG_3(7) = 70\% \times 90 = 63$.

Table 7.7. Available liquidity that can be invested in illiquid assets for maturities up to 10 years generated by the three funding sources

Maturity*	L_1	L_2	L_3	Total AVL_{NL}
1^-	16.00			16.00
2^-	12.80			12.80
3^-	10.24			10.24
4^-	8.19	48.00		56.19
5^-	6.55			6.55
6^-	5.24			5.24
7^-	4.19		50.40	54.59
8^-	3.36	28.80		32.16
9^-	2.68			2.68
10^-	13.42	54.00	27.00	94.42

* Maturity refers to the start of the survival period including the relevant rollover date.

Table 7.8. Available liquidity that can be invested in liquid assets for maturities up to 10 years generated by the three funding sources

Maturity*	L_1	L_2	L_3	Total AVL_L
1^-	4.00			4.00
2^-	3.20			3.20
3^-	2.56			2.56
4^-	2.05	12.00		14.05
5^-	1.64			1.64
6^-	1.31			1.31
7^-	1.05		12.60	13.65
8^-	0.84	7.20		8.04
9^-	0.67			0.67
10^-				

* Maturity refers to the start of the survival period including the relevant rollover date.

Performing computations for each funding source and for each rollover date, we come up with a complete term structure of available funding TSFu. The term structure of AVL_{NL} for investments in illiquid assets generated by each funding source, and the total amount, is shown in Table 7.7. Analogously, Table 7.8 presents the term structure for investments in liquid assets. The amount to be invested in maturities included in the survival periods relating to rollover dates is shown in Table 7.9.

It is interesting to see how assumptions about the funding gap on rollover dates strongly affect the entire TSFu and hence the liquidity available for investments in illiquid assets (i.e., typical banking contracts with retails customers or companies) and in liquid assets (i.e., in securities actively traded in the market). Extreme cases of a funding gap equal to the amount to be rolled over ($x\% = 100\%$) prevent any form of maturity transformation if the bank wants to implement a robust and balanced

Table 7.9. Available liquidity that has to be invested in liquid assets for maturities included in survival periods up to 10 years

Maturity	L_1	L_2	L_3	Total AVL_L
$1^-,1$	20.00			20.00
$2^-,2$	16.00			16.00
$3^-,3$	12.80			12.80
$4^-,4$	10.24	60.00		70.24
$5^-,5$	8.19			8.19
$6^-,6$	6.55			6.55
$7^-,7$	5.24		63.00	68.24
$8^-,8$	4.19	36.00		40.19
$9^-,9$	3.36			3.36
$10^-,10$				

investment and funding policy starting from the observation time. We will dwell more on the unintended (or even intended, we might think) consequences of the proposed international regulation on liquidity standards (see [101]).

7.6.1   The term structure of forward cumulated funding and how to use it

For practical purposes it is useful to build a term structure of forward cumulated funding (TSFCFu). This term structure shows the total funding available at each date, keeping in mind that it is always possible to safely use liquidity allocated to future expiries for shorter maturities.

The TSFu has been built based on the idea that the bank invests in illiquid assets according to investment in the longest possible maturity and to allocation of the resulting liquidity buffer. But this is not the only possible use of total available funding and we need a tool to effectively manage it: the TSFCFu serves this purpose.

For a given expiry, the bank can decide to use available funding for an illiquid asset as indicated by the TSFu, but it can also use all the funding allocated for longer expiries. For example, we know that the available funding for an asset expiring at time $T = 3$, funded with a liability expiring at $T = 1$ and of typical duration of one period, is $K(1 - x\%)^3$. Nevertheless, it is always possible to safely use the entire funding K for an investment in an illiquid asset expiring at $T = 1$, with no need to build any liquidity buffer since no rollover of the liability is needed.

When shorter expiry investments use the funding allocated for longer expiry investment, the need for a liquidity buffer decreases as a function of the number of rollovers no longer needed. Consequently, the need to allocate a fraction of the buffer to liquid assets should also correspondingly disappear. In practice, we can make two assumptions about investment in liquid assets:

1.   The bank still invests in liquid assets according to the TSFu produced using the methodology outlined above, assuming that investment in the illiquid asset with maturity T_b is the driving factor.

2. The bank considers the investment in liquid assets for each maturity as a consequence of the need to build a LB, so that it is not necessary when investment in illiquid assets implies a smaller number of (or even no) rollovers.

If the bank adopts the first assumption, then forward cumulated available liquidity (FCAVL_{NL}) from expiry T_i to the end of period T_b for the m-th funding source is computed as follows:

$$\text{FCAVL}_{NL}(T_i, T_b) = \sum_{j=i}^{N_m} \text{AVL}_{NL}(T_{j_m}, T_{N_m}) \tag{7.14}$$

Equation (7.14) indicates that for each expiry T_i the forward cumulated available liquidity for illiquid assets is equal to the sum of available liquidity for illiquid assets for each expiry date from T_i to the end of the considered horizon T_b.

When the bank decides to adopt the second assumption, then the FCAVL_{NL} also includes the fraction devoted to investment in liquid assets for each expiry. So we have:

$$\text{FCAVL}_{NL}(T_i, T_b) = \sum_{j=i}^{N_M} \text{AVL}_{NL}(T_{j_m}, T_{N_m}) + \text{AVL}_{L}(T_{j_m}, T_{N_m}) \tag{7.15}$$

The TSFCFu is then defined, for all M funding sources, as the following collection of FCAVL:

$$\text{TSFCFu}(T_0, T_b) = \left\{ \sum_{m=1}^{M} \text{FCAVL}_{NL}(T_0, T_b), \sum_{m=1}^{M} \text{FCAVL}_{NL}(T_1, T_b), \right.$$
$$\left. \dots, \sum_{m=1}^{M} \text{FCAVL}_{NL}(T_b, T_b) \right\} \tag{7.16}$$

Although both assumptions can have an economic and financial rationale backing them, we tend to favour the second option since the first is too conservative and not really justified by any real liquidity risk. We will present an example in which the bank chooses the second assumption.

Remark 7.6.1. *Although the two rules to build the TSFCFu have been presented as exclusively alternative, it should be noted that it is always possible to adopt a blended version of the two, by assuming that investment is the driver in the illiquid asset at expiry T_b, but that at the same time a fraction $1 - \beta$ of the AVL_L increments of the forward cumulated available liquidity $FCAVL_{NL}$. With respect to the second rule, there is a partial, instead of a total, contribution of liquidity devoted to liquid investments to the increase of available liquidity for illiquid investment.*

Once the bank has built the TSFCFu, it can easily check what is the maximum available funding for investments in illiquid assets, considering the possibility to use sums allocated to future expiries. Use of the TSFCFu is subject to the following rules:

- when a bank utilizes funds allocated to a given expiry, the corresponding amount is deducted from the funds referring to all the other expiry dates of the term structure;
- there is a floor at zero, so that any entry of the TSFCFu can never go negative;

- the updated term structure can be used for other investments if funding is still available.

Both the TSFu and the TSFCFu are necessary to manage available funding. The TSFCFu allows the bank to understand how much is globally available on any expiry, given the current amount of funding at time 0, considering investments in illiquid assets with a duration smaller than the longest expiry in the term structure. Once the investment is decided by means of the TSFCFu, the TSFu indicates how to allocate the remaining funds for shorter expiries, so as to guarantee the building of a LB. Example 7.6.2 will clarify this idea with a practical application.

Example 7.6.2. *We recall Example 7.6.1 and use all the data shown therein. We want to build the TSFCFu, given the TSFu shown in Tables 7.7–7.9. We work under the assumption that investments in illiquid assets for shorter dates require smaller amounts from the LB and hence smaller investments in liquid assets.*

In Table 7.10 we show the $FCAVL_{NL}$, broken down into its two components, and the TSFCFu, all of which include the three funding sources. The first entry in the column $TSFCFu_{NL}$ is the cumulated amount of column "Total AVL_{NL}" of Table 7.7 (i.e., 290.88), whereas the first entry of the second column shows the same for the column "Total AVL_L" of Table 7.8 (i.e., 49.12). The entry in the third column is the sum of entries of the first two columns. The rest of the table is built in exactly the same way.

In Figure 7.1 we compare that part of the TSFu that relates to illiquid investments using the TSFCFu: clearly, the two term structures converge at the same number at the end of the considered horizon T_b.

Assume the bank wants to invest the full amount available of 340 on expiry at time 1: this means that the bank uses all funds for an investment in illiquid assets maturing in 1 year. The available amounts for the following expiries are abated by the same amount, not going below zero for any expiry under any circumstances. In this case it is easy to check that available forward cumulated funding reduces to zero on every expiry. That would not be the case if the bank decided to invest a lower amount (say, 100), in an asset expiring at time 1, or an amount (say, 150) on expiry at time 5. In both these cases there would still be something left to invest for other expiries (as shown in Table 7.11).

Table 7.10. Term structure of forward cumulated funding and its components

Maturity	$\sum_j AVL_{NL}$	$\sum_j AVL_L$	$TSFCFu_{NL}$
1^-	290.88	49.12	340.00
2^-	274.88	45.12	320.00
3^-	262.08	41.92	304.00
4^-	251.84	39.36	291.20
5^-	195.65	25.31	220.96
6^-	189.10	23.67	212.77
7^-	183.86	22.36	206.21
8^-	129.26	8.71	137.97
9^-	97.11	0.67	97.78
10^-	94.42	0.00	94.42

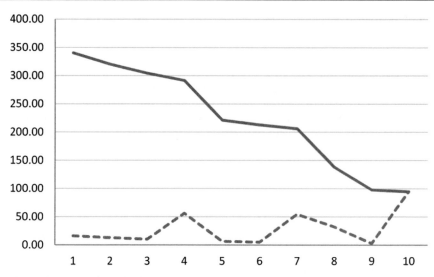

Figure 7.1. The TSFu for illiquid assets (dotted line) and the TSFCFu (continuous line). The x-axis shows the expiries whereas the y-axis the amount

Table 7.11. Term structure of forward cumulated funding after the bank decides to invest 340 or 100 in an asset expiring at time 1 (first and second column), or 150 in an asset expiring at time 5 (third column)

Maturity	340	100	150
1^-	0.00	240.00	190.00
2^-	0.00	220.00	170.00
3^-	0.00	204.00	154.00
4^-	0.00	191.20	141.20
5^-	0.00	120.96	70.96
6^-	0.00	112.77	62.77
7^-	0.00	106.21	56.21
8^-	0.00	37.97	0.00
9^-	0.00	0.00	0.00
10^-	0.00	0.00	0.00

Joint use of the TSFu and the TSFCFu can be illustrated by the third case of Table 7.11, when the bank decides to use 150 for an asset expiring at time 5, out of a total available of 220.96 (as can be read from Table 7.10): the used funds represent $\frac{150}{220.96} = 67.88\%$ of the total. This means that the bank needs to build a LB as indicated by the TSFu in Tables 7.7 and 7.8 (column "Total") for the corresponding percentage. In Table 7.12 we show the investment in illiquid and liquid assets necessary to preserve a LB for the investment of 150 expiring at time 5. The amount invested in liquid assets in the survival periods before expiry 5 is shown in Table 7.13.

Table 7.12. Liquidity allocated to illiquid and illiquid assets maturing before time 5 to build the liquidity buffer needed for an investment of 150 expiring at time 5

Maturity	AVL_{NL}	AVL_L
1^-	10.86	2.71
2^-	8.69	2.17
3^-	6.95	1.74
4^-	38.15	9.54

Table 7.13. Investment in liquid assets in the survival periods before time 5 for the liquidity buffer needed for an investment of 150 expiring at time 5

Maturity	AVL_L
$1^-, 1$	13.58
$2^-, 2$	10.86
$3^-, 3$	8.69
$4^-, 4$	47.68

7.7   NON-MATURING LIABILITIES

Among banks' main funding sources are non-maturing liabilities, typically sight deposits. In fact, although their duration is in theory nil because they can be closed (totally or partially) on demand by creditors,[10] in practice their actual duration is longer. In some cases, depending on the "stickiness" of the deposits, the duration can be around 5/7 years or longer.

Non-maturing liabilities can be seen as any other fixed maturity liability, except that the duration is stochastic and their rollover does not occur on predefined dates known at the observation time. In practice, the amount of non-maturing liabilities is assumed to follow some decaying pattern over time such that the bank can pretend they are rolled over on a periodic basis with a runoff factor, analogously to other liabilities we have analysed above. We investigate here how non-maturing liabilities are involved in the building of the TSFu and the size of the liquidity buffer needed to cover funding gaps brought about by their rollover.

Let $NML(T_0)$ be the amount at time T_0 of non-maturing liabilities the bank has in the balance sheet. Let T_b be the end of the period the bank considers necessary to determine the TSFu, and let the entire period $[T_0, T_b]$ be divided into N_{NML} subperiods. The bank can assume that a fraction of $x_{NML}\%$ of the total amount is lost during each subperiod,[11] so that it can actually assimilate the end of each subperiod to a rollover date, and the subperiod itself to a survival period of length equal to $\tau_{sv}(T_{n_{NML}}) = T_{n_{NML}} - T_{(n-1)_{NML}}$, for $n = 1, \ldots, N_{NML}$.

Under these assumptions, it is quite easy to apply the concepts introduced above for maturing liabilities to non-maturing liabilities. More specifically, the available liquidity

---

[10] Normally, creditors financing via sight deposits are termed "clients" by the bank.
[11] The same considerations on the nature and meaning of $x\%$ for a standard maturing liability can also be applied to $x_{NML}\%$.

for investments at the end of the considered horizon T_b is:

$$\text{AVL}_{NL}(T_0, T_b) = \text{NML}(T_0)(1 - x_{\text{NML}}\%)^{N_{\text{NML}}} \qquad (7.17)$$

The difference between this available liquidity and the initial amount $\text{NML}(T_0)$ is the liquidity buffer needed to cover funding gaps relating to the (fictitious) rollovers of non-maturing liabilities.

Since each survival period $\tau_{sv}(T_{n_{\text{NML}}})$ clashes with the entire period between two (fictitious) rollover dates, there is no investment available in non-liquid assets for that part of the liquidity buffer needed to cover each funding gap

$$\text{FG}(T_{n_{\text{NML}}}) = x_{\text{NML}}\%\text{NML}(T_0)(1 - x_{\text{NML}}\%)^{n_{\text{NML}}},$$

so that the entire amount is fully held in liquid assets:

$$\text{AVL}_L(T_{(n-1)_{\text{NML}}}, T_{n_{\text{NML}}}) = \text{FG}(T_{n_{\text{NML}}})$$

On the other hand, what has to be invested in fully liquid assets during a given survival period $\tau_{sv}(T_{n_{\text{NML}}})$ can be invested in less liquid assets expiring just before its start. In this case we have:

$$\text{AVL}_{NL}(T_0, T_{(n-1)_{\text{NML}}}) = (1 - \beta)\text{FG}(T_{n_{\text{NML}}})$$

where we have also included the preference of the bank for investment in liquid assets via the parameter β. The complementary part can also be invested in liquid assets so that the total amount of investment in them for each period is:

$$\text{AVL}_L(T_0, T_{(n-1)_{\text{NML}}}) = \beta\text{FG}(T_{n_{\text{NML}}})$$

Thus the term structures of funding and forward cumulated funding for the source of non-maturing liabilities can easily be derived in much the same way as above.

Example 7.7.1. *The bank wants to compute the TSFu and the TSFCFu for a period of 2 years. The entire period is divided into $N_{NML} = 24$ subperiods of length one month each. In each subperiod the bank supposes that $x_{NML}\% = 5\%$ of the outstanding amount is lost by depositor runoff. The one-month periods are also equal to the survival periods for each (fictitious) rollover. Assume that the bank has an amount of non-maturing liabilities equal to $NML(T_0) = 100$ and that its preference parameter for liquid investments is $\beta = 20\%$.*

It is straightforward to compute the available liquidity for non-liquid assets up to the 24th month:

$$AVL_{NL}(0, 24M) = 100(1 - 5\%)^{24} = 29.20$$

During each survival period, a quantity equal to the corresponding funding gap is invested in liquid assets. For the first period, which is a month in our example, we get:

$$AVL_L(0, 1M) = 100 \times 5\% = 5$$

For the second survival period, the amount of NML after runoff is $100 - 5\% \times 100 = 95$. The liquid investments for this period will be:

$$AVL_L(1M, 2M) = 95 \times 5\% = 4.75$$

Table 7.14. Term structure of available liquidity that can be invested in illiquid and liquid assets up to the end of each period of one month

Maturity	AVL_{NL}	AVL_L	Maturity	AVL_{NL}	AVL_L
1	4.75	0.00	13	2.57	0.00
2	4.51	0.00	14	2.44	0.00
3	4.29	0.00	15	2.32	0.00
4	4.07	0.00	16	2.20	0.00
5	3.87	0.00	17	2.09	0.00
6	3.68	0.00	18	1.99	0.00
7	3.49	0.00	19	1.89	0.00
8	3.32	0.00	20	1.79	0.00
9	3.15	0.00	21	1.70	0.00
10	2.99	0.00	22	1.62	0.00
11	2.84	0.00	23	1.54	0.00
12	2.70	0.00	24	29.20	

Up to expiry of the first survival period the bank can invest in illiquid assets an amount equal to the amount it needs for the subsequent survival period, keeping its preference for liquid assets in mind. For the first period we have:

$$AVL_{NL}(0, 1M) = 4.75 \times (1 - 20\%) = 3.80$$

For the same period the complementary fraction 20% is invested in liquid securities:

$$AVL_L(0, 1M) = 4.75 \times 20\% = 0.95$$

So that for the first period total $AVL_L(0, 1M) = 5.00 + 0.95 = 5.95$.
  The entire TSFu is shown in Tables 7.14 and 7.15. In Table 7.16 we show the TSFCFu.

Table 7.15. Term structure of available liquidity that can be invested in liquid assets in each survival period of one month

Maturity	AVL_L	Maturity	AVL_L
0–1	5.00	12–13	2.70
1–2	4.75	13–14	2.57
2–3	4.51	14–15	2.44
3–4	4.29	15–16	2.32
4–5	4.07	16–17	2.20
5–6	3.87	17–18	2.09
6–7	3.68	18–19	1.99
7–8	3.49	19–20	1.89
8–9	3.32	20–21	1.79
9–10	3.15	21–22	1.70
10–11	2.99	22–23	1.62
11–12	2.84	23–24	1.54

Table 7.16. Term structure of forward cumulated funding for non-maturing liabilities

Maturity	$FCAVL_{NL}$	Maturity	$FCAVL_{NL}$
1.00	95.00	13.00	51.33
2.00	90.25	14.00	48.77
3.00	85.74	15.00	46.33
4.00	81.45	16.00	44.01
5.00	77.38	17.00	41.81
6.00	73.51	18.00	39.72
7.00	69.83	19.00	37.74
8.00	66.34	20.00	35.85
9.00	63.02	21.00	34.06
10.00	59.87	22.00	32.35
11.00	56.88	23.00	30.74
12.00	54.04	24.00	29.20

7.7.1 Pricing of NML and cost of the liquidity buffer

Proposition 7.7.1. *The liquidity buffer cost incurred by the purchase of assets funded by NML is equal to zero if the bank can pay interest equal to a fraction of the risk-free interest rate that is applied for the repricing period. This fraction depends on the expected daily withdrawal rate on the outstanding NML. If the bank for some reason has to pay an interest rate greater than a fraction of the risk-free rate, then the liquidity buffer cost is greater than zero.*

Non-maturing liabilities can be typically withdrawn on demand by creditors (customers) as, for example, in the case of sight deposits. As such banks need to keep a liquidity buffer that is not only invested in liquid assets, at least a fraction of the buffer needs to be kept in cash so as to cover outflows that can be brought about by withdrawals on any day.

In practice, the bank estimates a daily withdrawal rate from the runoff rate $x_{NML}\%$. The simplest way to do this is to consider the number of days in a survival period and use the following relation:

$$(1 - x_{NML}^d\%)^{nd(n)} = (1 - x_{NML}\%)$$

where $x_{NML}^d\%$ is the daily withdrawal rate and $nd(n)$ the number of days in the n-th survival period; the daily withdrawal rate will then be:

$$x_{NML}^d\% = 1 - (1 - x_{NML}\%)^{1/nd(n)}$$

This basic method can be made much more sophisticated by analysing specific calendar dates and expected withdrawals for each of them, but this is beyond the scope of the current analysis. The assumption the bank is making in this simple case is that any drop in the $x_{NML}^d\%$ occurs daily at a constant rate consistent with the runoff rate over the entire survival period.

If $ed(n)$ have elapsed from the start of the n-th survival period and $NML(T_{n_{NML}})$ is the amount of NML at the beginning of the period, then the expected amount left is equal to:

$$\mathrm{NML}(T_{ed(n)}) = \mathrm{NML}(T_{n_{\mathrm{NML}}})(1 - x^d_{\mathrm{NML}}\%)^{ed(n)}$$

where $T_{ed(n)}$ is the date corresponding to $ed(n)$ after the start of the n-th survival period.

This information is useful to the bank when deciding the rate it is willing to pay on NML. It should be stressed that, since creditors providing funds via NML are typically retail customers, the bank benefits from having strong bargaining power in setting the rate to pay; on the other hand, competitive forces operating in the banking industry should not be completely overlooked, because they still play a role in setting the general level of the rate paid on such funding sources.

It is also worthy of mention that the rate is variable and repriced periodically to update it and put it in line with market interest rates. Usually, the repricing period is linked to a short-term rate such as the 3-month Libor/Euribor or Eonia rate.

When a bank has the bargaining power to set the rate paid freely, the fair level should consider the repricing period, the runoff rate $x_{\mathrm{NML}}\%$ and the daily withdrawal rate $x^d_{\mathrm{NML}}\%$. Assuming the repricing period clashes with the survival period (say, one month), then the bank can use the following relationship to compute the fair level to pay on NML between the start and the end of the period:

$$\mathrm{NML}(T_{n_{\mathrm{NML}}})d\frac{1}{365}\sum_{i=1}^{nd(n)}(1 - x^d_{\mathrm{NML}}\%)^i = \mathrm{NML}(T_{n_{\mathrm{NML}}})r\frac{1}{365}\sum_{i=1}^{nd(n)}(1 - x^d_{\mathrm{NML}}\%)^{i+1} \quad (7.18)$$

where $\mathrm{NML}(T_{n_{\mathrm{NML}}})$ is the amount of NML at the beginning of the period. Equation (7.18) states that the interest d that the bank pays on the amount of NML each day during the survival period (left-hand side), is equal to investment in liquid assets (whose expected return is the risk-free rate, as shown above) for an amount that is equal to NML available minus expected daily withdrawals (right-hand side).

Looking at this in greater detail, on every day the bank has an expected amount equal to $\mathrm{NML}(T_{n_{\mathrm{NML}}})d\frac{1}{365}\sum_{i=1}^{ed(n)}(1 - x^d_{\mathrm{NML}}\%)^i$ in its liabilities on which it pays the rate d; on the other hand, the bank can invest only $\mathrm{NML}(T_{n_{\mathrm{NML}}})\sum_{i=1}^{ed(n)}(1 - x^d_{\mathrm{NML}}\%)^{i+1}$ in risk-free liquid assets, since an amount equal to expected daily withdrawals, $(\mathrm{NML}(T_{n_{\mathrm{NML}}})\sum_{i=1}^{ed(n)}(1 - x^d_{\mathrm{NML}}\%)^i)x^d_{\mathrm{NML}}\%$, has to be kept as cash that earns 0. It is straightforward to compute the fair level that the bank should be willing to set on NML at the start of the repricing period:

$$d = \alpha r \quad (7.19)$$

where $\alpha = (1 - x^d_{\mathrm{NML}}\%)$, which is obviously smaller than 1. Equation (7.19) states that the fair rate on NML, which is refundable on demand, is the risk-free rate minus the amount of cash needed to cope with expected daily withdrawals. Consequently, the funding spread s^B that the bank pays is now computed over the fair risk-free return αr, and not simply r; so for NML the funding spread is $s^B = \max[d - \alpha r; 0]$. If the bank has reasonable bargaining power, then $d - \alpha r \leq 0$, which means the bank pays no funding spread for this source of funding. Sometimes the bank either has very weak bargaining power or competition in the banking industry is so fierce as to push NML rates above the fair level αr, such that a positive funding spread may result.

Assume the bank wants to finance the purchase of asset A expiring at T_b with NML and the number of related (fictitious) rollovers is N_{NML}; each rollover occurs on dates

T_{r_j}, with $j = 1, \ldots, N_{\text{NML}}$. The available amount $\text{AVL}_{NL}(T_0, T_b)$ that can be funded is given by equation (7.17).

To compute the LB, we can resort to equation (7.9) and adapt it to the specific case of NML. First, we note that since the survival period clashes with the entire period between two rollover dates, a fraction of the liquidity buffer equal to the funding gap for the relevant period is completely invested in liquid assets and/or in cash. Second, we need to keep in mind that this amount of the FG for each survival period varies with time. In fact, at date $T_{ed(n)}$ between the start and the end of a survival period, corresponding to $ed(n)$ days after the start of the n-th survival period, an amount needed to cover withdrawals on outstanding $\text{NML}_{T_{n_{\text{NML}}}}$ is held in cash:

$$\text{Cash}(T_{n_{\text{NML}}}, T_{ed(n)}) = \sum_{i=1}^{ed(n)} \text{NML}_{T_{n_{\text{NML}}}} (1 - x_{\text{NML}}^d \%)^i x_{\text{NML}}^d \%$$

which is the expected amount at time $T_{ed(n)}$ (considering a daily withdrawal rate of $x_{\text{NML}}^d \%$), multiplied by the withdrawal rate of $x_{\text{NML}}^d \%$. The amount of the buffer invested in liquid assets is:

$$\text{LAsset}(T_{n_{\text{NML}}}, T_{ed(n)}) = \sum_{i=1}^{ed(n)} \text{NML}_{T_{n_{\text{NML}}}} (1 - x_{\text{NML}}^d \%)^i (1 - x_{\text{NML}}^d \%)$$

$$= \sum_{i=1}^{ed(n)} \text{NML}_{T_{n_{\text{NML}}}} (1 - x_{\text{NML}}^d \%)^{i+1}$$

For the generic survival period $\tau(T_{r_j}) = \tau_{sv}(T_{r_j}) = T_{r_j} - T_{r_{j-1}}$ the cost of the buffer is:

$$\text{LBC}(T_{r_j}) = P^D(0, T_{r_j}) \beta s^B \text{LB}(T_{r_j}) \tau(T_{r_j}) + \sum_{i=1}^{nd_{\tau_{sv}}} P^D(0, T_{i(r_j)})$$

$$\times [(r + s^B)\text{Cash}(T_{r_{j-1}}, T_{i(r_j)}) + s^B \text{LAsset}(T_{r_{j-1}}, T_{i(r_j)})] \frac{1}{365} \quad (7.20)$$

where $T_{i(r_j)}$ is the date corresponding to i days after the start of the period $T_{r_{j-1}}$. It should be stressed that the LB does not include the fraction relating to the survival period, (so it is $\text{LB}(T_{r_j})$, instead of $\text{LB}(T_{r_{j-1}})$ as in equation (7.9)). The total cost of the liquidity buffer is as usual the sum of the LBC for all the survival periods until the maturity of asset A:

$$\text{LBC}^A(0) = \sum_{j=1}^{N_{\text{NML}}} \text{LBC}(T_{r_j}) \quad (7.21)$$

We can now examine the two cases of nil funding spread or positive funding spread on NML, and their effects on the cost of the liquidity buffer:

1. The bank has enough bargaining power to set $d = \alpha r$, or at an even lower level. In this case the funding spread s^B is zero, so that from (7.20) one immediately sees that the LBC to charge on asset A funded with NML is just the amount of cash kept in the buffer times the risk-free rate.
2. The bank has to pay some rate $d > \alpha r$ on its NML so that the LBC is not nil and its value is computed by means of equation (7.21).

Table 7.17. Amount invested in liquid assets and cash on each day of investment in an asset funded by non-maturing liabilities

Maturity	LAsset	Cash	Maturity	LAsset	Cash
1	94.68	0.1620	16	92.28	0.1579
2	94.51	0.1617	17	92.12	0.1576
3	94.35	0.1615	18	91.96	0.1574
4	94.19	0.1612	19	91.81	0.1571
5	94.03	0.1609	20	91.65	0.1568
6	93.87	0.1606	21	91.49	0.1566
7	93.71	0.1604	22	91.34	0.1563
8	93.55	0.1601	23	91.18	0.1560
9	93.39	0.1598	24	91.02	0.1558
10	93.23	0.1595	25	90.87	0.1555
11	93.07	0.1593	26	90.71	0.1552
12	92.91	0.1590	27	90.56	0.1550
13	92.75	0.1587	28	90.40	0.1547
14	92.59	0.1585	29	90.25	0.1544
15	92.44	0.1582	30	90.10	0.1542

Example 7.7.2. *Assume we are at the same outset as in Example 7.7.1 and that we want to compute the LBC related to the purchase of an asset expiring in one month, fully funded with the NML outstanding at time 0, which we recall is 100. Available funding can be obtained from the TSFCFu shown in Table 7.16: it is 95, which implies a $LB(T_{r_0}) = LB(0) = 5$. The daily withdrawal rate is $x^d_{NML}\% = 1 - (1 - 5\%)^{1/30} = 0.17\%$.*

Let us assume a constant risk-free interest rate equal to $r = 3\%$ p.a. for any maturity: the fair NML rate should be $d = 3\% \times (1 - 0.17\%) = (1 - 0.17\%) = 2.995\%$. We suppose the bank is unable to set this rate on NML at this level, but has to pay a higher rate so that $d - \alpha r = 2\%$. So the funding spread $s^B = 2\%$.

The liquidity buffer cost relating to this investment can easily be computed by considering the fact that we have just 1 period, so $N_{NML} = 1$; the period between the start and the first rollover is $\tau(T_{r_1}) = 30/365 = 0.0822$. In Table 7.17 we show the amount of LAsset and Cash that the bank holds on each day between the start and end of the investment. It is straightforward to calculate the single components of formula (7.20) and then of formula (7.21) (in this example we just have a single term to consider in the latter). Noting that $LB(T_{r_1}) = LB(1) = 0$ in this case, we just need to compute the two summations in the second part of (7.20) (i.e., $\sum_{i=1}^{nd_{\tau_{sv}}} (r + s^B)\text{Cash}(T_{r_j}, T_{i(r_j)})\frac{1}{365}$ and $\sum_{i=1}^{nd_{\tau_{sv}}} s^B \text{LAsset}(T_{r_j}, T_{i(r_j)})\frac{1}{365}.)$. The results are shown in Table 7.18, and we get $LBC^A(0) = 0.1525$.

Table 7.18. Calculations of the LBC for investment in an asset funded by non-maturing liabilities

$\sum P(0, T)s^B LAsset \times 1/365$	$\sum P(0, T)(r + s^B)Cash \times 1/365$	LBC
0.1516	0.0006	0.1523

7.8 THE SECOND CAUSE OF THE LIQUIDITY BUFFER: COLLATERAL MARGINING

In current financial markets, collateralization of derivative contracts, at least of those dealt between institutional investors, is the normal rule since it is considered the best way to mitigate or almost remove the counterparty credit risk. On the other hand, liquidity risk increases because there is a higher probability that cash or eligible (liquid) assets (typically bonds) are needed to post a collateral margin when the NPV of the contracts with a counterparty becomes increasingly negative. Moreover, one should not disregard the possibility of receiving cash or eligible assets when the NPV is positive: a positive windfall in liquidity risk management.

Derivatives contracts are subject to collateralization according to:

- CSA agreements: Thes are bilateral agreements between two institutional agents (generally banks) to periodically exchange collateral to cover the change in NPV of a derivative contract or a portfolio of contracts. It is almost standard practice today to have a daily exchange of collateral.
- Multilateral margining via central counterparties: Multilateral netting and margining of derivatives contracts is operated via clearing houses. In this case collateral is also exchanged once or more times a day.

The need for cash or eligible assets arises mainly when contracts cannot be replicated by a suitable strategy involving primary assets, as is the case for interest rate swaps and FRAs (see Chapter 12): hedging for those contracts is attained by reversing the same contract with another counterparty. If both trades (the original and the second traded for hedging purposes) are margined in the same way (say, daily) then there is no liquidity risk since the cash (or assets) needed to post collateral for one on them is precisely compensated by the collateral received on the other. When the two contracts are not collateralized in the same way, then the asymmetric behaviour of cash flows paid and received brings about liquidity risk. This situation usually occurs in banking activity when the bank trades with corporate clients (with whom there are agreements to post collateral on an infrequent basis or none at all) and hedges with other banks (with whom CSA agreements are typically signed on a daily basis).

7.8.1 A method to set the liquidity buffer for derivative collateral

Proposition 7.8.1. *The liquidity buffer to cover collateral margin calls is equal to the minimum negative value of the contract during its life. The minimum can be computed at an expected level, by expected negative exposure, or at a level with a given confidence level, by potential future exposure.*

We sketch a method to set the level of the LB when collateral agreements (such as a CSA) or multilateral margining via a clearing house is operating. We assume for simplicity's sake that collateral is posted daily, either in cash or eligible bonds, according to variations in the contract's NPV. The method consists of the following steps:

1. Determine the expected negative exposure (ENE) or the potential future exposure (PFE) of the contract until expiry. ENE is defined as expected negative NPV,

computed at time T_0, of the value V of a contract at time T_i, given that it expires at T_b,

$$\text{ENE}(T_0, T_i) = \mathbf{E}^Q[\min(V(T_i, T_b), 0)] \tag{7.22}$$

Expectation in this case is taken according to the risk-neutral measure, indicated by the superscript Q of the expectation operator, which takes forward levels quoted in the market as expected values and levels implied from quoted option prices as volatilities. Expectation can also be taken according to a real-world measure P, in which case we use means and variances estimated statistically from actual price movements.

The PFE is defined similarly as the minimum V^α reached by the value V at time T_i, such that the probability that the value is lower than $(1 - \alpha)$:

$$\text{PFE}(T_0, T_i) = \mathbf{E}^Q[\min(V^\alpha(T_i, T_b), 0)] \tag{7.23}$$

such that

$$\mathbf{P}[V(T_i, T_b) \geq V^\alpha(T_i, T_b)] \leq 1 - \alpha \tag{7.24}$$

2. Let period $[T_0, T_b]$ be divided into N subperiods. The LB that the bank needs to build is given by fraction γ, which depends on the risk aversion of the bank and on the minimum ENE of PFE for each of the subperiods:

$$\text{LB}(T_0) = \sum_{i=1}^{N} \gamma \Delta^- \text{ENE}(T_0, T_i) \tag{7.25}$$

or

$$\text{LB}(T_0) = \sum_{i=1}^{N} \gamma \Delta^- \text{PFE}(T_0, T_i) \tag{7.26}$$

where $\Delta^- = \min[\text{ENE}(T_0, T_i) - \text{ENE}(T_0, T_{i-1}); 0]$ is negative variation in ENE between the start and end of each subperiod (similar notation applies to the PFE). We implicitly assume here that ENE or PFE are constant during each subperiod $[T_{i-1}, T_i]$. Equations (7.25) and (7.26) state that the liquidity buffer is the minimum negative (expected or at a given confidence level) value of the contract.

The idea is that the bank wants to make sure that it is able to meet the requests for collateral by the counterparty. The collateral that will be posted during each period is given by ENE as the expected level, or by PFE at the maximum level with a given confidence level. The bank can adopt either measures, being more conservative with PFE and with a higher value of γ that could be set up to 100%.

3. The survival periods during the life of the contract are not determined according to (possibly fictitious) rollover dates, but they are simply contiguous subperiods, of a given length (say, one month), during which the liquidity buffer must be invested for an appropriate amount in liquid assets to meet collateral posting requirements. So, the N subperiods, for which we computed ENE or PFE, also clash with the survival periods included in the period $[T_0, T_b]$. In each survival period $\tau_{sv}(T_i)$ the LB is invested in liquid assets for an amount equal to variation in ENE, since they can be converted into cash or even used as collateral themselves.[12] The remaining buffer

---

[12] In this case a haircut on the market price is applied and the resulting value is considered equivalent to cash. We do not deal with these aspects here, but they have to be properly considered for full evaluation of the costs related to the liquidity buffer. See Chapter 8 for a possible solution on how to model haircuts.

can be invested in illiquid assets and liquid assets, according to parameter β, by suitably choosing their expiries such that at the start of each survival period an amount equal to γ times the variation in ENE or PFE is available for investment in liquid assets.

7.8.2   The cost of the liquidity buffer for derivative collateral

The cost of the LB can be derived from the principal ideas shown above for maturing and non-maturing assets, although we need to adapt them to the specific case.

In more detail, when collateral margining is the cause of the liquidity buffer it should be stressed that there is no expiring debt to be rolled over. The LB is built by the bank at the start of the contract by issuing debt and is supposed to be enough to cover the entire collateral needs. During the life of the contract, the collateral posted is adjusted according to cash flows paid/received from the derivative. Interest on the collateral account, accrued on the posted collateral, are paid periodically (typically on a monthly basis). At the end of the contract the collateral posted is returned, together with accrued interest. The collateral can be partially, or totally, returned also during the life of the contract if negative exposure declines or even turns into positive exposure. In either case, the debt used to built the LB is repaid with the collateral returned by the counterparty.

The part of the collateral that has to be invested in liquid assets (i.e., fraction β and an amount equal to γ times the exposure—however computed) will cause a loss equal to the funding spread of the bank s^B, similarly to what we have seen in the previous sections. Moreover, the amount that is posted as collateral is supposed to earn the risk-free rate[13] so that the bank still suffers a net cost equal to the funding spread s^B.[14]

From these considerations, one can write the formula for the cost of the liquidity buffer:

$$\mathrm{LBC}^{DC}(0) = \sum_{i=1}^{N} P(0, T_i)[\mathrm{LB}(T_i)\beta + \sum_{j=0}^{i} \gamma \mathrm{ENE}(T_0, T_j)]s^B \tau_{sv}(T_i) \qquad (7.27)$$

Equation (7.27) states that the total cost of the LB at time 0 is equal to the present value of the spread, paid over each survival period, applied to the amount of the remaining buffer invested in liquid assets ($\mathrm{LB}(T_i)\beta$) plus the amount used to post collateral up to time $\sum_{j=0}^{i} \gamma \mathrm{ENE}(T_0, T_j)$.

LBC^{DC} is a function of the duration of the contract and of the type of derivative. It is generally not a big quantity at the inception of the contract.

Example 7.8.1. *We show how to compute the LBC^{DC} for a FRA contract expiring in one year, when the bank pays the fixed rate K to receive the fixing of the Euribor, which we*

---

[13] This is consistent with the standard CSA agreements and collateral rules of clearing houses, whereby the agent posting collateral receives the OIS (Eonia for the Euro) rate, which is assumed to be the best approximation to a risk-free rate, and is the market remuneration rate for an unsecured investment of money on a one-day time horizon in any case.
[14] Basically, for the fraction β invested in liquid assets and the amount posted as collateral, the gain equal to the risk-free rate compensates only the risk-free part of the funding cost on the debt, leaving the bank with the net cost equal to the funding spread.

Table 7.19. Term structure of forward rates and discount factors rates for Eonia and 1-year Euribor fixings

Years	Eonia forward (%)	Spread forward (%)	Euribor (lin ACT / 360) (%)	DF Eonia	DF Euribor
0.00	0.95	0.60	1.55	1.00000	1.00000
0.08	0.95	0.60	1.55	0.99921	0.99871
0.17	0.95	0.60	1.55	0.99842	0.99742
0.25	0.95	0.60	1.55	0.99763	0.99613
0.33	0.95	0.60	1.55	0.99684	0.99485
0.42	0.95	0.60	1.55	0.99605	0.99357
0.50	0.95	0.60	1.55	0.99526	0.99228
0.58	0.95	0.60	1.55	0.99448	0.99100
0.67	0.95	0.60	1.55	0.99369	0.98973
0.75	0.95	0.60	1.55	0.99290	0.98845
0.83	0.95	0.60	1.55	0.99212	0.98717
0.92	0.95	0.60	1.55	0.99133	0.98590
1.00	0.95	0.60	1.55	0.99055	0.98463
2.00	0.95	0.60	1.55	0.98123	0.96960

assume to be a one-year rate as well. If we assume that the contract rate is $K = 1.55\%$, the terminal payoff to the bank is:

$$FRA = [L(1Y, 1Y) - 1.55\%]P^D(1Y, 1Y)$$

where $L(1Y, 1Y)$ is the Euribor fixing in one year for a period of one year, discounted by the risk-free discount factor $P^D(1Y, 1Y)$.

We assume for simplicity a flat term structure of Eonia (risk-free) forward rates and a spread over it to determine 1-year Euribor-fixing forward rates. The data are shown in Table 7.19.

If the volatility of the Euribor fixing is 30% (it is supposed to be estimated from historical levels or based on market quotes of caps and floors), then we can derive ENE and PFE (at the 99% c.l.): they are shown in Table 7.20, which assumes the FRA has a notional of EUR1,000,000, for each corresponding date at the end of the 12 monthly survival periods into which we divide the duration of the contract. A visual representation is given in Figure 7.2.

The resulting LB at inception is EUR159,975, if we set the percentage of coverage at $\gamma = 75\%$ (it is computed using (7.25)). Investment of the LB in liquid assets (for $\beta = 20\%$) and investment in liquid assets during each survival period are shown in Table 7.21, when the bank adopts ENE as a measure to predict negative exposures. If it chooses PFE, Table 7.22 shows the related liquidity buffer (computed using (7.26)) and the investment in liquid assets.

The LBC^{DC} for both cases, expressed in absolute terms and as a percentage of the notional, are given in Table 7.23: they are computed using a funding spread level constant that is equal to $s^B = 1\%$. In both cases of ENE and PFE they are significant for the contract we are considering.

Table 7.20. ENE and PFE at the 99% confidence level at the end of monthly survival periods for the FRA

Years	ENE payer	PFE (99%)
0.00	0	0
0.08	−61,863	−315,362
0.17	−87,450	−428,529
0.25	−107,058	−508,196
0.33	−123,568	−570,886
0.42	−138,094	−622,939
0.50	−151,210	−667,577
0.58	−163,256	−706,695
0.67	−174,454	−741,520
0.75	−184,958	−772,894
0.83	−194,881	−801,427
0.92	−204,306	−827,574
1.00	−213,300	−851,686

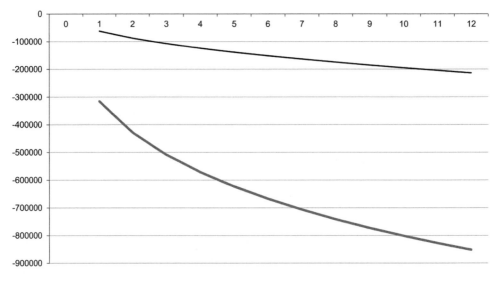

Figure 7.2. ENE (dark-grey line) and PFE (light-grey line) at the 99% confidence level at the end of monthly survival periods for the FRA

Table 7.21. Liquidity buffer evolution, fraction invested in liquid assets and investment in liquid assets during survival periods when ENE is used

Years	Buffer	Liquid assets	Liquid asset survival period
0.00	159,975	0	0
0.08	113,578	22,716	46,397
0.17	94,388	18,878	19,190
0.25	79,682	15,936	14,706
0.33	67,299	13,460	12,382
0.42	56,405	11,281	10,895
0.50	46,567	9,313	9,837
0.58	37,533	7,507	9,035
0.67	29,134	5,827	8,399
0.75	21,256	4,251	7,878
0.83	13,815	2,763	7,442
0.92	0	0	7,069
1.00	0	0	6,746

Table 7.22. Liquidity buffer evolution, fraction invested in liquid assets and investment in liquid assets during survival periods when PFE is used

Years	Buffer	Liquid assets	Liquid asset survival period
0.00	638,765	0	0
0.08	402,244	80,449	236,521
0.17	317,368	63,474	84,876
0.25	257,618	51,524	59,750
0.33	210,600	42,120	47,018
0.42	171,560	34,312	39,040
0.50	138,082	27,616	33,478
0.58	108,743	21,749	29,339
0.67	82,625	16,525	26,118
0.75	59,094	11,819	23,531
0.83	37,695	7,539	21,399
0.92	0	0	19,610
1.00	0	0	18,084

Table 7.23. Liquidity buffer costs in euros and as a percentage of the notional, when ENE or PFE is used

ENE		PFE	
Euros	% of notional	Euros	% of notional
1214.03	0.001	5153.05	0.005

7.9   THE THIRD CAUSE OF THE LIQUIDITY BUFFER: OFF-BALANCE-SHEET COMMITMENTS

The presence of off-balance-sheet (OBS) commitments is another cause of the need for a liquidity buffer. In theory, there are many OBS commitments, including contingent financial obligations deriving from derivative contracts. For the limited scope of liquidity buffer needs, we can restrict our analysis to cases where financial guarantees are called for:

- standby letters of credit
- bank loan commitments
- note issuance facilities

More specifically, we analyse the case of bank loan commitments: they are promises made by the bank to a counterparty to grant a loan on some date in the future under certain conditions. We can identify the following types of bank loan commitments:

- *Line of credit*: This is an informal commitment by a bank to lend funds to a client firm.
- *Revolving line of credit* and *committed credit lines*: These are formal agreement by a bank to lend funds on demand to a client firm under the terms of a contract.

Although the first case is in theory easier to manage in terms of liquidity risk, in practice they both bring about liquidity needs and hence the necessity to plan a funding strategy and build a suitable LB to cope with unexpected events related to withdrawals by the counterparty.

Proposition 7.9.1. *The liquidity buffer for a loan commitment is equal to its usage in excess, calculated at a given confidence level, with respect to expected usage by the counterparty.*

Let us assume the bank commits to granting a loan, under given conditions, at any time the counterparty chooses in a period $[T_0, T_b]$, up to a maximum amount L. The counterparty can also choose not to ask for the loan. The bank expects usage to be equal to $\overline{U}$: in other words, the bank expects that the counterparty will ask to have a loan for an amount $\overline{U} < L$. The bank also computes maximum usage at a given confidence level (say, 99%), such that a greater usage can only happen with a probability smaller than 1%: let U_{99} be such an amount. The bank can fund the commitment for average usage (as it would for a loan actually granted and not just a commitment) and can build a liquidity buffer for an amount equal to unexpected usage, defined as:

$$\text{LB}(0) = U_{99} - \overline{U} \tag{7.28}$$

$\text{LB}(0)$ must of necessity be invested in cash or in liquid securities earning the risk-free rate r, since it will be needed when the counterparty asks for the start of the loan.

Proposition 7.9.2. *The liquidity buffer cost for a loan commitment is proportional to the funding spread and to that part of the liquidity buffer not needed to cover unexpected usage.*

The bank has to pay a funding spread on the sum it raises in the market to build the LB at the reference time. When the LB is not needed to cover unexpected usage then it is invested in liquid assets, so that the bank suffers a net cost equal to s^B. On the other hand, if it is used to cover counterparty requests, it is reasonable to assume that the bank also included a charge for the funding spread in the contract terms, so that the expected return of the used amount is $r + s^B$, thus producing a net cost equal to 0 for the bank. In conclusion, we can write the formula for liquidity buffer costs as:

$$\text{LBC}^{LC}(0) = \int_{\overline{U}}^{U_{99}} (U_{99} - U)s^B(T_b - T_0)\mathbf{P}[U]dU \tag{7.29}$$

Equation (7.29) states that liquidity buffer costs are equal to the funding spread s^B applied over the period from T_0 to T_b to all possible usages of the commitment below the 99% confidence level U_{99}, but above the average level $\overline{U}$, with each case weighted by the probability of usage $\mathbf{P}[U]$. In fact, when usage is at some level U above the expected level, but below the maximum usage at the predefined confidence level, then the bank has built an unnecessary buffer for an amount equal to the difference between the two levels. The cost to keep this buffer is given by the funding spread.

From equation (7.29) it is clear that the bank needs a model for usage of the credit line to assign a given probability to different levels of usage of the commitment. Such a model can be very complex when trying to capture real features of the behaviour of the counterparty linked to its creditworthiness and how it evolves in time. This is beyond the scope of the current analysis though; more in-depth analysis is postponed to Chapter 9, where we present a sophisticated stochastic model to manage the risks related to credit lines.

Remark 7.9.1. *Equation (7.29) is based on several simplifying assumptions that need to be relaxed when building a realistic model for loan commitments. In fact, it is implicitly assumed that the counterparty chooses to use the line only once at the start of the commitment and then there is no further activity. In reality, if this behaviour can be reasonable for some kinds of commitments, in general it is not true because the counterparty can borrow money until the end of the commitment (within the limit of the notional amount obviously). Moreover, the possibility of having reimbursements during the life of the contract is not considered.*

In conclusion, equation (7.29) should be seen as a rough first approximation to spot the main factors affecting the cost of the liquidity buffer for loan commitments.

Example 7.9.1. *We show a credit line opened to a counterparty for a period of one year (so $T_b = 1$ and $T_0 = 1$) with a maximum amount of 100. Possible usage levels of the line and associated probabilities are indicated in Table 7.24 and a visual representation is given in Figure 7.3.*

Table 7.24. Usage levels of the credit line and associated probabilities

Usage	P[U] (%)
0	20
22	21
42	22
61	20
81	16
100	1

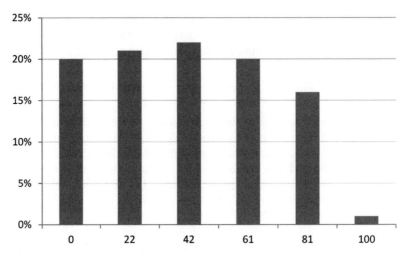

Figure 7.3. Usage levels of the credit line and associated probabilities

Table 7.25. Average usage, liquidity buffer and liquidity buffer costs as an absolute and as a percentage of the credit line amount

U	LB(0)	LBC(0)	LBC(0) (%)
40	41	0.1887	0.19

It is easy to compute expected usage, which is $\overline{U} = 40$, and the maximum usage level at the 99% confidence level, which is $U_{99} = 81$, so that $LB(0) = 41$. Assuming the bank has a funding spread equal to $s^B = 1.5\%$, then $LBC^{LC}(0)$ can easily be computed by applying a discrete version of equation (7.29). Looking at this in greater detail, we have:

$$\text{LBC}^{LC}(0) = (81 - 40) \times 22\% \times 1.5\%$$
$$+ (81 - 61) \times 20\% \times 1.5\%$$
$$+ (81 - 81) \times 16\% \times 1.5\%$$
$$= 0.1887$$

In Table 7.25 we recapitulate the results.

7.10   BASEL III REGULATION AND LIQUIDITY BUFFER

The document published by the Basel Committee in 2010 and amended in 2012 and 2013 (see [101] and [102]) introduced two main indicators to monitor and manage liquidity risk:[15]

- liquidity coverage ratio (LCR)
- net stable funding ratio (NSFR).

The LCR is important for impacts on the LB. It is defined as:

$$LCR = \frac{HLA}{NCO} \geq 100\%$$

where

- HLA is the stock of high liquidity assets available to the bank: it includes cash and unencumbered Treasury bonds and corporate bonds that fulfil some criteria of low credit risk, ease and certainty of valuation, and low correlation with risky assets (this will exclude bonds issued by financial institutions from the stock).
- NCO is total net cash outflow occurring during a period of 30 days following calculation of the index; the outflow is defined as:

$$NCO = CF^-(0, 30d) - \min[CF^+(0, 30d), 75\% \times CF^-(0, 30d)]$$

where $CF^-(0, 30d)$ is the cumulated negative cash flow (i.e., the outflow) and $CF^+(0, 30d)$ is the cumulated positive cash flow (i.e., the inflow), over a period of 30 days starting from the reference date in 0.

In this section to hark back to Chapter 4 where we discussed in detail how to build the LCR.

The LCR aims at ensuring that the bank holds a sufficient buffer for liquidity needs in a short period of 30 days. The denominator of the ratio NCO measures net outflows occurring during the next 30 days whereas the numerator HLA identifies the quantity of liquid assets and cash (i.e., the liquidity buffer) that must be held. It is worth stressing that the LCR limits inflows to an upper bound given by 75% of the outflows, which basically means that the bank has to keep a liquidity buffer equal to 25% of the negative cumulated cash flows over the period of the next 30 days in any case.

The regulation does not indicate how the liquidity buffer has to be built or how it has to be funded: it just focuses on the need for an adequate amount capable to cover outflows in the next 30 days. Nevertheless, the bank needs a more forward-looking approach so as to preserve a value of the LCR above 1 in the future as well.

We have already outlined a framework to build the liquidity buffer and the term structure of funding such that the bank can be sure that there is liquidity equilibrium in the future, within the limits under which stressed scenarios were designed, when it operates usual financial intermediation activity. We would now like to analyse the possibility of fitting the same framework to regulatory requirements and specifically to the LCR, so that this ratio is ensured to be above 1 in the future as well.

First, the period of 30 days considered in the LCR corresponds to the survival period we mentioned above, so we can set $\tau_{sv} = 30/365$: incidentally, this is what we have done in the examples in previous sections. Second, regulation prescribes a set of runoff factors to apply to different kinds of liabilities: they are the percentage of the expiring liability,

---

[15] See also Chapter 4 for an extensive discussion on the subject.

or of the outstanding amount of NML assumed not to be renewed. The runoff factors are equivalent to the factors $x\%$ we used in our framework applied to the different liabilities.

The basic criterion used by the Basel Regulation to disentangle liabilities is based on the relationship between the bank and its creditors. Let us show a few instances in greater detail:

- Retail deposit runoff—
  1. Stable deposits (runoff rate $= 3\%$ and higher): In the framework we presented above the monthly withdrawal rate $x_{NML}\% = 3\%$ at least, which means that the minimum daily withdrawal rate is $x_{NML}^d\% = 0.10\%$.
  2. Less stable deposits (runoff rates $= 10\%$ and higher): the monthly minimum withdrawal rate $x_{NML}\% = 10\%$, which amounts to a daily withdrawal rate of $x_{NML}^d\% \approx 0.351\%$.
- Unsecured wholesale funding runoff—
  1. Unsecured wholesale funding provided by small-business customers: 5% (stable funding), 10% (less stable funding) and higher; for these liabilities rollover risk is set in our framework at $x\% = 5\%$ or $x\% = 10\%$.
  2. Unsecured wholesale funding with operational relationships: 25% ($x\% = 25\%$).
  3. Unsecured wholesale funding provided by non-financial corporates and sovereigns, central banks and public sector entities: 75% ($x\% = 75\%$).
  4. Unsecured wholesale funding provided by other legal entity customers: 100% ($x\% = 100\%$). The regulator specifies that "all notes, bonds and other debt securities issued by the bank are included in this category regardless of the holder, unless the bond is sold exclusively in the retail market and held in retail accounts, in which case the instruments can be treated in the appropriate retail deposit category."
- Secured funding runoff—
  1. Loss of secured funding on short-term financing transactions: $x\% = 15\%$ is the rollover risk assigned to funding backed by assets that in the numerator are considered to be Level 2; $x\% = 25\%$ for secured funding transactions with the bank's domestic sovereign, domestic central bank, or domestic PSEs that have a 20% or lower risk weight, when the transactions are backed by assets other than Level 1 or Level 2 assets, in recognition that these entities are unlikely to withdraw secured funding from banks at a time of market-wide stress; finally, $x\% = 100\%$ for all other maturing transactions.
- Additional requirements—
  1. Derivative payables: 100% runoff. Derivatives that expire in 30 days cannot be rolled over. This has not been considered in our framework since there is no liquidity buffer to set aside for this occurrence. LCR construction rules simply forbid compensating negative cash flows with positive cash flows of a corresponding new contract rolled over for another period.
  2. Increased liquidity needs related to downgrade triggers embedded in financing transactions, derivatives and other contracts: 100% of the amount of collateral that would be posted for or contractual cash outflows generated by any downgrade up to and including a three-notch downgrade. This has not been considered in the framework above, although it can easily be handled by an

approach similar to that used to determine outflows due to collateralization of derivative contracts.

3. Increased liquidity needs related to the potential for valuation changes on posted collateral securing derivative and other transactions (20% of the value of non-Level 1 posted collateral). This too has not been considered in the framework, but it can be handled using the modelling tools we introduce in Chapter 8.

4. Loss of funding on asset-backed securities, covered bonds and other structured financing instruments and loss of funding on asset-backed commercial paper, conduits, securities investment vehicles and other such financing facilities. In both cases $x\% = 100\%$.

5. Drawdowns on committed credit and liquidity facilities. The undrawn portion of existing facilities has to be included in outflows as follows:
   —5% drawdowns on committed credit and liquidity facilities to retail and small-business customers: At the inception of the contract the buffer should be computed on unexpected usage equal to $U_{\mathrm{LCR}} = (1 - 5\%)^N L$, where N is the number of months until the end of the contract. Then $\mathrm{LB}(0) = U_{\mathrm{LCR}} - \overline{U}$ following the framework we presented above.
   —10% drawdowns on committed credit facilities to non-financial corporates, sovereigns and central banks, public sector entities and multilateral development banks: In this case $U_{\mathrm{LCR}} = (1 - 10\%)^N L$ and the liquidity buffer is computed accordingly.
   —30% drawdowns on committed liquidity facilities to non-financial corporates, sovereigns and central banks, public sector entities and multilateral development banks and 100% drawdowns on committed credit and liquidity facilities to other legal entities: In both cases $\mathrm{LB}(0) = L - \overline{U}$, since the full amount beyond the average level has to be assumed withdrawn during the period.

6. Increased liquidity needs related to market valuation changes on derivative or other transactions (non-0% requirement to be determined at national supervisory discretion): We can use in this case the approach sketched in Section 7.8, setting γ equal to the level decided by national authorities.

There are some other minor contingent outflows we have not included in the list, but can be included under a conceptual point of view in one of the cases above.

Following our approach to build the term structure of funding based on rollover (runoff) risk factors, it should be noted that bonds usually issued by banks in the market cannot be used to fund assets with expiries longer than their own. This is not strictly forbidden by regulation, but we showed that should a bank want to follow an equilibrium liquidity policy established since the beginning of the reference date, then a rollover risk factor $x\% = 100\%$ implies that available liquidity beyond the expiry of the liability is nil. In practice, the LCR implicitly forbids any maturity transformation activity insofar as liabilities with a runoff factor of 100% are concerned.

Regulation does not forbid non-equilibrium policies either, so that in theory the bank could follow a strategy like that described in Section 7.5 to fulfil the requirement that $\mathrm{LCR} \geq 1$. In practice, the bank can fund its LB in an inconsistent (according to our analysis) way relying on the low probability of occurrence of stressed scenarios. When this happens, though, it is much more likely that the LB is less effective to protect the bank.

In the following chapters we present models that enable the bank to simulate the main items on its balance sheet: this makes it possible to better manage and monitor the effectiveness of the LB. Moreover, it is possible to simulate the evolution of the LCR both for regulatory or risk management purposes as well.

8
Models for market risk factors

8.1 INTRODUCTION

In this chapter[1] we present some models for market risk factors: all market variables, such as interest rates, credit spreads, FX rates, stock prices and commodity prices, are affecting the payoff of most of the contracts a bank has on its balance sheet. Effective and parsimonious models are required to allow simulation of the cash flows of contracts linked to the different market variables, which become risk factors in themselves.

We first introduce models that can be used to model the evolution of FX rates and equities, then we dwell on interest rate models and default models, which are the basis for the modelling of credit spreads. We do not focus on all market variables (e.g., we do not analyse inflation modelling), but hopefully we will cover the vast majority of the market risk factors that affect the cash flows of contracts.

The second part of the chapter, from Section 8.5 on, is devoted to application of the models to liquidity risk management.

8.2 STOCK PRICES AND FX RATES

A standard way to model the evolution of stock prices and FX rates is to assume that they are commanded by a geometric Brownian motion. A process x_t follows a geometric Brownian motion if it described by the dynamics

$$\frac{dx_t}{x_t} = \mu \, dt + \sigma \, dW_t, \tag{8.1}$$

where μ and σ are, respectively, the constant drift and the volatility of the process, and W_t is a Brownian process. The differential equation (8.1) can be solved exactly. Given the value x_t at time t, the value of the process at any subsequent time T is

$$x_T = x_t \exp\left[\left(\mu - \frac{\sigma^2}{2}\right)(T - t) + \sigma \, W_T\right]. \tag{8.2}$$

Equation (8.1) is a real-world measure process, where the expected trend (μ) and the volatility of the process (σ) are supposed to be parameters reflecting historical realization of the observed equity prices of FX rates: as such they can be estimated by statistical techniques from actual time series. The process can also be written under the risk-neutral

---

[1] We are in grateful to Luca Visinelli for discussions with one of the authors in the development phase of the models presented in this chapter. Moreover, he gave invaluable support in implementing and testing them in the examples shown below.

measure,

$$\frac{dx_t}{x_t} = r_t \, dt + \sigma_t \, dW_t, \tag{8.3}$$

where r_t is the deterministic time-dependent instantaneous interest rate. The risk-neutral measure is used for pricing so that the volatility σ_t is extracted from market quotes of options backing out the implied volatility from the formula we will present below. The expected value of x_t at time T, assuming a constant interest rate and volatility parameter, is

$$\bar{x}_T = \mathbf{E}_t^Q[x_T] = e^{r(T-t)} x_t, \tag{8.4}$$

where, both here and in the following, we denote by $\mathbf{E}_t$ the expectation value with respect to filtration $\mathcal{F}_t$ under the risk-neutral measure (Q). In reality, we will see later (Chapter 12) that in many cases the proper drift under the risk-neutral measure (from a replication argument) is the repo rate in the case of equity, or the FX swap rate in the case of FX rates.

In the specific cases of an equity price S, equation (8.1) has to be extended to include the possibility of discrete dividends D_i paid on dates $\{t_1^D, t_2^D, \ldots, t_N^D\}$ over a predefined observed period as well. The price of the equity can be assumed to be composed of two parts: a stochastic part similar to (8.1) plus a deterministic component equal to the present value of the future dividends paid by the stock:

$$S_t = x_t + PVD_t \tag{8.5}$$

where $PVD_t = \sum_{i=1}^N e^{-r(t_i-t)} D_i$.

The evolution of the stock, as modelled by equation (8.5), evolves with jumps downwards on each dividend payment date with a a jump size equal to the lump sum paid. The evolution can also be applied to stock indices.

For FX rates there is no problem related to the payment of dividends, so that the dynamics in equations (8.1) and (8.3) do not need any adjustment. The risk-neutral dynamics have to be adjusted as follows:

$$d\mathcal{X}_t = r_t^{\mathcal{X}} \mathcal{X}_t dt + \sigma_t \mathcal{X}_t dW_t \tag{8.6}$$

where $\mathcal{X}$ is the FX rate and $r_t^{\mathcal{X}}$ is the implied FX swap rate implied from levels quoted in the market. The expected value is modified accordingly.

It is useful to show how to price a call option with strike K on a stock or an FX rate following the process x_t and maturity at time T:

$$\text{Call}(x_t, K, T, T, r, \sigma) = (x_T - K)^+, \tag{8.7}$$

has a value today equal to

$$\text{Call}(x_t, K, t, T, r, \sigma) = e^{-r(T-t)} \, \text{BlSc}(\bar{x}_T, K, \Sigma). \tag{8.8}$$

Here, we set $\Sigma = \sigma\sqrt{T-t}$ and we define the function

$$\text{BlSc}(F, K, \Sigma) = F \, N(d_1) - K \, N(d_2), \tag{8.9}$$

where

$$d_1 = \frac{\ln(F/K) + \Sigma^2/2}{\Sigma}, \quad \text{and} \quad \frac{\ln(F/K) - \Sigma^2/2}{\Sigma}, \tag{8.10}$$

while $N(x)$ is the cumulative probability distribution for a standardized normal distribution,

$$N(x) = \frac{1}{\sqrt{2\pi}} \int_{-\infty}^{x} e^{-u^2/2} \, du. \tag{8.11}$$

Put options can be priced via put–call parity:

$$\mathbf{Put}(x_t, K, t, T, r, \sigma) = (x_t, K, t, T, r, \sigma) - e^{-r(T-t)}((\bar{x}_T - K).$$

8.3 INTEREST RATE MODELS

We show here two one-factor short-rate models—the Vasicek model and the CIR model—as well as the Libor Market Model.

8.3.1 One-factor models for the zero rate

The (annual) risk-free zero rate r_t is the interest rate at which, at time t, money can be lent or borrowed for the infinitesimal amount of time dt: this is true if in the economy the default of economic agents is excluded. If r_t is modelled through a stochastic process, the price at time t of a zero-coupon bond maturing at time T is

$$P^D(t, T) = \mathbf{E}_t^Q \left[e^{-\int_t^T r_s \, ds} \right], \tag{8.12}$$

where the expectation is taken under the risk-neutral measure Q. The price in equation (8.12) coincides with the discount factor in the period $[t, T]$, with an instantaneous forward rate given by

$$f(t, T) = -\frac{\partial}{\partial T} \ln P^D(t, T). \tag{8.13}$$

The zero-rate is recovered as

$$r_t = \lim_{T \to t} f(t, T). \tag{8.14}$$

The expected return on a zero-coupon bond is under the risk-neural measure:

$$\mathbf{E}_t^Q \left[dP^D(t, T) \right] = r_t P^D(t, T) dt$$

The same expectation in the real measure is:

$$\mathbf{E}_t^P \left[dP^D(t, T) \right] = \left[r_t + \pi r_t \frac{\partial P^D(t, T)/\partial r_t}{P^D(t, T)} \right] P^D(t, T) dt$$

where π represents the market risk parameters and $\pi r_t \frac{\partial P^D(t,T)/\partial r_t}{P^D(t,T)}$ is the risk-premium required, which is proportional to the elasticity of the bond's value with respect to the risk factor r_t.

In one-factor models, the zero rate r_t is described by a single stochastic factor, depending on a Brownian process W_t. In the following, we briefly review two of the most popular one-factor models.

8.3.2   Vasicek model

In the Vasicek model [111], the zero rate follows the stochastic differential equation

$$dr_t = \kappa \left(\theta - r_t \right) dt + \sigma \, dW_t. \tag{8.15}$$

The parameter σ defines the volatility of the process, θ is a parameter defining the long-term mean to which trajectories evolve, and κ is the mean reversion speed, describing the velocity at which trajectories approach the long-term mean. Moreover, the quantity $\sigma^2/2\kappa$ defines the long-term variance possessed by trajectories after a time $\gg 1/\kappa$.

The risk-adjusted dynamics including the market risk parameter as well are:

$$dr_t = \kappa \left(\theta - r_t - r_t \pi \right) dt + \sigma \, dW_t.$$

We assume that the market risk parameter π is zero, so that the zero-rate r_T can be obtained at future times T when the process is known at time t, by solving equation (8.15), obtaining

$$r_T = r_t e^{-\kappa (T-t)} + \theta \left(1 - e^{-\kappa (T-t)} \right) + \sigma \int_t^T e^{\kappa (s-t)} dW_s. \tag{8.16}$$

Although the dynamics of the Vasicek model enjoy some nice properties, such as mean reversion towards the long-term means θ, unfortunately it does not prevent short-rate means from going below zero and thus assume negative values. While this might be seen as completely unrealistic,[2] it many cases it is preferred to have a boundary at the zero level. The CIR model allows such a feature to be introduced.

8.3.3   The CIR model

We will describe the CIR model extensively because it will be the main building block of most of the models we present in what follows. In a generic "mean-reverting" process, the interest rate r_t tends to be pulled towards a long-term average θ whenever the process deviates from it.

In the CIR model the process for r_t is:

$$dr_t = \kappa \left(\theta - r_t \right) dt + \sigma \sqrt{r_t} \, dW_t, \qquad r_{t=0} = r_0 > 0, \tag{8.17}$$

where θ is the long-term average, κ is a constant describing the speed of mean reversion, σ is the volatility of the process that causes deviations from a pure deterministic model and r_0 is the initial value (at time $t = 0$) of the interest rate.

In this case, we can also write the risk-adjusted dynamics we have to use when pricing contracts depending on the interest rates:

$$dr_t = \kappa \left(\theta - r_t - r_t \pi \right) dt + \sigma \sqrt{r_t} \, dW_t.$$

Furthermore in this case, we will assume in what follows that $\pi = 0$, so that drift under the risk-neutral and real measure is the same.

The short-rate dynamics in equation (8.17) were first suggested by Cox, Ingersoll and Ross in [55]. In the following, we indicate the CIR process in equation (8.17) as

$$r_t = \mathrm{CIR}(\kappa, \sigma, \theta, r_0, t). \tag{8.18}$$

---

[2] Some currencies such as the yen and the Swiss franc experienced negative levels of the interest rates for short expiries, typically up to one year.

When the parameters of the process satisfy the inequality

$$2\kappa\theta > \sigma^2, \tag{8.19}$$

it is ensured that the process r_t thus generated is always positive. Since the CIR model is of the mean-reverting type, both the expected value and the variance of r_t tend to a constant value when time tends to infinity. In fact, at time $t > 0$, the average value of the CIR process $CIR(\kappa, \sigma, \theta, r_0, t)$ is

$$\mathbf{E}_t\left[r_t \mid \mathcal{F}_t\right] = \theta + (r_0 - \theta)\, e^{-\kappa t}, \tag{8.20}$$

which shows explicitly that the long-term average of the CIR process tends to the value θ. To prove the formula in equation (8.20), one might take the average on both sides of equation (8.17), and use the fact that W_t has zero average. One is left with an ODE with initial condition $r = r_s$, leading to equation (8.20). With a similar technique, it can be shown that the variance of a CIR process is

$$\mathrm{Var}\left[r_t \mid F_t\right] = \frac{\sigma^2}{\kappa}\left(1 - e^{-\kappa t}\right)\left[r_0\, e^{-\kappa t} + \frac{\theta}{2}\left(1 - e^{-\kappa t}\right)\right]. \tag{8.21}$$

Zero-coupon bonds

A closed-form formula is available for zero-coupon bonds, alternatively named discount bonds or discount factors, in the CIR model. For a process r_t the moment-generating function over the time interval $[t; T]$ is defined as

$$m(q; t, T) = \mathbf{E}_t\left[e^{q\int_t^T r_s\, ds} \,\Big|\, \mathcal{F}_t\right]. \tag{8.22}$$

In the case of the CIR process in equation (8.17), $m(q; t, T)$ is known in a closed-form formula,

$$m(q; t, T) = A(q; t, T)\, e^{-B(q;t,T)\, r_t}, \tag{8.23}$$

where the coefficients $A(q; t, T)$ and $B(q; t, T)$ are defined as

$$\left.\begin{aligned}
A(q; t, T) &= \left[\frac{c_1 + d_1}{c_1\, e^{\gamma_1\,(T-t)} + d_1}\, e^{\frac{\kappa+\gamma_1}{2(T-t)}}\right]^{2\kappa\theta\sigma^2} , \\[2mm]
B(q; t, T) &= \frac{-2q\left[e^{\gamma_1\,(T-t)} - 1\right]}{(\gamma_1 + \kappa)(e^{\gamma_1\,(T-t)} - 1) + 2\gamma_1} ,
\end{aligned}\right\} \tag{8.24}$$

and with

$$\left.\begin{aligned}
\gamma_1 &= \sqrt{\kappa^2 - 2q\sigma^2}, \\[1mm]
c_1 &= \frac{\kappa + \gamma_1}{2q}, \\[1mm]
d_1 &= -\kappa + \gamma_1 2q.
\end{aligned}\right\} \tag{8.25}$$

The discount factor in the CIR model is then obtained from equation (8.23) when $q = -1$,

$$P_{\mathrm{CIR}}(r_t; t, T) \equiv m(-1; t, T). \tag{8.26}$$

The explicit expression for the discount factor is given in CIR (see [55]):

$$P_{\text{CIR}}(r_t; t, T) = A(t, T)\, e^{-B(t,T)\, r_t},$$

(8.27)

with

$$
\left.
\begin{aligned}
A(t, T) &= \left[\frac{2\gamma\, e^{(\kappa+\gamma)(T-t)/2}}{(\gamma + \kappa)\left(e^{\gamma(T-t)} - 1\right) + 2\gamma}\right]^{\frac{2\kappa\theta}{\sigma^2}}, \\
B(t, T) &= \frac{2\left(e^{\gamma(T-t)} - 1\right)}{(\gamma + \kappa)\left(e^{\gamma(T-t)} - 1\right) + 2\gamma},
\end{aligned}
\right\}
$$

(8.28)

and with $\gamma = \sqrt{\kappa^2 + 2\sigma^2}$.

Future and forward prices

Furthermore, futures and forward prices of zero-coupon bonds are available in closed-form formula in the CIR model.

At time t, the future price[3] of a future contract with maturity date $s > t$ on a discount bond paying one monetary unit at time $T > s$ is (see [53] for details):

$$\mathbf{H}_{\text{CIR}}(r_t; t, s, T) = \left(\frac{\eta}{\eta + B(s, T)}\right)^{2\kappa\theta/\sigma^2} A(s, T) \exp\left[-r_t\, \frac{\eta\, B(s, T)\, e^{-\kappa(s-t)}}{\eta + B(s, T)}\right],$$

(8.29)

where

$$\eta = \frac{2\kappa}{\sigma^2\left(1 - e^{-\kappa(s-t)}\right)}.$$

(8.30)

The forward price of a forward contract to deliver at the maturity date $s > t$ a discount bond paying one monetary unit at time $T > s$ is (see [53])

$$\mathbf{G}_{\text{CIR}}(r_t; t, s, T) = \frac{A(t, T)}{A(t, s)}\, e^{-[B(t,T) - B(t,s)]\, r_t}.$$

(8.31)

The future price of the bond can be seen as its expected value at time $s > t$, under the risk-neutral measure:

$$\mathbf{H}_{\text{CIR}}(r_t; t, s, T) = \mathbf{E}_t^Q\left[e^{-\int_s^T r_u\, du}\,\middle|\,\mathcal{F}_t\right].$$

(8.32)

On the other hand, the forward price of the bond can be considered as the expected value at time $s > t$ under the forward risk-adjusted measure, also called the s-adjusted measure (see [34]), in which equation (8.17) becomes:

$$dr_t = \left[\kappa\theta - (\kappa + B(t, s)\sigma^2)\, r_t\right] dt + \sigma\sqrt{r_t}\, dW_t^s, \qquad r_{t=0} = r_0 > 0,$$

(8.33)

where the notation is the same as that introduced above. The forward price of the bond is then:

$$\mathbf{G}_{\text{CIR}}(r_t; t, s, T) = \mathbf{E}_t^s\left[e^{-\int_s^T r_u\, du}\,\middle|\,\mathcal{F}_t\right] = \frac{P(r_t; t, T)}{P(r_t; t, s)}.$$

(8.34)

---

[3] The future price, as well as the forward price we show immediately below, should not be confused with the value of the contract. They are simply the price level making the value, respectively, of the the future or the forward contract equal to zero.

Probability distribution for a CIR process

In the CIR model, the process r_t is characterized by a non-central chi-squared distribution. In particular, the probability distribution of the process in equation (8.18) is (see [55]):

$$p_{r_0}(r_t) = \chi^2\left(2r_t c; 2q + 2, 2u\right) \tag{8.35}$$

where

$$c_t = 4\kappa \frac{\sigma^2}{(1 - e^{-\kappa t})},$$

$$v = c_t r_0,$$

$$u = c_t r_0 e^{-\kappa t},$$

$$q = \frac{2\kappa\theta}{\sigma^2} - 1$$

and $\chi^2(x; d, c)$ is the non-central chi-squared distribution, with d degrees of freedom and non-centrality parameter c.

It is also useful to give the CIR dynamics in the forward risk-adjusted measure, also called the t-adjusted measure: technically speaking, this is the measure under which the terminal payoff of a contract at time t is rescaled by dividing it by the value of a zero-coupon bond expiring at the time the probability distribution of the CIR process is:

$$p_{r_0}^t(r_t) = \chi^2\left(2r_t(\phi + \eta); \frac{4\kappa\theta}{\sigma^2}, \frac{2\phi^2 r_t e^{\gamma t}}{\phi + \eta}\right) \tag{8.36}$$

where

$$\gamma = \sqrt{\kappa^2 + 2\sigma^2}$$

$$\phi = \frac{2\gamma}{\sigma^2(e^{\gamma t} - 1)}$$

$$\eta = \frac{\kappa + \gamma}{\sigma^2}$$

As will be made clear in the models we will present, we will need both dynamics and distributions.

Options on bonds and interest rates

Following [55], the price of a European call option, with maturity s and strike K, on a zero-coupon bond with maturity $T > s$ and with a short interest rate $r_t = \text{CIR}(\kappa, \sigma, \theta, r_0, t)$ is

$$\text{Call}_{\text{CIR}}(t, s, T, K) = P_{\text{CIR}}(r_t; t, T) \chi^2\left(2r^*[\phi + \psi + B(s, T)], \frac{4\kappa\theta}{\sigma^2}, \frac{2\phi^2 e^{\gamma(s-t)} r_t}{\phi + \zeta + B(s, T)}\right)$$

$$- K P_{\text{CIR}}(r_t; t, s) \chi^2\left(2r^*[\phi + \zeta], \frac{4\kappa\theta}{\sigma^2}, \frac{2\phi^2 e^{\gamma(s-t)} r_t}{\phi + \zeta}\right), \tag{8.37}$$

where

$$\phi = \frac{2\gamma}{\sigma^2(e^{\gamma(s-t)} - 1)}, \qquad \zeta = \frac{\kappa + \gamma}{\sigma^2}, \tag{8.38}$$

and with the quantity r^* expressed in terms of the strike K by

$$r^* = \frac{\ln[A(s, T)/K]}{B(s, T)}. \tag{8.39}$$

Note that $K = A(s, T) e^{-B(s,T)r^*} < A(s, T)$.

The value of the corresponding European put on the zero-coupon bond is found by put–call parity:

$$\text{Put}(t, s, T, K) = \text{Call}_{\text{CIR}}(t, s, T, K) - P_{\text{CIR}}(r_t; t, T) + K\, P_{\text{CIR}}(r_t; t, s). \tag{8.40}$$

Although zero-coupon options are not actively traded in the market, equations (8.37) and (8.40) can be used to price much more common contracts such as cap and floor options on a discrete interest rate $L(t, s, T) = L_T(t)$, simply compounded and applied for a period starting at s and ending in T with strike rate X (e.g., a cap on a 3-month Eonia).[4]

The formula to evaluate a caplet with unit notional amount is:

$$\text{Cap}(t, s, T, X) = (1 + X(T - s))\,\text{Put}_{\text{CIR}}(t, s, T, K_X), \tag{8.41}$$

A floorlet's value is given by the formula:

$$\text{Floor}(t, s, T, X) = (1 + X(T - s))\,\text{Call}_{\text{CIR}}(t, s, T, K_X), \tag{8.42}$$

where the strike is

$$K_X = \frac{1}{1 + X(T - s)}. \tag{8.43}$$

Let us now consider a cap or floor option, with maturity T and fixing schedule t_i, $i = \{0, \ldots, n-1\}$, where n is the number of caplets or floorlets, and $t_n = T$. The cap option is a sum of the caplets between fixing dates t_i and payment dates t_{i+1}, hence:

$$\text{Cap}(t, T, X) = \sum_{i=1}^{n-1} (1 + X \tau_i)\,\text{Put}_{\text{CIR}}(t, t_i, t_{i+1}, K_{X_i}), \tag{8.44}$$

where we define the time intervals $\tau_i = t_{i+1} - t_i$, and

$$K_X = \frac{1}{1 + X \tau_i}. \tag{8.45}$$

Similarly, the floor is

$$\text{Floor}(t, T, X) = \sum_{i=1}^{n-1} (1 + X \tau_i)\,\text{Call}_{\text{CIR}}(t, t_i, t_{i+1}, K_{X_i}). \tag{8.46}$$

Even if quotes on caps and floors on Eonia or OIS rates are not very liquid in the current financial markets, equations (8.41) and (8.42) can be useful to drive the distributions of

---

[4] If we assume that the Libor and Euribor rates are not risk-free rates and we model them using a CIR model, then we can also price caps and floors on Libor or Euribor fixings. In the current market environment the assumption that Libor/Euribor fixings are risk-free rates is believed to be too strong and the model will work poorly to price this type of contract. Anyway, the example we suggest of caps and floors on Eonia rates admittedly refers to unusual contracts traded in the market.

discrete period rates that form the risk-free (Eonia or OIS) component of a Euribor or Libor fixing, if we model these as $F_i(t) = L_i(t) + S_i(t)$, (i.e., as the sum of the risk-free rate plus a credit spread S). We will dwell more on this later on in this chapter.

Summing two CIR processes

It is useful to study some properties of the CIR process since we will exploit them heavily in the models we present in this book. We start by analysing the sum of two CIR processes.

Let us consider two independent CIR processes,

$$\left. \begin{aligned} r_t^{(1)} &= \mathrm{CIR}(\kappa^{(1)}, \sigma^{(1)}, \theta^{(1)}, r_0^{(1)}, t), \\ r_t^{(2)} &= \mathrm{CIR}(\kappa^{(2)}, \sigma^{(2)}, \theta^{(2)}, r_0^{(2)}, t), \end{aligned} \right\} \tag{8.47}$$

We wish to know under which restrictions of the CIR parameters for $r_t^{(1)}$ and $r_t^{(2)}$ the process $r_t = r_t^{(1)} + r_t^{(2)}$ is still a CIR process.[5] To answer this, we consider the two CIR processes in the form given in equation (8.17),

$$\left. \begin{aligned} dr_t^{(1)} &= \kappa^{(1)}(\theta^{(1)} - r_t^{(1)})dt + \sigma^{(1)}\sqrt{r_t^{(1)}}\, dW_t^{(1)}, && r_{t=0}^{(1)} = r_0^{(1)} > 0, \\ dr_t^{(2)} &= \kappa^{(2)}(\theta^{(2)} - r_t^{(2)})dt + \sigma^{(2)}\sqrt{r_t^{(2)}}\, dW_t^{(2)}, && r_{t=0}^{(2)} = r_0^{(2)} > 0, \end{aligned} \right\} \tag{8.48}$$

so that the expression for dr_t is, considering the two processes $r_t^{(1)}$ and $r_t^{(2)}$ as independent,

$$dr_t = \left(\kappa^{(1)}\theta^{(1)} + \kappa^{(2)}\theta^{(2)} - \kappa^{(1)}r_t^{(1)} - \kappa^{(2)}r_t^{(2)}\right)dt + \sigma^{(1)}\sqrt{r_t^{(1)}}\, dW_t^{(1)} + \sigma^{(2)}\sqrt{r_t^{(2)}}\, dW_t^{(2)}, \tag{8.49}$$

with the initial condition $r_0 = r_0^{(1)} + r_0^{(2)} > 0$. We can write the expression for r_t in equation (8.49) in the form

$$dr_t = \kappa(\theta - r_t)dt + \sigma\sqrt{r_t}\, dW_t, \qquad r_{t=0} = r_0 > 0, \tag{8.50}$$

if we constrain the parameters as

$$\left. \begin{aligned} \kappa^{(1)} &= \kappa^{(2)} = \kappa, \\ \sigma^{(1)} &= \sigma^{(2)} = \sigma, \\ \theta^{(1)} + \theta^{(2)} &= \theta, \\ r_0^{(1)} + r_0^{(2)} &= r_0, \end{aligned} \right\} \tag{8.51}$$

with the new Brownian motion W_t defined through

$$\sqrt{r_t^{(1)}}\, dW_t^{(1)} + \sqrt{r_t^{(2)}}\, dW_t^{(2)} = \sqrt{r_t}\, dW_t. \tag{8.52}$$

---

[5] See also [59] on this point.

Summing up, if the CIR parameters for r_t are defined as in equation (8.51), then

$$r_t = r_t^{(1)} + r_t^{(2)} = \text{CIR}(\kappa, \sigma, \theta, r_0, t). \tag{8.53}$$

Multiplying a CIR process by a constant

We now consider how the process $r_t = \text{CIR}(\kappa, \sigma, \theta, r_0, t)$ is related to αr_t, where α is a positive constant. For this, we multiply equation (8.17) by α,

$$\alpha \, dr_t = \alpha \kappa (\theta - r_t) dt + \alpha \sigma \sqrt{r_t} \, dW_t, \tag{8.54}$$

or

$$\alpha r_t = \alpha \, \text{CIR}(\kappa, \sigma, \theta, r_0, t) = \text{CIR}(\kappa, \sqrt{\alpha} \sigma, \alpha \theta, \alpha r_0, t). \tag{8.55}$$

Estimation of the CIR model using the Kálmán filter

Since we will also use the CIR model for risk management purposes and not only for pricing purposes (in which case we would just calibrate the model to market prices to infer risk-neutral parameters), we need a robust procedure to estimate the parameters according to historical prices. In this section, we outline a technique for estimating the parameters κ, θ and σ of the CIR model. For this, we use a maximum likelihood estimation based on the Kálmán filtering technique.

The basis of the procedure we present is to extract zero rates from market prices of zero-coupon prices: these prices are often embedded in coupon bonds that can be seen as portfolios of discount bonds. In the CIR model, the prices of a zero-coupon bond are related to the zero rate r_t (here referred to as the latent variable) through the discount factor in equation (8.27). Indicating the bond maturity date by T, and setting

$$z_t = -\frac{1}{T - t} \ln P(t, T), \tag{8.56}$$

where $P(t, T)$ is the market price of a discount bond. The relation between the latent variable and z_t is

$$z_t = \alpha_t + \beta_t r_t, \tag{8.57}$$

and is referred to as the observation equation. For the CIR model we have:

$$z_t = -\frac{\ln A(t, T)}{T - t} + \frac{B(t, T)}{T - t} r_t, \tag{8.58}$$

where $A(t, T)$ and $B(t, T)$ are the CIR factors defined in equation (8.28).

The Kálmán filter technique has become the standard tool for estimating the parameters of a short-rate model (not only the CIR model), given the term structure of a portfolio of bonds. Kálmán filters are based on time discretization of the equations describing the evolution of the interest rate r_t (the latent variable) and of the bond price. If the time series of bond prices is considered from a date t_0 to an end date t, we discretize the time interval $[t_0, t]$ by introducing the time step $\delta = (t - t_0)/N$, where N is the number of dates in the interval, and the dates are

$$t_i = t_0 + i\delta, \qquad \text{with } i \in \{0, \dots, N\}. \tag{8.59}$$

Given the market price of the bond at time t_i as $P^{MKT}(t_i, t)$, we define

$$\hat{z}_i = -\frac{1}{T - t_i} \ln P^{MKT}(t_i, t),$$ (8.60)

The discretized version of equation (8.57) is

$$z_i = \alpha_i + \beta_i r_i,$$ (8.61)

where $z_i = z_{t_i}$, $r_i = r_{t_i}$, $\alpha_i = \alpha_{t_i}$ and $\beta_i = \beta_{t_i}$. A second equation is obtained by considering the time evolution of the rate, according to equation (8.17),

$$r_i = C + F r_{i-1} + \omega_i,$$ (8.62)

where, for a CIR process, $C = \theta (1 - e^{-\kappa \delta})$ and $F = e^{-\kappa \delta}$, while ω_i is a Gaussian noise with mean equal to zero and variance equal to

$$\text{Var}\,\omega_i = \frac{\sigma^2}{\kappa}\left(1 - e^{-\kappa\delta}\right)\left[\frac{\theta}{2}\left(1 - e^{-\kappa\delta}\right) + r_{i-1} e^{-\kappa\delta}\right].$$ (8.63)

With the Kálmán filter technique, equations (8.61) and (8.62) are simultaneously solved for r_i and z_i at step i, given the values of the variables at the $i - 1$-th step and the knowledge of z_i from the market data at time t_i, $\hat{z}_i$. As additional outcomes, the procedure produces values of the error $\epsilon_i = z_i - \hat{z}_i$, and the variance associated with the error $\text{Var}\,z_i$. At each step, we construct the logarithm of the likelihood function

$$\mathcal{L}_i = -\frac{\delta}{2}\ln 2\pi - \ln \sqrt{\text{Var}\,z_i} - \frac{\epsilon_i^2}{2}\text{Var}\,z_i.$$ (8.64)

The log-likelihood function of the process is the sum

$$\mathcal{L} = \sum_{i=1}^{N} \mathcal{L}_i.$$ (8.65)

The parameters κ, θ and σ are obtained by requiring that the function $\mathcal{L}$ be maximized with respect to these parameters. In practical numerical codes, since minimization techniques are easier to implement, one looks for the parameters that minimize the function $-\mathcal{L}$.

8.3.4   The CIR++ model

The CIR model is a parsimonious way to model the entire term structure of interest rates and also prevents negative values, in contrast to the Vasicek model. Nonetheless, it is often not rich enough to allow a perfect fit to observed market prices. On the other hand, when parameters are estimated from the historical time series, the model is unable in most cases to exactly reproduce observed market prices, even if they could be perfectly matched to them by means of single-time calibration.

In these cases it is convenient to extend the CIR model so as to allow perfect fitting to the initial term structure of (risk-free) interest rates, and a time-dependent deterministic extension is the easiest approach to adopt.

The CIR++ process

In the CIR++ model,[6] the short-rate dynamics for r_t are described as

$$r_t = x_t + \psi_t, \tag{8.66}$$

where x_t is a CIR process,

$$x_t = \mathrm{CIR}(\kappa, \sigma, \theta, x_0, t), \tag{8.67}$$

and ψ_t is a deterministic function that can be chosen so as to exactly match the initial term structure of interest rates. We denote the CIR++ model in equation (8.66) as

$$r_t = \mathrm{CIR}{++}(\psi_t, \kappa, \sigma, \theta, x_0, t), \tag{8.68}$$

The price at time t of a zero-coupon bond expiring at T under a CIR++ process is (see [35]):

$$P_{\mathrm{CIR}{++}}(r_t; t, T) = \exp\left(-\int_t^T \psi_s\, ds\right) P_{\mathrm{CIR}{++}}(x_t; t, T), \tag{8.69}$$

where $P^D_{\mathrm{CIR}}(r_t; t, T)$ is the discount factor defined in equation (8.27).

The average value of the CIR++ process in equation (8.27) over the period $[t, T]$ is

$$\mathbf{E}_t[r_t] = \mathbf{E}_t[r_t] + \mathbf{E}_t[\psi_t] = \theta + (x_t - \theta)\, e^{-\kappa(T-t)} + \frac{1}{T-t}\int_t^T \psi_{t'}\, dt', \tag{8.70}$$

while, since ψ_t is a deterministic process, the variance of r_t is given by the variance of the CIR process x_t alone,

$$\mathbf{Var}[r_t] = \frac{\sigma^2}{\kappa}\left(1 - e^{-\kappa(T-t)}\right)\left[x_t\, e^{-\kappa(T-t)} + \frac{\theta}{2}\left(1 - e^{-\kappa(T-t)}\right)\right]. \tag{8.71}$$

In a CIR++ model, we define the future in t, with expiry S and bond maturity T, as

$$\mathrm{H}_{\mathrm{CIR}}(t, S, T) = \exp\left(-\int_t^T \psi_s\, ds\right) \mathrm{H}_{\mathrm{CIR}}(t, S, T), \tag{8.72}$$

where $\mathrm{H}_{\mathrm{CIR}}(t, S, T)$ is the future of the CIR process defined in equation (8.29).

Typically, the deterministic function ψ_t will be stepwise constant: we will see below how to fit it to actual market prices.

Options on bonds and interest rates

In the CIR++ model, the price of a European call option with maturity s and strike K on a zero-coupon bond with maturity $T > s$ and interest rate $r_t = \mathrm{CIR}{++}(\psi_t, \kappa, \sigma, \theta, x_0, t)$ is

$$\mathrm{Call}_{\mathrm{CIR}{++}}(t, s, T, K) = P_{\mathrm{CIR}}(r_t; t, T)\, \chi^2\left(2\hat{r}\left[\phi + \zeta + B(s, T)\right], \frac{4\kappa\theta}{\sigma^2}, \frac{2\phi^2\, e^{\gamma(s-t)} x_t}{\phi + \zeta + B(s, T)}\right)$$

$$- K\, P_{\mathrm{CIR}}(r_t; t, s)\, \chi^2\left(2\hat{r}\left[\phi + \zeta\right], \frac{4\kappa\theta}{\sigma^2}, \frac{2\phi^2\, e^{\gamma(s-t)} x_t}{\phi + \zeta}\right), \tag{8.73}$$

---

[6] The model was introduced and analysed in [34], to which we refer the reader for more details.

where ϕ and ζ are as defined in equation (8.38), while

$$\hat{r} = \frac{1}{B(s,T)} \left[\ln \frac{A(s,T)}{K} + \int_s^T \psi_u \, du \right]. \tag{8.74}$$

The value of the corresponding put on the European bond is found from the formula

$$\text{Put}_{\text{CIR}++}(t,s,T,K) = \text{Call}_{\text{CIR}++}(t,s,T,K) - P_{\text{CIR}}(r_t; t,T) + K \, P_{\text{CIR}++}(r_t; t,s). \tag{8.75}$$

Caps and floors in the CIR++ model are related to the call and put bond options as in equations (8.41) and (8.42).

8.3.5 The Basic Affine Jump Diffusion Model

An extension of the CIR model, which can be applied also to the CIR++ model, is the inclusion of jumps in the process of the short rate r_t.[7]

A stochastic process Z_t is a basic affine jump diffusion (bAJD) model if it follows the process

$$dZ_t = \kappa(\theta - Z_t)dt + \sigma\sqrt{Z_t}\,dW_t + dJ_t, \qquad Z_{t=0} = Z_0 > 0. \tag{8.76}$$

where W_t is a standard Brownian motion, and J_t is an independent compound Poisson process with constant jump intensity $l > 0$, so that jumps occur more frequently with increasing l. We assume that each jump is exponentially distributed, with mean $\mu > 0$: the larger μ is the larger the size for a given jump. We also require $\kappa\theta \geq 0$ in order for the process to be well defined. We indicate the process Z_t in much the same way as the process in equation (8.76) as

$$Z_t = \text{bAJD}(\kappa, \sigma, \theta, l, \mu, Z_0, t). \tag{8.77}$$

Following [59] and [64], but with the notation as in [55], the moments of the bAJD in equation (8.77) are defined as

$$m(l,q;t,T) = \mathbf{E}_t\left[e^{q \int_t^T Z_s ds} \Big| \mathcal{F}_t \right] = A(l,q;t,T)\, e^{-B(q;t,T)\,Z_t}, \tag{8.78}$$

where

$$\left.\begin{array}{l} A(l,q;t,T) = A(q;t,T) \left[\dfrac{c_2 + d_2}{c_2\, e^{\gamma_1(T-t)} + d_2}\, e^{\frac{\kappa+\gamma_1-2q\mu}{2}(T-t)} \right]^{\frac{-\mu}{q(d_1+\mu)(c_1-\mu)}}, \\[4mm] c_2 = 1 - \dfrac{\mu}{c_1}, \\[4mm] d_2 = \dfrac{d_1 + \mu}{c_1}, \end{array}\right\} \tag{8.79}$$

and where $A(q;t,T)$ and $B(q;t,T)$ are the CIR factors given in equation (8.24). In particular, all moments for the bAJD process reduce to the moments for the CIR process when either $l = 0$ or $\mu = 0$, corresponding to the case in which either the intensity or the frequency of jumps is zero. In formulas, we have

$$\text{bAJD}(\kappa, \sigma, \theta, 0, \mu, Z_0, t) = \text{bAJD}(\kappa, \sigma, \theta, l, 0, Z_0, t) = \text{CIR}(\kappa, \sigma, \theta, Z_0, t), \tag{8.80}$$

---

[7] These types of processes are studied in [59] and [82]. See also [33] for an application to credit derivatives pricing.

as can be seen explicitly from the fact that when we set either $\mu = 0$ or $l = 0$ in equation (8.79), the expression for $m(l, q; t, T)$ reduces to $m(q; t, T)$ in equation (8.23).

The discount factor in the bAJD model can be written in exponential form as

$$P_{bADJ}(l; t, T) = A(l; t, T) e^{-B(t,T) Z_t}, \tag{8.81}$$

where

$$A(l; t, T) = A(t, T) \left[\frac{2\gamma \, e^{\frac{\kappa+\gamma+2\mu}{2}(T-t)}}{2\gamma + (\kappa + \gamma + 2\mu) \left(e^{\gamma (T-t)} - 1\right)} \right]^{\frac{2l\mu}{\sigma^2 - 2\kappa\mu - 2\mu^2}}, \tag{8.82}$$

and where $A(t, T)$ and $B(t, T)$ are the CIR coefficients in equation (8.28).

8.3.6 Numerical implementations

We now focus on some numerical issues related to the CIR model and its extensions. More specifically, the CIR process has to be handled with care in its discrete version, used to simulate paths for the short-rate r_t in Monte Carlo simulations.

8.3.7 Discrete version of the CIR model

Consider a short-rate factor r_t described by a CIR process, as in equation (8.17), and a security that depends on r_t. In order to evaluate the price of a contract at a future time $s > t$, or to simulate its cash flows, the value of r_s has to be known. This can be done by numerically evolving r_t using equation (8.17) in steps, from time t to time s. In greater detail let us introduce N discretization points t_i, equally spaced by

$$\Delta_t = \frac{s - t}{N}, \tag{8.83}$$

so that

$$t_i = t + i\Delta_t, \quad \text{and} \quad i = 0 \cdots N, \tag{8.84}$$

so that $t_0 = t$ and $t_N = s$.

For the Brownian motion term dW_t, we first note that

$$W_t \sim \sqrt{t} \mathcal{N}_{0,1}, \quad \text{and} \quad dW_t \sim \sqrt{\Delta_t} \mathcal{N}_{0,1}, \tag{8.85}$$

where the notation $A \sim B$ means that the two distributions A and B are equivalent, and $\mathcal{N}_{0,1}$ is a Gaussian random variable of zero mean and variance equal to one. We generate a sample of N values $\sim \mathcal{N}_{0,1}$ and call them Z_i, so that

$$dW_{t_i} \sim \sqrt{\Delta_t} Z_i. \tag{8.86}$$

Setting $r(t_i) = r_{t_i}$, equation (8.17) is discretized as

$$r(t_{i+1}) = r(t_i) + \kappa \left[\theta - r(t_i)\right] \Delta_t + \sigma \sqrt{r(t_i) \Delta_t} Z_i. \tag{8.87}$$

Given the initial value $r(t_0) = r_0$, the entire solution is reconstructed in steps. The procedure in equation (8.87) goes under the name of the Euler scheme. A major failure of the Euler scheme is that it cannot guarantee that the process r_t is always positive.

Of the various alternative schemes that have been proposed to mend this problem, [4] showed that the most suitable discretization for generating the process $CIR(\kappa, \sigma, \theta, r_0, t)$

is

$$r(t_{i+1}) = \left[\left(1 - \tfrac{1}{2}\kappa\Delta_t\right)\sqrt{r(t_i)} + \frac{\sigma\sqrt{\Delta_t}\,Z_i}{(2 - \kappa\Delta_t)} \right]^2 + \left(\kappa\theta - \frac{\sigma^2}{4}\right)\Delta_t, \qquad (8.88)$$

which provides a positive-definite process whenever the CIR condition in equation (8.19), $2\kappa\theta > \sigma^2$, is satisfied.

The same approach can be used to derive robust discretization for the forward risk-adjusted CIR process. A numerical implementation of the CIR process in this measure is (see [4]):

$$r(t_{i+1}) = \left[\left(1 - \tfrac{1}{2}\hat{\kappa}\Delta_t\right)\sqrt{r(t_i)} + \frac{\sigma\sqrt{\Delta_t}\,Z_i}{(2 - \hat{\kappa}\Delta_t)} \right]^2 + \left(\kappa\theta - \frac{\sigma^2}{4}\right)\Delta_t, \qquad (8.89)$$

where $\hat{\kappa} = \kappa + B(t, T)\sigma^2$.

We know that in the CIR++ model the short-rate r_t is modeled as a sum of a stochastic term x_t and a deterministic function ψ_t,

$$r_t = x_t + \psi_t. \qquad (8.90)$$

For the stochastic term, the same numerical procedures used for the CIR model can be employed. Instead, the deterministic function ψ_t can be modelled by a step function, with constant steps over some given time intervals. If the function is defined over the interval $[t, T]$, we introduce a set of times T_i, $i = \{0, \ldots, n\}$, with $T_0 = t$ and $T_n = T$, and we discretize the function $\psi_{T_i} = \psi_i$ with $i = \{1, \ldots, n\}$ so that ψ_i is constant over the corresponding step size $\tau_i = T_i - T_{i-1}$. An integral over $[t, T]$ is then approximated by

$$I(t, T) = \int_t^T \psi_u\, du \approx \sum_{i=1}^n \tau_i \psi_i. \qquad (8.91)$$

A little more care is needed if we wish to discretize an integral on the subinterval $[t_1, t_2]$, with $t < t_1 < t_2 < T$. In this case, we first need to find the integer n_1 for which $T_{n_1} < t_1 \le T_{n_1+1}$ and similarly the integer n_2 for which $T_{n_2} < t_2 \le T_{n_2+1}$. The integral is then discretized as

$$\int_{t_1}^{t_2} \psi_u\, du \approx \sum_{i=n_1+1}^{n_2+1} \tau_i' \psi_i \qquad (8.92)$$

where

$$\left. \begin{array}{l} \tau_{n_1+1}' = \displaystyle\sum_{i=1}^{n_1+1} \tau_i - t_1, \\[2mm] \tau_i' = \tau_i, \qquad \text{for } i \ne n_1 + 1 \text{ and } i \ne n_2 + 1, \\[2mm] \tau_{n_2+1}' = t_2 - \displaystyle\sum_{i=1}^{n_2} \tau_i. \end{array} \right\} \qquad (8.93)$$

8.3.8 Monte Carlo methods

Consider a contract with maturity T and payoff $H(r(T))$. The value at time t of this contract is

$$\mathbf{O}(t) = \mathbf{E}_t\left[e^{-\int_t^T r(s)\,ds} H(r(T))\right] = P^D(t, T)\, \mathbf{E}_t^T[H(r(T))], \tag{8.94}$$

where $\mathbf{E}_t$ is the expectation value in the risk-neutral measure, while $\mathbf{E}_t^T$ is the expectation value taken in the T-forward risk-adjusted measure (see Section 8.3.3). The discount factor $P^D(t, T)$ is obtained analytically, while the expected value of the payoff depends on the unknown value $r(T)$ of the short rate at maturity.

To compute the value of $\mathbf{E}_t^T[H(r_T)]$, we use the following Monte Carlo method. We generate p different paths of the discretized short rate, each path obtained by using the method in equation (8.89) for the forward risk-adjusted measure. In particular, for each path we obtain the value of the short rate at maturity and call it $r_j(T)$, with $j \in \{1, \dots, p\}$. The expectation value is approximated as

$$\mathbf{E}_t^T[H(r(T))] = \frac{1}{p} \sum_{j=1}^p H(r_j(T)), \tag{8.95}$$

so that the price of the contract is

$$\mathbf{O}_t \approx \frac{1}{p} P^D(t, T) \sum_{j=1}^p H(r_j(T)), \tag{8.96}$$

Pricing using a Monte Carlo method can be generalized to the case of path-dependent options. We consider the discretization of the short rate on the grid t_i, $\{i = 0, \dots, N\}$, with $t_0 = t$ and $t_N = T$, as discussed in Section 8.3.7. Defining

$$H(t_i) = H(r(t), \dots, r(t_i)), \tag{8.97}$$

the price of the path-dependent contract is

$$\mathbf{O}(t) = \sum_{i=1}^N \mathbf{E}_t\left[e^{-\int_t^{t_i} r(s)\,ds} H(t_i)\right] = P^D(t, T)\, \mathbf{E}_t^T\left[\frac{H(t_i)}{P^D(t_i, T)}\right]. \tag{8.98}$$

The expectation value is computed by considering p realizations of the short rate in the T-forward measure. For a given realization $j \in \{1, \dots, p\}$, the value of the short rate at the discretized time t_i is $r_j(t_i)$. Setting

$$H_j(t_i) = \frac{H(r_j(t), \dots, r_j(t_i))}{P^D(t_i, T)}, \tag{8.99}$$

the price of a path-dependent contract is

$$\mathbf{O}(t) \approx \frac{1}{p} P^D(t, T) \sum_{j=1}^p \sum_{i=1}^N H_j(t_i). \tag{8.100}$$

8.3.9   Libor market model

The Libor market model (LMM) [31] approaches the problem by using forward rates that are directly observable in the market, such as Libor or Euribor fixings. While these rates could basically be considered as risk free up until 2008, in current markets they are actually traded as rates referred to default-risky countrparties, since even major banks are subject to this risk.

These considerations imply that the LMM can no longer be used to model Libor (or Euribor) fixing rates, but it is more appropriate to model Eonia forward rates, applying then a spread on these to derive the value of fixing rates. Anyway, for the moment we disregard this complication and we present the LMM in its standard version.

In the LMM, the quantities that are modelled are a set of forward rates rather than the instantaneous short rate or instantaneous forward rates. Consider a set of maturities $\{T_i \mid i = 1, \ldots, N\}$ describing the reset dates for traded caps or floors on the market. By including the additional date $T_0 = t$, we define the time intervals $\tau_i = T_i - T_{i-1}$, $i = \{1, \ldots, N\}$ and the forward rates $L_i(t)$ observed at time t for the period $(T_{i-1}, T_i]$. In this model, the market has maturity $T_N = T$.

Here, for each date i, we model the Libor rate $L_i(t)$ by a stochastic process under its forward measure, over the period $[T_{i-1}, T_i]$. Assuming that the Libor rate $L_i(t)$ is a martingale under the T_i-forward measure, we have

$$dL_i(t) = \sigma_i(t)\, L_i(t)\, dW_{i,t}^{Q_{T_i}}, \qquad (8.101)$$

where $\sigma_i(t)$ is the volatility of $L_i(t)$ at time t, and $W_t^{Q_{T_i}}$ is an N-dimensional Brownian motion under the measure Q_{T_i}, with instantaneous covariance matrix ρ_t.

It is possible to link different T_i-forward measures with different values of i through a change of measure. As an example, we first consider the process for $L_i(t)$ in the T_1-forward measure. Denoting by $v_i(t)$ the volatility of the zero-coupon bond price $P^D(t, T_i)$ at time t, we find

$$dL_i(t) = \sigma_i(t)\, [v_1(t) - v_i(t)]L_i(t)\, dt + \sigma_i(t)\, L_i(t)\, dW_{i,t}^{Q_{T_1}}. \qquad (8.102)$$

Forward rate agreement and caps&floors

In a forward rate agreement (FRA), at the inception time t, counterparties fix the expiry date $S > t$ and the maturity of the contract $T > S$, to lock the interest rate over the period $[S, T]$. More specifically, at the maturity T, a payment with fixed interest rate K previously defined is exchanged in return for a floating payment based on the value of the Libor rate at time S, $L(S, T)$. At time S, the value of the contract on a unit notional value is then

$$V_S = (T - S)\,(K - L(S, T)). \qquad (8.103)$$

The value at time t of a FRA contract is

$$V_t = (T - S)\, P^D(t, T)\, \mathbf{E}_t^T\left[(L(S, T) - K)^+\right], \qquad (8.104)$$

where the expectation value is taken in the T-forward measure, denoted by $\mathbf{E}_t^T$. It should be noted that the discount bond $P^D(t, T)$ is taken from a curve different from the Libor (or Euribor) one. This numeraire bond is calculated out of a risk-free interest rate curve: in the current financial environment the best approximation to a risk-free rate is considered the OIS (or Eonia) rate, so that $P^D(t, T)$ is in practice derived from the OIS (or Eonia) swap prices quoted in the market.

A forward rate agreed at time t is defined as the fixed rate to be exchanged at time T for the Libor rate $L(S, T)$ so that the contract has zero value at time t. We denote the value of the forward rate as

$$\text{FRA}(t, S, T) = \mathbf{E}_t^T[L(S, T)]. \tag{8.105}$$

When the Libor curve $L(S, T)$ corresponds to the risk-free discount curve, we have an equality between the FRA rate and the forward rate computed out of the curve:

$$\text{FRA}(t, S, T) = F(t, S, T) = \left(\frac{P(t, S)}{P(t, T)} - 1 \right) \frac{1}{T - S}. \tag{8.106}$$

where $P(t, \cdot)$ are zero-coupon bonds extracted by Libor fixing curves. However, as mentioned above, this has no longer been the case since 2008, and Libor curves are treated independently of the discount (OIS or Eonia) curves, see the discussion above.

Caps and floors are options of forward rates. We consider the set of payment dates $\{T_i | i = 1, \ldots, N\}$ and corresponding periods $\tau_i = T_i - T_{i-1}$, with $i = 1, \ldots, N$, as discussed before, and we set $T_0 = S$.

An interest rate cap is a contract in which the buyer receives a flow of payments at the end of each period in which the interest rate has exceeded an agreed strike price K. The price at time t of a cap option can be viewed as the sum of individual caplets,

$$\text{Cap}(t, T) = N \sum_{i=1}^{N} \text{Cpl}_i(t, T_{i-1}, T_i). \tag{8.107}$$

At each time T_i, the option pays off the difference between the Libor rate and the strike X. Each caplet has a payoff

$$H_i = \tau_i \left(L(T_{i-1}, T_i) - X \right)^+, \tag{8.108}$$

When the expectation value is taken in the T_i-forward measure, denoted by $\mathbf{E}_t^{T_i}$, we find

$$\text{Cpl}_i(t, T_{i-1}, T_i) = \tau_i P^D(t, T_i) \mathbf{E}_t^{T_i}[(L(T_{i-1}, T_i) - X)^+], \tag{8.109}$$

The pricing of floor options relies on similar techniques to those used for pricing caps. A floor is a contract in which the buyer receives payments whenever the interest rate falls below a strike price X. Decomposing the floor option as a sum of floorlets,

$$\text{Floor}(t, T) = N \sum_{i=1}^{n} \text{Fll}_i(t, T_{i-1}, T_i), \tag{8.110}$$

where each floorlet has the value in the T_i-forward measure of

$$\text{Fll}_i(t, T_{i-1}, T_i) = \tau_i P^D(t, T_i) \mathbf{E}_t^{T_i}[(X - L(T_{i-1}, T_i))^+]. \tag{8.111}$$

The price of cap and floor options can be given in a closed-form formula using Black's formula [23], assuming that forward rates are lognormally distributed under the risk-neutral measure. The price of the cap option is

$$\text{Cap}(t, T) = N \sum_{i=1}^{n} P^D(t, T_i) \tau_i \, \text{BlSc}(F(t, T_{i-1}, T_i), X, \hat{\sigma}_i), \tag{8.112}$$

where

$$\hat{\sigma}_i = \sqrt{\int_t^{T_i} \sigma_i^2(s)\, ds}, \quad \text{for } i = \{1, \ldots, n\}, \tag{8.113}$$

and the function $\mathrm{BlSc}(F, K, \Sigma)$ is as defined in Section 8.2. The value of $\hat{\sigma}_i$ is retrieved from the market quote $\sigma_{\mathrm{MKT},i}$ for each i, as

$$\sigma_{\mathrm{MKT},i}^2 = \frac{\hat{\sigma}_i^2}{T_i - t} = \frac{1}{T_i - t} \int_t^{T_i} \sigma_i^2(s)\, ds, \tag{8.114}$$

and determines the price of the caplet through equation (8.112).

Swaps and swaptions

An interest rate swap (IRS) is a contract in which two parties agree to exchange one stream of cash flows against another stream. In a fixed-for-floating IRS, one party agrees to exchange a payment stream at a fixed interest rate K (the fixed leg of the contract) with a counterparty who in turn agrees to pay a flow of floating amounts (the floating leg).

In the following, we consider the term structure of payments for the floating leg given by the set $\{T_i \,|\, i = 1, \ldots, n\}$ defined above, together with the set $\{T_j^S\}, j = 1, \ldots, n^S$, for the payment stream of the fixed leg of the contract. We define the time interval

$$\tau_j^S = T_j^S - T_{j-1}^S \tag{8.115}$$

and

$$\tau_i = T_i - T_{i-1} \tag{8.116}$$

for the floating leg. Usually, the floating rate is fixed at the beginning of each period and both payments are due at the end of the period.

At time T_i, the floating leg pays the Libor rate $L_i(T_{i-1})$, where we set

$$L_i(t) = \mathrm{FRA}(t, T_{i-1}, T_i), \tag{8.117}$$

while the fixed leg pays a fixed rate. The value of the swap contract at time t is

$$V(t) = \sum_{i=1}^n \tau_i\, P^D(t, T_i)\, L_i(t) - K \sum_{j=1}^{n^S} \tau_j^S\, P^D(t, T_j^S). \tag{8.118}$$

The forward rate swap $S_{1,n}(t)$ is the unique fixed rate for which the two payment flows from the floating and the fixed legs in equation (8.118) coincide,

$$S_{1,n}(t) = \frac{\sum_{i=1}^n \tau_i\, P^D(t, T_i)\, L_i(t)}{\sum_{j=1}^{n^S} \tau_j^S\, P^D(t, T_j^S)}. \tag{8.119}$$

Defining the weights

$$\omega_i(t) = \frac{\tau_i\, P^D(t, T_i)}{\sum_{j=1}^{n^S} \tau_j^S\, P^D(t, T_j^S)}, \tag{8.120}$$

the price of the swap in equation (8.119) is written as a linear combination of Libor rates,

$$S_{1,n}(t) = \sum_{i=1}^{n} w_i(t) L_i(t).$$ (8.121)

A European payer swaption is an option on interest rates swaps giving the right to enter an interest rate swap contract at a future time T_e, when the fixed rate is K. In contrast, a receiver option gives the right to enter a receiver swap at time S. The payer swaption payoff at time S is

$$H^e = \left(S_{e,n}(T_e) - K\right)^+ C(T_e),$$ (8.122)

where we have defined the annuity

$$C(t) = \sum_{j=1}^{n^S} \tau_j^S P^D(t, T_j^S).$$ (8.123)

Using equation (8.119), we rewrite the swaption payoff as

$$H^e = \left(\sum_{i=e}^{n} \tau_i P^D(T_e, T_i) L_i(T_e) - K C(T_e)\right)^+.$$ (8.124)

Contrary to the cap option case, a swaption payoff cannot be decomposed into a sum of options on each period τ_i. Moreover, in [35] it is shown that the price of a swaption depends not only on the evolution of each Libor rate, but also on their joint behaviour.

To price the payoff in equation (8.124), we consider the measure Q_C in which the annuity is the numeraire. In this measure, the formula for the price of a swaption of expiry S and maturity T is (see [89])

$$\text{Swpt}(t, T) = \sum_{j=e}^{n^S} \tau_j^S P^D(t, T_j^S) \, \mathbf{E}_t^{Q_C}\left[S_{e,n}(T_e) - K\right]^+.$$ (8.125)

A closed-form formula is in theory unavailable. In practice, one may resort to the assumption of a lognormal distribution for the forward swap rate and thus obtain a pricing formula for payer swaptions of the type:

$$\text{Swpt}(t, T_e, T_n, S_{e,n}(t), K, \sigma_{e,n}, 1) = \sum_{j=e}^{n^S} \tau_j^S P^D(t, T_j^S) \, \text{Bl Sc}(S_{e,n}(T_e), K, \sigma_{e,n})$$ (8.126)

For a corresponding receiver swaption $\text{Swpt}(t, T_e, T_n, S_{e,n}(t), K, \sigma_{e,n}, -1)$ we can resort to put–call parity.

Modelling the Libor rate with a spread over the forward rate

As already anticipated above, after the 2008 crisis, a spread $S_i(t)$ at time t between the risk-free rate (approximated by the OIS or Eonia rate) and the Libor or Euribor fixing rate is experienced in the market,

$$S_i(t) = F_i(t) - L_i(t),$$ (8.127)

where $F_i(t) = F(t, T_{i-1}, T_i)$ is the Libor (or Euribor) forward (FRA) rate and

$F_i(t) = F(t, T_{i-1}, T_i)$ is the risk-free OIS (or Eonia) forward rate. In general, we can decide to model using two stochastic processes two variables from $S_i(t)$, $F_i(t)$ and $L_i(t)$, leaving the third determined by equation (8.127).

For swap rates, we use the fact that the swap $s(t)$ is written in equation (8.121) as a linear combination of Libor foward rates. Writing the Libor rate as a sum of the forward rate plus a spread as in equation (8.127), we obtain

$$S_{1,n}(t) = \bar{F}(t) + \bar{S}(t), \tag{8.128}$$

where we defined the processes

$$\bar{F}(t) = \sum_{i=1}^{n} w_i(t) \, F_i(t), \quad \text{and} \quad \bar{S}(t) = \sum_{i=1}^{n} w_i(t) \, S_i(t). \tag{8.129}$$

In particular, $\bar{F}(t)$ is a martingale under the measure Q_C. Following [89] and [68], the process $\bar{F}(t)$ can be treated, under generic assumptions, as a driftless process. In contrast, the pricing of the spread part $\bar{S}(t)$ needs an additional assumption, since it depends on both the collection of spread rates $S_i(t)$ and on discount factors as a result of weights $w_i(t)$. For this, we approximate the process as

$$\bar{S}(t) \approx \sum_{i=1}^{n} w_i(t_0) \, S_i(t), \tag{8.130}$$

where we replaced the time dependence on the weight with the value at t_0. With this approximation, $\bar{S}(t)$ is a martingale under Q_C and can be described, analogously to $\bar{F}(t)$, by a driftless process.

8.4 DEFAULT PROBABILITIES AND CREDIT SPREADS

In the credit risk literature, two different approaches to evaluating the probability of default have been developed; namely, the structural model and the reduced model. In a structural approach, the performance of the firm is governed by structural variables like the asset or the debt value, and a default is the result of poor operations of the firm. In reduced (or statistical) approach, the default intensity is modelled by a stochastic process, which might include jumps in the intensity of default λ_t.

The structural model and the reduced model are also referred to as endogenous and exogenous approaches, respectively, because in structural models the time of default is determined through the value of the firm, while in reduced models it is the jump of a stochastic process that determines bankruptcy.

We will mainly use reduced models, but we also quickly review structural models.

8.4.1 Structural models

In structural approaches, we model the structural variables of a firm (i.e., the assets and the debt value) using a stochastic or a deterministic process, in order to determine the time of default. Earlier literature on the subject includes [25], [91] and [24]. For example, in Merton's model, a firm defaults if its assets are below its debt when servicing the debt. In the Black and Cox model, a default occurs when the value V of the firm reaches a default boundary K.

Merton formula

Merton [91] proposed a model in which the firm value is treated as an option on the asset V. Suppose for simplicity that, at time t, the firm issues a bond with maturity T. We define the variables and parameters in Merton's model as in Table 8.1.

Table 8.1. Variables and parameters in Merton model

V_t	Firm asset at time t
V_T	Firm asset at time T
E_t	Firm equity at time t
E_T	Firm equity at time T
B_t	Value of the bond at time t
D	Debt repayment due at time t
σ_V	Volatility of the asset

In the Merton model, the firm is financed through a single bond paying no coupons and a single equity issue. At any intermediate time $t < s < T$, the asset of the firm is

$$V_s = E_s + B_s. \tag{8.131}$$

We assume that the asset follows the geometric Brownian motion described in Section 8.2,

$$dV_t = V_t \mu \, dt + V_t \sigma_V \, dW_t, \tag{8.132}$$

where μ is the instantaneous expected rate of return, and W_t is a Brownian motion.

At time T, the firm repays its debt D. When $V_T < D$, the firm defaults, and the value of the equity is zero. Conversely, if $V_T > D$, the firm repays the debt and the equity has value $E_T = V_T - D$. At time T, the value of the equity is then

$$E_T = (V_T - D)^+, \tag{8.133}$$

which resembles the payoff of a call option of the firm's asset V_t with strike price D. Using the Black–Scholes formula, we find the value of the equity at time t as

$$E_t = V_t N(d_1) - D e^{-r(T-t)} N(d_2), \tag{8.134}$$

where r is the risk-free rate, $N(x)$ is the cumulative probability distribution function for a normal distribution, and

$$d_1 = \frac{\ln V_t/D + (\mu + \sigma_V^2/2)(T-t)}{\sigma_V \sqrt{T-t}}, \quad \text{and} \quad d_2 = d_1 - \sigma_V \sqrt{T-t}. \tag{8.135}$$

Setting $\Sigma_V = \sigma_V \sqrt{T-t}$ and using the notation in Section 8.2, we have

$$E_t = e^{-r(T-t)} \, \text{BlSc}(V_T, D, \Sigma_V). \tag{8.136}$$

Although the structural approach is theoretically fascinating, it is hard to be satisfactorily calibrated to all available market data. The reduced-form approach we will sketch below is much more flexible, even if less linked to the microeconomic factors triggering the default event.

8.4.2 Reduced models

In a reduced-form approach, the event of default is modelled via an intensity of default λ. In this perspective, default intensities are modelled similarly to default-free interest rates, allowing us to use the same results and formulae previously described. In fact, it can be proved (see [62]) that, remarkably, defaultable bonds can be priced by adjusting the discount rate: this effective rate is the sum of the risk-free rate r_t and the intensity of default λ_t, and both components can be treated with the mathematical tools we have shown before.

Given that the firm has not defaulted up to time t, the time of default τ is defined as the probability of a default occurring in the next instant dt,

$$\text{PD}(t, t+dt) = \text{Prob}(\tau \in [t, t+dt]|\tau > t) = \lambda_t\, dt. \tag{8.137}$$

The intensity of default can be modelled differently as a

- constant (τ is the first jump of a time-homogeneous Poisson process);
- deterministic function (τ is the first jump of a time-inhomogeneous Poisson process);
- stochastic function (τ is the first jump of a Cox process).

In particular, the second and third approaches can be used to model the term structure of credit spreads, and the third approach can be used to model credit spread volatilities.

The probability that the firm survives to time T, given we are at time t, equates

$$\text{SP}(t, T) = \mathbf{E}_t\left[\exp\left(-\int_t^T \lambda_s\, ds\right)\right]. \tag{8.138}$$

This definition is consistent with the expression in equation (8.137), by setting

$$\text{PD}(t, T) = 1 - \text{SP}(t, T). \tag{8.139}$$

In fact, equation (8.137) can be proved using the definitions in equations (8.138) and (8.139).

Modelling default intensities with a CIR process

We model the intensity of default by a CIR process

$$d\lambda_t = \kappa\,(\theta - \lambda_t)dt + \sigma\sqrt{\lambda_t}\,dW_t, \tag{8.140}$$

where we impose the additional constraint on the parameters $2\kappa\theta > \sigma^2$ in order to ensure positiveness of the process.[8] At time t, the probability that the firm has not defaulted up to time T is given by equation (8.138) which, in the CIR model, can be written in the form of equation (8.27)

$$\text{SP}(t, T) = A(t, T)\, e^{-B(t,T)\,r_t}, \tag{8.141}$$

with the factors $A(t, T)$ and $B(t, T)$ as defined in equation (8.28). The corresponding probability of default is $\text{PD}(t, T) = 1 - \text{SP}(t, T)$.

We can also suppose that the intensity of default is a CIR++ process, with the dynamics and the formula for the SP modified accordingly as described in Section 8.3.4.

---

[8] For the default intensity process we further assume that the market risk parameter is equal to zero, so that risk-neutral and real measure drifts are the same.

Multiple defaults of correlated firms

For multiple issuers, we can assume that each default intensity process is the sum of an idiosyncratic component plus a common intensity of default. In this model, the default of the i-th issuer can be triggered by either the i-th idiosyncratic component or by the common component. Both the idiosyncratic and the common parts are described by independent CIR processes

$$\lambda_{t,i}^I = \mathrm{CIR}(\kappa_i^I, \sigma_i^I, \theta_i^I, \lambda_{0i}^I, t), \quad \text{with} \quad i \in \{1, ..., m\}, \tag{8.142}$$

where m is the total number of firms, and

$$\lambda_t^C = \mathrm{CIR}(\kappa^C, \sigma^C, \theta^C, \lambda_0^C, t). \tag{8.143}$$

The CIR process for the i-th firm is

$$\lambda_{t,i} = \lambda_{t,i}^I + p_i \lambda_t^C, \tag{8.144}$$

where $p_i \in [0, 1]$ operates as a correlation of the i-th issuer with the probability of a common default: this approach to modelling is termed "affine correlation".

The intensity is decomposed into an idiosyncratic term $\lambda_{i,t}^I$ and a common intensity of default λ_t^C. The idiosyncratic term is related to the probability that the default of the i-th issuer occurs independently of all other firms, while the process λ_t^C accounts for the probability that all firms default simultaneously. A common default affects the i-th issuer with a probability p_i.

The sum of the two CIR processes in equation (8.144) does not automatically imply that $\lambda_{t,i}$ is a CIR process. To find the constraints on the parameters, we first use the results in Section 8.3.3, to write the common process of default as

$$p_i \lambda_t^C = \mathrm{CIR}(\kappa^C, \sqrt{p_i}\, \sigma^C, p_i \theta^C, p_i \lambda_0^C, t), \tag{8.145}$$

and (again from Section 8.3.3) the sum of the two CIR processes $\lambda_{t,i}^I$ and $p_i \lambda_t^C$ is a CIR process $\lambda_{t,i}$ if we impose the constraints in equation (8.51),

$$\left. \begin{array}{c} \kappa_i^I = \kappa^C = \kappa, \\[4pt] \sigma_i^I = \sqrt{p_i}\,\sigma^C = \sigma_i, \\[4pt] \theta_i^I + p_i \theta^C = \theta_i, \\[4pt] \lambda_{0i}^I + p_i \lambda_0^C = \lambda_{0i}. \end{array} \right\} \tag{8.146}$$

For the correlated default intensities considered, the constraint in equation (8.19) reads

$$2\kappa \left(\theta_i^I + p_i \theta^C\right) > p_i (\sigma^C)^2, \quad \text{for } i = 1, \ldots, m. \tag{8.147}$$

Likewise, the intensity process can follow the CIR++ process in equation (8.67). The deterministic part of $\lambda_{i,t}$ is a function $\phi_{i,t}$, and we have

$$\lambda_{i,t} = \lambda_{i,t}^I + p_i \lambda_t^C + \phi_{i,t}, \tag{8.148}$$

8.4.3   Credit spreads

In Chapter 7 we quickly sketched how to set a fair credit spread for a loan contract, given the counterparty's probability of default and the loss given default. In this section we will try to show in more depth how to model credit spreads.

The modelling of credit spreads critically depends on assumptions made about recovery from the borrower's default: recovery is just complementary to loss given default. Let us assume that the loan has a face value of 1 which the borrower has to repay at expiry T, with (simply compounded) interest $(r + s) \times T$, where r is the risk-free rate and s is the credit spread. The default can occur at any time between the evaluation time $t = 0$ and the expiry $t = T$, but is only observed by the lender at expiry when the repayment should be made.

There are different possible choices for recovery, two of which are most relevant for practical purposes:

- Recovery of market value (RMV): upon the borrower's default, the lender recovers a fraction $R = 1 - L_{GD}$ of the market value of the loan. This means that the expected value V_T at expiry (i.e., $(1 + (r + s)T)$) is:

$$\mathrm{E}[V_T] = (1 + (r + s)T) \times (1 - \mathrm{PD}(0, T)) + (1 + (r + s)T)R \times \mathrm{PD}(0, T) \quad (8.149)$$

At time 0, the expected value is:

$$V_0 = \mathrm{E}\left[\frac{1}{1 + rT} V_T\right]$$

$$= [(1 + (r + s)T) \times (1 - \mathrm{PD}(0, T)) + (1 + (r + s)T)R \times \mathrm{PD}(0, T)]\frac{1}{1 + rT}$$

$$= (1 + \frac{sT}{1 + rT}) \times (1 - \mathrm{PD}(0, T)) + (1 + \frac{sT}{1 + rT})R \times (0, T) \quad (8.150)$$

Since the face value of the loan is 1 which is also the fair value it should have at inception when the amount is lent to the borrower ($V_0 = 1$), from equation (8.150) we have:

$$s = \frac{L_{GD}\mathrm{PD}(0, T)(1 + rT)}{1 - L_{GD}\mathrm{PD}(0, T)}\frac{1}{T}$$

Setting $L_{GD}{}^1 = L_{GD}(1 + rT)$,   recalling   that $\mathrm{PD}(0, T) = 1 - \mathrm{SP}(0, T) =$
$1 - E[e^{-\int_0^c \lambda_s ds}]$, and using the approximation $e^c = 1 + c$ for small c, after a few manipulations we obtain:

$$s = \frac{1 - P(L_{GD}{}^1\lambda_t; 0, T)}{P(L_{GD}{}^1\lambda_t; 0, T)}\frac{1}{T} \quad (8.151)$$

where $P(L_{GD}{}^1\lambda_t; 0, T)$ is the price of a zero-coupon bond expiring in T and with a discounting rate equal to $L_{GD}{}^1\lambda_t$. If λ_t follows a CIR model, it is possible to use formula (8.27) for a modified CIR process as shown in equation (8.54).

- Recovery of face value (RFV): upon the borrower's default, the lender recovers a fraction $R = 1 - L_{GD}$ of the face value (in our case, 1) of the loan. The expected value

V_T is:

$$E[V_T] = (1 + (r+s)T) \times (1 - PD(0, T)) + 1 \times R \times PD(0, T) \qquad (8.152)$$

At time 0, the expected value is:

$$V_0 = E\left[\frac{1}{1 + rT} V_T\right]$$

$$= [(1 + (r+s)T) \times (1 - PD(0, T)) + R \times PD(0, T)]\frac{1}{1 + rT}$$

$$= (1 + \frac{sT}{1 + rT}) \times (1 - PD(0, T)) + \frac{R}{1 + rT} \times PD(0, T) \qquad (8.153)$$

Furthermore in this case, since $V_0 = 1$, after a few manipulations we get:

$$s = \frac{PD(0, T)[(1 + rT) - R]}{1 - PD(0, T)}\frac{1}{T} = \frac{PD(0, T)(L_{GD} + rT)}{1 - (0, T)}\frac{1}{T}$$

Setting $L_{GD}^2 = L_{GD} + rT$, we can write the spread as

$$s = \frac{1 - P(L_{GD}^2\lambda_t; 0, T)}{P(\lambda_t; 0, T)}\frac{1}{T} \qquad (8.154)$$

For loans with a short maturity and for a counterparty with a reasonably low PD (say, 3%), the denominator of both equations (8.151) and (8.154) can be set approximately equal to 1. Moreover, it is also easy to check that for small rT, $L_{GD}^1 \approx L_{GD}^2$, so that for short-term loans, such as deposits in the interbank market, the two assumptions produce very similar spreads.

In conclusion, the credit spread between time t and T can be written as:

$$s(t, T) = E[L_{GD}PD(t, T)] \approx 1 - E\left[e^{-\int_t^T L_{GD}\lambda_s ds}\right] \qquad (8.155)$$

Equation (8.155) is a good approximation for both assumptions regarding recovery.

8.5 EXPECTED AND MINIMUM LIQUIDITY GENERATION CAPACITY OF AVAILABLE BONDS

Liquid assets are used to generate BSL and they can be considered as a component of the liquidity buffer, as seen in Chapter 7. We introduced the TSAA in Chapter 6 and showed how it is built and its connection with the TSLGC. We have left the problem of how to determine the future expected value of the assets, the unexpected minimum (stressed) values and the haircuts that can be applied unsolved. All this information is useful to the LGC because it is affected by the actual price of the assets on the balance sheet that can be used to extract liquidity and to match negative TSECCF.

In what follows we show how to monitor the LGC of one bond's holding and of a bond portfolio. Other assets, such as stocks, are less important as far as the LGC is concerned and they also require less sophisticated modelling. The main tool to monitor the LGC related to bonds is to build a term structure of minimum liquidity that can be generated at future dates within a chosen period at a given confidence level (e.g., 99%).

To build a term structure, we take the following steps:

1. Divide the chosen period into a number of M subperiods;
2. At the end of each subperiod t_m compute the minimum value of the bond's holding or of the portfolio of bonds;
3. Include the haircut either according to the approach outlined above or according to some predefined rules (e.g., ECB haircuts).

The building blocks we need to price the bonds and to compute the expected value and the stressed levels at future dates are:

- An interest rate model—we opt for the CIR++.
- A default model for multiple issuers—we opt for a reduced-form approach, with the default intensities depending on idiosyncratic and common factors (to account for the correlation between defaults and credit spreads). All intensities have CIR dynamics and a deterministic time function is added.
- A model for haircuts.
- A parameter to account for the specialness of single bonds.

8.5.1   Value of the position in a defaultable coupon bond

A defaultable coupon bond is a bond issued by an agent m that can default at some date in the future. Consider a bond held by the bank with the following characteristics:

- notional amount N;
- annual coupon rate c;
- coupon calendar $\{t_i\}$, with coupon periods $\tau_i = t_i - t_{i-1}$;
- maturity T;
- loss-given-default rate L_{GD}.

The value of the position in the bond with the specifics above is acquired at time t. We define the accrued time as the time between the last coupon payment and the acquisition,

$$T_{\text{accr}} = t - \max(t_i : t_i \le t). \tag{8.156}$$

The price of the coupon bond is

$$\mathbf{B}(t, T) = N\, P^{D\,\ell}(t, T)\, \text{SP}_m(t, T) + N \sum_{i:t_i > t} c\, \tau_i\, P^{D\,\ell}(t, t_i)\, \text{SP}_m(t, t_i)$$

$$+ N\,(1 - L_{GD}) \sum_{i:t_i > t} P^{D\,\ell}(t, t_i) \left[\text{SP}_m(t, t_{i-1}) - \text{SP}_m(t, t_i) \right] - N\, c\, T_{\text{accr}}. \tag{8.157}$$

In the first line we have the sum of all coupon flows, discounted by the risk-free discount factors over the period $[t, t_i]$. The third term accounts for the recovery paid in case of default, while the last term subtracts the accrual amount, which is the amount paid from the last coupon date to the time of acquisition. Obviously, setting $N = 100$ we get the market price of the bond.

We assume that the short rate follows CIR++ dynamics as in equation (8.66), so the function $P^{D\,\ell}(t, t_i)$ is given by the formula:

$$P^{D\,\ell}(t, t_i) = e^{-\ell(T - s)} P^D(t, t_i)$$

where ℓ is a bond-specific parameter to capture liquidity specialness and $P^{D\ell}(t, t_i)$ is defined in equation (8.27).

8.5.2 Expected value of the position in a coupon bond

The expected value of the bank's position in a coupon bond can be easily computed, since it is the future price calculated according to the model we use for interest rates.[9] We are interested in also computing the expected value net of the haircut, so we write the expected value of the position in a coupon bond as

$$\mathrm{CH}^{\mathcal{H}}(t, s, T) = [1 - \mathcal{H}_t(s)]\,\mathrm{CH}(t, s, T),\tag{8.158}$$

where $H_t(s)$ is the expected haircut at time s, see equation (8.166), while the future without including the haircut is

$$\mathrm{CH}(t, s, T) = N\,\mathbf{H}^\ell(r; t, s, T)\,\mathbf{H}(\lambda; t, s, T) + N\,c\sum_{i:t_i > s}(t_i - t_{i-1})\,\mathbf{H}^\ell(r; t, s, t_i)\,\mathbf{H}(\lambda_t; t, s, t_i)$$

$$+ N\,(1 - \mathrm{L_{GD}})\sum_{i:t_i > s}\mathbf{H}^\ell(r; t, s, t_i)\left[\mathbf{H}(\lambda_t; t, s, t_{i-1}) - \mathbf{H}(\lambda_t; t, s, t_i)\right] - N\,c\,T_{\mathrm{accr}},$$

$$\tag{8.159}$$

and

$$T_{\mathrm{accr}} = s - \max(t_l : t_l \le s).\tag{8.160}$$

In this case $\mathbf{H}^\ell(r; t, s, T)$ is also given by the formula:

$$\mathbf{H}^\ell(r; t, s, T) = e^{-\ell(T-s)}\mathbf{H}_{\mathrm{CIR}++}(r; t, s, T)$$

where ℓ is the bond-specific parameter to capture liquidity specialness and $\mathbf{H}_{\mathrm{CIR}++}(r; t, s, T)$ is defined in equation (8.72).

Equations (8.158) and (8.159) do not consider the possibility of default of the bond's issue between t and s. If the issuer goes bankrupt, the bank will not have a bond worth $\mathrm{CH}(t, s, T)$ but $\mathrm{CH}(t, s, T) - \mathrm{L_{GD}}$, where $\mathrm{L_{GD}}$ is the amount lost given the default. If we introduce the assumption the $\mathrm{L_{GD}} = x\%N$, or a constant fraction of the par value of the bond, times the notional amount, then it is easy to consider the loss potentially suffered as well since in this case the expected value at time s would be:

$$\mathrm{CH}^{DI}(t, s, T) = \mathrm{CH}(t, s, T) - \mathrm{L_{GD}}\mathrm{PD}(t, s)$$

or, put into words, the expected value including the default event $\mathrm{CH}^{DI}(t, s, T)$ is equal to the corresponding expected value without considering the default $\mathrm{CH}(t, s, T)$ minus the expected loss on default $\mathrm{L_{GD}}\mathrm{PD}(t, s)$.

The SP and the PD are modelled by a reduced-form approach where the default intensity of the n-th issuer is λ_t follows a CIR++ process too, so that formula (8.66) can also be used in this case:

$$\mathbf{E}_t[\mathrm{SP}_m(s, T)] = \mathbf{H}_{\mathrm{CIR}++}(\lambda_t; t, s, T)$$

When a portfolio of bonds is considered, then the intensities of default are defined as in

---

[9] Under the assumption that the the market risk parameter is zero, the future price formula can also be used to calculate the expected price in the real measure, provided that we use a volatility parameter estimated from the historical time series and not implied from quoted caps, floors or swaptions.

equation (8.148), where an idiosyncratic and common intensity and a deterministic time function ϕ_t appear.

We would like to stress the fact that for some issuers (typically sovereign) the PD can be zero and the bonds issued by them may even incorporate a liquidity discount (i.e., $\ell \leq 0$), so that their yield could even end up being lower than a corresponding risk-free bond.

8.5.3 Haircut modelling

At the present time t, the value $H(t)$ of the haircut to be applied to the bond's market value is typically a function of the probability of default PD of the issuer. This can be inferred from the bond's price or from the rating the bond's issuer has.

An approach based on the maturity T and credit rating has also been adopted by the ECB.[10] For a given maturity, the bond can be Step 1 and 2 if the harmonized rating is between AAA to A$-$, so that it has a haircut depending on the maturity and the category H_1; otherwise, the bond can be Step 3 if the rating is between BBB+ and BBB$-$, with a haircut H_2; finally, the bond can be out of the eligible set that is accepted by the ECB as collateral and implicitly has a haircut $H_3 = 100\%$, since no liquidity can be extracted from it by a repo transaction with the central bank.

A similar approach can be followed when simulating the haircut of a bond, since in the end a bond can always be pledged in a collateralized loan with the ECB. For the haircut to be applied at a future time s, we model $H(s)$ with a three-step function. Given two levels of the survival probability in the next period (say, 1 year) K_1 and $K_2 < K_1$, the bond at time s is Step 1 and 2 (first quality according to the ECB's classification) if its default probability is below $1 - K_1$; it is Step 3 if its default probability is between $1 - K_1$ and $1 - K_2$; finally, it is considered ineligible if its default probability is higher than $1 - K_2$.

We adopt a reduced-form approach to model the default probability of the issuer, and we assume that the default intensity follows a CIR process as in equation (8.140), using equations (8.139) and (8.141):

$$\lambda_t = \phi_t + \lambda_t^D$$

where ϕ_t is a deterministic function and the CIR stochastic function is defined as

$$\lambda_t^D = \mathrm{CIR}(\kappa, \sigma, \theta, \lambda_0^D, t).$$

We can derive the probability that the bond falls in the first, second or third of the groups described above. In particular, the probability at time t that the bond at time s falls in the first (Step 1 and 2) group is

$$p_1(t) = \chi^2 \left(2(\eta + \zeta) \lambda_1^D, \frac{4\kappa\theta}{\sigma^2}, \frac{2\eta^2 e^{\gamma(s-t)} \lambda_t^D}{\eta + \zeta} \right) \tag{8.161}$$

where, $\gamma = \sqrt{\kappa^2 + 2\sigma^2}$. We define the parameters

$$\eta = \frac{2\gamma}{\sigma^2(e^{\gamma(s-t)} - 1)}, \quad \text{and} \quad \zeta = \frac{\kappa + \gamma}{\sigma^2}, \tag{8.162}$$

---

[10] See the ECB's guidelines on liquidity policy [17].

and, by making the trigger K_1 equal to the discount factor on $[s, s + T_{\text{Hor}}]$ computed from the CIR++ intensity λ_t, we find

$$\lambda_1^D = \frac{1}{B(s, s + T_{\text{Hor}})} \left[\ln \frac{A(s, s + T_{\text{Hor}})}{K_1} - \int_s^{s+T_{\text{Hor}}} \phi_s \, ds \right] \tag{8.163}$$

where T_{Hor} sets the default time horizon from the time at which we compute the haircut. We can set $T_{\text{Hor}} = 1$ year, for example, or we can link the function to a longer term PD by setting $T_{\text{Hor}} = 5$ years.

Similarly, the probability that the PD at time s is between $1 - K_1$ and $1 - K_2$ is

$$p_2(t) = \chi^2 \left(2(\eta + \zeta) \lambda_2^D, \frac{4\kappa\theta}{\sigma^2}, \frac{2\eta^2 \, e^{\gamma(s-t)} \, \lambda_t^D}{\eta + \zeta} \right) - p_1(t), \tag{8.164}$$

with

$$\lambda_2^D = \frac{1}{B(s, s + T_{\text{Hor}})} \left[\ln \frac{A(s, s + T_{\text{Hor}})}{K_2} - \int_s^{s+T_{\text{Hor}}} \phi_s \, ds \right]. \tag{8.165}$$

Finally, the probability that the PD lies above $1 - K_2$ is $p_3(t) = 1 - p_1(t) - p_2(t)$.

The expected haircut at time s is then

$$\mathcal{H}_t(s) = p_1(t) \, H_1 + p_2(t) \, H_2 + p_3(t) \, H_3. \tag{8.166}$$

Since we presented a model for stochastic default intensities in Section 8.4, we can use it to model stochastic haircuts evolving in the future according to changes in the issuer's PD.

8.5.4   Future value of a bond portfolio

We are able to calculate the expected value of a bond's position at future dates; it is not a major problem to compute the expected value of a portfolio of bonds as well, since it is the sum of the single expected values. We are interested in finding a way to determine which is a stressed minimum level that the bond, or the portfolio of bonds, can reach at different dates in the future at a defined confidence level, say, 99%. In this case the correlation between issuers plays a major role in reducing the distance between the expected and the stress level, or the unexpected variation of the bond or portfolio of bonds.

8.5.5   Calculating the quantile: a $\Delta - \Gamma$ approximation of the portfolio

We consider a portfolio comprising N_B bonds and issued by N_f issuers. For each issuer i, there are N_i bonds in the bank's portfolio; each bond's position has value $\mathbf{B}^i(t, T_j)$ and expected $\text{CH}^i(t, s, T_j)$, $1 \leq j \leq N_i$. For numerical reasons, if a liquidity discount for the i-th bond exists (i.e., $\ell \leq 0$), then the corresponding value of the process $\lambda_{i,t}$ for the i-th issuer is theoretically zero, although we set it to 1e-10, and so is the value of the function ϕ_t.

Defining the vector of intensities[11]

$$Y_t = (r_t, \lambda_{1,t}, \ldots, \lambda_{N_f,t})^{\text{T}}, \tag{8.167}$$

---

[11] The model we present is based on [60]. We refer to it for technical details.

the expected value of the position for all bonds at time s is

$$V(Y_t) = \sum_{i=1}^{N_f} \sum_{j=1}^{N_i} \mathrm{CH}^i(t, s, T_j). \tag{8.168}$$

We perform a $\Delta - \Gamma$ approximation of the value of the portfolio at time s, around the value Y_s, as

$$V(Y_s) \approx V(Y_t) + \Delta^{\mathrm{T}} \cdot (Y_s - Y_t) + \tfrac{1}{2} (Y_s - Y_t)^{\mathrm{T}} \Gamma (Y_s - Y_t). \tag{8.169}$$

The vector Δ and the symmetric matrix Γ are computed by taking the numeric first and second derivatives of the portfolio $V(Y_t)$ with respect to r_t and $\lambda_{i,t}$. We recall that, given a function $f(x, y)$, the first derivative along x is approximated as

$$\frac{\partial f(x, y)}{\partial x} \approx \frac{f(x + h, y) - f(x - h, y)}{2h}, \tag{8.170}$$

the second derivative along x is

$$\frac{\partial^2 f(x, y)}{\partial x^2} \approx \frac{f(x + h, y) + f(x - h, y) - 2f(x, y)}{h^2}, \tag{8.171}$$

and the mixed derivative is

$$\frac{\partial^2 f(x, y)}{\partial x \, \partial y} \approx \frac{f(x + h, y + k) + f(x - h, y - k) - f(x + h, y - k) - f(x - h, y + k)}{4hk}. \tag{8.172}$$

The dimension of Δ and the rank of Γ both equate to $N_f + 1$. Setting

$$\alpha = V(Y_t) - \Delta^{\mathrm{T}} \cdot Y_t + \tfrac{1}{2} Y_t^{\mathrm{T}} \Gamma Y_t, \tag{8.173}$$

and

$$\beta = \Delta - \Gamma Y_t, \tag{8.174}$$

we rewrite equation (8.169) as

$$V(Y_s) \approx \alpha + \beta^{\mathrm{T}} \cdot Y_s + \tfrac{1}{2} Y_s^{\mathrm{T}} \Gamma Y_s. \tag{8.175}$$

This assumes that Y_s has a Gaussian distribution, with mean $M = (M^r, M^\lambda)^{\mathrm{T}}$ and a covariance matrix

$$\Omega = \begin{pmatrix} \Omega_r & 0 \\ 0 & \Omega_\lambda \end{pmatrix}. \tag{8.176}$$

For the CIR++ processes in equation (8.67), and the intensity $\lambda_{i,t}^D$ decomposed as in equations (8.142), and (8.143), at time s we have the mean

$$M^r = r_t + (1 - e^{-k(s-t)})(\theta_r - r_t) + \bar{\phi}, \tag{8.177}$$

$$M_i^\lambda = \lambda_{i,t} + (1 - e^{-k(s-t)})(\theta_i - \lambda_{i,t}) + \bar{\psi}_i, \tag{8.178}$$

while the covariance matrix is

$$\Omega_r = \frac{\sigma_r^2}{k_r}\left(1 - e^{-k_r\,(s-t)}\right)\left[r_t\,e^{-k_r\,(s-t)} + \frac{\theta_r}{2}\left(1 - e^{-k_r\,(s-t)}\right)\right], \tag{8.179}$$

$$(\Omega_\lambda)_{ii} = \frac{\sigma_i^2}{k_\lambda}\left(1 - e^{-k_\lambda\,(s-t)}\right)\left[\lambda_{i,t}\,e^{-k_\lambda\,(s-t)} + \frac{\theta_i}{2}\left(1 - e^{-k_\lambda\,(s-t)}\right)\right], \tag{8.180}$$

$$(\Omega_\lambda)_{ij} = \frac{\sigma_i\,\sigma_j}{k_\lambda}\left(1 - e^{-k_\lambda\,(s-t)}\right)\left[\lambda_t^C\,e^{-k_\lambda\,(s-t)} + \frac{\theta^C}{2}\left(1 - e^{-k_\lambda\,(s-t)}\right)\right]. \tag{8.181}$$

We recall that $\sigma_i = \sigma^C\sqrt{p_i}$ and $\theta_i = \theta_i^I + p_i\,\theta^C$. For N_f firms, the dimension of the vector M and the rank of the covariance matrix Ω are both $N_f + 1$.

Now we are able to compute the value of the quantile v for which there is a probability $p = P(V(Y_s) < v)$ that the value of the portfolio at time $s > t$ falls below v. To obtain $P(V(Y_s) < v)$, we first Fourier-transform $V(Y_s)$, defining the function

$$\phi(u) = E[\exp(iu\,V(Y_s))]. \tag{8.182}$$

The probability relates to $\phi(u)$ according to the formula of Gil-Pelaez [72],

$$P(V(Y_s) < v) = \frac{1}{2} - \frac{1}{2\pi}\int_{-\infty}^{+\infty}\frac{\mathrm{Im}\left(\phi(u)\,e^{-iuv}\right)}{u}\,du. \tag{8.183}$$

To perform the integration numerically, we first rewrite it as

$$P(V(Y_s) < v) = \frac{1}{2} - \frac{1}{\pi}\int_0^{+\infty}\frac{\mathrm{Im}\left(\phi(u)\,e^{-iuv}\right)}{u}\,du, \tag{8.184}$$

then we introduce a grid with equally spaced abscissae $u \to u_j = (j + 1/2)\delta x$, with step size δx and j running from one to an integer K. The integral is then truncated from zero to $K\,\delta x$, and equation (8.184) is approximated by

$$P(V(Y_s) < v) \approx \frac{1}{2} - \frac{1}{\pi}\sum_{j=0}^{K}\frac{\mathrm{Im}\left[\phi(u_j)\exp\left(-i\,u_j\,v\right)\right]}{j + 1/2}. \tag{8.185}$$

Fixing the time horizon s and the probability p that the portfolio falls below the level v, we invert equation (8.183) to obtain the quantile v; namely, we invert

$$\frac{1}{2} - \frac{1}{\pi}\sum_{j=0}^{K}\frac{\mathrm{Im}\left[\phi(u_j)\exp\left(-i\,u_j\,v\right)\right]}{j + 1/2} = p. \tag{8.186}$$

To find v numerically, we use a bisection method.

Since v only accounts for the market value of the portfolio of bonds given that no default of the issuers occurs during the period $[t, s]$, if we are interested in considering the quantile that also includes the losses suffered if one or more issuers go bankrupt we can compute the expected loss for the portfolio in the event of defaults,

$$\bar{v} = \sum_{i=1}^{m} N_i \left(1 - \mathrm{SP}_i(t, s)\right). \tag{8.187}$$

so that the quantile with default included is:

$$v^{DI} = v - \bar{v}. \tag{8.188}$$

The minimum level of a portfolio of bonds at the 99% c.l. corresponds to the first quantile of the distribution and is derived as described above.

8.5.6   Estimation of the CIR++ model for interest rates

To estimate the parameters of the process x_t in equation (8.66) (the process for the instantaneous interest rate) from market data, we can consider a series of discount factors bootstrapped from the Eonia swap quotes. We mentioned above that the Eonia rate can be considered virtually risk free, since it embeds the credit risk related to lending money to a bank for one day; moreover, swap rates with the Eonia rate as the underlying are assumed to be fully and continuously margined, so that counterparty credit risk is almost totally eliminated. In the end the Eonia rate and swaps on Eonia can be supposed to be the contracts from which it is possible to extract the risk-free term structure of interest rates.

The estimation involves two steps:

1. Estimate the parameters of the process x_t with the Kálmán filter, as explained in Section 8.3.3.
2. Calibrate a time-dependent function ψ_t with the market data of each date of the time series, so as to have a best fit of the model.

Let us now provide a practical example of estimating the parameters using real market data.

Example 8.5.1. *We consider a panel of bootstrapped discount factors, obtained from the Eonia swap rate quotes with maturities given in Table 8.2. The time series of the term structures of the swap rates is considered in the period running from 31/12/2010 to 4/6/ 2012. We plot the 1W, 1Y, 5Y, 10Y and 30Y swap rates in Figure 8.1.*

Table 8.2. Maturities of Eonia swap rates used in the estimation procedure

1w	1m	2m	3m	4m	5m	6m
7m	8m	9m	10m	11m	1y	2y
3y	4y	5y	6y	7y	8y	9y
10y	11y	12y	15y	20y	25y	30y

Discount factors on the same set of maturities as in Table 8.2 are derived for each date and used for the estimation with the help of the Kálmán filter technique, obtaining the results in Table 8.3.

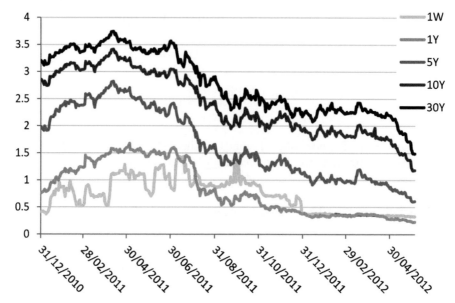

Figure 8.1. Eonia swap rates from 31/12/2010 to 4/6/2012

Table 8.3. Values of the parameters of the CIR model for the zero rate, obtained using the Kálmán filtering technique described

Parameter	Value
κ^r	0.08178
θ^r	6.23%
σ^r	10.1%

The deterministic function in equation (8.66) is found by requiring, for any date t_m in the panel data, a perfect match between the swap rate data of the time series with maturity τ_i, $P^{\text{data}}(t_m, \tau_i)$, and the value of the discount factor $P(x; t_m, \tau_i)$ from equation (8.69), imposing

$$P^{\text{data}}(t_m, \tau_i) = \exp\left(-\int_t^T \psi_s ds\right) P_{\text{CIR}}(x; t_m, \tau_i). \qquad (8.189)$$

$P_{\text{CIR}}(x; t_m, \tau_i)$ is known since we have already calibrated the CIR process for x_t (we approximate the value of x_0 using the Eonia overnight). We use the other $N_\phi = N_{\text{Eonia}} - 1$ series of Eonia maturities to construct the function ψ_t. We define a series of N_ϕ time steps $\Delta\tau_i$ as

$$\begin{cases} \Delta\tau_i = \tau_2, & \text{if } i = 1, \\ \Delta\tau_i = \tau_i - \tau_{i-1}, & \text{if } i \neq 1. \end{cases}$$

We ignore the first value τ_1 that refers to the maturity at one week. Assuming that ψ_t is a

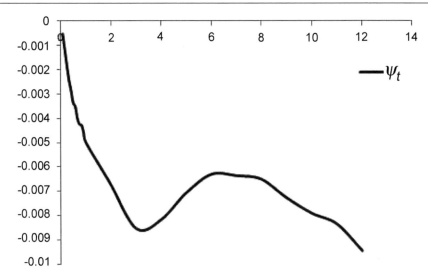

Figure 8.2. The function ψ_t, obtained with the method described in the main text, as a function of maturity

step function, of step size $\Delta\tau_i$, the integral of ψ_t is

$$\int_t^{\tau_i} \psi_s\,ds = \Delta\tau_1\psi_1 + \Delta\tau_2\psi_2 + \cdots + \Delta\tau_i\psi_i, \qquad (8.190)$$

the values for ψ_t are then built iteratively. The first value of the step function is

$$\psi_1 = -\frac{1}{\tau_1}\ln\frac{P^{\text{data}}(t_m, \tau_1)}{P_{\text{CIR}}(x; t_m, \tau_i)}, \qquad (8.191)$$

while the i-th value is

$$\psi_i = -\frac{1}{\Delta\tau_i}\left(\psi_1\,\Delta\tau_1 + \psi_2\,\Delta\tau_2 + \cdots + \psi_{i-1}\Delta\tau_{i-1} + \ln\frac{P^{\text{data}}(t_m, \tau_i)}{P_{\text{CIR}}(x; t_m, \tau_i)}\right). \qquad (8.192)$$

Note that, if there are M days of observation, this technique results in M step functions ψ_t.

Example 8.5.2. *We use the panel data described in Example 8.5.1 with the calibrated parameters for the zero rate in Table 8.3 to construct the function ψ_t. We show a plot of ψ_t as a function of maturity in years in Figure 8.2.*

8.5.7   Estimation of the CIR++ model for default intensities

In order to calibrate the parameters describing the intensities of default, we need to modify somewhat the Kálmán filter procedure described in Section 8.3.3 for the zero rates. Intensities of default are calibrated using a time series of coupon bonds, in which we consider a total of N_B coupon bonds and N_f issuers.

The number of CIR processes to be calibrated is $N_f + 1$, corresponding to the number of idiosyncratic processes N_f (one for each firm), plus the common process. For each day

Table 8.4. Specifics for the bonds issued by Italy, France and Spain

Bond	Issue date	Maturity	Coupon (%)
ITA1	28/03/2011	01/04/2014	3.00
ITA2	14/03/2012	01/03/2015	2.50
ITA3	01/01/2012	01/05/2017	4.75
ITA4	30/12/2010	01/03/2019	4.50
ITA5	26/08/2011	01/03/2022	5.00
FRA1	17/04/2012	25/09/2014	0.75
FRA2	30/12/2010	15/01/2015	2.50
FRA3	02/02/2012	25/02/2017	1.75
FRA4	30/12/2010	25/10/2018	4.25
FRA5	31/01/2012	25/04/2022	3.00
SPA1	05/04/2011	30/04/2014	3.40
SPA2	10/01/2012	30/07/2015	4.00
SPA3	31/08/2011	31/10/2016	4.25
SPA4	30/12/2010	30/07/2019	4.60
SPA5	11/11/2011	31/01/2022	5.85

t, we store this information into the vector $y_{k,t}$, where the first entry $y_{0,t}$ is for the common intensity of default, and the remaining N_f entries are for each idiosyncratic process. The total number of parameters to be calibrated is

$$N_{\text{parms}} = 3 + 2N_f, \tag{8.193}$$

corresponding to κ, θ^C, σ^C plus p_i and θ_i^I for each firm i.

Example 8.5.3. *We consider a portfolio of 15 bonds, issued by Italy (ITA), France (FRA) and Spain (SPA), respectively, over the period from 31/12/2010 to 25/05/2012 and with the specifics in Table 8.4. For each bond, we take into account the time series of prices from the beginning of the period, or the issue date if later, to the end of the period. We estimate the values of the parameters from the time series of bond prices using the Kálmán filter technique, obtaining the results in Table 8.5. In Figure 8.3, we plot the intensity of default λ_t for each issuer ITA, FRA, SPA, over the period 31/12/2010 to 25/5/2012, obtained by the Kálmán filter.*

Having calibrated the parameters of the CIR processes commanding the intensity of default of each issuer, we need to calibrate at the reference time $t = t_0$. We choose to use the model of the value of the intensity $\lambda_{0,i}$ for the i-th issuer, which can be decomposed into an idiosyncratic term $\lambda_{0,i}^I$ and a common term λ_0^C as

$$\lambda_{0,i} = \lambda_{0,i}^I + p_i \lambda_0^C, \quad i \in \{1, \ldots, N_f\}. \tag{8.194}$$

Defining the total number of bonds in the portfolio N_B as in equation (8.168), we construct the function

$$f(\lambda_0^C, \lambda_{0,1}^I, \ldots, \lambda_{0,N_f}^I) = \sum_{j=1}^{N_B} \left(\frac{\mathbf{B}_j - \mathbf{B}_j(\text{MKT})}{\mathbf{B}_j(\text{MKT})} \right)^2, \tag{8.195}$$

Table 8.5. Values of the parameters of the CIR model for the intensity of default process for the three issuers Italy, France and Spain, obtained with the Kálmán filtering technique

Parameter	Value
κ^r	0.0465
θ^C	1.1257%
θ^{ITA}	11.477%
θ^{FRA}	4.974%
θ^{SPA}	11.835%
σ^C	6.634%
p_{ITA}	0.883
p_{FRA}	0.668
p_{SPA}	0.867

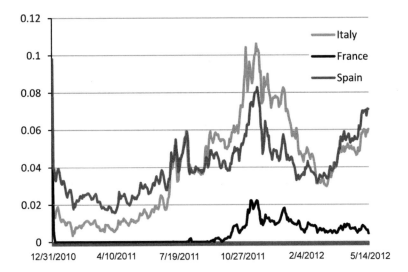

Figure 8.3. The value of the default intensity as a function of time, for the three issuers Italy, France and Spain, obtained from the Kálmán filter technique

where $\mathbf{B}_j(\text{MKT})$ is the market price for the j-th bond and $\mathbf{B}_j$ is the model price for the same bond according to equation (8.157). At this stage, we have set to zero the values of the functions $\phi_{i,t}$ for all firms, while we consider the calibrated function ψ_t for the zero-rate process. The values of $\lambda_{0,i}^I$ and λ_0^C are found by requiring that the above function be minimized.

After estimating the initial values $\lambda_{0,i}$, for each issuer i, we model the time-dependent $\phi_{i,t}$ with a step function of step size ΔT_ϕ, for a total of N_ϕ steps. For the i-th issuer, N_ϕ is fixed by the bond with the longest maturity, say T_J, so that

$$N_\phi = \left[\frac{T_J - t_0}{\Delta T_\phi} \right], \tag{8.196}$$

where t_0 is the last day considered and $[x]$ is the integer part of x.

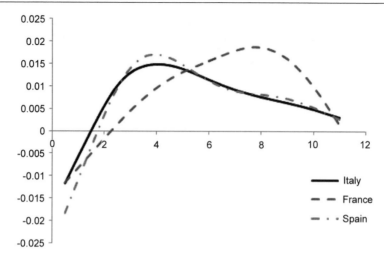

Figure 8.4. The value of the function ϕ_t as a function of time, for the three issuers Italy, France and Spain

The function $\phi_{i,t}$ is calibrated to the market data by a least squares procedure. We consider the function

$$f_i(\phi_{i,t}) = \sum_{j=1}^{N_i} \left(\frac{\mathbf{B}_j - \mathbf{B}_j(\text{MKT})}{\mathbf{B}_j(\text{MKT})} \right)^2. \tag{8.197}$$

In equation (8.197), the sum runs over the N_i bonds issued by the i-th firm, $\mathbf{B}_j$ is the price of the j-th defaultable coupon bond according to equation (8.157) and $\mathbf{B}_j(\text{MKT})$ is the corresponding market price for the same bond.

We demand the function $f_i(\phi_{i,t})$ to be minimized with respect to ϕ_t, under the additional constraint that the second derivative of $\phi_{i,t}$ be minimized at each step as well.

Example 8.5.4. *We consider the market bond prices of the portfolio described in Example 8.5.3, on the reference date 25/5/2012. Using CIR parameters for the zero rate and the default intensities in Tables 8.3 and 8.5, and using the function ψ_t obtained in Example 8.5.2, we obtain the model price in equation (8.157) for each issuer as a function of $\phi_{i,t}$ for that issuer. Using the methods described in this section, we calibrate the functions $\phi_{i,t}$ with the market data, obtaining the results shown in Figure 8.4.*

The model bond prices resulting from the estimated parameters and the deterministic function are shown in Table 8.6: for each bond we also show the theoretical price obtained only by the CIR component of the default intensity model and the price obtained by adding the time-dependent function.

Example 8.5.5. *We consider the market bond prices of the portfolio described in Example 8.6.1, on the reference date 4/6/2012. Using CIR parameters for the zero rate and the default intensities in Table 8.3 and 8.21, and using the function ψ_t obtained in Example 8.5.2, we obtain the model price in equation (8.157) for each issuer as a function of $\phi_{i,t}$ for that issuer. Using the methods described in this section, we calibrate the functions $\phi_{i,t}$ with the market data, obtaining the results shown in Figure 8.5.*

Table 8.6. Model bond prices in Example 8.5.3

Bond	MKT	CIR	CIR + ϕ
ITA1	98.913	97.675	98.310
ITA2	95.585	95.112	95.613
ITA3	99.128	99.392	99.357
ITA4	95.637	96.139	95.855
ITA5	95.703	95.717	95.561
FRA1	100.725	99.563	100.488
FRA2	105.088	103.881	104.974
FRA3	101.893	101.467	101.994
FRA4	114.858	114.704	114.923
FRA5	104.253	105.426	104.264
SPA1	98.403	97.041	97.640
SPA2	96.848	96.577	96.935
SPA3	94.982	95.392	95.382
SPA4	92.278	92.582	92.315
SPA5	96.845	92.872	96.734

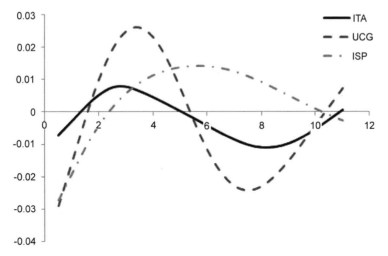

Figure 8.5. The value of the function ϕ_t as a function of time, for the three issuers Italy, Unicredit and Intesa Sanpaolo Bank

Finally, we need to compute the bond-specific parameter ℓ to perfectly match market bonds priced with model prices obtained with the estimated parameters. The value of ℓ can easily be found with a numerical procedure like the Newton–Rahpson method or bisection.

Example 8.5.6. *We refer to the portfolio described in Example 8.5.3. Using the method described in this section, we find the liquidity parameter for each bond as in Table 8.7.*

Table 8.7. Liquidity parameters for each bond considered in Example 8.5.3

Bond	Liquidity (%)
ITA1	−0.3374
ITA2	0.0112
ITA3	0.0540
ITA4	0.0347
ITA5	−0.0215
FRA1	−0.1000
FRA2	−0.0412
FRA3	0.0212
FRA4	0.0097
FRA5	0.0013
SPA1	−0.4086
SPA2	0.0299
SPA3	0.1057
SPA4	0.0070
SPA5	−0.0169

It is worthy of note that not all issuers have to be given a default probability. In some cases the bond prices show that the theoretical price can match market quotes only if the default intensity is set equal to zero and the process does not depart from this value. It is also likely that in these situations a liquidity premium (i.e., $\ell \leq 0$) is implied in market quotes, as we will see in the next example.

Example 8.5.7. *To the portfolio in Example 8.5.3 we add five additional bonds issued by Germany (GER). the specifics for the GER bonds are given in Table 8.8. Since the market price of these bonds is above the price obtained using the bond formula in equation (8.157) with the intensity parameter $\lambda_t = 0$, there is only a liquidity premium to be attached to these bonds. We obtain the liquidity parameter ℓ for each bond in Table 8.9.*

Table 8.8. Specifics for the GER bonds considered

Bond	Issue date	Maturity	Coupon (%)
GER1	22/05/2012	13/06/2014	0.00
GER2	30/12/2010	10/04/2015	2.25
GER3	08/05/2011	07/04/2017	0.50
GER4	30/12/2010	04/07/2019	3.50
GER5	10/04/2012	04/07/2022	1.75

Table 8.9. Liquidity parameter for the GER bonds in Table 8.8

GER1	−0.2371%
GER2	−0.2195%
GER3	−0.2297%
GER4	−0.1140%
GER5	−0.0257%

Example 8.5.8. *We consider the portfolio of bonds with the specifics in Table 8.20. Using the method described in this section, we find the liquidity parameter for each bond as in Table 8.10.*

Table 8.10. Liquidity parameters for each bond considered in Example 8.6.1

Bond	Liquidity (%)
ITA1	−0.3047
ITA2	0.0273
ITA3	0.0461
ITA4	0.0452
ITA5	0.0196
UCG1	−1.0417
UCG2	−0.2640
UCG3	−0.3605
UCG4	0.3014
UCG5	−0.0883
ISP1	−1.1025
ISP2	−0.7156
ISP3	−0.0064
ISP4	0.0231

8.5.8   Future liquidity from a single bond

We now have all the information to forecast the expected and minimum (at a given confidence level) liquidity that can be extracted form a bond: in fact, we can obtain liquidity as analysed in Chapter 6 when describing the TSAA, by selling or pledging the bond in a collateralized loan (which is in practice the same as repoing it).

If we know the expected and minimum levels of the price, with or without the haircut, we can build a term structure of liquidity that can be generated by the bond by adding this information to the TSAA. In the next example we show how the model we have calibrated in this section can help produce these data.

Example 8.5.9. *We consider a portfolio of EUR30 million notional containing only the bond issued by Italy maturing in 2017, see Example 8.5.3. We compute a term structure of expected price levels and of minimum levels at the 99% quantile over a period of one year,*

Table 8.11. Term structure of expected and minimum (99% c.l.) levels of liquidity (million), with and without credit event, generated by EUR30 million invested in the bond issued by Italy and maturing in 2017. The term structure is considered over one year, in monthly steps. No haircut has been applied

Months	Expected	99 Quantile (no credit event)	99 Quantile (with credit event)
1	29.6454	28.8239	28.7278
2	29.6127	28.5764	28.3846
3	29.5750	28.3115	28.0242
4	29.5414	28.0436	27.6612
5	29.5039	27.7768	27.2995
6	29.4711	27.5389	26.9671
7	29.4435	27.3409	26.6749
8	29.4188	27.1769	26.4171
9	29.3925	27.0338	26.1804
10	29.3628	26.9045	25.9579
11	29.3400	26.7953	25.7560
12	29.3096	26.6904	25.5585

in monthly steps. We also compute this stressed minimum level by considering and excluding the default event: in the latter case the intensity of default affects the price but does not trigger any jump event. When a haircut is not applied, we obtain the values in Table 8.11 and Figure 8.6 indicating the different levels of future liquidity.

The information contained in Table 8.11 can be used when building the TSAA and the TSLGC to estimate how much liquidity can be obtained by selling the bond in the next year.

The same type of analysis can be conducted by including the haircut so as to forecast the potential liquidity obtainable by repo transactions. We assume that the haircuts are determined by an approach such as the one explained above, and that the bond in the Step 1 and 2 group of the PD over one year is below 5%, whereas it falls in the Step 3 group when the PD is below 15% (above 15% it is no longer eligible for repo transactions). We obtain the term structure of expected and stressed levels at the 99% c.l. in Table 8.12 and Figure 8.7.

We can also set the trigger for the passage from Step 1 and 2 to Step 3 at lower PD levels. For example, we can leave the first trigger at 5% PD over one year and lower the second trigger to 7.5%. In this case we obtain the term structure in Table 8.13 and Figure 8.8.

8.5.9   Future liquidity from more bonds

The framework we have designed can also cope with a portfolio of many bonds with different maturities: in this case the bank can take advantage of the diversification effects that can be attained by buying bonds with different exposures to interest rates and to the evolution of the PD. It is clear that in this case the TSAA needs to be built while considering the aggregated position the bank has on a single issuer as well, since information on just one bond can be useful but is only a small part of the entire picture of the BSL.

Table 8.12. Term structure of expected and minimum (99% c.l.) levels of liquidity (million), with and without credit event, generated by EUR30 million invested in the bond issued by Italy and maturing in 2017. The term structure is considered over one year, in monthly steps. We applied a haircut with triggers at 5% and 15% for the PD over one year

Months	Expected	99 Quantile (no credit event)	99 Quantile (with credit event)
1	27.2747	26.5322	26.4361
2	27.2595	26.3030	26.1111
3	27.2524	26.1168	25.8295
4	27.2519	25.9366	25.5541
5	27.2463	25.7602	25.2829
6	27.2424	25.5983	25.0265
7	27.2406	25.4510	24.7850
8	27.2388	25.3164	24.5565
9	27.2334	25.1898	24.3364
10	27.2230	25.0699	24.1234
11	27.2173	24.9655	23.9262
12	27.2031	24.8632	23.7313

Table 8.13. Term structure of expected and minimum (99% c.l.) levels of liquidity (million), with and without credit event, generated by EUR30 million invested in the bond issued by Italy and maturing in 2017. The term structure is considered over one year, in monthly steps. We applied a haircut with triggers at 5% and 15% for the PD over one year

Months	Expected	99 Quantile (no credit event)	99 Quantile (with credit event)
1	26.7434	25.9727	25.8766
2	26.1191	25.0282	24.8363
3	25.2979	23.9671	23.6797
4	24.5307	23.0046	22.6222
5	23.8566	22.1659	21.6886
6	23.2768	21.4447	20.8729
7	22.7788	20.8229	20.1569
8	22.3456	20.2812	19.5213
9	21.9627	19.8037	8.9503
10	21.6214	19.3794	18.4328
11	21.3205	19.0065	17.9671
12	21.0448	18.6693	17.5374

Example 8.5.10. *Consider a portfolio of EUR30 million, equally distributed among the five bonds issued by Italy and with the specifics given in Example 8.5.3. The term structure of expected price levels and of minimum levels at the 99% quantile over a period of one year, in monthly steps, can be computed with the approach described in the main text. In this example we also compute this stressed minimum level by considering and excluding the default event, as in Example 8.5.9. When a haircut is not applied, we obtain the liquidity*

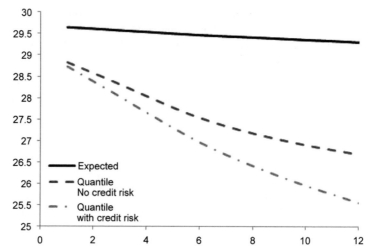

Figure 8.6. Term structure of expected and minimum (99% c.l.) levels of liquidity, with and without credit event, generated by EUR30 million invested in the bond issued by Italy and maturing in 2017, as in Table 8.11

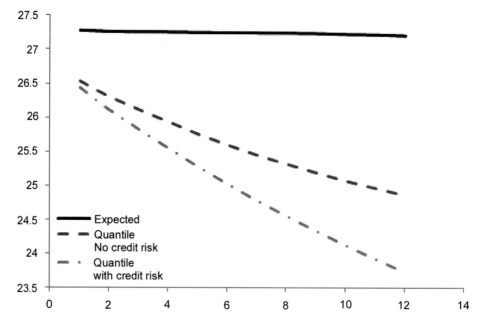

Figure 8.7. Term structure of expected and minimum (99% c.l.) levels of liquidity, with and without credit event, generated by EUR30 million invested in the bond issued by Italy and maturing in 2017, as in Table 8.12

that can be generated by selling the portfolio at future dates, both at an expected and at a minimum level (99% c.l.), as shown in Table 8.14 and Figure 8.9.

Moreover, bond portfolios can be repoed out, so we can compute the expected and minimum liquidity by including the haircuts too. As in Example 8.5.9, we assume two

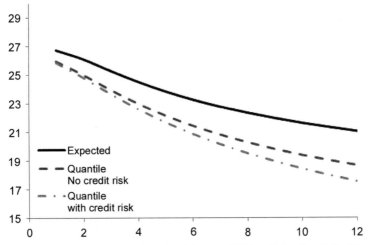

Figure 8.8. Term structure of expected and minimum (99% c.l.) levels of liquidity, with and without credit event, generated by 30 million euros invested in a portfolio of five bonds issued by Italy, as in Table 8.13

Table 8.14. Term structure of expected and minimum (99% c.l.) levels of liquidity (million), with and without credit event, generated by EUR30 million invested in a portfolio of five bonds issued by Italy and maturing. The term structure is considered over one year, in monthly steps. No haircut has been applied

Months	Expected	99 Quantile (no credit event)	99 Quantile (with credit event)
1	29.0883	28.3176	28.2215
2	29.0701	27.9792	27.7873
3	29.0478	27.7170	27.4297
4	29.0291	27.5030	27.1206
5	29.0070	27.3164	26.8391
6	28.9890	27.1570	26.5852
7	28.9765	27.0211	26.3551
8	28.9664	26.9026	26.1427
9	28.9551	26.7961	25.9427
10	28.9411	26.6991	25.7525
11	28.9333	26.6192	25.5798
12	28.9186	26.5431	25.4112

levels of PD triggering the passage from the ECB's Step 1 and 2 to Step 3 at 5%, whereas above 15% the bonds are no longer eligible for repo transactions. Table 8.15 and Figure 8.10 show the results.

Haircuts play a major role on the liquidity that can be obtained by repo transactions when a portfolio of bonds is also considered. In fact, when a higher haircut is triggered with higher probabilities, the minimum liquidity is strongly affected as shown in Table 8.16 and Figure 8.11: in this case triggers are set at 5 and 7.5% of the PD at one year.

Table 8.15. Term structure of expected and minimum (99% c.l.) levels of liquidity (million), with and without credit event, generated by EUR30 million euros invested in a portfolio of five bonds issued by Italy and maturing. The term structure is considered over one year, in monthly steps. We applied a haircut with triggers at 5% and 15% for the PD over one year

Months	Expected	99 Quantile (no credit event)	99 Quantile (with credit event)
1	26.8228	26.1314	26.0353
2	26.8208	25.9346	25.7428
3	26.8278	25.7790	25.4917
4	26.8406	25.6278	25.2454
5	26.8490	25.4806	25.0033
6	26.8586	25.3467	24.7749
7	26.8705	25.2275	24.5615
8	26.8822	25.1203	24.3605
9	26.8908	25.0215	24.1682
10	26.8949	24.9299	23.9833
11	26.9031	24.8529	23.8135
12	26.9035	24.7784	23.6465

Table 8.16. Term structure of expected and minimum (99% c.l.) levels of liquidity (million), with and without credit event, generated by EUR30 million invested in a portfolio of five bonds issued by Italy and maturing. The term structure is considered over one year, in monthly step. We applied a haircut with triggers at 5 and 7.5% for the PD over one year

Months	Expected	99 Quantile (no credit event)	99 Quantile (with credit event)
1	27.1940	26.3725	26.2764
2	26.5463	25.5100	25.3181
3	25.6983	24.4348	24.1475
4	24.9066	23.4088	23.0264
5	24.2096	22.4825	22.0052
6	23.6095	21.6772	21.1054
7	23.0921	20.9894	20.3235
8	22.6415	20.3996	19.6397
9	22.2427	19.8840	19.0306
10	21.8853	19.4270	18.4805
11	21.5697	19.0250	17.9856
12	21.2793	18.6600	17.5282

The BSL needs to be considered at an aggregated level when bonds are issued by several debtors as well. In this case we should also take into account the correlations between the probabilities of default that affect not only the losses suffered by the holder (the bank in our case) when the issuers go bankrupt, but also the price of the bonds in the portfolio.

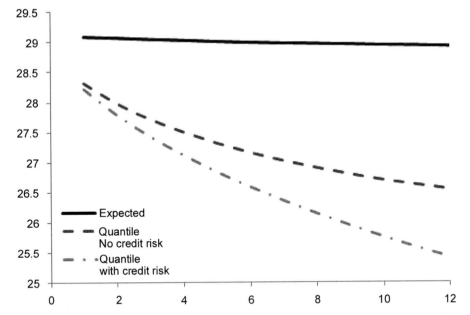

Figure 8.9. Term structure of expected and minimum (99% c.l.) levels of liquidity, with and without credit event, generated by EUR30 million invested in a portfolio of five bonds issued by Italy, as in Table 8.14

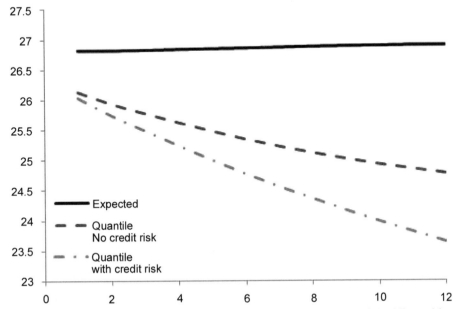

Figure 8.10. Term structure of expected and minimum (99% c.l.) levels of liquidity, with and without credit event, generated by EUR30 million invested in a portfolio of five bonds issued by Italy, as in Table 8.15

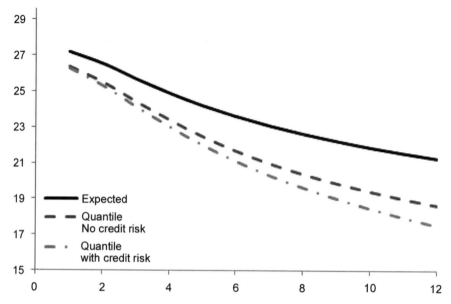

Figure 8.11. Term structure of expected and minimum (99% c.l.) levels of liquidity, with and without credit event, generated by EUR30 million invested in a portfolio of bonds issued by Italy, as in Table 8.16

The model we have introduced is capable of accounting for the correlation by using the composite CIR++ process: this correlation affects the liquidity that can be generated by the portfolio in two ways:

1. Prices are more correlated if the default intensities of the issuers are more correlated.
2. The haircuts of the bonds increase jointly with higher probability if the intensities are more correlated, since they are linked to the credit rating and we assumed that this is dependent on the probability of default, as explained above.

In both cases the liquidity that can be generated at future dates by the portfolio of bonds is smaller.

Example 8.5.11. *We consider a portfolio of EUR30 million, equally distributed among 20 bonds, 15 of which are those considered in Example 8.5.3, while the other 5 are the GER bonds in Example 8.5.7. We compute the term structure of the expected and minimum liquidity (99% c.l.) that can generated by the portfolio. We start by considering the case the when the portfolio is sold, so we exclude the haircuts. The results are in Table 8.17 and Figure 8.12.*

If the bank wants to compute the expected and minimum liquidity that can be extracted from the bond portfolio by repo transactions, the haircut has to be included. We assume that the levels at which the PD triggers passages between haircuts, modelled on the ECB's approach as explained in the main text, are set at 5 and 15% for all issuers. We obtain the term structure of liquidity in Table 8.18 and Figure 8.13.

When higher haircuts are more likely, such as when they are triggered by PD levels set at 5 and 7.5%, we obtain the term structure of liquidity in Table 8.19 and Figure 8.14.

Table 8.17. Term structure of expected and minimum (99% c.l.) levels of liquidity (million), with and without credit event, generated by EUR30 million invested in a portfolio equally distributed among 20 bonds issued by ITA, GER, FRA, SPA. The term structure is considered over one year, in monthly steps. No haircut has been applied

Months	Expected	99 Quantile (no credit event)	99 Quantile (with credit event)
1	30.4000	29.6310	29.5759
2	30.3845	29.4152	29.3053
3	30.3657	29.2380	29.0733
4	30.3495	29.0879	28.8687
5	30.3306	28.9547	28.6811
6	30.3147	28.8349	28.5072
7	30.2889	28.7582	28.3764
8	30.2658	28.6827	28.2470
9	30.2421	28.6069	28.1175
10	30.2160	28.5309	27.9881
11	30.1952	28.4572	27.8611
12	30.1676	28.3925	27.7432

Table 8.18. Term structure of expected and minimum (99% c.l.) levels of liquidity (million), with and without credit event, generated by EUR30 million invested in a portfolio equally distributed among 20 bonds issued by ITA, GER, FRA, SPA. The term structure is considered over one year, in monthly steps. We applied a haircut with triggers at 5 and 15% for the PD over one year

Months	Expected	99 Quantile (no credit event)	99 Quantile (with credit event)
1	28.6274	28.1105	28.0555
2	28.5981	27.8559	27.7459
3	28.5689	27.6487	27.4841
4	28.5432	27.4708	27.2516
5	28.5152	27.3095	27.0359
6	28.4896	27.1656	26.8378
7	28.4669	27.0366	26.6548
8	28.4463	26.9203	26.4847
9	28.4246	26.8126	26.3233
10	28.4003	26.7109	26.1681
11	28.3805	26.6217	26.0256
12	28.3539	26.5333	25.8841

8.6   FAIR HAIRCUT FOR REPO TRANSACTIONS AND COLLATERALIZED LOANS

In the previous section we introduced a tool to monitor the LGC of a portfolio of bonds held by the bank. In the case of liquidity generated by repo transactions, we have modelled the haircut to apply to the market price of the bonds following the approach

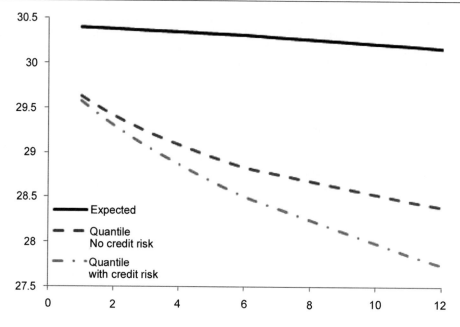

Figure 8.12. Term structure of expected and minimum (99% c.l.) levels of liquidity, with and without credit event, generated by EUR30 million invested in a portfolio of bonds issued by ITA, GER, FRA, SPA, as in Table 8.17

Table 8.19. Term structure of expected and minimum (99% c.l.) levels of liquidity (million), with and without credit event, generated by EUR30 million invested in a portfolio equally distributed among 20 bonds issued by ITA, GER, FRA, SPA. The term structure is considered over one year, in monthly steps. We applied a haircut with triggers at 5 and 7.5% for the PD over one year

Months	Expected	99 Quantile (no credit event)	99 Quantile (with credit event)
1	26.5448	25.6410	25.5859
2	26.0043	22.6308	22.5209
3	25.6040	20.2846	20.1199
4	25.2840	18.7317	18.5125
5	25.0177	17.6887	17.4151
6	24.7949	16.9663	16.6385
7	24.6054	16.4496	16.0678
8	24.4419	16.0710	15.6353
9	24.2967	15.7864	15.2971
10	24.1648	15.5680	15.0252
11	24.0492	15.4011	14.8050
12	23.9387	15.3366	14.6873

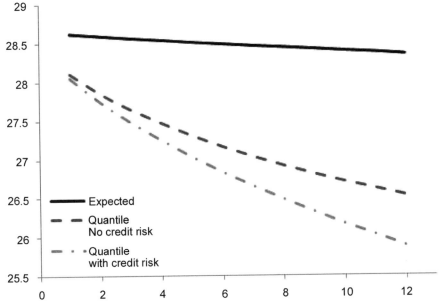

Figure 8.13. Term structure of expected and minimum (99% c.l.) levels of liquidity, with and without credit event, generated by EUR30 million invested in a portfolio of bonds issued by ITA, GER, FRA, SPA, as in Table 8.18

adopted by the ECB since, first, the central bank is the main counterparty for European banks[12] and, second, because the ECB's haircuts are often used as a guide to set haircuts for transactions not involving the central bank itself.

Nonetheless, we would like to design an approach to set fair haircut levels for repo transactions and collateralized repos which is somehow different and possibly more robust than that devised by the ECB. In fact, one of the main flaws of the ECB's approach to set haircuts is that it does not consider wrong-way risk in any way: this increases the probability of there being a joint default of the counterparty borrowing money in the deal and the issuer of the bond pledged as collateral. This situation clearly makes the collateral lose its risk mitigation feature and the credit risk to the lender approaches that of a non-collateralized loan.

We would like to stress the fact that wrong-way risk is very common for the following reason: collateral bonds are often Treasuries issued by the government of the country of the borrower bank. Typically, there is a strong correlation between the credit spreads (which reflects the PDs) of the Treasuries and the banks, for the circular fact that banks have huge quantities of Treasury bonds on their balance sheets to build the liquidity buffers. So, when crises occur with sovereign debts, such as the one experienced in 2011–2012 in Europe,[13] the PD of the banks of the countries under pressure increase as a result of the higher probability of default of the sovereign debt they hold as assets. Banks of countries such as Greece, Spain, Portugal, Ireland and Italy pay high credit spreads over

---

[12] We are absolutely aware we are restricting the analysis to a limited number of banks with respect to all financial institutions operating worldwide.
[13] At the time of this writing, the crisis is still not over.

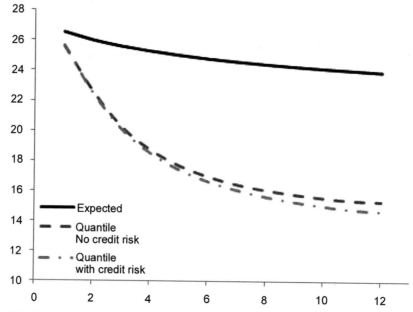

Figure 8.14. Term structure of expected and minimum (99% c.l.) levels of liquidity, with and without credit event, generated by EUR30 million invested in a portfolio of bonds issued by ITA, GER, FRA, SPA, as in Table 8.19

the risk-free rate (however we define it) because they are perceived as high risk for the Treasury bonds they hold (and for the more general country risk).

The framework we have introduced above is rich enough to effectively cope with this problem as well. Assume that counterparty d posts a portfolio of N_B bonds, issued by N_f issuers as collateral for a loan (or for a repo transaction). For each issuer there are N_i bonds in the portfolio: the notional of the loan at inception is the same as the value of the portfolio minus a fair haircut. This includes, at a given date T:

- market risk: the probability of having, on the counterparty's default, a value of the portfolio lower than the loan still outstanding because of market risk factor movements (interest rates and credit spreads);
- credit risk: the probability of having, on the counterparty's default, a value of the portfolio lower than the loan still outstanding because one or more issuers went bankrupt;
- wrong-way risk: as defined above, the higher probability that the counterparty's default and the issuers' default occur simultaneously.

The default of the counterparty i is modelled by a composite CIR++ process and a deterministic time-dependent function as seen in Section 8.5. We introduce an indicator function $D_d(0, T)$ equal to 1 if the default of the counterparty occurred between times 0 and T; it is equal to 0 otherwise. We take the approximation

$$D_d(0, T) = D_d^I(0, T) + \xi_d D_d^C(0, T)$$

where $D_d^I(0, T)$ is an indicator that the idiosyncratic default process for d has jumped by

T, whereas $D_D^C(0, T)$ is the indicator that the common default process has jumped by T; finally, ξ_i is the indicator of the event that d goes bust at the first common credit event.[14] In the framework we introduced above $\mathbf{P}(\xi_d = 1) = p_d$, where p_d is the factor linking the intensity of the common default event to the total intensity of the counterparty d, and

$$\mathrm{PD}_d^I(0, T) = \mathbf{P}[D_d^I(0, T) = 1] = 1 - \mathrm{SP}_d^I(0, T)e^{-\int_0^T \phi_d(s)ds}$$

$$\mathrm{PD}_d^C(0, T) = \mathbf{P}[D_d^C(0, T) = 1] = 1 - \mathrm{SP}_d^C(0, T)$$

where $\mathrm{SP}_d^I(t, T) = P_{\mathrm{CIR}}(\lambda_{d,t}^I; t, T)$ and $\mathrm{SP}^C(t, T) = P_{\mathrm{CIR}}(\lambda_t^C; t, T)$. It is worth noting that we included the effect of the time-dependent function $\phi_{d,t}$ within the idiosyncratic default event.

Let $V^{\mathrm{Coll}}(t)$ be the value of the portfolio of bonds used as collateral, formed as:

$$V^{\mathrm{Coll}}(T) = \sum_{i=1}^{N_f} \sum_{j=1}^{N_i} \mathbf{B}^i(0, T_j).$$

In a repo transaction or collateralized loan, the lender seeks to make the expected loss equal to zero over a given period from 0 to T. The expected loss (EL) is equal to the expected exposure at default (EAD) minus the value of the collateral, in the event of default of the counterparty i. The EAD is simply the amount lent (assuming no scheduled repayments between 0 and T), so that:

$$\mathrm{EL}(0, T) = \mathbf{E}[\mathrm{EAD} - V^{\mathrm{Coll}}(T)|D_d(0, T) = 1] \tag{8.198}$$

It is straightforward to check that:

$$\mathbf{E}[\mathrm{EAD}|D_d(0, T) = 1] = \mathrm{EAD}$$

If the amount lent is L then $\mathbf{E}[\mathrm{EAD}] = L$. Then we have:

$$\mathbf{E}[V^{\mathrm{Coll}}(T)|D_d(0, T) = 1]$$
$$= \mathbf{E}[V^{\mathrm{Coll}}(T)(1 - D_{\mathrm{Coll}}(0, T)) + (V^{\mathrm{Coll}}(T)-)D_{\mathrm{Coll}}(0, T)|D_d(0, T) = 1]$$

where $D_{\mathrm{Coll}}(0, T)$ is the indicator function equal to 1 if at least one issuer of the bonds in the collateral portfolio has gone bankrupt by time T, and $\mathrm{L_{GD}}$ is the loss generated by the default events. The equation can be rewritten as:

$$\mathbf{E}[V^{\mathrm{Coll}}(T)(1 - D_{\mathrm{Coll}}(0, T)) + (V^{\mathrm{Coll}}(T)-)D_{\mathrm{Coll}}(0, T)|D_d(0, T) = 1]$$
$$= \mathbf{E}[V^{\mathrm{Coll}}(T) - D_{\mathrm{Coll}}(0, T)|D_d(0, T) = 1]$$

We split this equation into two parts. In this case it is also clear that:

$$\mathbf{E}[V^{\mathrm{Coll}}(T)|D_d(0, T) = 1] = \sum_{i=1}^{N_f} \sum_{j=1}^{N_i} \mathrm{CH}^i(T, T_j)$$

since $V^{\mathrm{Coll}}(T)$ is the value of the portfolio at time T given that no default event has occurred. $\mathrm{CH}^i(T, T_j)$ is the expected price at time T of a coupon bond issued by i

---

[14] This approximation was used by Duffie and Pan [60]. We ignore the double-counting of defaults that occurs with both common and idiosyncratic credit events. The approximation also undercounts defaults associated with multiple common credit events before time T. These two effects partially offset each other.

expiring at time $T_j > T$, defined as in (8.158). We assume that an issuer does not have more than one bond expiring on a specific date. The second part is:

$$\mathbf{E}[\mathbf{L}_{\mathrm{GD}}D_{\mathrm{Coll}}(0, T)|D_d(0, T)=1] = (1 - \mathrm{PD}^C(T)(0, T))\mathrm{PD}_d^I(0, T)\sum_{i=1}^{N_f}\sum_{j=1}^{N_i}\mathbf{L}_{\mathrm{GD}j}^i\mathrm{PD}_i^I(0, T)$$

$$+ \mathrm{PD}^C(0, T)((1 - p_d)\mathrm{PD}_d^I(0, T) + p_d)$$

$$\times ((1 - p_i)\mathrm{PD}_i^I(0, T) + p_i)\sum_{i=1}^{N_f}\sum_{j=1}^{N_i}\mathbf{L}_{\mathrm{GD}j}^i \qquad (8.199)$$

The first part of the right-hand side considers the expected value of the loss on bonds in the event of the counterparty's default, given that the common default event is not triggered (the amount is weighted by the probability that the common event does not occur: $1 - \mathrm{PD}^C(T)(0, T)$); the second part is the expected value of the loss when the counterparty goes bankrupt and a common default event occurs (the amount is weighted by the probability that the common event occurs: $\mathrm{PD}^C(T)(0, T)$).

Making the simplifying assumption that $\mathbf{L}_{\mathrm{GD}j}^i = x\% \times N_j^i$ with N_j^i equal to the notional amount in the portfolio is a constant percentage of the par value of the bond, then we can rewrite the equation for the expected loss on the repo as:

$$\mathrm{EL}(T) = L - \mathbf{E}[V^{\mathrm{Coll}}(T)|D_d(0, T) = 1] + \mathbf{E}[\mathbf{L}_{\mathrm{GD}}D_{\mathrm{Coll}}(0, T)|D_d(0, T) = 1] \quad (8.200)$$

By the same token we can also compute the maximum loss at a defined confidence level, say 99%. This is quite easy to obtain since we already showed how to compute the minimum level of a portfolio of bonds at a given quantile by a $\Delta - \Gamma$ approximation; let the minimum value at the 99% c.l. of the portfolio at time T be:

$$\min_{99\%}[V^{\mathrm{Coll}}(T)] = v$$

where v is the quantile calculated as shown in Section 8.5. Then the maximum loss is:

$$\mathrm{ML}(T) = L - v + \mathbf{E}[\mathbf{L}_{\mathrm{GD}}D_{\mathrm{Coll}}(0, T)|D_d(0, T) = 1]$$

The fair haircut to apply to the value of the portfolio of bonds at the inception of the repo or collateralized loans is the level that makes the EL or the ML zero, depending on whether the bank wants to be more or less conservative. If the bank chooses to make the EL zero, considering that the amount lent at time 0 is equal to the value of the portfolio $V(t)$ minus the haircut, $L = (1 - \mathcal{H})V(0)$, the level of $\mathcal{H}$ is chosen so that:

$$\mathrm{EL}(T) = \mathbf{E}[(1 - \mathcal{H})V(0) - V(T)|D_d(0, T) = 1]$$

$$= (1 - \mathcal{H})V(0) - \mathbf{E}[V^{\mathrm{Coll}}(T)|D_d(0, T) = 1] + \mathbf{E}[\mathbf{L}_{\mathrm{GD}}D_{\mathrm{Coll}}(T)|D_d(0, T) = 1] = 0$$
$$(8.201)$$

If the bank wants to compute the haircut based on the minimum level of the portfolio of bonds, then:

$$\mathrm{ML}(T) = \mathbf{E}[(1 - \mathcal{H})V(0) - v^{DI}|D_d(0, T) = 1]$$

$$= (1 - \mathcal{H})V(0) - v + \mathbf{E}[\mathbf{L}_{\mathrm{GD}}D(0, T)|D_d(0, T) = 1] = 0 \qquad (8.202)$$

where v^{DI} is the quantile of the portfolio including default events as defined in Section 8.5.5.

It is interesting to measure the degree to which wrong-way risk impacts on the haircut. To this end we have to apply the formulae above assuming that no correlation exists between the counterparty and the issuer of the bond. In our setup this means that the parameter p is equal to zero for each debtor, or that the probability of a common credit event $PD^C = 0$. Nonetheless, we still want the total PD of each debtor to be the same as that produced by the combined effect of both the idiosyncratic and common factors. This means that in the absence of wrong-way risk it is

$$\left.\begin{array}{l} PD_d(t,s) = 1 - SP(\lambda_d^I + p_d \lambda^C, t, s), \\ PD_i(t,s) = 1 - SP(\lambda_i^I + p_i \lambda^C, t, s), \end{array}\right\} \tag{8.203}$$

where SP is the zero-coupon bond in equation (8.27). Equation (8.199) modifies as follows:

$$E[L_{GD} D_{Coll}(0,T)|D_d(0,T) = 1] = PD_d(0,T) \sum_{i=1}^{N_f} \sum_{j=1}^{N_i} L_{GD}{}_j^i PD_i(0,T)$$

The haircut is then computed as indicated in equations (8.201) and (8.202).

Example 8.6.1. *We consider a portfolio of Italian bonds, used as collateral for two firms (UCG, ISP), on June 6, 2012. The specifics for the ITA bonds (collateral) and the UCG, ISP bonds (portfolios) are given in Table 8.20.*

Assume that the bank has to lend money to another bank and that it accepts as collateral Treasury bonds. Let the counteparty borrowing money be either Intesa Sanpaolo (ISP), an Italian bank, or Unicredit Group (UCG), a European international bank. Moreover, we assume that the collateral comprises bonds issued by the Italian Treasury (ITA). The collateral is posted at the start of the contact and is not updated until maturity.

The interest rate process follows a CIR++ model and the parameters are those estimated in Example 8.5.1. To estimate the parameters of the default intensities of the two possible counterparties and of the Italian Treasury, we consider the prices of the bonds issued, respectively, by ITA, UCG and ISP, with the specifics in Table 8.20, over the period from 12/31/2010 to 6/4/2012; we set the reference date as 4/6/2012. For each bond, we take into account the time series of prices from the issue date to the reference date. We calibrate the values of the parameters with the term structure of bond prices using the Kálmán filter technique, obtaining the results in Table 8.21.

In Figure 8.15, we plot the intensity of default λ_t for each issuer ITA, UCG and ISP, over the period 12/31/2010 to 6/4/2012.

In Tables 8.22–8.24, we show the fair haircut (based on the EL and the ML) that the bank should apply for a repo or a loan secured with UCG or ISP maturing, respectively, in $s = 3M$, 6M and 1Y, for the three cases in which the collateral is a portfolio of the five Italian bonds above, the Italian bond maturing on 01/05/2017, and the other Italian bond maturing on 01/03/2022. We show the results both when we include wrong-way risk (WWR) and when we exclude it.

Haircuts are typically revised periodically to get the credit risk of the repo or collateralized loan back to as close to zero as possible. If the life of the contract is the period

Table 8.20. Specifics for the bonds issued by the Italian Treasury, Unicredit and Intesa Sanpaolo bank

Bond	Issue date	Maturity	Coupon (%)
ITA1	28/03/2011	01/04/2014	3.00
ITA2	14/03/2012	01/03/2015	2.50
ITA3	01/01/2012	01/05/2017	4.75
ITA4	30/12/2010	01/03/2019	4.50
ITA5	26/08/2011	01/03/2022	5.00
UCG1	30/12/2010	12/02/2013	4.825
UCG2	30/12/2010	14/01/2014	5.250
UCG3	30/12/2010	10/02/2014	4.375
UCG4	02/03/2012	07/03/2017	4.875
UCG5	30/12/2010	29/01/2020	4.375
ISP1	30/12/2010	04/12/2012	2.625
ISP2	25/02/2011	01/02/2013	3.250
ISP3	21/02/2012	28/02/2017	5.000
ISP4	30/12/2010	14/04/2020	4.125

Table 8.21. Values of the parameters of the CIR model for the intensity of default process for the issuers Italy, Unicredit and Intesa Sanpaolo Bank, obtained with the Kálmán filtering technique

Parameter	Value
κ	0.0276
θ^C	4.517%
θ^{ITA}	9.075%
θ^{UCG}	9.505%
θ^{ISP}	9.505%
σ^C	5.679%
p_{ITA}	0.8394
p_{UCG}	0.7984
p_{ISP}	0.8175

$[0, T]$, divided into n subperiods of length $[T_{i-1}, T_i]$, for $0 \geq i \leq n$ and $T_0 = 0$, then the haircut has to be calculated every time according to the methodology we have sketched above, with the default risk referring to the subperiod $[T_{i-1}, T_i]$, instead of the total period $[0, T_i]$. So, at the inception of the contract, the haircut is obtained, according to the expected or maximum loss, by solving the equations:

$$\text{EL}(T_1) = \mathbf{E}[(1 - \mathcal{H})V(0) - V(T_1)|D_d(0, T_1) = 1]$$

$$= (1 - \mathcal{H})V(0) - \mathbf{E}[V^{\text{Coll}}(T_1)|D_d(0, T_1) = 1] - \mathbf{E}[L_{\text{GD}}D_{\text{Coll}}(T_1)|D_d(0, T_1) = 1] = 0$$

Figure 8.15. The value of the default intensity as a function of time, for the three issuers Italy, Unicredit and Intesa Sanpaolo bank, obtained from the Kálmán filter technique described

Table 8.22. Haircuts based on the EL and ML. The collateral is the portfolio of Italian bonds

Expiry	Counterparty	With WWR		No WWR	
		EL (%)	ML (%)	EL (%)	ML (%)
3M	UCG	0.65	4.88	0.02	4.26
	ISP	0.66	4.89	0.02	4.26
6M	UCG	1.31	7.19	0.08	5.96
	ISP	1.34	7.22	0.08	5.95
1Y	UCG	2.52	10.23	0.10	7.82
	ISP	2.56	10.28	0.10	7.82

and

$$\mathrm{ML}(T_1) = \mathbf{E}[(1 - \mathcal{H})V(0) - v^{DI}|D_d(0, T_1) = 1]$$
$$= (1 - \mathcal{H})V(0) - v - \mathbf{E}[\mathrm{L}_{\mathrm{GD}}D_{\mathrm{Coll}}(0, T_1)|D_d(0, T_1) = 1] = 0$$

Then in T_1 the haircut is revised using new-market data and PD data by computing $\mathrm{EL}(T_2)$ or $\mathrm{ML}(T_2)$, and so on until the end of the contract.

Table 8.23. Haircuts based on the EL and ML. The collateral is the bond maturing on 01/05/2017

Expiry	Counterparty	With WWR		No WWR	
		EL (%)	ML (%)	EL (%)	ML (%)
3M	UCG	0.79	5.20	0.18	4.59
	ISP	0.80	5.21	0.18	4.59
6M	UCG	1.62	7.78	0.41	6.57
	ISP	1.64	7.81	0.41	6.57
1Y	UCG	3.16	11.37	0.79	9.00
	ISP	3.21	11.41	0.79	9.00

Table 8.24. Haircuts based on the EL and ML. The collateral is the bond maturing on 01/03/2022

Expiry	Counterparty	With WWR		No WWR	
		EL (%)	ML (%)	EL (%)	ML (%)
3M	UCG	0.94	7.67	0.32	7.05
	ISP	0.95	7.68	0.32	7.05
6M	UCG	1.88	11.45	0.65	10.22
	ISP	1.91	11.48	0.65	10.21
1Y	UCG	3.67%	17.05	1.26	14.64
	ISP	3.72%	17.10	1.25	14.63

8.7   ADJUSTMENTS TO THE VALUE OF ILLIQUID BONDS

Banks do not only have liquid bonds on their balance sheet for liquidity management purposes. Often some assets are liquid and actively traded in the market in the first part of their life, but afterwards the trading activity becomes scant and they no longer can be considered liquid. In these cases the bank will likely hold the assets until their maturity, but it is always possible that they can be sold to extract liquidity, although the trading process takes much longer to complete (maybe weeks or even months).

The problem with illiquid assets is twofold:

1. A fair value has to be attached to them which cannot directly be retrieved from the market, for the very fact that they are not actively traded. The fair value does not consider any difficulty in trading the bond such that it only refers to the case when it is perfectly liquid. So, attributing a fair value to an illiquid asset can only be carried out by disregarding any liquidity effects and by pretending that the asset is liquid.
2. An adjustment should be added to the fair value to reflect the actual capacity of the asset to generate liquidity, in terms of the amount and time needed.

Limiting our analysis to bonds, the fair value can easily be computed if other liquid bonds issued by the same debtor are actively traded in the market. In fact, based on them, it is possible to estimate the parameters of a model of the credit risk run by the issuer, such as the composite intensity framework we have used above to predict the LGC of a bond portfolio. Applying the credit model to illiquid bonds jointly with an interest rate model that has been also properly calibrated, allows computing the fair value with a relatively good degree of accuracy and reliability.

The liquidity adjustment to the fair value requires more care. The adjustment, as will be clear from what follows, is not an objective correction to the value, meaningful for any holder. It depends on subjective factors, such as the funding spread of the holder, the amount of the bond held on the balance sheet and, finally, the probability of selling the bond before its expiry. On the other hand, objective factors also play a role in defining the adjustment to the fair value: the trading activity of the bond, identified by the number of times it trades in the market in a given period and average amount. The combination of these two types of factors determine the liquidity adjustment to the fair value of the bond that refers to the specific holder—not a quantity that can be applied "objectively" to the bond.

The model we present hinges on two considerations:

1. A long position in an illiquid bond that cannot be sold immediately, but only over a certain period that depends on its trading activity, can be made comparable, in terms of generation liquidity, with a position in a liquid bond that can be immediately sold, if the bank borrows the amount that it would receive if the position were in the liquid bond, and then repay the loan as it receives the money from the selling of the illiquid bond during the period that is required to complete the trade. This strategy has clearly a cost that depends on the funding spread that the bank has to pay for the period needed to fully dismantle the position. We name the correction to the fair value of the bond due to this cost as liquid equivalent adjustment (LEA).
2. During the time required to completely sell the amount of the bond, the price of the bond can move up and down. The bank is interested in forecasting adverse movements and then computing the maximum loss (at a certain confidence level) it could suffer for not being able to sell immediately the amount held. The loss is given by the difference between the value of the position in the bond at the time the bank decides to sell it, and the minimum value of the position during the period required to completely sell it. We term the correction to the fair value of the bond due to this loss as price volatility adjustment (PVA).

Both adjustments have to take into account the fact that the costs (for LEA) and the loss (for PVA) are borne by the bank only if it decides to sell the position in the future. So they have to be weighted by a selling probability that will then be included in the model. The sum of the two adjustments is the liquidity adjustment (LA) to the fair value. The adjusted price is the liquidity that can be expected to be extracted from the position in an illiquid bond.

Remark 8.7.1. *The model we present produces the LA assuming that the bank wants to sell the entire amount held when it decides to do so. In reality, it is possible to consider cases when only partial liquidation of the position is planned as well. In this case the adjustment has to be computed with respect to this amount, smaller than the total amount on the* *balance sheet, so that it will be different. It is then possible to calculate a range of LAs depending on the different fractions of the total amount that have to be sold.*

8.7.1 Liquid equivalent adjustment

Let us focus on the LEA component of the LA. Assume that at time t we wish to compute the liquidity adjustment for a bond maturing at T. Let $\mathbf{B}(t, T)$ be the fair value at time t; the expected price of the bond at a future date s is $\mathrm{CH}(t, s, T)$. We work within the framework described in Section 8.5 to evaluate the bond and we use the same notation. The amount held by the bank on its balance sheet is N.

The bond is not actively traded in the market: we first need to model the trading activity. Let the average traded amount of the notional of the bond be $\bar{N}$, and let the trades occur with a trading intensity at time t equal to $\lambda^T(t)$. Trading intensity indicates how many trades occur in a short period dt; the inverse of the intensity $1/\lambda^T(t)$ gives the expected time elapsing before a new trade occurs.

For example, assume that $\bar{N} = 1{,}000{,}000$ and that $\lambda^T(t) = 365$. This means that the bank can expect to trade 1,000,000 notional every $\lambda^T(t) = 1/365$ of a year, or every day. If $\lambda^T(t) = 182$, then 1,000,000 notional is expected to trade approximately every 2 days.

Trading intensity is modelled as a deterministic function of the kind

$$\lambda^T(t) = \lambda^T e^{-\kappa^T t} + \bar{\lambda}^T (1 - e^{-\kappa^T t}), \tag{8.204}$$

where λ_0^T is the trade intensity at $t = 0$, $\bar{\lambda}^T$ is the long-term average trading intensity. Usually, bonds start with good trading activity after their issuance, then the number of deals gradually fade away during the life and, finally, the market becomes scant as the maturity approaches. This pattern can be modelled by setting a high trading intensity just after issuance of the bond (e.g., $\lambda^T(0) \geq 365$ for trades occurring at least once a day), and a low long-term average intensity (e.g., $\bar{\lambda}^T \leq 25$ for trades occurring less than once a fortnight). The speed at which trading activity is pushed towards the long-term average is commanded by the parameter κ^T.

The probability that the bank decides to sell the bond can be modelled by an intensity process as well: in this case we want to make the probability dependent on the default probability of the bank, since when the latter increases there is a higher probability that the bank may wish to sell less liquid assets to avoid paying high credit spreads over the risk-free rate. Thus, the selling intensity is:

$$\mu(t) = f(t) + \alpha \lambda_B^D(t), \tag{8.205}$$

where $f(t)$ is a deterministic function and $\lambda_B^D(t)$ is the bank's default intensity, which is in turn a composite intensity as in Section 8.5. This formulation will also allow wrong-way risk to be considered (i.e., a higher probability to sell the bond when its value is lower due to the higher default probabilities of the issuer). Using the property of the CIR process, we write the selling intensity as

$$\mu(t) = f(t) + \mathrm{CIR}(\alpha \lambda_B^D(t_0), \kappa, \alpha \theta, \sqrt{\alpha} \sigma, t - t_0), \tag{8.206}$$

so that $\mu(t)$ is a process. Here, for the function $f(t)$, we take a deterministic function of the type

$$f(t) = f(t_0) e^{-k(t-t_0)} + \bar{f}(1 - e^{-k(t-t_0)}), \tag{8.207}$$

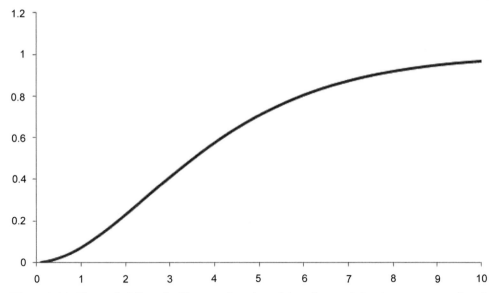

Figure 8.16. The probability of selling as a function of time (in years) for the parameters given in Table 8.25

so that the integral is

$$F(t_0, t) = \int_{t_0}^{t} f(u)du = (t - t_0)\bar{f} + \frac{1 - e^{-k(t-t_0)}}{k}\left[f(t_0) - \bar{f}\right]. \qquad (8.208)$$

It is also easy to check that when the PD of the bank (i.e., the holder of the bond) increases, selling intensity increases as well by a factor α. The probability of selling the bond between two times s and T is

$$PS(s, T) = PNS(t, s) - PNS(t, T). \qquad (8.209)$$

where $PNS(t_0, t)$ is the probability that the bond is *not* sold within $[t_0, t]$, which is available in a closed-form formula in our setting:

$$PNS(t_0, t) = e^{-\int_{t_0}^{t} f(s)ds} P_{CIR}(\lambda_B^D(t), t_0, t) \qquad (8.210)$$

where $P(\lambda_B^D(t), t_0, t)$ is given in (8.27). In Figure 8.16 we show the probability of selling as a function of time for the selling parameters in Table 8.25.

Table 8.25. The selling parameters used for Figure 8.16

Parameter	Value
$f(t_0)$	1%
k	0.3
$\bar{f}$	50%
α	0.00

Given this setting, at time t the bank has to operate an expected number of $N/\bar{N}$ transactions to sell the entire position it holds; with selling intensity equal to $\lambda^T(t)$, the average time $\text{Tl}(t)$ to close out the position is:

$$\text{Tl}(t) = \frac{N}{\bar{N}\,\lambda^T(t)}. \tag{8.211}$$

If the bank wants to have the money it would receive if the bond were liquid immediately, it has it to borrow an amount of money equal to $N \times \mathbf{B}(t, T)$. The borrowed amount is gradually paid back as the selling process completes; meanwhile the bank pays interest on the outstanding debt it has. The total interest rate the bank pays is composed of the risk-free rate plus a funding (credit) spread; on the other hand, the bank still earns the yield on the part of the position in the bond that has not yet been sold (which equals the outstanding debt). For equilibrium the yield on the bond's position should match the risk-free rate so we assume that on an expectation basis the net cost paid by the bank is the funding spread.

Over the period $[t, t + \text{Tl}(t)]$ the annualized funding spread required of the bank is:[15]

$$s^B(t, t + \text{Tl}(t)) = L_{\text{GD}}\,\frac{\text{PD}_B(t, t + \text{Tl}(t))}{\text{Tl}(u)}, \tag{8.212}$$

where L_{GD} is the loss given default percentage (e.g., $L_{\text{GD}} = 60\%$) and PD_B is the default probability of the bank.

The LEA is the present value of the expected costs paid by the bank in case it decides to sell the bond, weighted by the probability of selling:

$$\text{LEA}(t_0, T) = \mathbf{E}\Bigg[\int_{t_0}^{T} P^D(t_0, t)$$
$$\times \left(\int_{t}^{t+\text{Tl}(t)} s^B(u, u + \text{Tl}(t))\,(N - \bar{N}\,\lambda^T(u)\,(u - t))\mathbf{B}(u, T)\,du\right) d\text{PNS}(t_0, t)\Bigg], \tag{8.213}$$

where $s^B(u, u + \text{Tl}(t))$ is the stochastic spread rate applied for the period $[u, u + \text{Tl}(t)]$ and $P^D(t, u)$ is the discount factor for the short-rate r_t over the period $[t, u]$.

Over the period $[t, t + \text{Tl}(t)]$, we approximate the spread and the price of the bond with its value in t. This is a good numeric approximation, since the liquidation time ranges from one day to a few months, and the integral over du can be performed numerically by using a few integration points. The integral in equation (8.213) is then approximated as

$$\text{LEA}(t_0 T) = N\,\mathbf{E}\Bigg[\int_{t_0}^{T} P^D(t_0, t)\,s^B(t)\,\mathbf{B}(t, T)$$
$$\times \left(\int_{t}^{t+\text{Tl}(t)} \left(1 - \frac{u - t}{(t)}\right) du\right) d\text{PNS}(t_0, t)\Bigg]. \tag{8.214}$$

---

[15] See Section 8.4.

where $s^B(t) = s^B(t, t + \text{Tl}(t))$. The integration over du is

$$\int_t^{t+\text{Tl}(t)} \left(1 - \frac{u - t}{\text{Tl}(t)}\right) du = \text{Tl}(t) - \frac{\text{Tl}(t)^2}{2} = \frac{1}{2}\text{Tl}(t). \tag{8.215}$$

The liquidity adjustment in equation (8.214) is then

$$\text{LEA}(t_0, T) = N\,\mathbf{E}\left[\int_{t_0}^T P^D(t_0, t)\, s(t)\, \mathbf{B}(t, T)\, \frac{\text{Tl}(t)}{2}\, d\text{PNS}(t_0, t)\right]. \tag{8.216}$$

Numerical evaluation

To compute the value of the LEA, we consider a set of n dates T_i at which the selling of the bond might occur. We define the liquidation time at T_i with $\text{Tl}_i = \text{Tl}(T_i)$. The liquidity adjustment in equation (8.216) reads

$$\text{LEA}(t_0, T) = N\,\mathbf{E}\left[\sum_{i=1}^n P^D(t_0, T_i)\, s^B(T_i, T_i + \text{Tl}_i)\, (T_i, T)\, \frac{\text{Tl}_i}{2}\, (\text{PNS}(t_0, T_{i-1}) - \text{PNS}(t_0, T_i))\right].$$
$$\tag{8.217}$$

Taking the expression for the spread as in equation (8.212), the expression for $\text{LEA}(t_0, T)$ reads

$$\text{LEA}(t_0, T) = \frac{N}{2}\,\text{L}_{\text{GD}}\,\mathbf{E}\left[\sum_{i=1}^n P^D(t_0, T_i)\, \mathbf{B}(T_i, T)\, \text{PD}_B(T_i, T_i + \text{Tl}_i)\right.$$

$$\left. \times (\text{PNS}(t_0, T_{i-1}) - \text{PNS}(t_0, T_i))\right]. \tag{8.218}$$

Defining the function

$$\mathcal{SB}(t_0, T_i, T) = \mathbf{E}\left[P^D(t_0, T_i)\, \mathbf{B}(T_i, T)\, \text{PD}_B(T_i, T_i + \text{Tl}_i) \times (\text{PNS}(t_0, T_{i-1}) - \text{PNS}(t_0, T_i))\right],$$
$$\tag{8.219}$$

the expression for the $\text{LEA}(t_0, T)$ is

$$\text{LEA}(t_0, T) = \frac{N}{2}\sum_{i=1}^n \mathcal{SB}(t_0, T_i, T).$$

The expression for $\mathcal{SB}(t_0, T_i, T)$ can be cast in a closed form (details are given in Appendix 8.A).

8.7.2 Price volatility adjustment

The second component of LA is the adjustment due to the losses the bank can incur during the liquidation period, since the bond price can divert from the level at the time the selling process starts. We define this as Price Volatility Adjustment (PVA). Consider a bond of maturity T. At time t_0, let the expected (future) in t be $\text{CH}(t_0, t, T)$; the value of the portfolio can also drop, at time t, to $V_p(t_0, t)$ for a certain confidence level p.

To compute PVA, we cannot apply the procedure in Section 8.7.1 to separate the expected value of the product from the probability of selling and the quantile. In the present case, we need to compute the expectation value in the forward risk-adjusted measure with respect to the short rate r and to the default intensity processes. Let us define PVA as

$$\text{PVA}(t_0, T) = \mathbf{E}\left[\int_{t_0}^{T} P^D(t_0, t)\right.$$

$$\left. \times \left(\int_{t}^{t+\text{TI}(t)} \left[N - \bar{N}\,\lambda^T(t)\,(t-u)\right] \left[\mathbf{B}(u, T) - V_p(t, u)\right] du\right) d\text{PNS}(t_0, t)\right]. \quad (8.220)$$

Similarly to the case of $\text{LEA}(t_0, T)$, we assume that the selling of the bond can happen only at specific dates T_i. The expression in equation (8.220) reads

$$\text{PVA}(t_0, T) = N\,\mathbf{E}\left[\sum_{i=1}^{n} P^D(t_0, T_i)\,(\text{PNS}(t_0, T_{i-1}) - \text{PNS}(t_0, T_i))\right.$$

$$\left. \times \int_{T_i}^{T_i + \text{TI}_i} \left[1 - \frac{T_i - u}{\text{TI}_i}\right] \left[\mathbf{B}(u, T) - V_p(T_i, u)\right] du\right]. \quad (8.221)$$

To evaluate $\text{PVA}(t_0, T)$ numerically, we first consider the expectation value appearing in equation (8.221). We take this expectation value in the forward measure $\mathbf{E}^{T_i, T_i}$, where the first index refers to the T_i-forward measure with respect to r_t, and the second index refers to the T_i-forward measure with respect to λ. We obtain

$$\mathbf{E}\left[P^D(t_0, T_i)\,\mathbf{B}(u, T)\,(\text{PNS}(t_0, T_{i-1}) - \text{PNS}(t_0, T_i))\right]$$

$$= P^D(t_0, T_i)\,\text{PNS}(t_0, T_{i-1})\,\mathbf{E}^{T_i, T_i}[\mathbf{B}(u, T)] - P^D(t_0, T_i)\,\text{PNS}(t_0, T_i)\,\mathbf{E}^{T_i, T_i}[\mathbf{B}(u, T)]$$

$$= P^D(t_0, T_i)\,\text{CG}(T_i, u, T)\,[\text{PNS}(t_0, T_{i-1}) - \text{PNS}(t_0, T_i)] \quad (8.222)$$

where $\text{CG}(t, s, T)$ indicates the forward at time t for a bond with expiry s and maturity T, in the measure described above. Explicitly, it is

$$\text{CG}(t, s, T) = N\,\mathbf{G}^\ell(r; t, s, T)\,\mathbf{G}(\lambda_{A,t}^D; t, s, T) + N\,c\sum_{i: t_i > s} (t_i - t_{i-1})\,\mathbf{G}^\ell(r; t, s, t_i)\,\mathbf{G}(\lambda_{A,t}^D; t, s, t_i)$$

$$+ N\,(1 - \text{L}_{\text{GD}})\sum_{i: t_i > s} \mathbf{G}^\ell(r; t, s, t_i)\left[\mathbf{G}(\lambda_{A,t}^D; t, s, t_{i-1}) - \mathbf{G}(\lambda_{A,t}^D; t, s, t_i)\right]$$

$$- N\,c\,T_{\text{accr}}, \quad (8.223)$$

where $\lambda_{A,t}^D$ is the default intensity of the bond's issuer, which follows the usual composite CIR++ dynamics, and the accrued time is

$$T_{\text{accr}} = s - \max(t_l : t_l \le s),$$

and $\mathbf{G}^\ell(r; t, s, T)$ is given by

$$\mathbf{G}^\ell(r; t, s, T) = e^{-\ell(T-s)}\mathbf{G}(r; t, s, T)$$

where ℓ is the bond-specific parameter to capture liquidity specialness and $\mathbf{G}$ is the zero-coupon bond forward price given in equation (8.31). The expression in equation (8.221) reads

$$\mathrm{PVA}(t_0, T) = N \sum_{i=1}^{n} P^D(t_0, T_i) \left[\mathrm{PNS}(t_0, T_{i-1}) - \mathrm{PNS}(t_0, T_i)\right]$$

$$\times \int_{T_i}^{T_i+\mathrm{Tl}_i} \left[1 - \frac{T_i - u}{\mathrm{Tl}_i}\right] \left[\mathrm{CG}(T_i, u, T) - V_p(T_i, u)\right] du. \qquad (8.224)$$

To compute the quantile, we refer to the procedure outlined in Section (8.5.5), with the following modification. First, all futures appearing in the formulae are replaced by the corresponding expressions for the forwards in equation (8.223). Second, the mean and the covariance matrix of the short rate and of the default intensities are taken in the forward risk-adjusted measure. Following the result in Appendix 8.A, the mean is

$$M^r = e^{-I_0(t)} \left[r_0 + \theta_r I_1(t)\right],$$

$$M_i^\lambda = e^{-I_0(t)} \left[\lambda_0 + \theta_i I_1(t)\right],$$

while the covariance matrix is

$$\Omega_r = \frac{\sigma_r^2}{\kappa_r} e^{-2I_0(t)} I_1(t) \left[r_{i,t} + \frac{\theta_r}{2} I_1(t)\right],$$

$$(\Omega_\lambda)_{ii} = \frac{\sigma_i^2}{\kappa_\lambda} e^{-2I_0(t)} I_1(t) \left[\lambda_{i,t} + \frac{\theta_i}{2} I_1(t)\right],$$

$$(\Omega_\lambda)_{ij} = \frac{\sigma_i \sigma_j}{\kappa_\lambda} e^{-2I_0^C(t)} I_1^C(t) \left[\lambda_t^C + \frac{\theta^C}{2} I_1^C(t)\right].$$

We defined the integrals

$$I_0(t) = \int_0^t \tilde{\kappa}(u)\, du, \quad \text{and} \quad I_1(t) = \kappa \int_0^t e^{I_0(u)}\, du, \qquad (8.225)$$

while $I_0^C(t)$ and $I_1^C(t)$ are the same as the CIR parameters for the common intensity of the default process $\lambda^C(t)$ used. Explicit formulae for the integrals are given in Appendix 8.A.

Numerical evaluation of the integral in equation (8.224)

In computing the value of $\mathrm{PVA}(t_0, T)$, we cannot approximate the function $\mathrm{CG}(T_i, u, T) - V_p(T_i, u)$ appearing in equation (8.224) to its value in T_i, because at the selling time the quantile equals the value of the bond and the expected loss is zero. In order to include the expected loss in the numerical computation of the integral over du, we use the following procedure

- we divide the period $[T_i, \mathrm{Tl}_i]$ into m fractions;
- we introduce the time step

$$\delta t_i = \frac{\mathrm{Tl}_i}{m}; \qquad (8.226)$$

- we introduce the integration points

$$t_k = T_i + k\, \delta t_i, \quad \text{with } k = 1, \ldots, m. \qquad (8.227)$$

- At the integration point $u = t_k$, we substitute

$$\frac{t_k - T_i}{\text{Tl}_i} = \frac{k}{m}.$$

The integral over du in equation (8.224) is then approximated by

$$\int_{T_i}^{T_i + \text{Tl}(T_i)} \left(1 - \frac{u - T_i}{\text{Tl}_i}\right) \left(\text{CG}(T_i, u, T) - V_p(T_i, u)\right) du$$

$$\approx \sum_{k=1}^{m} \left(1 - \frac{k}{m}\right) \left(\text{CG}(T_i, t_k, T) - V_p(T_i, t_k)\right) \delta t_i. \quad (8.228)$$

With this approximation, the expression in equation (8.224) reads

$$\text{PVA}(t_0, T) = N \sum_{i=1}^{n} P^D(t_0, T_i) \left(\text{PNS}(t_0, T_{i-1}) - \text{PNS}(t_0, T_i)\right)$$

$$\times \sum_{k=1}^{m} \left(1 - \frac{k}{m}\right) \left(\text{CG}(T_i, t_k, T) - V_p(T_i, t_k)\right) \delta t_i. \quad (8.229)$$

Total liquidity adjustment for the bond is then:

$$\text{LA}(t_0, T) = \text{LEA}(t_0, T) + \text{PVA}(t_0, T). \quad (8.230)$$

Example 8.7.1. *In the following example, we consider a bank with characteristics similar to Unicredit (UCG, see above) wants to value a bond issued by Intesa Sanpaolo (ISP) with the specifics in Table 8.26. In Table 8.27, we show the CIR parameters used to describe the default intensity of UCG and ISP. We assume that the bond can be sold only*

Table 8.26. Specifics of the ISP bond for which the liquidity adjustment is computed

Parameter	Value
Maturity	14/4/2020
Coupon rate	4.1250%
Market price	87.5480

Table 8.27. Parameter values of the model for the intensity of default process for UCG and ISP

Parameter	Value
λ^C	6.06%
λ^{UCG}	3.51%
λ^{ISP}	3.99%
κ	0.0276
θ^C	4.517%
θ^{UCG}	9.505%
θ^{ISP}	9.505%
σ^C	5.679%
ρ_{UCG}	0.7984
ρ_{ISP}	0.8175

Table 8.28. Parameters used for the results in Table 8.29

Parameter	Value
$\bar{N}$	2,000,000
λ^T	50
κ^T	1
$\bar{\lambda}^T$	10
$f(t_0)$	1%
k	0.05
$\bar{f}$	80%
α	0.00

Table 8.29. The term structure of liquid equivalent adjustment (LEA), liquid volatility adjustment (PVA) and total liquidity adjustment LA = LEA + PVA, for the parameters used in Table 8.28

T_i	PS(T_{i-1}, T_i) (%)	$T_{\text{liquidation}}$ (days)	Expected loss	LEA	PVA	LA
0.5	0.98	53.30	4.0933	0.0030	0.0020	0.0050
1.0	1.91	73.89	5.2729	0.0092	0.0065	0.0158
1.5	2.77	96.50	6.4234	0.0182	0.0146	0.0328
2.0	3.53	118.48	7.4070	0.0283	0.0258	0.0542
2.5	4.17	137.48	8.1346	0.0372	0.0388	0.0759
3.0	4.70	152.30	8.4752	0.0426	0.0509	0.0935
3.5	5.10	162.94	8.4820	0.0441	0.0601	0.1042
4.0	5.38	170.16	8.1484	0.0421	0.0654	0.1075
4.5	5.53	174.86	7.5734	0.0381	0.0667	0.1048
5.0	5.58	177.83	6.7913	0.0335	0.0642	0.0977
5.5	5.53	179.69	5.8403	0.0294	0.0585	0.0879
6.0	5.40	180.83	4.8395	0.0262	0.0506	0.0768
6.5	5.19	181.53	3.8231	0.0240	0.0418	0.0659
7.0	4.93	181.96	2.8066	0.0226	0.0318	0.0544
7.5	4.62	182.22	1.6078	0.0221	0.0227	0.0447
7.9	3.12	182.34	1.2020	0.0147	0.0134	0.0281
				0.4354	0.6138	1.0492

at specific dates T_i, with constant semiannual intervals $T_i - T_{i-1} = 6M$. In Table 8.29, we show results for the term structure of the probability of selling at each T_i the LEA, the liquidation time in days, the expected loss over $[T_i, T_i + Tl_i]$ and the values of PVA and total liquidity adjustment LA = LEA + PVA, when the parameters in Table 8.28 are used.

Example 8.7.2. *Keeping Example 8.7.1 in mind, we consider the case in which the liquidation time is much shorter when the bond is sold in the first years. Table 8.30 gives the entire set of parameters used. $\lambda^T = 730$ indicates that the bond trades in the market on average three times a day, in an amount of $\bar{N} = EUR2$ million. The results are in Table 8.31.*

Example 8.7.3. *Keeping Example 8.7.1 in mind once again, we consider the case in which the parameter of mean reversion governing the selling probability of the bond is higher.*

Table 8.30. Parameters used for the results in Table 8.31

Parameter	Value
$\bar{N}$	EUR2 million
λ^T	730
κ^T	1
$\bar{\lambda}^T$	10
$f(t_0)$	1%
k	0.05
$\bar{f}$	80%
α	0.00

Table 8.31. The term structure of the liquid equivalent adjustment (LEA), the price volatility adjustment (PVA), and the total liquidity adjustment LA = LEA + PVA, for the parameters used in Table 8.33

T_i	$PS(T_{i-1}, T_i)$ (%)	$T_{\text{liquidation}}$ (days)	Expected loss	LEA	PVA	LA
0.5	0.98	4.09	2.5486	0.0002	0.0001	0.0003
1.0	1.91	6.64	3.0860	0.0008	0.0005	0.0013
1.5	2.77	10.70	3.6662	0.0020	0.0013	0.0033
2.0	3.53	17.00	4.2060	0.0041	0.0028	0.0070
2.5	4.17	26.43	4.8076	0.0073	0.0058	0.0131
3.0	4.70	39.83	5.3976	0.0113	0.0107	0.0221
3.5	5.10	57.53	5.9033	0.0158	0.0178	0.0336
4.0	5.38	78.76	6.2673	0.0197	0.0267	0.0465
4.5	5.53	101.47	6.3582	0.0223	0.0357	0.0579
5.0	5.58	122.97	6.1349	0.0233	0.0424	0.0657
5.5	5.53	141.11	5.5452	0.0232	0.0449	0.0681
6.0	5.40	154.97	4.7493	0.0225	0.0430	0.0656
6.5	5.19	164.79	3.8259	0.0219	0.0380	0.0598
7.0	4.93	171.37	2.8260	0.0213	0.0301	0.0514
7.5	4.62	175.63	1.6826	0.0213	0.0220	0.0432
7.9	3.12	177.69	1.2020	0.0143	0.0131	0.0273
				0.2314	0.3348	0.5662

This means that before expiry of the bond, there will be more chances that the bond will be sold by UGC. Table 8.32 gives the parameters and the results are shown in Table 8.33.

Example 8.7.4. *Keeping Example 8.7.1 in mind yet again, we show the impact of parameter α, which regulates the impact of the stochastic component of the probability of selling depending on the probability of default of the bank (UCG in this case). The results are shown in Figure 8.17 for the parameters in Table 8.34.*

Conditioned selling probability

In this section we will show how the results presented in the previous examples modify when we assume the bank will definitely sell the bond within the maturity T. To consider

Table 8.32. Parameters used for the results in Table 8.33

Parameter	Value
$\bar{N}$	EUR2 million
λ^T	50
κ^T	1
$\bar{\lambda}^T$	10
$f(t_0)$	1%
k	1
$\bar{f}$	80%
α	0.00

Table 8.33. The term structure of liquid equivalent adjustment (LEA), price volatility adjustment (PVA) and total liquidity adjustment LA = LEA + PVA, for the parameters used in Table 8.32

T_i	$PS(T_{i-1}, T_i)$ (%)	$T_{\text{liquidation}}$ (days)	Expected loss	LEA	PVA	LA
0.5	8.53	53.30	4.0933	0.0261	0.0170	0.0431
1.0	17.43	73.89	5.2729	0.0842	0.0593	0.1434
1.5	18.40	96.50	6.4234	0.1210	0.0971	0.2181
2.0	15.66	118.48	7.4070	0.1260	0.1147	0.2406
2.5	12.03	137.48	8.1346	0.1072	0.1118	0.2190
3.0	8.73	152.30	8.4752	0.0792	0.0946	0.1738
3.5	6.13	162.94	8.4820	0.0530	0.0723	0.1254
4.0	4.23	170.16	8.1484	0.0331	0.0515	0.0846
4.5	2.88	174.86	7.5734	0.0198	0.0348	0.0546
5.0	1.95	177.83	6.7913	0.0117	0.0225	0.0342
5.5	1.32	179.69	5.8403	0.0070	0.0139	0.0209
6.0	0.89	180.83	4.8395	0.0043	0.0083	0.0126
6.5	0.60	181.53	3.8231	0.0028	0.0048	0.0076
7.0	0.40	181.96	2.8066	0.0018	0.0026	0.0044
7.5	0.27	182.22	1.6078	0.0013	0.0013	0.0026
7.9	0.14	182.34	1.2020	0.0006	0.0006	0.0012
				0.6792	0.7070	1.3862

this case, we introduce the probability of selling conditional to the selling of the bond before expiry. We impose that the probability of not having sold the bond within T is given the value of zero or, equivalently, the probability of selling before T the value of one. To achieve this, we divide the probability of selling presented in equation (8.209) by the probability of selling the bond after T, so that it becomes a conditional probability:

$$PS'(t_0, t) = \frac{PS(t_0, t)}{1 - PNS(t_0, T)}. \tag{8.231}$$

The conditional probability of selling thus defined satisfies

$$PS'(t_0, T) = 1. \tag{8.232}$$

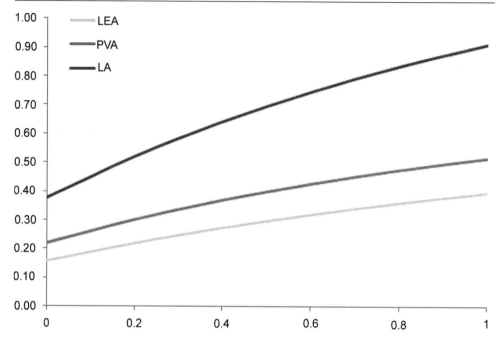

Figure 8.17. LA, LEA and PVA as a function of parameter α (x-axis). The other parameters are given in Table 8.34

Table 8.34. The selling parameters used for Figure 8.17

Parameter	Value
$\bar{N}$	EUR2 million
λ^T	50
κ^T	1
$\bar{\lambda}^T$	10
$f(t_0)$	1%
k	0.1
$\bar{f}$	10%

Example 8.7.5. *In this example we keep the results presented in Examples 8.7.1, 8.7.2 and 8.7.3 in mind, where UCG computes the liquidity adjustment on an ISP bond using the specifics in Table 8.26.*

When the conditional probability of selling $PS'(t_0, t)$ is used instead of $PS(t_0, t)$, the results obtained in the examples above modify as follows. In Table 8.35, we show the results when the trading and selling parameters are the same as in Table 8.28. In Table 8.36, we show the results when the trading and selling parameters are the same as in Table 8.30, where the initial value of trading intensity is higher than in the first example. Finally, in Table 8.37, we show the results when the trading intensity and the selling parameters are as given in Table 8.32. In Figure 8.17, LA, ELA and PVA are plotted as a function of parameter α.

Table 8.35. The term structure of liquid equivalent adjustment (LEA), price volatility adjustment (PVA) and total liquidity adjustment $LA = LEA + PVA$, for the parameters used in Table 8.28

T_i	(T_{i-1}, T_i) (%)	$T_{\text{liquidation}}$ (days)	Expected loss	LEA	PVA	LA
0.5	1.44	53.30	4.0933	0.0044	0.0029	0.0073
1.0	2.80	73.89	5.2729	0.0135	0.0095	0.0230
1.5	4.04	96.50	6.4234	0.0266	0.0213	0.0479
2.0	5.15	118.48	7.4070	0.0414	0.0377	0.0791
2.5	6.09	137.48	8.1346	0.0543	0.0566	0.1109
3.0	6.86	152.30	8.4752	0.0622	0.0743	0.1365
3.5	7.44	162.94	8.4820	0.0643	0.0877	0.1521
4.0	7.85	170.16	8.1484	0.0615	0.0955	0.1570
4.5	8.08	174.86	7.5734	0.0556	0.0974	0.1529
5.0	8.15	177.83	6.7913	0.0489	0.0937	0.1426
5.5	8.08	179.69	5.8403	0.0430	0.0854	0.1284
6.0	7.88	180.83	4.8395	0.0383	0.0738	0.1121
6.5	7.58	181.53	3.8231	0.0351	0.0611	0.0961
7.0	7.19	181.96	2.8066	0.0330	0.0465	0.0795
7.5	6.75	182.22	1.6078	0.0322	0.0331	0.0653
7.9	4.56	182.34	1.2020	0.0214	0.0196	0.0410
				0.6356	0.8961	1.5317

Table 8.36. The term structure of liquid equivalent adjustment (LEA), price volatility adjustment (PVA) and total liquidity adjustment LA = LEA + PVA, for the parameters used in Table 8.30

T_i	$PS(T_{i-1}, T_i)$ (%)	$T_{\text{liquidation}}$ (days)	Expected loss	LEA	PVA	LA
0.5	1.44	4.09	2.5486	0.0003	0.0002	0.0004
1.0	2.80	6.64	3.0860	0.0012	0.0007	0.0019
1.5	4.04	10.70	3.6662	0.0030	0.0018	0.0048
2.0	5.15	17.00	4.2060	0.0060	0.0041	0.0102
2.5	6.09	26.43	4.8076	0.0106	0.0085	0.0191
3.0	6.86	39.83	5.3976	0.0166	0.0157	0.0322
3.5	7.44	57.53	5.9033	0.0231	0.0261	0.0491
4.0	7.85	78.76	6.2673	0.0288	0.0391	0.0679
4.5	8.08	101.47	6.3582	0.0325	0.0521	0.0846
5.0	8.15	122.97	6.1349	0.0340	0.0618	0.0959
5.5	8.08	141.11	5.5452	0.0339	0.0655	0.0994
6.0	7.88	154.97	4.7493	0.0329	0.0628	0.0957
6.5	7.58	164.79	3.8259	0.0319	0.0554	0.0873
7.0	7.19	171.37	2.8260	0.0311	0.0439	0.0750
7.5	6.75	175.63	1.6826	0.0310	0.0321	0.0631
7.9	4.56	177.69	1.2020	0.0209	0.0191	0.0399
				0.3378	0.4888	0.8266

Table 8.37. The term structure of liquid equivalent adjustment (LEA), liquid volatility adjustment (PVA) and total liquidity adjustment LA = LEA + PVA, for the parameters used in Table 8.32

T_i	$PS(T_{i-1}, T_i)$ (%)	$T_{\text{liquidation}}$ (days)	Expected loss	LEA	PVA	LA
0.5	8.56	53.30	4.0933	0.0262	0.0171	0.0433
1.0	17.51	73.89	5.2729	0.0845	0.0595	0.1440
1.5	18.47	96.50	6.4234	0.1215	0.0975	0.2190
2.0	15.73	118.48	7.4070	0.1265	0.1151	0.2416
2.5	12.08	137.48	8.1346	0.1076	0.1123	0.2199
3.0	8.77	152.30	8.4752	0.0795	0.0950	0.1745
3.5	6.16	162.94	8.4820	0.0533	0.0726	0.1259
4.0	4.25	170.16	8.1484	0.0333	0.0517	0.0850
4.5	2.90	174.86	7.5734	0.0199	0.0349	0.0548
5.0	1.96	177.83	6.7913	0.0118	0.0225	0.0343
5.5	1.32	179.69	5.8403	0.0070	0.0140	0.0210
6.0	0.89	180.83	4.8395	0.0043	0.0083	0.0127
6.5	0.60	181.53	3.8231	0.0028	0.0048	0.0076
7.0	0.40	181.96	2.8066	0.0018	0.0026	0.0044
7.5	0.27	182.22	1.6078	0.0013	0.0013	0.0026
7.9	0.14	182.34	1.2020	0.0006	0.0006	0.0012
				0.6820	0.7099	1.3919

APPENDIX 8.A   EXPECTATION VALUE OF THE BOND WITH SELLING PROBABILITY AND SPREAD

In this section, we compute the expectation value in equation (8.219). We write this expression as

$$
SB(t_0, T_i, T) = \mathbf{E}_t \Bigg[\sum_{i=1}^n e^{-\int_{t_0}^{T_i} r(s)\,ds} B(T_i, T) \left(e^{-\int_{t_0}^{T_i} \lambda_B(t)\,dt} - e^{-\int_{t_0}^{T_i+Tl_i} \lambda_B(t)\,dt} \right)
$$
$$
\times \left(e^{-F_{i-1}} e^{-\int_{t_0}^{T_{i-1}} \alpha \lambda_B(t)\,dt} - e^{-F_i} e^{-\int_{t_0}^{T_i} \alpha \lambda_B(t)\,dt} \right) \Bigg]. \quad (8.233)
$$

In equation (8.233), we explained the expressions for $P^D(t_0, T_i)$ in terms of the stochastic short-rate $r(t)$, and the expressions for $PD_B(T_i, T_i + Tl_i)$ and $PNS(t_0, T_i)$ in terms of default intensities. Moreover, $B(T_i, T)$ is the expression for a defaultable coupon bond, see equation (8.157), before the expectation value is taken,

$$
B(T_i, T) = e^{-\int_{T_i}^{T} r(s)\,ds} e^{-\int_{T_i}^{T} \lambda_A(s)\,ds} + \sum_{j:t_j > T_i} c\,T_i e^{-\int_{T_i}^{t_j} r(s)\,ds} e^{-\int_{T_i}^{t_j} \lambda_A(s)\,ds}
$$
$$
+ (1 - L_{GD}) \sum_{j:t_j > T_i} e^{-\int_{T_i}^{t_j} r(s)\,ds} \left[e^{-\int_{T_i}^{t_{j-1}} \lambda_A(s)\,ds} - e^{-\int_{T_i}^{t_j} \lambda_A(s)\,ds} \right] - c\,T_{\text{accr}}. \quad (8.234)
$$

The quantity in equation (8.234) is the sum of four terms, so that $\mathcal{SB}(t_0, T_i, T)$ in equation (8.233) can be split into four terms as well. For example, we show explicitly the computation involving the term

$$\sum_{j:t_j > T_i} c\, \tau_i e^{-\int_{T_i}^{t_j} r(s)ds} \, e^{-\int_{T_i}^{t_j} \lambda_A(s)ds},$$

and the part in equation (8.233) containing this term reads

$$\mathbf{E}_{t_0}\left[\sum_{i=1}^{n} \sum_{j:t_j > T_i} c\, \tau_i e^{-\int_{T_i}^{t_j} r(s)ds} \, e^{-\int_{T_i}^{t_j} \lambda_A(s)ds} \left(e^{-\int_{t_0}^{T_i} \lambda_B(t)\,dt} - e^{-\int_{t_0}^{T_i + \Pi_i} \lambda_B(t)\,dt} \right) \right.$$

$$\left. \times \left(e^{-F_{i-1}} e^{-\int_{t_0}^{T_{i-1}} \alpha \lambda_B(t)\,dt} - e^{-F_i} e^{-\int_{t_0}^{T_i} \alpha \lambda_B(t)\,dt} \right) \right]$$

$$= \sum_{i=1}^{n} \sum_{j:t_j > T_i} c\, \tau_i \, \mathbf{E}_t\left[e^{-\int_{t_0}^{t_j} r(s)ds} \, e^{-\int_{T_i}^{t_j} \lambda_A(s)ds} \right.$$

$$\times \left(e^{-F_{i-1}} e^{-\int_{t_0}^{T_{i-1}}(1+\alpha)\lambda_B(t)\,dt} e^{-\int_{T_{i-1}}^{T_i} \lambda_B(t)\,dt} - e^{-F_{i-1}} e^{-\int_{t_0}^{T_{i-1}}(1+\alpha)\lambda_B(t)\,dt} e^{-\int_{T_{i-1}}^{T_i+i} \lambda_B(t)\,dt} \right.$$

$$\left. \left. - e^{-F_i} e^{-\int_{t_0}^{T_i}(1+\alpha)\lambda_B(t)\,dt} + e^{-F_i} e^{-\int_{t_0}^{T_i}(1+\alpha)\lambda_B(t)\,dt} e^{-\int_{T_i}^{T_i+i} \lambda_B(t)\,dt} \right) \right], \tag{8.235}$$

where we set the integral of the deterministic selling function $F_i = F(t_0, T_i)$. The expression in equation (8.235) is the sum of four distinct terms, coming from cross multiplication of the default probability times the probability of selling the asset over the period considered. For example, the first term in the sum in equation (8.235) is

$$\mathbf{E}_{t_0}\left[e^{-\int_{t_0}^{t_j} r(t)dt} \, e^{-\int_{T_i}^{t_j} \lambda_A(t)dt} \, e^{-\int_{t_0}^{T_{i-1}}(1+\alpha)\lambda_B(t)dt} \, e^{-\int_{T_{i-1}}^{T_i} \lambda_B(t)dt} \right].$$

We split processes λ_B and λ_A into an idiosyncratic and a common component and we arrange terms, thus obtaining

$$\mathbf{E}_{t_0}\left[e^{-\int_{t_0}^{t_j} r(t)dt} \, e^{-\int_{T_i}^{t_j} \lambda_A^I(t)dt} \right.$$

$$\times e^{-\int_{t_0}^{T_{i-1}}(1+\alpha)\lambda_B^I(t)dt - \int_{T_{i-1}}^{T_i} \lambda_B^I(t)dt} \, e^{-\int_{t_0}^{T_{i-1}}(1+\alpha)p_B\lambda^C(t)dt - \int_{T_{i-1}}^{T_i} p_B\lambda^C(t)dt - \int_{T_i}^{t_j} p_A\lambda^C(t)dt} \left. \right]. \tag{8.236}$$

We take the expectation value in the t_j-forward measure with respect to r_t and λ_A^I, so that the expression above is

$$P_{\text{CIR}}(r_0; t_0, t_j)\, \mathbf{G}(\lambda_A^I; t_0, T_i, t_j)\, \mathbf{E}_{t_0}^{t_j}\left[e^{-\int_{t_0}^{T_{i-1}}(1+\alpha)\lambda_B^I(s)ds - \int_{T_{i-1}}^{T_i} \lambda_B^I(s)ds} \right]$$

$$\times \mathbf{E}_{t_0}^{t_j}\left[e^{-\int_{t_0}^{T_{i-1}}(1+\alpha)p_B\lambda^C(s)ds - \int_{T_{i-1}}^{T_i} p_B\lambda^C(s)ds - \int_{T_i}^{t_j} p_A\lambda^C(s)ds} \right]. \tag{8.237}$$

Using the result

$$\mathbf{E}_{t_0}\left[e^{-\int_{t_0}^{T_{i-1}} a\lambda(s)ds}\, e^{-\int_{T_{i-1}}^{T_i} b\lambda(s)ds}\right] = P_{\mathrm{CIR}}(a\lambda(t_0); t_0, T_{i-1})\, \mathbf{G}(b\lambda(t_0); t_0, T_{i-1}, T_i), \quad (8.238)$$

we obtain

$$\mathbf{E}_{t_0}^{t_j}\left[e^{-\int_{t_0}^{T_{i-1}} (1+\alpha)\lambda_B^I(s)ds - \int_{T_{i-1}}^{T_i} \lambda_B^I(s)ds}\right] = P_{\mathrm{CIR}}((1+\alpha)\lambda_B^I(t_0); t_0, T_{i-1})\, \mathbf{G}(\lambda_B^I(t_0); t_0, T_{i-1}, T_i),$$

$$(8.239)$$

and

$$\mathbf{E}_{t_0}^{t_j}\left[e^{-\int_{t_0}^{T_{i-1}} (1+\alpha)p_B\lambda^C(s)ds - \int_{t_0}^{T_i} p_B\lambda^C(s)ds - \int_{T_i}^{t_j} p_A\lambda^C(s)ds}\right]$$

$$= P_{\mathrm{CIR}}((1+\alpha)p_B\lambda^C(t_0); t_0, T_{i-1})\, \mathbf{G}(p_B\lambda^C(t_0); t_0, T_{i-1}, T_i)\, \mathbf{G}(p_A\lambda^C(t_0); t_0, T_i, t_j). \quad (8.240)$$

Summing up, the expectation value is

$$P_{\mathrm{CIR}}(r; t_0, t_j)\, P_{\mathrm{CIR}}((1+\alpha)\lambda_B; t_0, T_{i-1})\, \mathbf{G}(\lambda_A; t_0, T_i, t_j)\, \mathbf{G}(\lambda_B; T_0, T_{i-1}, T_i). \quad (8.241)$$

Computing all four expectation values in equation (8.235), and repeating the computation for all four terms in the expression for the coupon bond in equation (8.234) and rearranging, we finally obtain the expression for the bond with the probability of selling and the spread in equation (8.219) as

$$\mathcal{SB}(t_0, T_i, T) = P_{\mathrm{CIR}}(r; t_0, T_i)\, F(T_i)\, \mathcal{B}(t_0, T_i, T),$$

where

$$\mathcal{F}(T_i) = e^{-F_{i-1}} P_{\mathrm{CIR}}((1+\alpha)\lambda_B; t_0, T_{i-1})\, \mathbf{G}(\lambda_B; t_0, T_{i-1}, T_i) - e^{-F_i} P_{\mathrm{CIR}}((1+\alpha)\lambda_B; t_0, T_i),$$

$$(8.242)$$

and we define the coupon bond when the selling probability is included as

$$\mathcal{B}(t_0, T_i, T) = \mathcal{P}(t_0, T_i, T) + \sum_{j=1}^{n} c\,\tau_i\, \mathcal{P}(t_0, T_i, t_j)$$

$$+ (1 - \mathrm{L_{GD}}) \sum_{j=1}^{n} \left[\mathcal{P}(t_0, T_i, S_{j-1}) - \mathcal{P}(t_0, T_i, t_j)\right] - c\, T_{\mathrm{accr}}\, \mathcal{P}(t_0, T_i, T_i).$$

$$(8.243)$$

We now introduce for notational convenience the function

$$\mathcal{P}(t_0, T_i, t_j) = \mathbf{G}_{\mathrm{CIR}}(r; T_i, t_j) \left[\mathbf{G}(\lambda_A; t_0, T_i, t_j) - \mathcal{G}(t_0, T_i, t_j)\right], \quad (8.244)$$

with, if $t_j > T_i + \mathrm{Tl}_i$,

$$\mathcal{G}(t_0, T_i, t_j) = \mathbf{G}(\lambda_A^I; t_0, T_i, t_j)\, \mathbf{G}(\lambda_B^I; t_0, T_i, T_i + \mathrm{Tl}_i)$$

$$\times \mathbf{G}((p_A + p_B)\lambda^C; t_0, T_i, T_i + \mathrm{Tl}_i)\, \mathbf{G}(p_A\lambda^C; t_0, T_i + \mathrm{Tl}_i, t_j), \quad (8.245)$$

or, if $t_j \leq T_i + \mathrm{Tl}_i$,

$$\mathcal{G}(t_0, T_i, t_j) = \mathbf{G}(\lambda_A^I; t_0, T_i, t_j)\, \mathbf{G}(\lambda_B^I; t_0, T_i, T_i + \mathrm{Tl}_i)$$

$$\times \mathbf{G}((p_A + p_B)\lambda^C; t_0, T_i, t_j)\, \mathbf{G}(p_B\, \lambda^C; t_0, t_j, T_i + \mathrm{Tl}_i)\,. \qquad (8.246)$$

Eventually, LEA is written in the more readable form

$$\mathrm{LEA}(t_0, T) = \frac{N}{2}\, \mathrm{L_{GD}} \sum_{i=1}^{n} \mathcal{SB}(t_0, T_i, T) = \frac{N}{2}\, \mathrm{L_{GD}} \sum_{i=1}^{n} P_{\mathrm{CIR}}(r; t_0, T_i)\, \mathcal{F}(T_i)\, \mathcal{B}(t_0, T_i, T).$$

$$(8.247)$$

The forward risk-adjusted measure

In the T-forward measure, a CIR process reads

$$dr(t) = (\kappa\,\theta - \tilde{\kappa}(t)\, r(t))\, dt + \sigma\, \sqrt{r(t)}\, dW_t^T. \qquad (8.248)$$

Brownian motion in the T-forward measure is

$$dW_t^T = dW_t + \sigma^2\, B(t, T),$$

and the mean reversion speed is

$$\tilde{\kappa}(t) = \kappa + \sigma^2\, B(t, T),$$

with the CIR factor

$$B(t, T) = \frac{2(e^{\gamma(T-t)} - 1)}{(\gamma + \kappa)(e^{\gamma(T-t)} - 1) + 2\gamma},$$

and $\gamma = \sqrt{\kappa^2 + 2\sigma^2}$.

Mean in the FRA measure

In the following, we indicate the mean value of r_t in the T-forward measure with

$$\mathbf{E}_1(t) = \mathbf{E}^T[r(t)]. \qquad (8.249)$$

Taking the expectation value of equation (8.248) in the T-forward measure, we find that $\mathbf{E}_1(t)$ satisfies the differential equation

$$\frac{d\mathbf{E}_1(t)}{dt} = \kappa\,\theta - \tilde{\kappa}(t)\, \mathbf{E}_1(t). \qquad (8.250)$$

To solve for $\mathbf{E}_1(t)$, we first compute a solution to the homogeneous part of the differential equation,

$$\frac{d\mathbf{E}_1^{\mathrm{Hom}}(t)}{dt} = -\tilde{\kappa}(t)\, \mathbf{E}_1^{\mathrm{Hom}}(t), \qquad (8.251)$$

or

$$\mathbf{E}_1^{\mathrm{Hom}}(t) = r_0\, e^{-\int_0^t \tilde{\kappa}(u)\, du}, \qquad (8.252)$$

where r_0 is the value at time $t = 0$ of the interest rate. To find a complete solution to equation (8.250), we use the method of the variation of constants. For this, we write

$$\mathbf{E}_1(t) = \mathbf{E}_1^{\mathrm{Hom}}(t) + r_0(t)\, e^{-\int_0^t \tilde{\kappa}(u)\, du}, \qquad (8.253)$$

where the function $r_0(t)$ follows a differential equation which is obtained by plugging equation (8.253) into equation (8.250), giving

$$\frac{dr_0(t)}{dt} e^{-\int_0^t \tilde{\kappa}(u)\, du} = \kappa\,\theta, \tag{8.254}$$

with the formal solution

$$r_0(t) = \kappa\,\theta \int_0^t e^{\int_0^u \tilde{\kappa}(v)\, dv}\, du. \tag{8.255}$$

Finally, a solution to the inhomogeneous equation (8.250) is given by the sum of the solution found by the methods of the variation of constants plus the homogeneous solution,

$$\mathbf{E}_1(t) = r_0\, e^{-\int_0^t \tilde{\kappa}(u)\, du} + \kappa\,\theta\, e^{-\int_0^t \tilde{\kappa}(u)\, du} \int_0^t e^{\int_0^u \tilde{\kappa}(v)\, dv}\, du. \tag{8.256}$$

As a check, we impose a constant $\tilde{\kappa}(t) = \kappa$, obtaining

$$\mathbf{E}_1(t) = r_0\, e^{-\kappa t} + \kappa\,\theta\, e^{-\kappa t} \int_0^t e^{\kappa u}\, du$$

$$= r_0\, e^{-\kappa t} + \theta\left(1 - e^{-\kappa t}\right), \tag{8.257}$$

which is precisely the expression for the average value of r_t in the risk-neutral measure. For the CIR model, this expression can be cast in a closed-form formula, since

$$\int_0^t \tilde{\kappa}(u)\, du = -\gamma\, t - 2\ln\left[\frac{(\gamma + \kappa)(e^{\gamma(T-t)} - 1) + 2\gamma}{(\gamma + \kappa)(e^{\gamma T} - 1) + 2\gamma}\right]. \tag{8.258}$$

It can be shown that, in the limit $\sigma \to 0$, the expression above reduces to $\kappa\, t$. We have

$$e^{-\int_0^t \tilde{\kappa}(u)\, du} = \left[\frac{(\gamma + \kappa)(e^{\gamma(T-t)} - 1) + 2\gamma}{(\gamma + \kappa)(e^{\gamma T} - 1) + 2\gamma}\right]^2 e^{\gamma t}, \tag{8.259}$$

and

$$\int_0^t e^{\int_0^u \tilde{\kappa}(v)\, dv}\, du = \frac{1}{\gamma\left[\frac{1}{e^{\gamma t} - 1} + \frac{\gamma - \kappa}{(\gamma + \kappa)(e^{\gamma T} - 1) + 2\gamma}\right]} \tag{8.260}$$

The complete expression for the mean of the CIR process in the T-forward measure is

$$\mathbf{E}_1(t) = e^{\gamma t}\left[\frac{(\gamma + \kappa)(e^{\gamma(T-t)} - 1) + 2\gamma}{(\gamma + \kappa)(e^{\gamma T} - 1) + 2\gamma}\right]^2 \left[r_0 + \frac{\kappa\,\theta}{\gamma\left[\frac{1}{e^{\gamma t} - 1} + \frac{\gamma - \kappa}{(\gamma + \kappa)(e^{\gamma T} - 1) + 2\gamma}\right]}\right]. \tag{8.261}$$

Volatility in the FRA measure

Let us try to find the value of the quantity

$$\mathrm{Vol} = \mathbf{E}^T\left[\left(r(t) - \mathbf{E}^T[r(t)]\right)^2\right]. \tag{8.262}$$

Setting

$$\mathbf{E}_2 = \mathbf{E}^T\left[r(t)^2\right], \tag{8.263}$$

we have

$$\text{Vol} = \mathbf{E}_2 - \mathbf{E}_1^2. \tag{8.264}$$

Using Ito's lemma, the quantity $r(t)^2$ follows the process

$$dr(t)^2 = 2 r(t) dr(t) + \sigma^2 r(t) dt$$

$$= 2 r(t) (\kappa \theta - \tilde{\kappa}(t) r(t)) dt + 2 r(t) \sigma \sqrt{r(t)} dW_t^T + \sigma^2 r(t) dt \tag{8.265}$$

where in the last equality we used the expression in equation (8.248) for the CIR process in the T-forward measure. Taking the expectation value on both sides, we obtain

$$d \mathbf{E}_2 = -2\tilde{\kappa}(t) \mathbf{E}_2 dt + (2\kappa \theta + \sigma^2) \mathbf{E}_1 dt. \tag{8.266}$$

The solution to the homogeneous equation is

$$\mathbf{E}_2^{\text{Hom}}(t) = r_0^2 e^{-2 \int_0^t \tilde{\kappa}(u) du}. \tag{8.267}$$

The solution to the inhomogeneous equation is the sum

$$\mathbf{E}_2(t) = r_0^2 e^{-2 \int_0^t \tilde{\kappa}(u) du} + v(t) e^{-2 \int_0^t \tilde{\kappa}(u) du}, \tag{8.268}$$

where the function $v(t)$ is fixed by using the method of the variation of constants. We find

$$\frac{dv(t)}{dt} e^{-2 \int_0^t \tilde{\kappa}(u) du} = (2\kappa \theta + \sigma^2) \mathbf{E}_1$$

$$= (2\kappa \theta + \sigma^2) \left[r_0 e^{-\int_0^t \tilde{\kappa}(u) du} + \kappa \theta e^{-\int_0^t \tilde{\kappa}(u) du} \int_0^t e^{\int_0^u \tilde{\kappa}(v) dv} du \right], \tag{8.269}$$

with the formal solution

$$v(t) = (2\kappa \theta + \sigma^2) \int_0^t \left[r_0 e^{\int_0^u \tilde{\kappa}(v) dv} + \kappa \theta e^{\int_0^u \tilde{\kappa}(v) dv} \int_0^u e^{\int_0^v \tilde{\kappa}(w) dw} dv \right] du. \tag{8.270}$$

Setting

$$I_1(t) = \kappa \int_0^t e^{\int_0^u \tilde{\kappa}(v) dv} du, \tag{8.271}$$

and

$$I_2(t) = \kappa \int_0^t e^{\int_0^u \tilde{\kappa}(v) dv} I_1(u) du, \tag{8.272}$$

we find that the volatility is

$$\text{Vol} = \frac{\sigma^2}{\kappa} e^{-2 \int_0^t \tilde{\kappa}(u) du} [r_0 I_1(t) + \theta I_2(t)] + \theta^2 \left[2 I_2(t) - I(1)^2 \right]. \tag{8.273}$$

However, the second term is unnecessary, since we find that

$$I_1(t) = \frac{\kappa \left[(\gamma + \kappa)(e^{\gamma T} - 1) + 2\gamma \right] (e^{\gamma t} - 1)}{\gamma [e^{\gamma t} (\gamma - \kappa) + e^{\gamma T} (\gamma + \kappa)]} \tag{8.274}$$

and

$$I_2(t) = \tfrac{1}{2} I_1(t)^2, \tag{8.275}$$

so $2\,I_2(t) - I(1)^2 = 0$. The volatility in the T-forward measure is then

$$\text{Vol} = \frac{\sigma^2}{\kappa}\,e^{-2\int_0^t \tilde{\kappa}(u)\,du}\,I_1(t)\left[r_0 + \frac{\theta}{2}\,I_1(t)\right]. \tag{8.276}$$

When $\sigma \to 0$, and $\gamma \to \kappa$, this equation reduces to the usual expression for the volatility in the risk-neutral measure,

$$\text{Vol} = \frac{\sigma^2}{\kappa}\,r_0\,e^{-\kappa t}\left(1 - e^{-\kappa t}\right) + \frac{\sigma^2}{2\kappa}\,\theta\left(1 - e^{-\kappa t}\right)^2. \tag{8.277}$$

9

Behavioural models

9.1 INTRODUCTION

Some items on the balance sheets of banks need to be modelled by a behavioural approach. By "behavioural" is generally meant a model that takes into account not only standard rationality principles to evaluate contracts, which basically means that economic agents prefer more wealth to less wealth, and that they prefer to receive cash sooner than later; behavioural models consider other factors as well, typically estimated by means of statistical analysis, which may produce effects that otherwise could not be explained. It should be stressed that in any event financial variables, such as interest rates or credit spreads, are the main driver of customer or, more generally, counterparty behaviour.

There are three main phenomena that need behavioural modelling: prepayment of mortgages, evolution of the amount of sight and saving deposits and withdrawals from credit lines. We will propose models for each focusing mainly on what we think is a good solution for liquidity management, without trying to offer a complete picture on the entire range of available models developed in theory or in practice. Anyway, as far as mortgage prepayments and withdrawals from credit lines are concerned, we introduce models that to our knowledge have never been proposed before, which aim at considering financial, credit and liquidity risk in a unified framework.

9.2 PREPAYMENT MODELLING

The prepayment of mortgages has to be properly taken into account in liquidity management, although many of the effects of the decision to pay back the residual amount of debt by the mortgagee are financial as they may cause losses to the financial institution. We will present a model to cope with the prepayment of fixed rate mortgages, because they combine both liquidity and financial effects.

9.2.1 Common approaches to modelling prepayments

There are two fundamental approaches to model prepayments

- *Empirical models (EMs)*: Prepayment is modelled as a function of some set of (non-model based) explanatory variables. Most of these models use either past prepayment rates or some other endogenous variables (such as burnout) or economic variables (such as GDP or interest rate levels) to explain current prepayment. Since they are just heuristic reduced-form representations for some true underlying process, it is not clear how they would perform in a different economic environment. Besides, no dynamic link between the prepayment rate and other explanatory variables has been established.

- *Rational prepayment models (RPMs)*: They are based on contingent claims pricing theory and as such the prepayment behaviour depends on interest rate evolution. Prepayment is considered as an option to close the contract at par (by repaying the nominal value of the outstanding amount), which will be exercised if the market value of the mortgage is higher than the nominal residual value. Although these models consistently link valuation of the mortgage and prepayment, their prepayment predictions do not closely match observed prepayment behaviour since not all debtors are skilled enough to evaluate the convenience of exercising the options. One of the drawbacks of rational models is that in their basic forms they imply that there will either be no prepayment or all mortgages with similar features will suddenly prepay, because all mortgagees will exercise their options.

Empirical features commonly attributed to mortgage prepayment are the following:

- some mortgages are prepaid even when their coupon rate is below current mortgage rates;
- some mortgages are not prepaid even when their coupon rate is above current mortgage rates;
- prepayment appears to be dependent on a burnout factor.

Since basic and simple RPMs are unable to fully take into account these features, most banks adopt EMs in an attempt to accurately predict prepayment rates. The prediction is the so-called CPR, or constant prepayment rate, which is used to project expected cash flows and which can be expressed as a function of different variables. For example, a well-known EM is the Richard and Roll [105] model adopted by Goldman Sachs and the US Office of Thrifts and Supervision; this model can be written in very simple form as:

$$CPR = f(\text{Refinance incentive})g(\text{Seasoning})h(\text{Month})l(\text{Burnout factor})$$

So the CPR depends on four functions of four different factors, the most important of which happens to be the refinance incentive or, in other words, exercising the option when it is convenient to do so. The refinance incentive (RI) function $f()$ is modelled as:

$$RI = 0.3124 - .020252 \times \arctan(8.157[-(C+S)/(P+F) + 1.20761])$$

where arctan is the arctangent function, C is the fixed rate of the coupon, S is the servicing rate of the pool,[1] P is the refinancing rate and F are additional costs due to refinancing.

In general, EMs perform quite well when predicting expected cash flows; they are also used to set up portfolios with hedging instruments with the notional adjusted according to the CPR. Since most model vendors plug EMs into their ALM systems and most banks use them, we examine how hedging with EMs works in practice.

9.2.2 Hedging with an empirical model

The refinance incentive is the most important factor, particularly in market environments with extremely low rates. In some countries mortgagees are charged no

---

[1] The original Richard and Roll model was conceived for MBS. $S = 0$ if the model is used for standard mortgage portfolios.

prepayment penalties, so they are more eager to exploit the prepayment option. More-over, some regulations allow mortgagees to transfer the mortgage to another bank at no cost: in this case competition amongst banks pushes the refinancing of mortgages with high contract rates when rates are low, thus increasing the "rationality" of prepayment. Even if the bank manages to keep the mortgagee, it is forced to refinance the mortgage at new market rates. In either case, in practical terms this is equivalent to a prepayment.

It goes without saying that, when the refinancing incentive is the major driver for prepayments, the bank suffers a loss that in very general terms can be set equal to the replacement cost of the prepaid contract.

For this reason we introduce a very simplified EM, and we use a function of the kind:

$$CPR = \alpha + \beta(C/P) \tag{9.1}$$

where C and P are defined as above. The CPR in equation (9.1) is a constant α plus a proportion β of the ratio between the mortgage rate C and the current rate level P. The lower the current rate P, the higher the CPR.

Let us create a laboratory environment and calibrate model (9.1) to empirical data reproduced by a random number generator. We assume that P is representative of a "general" level of interest rates (e.g., the average of the 5, 10 and 20-year swap rates). Moreover, C is the average fixed rate of the portfolio of mortgages, which we set equal to 3.95% (in line with the market rates we consider below). For each level of rates we have an annual CPR generated by the equation:

$$CPR = 0.75\% + 5\% \times \frac{C}{P} + 0.5\% \times \epsilon$$

where ϵ is a random number extracted from a normally distributed variable. The data are shown in Table 9.1.

We carry out linear regression to estimate the parameters and get $\alpha = 0.02881267$ and $\beta = 0.029949414$. A graphical representation of the fitting is given in Figure 9.1.

The simple model above seems able to capture the relevant factors affecting prepayment activity, which is strongly dependent on the level of the current interest

Table 9.1. Current level of rates P, ratio between fixed mortgage rate and current level of rates (C/P) and percentage of prepaid mortgages $PP\%$

Rates (%)	C/P	PP (%)
2.50	1.58	8.49
3.00	1.32	7.15
3.50	1.13	6.44
4.00	0.99	5.46
4.50	0.88	4.66
5.00	0.79	4.45
5.50	0.72	4.09
6.00	0.66	3.83
6.50	0.61	2.75
7.00	0.56	3.76
7.50	0.53	2.96

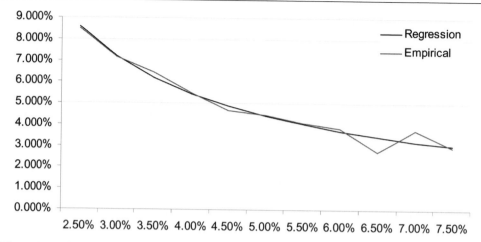

Figure 9.1. Linear regression estimation of prepayment data. The percentage of prepayments in one year is plotted against the current interest rate level

rate. Given this, we have the CPR to project expected cash flows and then to set up proper hedging strategies with other interest rate derivatives, typically IR swaps. The main problem with such an EM is that it is not dynamic and, unfortunately, does not allow for an effective hedge against *both* movements in interest rates *and* prepayment activity.

To see this, let us consider a mortgage that is representative of a bank's mortgage portfolio sold to clients at current market conditions. The mortgage expires in 10 years, it is linearly amortizing and its fair fixed rate, yearly paid, is 3.95%, given the 1Y Libor forward rates and associated discount factors shown in Table 9.2. In Table 9.3 the oustanding capital at the beginning of each year is shown. For simplicity's sake we also assume that no credit spread is applied, nor any markup to cover administrative costs, so that the mortgage rate is given only by Libor rates.

We can also compute expected cash flows given the prepayment activity forecast by the model we calibrated. If we assume that the current level of the interest rate is

Table 9.2. 1Y Libor forward rates and discount factors for maturities from 1 to 10 years

Year	Forward Libor (%)	Discount factor
1	3.25	0.96852
2	3.50	0.93577
3	3.75	0.90195
4	4.00	0.86726
5	4.25	0.83190
6	4.50	0.79608
7	4.75	0.75998
8	5.00	0.72379
9	5.25	0.68769
10	5.50	0.65184

Table 9.3. Outstanding capital at the beginning of each year for the representative mortgage

Year	Outstanding capital
1	100
2	90
3	80
4	70
5	60
6	50
7	40
8	30
9	20
10	10

summarized in the 10Y rate, 5.5%, the model provides a CPR of 4.02% p.a. Expected amortization and contract and expected cash flows are easily computed (see Table 9.4). In computing expected cash flows we used the convention that the CPR is a continuous rate such that, for a given year T, the percentage of prepaid mortgages is $(1 - e^{-CPR \times T})$.

The mortgage rate computed on expected cash flows, keeping in mind the prepayment effects, is slightly lower and equal to 3.89%. This is easy to understand, since we are in a steep-curve environment and the prepayment entails a shorter (expected) maturity of the contract, thus making the fair rate lower. In a very competitive market, it is tempting for the bank to grant such a lower rate to mortgagees, because after taking account of the costs related to hedging the bank appears not to be actually giving away value to customers.[2]

In fact, the ALM of the bank typically finances the mortgage portfolio by rolling over short-term debt or a similar maturity debt, but at a floating rate. The reason is easily understood, since as a result of floating rate indexation the duration of the bank debt is very short, and hence the volatility of balance sheet liabilities is reduced as well. As a consequence, the bank transforms its fixed rate mortgage portfolio into a floating rate mortgage portfolio (so that asset duration matches liability duration),[3] by taking expected cash flows instead of contract cash flows into account: in this way risk managers believe they have appropriately hedged prepayment risk as well, at least in average terms. The transformation, or hedge, is performed using liquid market instruments, usually swaps, by paying the fixed rate earned on the mortgage and receiving the Libor fixing (which is concurrently paid on financing).

In the example we are considering, the swap used for hedging purposes is not standard, but an amortizing swap with a decreasing notional equal to expected amortization as shown in the fourth column of Table 9.4, which reveals expected outstanding capital at the end of each year. Since we are not considering any credit spread on the mortgage, and assuming no credit issues in the swap market as well, we get the swap fair rate at inception as 3.89%, which is exactly the mortgage rate computed using expected

---

[2] What is more, some vendors advocate such a practice to bring about more competitive rates for mortgages than those of other banks. Needless to say, banks are giving away value if this policy is adopted, as we will show below.

[3] Actually, the ALM should match the basis point sensitivities of the assets and liabilities for each relevant maturity bucket. We do not go into detail since they are beyond the scope of the current analysis.

Table 9.4. Percentage of prepaid loans up to a given year, expected and contract cash flows and expected amortization

Year	Prepayment (%)	Expected cash flows	Contract cash flows	Expected amortization
1	3.95	17.346	13.95	86.45
2	7.74	15.918	13.56	73.81
3	11.38	14.575	13.16	62.04
4	14.87	13.314	12.77	51.08
5	18.23	12.129	12.37	40.88
6	21.46	11.018	11.98	31.42
7	24.55	9.976	11.58	22.63
8	27.53	8.998	11.19	14.49
9	30.39	8.083	10.79	6.96
10		7.356	10.40	0.00

(i.e., including the prepayment effect) cash flows, hence confirming that none of the hedging costs have been ignored when pricing the mortgage out of expected cash flows instead of contract cash-flows.

If the model is correctly predicting prepayment rates, then there would be no loss: at the end of each year the outstanding capital matches the expected capital (net of prepayments) and the hedging swap would still be effective in protecting against exposure to interest rate movements. The problem is that the very model we are using (which, we recall, is a simple version of the most common models included in the ALM applications of software vendors) actually links the level of the CPR to the level of interest rates. So, barring possible divergences due to normal statistical errors, variations in the CPR are also due to movement in the term structure of interest rates, although this cannot be dynamically included in risk management policies since the EM is static. If rates move, this means that swap hedging will no longer be effective and the bank will have to appropriately rebalance its notional quantities. But, interest rates do move, so we can be sure that the hedge has to be rebalanced in the future, even if the estimated parameters of model (9.1) prove to be correct and do not change after a new recalibration.

Being pretty sure that the bank will change the notional of the hedging swap in the future, the problem is now to understand if this rebalancing generates a loss or a profit (without considering transaction costs). Let us see what happens if the term structure of forward rates experiences a parallel shift downward or upward of 2% after 1 year. In this case, if the probabilities of prepayment are kept constant, the hedging swap portfolio would experience a positive, or negative, variation of its net present value (NPV), thus counterbalancing the negative, or positive, variation of the NPV suffered on the mortgage. The profit, or loss, can be approximated with very high accuracy, since we are assuming a parallel shift of the forward rates that would be equal to DV01 $\times \Delta r$, where DV01 is the discounted annuity of fixed rate payments of the swap, and Δr is variation of the swap fair rate due to the change in Libor forward rates.

In Table 9.5 we show the profit and loss due to unwinding of the original hedging swap for the two scenarios of parallel shift (upward and downward) of the forward rate term structure. When rates fall, the hedging swap suffers a loss, since it is a (fixed rate) payer and the new fair rate for a similar swap structure is 2.09%; the loss is given by the DV01 indicated in the second column times the $\Delta r = 2.09\% - 3.89\%$. On the other hand, when forward interest rates move upward by 2%, the unwinding of the swap generates a profit, computed as before considering the new fair swap rate 6.05%. As expected, the profit has the same order of magnitude as the loss. Moreover, since the swap is mimicking the mortgage, variation of the NPV of the latter is a mirror image of the former. The reason we have to unwind the original hedging swap and open a new one will be clear in what follows.

Table 9.5. Profit and loss due to closing of the original hedging swap position

	Fair rate (%)	DV01	P&L
Down 2%	2.09	364.67	−6.5462
Up 2%	6.05	321.39	6.9578

Actually, if the probabilities of prepayment change according to (9.1), we have two consequences: first, the original swap no longer perfectly hedges variations in the value of the mortgage; second, rebalancing of the notional of the swap is needed at least to bring it back into line with the new expected amortization schedule of the mortgage. We have then to unwind the original position and open a new one with a new swap with a notional amount matching the expected amortization schedule of the mortgage, with a fixed rate equal to the mortgage rate based on current market rates.[4]

First, let us examine what happens to expected repayments in the future when rates move. Table 9.6 shows the new expected amortization schedule after a change in the CPR due to a movement in interest rates: with a new level of the 10Y[5] at 3.5%, the CPR would be 8.49%. This means that the actual outstanding capital after one year will be less than that projected by the starting CPR (4.02%), and consequently future expected outstanding capital amounts will also be smaller (i.e., the expected amortization will be more accelerated).

The same reasoning also applies to a scenario where the term structure of forward rates experiences a shift upward of 2%, as shown in Table 9.7. In this case, from (9.1), we know that the new CPR rate will be 2.96%, in correspondence with the 10Y forward rate of 7.50%. Hence the oustanding amount after one year will be higher than the one previously projected, and thus all expected future capital amounts will also be revised upward (i.e., amortization will be slower).

We now have to compute the profit or loss produced by opening a position in a swap with the same rate as the original one (which is also the mortgage rate that we need to match on interest payment dates), with a reference capital schedule mirroring the revised expected amortization of the mortgage at current market rate levels. Table 9.8 summarizes the results for both scenarios. When rates are down 2%, the new swap generates a profit of 4.7119: this is easy to understand, since the bank still pays 3.89% on this

---

[4] Here we assume no transaction costs; hence, brute force replacement of the first swap by the second is chosen. Clearly, more cost-effective rebalancing strategies could be adopted to minimize transaction costs, since they are actually paid in the market.
[5] Actually, after one year it is the 9Y maturity. For the purposes of this analysis we try to project the new 10Y rate.

Table 9.6. New expected amortization schedule after the term structure of forward rates drops 2%. The CPR moves from 4.02 to 8.49% according to model (9.1)

Year	Prepayment (%)	Expected cash flows	Expected amortization	Variation of notional
1	8.14	20.96	82.67	−3.78
2	15.62	18.17	67.50	−6.31
3	22.49	15.70	54.26	−7.78
4	28.80	13.51	42.72	−8.36
5	34.60	11.57	32.70	−8.18
6	39.92	9.86	24.03	−7.39
7	44.82	8.35	16.55	−6.08
8	49.31	7.02	10.14	−4.36
9	53.44	5.85	4.66	−2.31
10			0.00	

Table 9.7. New expected amortization schedule after a shift upward for the term structure of forward rates of 2%. The CPR moves from 4.02 to 2.96% according to model (9.1)

Year	Prepayment (%)	Expected cash flows	Expected amortization	Variation of notional
1	2.92	16.46	87.36	0.93
2	5.75	15.33	75.40	1.59
3	8.50	14.24	64.05	2.01
4	11.17	13.21	53.30	2.22
5	13.76	12.22	43.12	2.23
6	16.28	11.28	33.49	2.07
7	18.72	10.39	24.38	1.75
8	21.10	9.54	15.78	1.29
9	23.40	8.73	7.66	0.70
0		8.06	0.00	0.00

Table 9.8. Profits and losses due to the opening of new hedging swaps and the net result of closing the original position

	Fair rate (%)	DV01	P&L	Net P&L
Down 2%	2.37	310.43	4.7119	−0.8185
Up 2%	6.05	332.57	−7.2329	−0.2752

contract, although the new fair swap rate is 2.37% (the profit is computed as above by means of the DV01 in the second column). Nevertheless, keeping the loss incurred in mind when closing the original swap position, the bank suffers a total net loss of −0.8185 (shown in the fourth column).

Surprisingly enough, a net loss is also suffered by the bank when prepayment activity slows down as a result of higher rates in the upward parallel shift scenario. Actually, notwithstanding the profit gained when closing the original swap position, the loss suffered when opening the new swap is even higher.

At this point we can be pretty certain that, unfortunately, the hedging strategy of a mortgage, based on taking a position in swaps with a notional schedule mimicking the mortgage's expected amortization, is flawed and produces losses unless rates do not change and consequently the CPR is fixed too. In reality, this rarely happens since interest rates move and EMs predict changing CPRs. We need to investigate further where the losses come from, so that we can hopefully come up with a more effective hedging strategy.

9.2.3 Effective hedging strategies of prepayment risk

To better understand how losses are produced when hedging expected cash flows, we consider the following case: a bank has a bullet mortgage with a mortgagee of amount A, which expires in two years. At the end of the first year the mortgagee pays fixed rate interest c and at the end of the second year she repays interest c and capital A. At the end of the first year, she also has the option to prepay the entire outstanding amount plus the interest accrued up to then: we assume that this option is exercised with probability p. Table 9.9 shows expected cash flows and expected and contract amortization at the beginning of each year.

Table 9.9. A simple 2-year bullet mortgage

Year	Interest	Expected cash flows	Expected amortization	Amortization
0				A
1	c	$c + A \times p$	$A - A \times p$	A
2	c	$c + A \times (1 - p)$	0	0

The bank closes a (fixed rate) payer swap with 2-year expiry and varying notional amount equal each year to the expected amortization. This is not a standard swap traded in the interbank market, but it is not difficult to get a quote on it by a market maker. Let us indicate by $\mathrm{Swp}(n, m)$ a swap starting at time n and expiring at m. We can decompose the 2-year swap in two single-period swaps, so that the hedging swap portfolio P is comprised of:

- $A \times \mathrm{Swp}(0, 1)$
- $(A - A \times p) \times \mathrm{Swp}(1, 2)$

It is very easy to check that the portfolio is

$$P = A \times \mathrm{Swp}(0, 2) - p \times A \times \mathrm{Swp}(1, 2)$$

since $\text{Swp}(0,1) + \text{Swp}(1,2) = \text{Swp}(0,2)$. The second component of the portfolio is a short position in a forward starting swap, whose notional is the mortgage notional amount weighted by the probability of prepayment at the end of the first year. The forward starting swap can be further decomposed, by means of put–call parity, as follows:

$$\text{Swp}(1,2) = \text{Pay}(1,2;c) - \text{Rec}(1,2;c)$$

where $\text{Pay}(n,m;K)$ ($\text{Rec}(n,m2;K)$) is the value of a payer (receiver) swaption struck at K, expiring at n, written on a forward swap starting at n and maturing at m. So, collecting results, we have that the hedging portfolio is:

$$P = A \times \text{Swp}(0,2) - p \times A \times (\text{Pay}(1,2;c) - \text{Rec}(1,2;c)) \qquad (9.2)$$

If the probability of prepayment p (the CPR approximately in practice) is invariant with the interest rate level,[6] equation (9.2) is just an alternative way of expressing a position in a swap with maturity and amortizing notional equal to that of the mortgage. So, the following two strategies are exactly equivalent:

1. Entering in a (fixed rate) payer swap, with an amortizing schedule equal to the mortgage's *expected* amortizing schedule, and with the same expiry as the mortgage.
2. Entering in a (fixed rate) payer swap, with a amortizing schedule equal to the mortgage's *contract* amortizing schedule, and with the same expiry as the mortgage; selling a payer swaption expiring in one year and written on a one-year swap, struck at the mortgage rate level c; buying a receiver swaption, otherwise identical to the payer swaption. The amount of the swap underlying the swaptions follows the *contract* amortizing schedule, whereas the quantity of swaptions to buy, or sell, is equal to the prepayment probability.[7]

Any equivalence between strategies (1) and (2) vanishes if the probability of prepayment p is not independent of the interest rate level, as is also the case in the very simple EM we presented in the previous section and generally the case in reality. If this is the case, decomposition allows for a more precise and effective hedge, provided we design a model capable of encompassing all these aspects.

Returning to our numerical example in the section above, it is now quite simple to understand the factors causing losses. In fact, in the numerical example the bank has decided to hedge the mortgage by strategy(1), assuming there is constant probability of prepayment (CPR). But the behaviour of the mortgagee (modelled via EM (9.1)) implies a higher probability when rates go down and lower when they go up. We can make the following points:

● When interest rates fall, the mortgage's NPV increases, and this is compensated by the payer swap with the same maturity. The loss originates from the fact that the probability of prepayment is higher than that guessed at the contract's inception. When seen from the perspective of strategy (2), it is as if the bank had bought a receiver swaption whose quantity is the probability of prepayment assumed at the beginning of the contract, but this is not enough to cover the loss of the mortgage

---

[6] It could be deterministically time dependent though.

[7] This very important distinction is not manifest in this simplified 2-year example, but it is much clearer by generalizing (see Appendix 9.A) the suggested decomposition of the hedge using arbitrary maturities and amortization schedules.

which implies being short a receiver swaption with a larger quantity equal to the new prepayment probability.

- When interest rates rise, the mortgage's NPV decreases, this being counterbalanced by an increase in the swap value. In this case the loss also originates from the fact that the short position in the payer swaption (equal to the starting probability of prepayment) turns out to be bigger than that needed by the lower prepayment probability concurrent with higher rates.
- A more general point relates to why a bank should also sell the payer swaption when hedging the mortgage? When the bank adopts strategy (1), it is implicitly replicating the short position in the payer swaption, with the even worse circumstance of doing so in a higher than needed quantity when its NPV is negative (i.e., when rates move upwards). Actually, if the bank adopts hedging strategy (2), it is able to disentangle the different instruments to be bought or sold, and then to decide which is worth trading or not.

The analysis in this section is very useful and in Appendix 9.A we break down the hedging portfolio for a generic mortgage with a given expiry and amortizing schedule. In summary, the hedging portfolio comprises:

1. A payer swap with the same fixed rate and expiry as the mortgage, and with the same amortizing schedule as the mortgage's contract amortization schedule.
2. A short position in a portfolio of payer swaptions, expiring on each repayment date and written on a swap whose maturity date is the same as the mortgage's and as the mortgage's contract amortization schedule.
3. A long position in a portfolio of receiver swaptions, expiring on each repayment date and written on a swap whose maturity date is the same as the mortgage's and as the mortgage's contract amortization schedule.

Each swaption has a quantity equal to the probability that prepayment occurs between the expiry dates of two contiguous swaptions.

Important implications can be drawn from the hedging portfolio:

- To properly hedge prepayment risk, a dynamic model of prepayment probability has to be designed, so as to allow for an increase in prepayments when rates go down.
- Making the probability higher when rates are low increases sensitivity to the value of the receiver swaptions that the bank has to buy to hedge the exposure. This yields more reliable hedging ratios and allows appropriate hedging against the costs incurred when prepayment activity increases.
- Moreover, making the probability higher when rates are low increases the price of the receiver swaption portfolio needed to hedge the exposure. This means that prepayment options are priced more accurately and can be included in the final rate to apply in the mortgage's contract.
- Selling the payer swaption portfolio is not needed: doing so unnecessarily offsets a mirror image long-option position on the mortgage that can grant some profits. We have seen that the standard strategy and other commonly adopted strategies do indeed mimic the selling of this swaption portfolio, very likely by an overdue amount.
- When including the effects of prepayments in the pricing of the loan, the bank does not have to price the long position in the payer swaption portfolio, which reduces the final contract rate. In fact, this is an obscure optionality that cannot easily be priced

by mortgagees, even in a very competitive environment with rather sophisticated players.

9.2.4   Conclusions on prepayment models

Some recipes can be provided for the design of a prepayment model:

- EMs can be useful, but they have to be integrated with a RPM: the decomposition shown above makes it clear that mortgagees are implicitly long a portfolio of receiver swaptions by a certain amount that has to be included in the pricing.
- Probabilities of prepayment must be dynamically linked to the level of interest rates.
- Since we need to include the valuation of options in the pricing, we need also to account for the volatility of interest rates, so that a prepayment model has to be designed *jointly* with an interest rate model.
- As a consequence we can hedge sensitivities not only to interest rates, but also to volatilities (i.e., Vega).

In Section 9.2.5, we develop a prepayment model[8] to hedge the prepayment risk of fixed rate mortgages which considers all the points above. It provides the ALM with a valuable tool to embed the costs of implied optionalities in the pricing of new mortgages, and to effectively hedge the exposures of an aggregated mortgage portfolio.

Undertaking the computation is a formidable challenge, so we come up with an accurate and quick solution that avoids resorting to Monte Carlo valuations, which are rather unstable when computing sensitivities and not suitable for a portfolio of hundred of thousands of contracts such as bank mortgage portfolios.

9.2.5   Modelling prepayment decisions

Assume that a bank closes a number of fixed rate mortgage contracts with clients who have the possibility to prepay the outstanding debt balance in the future. Further assume that mortgagees decide whether to prepay their mortgage at random discrete intervals, usually clashing with payment dates. The probability of a prepayment decision taken on the basis of the interest rate level is described by hazard function λ: the probability that the decision is made in a time interval of length dt is approximately λdt. Basically, this decision is taken when interest rates fall.

Besides prepayment (refinancing) for interest rate reasons, mortgagees may also prepay for exogenous reasons (e.g., job relocation or house sale). The probability of exogenous prepayment is described by hazard function ρ: this represents a baseline prepayment level (i.e., the expected prepayment level when no financially optimal (interest-driven) prepayment should occur).

We model the interest rate based prepayment within a reduced-form approach. This allows us to include prepayments in the pricing, interest rate risk management (ALM) and liquidity management consistently. We adopt a stochastic intensity of prepayment λ, assumed to follow CIR dynamics:

$$d\lambda_t = \kappa[\theta - \lambda_t]dt + \nu\sqrt{\lambda_t}dZ_t$$

---

[8] The model was proposed in [47].

This intensity provides the probability of the mortgage rationally terminating over time. We further assume that the intensity is correlated to interest rates, so that when rates move to lower levels, more rational prepayments occur: this stochastic framework allows for a wide variety of prepayment behaviours. Survival probability (i.e., the probability that no rational decision is taken up to time T, evaluated at time t) is:

$$\mathrm{SP}^R(t, T) = \mathrm{SP}^R(t, T; \lambda_0, \kappa, \theta, \nu) = E^Q\left[\exp\left(-\int_0^T \lambda_s ds\right)\right] = A(t, T)e^{-B(t,T)\lambda_t} \quad (9.3)$$

Functions $A(t, T)$ and $B(t, T)$ are given in equation (8.69). Parameter ψ is the market premium for prepayment risk and is assumed to be 0.[9]

Exogenous prepayment is also modelled in reduced-form fashion by constant intensity ρ: it can actually be time dependent as well. In this case the survival probability, or the probability that no exogenous prepayment occurs up to time T, evaluated at time t, is:

$$\mathrm{SP}^E(t, T) = e^{-\rho(T-t)} \quad (9.4)$$

Total survival probability (no prepayment for whatever reason occurs) is:

$$\mathrm{SP}(t, T) = \mathrm{SP}^R(t, T)\mathrm{SP}^E(t, T) \quad (9.5)$$

whereas total prepayment probability is:

$$\mathrm{PP}(t, T) = 1 - \mathrm{SP}^R(t, T)\mathrm{SP}^E(t, T) \quad (9.6)$$

Consider a mortgage with a coupon rate c expiring at time T. At each period, given current interest rates, the optimal prepayment strategy determines whether the mortgage holder should prepay and refinance at current rates. Loosely speaking, for a given coupon rate c, keeping transaction costs in mind, there is a critical interest rate level r^* such that if rates are lower ($r_t < r^*$) then the mortgagee will optimally decide to prepay. If it is not optimal to refinance, any prepayment is for exogenous reasons; otherwise, the mortgagee may prepay either for interest rate related or for exogenous reasons.

In order to make the model more analytically tractable, we assume that both types of decisions[10] may occur at any time, but the effects on prepayments by the rational decision are produced only when the rates are below critical levels. In other words, when a rational decision is taken and the rates are above critical level r^*, no prepayment actually occurs and no cost is borne by the bank. For such a mortgage, the rational decision produces no effects and cannot be taken again in the future, since both rational and exogenous decisions may occur only once, and as soon as one of the two occurs the mortgage is prepaid.

---

[9] Basically, parameter ψ is assumed to be included in parameter κ. They both occur in formula (9.3) (always as a sum), so they can jointly be estimated from historical data. We will also use the real measure for pricing; hence, we implicitly assume that the market premium for prepayment risk is zero so that the risk-neutral measure coincides with the real one.

[10] Decisions to prepay depend on the jump occurrence modelled by intensities.

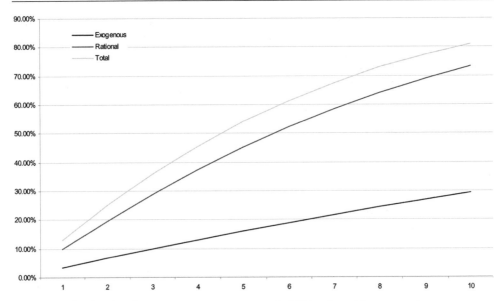

Figure 9.2. Rational and exogenous prepayment probabilities for a 10-year mortgage

Example 9.2.1. *Figure 9.2 plots prepayment probabilities for different times up to (fixed rate) mortgage expiry, assumed to be in 10 years. The three curves refer to:*

- *exogenous prepayment, given by constant intensity $\rho = 3.5\%$;*
- *rational (interest-driven) prepayment, produced assuming $\lambda_0 = 10.0\%$, $\kappa = 27\%$, $\theta = 50.0\%$ and $\nu = 10.0\%$.*
- *total prepayment, when it is rational to prepay the mortgage $(r_t < r^*)$.*

9.2.6 Modelling the losses upon prepayment

Assume at time t_0 the mortgage has the following contract terms:

- the mortgage notional is $A_0 = A$ and the mortgagee is not subject to credit risk;
- the mortgagee pays at predefined scheduled times t_j, for $j \in (0, 1, \ldots, b)$, a fixed rate c computed on the outstanding residual capital at the beginning of the reference period $\tau_j = t_j - t_{j-1}$, denoted by A_{j-1}. The interest payment will then be $c\tau_j A_{j-1}$;
- on the same dates, besides interest the mortgagee also pays I_j, which is a portion of the outstanding capital, according to an amortization schedule;
- the expiry is time $t_b = T$;
- the mortgagee has the option to end the contract by prepaying on payment dates t_j the remaining residual capital A_j, together with the interest and capital payments as defined above. The decision to prepay, for whatever reason, can be taken at any time, although the actual prepayment occurs on scheduled payment dates.

The assumption that the interest, capital, and the prepayment dates are the same is easily relaxed.

The fair coupon rate c can be computed by balancing the present value of future cash flows with the notional at time t_0:

$$\sum_j [c\tau_j A_{j-1} + I_j] P^D(t_0, t_j) = A$$

which immediately leads to:

$$c = \frac{A - \sum_j I_j P^D(t_0, t_j)}{\sum_j \tau_j A_{j-1} P^D(t_0, t_j)}$$

where $P^D(t_0, t_j)$ is the discount factor at time t_0 for date t_j. It should be noted that the quantity $A - \sum_j I_j P^D(t_0, t_j)$ can be replaced by $\sum_j \tau_j A_{j-1} F_j(t_0) P^D(t_0, t_j)$,[11] where $F_j(t_0)$ is the forward rate at time t_0 starting at time t_j.

Assume now that the mortgage is prepaid at a given time t_k (for $k \in \{0, 1, \ldots, b\}$); its current value will be:

$$\sum_j [c\tau_j A_{j-1} + I_j] P^D(t_k, t_j) = A^P$$

where A^P will almost surely be different from the residual capital amount A_{k-1}, unless the forward rates implied in the term structure at time t_0 actually occur in the market at time t_k. The prepayment can be either rational or exogenous.

After prepayment, to hedge its liabilities the bank closes a new mortgage similar to the prepaid one, so that this new one replaces all previous capital payments and yields new interest rate payments as well. The fair rate $c_{k,b}(t_k)$ of this new mortgage[12] will be determined by market rates at time t_k:

$$\sum_j [c_{k,b}(t_k)\tau_j A_{j-1} + I_j] P^D(t_k, t_j) = A_{k-1}$$

Hence, the bank will suffer a loss or earn a profit given by:

$$A^P - A_{k-1} = \sum_j P^D(t_k, t_j)\tau_j A_{j-1}(c - c_{k,b}(t_k)) \tag{9.7}$$

The bank is mainly interested in measuring (and managing) expected losses relating to the (rational) prepayment at times $\{t_k\}$, which we indicate as expected loss (EL) evaluated at time t_0:

$$EL(t_k, t_k) = E^Q \left[\max\left(\sum_j P^D(t_k, t_j)\tau_j A_{j-1}(c - c_{k,b}(t_k)); 0 \right) \right]. \tag{9.8}$$

Equation (9.8) can be computed under the forward mortgage rate measure $Q^{k,b}$ (where Q is the real measure), associated with the rate $c_{k,b}(t_k)$, as:

$$EL(t_0, t_k) = \frac{\sum_j P^D(t_0, t_j)\tau_j A_{j-1}}{P^D(t_0, t_k)} E^{k,b} \left[\max[c - c_{k,b}(t_k); 0] \right]. \tag{9.9}$$

The numeraire under this measure is $\sum_j P^D(t_k, t_j)\tau_j A_{j-1}$.

EL is a function of the term structure of risk-free rates.[13] We model risk-free rates in a market model framework:[14] each forward rate is lognormally distributed, with a given

---

[11] This is trivially obtained by considering the pricing equation of an amortizing floating rate mortgage.
[12] We will use the notation $c_{a,b}(t)$ to indicate the time-t fair rate of a mortgage with residual payments at t_j, with $j \in \{a, a+1, \ldots, b\}$.
[13] OIS (or Eonia for the euro) can be considered risk-free rates for practical purposes.
[14] See Chapter 8 for details on market models.

volatility that can be estimated historically, or extracted from market quotes for caps and floors and swaptions:

$$dF_j(t) = \sigma_j F_j(t) dW_t$$

Any prepayment causing a loss for the bank can be caused for both exogenous and rational reasons, such an occurrence is described by intensity λ_t: we assume that this intensity is negatively correlated to the level of interest rates. There is also a contribution arising from exogenous prepayment decisions, which may occur under any market condition, thus generating either a loss or a profit to the bank. It is then possible to compute the expected loss on prepayment (ELoP), defined as expected loss at time t_k when the decision to prepay (for whatever reason) is taken between t_{k-1} and t_k:

$$\text{ELoP}(t_0, t_k) = E^{k,b}\left[1_{\tau \in [t_{k-1}, t_k]} \max\left[\sum_j P^D(t_k, t_j) \tau_j A_{j-1}(c - c_{k,b}(t_k)); 0\right]\right] \quad (9.10)$$

where $1_{\tau \in [t_{k-1}, t_k]}$ is the indicator function equal to 1 when prepayment occurs within period of time $[t_{k-1}, t_k]$. Under the forward mortgage rate measure $Q^{k,b}$ we have

$$\text{ELoP}(t_0, t_k) = \frac{\sum_j P^D(t_0, t_j) \tau_j A_{j-1}}{P^D(t_0, t_k)} E^{k,b}\left[1_{\tau \in [t_{k-1}, t_k]} \max\left[c - c_{k,b}(t_k); 0\right]\right]. \quad (9.11)$$

Valuation of the EL

From (9.8) the EL at time t_k can easily be seen as the (undiscounted) value of a swaption written on a non-standard swap. A closed-form approximation for such contracts has been derived by Castagna et al. [49].

Let us start with a standard swaption (i.e., a swaption written on a standard swap). The fair swap rate at inception of the contract is:

$$K = S(t; T_a, T_b) = S_{a,b}(t) = \frac{P^D(t, T_a) - P^D(t, T_b)}{\sum_{i=a+1}^b \tau_i P^D(t, T_i)} \quad (9.12)$$

where τ_i is the year fraction between T_{i-1} and T_i fixed rate payment dates, and $P^D(t, T)$ is the price of a zero-coupon bond at time t expiring at time T. The rate is derived by setting the value of the swap at the start of the contract at zero:

$$\text{IRS}(t) = \sum_{i=a+1}^b \tau_i P^D(t, T_i)[F_i(t) - K] = 0 \quad (9.13)$$

where $F_i(t)$ is the forward risk-free rate

$$F_i(t) = \frac{P^D(t, T_{i-1}) - P^D(t, T_i)}{\tau_i P^D(t, T_i)}$$

We denote by $\text{Swpt}(t, s, T_b, S(t; s, T_b), K, \sigma_{s,T_b}, \omega)$ the value of a swaption at time t, expiring in s and struck at K, written on a forward swap rate $S(t; s, T_b)$; this value is calculated by the standard market (Black) formula with implied volatility σ_{s,T_b}, and the last argument indicates whether the swaption is a payer (1) or a receiver (−1). The formula is:

$$\text{Swpt}(t, T_a, T_b, S_{a,b}(t), K, \sigma_{a,b}, \omega) = C_{a,b}(t)\, \text{BlSc}(S_{e,n}(T_e), K, \sigma_{e,n}) \qquad (9.14)$$

The formula can be found in Section 8.3.9. We have used the notation $C_{a,b}(t)$ for an annuity that is equal to:

$$C_{a,b}(t) = \sum_{i=a+1}^{b} \tau_i P^D(t, T_i)$$

In the specific case of a non-amortizing mortgage of notional A, with fixed rate payments on dates $\{t_k\}$, starting at t_k and ending at T_b, the fair coupon rate can easily be shown to be equal to the fair swap rate, so $c_{k,b}(t_0) = S_{k,b}(t_0)$. This has to be compared with the original mortgage rate c (relating to a similar mortgage that started at t_0, see equation (9.7)), so the expected loss on prepayment dates $\{t_k\}$ is:

$$\text{EL}(t_0, t_k) = \frac{A}{P^D(t_0, t_k)} \text{Swpt}(t_0, t_k, T_b, c_{k,b}(t_0), c, \sigma_{k,b}, -1) \qquad (9.15)$$

Typically mortgages are amortizing, so we need a formula to price non-standard swaptions. We use the term "meta-swap" for a swap with unit notional and a time-varying fixed rate that is equivalent to the contract fixed rate times the notional amount for each date A_{i-1}^c (i.e., the one at the start of the calculation period).

Let us assume that the IRS floating leg pays at times $T_a, \ldots, T_b$, where T_a is the first payment time after the EL time t_k, and that the IRS fixed leg pays at times $T_{c_1}, \ldots, T_{c_J}$, where $c_1 \geq a$ and $c_J = b$ (fixed leg times are assumed to be included in the set of floating leg times, and in reference to a mortgage they will be assumed to be the same for both legs).

The fixed rate payment at each payment date T_{c_j} is:

$$R_j = \beta_j c \qquad (9.16)$$

where

$$\beta_j = A_{j-1}^c \tau_j^c \qquad (9.17)$$

and τ_j^c denotes the year fraction for the fixed leg.

The floating leg will exchange the future risk-free (OIS) forward times α_l, which is the year fraction times the notional A_{l-1}^L at the beginning of the calculation period:

$$\alpha_l = A_{l-1}^L \tau_l^L \qquad (9.18)$$

Note that despite the fact that the meta-swap has unit notional, both the total fixed rate and the fraction into which the year is divided contain the notional of the swap. Note also that the year fraction τ_i can be different for the floating and the fixed leg. When fixed rate mortgage c amortizes with an amortization schedule $A_i^c = A_i^L$, the expected loss on prepayment dates t_k can be calculated as follows:

$$\text{EL}(t_0, t_k) = \bar{C}_{k,b}(t_0) \text{Bl}\big(0, t_k, T_b, c_{k,b}(t_k), c, \varsigma(t_k), -1\big) / P^D(t_0, t_k) \qquad (9.19)$$

where

$$\bar{C}_{k,b}(t) = \sum_{l=k}^{b} \beta_j P^D(t, T_l),$$

is the DV01 of the forward (start date t_i) meta-swap. In case $\bar{C}_{k,b}(0) \leq 0$, the EL can be approximated with the (positive) value of the underlying forward swap (mortgage rate). Define:

$$w_l(t) = \frac{\alpha_l P^D(t, T_l)}{\bar{C}_{k,b}(t)} \tag{9.20}$$

We then have:

$$c_{k,b}(t) = \bar{S}_{k,b}(t) = \sum_{l=k+1}^{b} w_l(t) F_l(t) \tag{9.21}$$

which is the forward swap rate of the meta-swap and the forward fair amortizing mortgage rate. In a standard swap the forward swap rate is the average of the OIS forward rates F_l weighted by a function of the discount factors. In the case of the meta-swap the average of the OIS forward rates is weighted by a function of the notional and discount factors. We assume that $c_{k,b}(t_k)$ is lognormally distributed, with the mean equal to its forward value. The volatility of the meta-swap rate, or the amortizing mortgage rate, can be approximated by widely adopted "freezing" of the weights in (9.20), so that by setting $\bar{w}_l = w_l(0)$ we get:

$$\varsigma(t_k)^2 = \frac{1}{c_{k,b}(t)^2} \sum_{l=k}^{b} \sum_{m=k}^{b} \sigma_l \sigma_m \bar{w}_l \bar{w}_m F_l(0) F_m(0) \varphi(l, m) \tag{9.22}$$

which is the volatility of the forward rate of the meta-swap assuming that the volatility of OIS forward rates, σ, is constant through time and that $\varphi(l, m)$ is the correlation between $F_l(0)$ and $F_m(0)$.

Adding mortgagee credit risk

Assume that the default probability for the mortgagee between time t and T is $\mathrm{PD}(t, T)$ and that the loss-given default is a percentage of the outstanding capital equal to L_{GD}, which is equivalent to $(1 - R_{ec})$ with R_{ec} being the recovery rate.

It is relatively easy to infer a fair mortgage rate default risk adjusted $c_{k,b}^D(t)$. In fact, considering again that the mortgage rate is equivalent to the rate of a swap that perfectly matches cash flows and pays the Libor rate against receiving the fixed rate, the fair mortgage rate is derived by setting the floating leg equal to the fixed leg, this time keeping expected cash flows depending on the occurrence of default in mind:

$$\sum_{l=k}^{b} \left((I_l + c\tau_l A_{l-1})(1 - \mathrm{PD}(t_k, t_l)) + A_{l-1} R_{ec}(\mathrm{PD}(t_k, t_l) - \mathrm{PD}(t_k, t_{l-1})) \right) P^D(t_k, t_l)$$

$$= \sum_{l=k}^{b} \left((I_l + L_l \tau_l A_{l-1})(1 - \mathrm{PD}(t_k, t_l)) + A_{l-1} R_{ec}(\mathrm{PD}(t_k, t_l) - \mathrm{PD}(t_k, t_{l-1})) \right) P^D(t_k, t_l)$$

where I_l is the capital installment paid at time t_l. Simplifying we get:

$$c_{k,b}^D(t) = \sum_{l=k+1}^{b} w_l^D(t) F_l(t) \tag{9.23}$$

where

$$w_l^D(t) = \frac{\sum_{l=k}^{b} \left(\tau_l A_{l-1} \mathrm{R}_{ec}(1 - \mathrm{PD}(t_k, t_l))\right) P^D(t, t_l)}{\bar{C}_{k,b}^D(t)}$$

and

$$\bar{C}_{k,b}^D(t) = \sum_{l=k}^{b} \left(\tau_l A_{l-1}(1 - \mathrm{PD}(t_k, t_l))\right) P^D(t, t_l).$$

Typically, mortgages are quoted at spread Sp over a reference curve (say, Libor): the problem is not how to infer the PD from this information. It is possible to show[15] that the (assumed constant) default intensity $\gamma(t) = \gamma$ of a given reference entity can be extracted from the spread at time t_0 by means of the following approximation:

$$\gamma = \frac{Sp_{0,b}(0)}{\mathrm{L}_{GD}} \tag{9.24}$$

where $Sp_{0,b}(0)$ is the spread for a mortgage starting at time 0 expiring in T_b.

Formula (9.24), besides being quite simple and intuitive, is extremely convenient since it does not require knowledge of discount factors (to be extracted from the interest rate curve). One just needs the spread and an assumption on the L_{GD}. It is well known that the approximation works rather well even when the default intensity is far from being constant.

The survival probability of the credit entity can then be approximated in a straightforward manner:

$$\mathrm{SP}(0, T_b) = Q(\tau > T_b) \approx e^{-\gamma T_b} = e^{-\frac{S_{0,b}(0)T_b}{\mathrm{L}_{GD}}} \tag{9.25}$$

We can then infer, at each given date, an entire term structure of SPs from the spreads for mortgages with different expiries T_b. Even if the γ values for two maturities T_b and $T_{b'}$ are likely to be different, this does not create any inconsistency, since such γs must be viewed as average values over their respective intervals rather than constant (instantaneous) intensities.

Default probabilities are simply:

$$\mathrm{PD}(0, T) = Q(\tau < T) = 1 - \mathrm{SP}(0, T). \tag{9.26}$$

Valuation of the ELoP

Having derived valuation formulae for the EL, it is straightforward to value the ELoP, for prepayments in $\{t_k\}$. We indicate this expected loss on prepayment as ELoP_1, since we will afterward introduce a second type of rational prepayment. In the most general formulation, it is:

$$\mathrm{ELoP}_1(t_0, t_k) = \frac{1}{P^D(t_0, t_k)} E^Q\left\{ \int_{t_{k-1}}^{t_k} \bar{C}_{k,b}(t_k)\max[c - c_{k,b}(t_k); 0]1_{\tau \in [t_s + ds]} \right\}$$

Equation (9.27) is the most general form to value the ELoP_1 and includes both the amortizing and non-amortizing cases we have shown above. So we will focus on solving

---

[15] See, for example, [46].

this equation. We move to the forward mortgage rate $c_{k,b}(t_k)$ measure, so that:

$$\text{ELoP}_1(t_0, t_k) = \frac{\bar{C}_{k,b}(t_0)}{P^D(t_0, t_k)} E^{k,b}\left\{\int_{t_{k-1}}^{t_k} \max[c - c_{k,b}(t_k); 0]1_{\tau \in [t_s + ds]}\right\} \quad (9.27)$$

The first simplification we make is to assume that the prepayment decision (whose effects manifest themselves at the next payment date in any event) occurs at discrete times between $[t_{k-1}, t_k]$, which for our purposes are divided into J intervals whose length is $\Delta t = \frac{t_k - t_{k-1}}{J}$ so that we can write (by applying Fubini's lemma as well):

$$\begin{aligned}
\text{ELoP}_1(t_0, t_k) &= \frac{\bar{C}_{k,b}(t_0)}{P^D(t_0, t_k)} \int_{t_{k-1}}^{t_k} E^{k,b}\left\{\max[c - c_{k,b}(t_k); 0]1_{\tau \in [t_s + ds]}\right\} \\
&\approx \frac{\bar{C}_{k,b}(t_0)}{P^D(t_0, t_k)} \sum_{j=1}^{J}\left\{E^{k,b}\left[\max(c - c_{k,b}(t_k); 0)1_{\tau \leq t_k + j\Delta t}\right]\right. \\
&\qquad\qquad\left. - E^{k,b}\left[\max(c - c_{k,b}(t_k); 0)1_{\tau \leq t_k + (j-1)\Delta t}\right]\right\} \quad (9.28)
\end{aligned}$$

or equivalently

$$\begin{aligned}
\text{ELoP}_1(t_0, t_k) &= \frac{\bar{C}_{k,b}(t_0)}{P^D(t_0, t_k)} \sum_{j=1}^{J}\left\{E^{k,b}\left[\max(c - c_{k,b}(t_k); 0)1_{\tau \geq t_k + (j-1)\Delta t}\right]\right. \\
&\qquad\qquad\left. - E^{k,b}\left[\max(c - c_{k,b}(t_k); 0)1_{\tau \geq t_k + j\Delta t}\right]\right\}
\end{aligned}$$

More explicitly we have:

$$\begin{aligned}
\text{ELoP}_1(t_0, t_k) &= \frac{\bar{C}_{k,b}(t_0)}{P^D(t_0, t_k)} E^{k,b} \\
&\times \left\{\sum_{j=1}^{J} \max[c - c_{k,b}(t_k)]\left(e^{-\rho(t_{k-1} + (j-1)\Delta t - t_0)} e^{-\int_{t_0}^{t_{k-1} + (j-1)\Delta t} \lambda_s ds}\right.\right. \\
&\qquad\qquad\left.\left. - e^{-\rho(t_{k-1} + j\Delta t - t_0)} e^{-\int_{t_0}^{t_{k-1} + j\Delta t} \lambda_s ds}\right)\right\} \quad (9.29)
\end{aligned}$$

9.2.7   Analytical approximation for ELoP₁

Equation (9.29) does not admit an explicit analytical solution, but an analytical approximation is viable. We start from a more general case of the pricing of an option when the instantaneous interest rate is correlated with the underlying asset.[16] Let us focus first on valuing a payoff of the kind:

$$\text{Call}_1(0, T; K) = E\left[\exp\left\{-\int_0^T r_t^{(\varepsilon)} dt\right\}[S_T - K]^+\right], \quad (9.30)$$

---

[16] Derivation of the formula follows [81] in the specific case when the underlying asset is a pure martingale. Extensive tests on the accuracy of the formula using Monte Carlo simulation are shown therein.

where S_t is an exponential martingale:

$$dS_t = \sigma_t S_t \, dW_{1t}, \qquad (9.31)$$

with solution $S(t_0) = S_0$ equal to:

$$S_t = S_0 \exp\left\{ \int_0^t \sigma_s \, dW_s - \frac{1}{2} \int_0^t \sigma_s^2 \, ds \right\}, \qquad (9.32)$$

where σ_t is a deterministic function of t. Assume also that the stochastic interest rate $r_t^{(\varepsilon)}$ is described by the dynamics:

$$r_t^{(\varepsilon)} = r_0 + \int_0^t \varsigma\left(r_s^{(\varepsilon)}, s\right) ds + \varepsilon \int_0^t \nu\left(r_s^{(\varepsilon)}, s\right) dW_{2s}, \qquad (9.33)$$

with $0 \le \varepsilon \le 1$. We assume that dW_{1t} and dW_{2t} are correlated with the correlation parameter ϱ.

When the instantaneous interest rate follows CIR dynamics, we have that $r_t^{(\varepsilon)}$ is

$$dr_t^{(\varepsilon)} = \kappa\left(\bar{r} - r_t^{(\varepsilon)}\right) dt + \varepsilon \sqrt{r_t^{(\varepsilon)}} \, dW_{2t}, \qquad (9.34)$$

with expected value at time t:

$$r_t = r_0 e^{-\kappa t} + \bar{r}\left(1 - e^{-\kappa t}\right). \qquad (9.35)$$

We then get

$$dY_t = -\kappa Y_t \, dt \implies Y_t = e^{-\kappa t} \implies \int_t^T Y_s \, ds = e^{-\kappa T} - e^{-\kappa t}, \qquad (9.36)$$

and the underlying asset's dynamics is

$$S_t = S_0 \exp\left\{\sigma W_{1T} - \tfrac{1}{2}\sigma^2 T\right\}. \qquad (9.37)$$

Under this specification, it can be shown[17] that:

$$\text{Call}_1(0, T; K) = S_0 \exp\left\{-\int_0^T r_t \, dt\right\} N[d_1] - K \exp\left\{-\int_0^T r_t \, dt\right\} N[d_2]$$

$$- \varepsilon \left[S_0 \exp\left\{-\int_0^T r_t \, dt\right\} \Sigma_{12} N[d_1] + \exp\left\{-\int_0^T r_t \, dt\right\} \frac{c\Sigma_{12}}{\sqrt{\Sigma_{11}}} \right.$$

$$\left. \times \left[S_0 \phi(d_1) - K\phi(d_2)\right] \right] + o(\varepsilon). \qquad (9.38)$$

which can be seen as a standard BS formula plus a correction factor due to the correlation between the interest rate and the underlying asset. Terms Σ_{11} and Σ_{12} are:

$$\Sigma_{11} = \varsigma^2 T, \qquad (9.39)$$

---

[17] See [52] for complete derivation of the following formulae.

and

$$\Sigma_{12} = \varrho \varsigma \int_0^T dv \left(\int_v^T Y_t \, dt \right) Y_v^{-1} \nu(\lambda_v, v) \, dv$$

$$= -\frac{\varrho \varsigma}{\kappa} \int_0^T dv \left[e^{-\kappa T} - e^{-\kappa v} \right] e^{\kappa v} \sqrt{\lambda_v} \, dv$$

$$= -\frac{\varrho \varsigma}{\kappa} \int_0^T dv \left[e^{-\kappa(T-v)} - 1 \right] \sqrt{\lambda_v} \, dv$$

$$= \varrho \varsigma \frac{2\sqrt{\theta}\left((1 + 2e^{\kappa T})\sqrt{\theta} - 3\gamma \right) + \left(\lambda_0 - \theta(1 + 2e^{\kappa T}) \right)\psi}{2 e^{\kappa T} \kappa^2 \sqrt{\theta}}, \tag{9.40}$$

where

$$\gamma = e^{\kappa T/2}\sqrt{\lambda_0 - \theta[1 - e^{\kappa T}]}, \tag{9.41}$$

and

$$\psi = \log\left(\frac{(\sqrt{\lambda_0} + \sqrt{\theta})^2}{\lambda_0 - \theta[1 - 2e^{\kappa T}] + 2\gamma\sqrt{\theta}} \right). \tag{9.42}$$

Now, if we set $S_t = c_{k,b}(t)$ and we consider the interest rate as the stochastic prepayment intensity λ_t and include the exogenous rate ρ as well, we can rewrite (9.38):

$$\text{Call}_1(0, T; c) = E\left[1_{\tau \geq T} \left[c_{k,b}(T) - c \right]^+ \right]$$

$$= E\left[\exp\left\{ -\int_0^T (\lambda_t + \rho) \, dt \right\} \left[c_{k,b}(T) - c \right]^+ \right]$$

$$= c_{k,b}(t_0) \exp\left\{ -\int_{t_0}^T (\lambda_t + \rho) \, dt \right\} N[d_1] - c \exp\left\{ -\int_0^T (\lambda_t + \rho) \, dt \right\} N[d_2]$$

$$- \varepsilon \left[c_{k,b}(t_0) \exp\left\{ -\int_{t_0}^T (\lambda_t + \rho) \, dt \right\} \Sigma_{12} N[d_1] \right.$$

$$\left. + \exp\left\{ -\int_{t_0}^T (\lambda_t + \rho) \, dt \right\} \frac{\Sigma_{12}}{\sqrt{\Sigma_{11}}} \left[c_{k,b}(t_0)\phi(d_1) - c\phi(d_2) \right] \right] + o(\varepsilon). \tag{9.43}$$

where the remaining notation is the same as above.

In order to value (9.29), we first need to compute the expected loss over the entire interval $[t_{k-1}, t_k]$. To that end we consider the loss to be given by the terminal payoff, in terms of a put option and not a call. In this case the intensity process λ_t is correlated only up to each $t_{k-1} + j\Delta t$, and not over the entire interval. So we have to modify $\Sigma_{12} \to \Sigma_{12}^k$ as follows:

$$\Sigma_{12}^k = -\frac{\varrho \varsigma}{\kappa} \int_{t_0}^{t_k} dv \left[e^{-\kappa(t_k-v)} - 1 \right] \sqrt{\lambda_v} \, dv$$

$$= \varrho \varsigma \frac{2\sqrt{\theta}\left((1 + 2e^{\kappa(t_k-t_0)})\sqrt{\theta} - 3\gamma \right) + \left(\lambda_0 - \theta(1 + 2e^{\kappa(t_k-t_0)}) \right)\lambda}{2 e^{\kappa(t_k-t_0)} \kappa^2 \sqrt{\theta}}, \tag{9.44}$$

where

$$\gamma = e^{\kappa(t_k - t_0)/2}\sqrt{\lambda_0 - \theta\left[1 - e^{\kappa(t_k - t_0)}\right]}, \tag{9.45}$$

and

$$\lambda = \log\left(\frac{\left(\sqrt{\lambda_0} + \sqrt{\theta}\right)^2}{\lambda_0 - \theta\left[1 - 2e^{\kappa(t_k - t_0)}\right] + 2\gamma\sqrt{\theta}}\right). \tag{9.46}$$

The call option price is then:

$$\begin{aligned}
\text{Call}_1(t_0, t_k, t_{k-1} + j\Delta t; c) &= E\left[\exp\left\{-\int_{t_0}^{t_{k-1}+j\Delta t}(\lambda_t + \rho)\,dt\right\}\left[c_{k,b}(t_k) - c\right]^+\right]\\
&= c_{k,b}(t_0)\exp\left\{-\int_{t_0}^{t_{k-1}+j\Delta t}(\lambda_t + \rho)\,dt\right\}\mathcal{N}[d_1]\\
&\quad - c\exp\left\{-\int_{t_0}^{t_{k-1}+j\Delta t}(\lambda_t + \rho)\,dt\right\}\mathcal{N}[d_2]\\
&\quad - \varepsilon\left[c_{k,b}(t_0)\exp\left\{-\int_{t_0}^{t_{k-1}+j\Delta t}(\lambda_t + \rho)\,dt\right\}\Sigma_{12}^{t_{k-1}+j\Delta t}\mathcal{N}[d_1]\right.\\
&\quad + \exp\left\{-\int_{t_0}^{t_{k-1}+j\Delta t}(\lambda_t + \rho)\,dt\right\}\frac{\Sigma_{12}^{t_{k-1}+j\Delta t}}{\sqrt{\Sigma_{11}}}\\
&\quad \left.\times\left[c_{k,b}(t_0)\phi(d_1) - c\phi(d_2)\right]\right] + o(\varepsilon). \tag{9.47}
\end{aligned}$$

Basically, it provides the value of a call option subject to survival of the underlying process $c_{k,b}(t_0)$ up to t_k.

We also need to derive the put value via put–call parity:

$$\begin{aligned}
\text{Put}_1(t_0, t_k, t_{k-1} + j\Delta t; c) &= \text{Call}_1(t_0, t_k, t_{k-1} + j\Delta t; K) - \text{EF}_1(t_k, t_{k-1} + j\Delta t)\\
&\quad + c\text{SP}^D(t_0, t_{k-1} + j\Delta t)
\end{aligned}$$

where EF_1 is the expected value $c_{k,b}(t_0)$ in case a prepayment does not occur before t_k. It can be computed as a call option struck at 0: $\text{EF}_1(t_0, T, t_k) = \text{Call}_1(t_0, T, t_k; 0)$. The prepayment probability PP is calculated as in equation (9.6).

We now have all we need to compute (9.29), which can be rewritten as follows:

$$\text{ELoP}_1(t_0, t_k) = \bar{C}_{k,b}(t_0)\sum_{j=1}^{J}\left(\text{Put}_1(t_0, t_k, t_{k-1} + (j-1)\Delta t; c) - \text{Put}_1(t_0, t_k, t_{k-1} + j\Delta t; c)\right) \tag{9.48}$$

9.2.8 Valuing the ELoP using a VaR approach

Intensity λ cannot easily be hedged using market instruments, since no standard contract exists whose value depends on rational prepayment intensity. A possible conservative approach to valuation of the ELoP would be to consider an intensity process occurring at a high level with a given confidence level (say, 99%).

For our purposes, we need to use this distribution to determine the minimum survival probability from t_0 up to each date $\{t_k\}$, or equivalently the maximum prepayment probability up to $\{t_k\}$. But what we actually need is the forward risk-adjusted distribution for λ_t, which is given in equation (8.36).

Assume we want to build an expected survival probability curve up to expiry of the mortgage in $t_N = T$. Assume also that we divide the interval $[t_0, t_N]$ into N subintervals $\Delta t = [t_N - t_0]/N$. We follow Procedure 9.2.1 which is given in pseudocode.

Procedure 9.2.1. *This procedure derives the maximum expected levels of prepayment intensity $\lambda_{t_i}^*$, at discrete prepayment dates, with a confidence level (c.l.), say, of 99%:*

1. **For** $i = 1, \ldots, N$
2. $t_i = t_0 + i \cdot \Delta t$
3. $\lambda_{t_i}^* = \lambda_{t_i} : p_{\lambda_t}^{t_i}(\lambda_{t_i}) = c.l.$
4. **Next**

Having determined the maximum default intensity levels, we can compute the term structure of (minimum) survival probabilities $SP^R(0, t_i)$:

1. **For** $i = 1, \ldots, N$
2. $t_i = t_0 + i \cdot \Delta t$
3. $SP_{c.l.}^R(t_0, t_i) = SP_{c.l.}^R(t_0, t_i)SP_{c.l.}^R(t_i, t_{i+1}; \lambda_{t_i}^*, \kappa, \theta, \nu)$
4. **Next**

Having determined the minimum rational survival probability, the maximum (total) prepayment probability up to given time $\{t_i\}$ is straightforward:

$$PP_{c.l.}(0, t_i) = 1 - SP^E(t_0, t_i)SP_{c.l.}^R(t_0, t_i) \tag{9.49}$$

for $i = 1, \ldots, N$.

To evaluate the ELoP using a VaR-style approach we need to compute the conditional mean (drift) and conditional volatility of the mortgage rate process as well:[18] we know that it is assumed to be lognormally distributed with the mean equal to its forward level (so that the drift of the process of $c_{i,b}$ is zero) and with the volatility parameter the same as in (9.22). Conditional volatility for a mortgage rate at time T, and for a rational intensity process observed in $t_i \leq T$, is:

$$\bar{\varsigma}_i(T) = \sqrt{\frac{\varsigma^2(T)T - u_s}{(T - t_0)}} \tag{9.50}$$

where

$$u_s = (\rho\varsigma\sqrt{(T - t_0)})^2$$

The drift of the process is:

$$\bar{\mu}_i(T) = \bar{\mu}_{i-1}(T) + \sqrt{u_s}(\lambda_{t_i}^* - \bar{\lambda})\Delta t \tag{9.51}$$

with initial condition $\bar{\mu}_{i-1}(T) = 0$ and

$$\bar{\lambda} = \lambda_0 e^{-\kappa(t_i - t_0)} + \theta[1 - e^{-\kappa(t_i - t_0)}]$$

---

[18] For more details on how to compute conditional expected values in a VaR context see [48].

The ELoP can thus be computed with formula (9.48) by using the adjusted forward mortgage rate

$$\bar{c}_{i,b}(t_0) = c_{i,b}(t_0)e^{\bar{\mu}_i(T)}$$

and volatility parameter $\bar{\varsigma}_i(T)$.

Example 9.2.2. *Assume 1Y (risk-free) OIS forward rates with volatilities like those in Table 9.10. Assume further that exogenous prepayment intensity is 3% p.a. and rational prepayment intensity has the same dynamics parameters as presented above. We consider a 10Y mortgage, with a fixed rate paid annually of 3.95%. The fair rate has been computed without taking into account any prepayment effect (credit risk is not considered, although it can be included within the framework). The amortization schedule is in Table 9.11.*

Given the market and contract data above, we can derive the EL at each possible prepayment date, which we assume occurs annually. It is plotted in Figure 9.3. A closed-form approximation has been employed to compute the EL. In a similar way it is possible to calculate the ELoP. We also use in this case an analytical approximation that allows for correlation between interest rates and rational prepayment intensity.

In Figure 9.4 the ELoP is plotted for a zero correlation case and for a negative correlation set at −0.8. This value implies that, when interest rates decline, the default

Table 9.10. Volatilities of 1Y OIS forward rates

Years	Forward Libor (%)	Volatility (%)
1	3.50	18.03
2	3.75	18.28
3	4.00	18.53
4	4.25	18.78
5	4.50	18.43
6	4.75	18.08
7	5.00	17.73
8	5.25	17.38
9	5.50	17.03
10	5.75	16.78

Table 9.11. Amortization schedule of a 10Y mortgage

Years	Notional
1	100.00
2	90.00
3	80.00
4	70.00
5	60.00
6	50.00
7	40.00
8	30.00
9	20.00
10	10.00

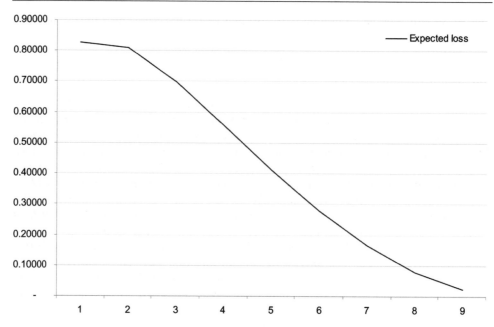

Figure 9.3. Expected loss for a 10-year mortgage

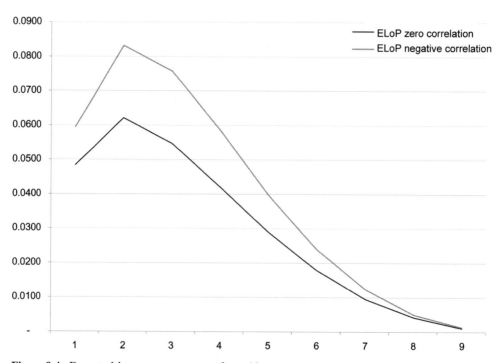

Figure 9.4. Expected loss on prepayment for a 10-year mortgage

intensity increases. Since the loss for the bank is bigger when rates are low, the ELoP in this case is higher than in the uncorrelated case.

9.2.9   Extension to double rational prepayment

The framework designed so far implicitly assumes that rational prepayment is driven by the convenience of closing a live fixed rate mortgage and opening a new one with a corresponding residual maturity and a lower contract rate. An alternative the mortgagor could pursue is to open a new mortgage with a floating rate: although from a theoretical financial perspective the two alternative choices are equivalent, from a behavioural perspective as a result of poor financial skills a comparison between the floating rate (e.g., the 3-month Libor) and the original fixed rate can produce a "rational" reason to prepay.

To model this behaviour, assume that the prepayment decision modelled before resembles a jump whose occurrence is described by an intensity rate π. The decision can be taken at any time, but it produces effects only when the Libor rate is lower than the contract rate $L_t < c$. The EL is the same as that subsequent to a rational prepayment, whereas the ELoP, which we indicate by ELoP_2 in this case, can be written as:

$$\text{ELoP}_2(t_0, t_k) = \frac{\bar{C}_{k,b}(t_0)}{P^D(t_0, t_k)} E^{k,b} \left\{ \sum_{j=1}^{J} \max[c - c_{k,b}(t_k)] 1_{\{F_k(t_{k-1}) < c\}} \right.$$

$$\left. \times \left(e^{-\rho(t_{k-1} + (j-1)\Delta t - t_0)} e^{-\int_{t_0}^{t_{k-1} + (j-1)\Delta t} \pi_s ds} - e^{-\rho(t_{k-1} + j\Delta t - t_0)} e^{-\int_{t_0}^{t_{k-1} + j\Delta t} \pi_s ds} \right) \right\}$$

$$(9.52)$$

where we have kept the effects of the exogenous prepayment that is operating in any case in mind.

The dynamics of rational intensity π, which only manifests its effects when the Libor rate $F_{k+1}(t_k) < c$, are specified as follows:

$$d\pi_t = \kappa_\pi(\theta_\pi - \pi_t)dt + \nu_\pi \sqrt{\pi_t} dZ_t$$

According to this intensity, the probability that no rational decision is taken up to time T, evaluated at time t, is:

$$\text{SP}_2^R(t, T) = \text{SP}_2^R(t, T; \pi_0, \kappa_\pi, \theta_\pi, \nu_\pi) = E^Q \left[\exp\left(-\int_0^T \pi_s ds \right) \right] = A(t, T) e^{-B(t,T)\pi_t} \quad (9.53)$$

where $A(t, T)$ and $B(t, T)$ are the same as in equation (8.27). ψ_π is the market premium for prepayment risk which is also assumed in this case to be 0. We indicate the survival probability in this case as:

$$\text{SP}_2(t, T) = \text{SP}_2^R(t, T) \quad (9.54)$$

and the total prepayment probability is:

$$\text{PP}_2(t, T) = 1 - \text{SP}_2^R(t, T) \quad (9.55)$$

To value (9.52) we first need to compute the following:[19]

$\text{Call}_2(t_0, t_k, t_{k-1} + j\Delta t; c)$

$$= E\left[e^{-\int_{t_0}^{t_{k-1}} \pi_s ds}\left[c_{k,b}(t_k) - c\right]^+ 1_{\{F_{k+1} < c\}}\right]$$

$$= \exp\left\{-\int_0^{T_1} \pi_t \, dt\right\}\left[c_{k,b}(t_0)\mathcal{N}_2(d_1, -f_1, -\rho_{c_{k,b}F_{k+1}(t_k)}) - c\mathcal{N}_2(d_2, -f_2, -\rho_{c_{k,b}F_{k+1}(t_k)})\right]$$

$$- \varepsilon \exp\left\{-\int_0^{T_1} \pi_t \, dt\right\}\left[ac_{k,b}(t_0)\sqrt{\tilde{\Sigma}_{22}}\left(\sqrt{\Sigma_{22}}\mathcal{N}_2(d_1, -f_1, -\rho_{c_{k,b}F_{k+1}(t_k)}) + \phi(d_1)\right.\right.$$

$$\left.- \rho_{c_{k,b}F_{k+1}(t_k)}\phi(f_1)\right)$$

$$+ bc_{k,b}(t_0)\sqrt{\tilde{\Sigma}_{33}}\left(-\rho_{c_{k,b}F_{k+1}(t_k)}\sqrt{\Sigma_{22}}\mathcal{N}_2(f_1, -d_1, -\rho_{c_{k,b}F_{k+1}(t_k)}) + \rho_{c_{k,b}F_{k+1}(t_k)}\phi(d_1) - \phi(f_1)\right)$$

$$\left.- ac\sqrt{\tilde{\Sigma}_{22}}\left(\phi(d_2) - \rho_{c_{k,b}F_{k+1}(t_k)}\phi(f_2)\right) - bc\sqrt{\tilde{\Sigma}_{33}}\left(\rho_{c_{k,b}F_{k+1}(t_k)}\phi(d_2) - \phi(f_2)\right)\right], \quad (9.56)$$

where $\mathcal{N}_2(.; .; .)$ is the bivariate normal distribution, and:

$$d_2 = \frac{\ln(c_{k,b}(t_0)/c) - \frac{1}{2}\Sigma_{22}}{\sqrt{\Sigma_{22}}}, \quad f_2 = \frac{\ln(F_{k+1}(t_0)/c) - \frac{1}{2}\Sigma_{33}}{\sqrt{\Sigma_{33}}} \quad (9.57)$$

and

$$d_1 = d_2 + \sqrt{\Sigma_{22}}, \quad f_1 = f_2 + \rho_{c_{k,b}F_{k+1}(t_k)}\sqrt{\Sigma_{22}}. \quad (9.58)$$

Furthermore

$$\Sigma_{22} = \varsigma^2(t_k - t_0), \quad \Sigma_{33} = \sigma_{k+1}^2(t_k - t_0), \quad \tilde{\Sigma}_{22} = \varsigma^2(t_{k-1} - t_0), \quad \tilde{\Sigma}_{33} = \sigma_{k+1}^2(t_{k-1} - t_0). \quad (9.59)$$

The other two covariances are more difficult to solve explicitly, but we can find an analytical expression for both of them in any case. We define

$$\gamma_\pi = e^{\kappa_\pi(t_{k-1}-t_0)/2}\sqrt{\pi_0 - \theta_\pi\left(1 - e^{\kappa_\pi(t_{k-1}-t_0)}\right)}, \quad (9.60)$$

and

$$\lambda_\pi = \log\left(\frac{\left(\sqrt{\pi_0} + \sqrt{\theta_\pi}\right)^2}{\pi_0 - \theta_\pi\left(1 - 2e^{\kappa_\pi(t_k-t_0)}\right) + 2\gamma_\pi\sqrt{\theta_\pi}}\right). \quad (9.61)$$

Hence the two covariances can be expressed as

$$\tilde{\Sigma}_{12} = \rho_{c_{k,b}\pi}\varsigma \frac{2\sqrt{\theta_\pi}\left(\left(1 + 2e^{\kappa_\pi(t_{k-1}-t_0)}\right)\sqrt{\pi_0} - 3\gamma_\pi\right) + \left(\pi_0 - \theta_\pi\left(1 + 2e^{\kappa_\pi(t_{k-1}-t_0)}\right)\right)\lambda_\pi}{2e^{\kappa_\pi(t_{k-1}-t_0)}\kappa_\pi^2\sqrt{\theta_\pi}}$$

$$(9.62)$$

---

[19] The complete proof is in [52].

and

$$
\tilde{\Sigma}_{13} = \rho_{F_{k+1}(t_k)\pi}\sigma_{k+1} \frac{2\sqrt{\theta}\left(\left(1 + 2e^{\kappa_\pi(t_{k-1}-t_0)}\right)\sqrt{\pi_0} - 3\gamma_\pi\right) + \left(\pi_0 - \theta_\pi\left(1 + 2e^{\kappa_\pi(t_{k-1}-t_0)}\right)\right)\lambda_\pi}{2e^{\kappa_\pi(t_{k-1}-t_0)}\kappa_\pi^2\sqrt{\theta_\pi}}
$$

$$(9.63)$$

and

$$
a := \frac{\tilde{\Sigma}_{12}\tilde{\Sigma}_{33} - \tilde{\Sigma}_{13}\tilde{\Sigma}_{23}}{\tilde{\Sigma}_{22}\tilde{\Sigma}_{33} - \tilde{\Sigma}_{23}^2}, \quad b := \frac{\tilde{\Sigma}_{13}\tilde{\Sigma}_{22} - \tilde{\Sigma}_{23}\tilde{\Sigma}_{12}}{\tilde{\Sigma}_{22}\tilde{\Sigma}_{33} - \tilde{\Sigma}_{23}^2},
$$

$$(9.64)$$

We denote by $\rho_{c_{k,b}\pi}$ the correlation between the mortgage rate at time t_k and the intensity π, by $\rho_{F_{k+1}(t_k)\pi}$ the correlation between the Libor rate fixing at time t_k and the intensity π and, finally, by $\rho_{c_{k,b}F_{k+1}(t_k)}$ the correlation between the mortgage rate and Libor at time t_k. The last quantity can be derived by means of the formula:

$$
\rho_{c_{k,b}F_{k+1}(t_k)} = \frac{\sum_{i=k+1}^{b} w_i F_i(t_0)\sigma_i\phi(i,k)}{\varsigma(t_k)c_{k,b}}
$$

$$(9.65)$$

where the notation is the same as that used above. We use the well-known procedure of freezing Libor rates at the level prevailing at time t_0.

We can derive the put via put–call parity:

$$
\text{Put}_2(t_0, t_k, t_{k-1} + j\Delta t; c) = \text{Call}_2(t_0, t_k, t_{k-1} + j\Delta t; c) - \text{EF}_2(t_0, t_k, t_{k-1} + j\Delta t; c)
$$
$$
+ c\mathcal{N}(-f_2)\text{SP}_2(t_0, t_{k-1} + j\Delta t)
$$

The quantity $\text{EL}_2(t_0, t_k, t_{k-1} + j\Delta t; c)$ is equal to $E[e^{-\int_{t_0}^{t_{k-1}} \pi_s ds}c_{k,b}(t_k)1_{\{F_{k+1}<c\}}]$ and can be computed as the price of $\text{Call}_2(t_0, t_k, t_{k-1} + j\Delta t; 0)$, forcing the following quantities in formula (9.56) (although the strike $c = 0$) to be:

$$
f_2 = \frac{\ln(c_{k,b}(t_0)/c) - \frac{1}{2}\Sigma_{33}}{\sqrt{\Sigma_{33}}}
$$

$$(9.66)$$

and

$$
f_1 = f_2 + \rho_{c_{k,b}F_{k+1}(t_k)}\sqrt{\Sigma_{22}}.
$$

$$(9.67)$$

Finally, we are able to compute the expected loss on prepayment

$$
\text{ELoP}_2(t_0, t_k) = \bar{C}_{k,b}(t_0)\sum_{j=1}^{J}(\text{Put}_2(t_0, t_k, t_{k-1} + (j-1)\Delta t; c) - \text{Put}_2(t_0, t_k, t_{k-1} + j\Delta t; c))
$$

$$(9.68)$$

Total ELoP of this extended version of the model is the sum of ELoP_1 in (9.48) and ELoP_2 in (9.68) ($\text{ELoP} = \text{ELoP}_1 + \text{ELoP}_2$). This will also be the ELoP used to compute total prepayment cost, that we define in the following section.

9.2.10   Total prepayment cost

The ELoP is a tool to measure expected losses a bank will suffer upon prepayment. For hedging and pricing purposes, though, it is more useful to compute total prepayment cost (TPC), defined as the sum of the present values of $\text{ELoP}(t_0, t_k)$ for all possible K prepayment dates in the interval $[t_0, t_b = T]$:

$$\text{TPC}(t_0, T) = \sum_{k=1}^{K} P^D(t_0, t_k)\text{ELoP}(t_0, t_k) \tag{9.69}$$

TPC can be hedged, since it is a function of Libor forward rates and related volatilities entering in the mortgage rate $c_{k,b}(t_0)$: $\text{TPC}(t_0, T) \to \text{TPC}(t_0, T; F(t_1), \ldots, F(t_{b-1}), \sigma_1, \ldots, \sigma_{b-1})$. As for its sensitivity to interest rates, we can bump a given amount (say, 10 bps) separately each forward and then calculate the change in TPC. Denoting by $\Delta_{\delta F(t_i)}\text{TPC}$ the sensitivity of TPC with respect to bump $\delta F(t_i)$ of the forward $F(t_i)$, we have that:

$$\Delta\text{TPC}_{\delta F(t_i)} = (\text{TPC}(t_0, T; F(t_1), \ldots, F(t_i) + \delta F(t_i), \ldots, F(t_{b-1}), \sigma_1, \ldots, \sigma_{b-1})$$
$$- \text{TPC}(t_0, T; F(t_1), \ldots, F(t_i), \ldots, F(t_{b-1}), \sigma_1, \ldots, \sigma_{b-1}))/\delta F(t_i)$$

In an analogous fashion we can compute its sensitivity to volatilities:

$$\Delta\text{TPC}_{\delta\sigma_i} = (\text{TPC}(t_0, T; F(t_1), \ldots, F(t_{b-1}), \sigma_1, \ldots, \sigma_i + \delta\sigma_i, \ldots, \sigma_{b-1})$$
$$- \text{TPC}(t_0, T; F(t_1), \ldots, F(t_i), \ldots, F(t_{b-1}), \sigma_1, \ldots, \sigma_i, \ldots, \sigma_{b-1}))/\delta\sigma_i$$

These sensitivities can easily be converted in hedging quantities of liquid market instruments, such as swaps and caps and floors.

9.2.11 Expected cash flows

The model can also be employed to project expected cash flows, taking into account the prepayment effect. More specifically, as already stated, the rational prepayment decision may occur at any time, but the actual effects both in terms of anticipated unwinding of the contract and of costs for the bank, manifest themselves only when the condition that the forward mortgage rate is lower than the contract rate $c_{k,b}(t_k) < c$ is verified. In the previous section we considered this condition, since we only calculate the P&L effects when $c_{k,b}(t_k) < c$. Actually, the bank always suffers a loss in this case.

When projecting expected cash flows, the probability of an anticipated inflow of the residual notional at a given time t_k has to be computed as follows:

$$\text{PP}_e(t_0, t_k) = 1 - \text{SP}_e^R(t_0, t_k)\text{SP}^E(t_0, t_k) \tag{9.70}$$

where $\text{SP}_e^R(t, T)$ is the survival probability jointly with condition $c_{k,b}(t_k) < c$, which we name "effective". The latter can be calculated by exploiting the approach described above for the ELoP: so we start with the effective rational prepayment probability in the interval $[t_{k-1}, t_k]$. Assume we divide this into J subintervals Δt

$$\text{PP}_{e,1}^R(\tau \in [t_{k-1}, t_k]) = \sum_{j=1}^{J} D_{j,1}(t_0, t_k; c) \tag{9.71}$$

where

$$D_{j,1}(t_0, t_k; c) = \Big((\text{Put}_1(t_0, t_k, t_{k-1} + (j-1)\Delta t; c) - \text{Put}_1(t_0, t_k, t_{k-1} + j\Delta t; c))$$

$$- (\text{Put}_1(t_0, t_k, t_{k-1} + (j-1)\Delta t; 0.999c)$$

$$- \text{Put}_1(t_0, t_k, t_{k-1} + j\Delta t; 0.999c)) \Big) / (0.001c) \tag{9.72}$$

The notation and pricing formulae for the put options are the same as above. In practice, we calculate the price of a digital option in case it terminates before expiry with a probability determined by rational prepayment intensity λ_t. The effective prepayment probability from t_0 up to a given time t_k can be obtained by summing all the probabilities relating to prepayment times occurring before t_k and including the latter as well:

$$\text{PP}_{e,1}^R(t_0, t_k) = \sum_{j=1}^{k} \text{PP}_{e,1}^R(\tau \in [t_{j-1}, t_j]) \tag{9.73}$$

This quantity is used in (9.70) since $\text{SP}_e^R(t_0, t_k) = 1 - \text{PP}_{e,1}^R(t_0, t_k)$.

The same can also be done if a second type of rational prepayment is introduced, so that:

$$\text{PP}_{e,1}^R(\tau \in [t_{k-1}, t_k]) = \sum_{j=1}^{J} D_{j,1}(t_0, t_k; c) \tag{9.74}$$

where

$$D_{j,2}(t_0, t_k; c) = \Big((\text{Put}_2(t_0, t_k, t_{k-1} + (j-1)\Delta t; c) - \text{Put}_2(t_0, t_k, t_{k-1} + j\Delta t; c))$$

$$- (\text{Put}_2(t_0, t_k, t_{k-1} + (j-1)\Delta t; 0.999c)$$

$$- \text{Put}_2(t_0, t_k, t_{k-1} + j\Delta t; 0.999c)) \Big) / (0.001c) \tag{9.75}$$

and

$$\text{PP}_{e,2}^R(t_0, t_k) = \sum_{j=1}^{k} \text{PP}_{e,2}^R(\tau \in [t_{j-1}, t_j]) \tag{9.76}$$

Total survival probability if we keep this additional rational prepayment in mind would be $\text{SP}_e^R(t_0, t_k) = 1 - \text{PP}_{e,1}^R(t_0, t_k)\text{PP}_{e,2}^R(t_0, t_k)$.

Expected total cash flow (interest + capital) at time t_0 for each scheduled payment time[20] $\{t_j = t_k\}$ is given by the formula:

$$\text{cf}^e(t_0, t_j) = (I_j + c\tau_j A_{j-1})(1 - \text{PP}_e(t_0, t_j)) + A_{j-1}(\text{PP}_e(t_0, t_j) - \text{PP}_e(t_0, t_{j-1})) \tag{9.77}$$

The expected outstanding amount at each time is given by:

$$A_j^e(t_0, t_j) = A_{j-1} - [I_j(1 - \text{PP}_e(t_0, t_j)) + A_{j-1}(\text{PP}_e(t_0, t_j) - \text{PP}_e(t_0, t_{j-1}))] \tag{9.78}$$

---

[20] Scheduled payment times are assumed to be equal to possible prepayment times.

It will be useful to define the prepayment-risky annuity, PRDV01:

$$\text{PRDV01}(t_0, t_b) = \sum_{j=1}^{b} \tau_j A_{j-1} P^D(t_0, t_j)(1 - \text{PP}_e(t_0, t_j)) \tag{9.79}$$

and the present value of the sum of expected capital cash flows PVECF:

$$\text{PVECF}(t_0, t_b) = \sum_{j=1}^{b} [I_j(1 - \text{PP}_e(t_0, t_j)) + A_{j-1}(\text{PP}_e(t_0, t_j) - \text{PP}_e(t_0, t_{j-1}))] P^D(t_0, t_j) \tag{9.80}$$

Both quantities can be computed with respect to standard prepayment probabilities or those derived by means of a VaR approach. Moreover, both can be compared with equivalent quantities when no prepayment risk is considered. Hence we have the DV01:

$$\text{DV01}(t_0, t_b) = \sum_{j=1}^{b} \tau_j A_{j-1} P^D(t_0, t_j) \tag{9.81}$$

and the present value of the sum of the contract capital cash flows CF:

$$\text{CF}(t_0, t_b) = \sum_{j=1}^{b} I_j P^D(t_0, t_j) \tag{9.82}$$

9.2.12 Mortgage pricing including prepayment costs

The fair rate of a mortgage at inception has to take into account two effects of prepayment. The first effect is due to the fact that prepayment is equivalent to accelerated amortization, so that the bank receives earlier than expected the amount lent to the mortgagee: this produces a lowering of the fair mortgage rate. This effect is gauged by weighting future cash flows with prepayment probabilities. The second effect is due to the cost that the bank bears when prepayment occurs when the replacement of the mortgage in the bank's assets can be operated at a rate lower than the original one: we have measured this cost using the TPC.

Let us start with the fair rate at time t_0 of a mortgage with notional A starting at t_0, ending at $T = t_b$, with a predefined amortization schedule:

$$c_{0,b}(t_0) = \frac{A - \text{CF}(t_0, t_b)}{\text{DV01}(t_0, t_b)} \tag{9.83}$$

This formula does not include any effect due to prepayment. We can include the first effect mentioned above by replacing the DV01 and the present value of the contract's capital cash flows by their expected value:

$$c_{0,b}^{pw}(t_0) = \frac{A - \text{PVECF}(t_0, t_b)}{\text{PRDV01}(t_0, t_b)} \tag{9.84}$$

where the superscript pw stands for *prepayment weighted*. The effect of anticipating the amortization implies that $c_{0,b}(t_0) \geq c_{0,b}^{pw}(t_0)$. To calculate a *full risk* fair rate that also includes the cost stemming from prepayment, formula (9.84) modifies as follows:

$$c_{0,b}^{fr}(t_0) = \frac{A - \text{PVECF}(t_0, t_b) - \text{TPC}}{\text{PRDV01}(t_0, t_b)} \tag{9.85}$$

Equation (9.85) acknowledges to the mortgagee both the benefits and costs for the bank in case of prepayment. A more conservative approach would be to include the TPC computed with a VaR approach, instead of the standard approach. An alternative would be to charge the TPC, split over the expected life of the contract, over the fair rate with no prepayment risk:

$$c_{0,b}^{pc}(t_0) = c_{0,b}(t_0) + \frac{\text{TPC}}{\text{PRDV01}(t_0, t_b)} \tag{9.86}$$

This rate can be considered the standard fair rate including *prepayment cost* but not the first prepayment effect (accelerated amortization).

Finally, to give an idea of the maximum rate that can be charged to the mortgagee, we consider *overhedging* the TPC, which is simply the summation of all the expected losses EL without any weighting for the prepayment probability. In this case the formula for the mortgage rate is:

$$c_{0,b}^{pwoh}(t_0) = \frac{A - \text{PVECF}(t_0, t_b) - \sum_{k=1}^{b-1} \text{EL}_k}{\text{PRDV01}(t_0, t_b)} \tag{9.87}$$

as long as we are only considering the first prepayment effect. Otherwise, we simply add total expected loss (split over the expected life of the contract) to the standard fair rate:

$$c_{0,b}^{oh}(t_0) = c_{0,b}(t_0) + \frac{\sum_{k=1}^{b-1} \text{EL}_k}{\text{PRDV01}(t_0, t_b)} \tag{9.88}$$

Example 9.2.3. *Considering the case in Example 9.2.2, we now compute the TPC related to the 10-year mortgage, which is equal to 48 bps.*

Table 9.12 shows the sensitivity of the TPC to a tilt of 10 bps for each forward rate. These sensitivities are then translated in an equivalent quantity of swaps, with expiries from 1 year to 10 years, needed to hedge them.

Table 9.13 shows the Vega of the TPC with respect to the volatilities of each forward rate. These exposures can hedged using caps and floors or swaptions in the Libor market

Table 9.12. Interest rate sensitivity of the TPC

Years	Sensitivity	Hedge quantity
1	0.02	16.82
2	0.02	9.07
3	0.02	5.58
4	0.01	3.45
5	0.01	2.19
6	0.01	1.38
7	0.01	0.92
8	0.00	0.64
9	0.00	0.40

Table 9.13. Vega of the TPC

Years	Vega
1	0.08
2	0.20
3	0.33
4	0.45
5	0.53
6	0.54
7	0.48
8	0.33
9	0.12

model setting we are working in (by calibrating the forward rate correlation matrix to the swaption volatility surface).

Let us now assume we want to include the prepayment cost in the 10-year mortgage. We first include exogenous prepayment, which is independent of the level of interest rates, so that on average its effects boil down to anticipated repayment of the outstanding notional: this will reduce the fair rate and, according to the data we used above, we have the fair rate modified as:

$$c = 3.95\% \rightarrow c = 3.89\%$$

Second, we include the TPC arising from rational prepayment (48 bps), which surely entails an increase of the fair rate:

$$c = 3.89\% \rightarrow c = 4.00\%$$

or the total effect of the prepayment of 5 bps in the fair rate.

For comparison purposes, we consider the overhedge strategy which consists in replication of the EL instead of the ELoP. In this case the fair mortgage rate would change as follows:

$$c = 3.89\% \rightarrow c = 4.78\%$$

As mentioned in the main text, while the interest rate and volatility risk can be hedged using standard (and liquid) market instruments, the prepayment risk related to the stochasticity of (rational prepayment) intensity cannot be eliminated. We suggest a VaR-like approach to resolve this. The corresponding TPC for the 10-year mortgage is 56 bps and the fair rate modifies as:

$$c = 3.89\% \rightarrow c = 4.02\%$$

which means that a generally higher prepayment probability has little impact on pricing. In Table 9.14 we show a comparison between expected and 99th percentile rational prepayment probabilities. Higher probability increases the costs but, since it also anticipates prepayment, the likelihood to have larger differences between current and mortgage rates is reduced.

Table 9.14. Expected and 99th percentile prepayment probabilities from the first to the last possible prepayment date

Years	PP (%)	PP at 99% (%)
1	14	19
2	32	42
3	49	62
4	64	77
5	75	86
6	83	90
7	89	92
8	93	93
9	95	94

Table 9.15. Sets of parameters, fair rates and TPC (using standard and VaR-like approaches)

Parameters	Fair rate (%)	Fair rate 99% (%)	TPC (bps)	TPC 99% (bps)
$\lambda_0 = 50\%, \nu = 0.10\%, \theta = 50\%$	4.01	4.03	50	56
$\lambda_0 = 50\%, \nu = 0.25\%, \theta = 50\%$	4.02	4.07	55	77
$\lambda_0 = 20\%, \nu = 0.25\%, \theta = 20\%$	4.01	4.04	49	65

To appreciate the effect of different parameters on the TPC, in Table 9.15 we show three sets of parameters of the intensity dynamics of rational prepayment and their effect on:

- *the fair rate;*
- *the fair rate at 99th percentile prepayment probabilities;*
- *the TPC;*
- *the TPC at 99th percentile prepayment probabilities.*

The total effect is rather limited for the mortgage fair rate. When considering the TPC, the differences between the base and VaR-like approach are bigger.

Example 9.2.4. *We now show how the model presented works for a portfolio of mortgages. The Eonia discount factors and zero rates (in percent), for years 1 to 30, that we have used have been extracted from deposits, FRAs and swaps on Euribor (shown in Table 9.16). In Table 9.17 we show volatilities for the forward rates needed to compute the EL.*

We consider a portfolio of 307,048 mortgages worth a total amount of EUR1 billion. The distribution of contract fixed rates within the portfolio is given in Table 9.18 and represented in Figure 9.5.

The distribution of notional amounts is shown in Table 9.19 and Figure 9.6. The vast majority of mortgage notional amounts were less than EUR200,000, and only 506 contracts were above 500,000 euros and 111 above EUR1 million.

Finally, we show the distribution of maturities within the portfolio in Table 9.20 and Figure 9.7. Mortgage maturity is mainly concentrated on 10 years and 20 years; fewer

Table 9.16. Eonia discocunt factors and zero rates for maturities from 1 to 30 years

Years	Discount factors	Zero rates
1	0.989472	1.05
1.5	0.983067	1.13
2	0.975769	1.22
3	0.958387	1.41
4	0.937119	1.62
5	0.912738	1.82
6	0.886029	2.01
7	0.857756	2.19
8	0.828951	2.34
9	0.800307	2.47
10	0.771627	2.59
12	0.714952	2.79
15	0.638621	2.98
20	0.536823	3.11
25	0.465364	3.06
30	0.416991	2.91
40	0.338455	2.71
50	0.263152	2.67

Table 9.17. Volatilities of Eonia forward rates for maturities from 1 to 30 years

Years	Volatility
1	44.41
1.5	51.01
2	53.38
3	47.99
4	45.87
5	42.64
6	39.27
7	36.31
8	33.86
9	31.93
10	30.35
12	27.80
15	25.50
20	23.77
25	23.59
30	24.40

contracts have shorter maturities and only 1.31% of the total portfolio has an expiry after 30 years.

Total prepayment cost (TPC), given market conditions at the evaluation date, is around EUR49 million (see Table 9.21). This is a not a small percentage of the outstanding notional amount (remaining capital) of the mortgages. TPC is the current value of

Table 9.18. Distribution of contract fixed rates for the mortgage portfolio

Contract rate	Number	%
<2.5%	42,569	13.86
2.5% < x < 5%	23,155	7.54
5% < x < 7%	225,457	73.43
>7%	15,867	5.17
Total	307,048	100.00

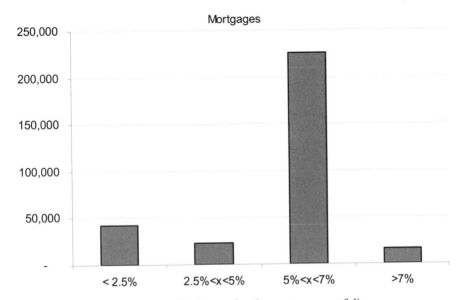

Figure 9.5. Distribution of contract fixed rates for the mortgage portfolio

expected losses incurred in the future from the prepayment decisions taken by mortgagees.

The possibility to hedge this quantity is crucial to minimize the costs related to prepayments. In a low-margin environment for the bank, such a cost is definitely not negligible. Prepayment exposures must be monitored and appropriate hedging strategies must be implemented.

Zero rate sensitivities are reported in Table 9.22 for different tenors from 1 year to 30 years: most exposures are between 10 years and 25 years. For a parallel shift in the zero rate curve of 1 basis point, variation in TPC is of about EUR145,000. The bank gains (i.e., TPC decreases) when rates move up.

Exposures to volatilities are shown for expiries running from 1 to 30 years in Table 9.23. Most sensitivity is on expiries between 10 and 20 years. An upward shift of the term structure of market implied volatilities produces an increase in TPC of about EUR420,000.

The expected cash flows and amortization of the pool of mortgages for each month, running from the calculation date to 41 years, are shown in Table 9.24. Expected cash flows include contract repayments (capital and interest) weighted by the probability of no

Table 9.19. Distribution of notional amounts for the mortgage portfolio

Amount (EUR)	Number	%
< 200,000	292,927	95.40
200,000 < x < 500,000	13,504	4.40
500,000 < x < 1,000,000	506	0.16
> 1,000,000	111	0.04
Total	307,048	100.00

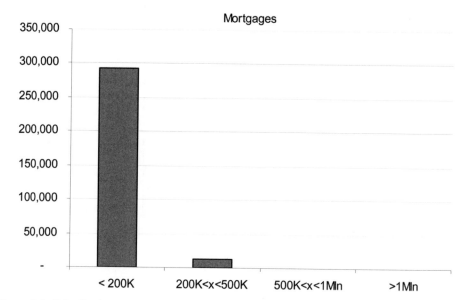

Figure 9.6. Distribution of notional amounts for the mortgage portfolio

Table 9.20. Distribution of maturities for the mortgage portfolio

Maturity (years)	Number	%
< 5	39,655	12.91
5 < x < 10	57,349	18.68
10 < x < 20	118,226	38.50
20 < x < 30	87,797	28.59
> 30	4,021	1.31
Total	307,048	100.00

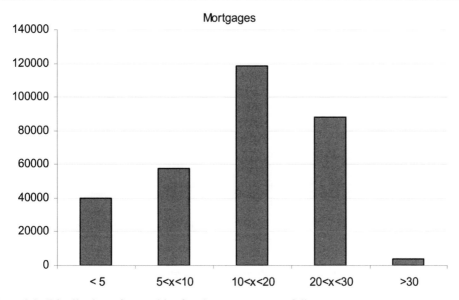

Figure 9.7. Distribution of maturities for the mortgage portfolio

Table 9.21. Total prepayment cost of the portfolio of mortgages

Total	Percent
48,736,032	4.874

Table 9.22. Zero rate sensitivities of the TPC of the portfolio of mortgages

Years	Zero rate sensitivity
1	−2,203.03
2	−1,462.35
3	−2,336.41
4	−1,652.77
5	−1,068.93
6	−575.21
7	2,289.25
8	5,928.28
9	7,129.96
10	9,665.28
12	16,813.30
15	33,398.23
20	46,136.98
25	31,621.84
30	3,291.74
Total	146,976.18

Table 9.23. Volatility sensitivities of the TPC of the portfolio of mortgages

Years	Vega
1	−361.1
1.5	−705.2
2	−2,375.5
3	−10,554.2
5	−31,045.8
7	−51,706.8
10	−119,649.7
15	−121,675.8
20	−67,321.9
30	−13,647.9
Total	−419,043.9

prepayment and the full reimbursement of the remaining capital, plus interest for the last period, weighted by the probability of prepayment. Expected amortization includes the amount of capital to be repaid weighted by the no prepayment probability and the amount of remaining capital paid back when the mortgage ends before expiry, wighted by the prepayment probability.

9.3 SIGHT DEPOSIT AND NON-MATURING LIABILITY MODELLING

The modelling of deposits and non-maturing liabilities is a crucial task for liquidity management of a financial institution.[21] It has become even more crucial in the current environment after the liquidity crisis that affected the money market in 2008/2009.

Typically, the ALM departments of banks involved in the management of interest rate and liquidity risks face the task of forecasting deposit volumes, so as to design and implement consequent liquidity strategies.

Moreover, deposit accounts represent the main source of funding for the bank, primarily for those institutions focused on retail business, and they heavily contribute to the funding available in every period for lending activity (see Chapter 7). Of the different funding sources, deposits have the lowest costs, so that in a *funding mix* they contribute to reducing the total cost of funding.[22]

Indeed, deposit contracts have the peculiar feature of not having a predetermined maturity, since the holder is free to withdraw the whole amount at any time. The liquidity risk for the bank arises from the mismatch between the term structures of assets and liabilities of the bank's balance sheet, since liabilities are mostly made up of non-maturing items and assets by long-term investments (such as mortgage loans). We extensively analysed this problem in Chapter 7.

The optionality embedded in non-maturing products, relating to the possibility for the

---

[21] We would like to thank Francesco Manenti for the help preciously provided in implementing and testing the models outlined in this section.
[22] We will extend the analysis of the funding mix in Chapter 11.

Table 9.24. Expected cash flows and amortization schedule of the portfolio of mortgages

Months	Expected amounts	Expected amortization	Months	Expected amounts	Expected amortization
1	10.064	958.729	131	67.517	388.549
2	13.51	982.178	143	62.102	347.832
3	13.089	974.546	155	55.119	311.9
4	13.088	966.976	167	51.84	277.291
5	12.896	959.503	179	49.695	242.799
6	12.184	952.218	191	47.02	209.019
7	12.548	944.912	203	41.844	178.534
8	12.203	937.725	215	33.747	154.582
9	12.155	930.642	227	30.58	132.45
10	11.652	923.843	239	29.146	110.465
10	11.58	917.18	251	26.928	89.438
11	11.376	910.655	263	23.668	70.509
12	11.047	904.253	275	18.843	55.388
13	11.022	897.953	287	16.972	41.293
14	10.669	891.806	299	16.053	27.292
15	10.699	885.713	311	14.655	13.884
16	10.528	879.736	323	11.371	3.012
17	10.063	873.902	335	2.698	0.382
18	10.263	868.089	347	0.157	0.244
19	9.957	862.401	359	0.115	0.14
20	9.977	856.783	371	0.067	0.08
21	9.689	851.278	383	0.033	0.051
22	9.746	845.808	395	0.02	0.033
23	9.65	840.394	407	0.013	0.021
35	104.138	782.604	419	0.012	0.011
47	99.169	726.583	431	0.007	0.004
59	94.512	672.11	443	0.003	0.001
71	89.91	619.321	455	0.001	0
83	84.179	569.249	467	0	0
95	78.139	522.589	479	0	0
107	74.318	477.166	491	0	0
119	71.312	432.257			

customer to arbitrarily choose any desired schedule of principal cash flows, has to be understood and accounted for when performing liability valuation and hedging market and liquidity risk. Thus, a sound model is essential to deal with embedded optionality for liquidity risk management purposes.

9.3.1 Modelling approaches

Two different approaches can be found in the financial literature and in market practice to model the evolution of deposit balances:

- bond portfolio replication
- OAS models.

Bond portfolio replication, probably the most common approach adopted by banks, can be briefly described as follows. First, the total deposit amount is split into two components:

- a *core* part that is assumed to be insensitive to market variable evolution, such as interest rates and deposit rates. This fraction of the total volume of deposits is supposed to decline gradually over a medium to long-term period (say, 10 or 15 years) and to amortize completely at the end of it.
- a *volatile* part that is assumed to be withdrawn by depositors over a short horizon. This fraction basically refers to the component of the total volume of deposits that is normally used by depositors to match their liquidity needs.

Second, the core part is hedged using a portfolio of vanilla bonds and money market instruments, whose weights are computed by solving an optimization problem that could be set according to different rules. Typically, portfolio weights are chosen so as to replicate the amortization schedule of deposits or, in other words, their duration. In this way the replication portfolio protects the economic value of the deposits (as defined later on) against market interest rate movements. Another constraint, usually imposed in the choice of portfolio weights, is target return expressed as a certain margin over market rates.

Since deposit rates are updated, with relatively large freedom of action, by banks to align them with market rates, the replication portfolio can comprise fixed rate bonds, to match the inelastic part of deposit rates that do not react to changes in market rates, and floating rate bonds, to match the elastic part of deposit rates. The process to rebalance the bond portfolio, although simple in theory, is quite convoluted in practice. For a more detailed explanation of the mechanism see [86].

Third, the volatile part is invested in very short term assets, typically overnight deposits, and represents a liquidity buffer to cope with daily withdrawals by depositors.

The critical point of this approach is estimation of the amortization schedule of non-maturing accounts, which is performed on a statistical basis and has to be reconsidered periodically. One of the flaws of the bond replica approach is that risk factors affecting the evolution of deposits are not modelled as stochastic variables. So, once statistical analysis is performed, the weights are applied by considering the current market value of the relevant factors (basically, market and deposit rates) without considering their future evolution.

This flaw is removed, at least partially, by the so-called option-adjusted spread (OAS) approach, which we prefer to call the stochastic factor (SF) approach.[23] In principle, the approach is little different from the bond portfolio replica approach: it identifies statistically how the evolution of deposit volumes is linked to risk factors (typically, market and interest rates) and then sets up a hedge portfolio that covers their exposures.

The main difference lies in that, in contrast tobond portfolio replication, in the SF approach the weights of hedging instruments are computed keeping the future random evolution of risk factors in mind, so that the hedging activity resembles the dynamic

---

[23] We think the term OAS is misleading for a number of reasons: it does not explicitly model any optionality and does not adjust any spread, as will be clear from what we show below. The name is likely derived from suspect practice in the fixed income market, which uses an effective discount rate to price assets by taking into account embedded optionalities (whence the name).

replication of derivatives contract. The hedging portfolio is revised based on the market movements of risk factors, according to the stochastic process adopted to model them.

We prefer to work with a SF approach to model deposit volumes for several reasons. First, we think the SF approach is more advanced from the modelling perspective, explicitly taking into account the stochastic nature of risk factors. Second, if bond portfolio replication can be deemed adequate to hedge the interest rate margin and the economic value of deposits, from the liquidity risk management point of view the SF approach is superior, by the very fact that it is possible to jointly evaluate within a unified consistent framework the effects of risk factors both on the economic value and on future inflows and outflows of deposits. Third, it is easier to include complex behavioural functions linking the evolution of volumes to risk factors in the SF approach. Finally, bank-run events can also be considered and properly taken into account in the SF approach, whereas their inclusion seems quite difficult within the bond portfolio replication approach.

9.3.2 The stochastic factor approach

The first attempt to apply the SF approach, within an arbitrage-free derivatives-pricing framework, to deposit accounts was made by Jarrow and van Deventer [78]. They derived a valuation framework for deposits based on the analogy between these liabilities and an exotic swap whose principal depends on the past history of market rates. They provide a linear specification for the evolution of deposit volumes applied to US federal data.

Other similar models have been proposed[24] within the SF approach: it is possible to identify three building blocks common to all of them:

1. A stochastic process for interest rates: in [78], for example, it is the Vasicek model (see Chapter 8).
2. A stochastic model for deposit rates: typically, these are linked to interest rates by means of a more or less complex function.
3. A model for the evolution of deposit volumes: since this is linked by some functional forms to the two risk factors in points 1 and 2, it too is a stochastic process.

Specification of the dynamics of deposit volumes is the crucial feature distinguishing the different SF models: looking at things from the microeconomic perspective, volumes depend on the liquidity preference and risk aversion of depositors, whose behaviour is driven by opportunity costs between alternative allocations. When market rates rise, depositors have a greater temptation to withdraw money from sight deposits and invest them in other assets offered in the market.

SF models can be defined *behavioural* in the sense that they try to capture the dynamics of depositor behaviour with respect to market rates and deposit rates movements. In doing this, these models exploit option-pricing technology, developed since the 1970s, and depend on stochastic variables, in contrast to the previously mentioned class on simpler statistical models.

Depositor behaviour can be synthesized in a behavioural function that depends on risk factors and determines their choice in terms of the amount allocated in deposits.

---

[24] See, amongst others, [86], [57], [80] and [26].

This function could be specified in various forms, allowing for different degrees of complexity. Given their stochastic nature, those models are suitable for implementation in simulation-based frameworks like Monte Carlo methods.

Since closed-form formulae for the value of deposits are expressed as risk-neutral expectations, the scenario generation process has to be accomplished with respect to the equivalent martingale probability measure. For liquidity management purposes, it is more appropriate to use real-world parameter processes. In what follows we will not distinguish between them: as we have also assumed in other parts of this book, with a risk premium parameter equal to zero, real-world processes for interest rates clash with risk-neutral ones.

We propose a specification for the SF approach which we think is parsimonious enough, yet effective.

Modelling of market interest rates

The dynamics of market interest rates can be chosen rather arbitrarily: the class of short-rate models we introduced in Chapter 8 is suitable and can be effectively used. In our specification we adopted a single-factor CIR++ model (see Section 8.3.4): we know that such a model is capable of perfectly matching the current observed term structure of risk-free zero rates. The market instantaneous risk-free rate is thus given by

$$r_t = x_t + \phi_t$$

where x_t has dynamics

$$dx_t = k(\theta - x_t)dt + \sigma\sqrt{x_t}dW_t$$

and ϕ_t is a deterministic function of time.

Modelling of deposit rates

Deposit rate evolution is linked to the pricing policy of banks, providing a tool that can be exploited to drive deposit volumes across time. It is reasonable to think that an increase in the deposit rate will work as an incentive for existing depositors not to withdraw from their accounts or to even increase the amount deposited.

The rate paid by the bank on deposit accounts can be determined according to different rules. Here are some examples:

1. Constant spread below market rates:

$$d_t = \max[r_t - \alpha, 0] \tag{9.89}$$

    to avoid having negative rates on the deposit, there is a floor at zero.
2. A proportion α of market rates:

$$d_t = \alpha r_t \tag{9.90}$$

    We analysed the fair pricing of sight deposits and non-maturing liabilities in Chapter 7, where we also derived the fair rate that a bank should pay on these contracts, discovering that it is a functional form of the kind in equation (9.90).
3. A function similar to the two above but also dependent on the amount deposited:

$$d_t = \sum_{j=1}^{m} i_j(r_t) \, 1_{\{D_t^j, D_t^{j+1}\}} D_t \tag{9.91}$$

where D^j and D^{j+1} are the range of deposit volumes D producing different levels of deposit rates.

We adopt a rule slightly more general than equation (9.90) (i.e., a linear affine relation between the deposit rate and the market short rate):

$$d_t = \alpha + \beta r_t + u_t \tag{9.92}$$

where $E(u_t) = 0, \forall t$.

As will be manifest in what follows, the evolution of deposit volumes depends on the deposit rate, so in this framework the pricing policy function, which is obviously discretionary for the bank, represents a tool to drive deposit volumes and, consequently, can be used to define liquidity strategies.

Modelling of deposit volumes: linear behavioural functions

We can model the evolution of total deposit volumes by establishing a linear relationship between its log variations and risk factors (i.e., market interest and deposit rates): this is the simplest behavioural functional form we can devise. Moreover, we add an auto-regressive component, by imposing the condition that log variation of the volume at a given time is linked to log variation of the previous period with a given factor and, finally, we also include a relationship with time, so as to detect time trends. Volume evolution in this case is given by the equation:

$$\log D_t = \gamma_0 + \gamma_1 \log D_{t-1} + \gamma_2 t + \gamma_3 \Delta r_t + \gamma_4 \Delta d_t + \epsilon_t \tag{9.93}$$

with Δ being the first-order difference operator and ϵ_t the idiosyncratic error term with zero mean. This formula is in practice the same as the one given in [78].

Model (9.93) is convenient because the parameters can easily be estimated on historical data via the standard OLS algorithm.

The presence of a time component in equation (9.93) is justified by empirical evidence on deposit series, which exhibits a trend component. This factor could be modelled in alternative ways, substituting the linear trend with a quadratic or exponential one.

For interest rate risk management purposes, it is interesting to understand how deposit evolution can be explained only by market and deposit rate movements. To this end, we introduce a reduced version of the model that can be estimated minus the trend component; that is:

$$\log D_t = \gamma_0 + \gamma_1 \log D_t + \gamma_2 \Delta r_t + \gamma_3 \Delta d_t \tag{9.94}$$

Empirical analysis of both model forms will be presented below.

Modelling of deposit volumes: nonlinear behavioural models

The behavioural function linking the evolution of deposit volume to risk factors can also be nonlinear, possibly involving complex forms. In recent years some efforts have been made to formulate this relation according to more sophisticated functions that describe peculiar features of deposit dynamics. The main contribution in this direction was provided by Nystrom [97], who introduced a nonlinear dependency of the dynamics of deposit volumes on interest rates in the valuation SF framework we are discussing.

Formalization of such dynamical behaviour is not trivial and we propose a model specification, inspired by [97].

The main reason nonlinear behavioural functions have been proposed is equation (9.93) has a drawback: it does not allow empirically observed depositor reactions to market and deposit rate movements to be fully captured. Actual behaviour exhibits high nonlinearity with respect to these, in the sense that it depends not only on variations, as implied by equation (9.93), but also on the levels of market and deposit rates.

The main idea behind modelling nonlinear behaviour is based on the microeconomic liquidity preference theory: depositors (and, generally speaking, investors) prefer to keep their investments liquid when market rates are low. As market rates increase, the preference for liquidity is counterbalanced so that depositors transfer higher fractions of their income and wealth to less liquid investments.

Looking at this in greater detail, the first variable to consider is total depositor income I, growing at an annual rate ρ: on an aggregated base we could regard it as the growth rate of the economy (GDP) or simply the growth rate of the income for each depositor (customer).

Second, allocation of the income between deposits and other (less liquid) investments hinges on the following assumptions:

- each depositor modifies his balance in the deposit account by targeting a given fraction $\overline{\lambda}$ of his income I. This level can be interpreted as the amount needed to cover his short-time liquidity needs. At any time t, given the current fraction λ_t of the income invested in deposits, adjustment toward the target $\overline{\lambda}$ occurs at speed ζ;
- there is an interest rate strike level E, specific to the customer, such that when the market rate is higher he then reconsiders the target level and redirects a higher amount to other investments (i.e., fraction γ of his income);
- there is a deposit rate strike level F, specific to the customer, such that when the rate received on deposits is higher he then is more reluctant to withdraw money (i.e., fraction δ of his income).

Under these assumptions, evolution of fraction λ_t of the income allocated in sight deposits is:

$$\lambda_{t+\Delta t} - \lambda_t = \zeta(\overline{\lambda} - \lambda_t)\Delta t + \gamma 1_{[E,\infty)}(r_t) + \delta 1_{[F,\infty)}(d_t) \qquad (9.95)$$

where $1_{[E,\infty)}$ is the indicator function equal to 1 when the condition in the subscript is verified. Income I grows as follows:

$$I_{t+\Delta t} - I_t = I_t \rho \Delta t \qquad (9.96)$$

and the deposit volume at time t is:

$$D_t = \lambda_t I_t \qquad (9.97)$$

In reality, since each depositor has different levels of strike rates E and F, due to their preferences for liquidity, on an aggregated basis that considers all the bank's customers there is a distribution of strike rates that reflects their heterogeneity in behaviour. So, when we pass from evolution of single deposits to evolution of the total volume of deposits on a bank's balance sheet, strike rates can be thought to be distributed according to any suitable probability function $h(x)$: in the specification we present here

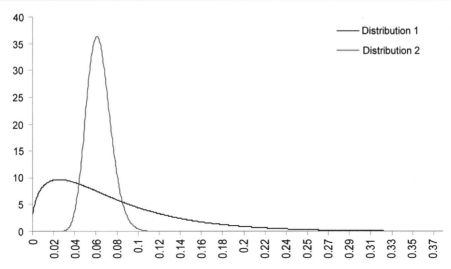

Figure 9.8. Two possible distributions produced by the gamma function (the *x*-axis shows the interest rate level and the *y*-axis shows the value of the function $h(x)$).

we choose a gamma function; that is:

$$h(x; \alpha, \beta) = \frac{(x/\beta)^{\beta-1} \exp(-x/\beta)}{\beta \Gamma(\alpha)}$$

The gamma function is very flexible and allows the distribution to have a wide range of possible shapes.[25]

Example 9.3.1. *As just said, the Gamma function is very flexible and allows for a wide range of possible shapes for the distribution. If we set $\alpha = 1.5$ and $\beta = 0.05$, for example, we have a distribution labelled as "1" in Figure 9.8. If $\alpha = 30$ and $\beta = 0.002$ we have a distribution labelled as "2". It is possible to model aggregated customer behaviour, making it more or less concentrated around specific levels.*

Alternatively, we can use the equivalent functional form of the gamma distribution written as:

$$h(x; k, \theta) := \frac{1}{\theta^k \Gamma(k)} x^{k-1} e^{-\frac{x}{\theta}}$$

This is actually what we will use to estimate the parameters from historical data shown below.

Evolution of the total volume of deposits can be written by modifying equation (9.95) and considering the distributions of strike rates instead of the single strike rates for each depositor:

$$\lambda_{t+\Delta t} - \lambda_t = \zeta(\overline{\lambda} - \lambda_t)\Delta t + \gamma H(r_t, k_1, \theta_1) + \delta H(d_t, k_2, \theta_2) \tag{9.98}$$

where $H(x, k, \theta) = \int_0^x h(u; k, \theta) du$ is the gamma cumulative distribution function.

---

[25] The gamma function was also chosen for the behavioural function in [97].

To make econometric estimation of parameters easier, we rewrite equation (9.98) in the following way:

$$\lambda_t = \alpha + \beta\lambda_{t-1} + \gamma H(r_t, k_1, \theta_1) + \delta H(d_t, k_2, \theta_2) \tag{9.99}$$

where $\alpha = \zeta\bar{\lambda}\Delta t$ and $\beta = \zeta\Delta t$.

Equation (9.99) can be applied by the bank to the "average customer". Given the heterogeneity of behaviours, given current market and deposit rates, the incentive to change income allocation by increasing less liquid investments, balanced by the incentive to keep the investment in deposits provided by deposit rates, can be synthesized in gamma distribution functions, so that $H(x, k, \theta)$ turns out to be the cumulative density of the average customer's strike.

9.3.3 Economic evaluation and risk management of deposits

The three building blocks employed to model deposits can be used to compute the economic value to the bank of the total amount held on the balance sheet.

At time $t = 0$, for a time horizon T, the economic value is the expected margin that can be earned by the bank on the present and future volume of deposits. In fact, the amount of funds raised by the bank in the form of deposits can be invested in short-expiry risk-free investments yielding r_t; on the other hand, the deposit cost to the bank is the rate d_t that it has to pay to depositors. Mathematically, this is:

$$V^D(0, T) = \sum_{j=1}^{n} \int_0^T E^Q\left[(r_t - d_{j,t})D_{j,t}P^D(0, t)\right]dt \tag{9.100}$$

where $D_{j,t}$ is the amount deposited in account j at time t and n is the number of deposit accounts. Expectation is taken under the equivalent martingale risk-neutral measure Q. Equation (9.100) is the expected net interest margin to the bank over the period $[0, T]$, for all deposit accounts, discounted at 0 by the risk-free discount factor P^D.

As suggested in [78], the value of deposits can be regarded as the value of an exotic swap, paying floating rate $d_{j,t}$ and receiving floating rate r_t, on the stochastic principal $D_{j,t}$ for the period between 0 and T.

The approach we outlined above is also a good tool for liquidity risk management, since it can be used to predict expected or stressed (at a given confidence level) evolution of deposit volumes. To compute these metrics, we need to simulate the two risk factors using a Monte Carlo method (i.e., the risk-free instantaneous interest rate and the deposit rate).[26] We undertake the following steps:

- given time horizon T, divide the period $[0, T]$ into M steps;
- simulate N paths for each risk factor;
- compute the expected level of deposit volumes $V(0, T_i)$ at each step $i \in \{0, 1, \ldots, M\}$, by averaging out N scenarios, by means of equation (9.93) or (9.99):

$$D^e(T_i) = \mathbf{E}[D(T_i)] = \frac{\sum_{m=1}^{M} D^m(T_i)}{M}$$

- compute the stressed level of deposit volumes at confidence level p, $V^p(0, T_i)$ at each

---

[26] See Chapter 8 for discretization schemes for CIR processes.

step $i \in \{0, 1, \ldots, M\}$, based on M scenarios. For liquidity risk management purposes the bank is interested in the minimum levels of deposit volumes at a given time T_i, hence we define the stressed level at the p confidence level as:

$$D^p(T_i) = \inf\{D(T_i) : \mathbf{P}[D(T_i) < D^p(T_i)] \geq p\}$$

In Chapter 7 we learned how to build the term structure available of funding (TSFu) for non-maturing liabilities. We assumed there that the total amount of deposits dropped by a given percent $x_{\mathrm{NML}}\%$ in each division of the horizon considered. Actually, the parameter $x_{\mathrm{NML}}\%$ can also be derived from the model we are using, since it can be inferred by computing the minimum amount of deposit volumes D^p at each time T_i, for $i \in \{1, \ldots, N\}$, at confidence level p (say, 99%).

Banks may be interested in computing the minimum level of deposits during the entire period between the reference time (say, 0) and a given time T_i: this is actually the value that corresponds to the actual available liquidity that can be used for investments expiring at T_i. To this end it is useful to introduce the process of minima for deposit volumes, defined as:

$$D^{\mathrm{min}}(T_i) = \lim_{0 \leq s \leq T_i} D(s)$$

Basically, the process excludes all growth in deposit volumes due to new deposits or to an increase in the amount of the existing ones; it only considers the abating effects produced by risk factors. The metric is also consistent with the fact that in any event the bank can never invest more than the existing amount of deposits it has on its balance sheet.

The SF approach can also be used for interest rate management purposes. Once we have the computed the economic value of deposits, it is straightforward to compute their sensitivity to risk factors by setting up hedging strategies using liquid market instruments such as swaps. To this end, we can calculate the sensitivity of the economic value of deposits to perturbations in the market zero-rate curve. Sensitivity to the forward rate $F(0; t_i, t_{i+1}) = F_i(0)$ is obtained numerically by means of the following:

$$\Delta V(0, T; F_i(0)) = V(0, T; \tilde{F}_i(0)) - V(0, T; F_i(0)) \tag{9.101}$$

where $V(\cdot)$ is provided by (9.100) and $\tilde{F}_i(0)$ is the relevant forward rate bumped by a given amount (e.g., 10 bps).

In Section 9.3.2, we assumed the instantaneous short rate follows single-factor CIR++ dynamics. Let us now assume that the initial zero-rate curve generated by the model (i.e., the series $\{P^D(0, T_i)\}_{i=1}^n$) perfectly matches the market-observed term structure, and that we have to modify the short-rate dynamics in a way that produces the desired bump on forward rates at time 0, by suitably modifying the deterministic time-dependent term $\phi(t)$ of the CIR++ process. This is easily done: let bmp be the size of the bump given to the term structure of the starting forward rate $F_i(0)$; in the CIR++ process the tilted forward $\tilde{F}_i(0)$ is obtained by modifying the integrated time-dependent function $\phi(t)$ as:

$$\int_{T_i}^{T_{i+1}} \phi(s)ds \quad \rightarrow \quad \int_{T_i}^{T_{i+1}} \phi(s) + \frac{\ln(bmp)}{\tau_i} ds$$

where $\tau_i = T_{i+1} - T_i$.

We present below some practical applications of the approach just sketched.

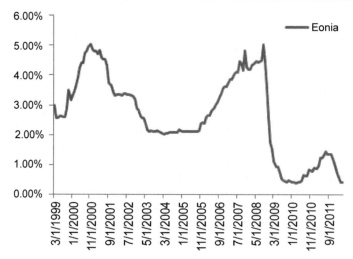

Figure 9.9. Time series of 1-month Eonia swap rates for the period 3/1999:4/2012

Example 9.3.2. *We empirically estimate and test the SF approachusing the two behavioural functions presented above, based on public aggregated data for sight deposits in Italy. We considered a sample of monthly observations in the period 3/1999:4/2012 for the total volumes of sight deposits and the average deposit rates paid by the bank. Deposit data are published by the Bank of Italy (see its* Bollettino Statistico).[27]

We consider the euro 1-month overnight index average (Eonia swap) rate as a proxy for the market short risk-free rate: values for the analysis period are plotted in Figure 9.9.

The CIR model for the market rate was calibrated on a time series of Eonia rates via the Kálmán filter,[28] and the resulting values for the parameters were:

$$\kappa = 0.053, \quad \theta = 7.3, \quad \sigma = 8.8\%$$

For the second building block (deposit rates), the linear relation between market rates and deposit rates in equation (9.92) was estimated via the standard OLS algorithm (results are shown in Table 9.25). Figure 9.10 plots the actual time series of deposit rates and fitted values from estimated regression. The model shows the time series to be a good fit and we can observe that the linear affine relation is strongly consistent with the data.

Finally, we need to adopt a behavioural function. We start with the linear model for deposit volumes in equation (9.93). The estimation results shown in Table 9.26 prove the model to be a good explanation of the data in this case. We note that the signs of coefficients multiplying, respectively, variations in the market rate and variations in the deposit rate, are opposite as expected. Figure 9.11 plots actual and fitted time series of deposit volumes.

We can now use estimated parameters to compute the economic value of deposits via Monte Carlo simulations of the formula (9.100). The standard approach requires generation of a number of simulated paths for risk factors by means of the estimated dynamics,

---

[27] Data are also available at www.bancaditalia.it
[28] See Chapter 8 for details.

Table 9.25. Regression results for the deposit rate equation (9.92)

	Coefficient	Significance (p-values)
Intercept α	1.05	0.042
Market rate r_t	0.92	1.86E-51
R^2	0.92	
F statistics	1773	
F significance	4.23E-87	

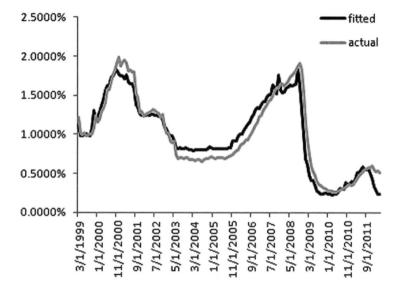

Figure 9.10. Actual time series of deposit rates vs fitted values

Table 9.26. Regression results for the linear behavioural equation (9.93).

	Coefficient	Significance (p-values)
Intercept	1.05	0.042
Lagged D_{t-1}	0.92	1.86E-51
Time t	0.4E-3	0.093
Market rate variations Δr_t	−3.45	0.001
Deposit rate variations Δd_t	7.54	0.009
R^2	0.99	
F statistics	4518	
F significance	1.17E-157	

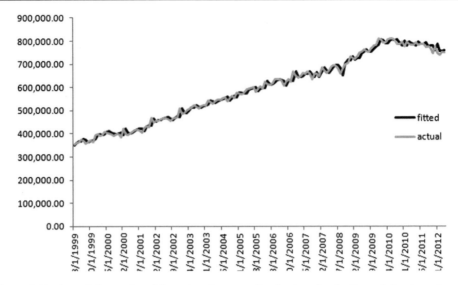

Figure 9.11. Actual time series of deposit volumes vs fitted values for the linear behavioural model

following these steps:

- *compute 10,000 paths for market rate evolution, simulated using CIR dynamics;*
- *for each path, compute the corresponding path for the deposit rate and deposit volumes according to estimated regressions (equations (9.92) and (9.93));*
- *compute the deposit value at each time step in the simulation period;*
- *sum discounted values path by path and average them to obtain the present value of the total amount of deposits.*

Figure 9.12 shows simulated paths for state variables, using the CIR process with the estimated parameters, starting from the first date after the end of the sample period, the average path of deposit volumes and the minimum amount computed at the 99% c.l. With initial total deposit volumes of EUR834,468 billion and a simulation period of 10 years, the estimated economic value to the bank of holding deposits is EUR121,030 billion.

We also provide empirical results for the reduced version of the linear behavioural model given in equation (9.94). Table 9.27 reports regression parameters for this model, and simulated paths are plotted in Figure 9.13. As expected, excluding the time trend, the forecast for deposit volumes is much more conservative, and the minimum volume at the 99% c.l. rapidly decreases.

We now estimate the parameters of the nonlinear behavioural model in equation (9.99), via a nonlinear least squares algorithm; we still use the same dataset as above (i.e., the sample 3/1999:4/2012 of monthly data for non-maturing deposit volumes, 1-month Eonia swap rates and deposit rates).

In this case, what we actually model is the evolution of proportion λ of depositor income held in sight deposits. At an aggregated level, we approximate the total income to nominal GDP, so that fraction λ will relate to this quantity. Since we are working with Italian deposits, we take Italian GDP data that are published quarterly and undertake linear

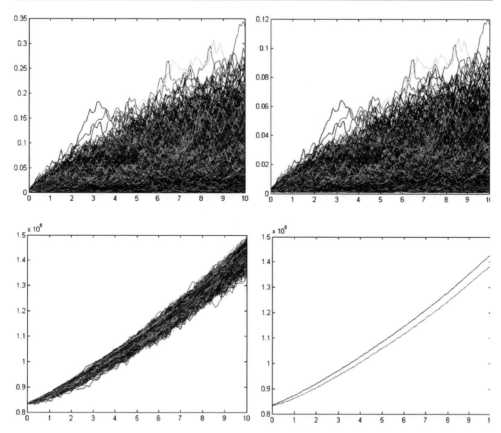

Figure 9.12. (From the top left clockwise) Simulated paths for 1-month Eonia swap rate, deposit rate and deposit volume, term structure of expected future volumes, and minimum (99% c.l.) future volumes

Table 9.27. Regression results for the reduced version of the linear behavioural equation (9.94)

	Coefficient	Significance (p-values)
Intercept	0.19	0.048
Lagged D_{t-1}	0.98	2.34E-159
Market rate variations Δr_t	−4.1	2.57E-04
Deposit rate variations Δd_t	6.52	0.04
R^2	0.99	
F statistics	5837	
F significance	1.66E-157	

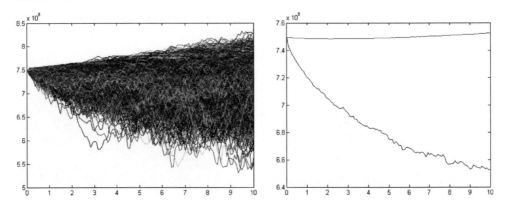

Figure 9.13. (Left) Simulated paths for deposit volumes. (Right) Term structure of expected and minimum (99% c.l.) future volumes

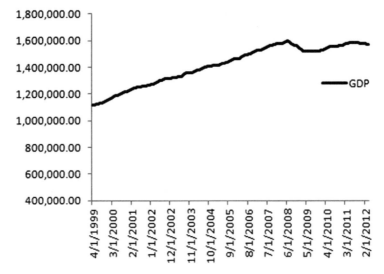

Figure 9.14. Time series of Italian nominal GDP for the sample 3/1999:4/2012. Quarterly data are linearly interpolated to obtain the monthly time series

interpolation to obtain monthly values.[29] *The reconstructed nominal GDP time series, for the estimation period we consider, is shown in Figure 9.14.*

Estimated coefficients and their significance are shown in Table 9.28. Figure 9.16 plots the probability density function (PDF) of the strike, respectively, for market (E) and deposit (F) rates. We can see that the cumulative density functions are at their highest when the market rate exceeds 3.55% and the deposit rate exceeds 4.25%. These should be considered the levels for market interest rates and deposit rates when most customers are considering reallocating the fraction of income held in deposits in other investments.

---

[29] We are aware this is likely not the most sound way to interpolate GDP data, but we think it is reasonably good for the limited purpose of our analysis.

Table 9.28. Regression results for the nonlinear behavioural equation (9.99)

	Coefficient	*Significance (p-values)*
Intercept	0.25	1.09e-167
Lagged λ_{t-1}	0.53	1.20e-158
Gamma market rates $H(r_t)$	−0.09	4.12e-083
Gamma market rates θ_1	18.77	1.13e-077
Gamma market rates k_1	0.001	3.86e-081
Gamma deposit rates $H(d_t)$	0.14	0.0054
Gamma deposit rates θ_2	24.26	1.67e-066
Gamma deposit rates k_2	0.001	3.01e-056
R^2	0.97	
F statistics	4,518	
F significance	1.1767E-157	

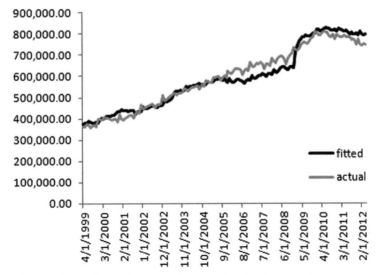

Figure 9.15. Actual time series of deposit volumes vs fitted values for the nonlinear behavioural model

Regression has an R^2 value lower than the linear model tested before: this is also confirmed by the plot of actual vs fitted deposit volumes in Figure 9.15.

As already done for the linear model, we can compute the economic value of deposits using a Monte Carlo simulation. Figure 9.17 shows simulated paths of deposit volumes and the term structure of expected and minimum volumes. With a simulation period of 10 years and an initial volume of EUR834,467 billion, the economic value of estimated deposits is EUR88,614, so the nonlinear model is more conservative than the linear one.

We can also run Monte Carlo simulations for the nonlinear model after freezing the time trend (which in this case means keeping the GDP constant with the initial level) and the

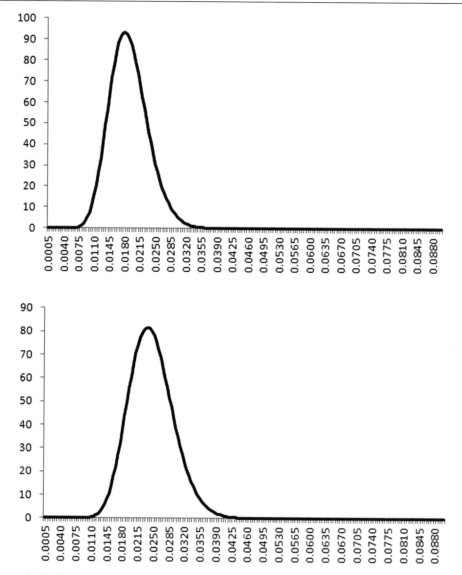

Figure 9.16. Gamma probability density function of the strike level for market interest rates (upper graph) and for deposit rates (lower graph), given the estimated parameters

deposit rate. In this way we isolate the effect produced by market interest rates on deposit volumes.

When just the time trend is frozen we get the results shown in Figure 9.18. It is worthy of note that without the time trend, the fraction of income held in deposits rapidly reaches a minimum and then, given the autoregressive nature of the model in equation (9.99), it keeps constant at this level.

Figure 9.19 shows the results when both the time trend and the deposit rate are frozen: qualitatively, they are the same as when just the time trend is frozen.

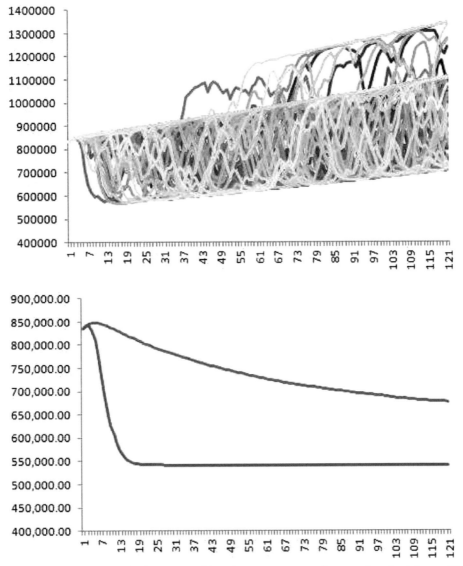

Figure 9.17. Simulated paths (upper graph) and term structure of expected and minimum (99% c.l.) future volumes (lower graph) derived by the estimated nonlinear model

A comparison between the linear and nonlinear model, as far as the expected and minimum level of deposit volumes is concerned, is shown in Figure 9.20. It is quite clear that the nonlinear model seems to be much more conservative in terms of expected and minimum levels of volumes.

We also present a comparison of the market rate sensitivities of the economic value of deposits obtained by the linear and nonlinear model. In Table 9.29 sensitivities to the 1-year forward (risk-free) Eonia rates, fixed every year up to 10 years, are shown. Sensitivities relate to a bump in the relevant forward rate of 10 bps. The linear model has bigger

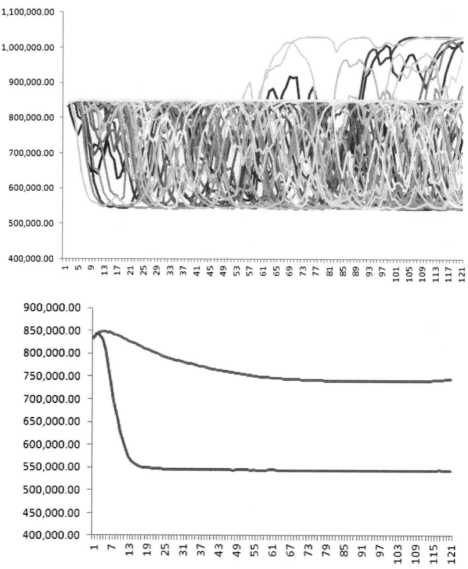

Figure 9.18. Simulated paths (upper graph) and term structure of expected and minimum (99% c.l.) future volumes (lower graph) derived by the estimated nonlinear model when the time trend is frozen

sensitivities due to the higher volumes, and hence higher economic value, expected in the future.

9.3.4 Inclusion of bank runs

It can be interesting to include the possibility of a bank run in the future, due to a lack of confidence by depositors in the creditworthiness and accountability of the bank. If this occurs, it is reasonable to expect a sharp and sudden decline in deposit volumes.

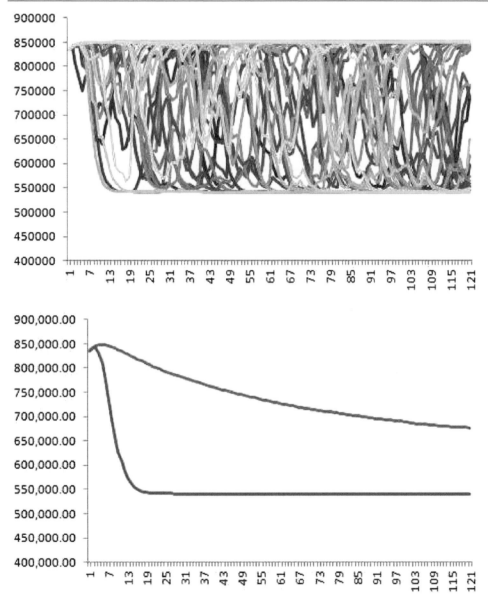

Figure 9.19. Simulated paths (upper graph) and term structure of expected and minimum (99%
c.l.) future volumes (lower graph) derived by the estimated nonlinear model when both the time
trend and the deposit rate are frozen

To consider a bank run fully, we needs to find some variable that is linked to the
bank's credit robustness (or lack of it). The credit spread of the bank on short or long-
term debt could be a possible solution: it can either be extracted from market quotes of
the bonds issued by the bank or from bank's CDS quotes.

As for the model necessary to simulate this, the very nature of a bank run makes the
nonlinear behavioural model more suitable. In fact, it is possible to add an additional

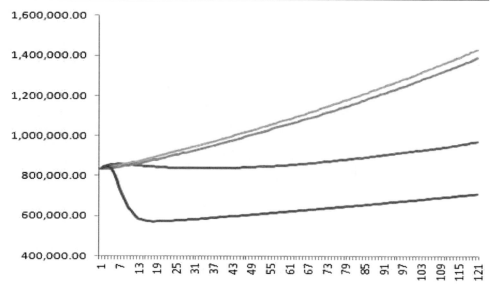

Figure 9.20. Term structure of expected and minimum (99% c.l.) future volumes (lower graph) derived by the linear (equation (9.93)) and the nonlinear (equation (9.99)) model

Table 9.29. Sensitivities to 1Y1Y forward Eonia swap rates of 10 bps up to 10 years for the linear and nonlinear model

Years	Sensitivity of linear model	Sensitivity of nonlinear model
1	730	524
2	770	683
3	810	663
4	860	657
5	910	659
6	960	664
7	1,000	678
8	1,050	689
9	1,090	703
10	1,100	723

behavioural function, related to the bank's credit spread, which will likely be densely concentrated at a high level (denoting an idiosyncratic critical condition). The inclusion of a bank run can be covered by extending formula (9.99) as follows:

$$\lambda_t = \alpha + \beta\lambda_t + \gamma H(r_t; k_1, \theta_1) + \delta H(i_t, k_2, \theta_2) + \eta H(s_t^B; k_3, \theta_3) \qquad (9.102)$$

The new behavioural function $H(s_t^B; k_3, \theta_3)$ is another gamma function taking the bank's spread s^B as input.

It is quite difficult to estimate the parameters of this function, since it is pretty unlikely the bank has experienced many bank runs. We can resort to bank runs experienced by comparable banks, but even here insufficient events can be observed for robust estimation of the parameters. Nonetheless, the bank can include bank runs on a judgmental basis by assigning given values to the behavioural function according to its hypothesis of stressed scenarios.

Example 9.3.3. *We extend the nonlinear model we estimated in Example 9.3.2 to include the possibility of a bank run.*

To compute the term structure of expected and minimum deposit volumes we use equation (9.102), using the parameters shown in Table 9.28. The parameters of the additional behavioural function are set as follows:

$$\eta = 0.2, \quad k_3 = 32, \quad \theta_3 = 0.002$$

Given parameters k_3 and θ_3 of the gamma function, when the credit spread of the bank reaches a level above 800 bps, then a drop of 20% in the level of deposits is experienced in each period (remember, we use monthly steps in our examples).

To model the credit spread and simulate its evolution in the future, we assume that the default intensity of the bank is given by a CIR process as in equation (8.140), with parameters:

$$\lambda_0 = -0.2, \quad \kappa = 0.5, \quad \theta = 5\%, \quad \sigma = 12\%$$

Moreover, we assume $L_{GD} = 60\%$ upon a bank's default. We further assume that the spread entering the behavioural function is the 1-month one for short-term debt.

Figure 9.21 shows the simulated paths and the term structure of expected and minimum deposit volumes: when compared with Figure 9.17 the lower levels projected by the model become evident.

9.4   CREDIT LINE MODELLING

Loan commitments or credit lines are the most popular form of bank lending representing a high percentage of all commercial and industrial loans by domestic banks. Various models exist in the literature for pricing loan commitments: amongst those most recently published are [50], [79] and [12]. These three articles model credit lines by considering as many empirical features as possible, although admittedly many factors enter the valuation and risk management of these types of contracts. In fact, [12] allows for partial usage of credit lines, but the authors do not include in the analysis any dependence between default probability and withdrawals; [50] allows for stochastic interest rates and intensity of default, the probability of using credit lines is linked to default probability, but unfortunately (at least in the specified model) partial and multiple withdrawals are not allowed for; finally, [79] models credit line usage as a function of default probability, with an average deterministic withdrawal that is due to causes other than debtor creditworthiness.

The effects on withdrawals by the default probability and, hence, the spread of the debtor is well documented. This is quite understandable, since when credit lines are committed and no updating clause is included in the contract, the debtor is long an option on its own credit spread struck at the contract spread level specified at inception. This highlights the necessity of using a stochastic model for the probability of default in order to price and monitor financial and liquidity effects appropriately.

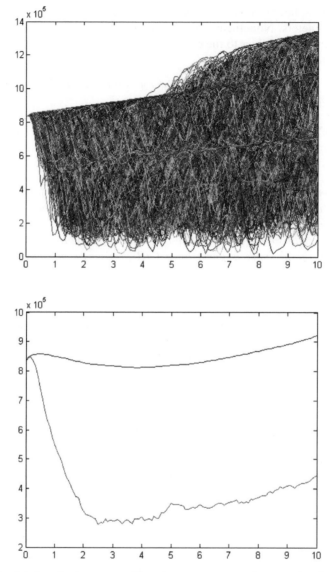

Figure 9.21. Simulated paths (upper graph) and term structure of expected and minimum (99% c.l.) future volumes when bank runs are included

In what follows we present a doubly stochastic intensity-based model for the joint behavior of loan commitments, one that is simple and analytically tractable and incorporates the critical features of loan commitments observed in practice:

- multiple withdrawals by the debtor;
- interaction between the probability of default and level of usage of credit lines;
- impacts on the funding and liquidity buffers to back up the withdrawals.

Furthermore, we design a specific tractable dynamic common factor model for the defaults of several debtors by allowing them to be correlated. Although the Gaussian copula model is an industry standard, it is not easy to adapt this framework to cope with credit lines. We prefer to adopt a reduced-form approach to model defaults. In our analysis, we focus on the doubly stochastic model for default intensity and we assume a common factor affecting the default intensity of all debtor models, thus producing some dependency amongst them. Accordingly, the correlation of withdrawal times and level of withdrawals can be captured by this common component.

We will introduce withdrawal intensity as a function of default intensity. We will achieve two results with such a specification: first, withdrawal intensity increases as default intensity increases, hence accounting for the positive correlation between credit line usage and the level of debtor spread (both of which are functions of default intensity). Second, the joint distribution of the portfolio of credit lines of a financial institution depends on the degree of concentration (or diversification) of the credit risk of debtors. We demonstrate the significant impact resulting from the correlation between default intensity and joint withdrawal distribution.

9.4.1 Measures to monitor usage of credit lines

There are two main measures used in practice to monitor and model credit lines:

- *Usage*: This is simply defined as the (expected) percentage of the credit line drawn down at any time s (possibly coinciding with the maturity of the credit line) given the observation time t. Mathematically, it can be expressed as:

$$\text{USG}_t(s) = \mathbf{E}_t[\text{DA}(s)/\text{CrLn}_0] \tag{9.103}$$

where $\text{DA}(s)$ is the amount drawn at s and CrLn_0 is the amount of the credit line opened at inception of the contract at time 0.

- *Loan equivalent*: This is the percentage of the available amount left, after past withdrawals, which is expected at time t to be used up to time s:

$$\text{LEQ}_t(s) = \mathbf{E}_t\left[\frac{\text{DA}(s) - \text{DA}(t)}{\text{CrLn}_0 - \text{DA}(t)}\right] \tag{9.104}$$

The LEQ metric is commonly used to estimate exposure at default at time τ ($\text{EAD}(\tau)$). It is common practice to assume that usage up to time t is an integral part of exposure at default and the LEQ for the unused portion is added to give total EAD; then, from (9.104), it is quite easy to derive:

$$\text{EAD}_t(\tau) = \text{DA}(s) + \text{LEQ}_t(\tau)(\text{CrLn}_0 - \text{DA}(t))$$

The LEQ has the useful property of allowing the unused portion of a credit line to be modelled separately from the withdrawn portion. It is interesting to note that in empirical studies (see, for example, [115], amongst many others) that both the USG and the LEQ or credit lines lent to defaulted debtors are higher than those lent to surviving debtors.

9.4.2 Modelling withdrawal intensity

The model we present focuses on the usage metric (USG). Consider a bank with a portfolio of m different credit lines, each one with a given expiry T_i ($i = 1, 2, \ldots, m$). Each credit line can be drawn within limit L_i at any time s between today (time $t = 0$) and its expiry. To model the usage of the line, we introduce withdrawal intensity, which indicates the percentage of the total amount of the line L_i drawn down in the infinitesimal interval of time dt.

For credit line i, between today and the maturity T_i, we assume that a debtor can withdraw portions in multiples of 1% of the total amount. Each withdrawal is modelled as a jump from a Poisson distribution $N_i(t)$ with time-varying default intensity λ_t^W. By construction, it is not possible to consider the effect of more than 100 jumps, since it would represent more than the total amount of the specific credit line, unless we allow for an overdraft. In this case we can set the total number of possible jumps at more than 100. There are several ways to address this problem, but we present two methods: proportional redistribution or cumulated attribution to the last (typically 100th) jump. More details on both methods will be given in Section 9.4.3.

Consider a probability space $(\Omega, \mathcal{F}, \mathcal{F}_t, P)$: since it is not possible to really hedge usage of the line, P represents the physical probability measure. Stochastic withdrawal intensity $\lambda_i^W(t)$ for the i-th borrower is a combination of three terms:

$$\lambda_i^W(t) = \alpha_i(\rho_i(t) + \lambda_i^D(t)), \tag{9.105}$$

where α_i is a constant, $\rho_i(t)$ is a time-dependent deterministic variable and $\lambda_i^D(t)$ is default intensity. The specification is rich enough to allow for precise modelling of expected usage at any time t, via functions α_i and $\rho_i(t)$, while the dependence on default intensity $\lambda_i^D(t)$ introduces a correlation between the worsening creditworthiness of the debtor and higher usage of the credit line.

To model the joint usage of m credit lines, it is useful to allow for correlation between the default intensities (and hence default events) of the m debtors as well. We model this by means of an affine correlation: the default intensity of debtor i, for $i = 1, 2, \ldots, m$, is the sum of two separate intensities:

$$\lambda_i^D(t) = \lambda_i^I(t) + p_i \lambda^C(t), \tag{9.106}$$

where $\lambda_i^I(t)$ is the i-th debtor's idiosyncratic component, $\lambda^C(t)$ is a common factor and p_i is a scalar parameter, ranging from 0 to 1, controlling the degree of correlation between debtor default intensities and default events. This model was presented in Chapter 8 and we refer the reader to it for more details. Intuitively, λ_i^I is the arrival intensity of default specific to a debtor of line i, while λ^C is the arrival intensity of a common event which, with some conditional probabilities, causes the default of all debtors in the set of m credit lines, each one with probability p_i.[30] Given this setting, the borrower may withdraw at any time $t \in (0, T]$ with maturity T.

Equation (9.106) implies that correlation is induced both through a common factor λ^C in intensities and through a common event. More specifically, conditional on all the independent processes $\lambda_1^I, \ldots, \lambda_m^I, \lambda^C$, there are independent Poisson processes $N_1^I, \ldots, N_m^I, N^C$ with these time-varying deterministic intensities. Whenever N^C jumps,

---

[30] The specification of default intensity is the same as in [60].

any borrower i defaults with probability p_i, and the default events of the various borrowers, at any such common event time, are conditionally independent. This means there is the potential for more than one borrower to default simultaneously.

We assume all components of the default process are independent and follow a (pure) Cox–Ingersoll–Ross (CIR) process, which is,

$$\left.\begin{aligned} d\lambda_i^I(t) &= \kappa_i^I[\theta_i^I - \lambda_i^I(t)]dt + \sigma_i^I\sqrt{\lambda_i^I(t)}dW_i^I(t), \\ d\lambda^C(t) &= \kappa^C[\theta^C - \lambda^C(t)]dt + \sigma^C\sqrt{\lambda^C(t)}dW^C(t), \end{aligned}\right\} \tag{9.107}$$

where W^i and W^c are Wiener processes. The drift factor $\kappa_i^I[\theta_i^I - \lambda_i^I(t)]$ (respectively, $\kappa^C[\theta^C - \lambda^C(t)]$) ensures mean reversion of intensity component λ_i^I (λ^C) towards its long-run value θ_i^I (θ^C), with the speed of adjustment governed by a strictly positive parameter κ_i^I (κ^C). The standard deviation factor $\sigma_i^I\sqrt{\lambda_i^I(t)}$ ($\sigma^C\sqrt{\lambda^c(t)}$) avoids the possibility of there being a negative intensity component λ_t^i (λ_t^c).

We set the following parameter constraints:[31]

- $\kappa^I = \kappa^C = \kappa$
- $\sigma^i = \sqrt{p_i}\sigma^c = \sigma, \quad i = 1, 2, \cdots, m$

so that the default intensity λ_i^D is still a CIR process. In particular,

$$d\lambda_i^D(t) = \kappa[\theta_i^D - \lambda_i^D(t)]dt + \sigma\sqrt{\lambda_i^D(t)}d\tilde{W}_i(t), \tag{9.108}$$

where $\theta_i^D = \theta_i^I + p_i\theta^C$ and the initial value $\lambda_i^D(0) = \lambda_i^I(0) + p_i\lambda^C(0)$, $i = 1, 2, \ldots, m$. In short,

$$\lambda_i^D(t) = \text{CIR}(\kappa, \sigma, \theta_i^D, \lambda_i^D(0), t) = \text{CIR}(\kappa, \sqrt{p_i}\sigma^C, \theta_i^I + p_i\theta^C, \lambda_i^I(0) + p_i\lambda_i^C(0), t). \tag{9.109}$$

where CIR indicates a Cox–Ingersoll–Ross process defined by the arguments within brackets.

Based on equation (9.105), default intensity $\lambda_i^D(t)$ is multiplied by a deterministic variable α_i. A convenient formula allows the formulae for CIR process parameters to be retained, as seen in Chapter 8, by adjusting the parameters of the process. Equation (9.109) can be rewritten as

$$\lambda_i^D(t) = \text{CIR}\left(\kappa/\alpha_i, \sigma/\sqrt{\alpha_i}, \theta, \lambda(0), t\alpha_i\right). \tag{9.110}$$

Note that the stochastic processes $\lambda_i^I(t)$, $\lambda^C(t)$, $\lambda_i^W(t)$ can be considered special cases of basic affine jump diffusions (basic AJD) using a zero-compound Poisson process. The basic AJD model has a closed form that can be used for both the generating function and the characteristic function (for more details see [64]).

9.4.3 Liquidity management of credit lines

The framework sketched can be used to derive the usage distribution of a credit line and joint usage of the portfolio of credit lines the bank has. We show how the model is capable of catching the diversification effects produced by the lower or higher correlation between the default probabilities of borrowers. The link between credit risk and

---

[31] See Section 8.4.

usage is also due to default events: these clearly distort the usage distribution, which obviously impacts liquidity management as well.

We will first focus on a single credit line, then we will extend the result to a portfolio of two credit lines: the results can easily be generalized to the case when more lines are involved. We will also see how to derive usage distributions at different times. Finally, the introduction of default events will complete the analysis.

Single credit line

We derive the probability distribution of the usage of one credit line at given time T, given we are at time t. Let us consider a portfolio of a single credit line i and assume for the moment that the time-dependent parameter $\rho_i(t) = 0$ for all t. In this case we can combine the two factors for credit risk into one, as as explained above, so that the common component can be neglected. Total withdrawal intensity is then $\lambda_i^W(t) = \alpha_i \lambda_i^D(t)$: we can treat the rescaling parameter α_i by making the change of variable in (9.110). The probability that no withdrawal happens (i.e., that no jumps occur) up to time T is given by:

$$P\big[N^i(T) = 0\big] = 1 - P\big[N^i(T) \geq 1\big]$$

$$= \mathbf{E}\left[\exp\left\{-\int_0^T \lambda_i^W(t)\,dt\right\}\right] = A(t, T)\,e^{-B(t,T)\lambda_i^W(0)}, \quad (9.111)$$

where $A(t, T)$ and $B(t, T)$ have the following forms:

$$A(t, T) = \left(\frac{2\xi_i\, e^{\frac{(\xi_i+\kappa_i)(T-t)}{2}}}{(\xi_i + \kappa_i)\big(e^{\xi_i(t,T)} - 1\big) + 2\xi_i}\right)^{\frac{2\kappa\theta_i}{\sigma_i}} \quad (9.112)$$

and

$$B(t, T) = \frac{2\big(e^{\xi_i(T-t)} - 1\big)}{(\xi_i + \kappa_i)\big(e^{\xi_i(T-t)} - 1\big) + 2\xi_i}, \quad (9.113)$$

where $\xi_i = \sqrt{\kappa^2 + 2\sigma_i^2}$.

We now need to derive the probability of the number of withdrawals being greater than zero. Based on [64], we numerically know the probability distribution of $\Lambda_i^W(s, T) = \int_s^t \lambda_i^W(u)\,du$. The characteristic function is actually known in closed form.[32] The distribution of the integrated factor can therefore be efficiently calculated by Fourier inversion, which is done by carrying out the following steps:

1. Evaluate the characteristic function $\Lambda_i^W(s, T)$ on an unequally spaced grid of length 1,024 whose mesh size is smallest for grid points close to 0 (e.g., by using an equally spaced grid on a logarithmic scale).
2. Fit a complex-valued cubic spline to the output from step 1 and evaluate the cubic spline on an equally spaced grid with 2^{18} points.
3. Apply a fast Fourier transform (FFT) to the output from step 2 to obtain the density of $\Lambda_i^W(t)$ evaluated on a equally spaced grid.

Figure 9.22 displays the the probability distribution of $\Lambda_i^W(0, T) = \int_0^T \lambda_i^W(u)\,du$.

---

[32] See Appendix 9.C.

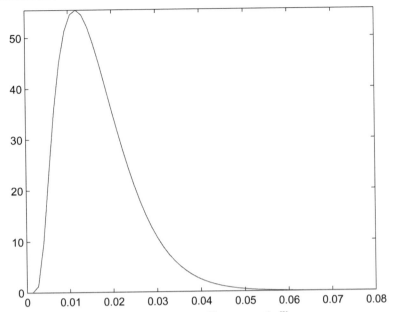

Figure 9.22. The probability distribution of $\Lambda_i^W(s,T) = \int_s^t \lambda_i^W(u)\,du$. Parameters are set at $\kappa_i^W = \kappa_i^D/\alpha_i = 0.8$, $\sigma = 15\%$, $\theta_i^W/\theta_i^D/\alpha_i = 2.0\%$, $\alpha_i = 1$, $\lambda_i^W = 1.5\%$ and $T = 1$ year

Having numerically evaluated the probability distribution of $\Lambda_i^W(s,T)$, we can evaluate the probability distribution of the Poisson process using the following formula:

$$\mathbf{P}\big[N^i(t) = K\big] = \int \mathbf{P}\big[N^i(t) = K \,\big|\, \Lambda_i^W(t)\big]\,dQ\big(\Lambda_i^W(t)\big)$$

$$\cong \sum_{j=1}^{N} \mathbf{P}\big[N^i(t) = K \,\big|\, \tilde{y}_j\big] f_{\Lambda_i^W}(\tilde{y}_j)\,\Delta\tilde{y}_j, \quad (9.114)$$

where $\tilde{y}_j = j\Delta y$ ($0 \leq j < N$), $\Delta\tilde{y}$ is the spacing of the grid and N the number of points, $i = 1, \ldots, m$. The term $\mathbf{P}\big[N^i(t) = K \,\big|\, \tilde{y}_j\big]$ is simply given by the Poisson density function:

$$\mathbf{P}\big[N^i(t) = K \,\big|\, \tilde{y}_j\big] = e^{-\tilde{y}_j} \frac{\tilde{y}_j^K}{K!}. \quad (9.115)$$

Adding the time-dependent parameter is also easy, since it means increasing the jump intensity by the quantity $\pi_i = \alpha_i \int_0^T \rho_i(s)\,ds$, so that (9.115) becomes:

$$\mathbf{P}\big[N^i(t) = K \,\big|\, \tilde{y}_j\big] = e^{-(\tilde{y}_j + \pi_i)} \frac{(\tilde{y}_j + \pi)^K}{K!}. \quad (9.116)$$

Example 9.4.1. *We plot the usage (USG) distribution after 1 year of a credit line. As seen above, this is tantamount to computing a Poisson process distribution with jumps from 0 to 100. We assume that the default intensity λ_i^D is composed of two CIR processes $CIR_i^I(0.015, 0.8, 0.15, 0.02, 1)$ and $CIR^C(0.015, 0.8, 0.2, 0.015, 1)$, such that $CIR_i^D(0.8, 0.1789, 0.0320, 0.015, 1)$. Furthermore, we suppose a coefficient $\alpha_i = 1{,}500$. Figure 9.23 represents the three plots having a value for the p_i coefficient equal to 0.8:*

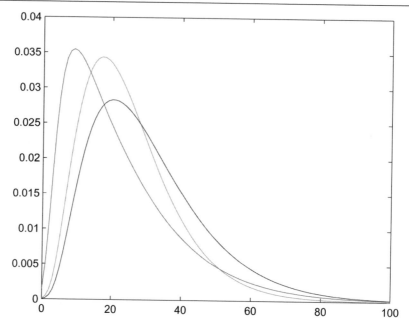

Figure 9.23. In this figure we plot the probability distributions of (i) $N_i^I(t)$ in light grey, (ii) $N^C(t)$ in grey and (iii) $N_i(t)$ in dark grey. These processes are characterized by the following parameters: $\mathrm{CIR}_i^I(0.8, 0.15, 0.02, 0.015, 1)$, $\mathrm{CIR}^C(0.8, 0.2, 0.015, 0.015, 1)$ and hence $\mathrm{CIR}_i^D(0.8, 0.1789, 0.0320, 0.015, 1)$ since we have $p_i = 0.8$

the light-grey line is the plot of $N_i^I(t)$, the grey line is $N^C(t)$ and the dark-grey line $N_i(t)$ is the total distribution, which is defined as total withdrawal intensity. In Figure 9.24 we show the withdrawal distribution when $p_i = 0.2$, with the other parameters as before.

Percentile evaluation

It is useful to compute the highest withdrawal within the chosen period, at a given confidence level *c.l.* (e.g., 99%), when pricing and managing the liquidity risk of the credit line. We evaluate the *c.l.*-percentile of the withdrawal distribution as follows:

1. We find the *c.l.*-percentile of the $\Lambda_i^W(t)$ distribution. We indicate this value by $\tilde{\Lambda}_i^W$;
2. Using equation (9.116), we evaluate the Poisson distribution of withdrawals using $\tilde{\Lambda}_i^W$ as the new deterministic intensity.
3. We calculate the *c.l.*-percentile of the distribution obtained in the previous step.

Example 9.4.2. *Let us consider, for instance, a CIR process characterized by the following parameters: $CIR(0.8, 0.15, 0.02, 0.015, 1)$, which have a multiplying factor equal to $\alpha_i = 1,500$. Let us consider a confidence level of 99%. We find a value for $\tilde{\Lambda}_i^W$ equal to 62.2217 (as shown in Figure 9.25). This plot is in jump basis, which means that the x-axis goes from 0 to 100 jumps. What we actually need is a different basis: 1% amounts of borrowed money on that specific credit line (as previously specified in Section 9.4.2). If the*

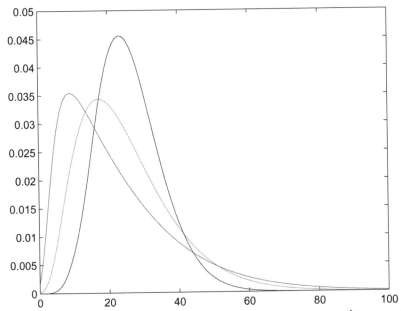

Figure 9.24. In this figure we plot the probability distributions of (i) $\Lambda_i^I(t)$ in light grey, (ii) $\Lambda^C(t)$ in grey and (iii) $\Lambda_i^W(t)$ in dark grey. These processes are characterized by the following parameters: $\mathrm{CIR}_i^I(0.8, 0.15, 0.02, 0.015, 1)$, $\mathrm{CIR}(0.8, 0.2, 0.015, 0.015, 1)$ and hence $\mathrm{CIR}_i(0.8, 0.0894, 0.0230, 0.015, 1)$ since we have $p_i = 0.2$

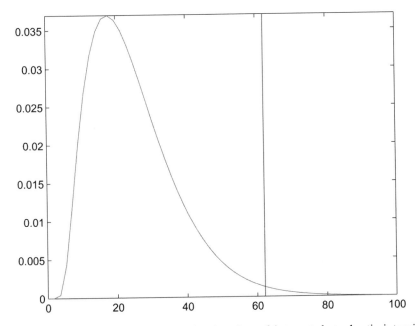

Figure 9.25. The curve represents the density function of integrated stochastic intensity $\Lambda_i(t)$ characterized by the following parameters: $\mathrm{CIR}(0.8, 0.15, 0.02, 0.015, 1)$. The vertical line represents the 99th percentile of this distribution, which in this case is equal to 62.2217

credit line, for example, has a value of EUR5,000,000, then the largest usage at the 99th percentile is 5,000,000 × 62.2217/100 = EUR3,111,085.

Dealing with jumps over 100

As already mentioned, if we do not allow an overdraft on the credit line, then we have to deal with jumps above 100 of the Poisson process used to define the withdrawal distribution. Basically, we need to redistribute the probability of jumps above 100 over the full range of jumps between 0 and 100. We here show two methods to cope with this problem: one is the proportional approach, the other is to put all the probability on the last possible jump (i.e., 100).

Looking at this in greater detail, the proportional approach splits the probability of an overdraft on the credit line (i.e., more than 100 jumps) proportionally over the probabilities of the number of jumps from 0 to 100. This redistribution is operated via the formula:

$$\mathbf{P}'_i[N^i(t) = K] = \mathbf{P}_i[N^i(t) = K] + \frac{\mathbf{P}_i[N^i(t) = K]}{\mathbf{P}(L)} \mathbf{P}(R), \tag{9.117}$$

where $k = 1, \ldots, 100$, $\mathbf{P}(L) = \sum_{k=0}^{100} \mathbf{P}[N^i(t) = K]$ is the cumulated probability of the first 100 jumps and $\mathbf{P}(R) = 1 - \mathbf{P}(L)$ is the probability of the overdrawn part of the credit line. So, the probability of there being K jumps is adjusted by the fraction of the total probability that has more than 100 jumps, this fraction being proportional to its weight in the cumulated probability of the first 100 jumps. In other words, the method calculates jump probabilities conditioned to having fewer than 100 jumps.

The second approach simply assigns to the 100th jump probability the cumulated probability of there being an overdraft of the line, according to the formula:

$$\mathbf{P}'_i[N^i(t) = K] = \mathbf{P}'_i[N^i(t) = K] + \mathbf{P}(R), \tag{9.118}$$

where the notation is the same as in the first approach.

Figure 9.26 shows the two redistribution methods we have sketched: (a) represents the proportional approach and (b) shows the last point approach. Of course, expected usage of the credit line is different depending on the method adopted: in fact, expected usage with the proportional method is 28.2877% while it is 29.6318% with the second approach.

Although the first (proportional) approach seems more sensible, the second (last jump) approach allows capturing an effect that has been documented in empirical studies (see, for example, [77]). More specifically, empirical withdrawal distributions seem to be bimodal peaking at around average usage and at full (100%) usage. The second method is best at addressing this situation. However, in what follows we will use only the first method.

Example 9.4.3. *We consider usage of a credit line on an amount of L =5,000,000, using the parameters given in Table 9.30. The probability distribution can be normalized using the procedure described in this section. The results are shown in Figure 9.27. In Table 9.31, we show the values of the 1st and 99th percentiles and the average distribution.*

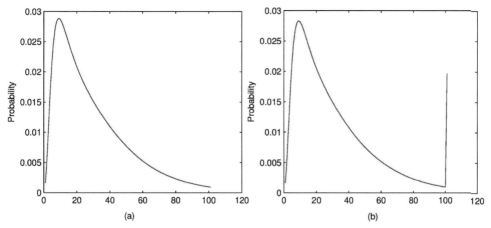

Figure 9.26. (a) Adjusted distribution of jumps (withdrawal percentages of the line) according to the proportional approach. (b) The same distribution adjusted according to the last point approach. Both figures are based on the withdrawal intensity given by a process $\mathrm{CIR}(0.8/4000, 15\%/\sqrt{4000}, 0.2\%/4000, 1\%, 1 \times 4000)$ and $\rho = 0$

Table 9.30. Parameters used for the single credit line used in Example 9.4.3

	Credit line
L	5,000,000
κ	0.8
α	2,500
λ	1.735%
θ	1.735%
σ	10.00%

Joint usage of a portfolio of credit lines

The joint distribution of usage of more than one line is more complex to derive than when dealing with a single credit line. Moreover, in this case the common factor of the default intensity of each debtor, λ^C, plays a crucial role since not only does it drive the (affine) correlation amongst defaults, but it also affects the probability of simultaneous withdrawals from different lines.

Considering this in greater detail, when a jump given the common intensity process λ^C occurs, all debtors withdraw a given percentage of their line. The higher the intensity of the common component, the larger the amount withdrawn from each line at the same time. It is clear that in this setting a portfolio more concentrated in terms of credit risk is also riskier in terms of unexpected liquidity needs (as we will see below).

We will outline a numerical procedure that approximates the joint distribution, which unfortunately is not available in analytical form. First, along the lines of [60], we set the

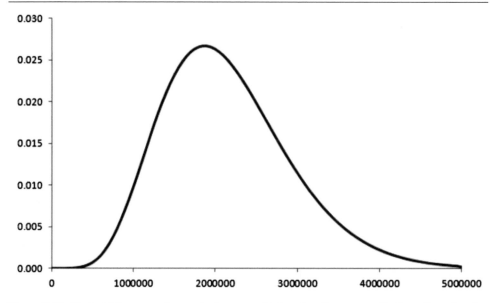

Figure 9.27. Probability usage for a single user withdrawing from a credit line of total value $L = 5{,}000{,}000$. The distribution parameters are specified in Table 9.30

Table 9.31. Values of the 1st and 99th percentiles U_{01} and U_{99}, and of average usage $\bar{U}$, for the calculation of usage probability in Figure 9.27

U_{99} (million)	U_{01} (million)	$\bar{U}$ (million)
4.2500	0.7500	2.1405

following approximation:

$$N_t^i \sim N_i^I(t) + p_i N^C(t), \tag{9.119}$$

where $N_i^I(t)$ is the i-th idiosyncratic event-counting process indicating the number of times it has jumped by time t, while $N^C(t)$ is the common event-counting process indicating the number of times it has jumped by time t; p_i indicates the weight (or the probability) by which the common event affects single debtor i. So, we can either have a withdrawal specific for each debtor, or a common withdrawal for all debtors, although in the latter case every debtor has probability p_i to actually withdraw.[33]

To illustrate the procedure, consider for simplicity two credit lines of amounts, respectively, L_1 and L_2, so that the total portfolio of credit lines of the bank is $L = L_1 + L_2$. Let w_1 (w_2) be the value of 1% of the first (respectively, second) credit line, $w_1 = L_1 \times 1\%$.

Let us divide the usage percentage of the total credit line L into G discrete intervals of

---

[33] As noted in [60] and analogously for the "default" event, the approximation overestimates the number of occurrences since the sum of the idiosyncratic and common jumps can be above 100. On the other hand, it underestimates the probability of events related to multiple common events. The two effects somehow cancel each other out.

Table 9.32. Withdrawal model specification. Columns represent individual components and rows common components. Each withdrawal is a combination of jumps of two components

$N^C = 0$		$N^C = 1$		$\cdots$	$N^C = 100$	
Line 1	Line 2	Line 1	Line 2	$\cdots$	Line 1	Line 2
0	0	$(0 + p_1)w_1$	$(0 + p_2)w_2$	$\cdots$	$(0 + p_1 100)w_1$	$(0 + p_2 100)w_2$
$1w_1$	$1w_2$	$(1 + p_1)w_1$	$(1 + p_2)w_2$	$\cdots$	$(1 + p_1 100)w_1$	$(1 + p_2 100)w_2$
$2w_1$	$2w_2$	$(2 + p_1)w_1$	$(2 + p_2)w_2$	$\cdots$	$(2 + p_1 100)w_1$	$(2 + p_2 100)w_2$
$\cdots$	$\cdots$	$\cdots$	$\cdots$	$\cdots$	$\cdots$	$\cdots$
$100w_1$	$100w_2$	$(100 + p_1)w_1$	$(100 + p_2)w_2$	$\cdots$	$(100 + p_1 100)w_1$	$(100 + p_2 100)w_2$

size $\delta = 1/G$. For example, we divide total usage into 100 intervals from 0 to 100% of equal size $\delta = 1\%$. A given usage is assigned to each interval (e.g., usage corresponding to the midpoint or the upper bound of the interval). Let $U(k)$ be the usage of the two lines for the interval $[l_{k-1} \times L, l_k \times L]$, where $l_k = k\delta = k/100$. The probability of usage $U(k)$ can be expressed as

$$\mathbf{P}[U(k)] = \sum_{i=0}^{100} \mathbf{P}[l_{k-1} \times L < U(k) \leq l_k \times L | N^C = i] \, \mathbf{P}[N^C = i], \tag{9.120}$$

To evaluate (9.120) in practice, we can build a table like that in Table 9.32. Each column records the number of times N^C the common event occurred. Given this, each row shows withdrawal from the two lines. For example, the second row in the second column shows withdrawal from line 1 when there is one idiosyncratic jump and one common jump (i.e., $(1 + p_1 \times 1) \times w_1$), since we only have probability p_1 that the common jump actually translates into withdrawal from line 1.

The probability that each idiosyncratic jump occurs can be computed by (9.116), by setting $\lambda_i^W(t) = \alpha_i \lambda_i^I(t)$ and using the related CIR process. The probability $\mathbf{P}[N^C = K]$ is similarly derived as in (9.116), by setting $\lambda_i^W(t) = \alpha_i \lambda^C(t)$ (using parameters of the corresponding CIR process) and $\pi_i = 0$.

After building the matrix, we start the following procedure.

Procedure 9.4.1. *Set all probabilities* $\mathbf{P}(U(k)) = 0$, *for* $k = 1, \ldots, 100$.

1.   **For** $c = 0, \ldots, 100$
2.   **For** $k = 1, \ldots, 100$
3.   *find all the combinations such that*

$$l_{k-1} L \leq (n + p_1 c)w_1 + (m + p_2 c)w_2 \leq l_k L$$

4.   *assign to these combinations the probability*

$$\mathbf{P}[U(k)] = \mathbf{P}[U(k)] + \mathbf{P}[N_1^I = n] \, \mathbf{P}[N_2^I = m] \, \mathbf{P}[N^C = c]$$

5.   **Next**
6.   **Next**

The procedure produces the discrete distribution of absolute usage U of lines $L = L_1 + L_2$.

In a compact formula, the joint probability of usage $\mathbf{P}[U(k)]$ for withdrawal of amount $U(k)$ is given by

$$\mathbf{P}[U(k)] = \sum_{c,n,m} \mathbf{P}[N_1^I = n]\,\mathbf{P}[N_2^I = m]\,\mathbf{P}[N^C = c], \tag{9.121}$$

where the sum runs over all values of c, n, m that satisfy the condition $l_{k-1}L \leq (n + p_1 c)w_1 + (m + p_2 c)w_2 \leq l_k L$. We write this condition in compact form as

$$\mathbf{P}[U(k)] = \sum_{c,n,m} \mathbf{P}[N_1^I = n]\,\mathbf{P}[N_2^I = m]\,\mathbf{P}[N^C = c]\,\mathbf{1}_{\{l_{k-1}L \leq (n+p_1 c)w_1 + (m+p_2 c)w_2 \leq l_k L\}}, \tag{9.122}$$

where the indicator function for an element x over a set $(a, b]$ is

$$\mathbf{1}_{\{a < x \leq b\}} = \begin{cases} 1 & \text{if } x \in (a, b], \\ 0 & \text{if } x \notin (a, b]. \end{cases} \tag{9.123}$$

Procedure 9.4.1 can easily be generalized to the case when the bank has a portfolio of M credit lines. All the combinations that generate usage $U > L$ have a probability that can be summed to probability $\mathbf{P}(R)$ in equation (9.117) (i.e., to have an overdraft on the lines). This probability can be dealt with using the normalization approach outlined in Section 9.4.3.

Example 9.4.4. *We consider joint usage of a credit line from two identical credit lines, each of total value $L_1 = L_2 = 5{,}000{,}000$, using the parameters in Table 9.33. We consider extreme cases when the common process $p_{\text{low}} = 0.01$ (lowly correlated) and when the common process $p_{\text{high}} = 0.99$ (highly correlated). We have chosen parameters such that both intensities have the same CIR parameters for the total process*

$$CIR(\kappa,\, \sqrt{p}\sigma^C,\, \theta^I + p\,\theta^C,\, \lambda^I(0) + p\,\lambda^C(0),\, t),$$

and equate the CIR parameters used in the case of the single credit line in Example 9.4.3. The results are shown in Figure 9.28.

Marginal distributions of the usage of credit lines

For each debtor withdrawing from the total of credit lines L, we can obtain the marginal probability distribution of usage of its line by following the methods outlined in Section 9.4.3. Assuming that the i-th debtor can withdraw a maximum amount L_i from the total of lines L, the marginal probability $\mathbf{P}_i[U_i(k)]$ of usage of the $U_i(k)$ bucket in terms of the common and idiosyncratic distributions is

$$\mathbf{P}_i[U_i(k)] = \sum_{c=0}^{100} \sum_{n=0}^{100} \mathbf{P}[N_i^I = n]\,\mathbf{P}[N^C = c]\,\mathbf{1}_{\{l_{k-1} < U_i(k) \leq l_k\}}, \tag{9.124}$$

where $l_k = k\,L_i/100$. Equation (9.124) is obtained using Procedure 9.4.1 when only one credit line is present. Since, for a single credit line, the probability of usage for bucket $U_i(k)$ is given by all processes with $k - 1 < n + p_i c \leq k$, we obtain

$$\mathbf{P}_i[U_i(k)] = \sum_{c=0}^{100} \sum_{n=0}^{100} \mathbf{P}^I[N_i^I = n]\,\mathbf{P}^C[N^C = c]\,\mathbf{1}_{\{k-1 < n+p_i c \leq k\}}. \tag{9.125}$$

Table 9.33. Parameters used for the joint probability of usage when $p_{high} = 0.99$ (highly correlated) and when $p_{low} = 0.01$ (lowly corelated)

	Line 1	Line 2
L	5,000,000	5,000,000
κ	0.8	0.8
α	2500	2500
λ^C	1.00%	1.00%
λ^I_{high}	0.745%	0.745
λ^I_{low}	1.725%	1.725%
θ^C	1.00%	1.00%
θ^I_{high}	0.745%	0.745%
θ^I_{low}	1.73%	1.73%
σ	10.00%	10.00%

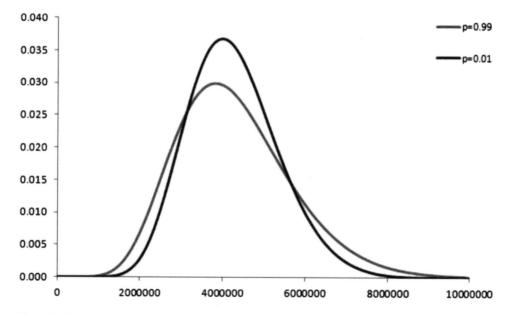

Figure 9.28. The joint probability of usage when $p = 0.01$ (lowly correlated) and when $p = 0.99$ (highly correlated), using the parameters in Table 9.33. Also shown are the averages, the 1st and the 99th percentile of the two distributions

Using the results in Section 9.4.3, the probability $\mathbf{P}_i[R]$ of having an overdraft on the single credit line i is

$$\mathbf{P}_i[R] = 1 - \sum_{k=0}^{100} \mathbf{P}[U_i(k)], \tag{9.126}$$

from which we obtain the normalized marginal distribution as

$$\mathbf{P}[U_i(k)] \rightarrow \frac{\mathbf{P}[U_i(k)]}{1 - \mathbf{P}_i[R]}. \tag{9.127}$$

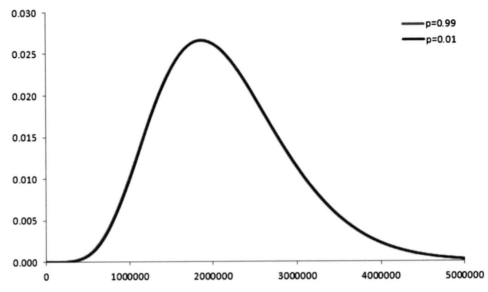

Figure 9.29. The marginal usage probability distribution for a 5,000,000 credit line, given the joint usage distribution arrived at through the parameters in Table 9.33. We show the case when there is high correlation ($p = 0.99$) and low correlation ($p = 0.01$) with the process of common usage

Example 9.4.5. *In Example 9.4.4, we considered the case of the joint usage distribution of two identical credit lines, respectively with a low $(p = 0.01)$ or a high $(p = 0.99)$ correlation with the common withdrawal process. Here, we construct the marginal usage distributions for each credit line. The parameters are given in Table 9.33. Since correlation parameter p also occurs in the indicator function, when $p = 0.01$, the common jump does not affect the sum $n + pc$ in the indicator function, and the probability of usage coincides with the idiosyncratic probability; for $p = 0.99$, the probability of usage is the convolution of idiosyncratic and common components. In the case considered, the two distributions coincide because we assumed the same process for intensity in both cases, see Figure 9.29.*

For both $p = 0.99$ and $p = 0.01$, we find that the 99th percentile of the joint distribution lies below the 99th prcentile of two identical single credit lines. For example, for $p = 0.99$, the value of the 99th percentile for the joint distribution is $L_{99,\text{joint}} = 8{,}100{,}000$, while each single line with the same parameters has a 99th percentile at $L_{99,\text{single}} = 4{,}300{,}000$. We thus have $L_{99,\text{joint}} < 2L_{99,\text{single}}$. Similarly, for $p = 0.01$, the value of the 99th percentile for the joint distribution is $L_{01,\text{joint}} = 5{,}400{,}000$, while each single line with the same parameters has a 99th percentile at $L_{01,\text{single}} = 3{,}000{,}000$. We thus have $L_{01,\text{joint}} < 2L_{01,\text{single}}$.

Term structure of usage

We study how the probability distribution evolves in time when future times at which usage is computed are changed. We make the simplifying assumption that the borrower withdraws the line only on a predefined number of dates T_j, with $j \in \{1, \ldots, n\}$. As in the examples below, we consider usage over the period of one year divided into 12 months

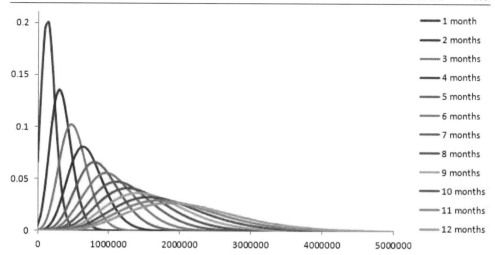

Figure 9.30. The term structure of usage probability of a single credit line, using the parameters given in Table 9.30

$(n = 12)$, and we take monthly steps

$$T_j = \frac{j}{12}, \quad \text{with } j = 1, \dots, 12, \tag{9.128}$$

at which usage is computed.

Example 9.4.6. *We consider the term structure of usage of a single credit line, using the parameters given in Table 9.30, and the term structure of time steps defined in equation (9.128). To model the term structure of usage numerically, we build a cycle going from $j = 1$ to $j = 12$ in which, at each step, we generate probability of usage $\mathbf{P}[N = n]$, at withdrawal date T_j. We obtain the plot in Figure 9.30. In Table 9.34 we show the average and the 99th percentile of the term structure of distributions.*

Table 9.34. The term structure of the 1st percentile, the 99th percentile and the average usage of a single credit line arrived at through the parameters given in Table 9.30

Date	U_{01} (million)	U_{99} (million)	Average (million)
1	0.0000	0.4000	0.1590
2	0.0500	0.7500	0.3374
3	0.1500	1.0500	0.5184
4	0.2000	1.3500	0.6998
5	0.3000	1.7000	0.8810
6	0.3500	2.0500	1.0617
7	0.4000	2.4500	1.2430
8	0.5000	2.8000	1.4241
9	0.5500	3.2000	1.6051
10	0.6000	3.5500	1.7857
11	0.6500	3.9500	1.9649
12	0.7500	4.2500	2.1405

Example 9.4.7. *We consider the term structure of joint usage of two identical credit lines, using the parameters given in Table 9.33, and the term structure of withdrawal dates as in equation (9.128). To model the term structure of usage numerically, we build a cycle going from $j = 1$ to $j = 12$ in which, at each step, we generate the probability of usage distribution for both the common component $\mathbf{P}[N^C = c]$ and each idiosyncratic one $\mathbf{P}[N^I = n]$, at time horizon T_j. Since the two lines in Table 9.33 are identical, we do not need to distinguish between the two idiosyncratic probabilities. In the case of high correlation ($p = 0.99$), joint usage evolves in time as shown in Figure 9.31. In the case of weak correlation ($p = 0.01$), we obtain the plot in Figure 9.32.*

Example 9.4.8. *We build the term structure of the marginal usage distribution of a credit line associated with the portfolio of credit lines in Example 9.4.4, for the case when there is high correlation with the common default probability and for the case when there is low correlation. We build a cycle going from $j = 1$ to $j = 12$ in which, at each step, we generate the probability of usage distribution for both the common component $\mathbf{P}[N^C = c]$ and the idiosyncratic one $\mathbf{P}[N^I = n]$, at time horizon T_j. After we normalize these distributions according to the procedure in Section 9.4.3, we find the probability of usage $\mathbf{P}[U(k)]$ from equation (9.124).*

The term structure of the marginal distribution for the joint probability distribution in Example 9.4.7 is shown in Figure 9.33 and Table 9.35 when $p = 0.99$, and in Figure 9.34 and Table 9.36 when $p = 0.01$.

Adding default events

The intensity of default of the i-th credit line, $\lambda_i^D(t)$, is related to the stochastic withdrawal intensity for the i-th borrower $\lambda_i^W(t)$ by equation (9.105), and follows the CIR process defined in equation (9.109). At time t, the probability of survival to

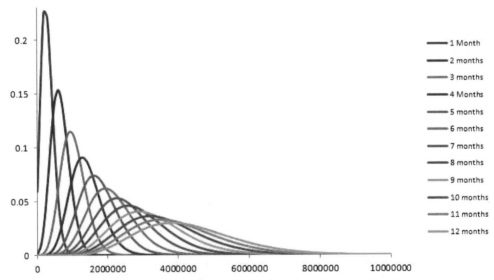

Figure 9.31. The term structure of joint usage probability of two identical credit lines when $p = 0.99$ and the other parameters are as in Table 9.33

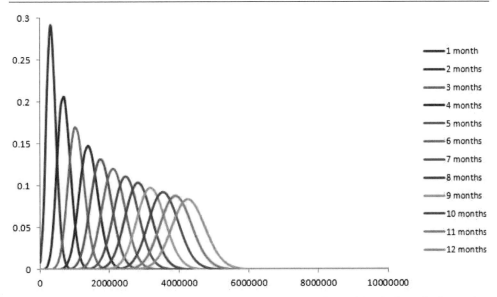

Figure 9.32. The term structure of joint usage probability of two identical credit lines when $p = 0.01$ and the other parameters are as in Table 9.33

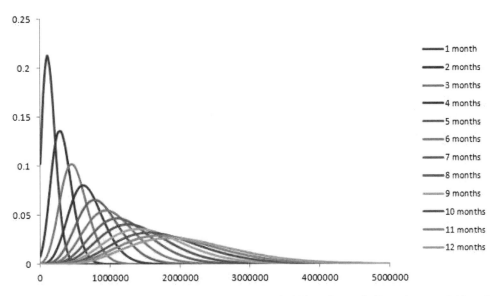

Figure 9.33. The term structure of marginal usage probability of a credit line when $p = 0.99$ and the other parameters are as in Table 9.33

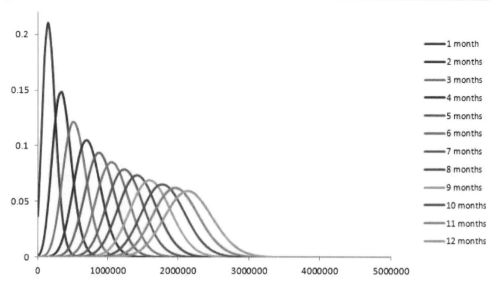

Figure 9.34. The term structure of marginal usage probability of a credit line when $p = 0.01$ and the other parameters are as in Table 9.33

Table 9.35. The term structure of the 1st percentile, the 99th percentile, and average usage from the marginal distribution of the usage probability of a credit line when there is high correlation ($p = 0.99$) with the common default probability (the parameters are given in Table 9.33)

Date	U_{01} (million)	U_{99} (million)	Average (million)
1	0.0000	0.4000	0.1377
2	0.0500	0.7000	0.3151
3	0.1000	1.0000	0.4969
4	0.2000	1.3500	0.6792
5	0.2500	1.7000	0.8615
6	0.3500	2.0500	1.0438
7	0.4000	2.4000	1.2260
8	0.4500	2.8000	1.4083
9	0.5500	3.2000	1.5906
10	0.6000	3.5500	1.7725
11	0.6500	3.9500	1.9531
12	0.7000	4.2500	2.1302

time T is

$$SP_i(t, T) = A(t, T) e^{-B(t,T) \lambda_i^P(t)}, \tag{9.129}$$

where $A(t, T)$ and $B(t, T)$ are functions entering the CIR discount factor defined in equation (8.27). Similarly, the probability of default is

$$PD_i(t, T) = 1 - SP_i(t, T). \tag{9.130}$$

Table 9.36. The term structure of the 1st percentile, the 99th percentile and average usage from the marginal distribution of the usage probability of a credit line when there is low correlation ($p = 0.01$) with the common default probability (the parameters are given in Table 9.33)

Date	U_{01} (million)	U_{99} (million)	Average (million)
1	0.0000	0.4500	0.1749
2	0.1000	0.7000	0.3601
3	0.2000	0.9500	0.5412
4	0.3000	1.2000	0.7217
5	0.4500	1.4500	0.9021
6	0.6000	1.6500	1.0826
7	0.7000	1.9000	1.2622
8	0.8500	2.1000	1.4423
9	1.0000	2.3000	1.6225
10	1.1500	2.5500	1.8029
11	1.3000	2.7500	1.9832
12	1.4500	2.9500	2.1636

Since $\lambda_i^D(t) = \lambda_i^I(t) + p_i \lambda^C(t)$, we use an approximation[34] to find usage in the case of default. We introduce the indicators D_i^I and D^C, which take the value one in the case of default and zero in the case of survival to time T. The indicator for process $\lambda_i^D(t)$ is then $D_i = D_i^I + \xi_i D^C$, where ξ_i is one with probability p_i and zero with probability $1 - p_i$. The probability of usage $\mathbf{P}[U_k]$ for the total credit line L, with $l_{k-1}L < U_k \leq l_k L$ and with a total of N credit lines, can be written as

$$\mathbf{P}[U(k)] = \mathbf{P}(U_k|D^C = 1)\,\mathrm{PD}^C(t,T) + \mathbf{P}(U_k|D^C = 0)\,(1 - \mathrm{PD}^C(t,T))$$

$$= \mathrm{PD}^C(t,T) \sum_{i=1}^{N} \mathbf{P}(U_k|D_i^I = 1, D^C = 1, \xi_i = 1)\mathrm{PD}_i^I(t,T)\,p_i$$

$$+ \mathrm{PD}^C(t,T) \sum_{i=1}^{N} \mathbf{P}(U_k|D_i^I = 1, D^C = 1, \xi_i = 0)\mathrm{PD}_i^I(t,T)\,(1 - p_i)$$

$$+ (1 - \mathrm{PD}^C(t,T)) \sum_{i=1}^{N} \mathbf{P}(U_k|D_i^I = 1, D^C = 0, \xi_i = 1)\mathrm{PD}_i^I(t,T)\,p_i$$

$$+ (1 - \mathrm{PD}^C(t,T)) \sum_{i=1}^{N} \mathbf{P}(U_k|D_i^I = 1, D^C = 0, \xi_i = 0)\mathrm{PD}_i^I(t,T)\,(1 - p_i)$$

$$+ \mathrm{PD}^C(t,T) \sum_{i=1}^{N} \mathbf{P}(U_k|D_i^I = 0, D^C = 1, \xi_i = 1)(1 - \mathrm{PD}_i^I(t,T))\,p_i$$

$$+ \mathrm{PD}^C(t,T) \sum_{i=1}^{N} \mathbf{P}(U_k|D_i^I = 0, D^C = 1, \xi_i = 0)(1 - \mathrm{PD}_i^I(t,T))\,(1 - p_i)$$

---

[34] The approximation was first suggested in [60] and has already been used in Chapter 8.

$$+ (1 - \text{PD}^C(t, T)) \sum_{i=1}^{N} \mathbf{P}(U_k | D_i^I = 0, D^C = 0, \xi_i = 1)(1 - \text{PD}_i^I(t, T)) \, p_i$$

$$+ (1 - \text{PD}^C(t, T)) \sum_{i=1}^{N} \mathbf{P}(U_k | D_i^I = 0, D^C = 0, \xi_i = 0)(1 - \text{PD}_i^I(t, T)) \, (1 - p_i).$$

When the i-th firm defaults, its probability of usage is zero, $\mathbf{P}(U_k | D_i^I = 1) = 0$, independently of the value of the other indicators D^C and ξ_i. We also have a default event if both $\xi_i = 1$ and $D^C = 1$. These cases correspond to the first five sums above, which give a probability of zero usage, while the remaining three probabilities are

$$\mathbf{P}[U(k)] = \sum_{i=1}^{N} \mathbf{P}(U_k | D_i^I = 0, D^C = 1, \xi_i = 0)(1 - \text{PD}_i^I(t, T)) \text{PD}^C(t, T)(1 - p_i)$$

$$+ \sum_{i=1}^{N} \mathbf{P}(U_k | D_i^I = 0, D^C = 0, \xi_i = 1)(1 - \text{PD}_i^I(t, T))(1 - \text{PD}^C(t, T)) p_i$$

$$+ \sum_{i=1}^{N} \mathbf{P}(U_k | D_i^I = 0, D^C = 0, \xi_i = 0)(1 - \text{PD}_i^I(t, T))(1 - \text{PD}^C(t, T))(1 - p_i).$$

The three terms in the summation correspond to default of the common line with $\xi_i = 0$ (with probability $1 - p_i$, first line in the equation) and to survival of both the idiosyncratic and common terms (last two lines of the equation).

In case of no default of the i-th line, all three probabilities $\mathbf{P}(U_k | D_i^I = 0, D^C = 1, \xi_i = 0)$, $\mathbf{P}(U_k | D_i^I = 0, D^C = 0, \xi_i = 1)$, $\mathbf{P}(U_k | D_i^I = 0, D^C = 0, \xi_i = 0)$ are equal and equate to the probability of usage computed without assuming default, call it $\mathbf{P}(U_k, D_i = 0)$, where D_i is a new indicator that states whether the i-th firm has defaulted or not at time T, independently of the cause. Summing up all three probabilities, we obtain the idiosyncratic usage from the i-th line including the survival probability,

$$\mathbf{P}_i^{\text{surv}}(N^I = n) = \left(1 - \text{PD}_i^I(0, T)\right) \left(1 - p_i \, \text{PD}^C(0, T)\right) \mathbf{P}_i^I(N^I = n). \quad (9.131)$$

Similarly, we define

$$\mathbf{P}_i^{\text{def}}(N^I = n) = \left[1 - \left(1 - \text{PD}_i^I(0, T)\right) \left(1 - p_i \text{PD}^C(0, T)\right)\right] \mathbf{P}_i^I(N^I = n)$$

$$= \left(\text{PD}_i^I(0, T) + p_i \, \text{PD}^C(0, T) - p_i \, \text{PD}_i^I(0, T) \, \text{PD}^C(0, T)\right) \mathbf{P}_i^I(N^I = n).$$

$$(9.132)$$

Joint usage with probability of default

We now introduce the possibility that the entirety of credit lines L is drawn by two defaultable debtors. The case of m users can easily be derived from this case. To obtain the joint usage from two credit lines, we modify equation (9.121) as

$$\mathbf{P}^{\text{def}}(U(k)) = \sum_{c,n,m} \mathbf{P}(N^C = c) \, \mathbf{P}_1^{\text{surv}}(N_1^I = n) \, \mathbf{P}_2^{\text{surv}}(N_2^I = m), \quad (9.133)$$

with the triplet (c, n, m) satisfying $l_{k-1} L \le (n + p_1 c) w_1 + (m + p_2 c) w_2 \le l_k L$, $l_k = k/100$, $w_i = L_i/100$.

To obtain the marginal probability of usage from a single credit line of total usage L_i, we modify equation (9.124) by considering the idiosyncratic probability of default $\mathbf{P}^{\text{surv}}[N^I = n]$ in equation (9.131) for the idiosyncratic process. We have

$$\mathbf{P}_i^{\text{def}}[U_i(k)] = \sum_{c=0}^{100} \sum_{n=0}^{100} \mathbf{P}^{\text{surv}}[N_i^I = n] \, \mathbf{P}^C[N^C = c] \, \mathbf{1}_{\{k-1<n+p_i\,c<k\}}, \qquad (9.134)$$

where the suffix "def" indicates that the probability distribution takes into account the probability of default.

Example 9.4.9. *In Figure 9.35, we show the results for the joint probability of usage for two credit lines using the parameters in Table 9.33, obtained from equation (9.133). We considered the case when there is low correlation with the common default process ($p = 0.01$) and the case when there is high correlation with the common default process ($p = 0.99$). Figure 9.35 further compares the joint probability of usage without considering the probability of default, equation (9.121). We have collected the relevant information on the distributions in Table 9.37 and in Table 9.38 we show the term structures of expected usage for all the cases..*

The marginal probability distribution for a single credit line of the joint distribution considered above is shown in Figure 9.36 and Table 9.38 for both cases $p = 0.01$ and $p = 0.99$. Figure 9.36 further shows the marginal usage probabilities when the probability of default is not considered, equation (9.124). We find the probability of zero usage for $p = 0.99$ equal to $\mathbf{P}^{\text{def}}(0) = 1.94\%$, and for $p = 0.99$ equal to $\mathbf{P}^{\text{def}}(0) = 1.72\%$.

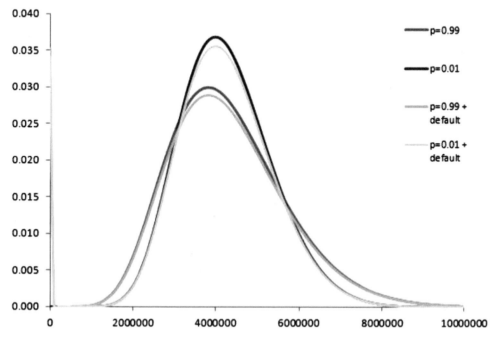

Figure 9.35. The joint usage probability of two credit lines for $p = 0.99$ and $p = 0.01$ and the corresponding joint usage probability including the probability of default for $p = 0.99$ and $p = 0.01$

Table 9.37. Relevant data for the distributions in Figure 9.35

	$p = 0.99$	$p = 0.01$	$p = 0.99 + default$	$p = 0.01 + default$
Average (million)	4.2913	4.2892	4.1404	4.1430
Probability of zero usage	0%	0%	3.52%	3.41%

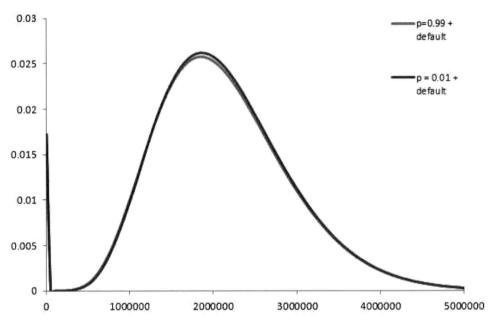

Figure 9.36. The marginal usage probability for a single credit line using the parameters as in Table 9.33 for the case of high correlation ($p = 0.99$) and that of low correlation ($p = 0.01$) with the common default process

9.4.4 Pricing of credit lines

The setup we introduced above is useful to monitor the withdrawal distribution of a portfolio of credit lines and thus allow for effective liquidity management. Nonetheless, it is also rich enough to allow pricing of a credit line featured by a notional amount of L, by a probability of usage $\mathbf{P}[U]$ and by a term structure of usage at times T_j, $j \in \{1, \ldots, n\}$, defined in Section 9.4.3. We indicate average usage of the credit line up to time T_j with $\bar{U}_j$, the liquidity buffer with $\mathbf{LB}_j$ and we define

$$\tau_j = T_j - T_{j-1}, \tag{9.135}$$

where $T_0 = t$.

Assume that at time T_j the funding cost (expressed as a simply compounded rate) that the bank has to pay for the period $[T_{j-1}, T_j]$ is a sum of constant funding spread s^B

Table 9.38. Average usage with the parameters in Table 9.33, for $p = 0.99$ and $p = 0.01$. We also separately show the case of no default (first two columns) and the case of default (last two columns)

Time	Average usage			
	Usage $p = 0.99$ (million)	Usage $p = 0.01$ (million)	Usage $p = 0.99 + default$ (million)	Usage $p = 0.01 + default$ (million)
(months)				
1	0.2920	0.3285	0.3067	0.3298
2	0.6542	0.6940	0.6521	0.6900
3	1.0188	1.0545	1.0102	1.0454
4	1.3833	1.4142	1.3674	1.3979
5	1.7479	1.7739	1.7228	1.7484
6	2.1125	2.1340	2.0761	2.0973
7	2.4771	2.4921	2.4273	2.4422
8	2.8416	2.8513	2.7765	2.7861
9	3.2060	3.2107	3.1236	3.1282
10	3.5701	3.5702	3.4688	3.4685
11	3.9328	3.9299	3.8132	3.8069
12	4.2916	4.2897	4.1588	4.1434

and risk-free r_j, the latter derived from the term structure of risk-free[35] discount factors by

$$r_j = \left(\frac{P^D(t, T_{j-1})}{P^D(t, T_j)} - 1 \right) \frac{1}{\tau_j}. \tag{9.136}$$

Let us define total usage of the credit line as:

$$\mathbf{U}_j = \bar{U}_j + \mathrm{LB}_j - \max\left[\bar{U}_j + \mathrm{LB}_j - U, 0\right], \tag{9.137}$$

Absolute usage $\mathbf{U}_j$ is split into three parts:

1. Expected (average) usage $\bar{U}_j$.
2. Liquidity buffer LB_j to cope with usage beyond the expected level.[36]
3. A liquidity option, $\max\left[\bar{U}_j + \mathrm{LB}_j - U, 0\right]$, sold to the borrower equal to the maximum usage the bank can cover (expected plus LB) minus actual usage U.

The LB is set at a level that covers maximum usage in excess of the expected level at a given confidence level (say, 99%).

Expected usage, given that maximum usage is within the confidence level chosen when setting the LB, can be found with the formula:

$$\overline{U}_j = \left[\bar{U}_j + \mathrm{LB}_j - \int_0^{\bar{U}_j + \mathrm{LB}_j} \left(\bar{U}_j + \mathrm{LB}_j - U \right) P[U]\, dU \right], \tag{9.138}$$

which makes use of the distribution of usage derived above.

---

[35] As noted several times already, the best approximation to the risk-free rate is given by the OIS (Eonia for the euro) swap rates.

[36] See Chapter 7 for a discussion on how to set the LB for credit lines.

When a counterparty withdraws a given amount from the line, it will pay interest for the period. Just for modelling purposes, we assume that the borrower decides to use the line at the beginning of each period (T_{j-1}) and repays the amount plus interest at T_j; then it can choose to withdraw a given amount from the credit line for all periods until expiry of the contract.

Assume for the moment that the borrower is not subject to credit risk, so that the bank does not have to worry about being compensated for the default. The interest required should only be enough to cover the total funding cost of the bank (i.e., the risk-free rate plus the bank's funding spread). Over the period $[T_{j-1}, T_j]$ the bank can expect to receive interest equal to:

$$C_j = \tau_j \left(r_j + s^B \right) \overline{\mathbf{U}}_j. \tag{9.139}$$

which is simply the total funding cost charged for the duration of the period for expected usage (given maximum usage).

Given maximum usage of the line at time T_j, at a confidence level that we assume the bank sets at 99%, the liquidity buffer is:

$$LB_j = U_{99,j} - \bar{U}_j, \tag{9.140}$$

where $U_{99,j}$ is the 99th quantile of the distribution at time T_j. Total usage in equation (9.137) is

$$\mathbf{U}_j = U_{99,j} - \max \left[U_{99,j} - U_j, 0 \right], \tag{9.141}$$

usage up to the value $U_{99,j}$ is

$$\overline{\mathbf{U}}_j = \left[U_{99,j} - \int_0^{U_{99,j}} \left(U_{99,j} - U \right) \mathbf{P}[U] \, dU \right], \tag{9.142}$$

So, expected interest received, given maximum usage of the credit line at the 99% c.l., is

$$C_j = \tau_j \left(r_j + s^B \right) \bar{\mathbf{U}}_j. \tag{9.143}$$

9.4.5 Commitment fee

In credit line contracts the bank applies a fee that has to be paid periodically by the counterparty. This fee remunerates the bank for providing liquidity on demand and is applied to the unused part of the line: The level of the fee can be determined in such a way that the contract is fair at inception, as we explain below.

The bank funds maximum usage of the credit line over period τ_j by borrowing quantity $U_{99,j}$ at time T_{j-1}, and repaying the amount $\left[1 + \tau_j \left(r_j + s^B \right) \right] U_{99,j}$ (i.e., notional plus total funding cost at time T_j). This amount should equate to earnings from:

1. Expected interest received (as given in equation (9.143)) and repayment of the amount withdrawn.[37]
2. Reinvesting the unused amount $\left(U_{99,j} - \overline{U}_j \right)$ in risk-free liquid investments earning r_j.
3. The commitment fee Fee$_j$ applied to the unused amount $L - \overline{\mathbf{U}}_j$.

---

[37] Remember, this is only a modelling assumption that might not actually occur in reality. It allows for the amount to be repaid and immediately withdrawn again.

Put mathematically,

$$\left[1 + \tau_j \left(r_j + s^B\right)\right] U_{99,j} = \overline{U}_j + C_i + \left(1 + \tau_j r_j\right) \left(U_{99,j} - \overline{U}_j\right) + \text{Fee}_j, \quad (9.144)$$

from which, using equation (9.143), we obtain the fair commitment fee

$$\text{Fee}_j = \tau_j s^B \left(U_{99,j} - \overline{U}_j\right). \quad (9.145)$$

Introducing the fee rate c_j for the commitment fee over the unused amount,

$$\text{Fee}_j = \tau_j c_j \left(L - \overline{U}_j\right), \quad (9.146)$$

and equating equations (9.145) and (9.146), we obtain

$$c_j = s^B \frac{U_{99,j} - \overline{U}_j}{L - \overline{U}_j}. \quad (9.147)$$

The commitment fee is determined once and for all at the inception of the contract, so we need to find the unique rate c that ensures the present value of the total amount paid by the bank over all periods $[T_{j-1}, T_j]$, until the expiry of the contract, equates to the present value of inflows previously described, received from all periods $[T_{j-1}, T_j]$ as well. We then have:

$$c = s^B \frac{\sum_{j=1}^n \tau_j \left(U_{99,j} - \overline{U}_j\right) P^D(t, T_j)}{\sum_{j=1}^n \tau_j \left(L - \overline{U}_j\right) P^D(t, T_j)} = \frac{\sum_{j=1}^n c_j \tau_j \left(L - \overline{U}_j\right) P^D(t, T_j)}{\sum_{j=1}^n \tau_j \left(L - \overline{U}_j\right) P^D(t, T_j)}. \quad (9.148)$$

where $P^D(t, T_j)$ is the risk-free discount factor for cash flows occurring at T_j.

An example should clarify the ideas presented so far.

Example 9.4.10. *We consider the term structure of a single credit line using the parameters in Table 9.30. In Table 9.39, we give values for U_{99}, average usage up to U_{99} $(\overline{U})$, average unused line $L - \overline{U}$, and commitment rate c_j for usage of the single credit line, obtained from*

Table 9.39. Values for the 99th percentile (U_{99}), usage up to U_{99} $(\overline{U})$, unused line $(L - \overline{U})$ and the commitment fee rate c_j for a single credit line, obtained from equation (9.144) using the parameters in Table 9.30. We assumed $s^B = 1\%$ and chose the other parameters from Table 9.30

Months	U_{99} (million)	$\overline{U}$ (million)	$L - \overline{U}$ (million)	Fee rate (%)	Fee
1	0.4000	0.1590	0.2410	0.05	201.10
2	0.7500	0.3374	0.4126	0.09	344.38
3	1.0500	0.5184	0.5316	0.12	443.60
4	1.3500	0.6998	0.6502	0.15	542.65
5	1.7000	0.8810	0.8190	0.20	683.49
6	2.0500	1.0617	0.9883	0.25	824.85
7	2.4500	1.2430	1.2070	0.32	1,007.23
8	2.8000	1.4241	1.3759	0.39	1,148.16
9	3.2000	1.6051	1.5949	0.47	1,331.06
10	3.5500	1.7857	1.7643	0.55	1,472.28
11	3.9500	1.9649	1.9851	0.65	1,656.56
12	4.2500	2.1405	2.1095	0.74	1,760.36

equation (9.147). We used the value $s^B = 1\%$, over a period of a year divided into $n = 12$ months. The unique rate ensuring that bank outflow and inflow equate, equation (9.148), is $c = 0.3\%$.

9.4.6   Adding the probability of default

We consider the pricing of a credit line subject to default risk of the borrower over the life of the contract and relating to the term structure of usage described in Section 9.4.4. When the possibility of default is taken into account, the expected value of usage $\mathbf{U}$ in equation (9.142) is computed using the probability of usage $\mathbf{P}^{\text{def}}[U]$ (see equation (9.134)) in place of $\mathbf{P}[U]$. Put mathematically,

$$\overline{\mathbf{U}}_j^{\text{def}} = \left[U_{99,j}^{\text{def}} - \int_0^{U_{99,j}^{\text{def}}} \left(U_{99,j}^{\text{def}} - U \right) \mathbf{P}^{\text{def}}[U] \, dU \right], \tag{9.149}$$

where $U_{99,j}^{\text{def}}$ is the 99th quantile of $\mathbf{P}_i^{\text{def}}[U]$ at time T_j.

For the i-th credit line, the probability of withdrawal $\mathbf{P}^{\text{def}}[U]$ is given by equation (9.134), whereas the probability the line has survived to time T_{j-1} is

$$\mathbf{P}_i^{\text{surv}}[N^I = n] = \left(1 - \text{PD}_i^I(t, T_{j-1}) \right) \left(1 - p_i \, \text{PD}^C(t, T_{j-1}) \right) \mathbf{P}_i^I(N^I = n). \tag{9.150}$$

When the possibility of default is not considered, balancing between the costs of the bank and the corresponding profits leads to equation (9.144). To find an analogy to equation (9.144) when the probability of default is included, we have to consider that expected interest and the commitment fee are repaid in the case the borrower survives, while in the case of default the bank receives only recovery amount $(1 - \text{L}_{\text{GD}}) \overline{\mathbf{U}}_j^{\text{def}}$. To compensate for this risk, the bank adds credit spread s^c to the total interest applied over the average used amount. Put mathematically,

$$\left[1 + \tau_j \left(r_j + s^B \right) \right] U_{99,j}^{\text{def}} = \left(1 + \tau_j \, r_j \right) \left(U_{99,j}^{\text{def}} - \overline{\mathbf{U}}_j^{\text{def}} \right)$$

$$+ \left\{ \overline{\mathbf{U}}_j^{\text{def}} + C_j^{\text{def}} + \text{Fee}_j^{\text{def}} + \tau_j \, s_j^c \, \overline{\mathbf{U}}_j^{\text{def}} \right\} \text{SP}_i^D(T_{j-1}, T_j)$$

$$+ \left(1 - \text{L}_{\text{GD}} \right) \overline{\mathbf{U}}_j^{\text{def}} \left(1 - \text{SP}_i^D(T_{j-1}, T_j) \right), \tag{9.151}$$

where the expected interest earned by the bank is

$$C_j^{\text{def}} = \tau_j \left(r_j + s^B \right) \overline{\mathbf{U}}_j^{\text{def}}, \tag{9.152}$$

the commitment fee is

$$\text{Fee}_j^{\text{def}} = \tau_j \, c_j \left(L - \overline{\mathbf{U}}_j^{\text{def}} \right), \tag{9.153}$$

Equation (9.151) states that the total funding cost plus repayment of the capital ($\left[1 + \tau_j \left(r_j + s^B \right) \right] U_{99,j}^{\text{def}}$) equates to:

1. The interest earned by investing the unused amount in a risk-free liquid asset: $\left(1 + \tau_j \, r_j \right) \left(U_{99,j}^{\text{def}} - \overline{\mathbf{U}}_j^{\text{def}} \right)$.
2. The expected amount received from the counterparty in case it survives: $\left\{ \overline{\mathbf{U}}_j^{\text{def}} + C_j^{\text{def}} + \text{Fee}_j^{\text{def}} + \tau_j \, s_j^c \, \overline{\mathbf{U}}_j^{\text{def}} \right\} \text{SP}_i^D(T_{j-1}, T_j)$.
3. Recovery of the used amount in case the counterparty defaults: $\left(1 - \text{L}_{\text{GD}} \right) \overline{\mathbf{U}}_j^{\text{def}} \left(1 - \text{SP}_i^D(T_{j-1}, T_j) \right)$.

The credit spread that the bank should apply, s_j^c, satisfies

$$\left[1 + \tau_j\left(r_j + s^B\right)\right] \overline{\mathbf{U}}_j^{\text{def}} = \left[1 + \tau_j(r_j + s^B + s_j^c)\right] \overline{\mathbf{U}}_j^{\text{def}} \, \text{SP}_i(T_{i-1}, T_j)$$

$$+ (1 - \text{L}_{\text{GD}}) \overline{\mathbf{U}}_j^{\text{def}} \left(1 - \text{SP}_i(T_{j-1}, T_j)\right). \quad (9.154)$$

So we find:

$$s_j^c = \left[(r_j + s^B) + \frac{\text{L}_{\text{GD}}}{\tau_j}\right] \frac{1 - \text{SP}_i(T_{j-1}, T_j)}{\text{SP}_i(T_{j-1}, T_j)}, \quad (9.155)$$

Furthermore, in this case the bank does not apply different spreads for each period, but sets at inception a single spread valid for the entirety of the contract, $\overline{s}^c$, which is determined as:

$$\overline{s}^c = \frac{\sum_{j=1}^{n} s_j^c \, \tau_j \, \overline{\mathbf{U}}_j^{\text{def}} \, P^D(t, T_j) \, \text{SP}_i(T_{j-1}, T_j)}{\sum_{j=1}^{n} \tau_j \, \overline{\mathbf{U}}_j^{\text{def}} \, P^D(t, T_j) \, \text{SP}_i(T_{j-1}, T_j)}. \quad (9.156)$$

The commitment fee has to be recalculated considering the probability of default of the borrower: using equation (9.151) we obtain an expression for fee rate c_j over period τ_j as:

$$c_j = s^B \frac{U_{99,j}^{\text{def}} - \overline{\mathbf{U}}_j^{\text{def}}}{L - \overline{\mathbf{U}}_j^{\text{def}}} \frac{1}{\text{SP}_i^D(T_{j-1}, T_j)}, \quad (9.157)$$

to be compared with the value in equation (9.147) obtained when the probability of default is not added. The unique value of c that has to be applied for the entire duration of the contract is:

$$c = \frac{\sum_{j=1}^{n} c_j \tau_j \left(L - \overline{\mathbf{U}}_j^{\text{def}}\right) P^D(t, T_j) \, \text{SP}_i^D(T_{j-1}, T_j)}{\sum_{j=1}^{n} \tau_j \left(L - \overline{\mathbf{U}}_j^{\text{def}}\right) P^D(t, T_j) \, \text{SP}_i(T_{j-1}, T_j)}, \quad (9.158)$$

Example 9.4.11. *Referring to the discussion in Example 9.4.10, in Table 9.40 we show the value of the fee rate for usage of a single credit line when the probability of default is added. The probability of default is modelled by a CIR process using the parameters in Table 9.30.*

The numerical value of the fee rate in equation (9.158) is $c = 0.30\%$ and the credit spread in equation (9.156) is $\overline{s}^c = 1.03\%$.

9.4.7 Spread option

The fact that the credit spread for the borrower is set once for the entire life of the contract at inception implicitly means that the bank is selling a spread option to the counterparty. The borrower will find it attractive to withdraw the line if its credit-worthiness worsened, since it can always pay the spread fixed in the contract. This is the reason we introduced a dependenc of the withdrawal intensity of the line on the probability of default of the borrower: this contributes to building the marginal and joint distribution of withdrawals and as such it is useful for liquidity management purposes. On the other hand, the bank has not yet considered how much the option is worth financially, so we now have to include in the pricing.

Table 9.40. Values for the 99th percentile (U_{99}), usage up to U_{99} ($\bar{U}$), unused line ($L - \bar{U}$) and the commitment fee rate c_j for a single credit line, obtained from equation (9.144) using the parameters in Table 9.30. We assumed $s^B = 1\%$ and chose the other parameters from Table 9.30

Months	U_{99} (million)	$\bar{U}$ (million)	$L - \bar{U}$ (million)	Fee rate (%)	Fee
1	0.0000	0.4000	0.1565	0.05	203.22
2	0.0500	0.7500	0.3362	0.09	345.38
3	0.1500	1.0500	0.5161	0.12	445.50
4	0.2000	1.3500	0.6957	0.15	546.03
5	0.3000	1.7000	0.8746	0.20	688.80
6	0.3500	2.0500	1.0525	0.25	832.52
7	0.4000	2.4500	1.2305	0.32	1,017.70
8	0.5000	2.8000	1.4077	0.39	1,161.86
9	0.5500	3.2000	1.5843	0.47	1,348.41
10	0.6000	3.5500	1.7601	0.55	1,493.71
11	0.6500	3.9500	1.9339	0.66	1,682.47
12	0.7500	4.2500	2.1037	0.74	1,791.13

For a given time T_j, the payout of the spread option to the counterparty is:

$$\mathbf{S}_j^o = E_j \left[\tau_j \, U \left(s^c - \overline{s^c} \right)^+ \right], \tag{9.159}$$

The payoff is the same as a call option on the level of the credit spread where the strike $\overline{s^c}$ is the value that satisfies equation (9.157) (i.e., the level of the credit spread set for the entire duration of the contract). The value is obviously greater when the credit spread increases with respect to the strike level, since the borrower finds it more convenient to withdraw the line rather than borrowing money by a new debt contract.

To compute equation (9.159), we replace the expectation value by weighted integration over the possible values of default intensity λ, where the weight $p_i(\lambda)$ is the CIR probability of obtaining a value λ at time T_j if the value at time t is λ_t. Mathematically, the probability is

$$p_i(\lambda) = \chi^2 \left(2(\phi + \psi) \, \lambda, \frac{4 \, \kappa \, \theta}{\sigma^2}, \frac{2\phi^2 \, e^{\gamma(T_{j-1}-t)} \, \lambda_t}{\phi + \psi} \right), \tag{9.160}$$

where

$$\gamma = \sqrt{\kappa^2 + 2\sigma^2}, \quad \phi = \frac{2\gamma}{\sigma^2(e^{\gamma(T_{j-1}-t)} - 1)}, \quad \psi = \frac{\kappa + \gamma}{\sigma^2}. \tag{9.161}$$

The spread option formula is

$$\mathbf{S}_j^o = \tau_j \int_0^{+\infty} U(\lambda) \left(s^c(\lambda) - \overline{s^c} \right)^+ p_i(\lambda) \, d\lambda, \tag{9.162}$$

where we have made the dependence of usage U and s^c on λ explicit. Looking at this in greater detail, $s^c(\lambda)$ depends on λ through survival probability $\mathrm{SP}_i(T_{j-1}, T_j)$, as is clear from (9.157). The term $\left(s^c(\lambda) - \overline{s^c} \right)^+$ limits the range of integration to $(\lambda_j^*, +\infty)$, where

λ_j^* is the value of λ at time T_j that satisfies

$$s^c(\lambda_j^*) = \overline{s}^c. \tag{9.163}$$

Usage $U(\lambda)$ depends on λ through the probability distribution of the Poisson process $\mathbf{P}^{\mathrm{def}}[N = k]$, see equation (9.134), and the relation between the probability of the i-th debtor $\lambda_i^W(t)$ making a withdrawal and default of the i-th credit line expressed in equation (9.105). Conditioning the probability of usage to $\lambda_i^W(t)$ gives

$$\mathbf{S}_j^o = \tau_j \sum_{k=0}^{100} U_k \int_{\lambda_j^*}^{+\infty} \mathbf{P}^{\mathrm{def}}[N = k|\lambda^W] f_{\Lambda^W}(\lambda^W) \left[s^c(\lambda) - \overline{s}^c\right] p_i(\lambda) \, d\lambda, \tag{9.164}$$

where $U_k = k\,L/100$.

The spread option is sold by the bank to the counterparty, so it is an additional cost that has to be considered besides total funding, for each period the life of the contract has been divided into. We charge this additional cost $\mathbf{S}_i^o$ to the commitment fee in equation (9.151), by solving the following equation:

$$\left[1 + \tau_j\left(r_j + s^B\right)\right] U_{99,j}^{\mathrm{def}} + \mathbf{S}_j^o = \left(1 + \tau_j r_j\right)\left(U_{99,j}^{\mathrm{def}} - \overline{\mathbf{U}}_j^{\mathrm{def}}\right)$$

$$+ \left\{\tau_j c_j \left(L - \overline{\mathbf{U}}_j^{\mathrm{def}}\right) + \left[1 + \tau_j(r_j + s^B + s_j^c)\right] \overline{\mathbf{U}}_j^{\mathrm{def}}\right\} \mathrm{SP}_i(T_{j-1}, T_j)$$

$$+ \left(1 - \mathbf{L}_{\mathrm{GD}}\right) \overline{\mathbf{U}}_j^{\mathrm{def}} \left(1 - \mathrm{SP}^D(T_{j-1}, T_j)\right), \tag{9.165}$$

where s_j^c satisfies equation (9.154). We obtain

$$c_j = \frac{s^B\left(U_{99,j}^{\mathrm{def}} - \overline{\mathbf{U}}_j^{\mathrm{def}}\right) + \mathbf{S}_i^o/\tau_j}{L - \overline{\mathbf{U}}_j^{\mathrm{def}}} \frac{1}{\mathrm{SP}_i(T_{j-1}, T_j)}. \tag{9.166}$$

To compute the value of the spread option, we use a numerical approximation of the integral over λ in equation (9.164). We first truncate the range of integration to $[\lambda_i^*, \lambda^{\max}]$, we divide the interval $\lambda^{\max} - \lambda_i^*$ into N intervals, setting

$$\Delta\lambda = \frac{\lambda^{\max} - \lambda_i^*}{N}, \tag{9.167}$$

and we define integration points $\lambda_j = \lambda_i^* + j\,\Delta\lambda$. Equation (9.164) is then approximated as

$$\mathbf{S}_i^o = \tau_j \sum_{k=0}^{100} U_k \sum_{j=0}^{N} \mathbf{P}^{\mathrm{def}}[N = k|\lambda_j] f_{\Lambda^W}(\lambda_j) \left[s^c(\lambda_j) - \overline{s}_j^c\right] p_i(\lambda_j) \, \Delta\lambda. \tag{9.168}$$

Example 9.4.12. *In Table 9.41, we show spread options $\mathbf{S}_j^o$, fee rate c_j and the commitment fee for a single credit line using the parameter in Table 9.30. Using equation (9.158) with the values of c_j as in equation (9.166), we obtain the new value $c = 0.42\%$, higher than $c = 0.30\%$ obtained without considering spread options.*

Table 9.41. Values for spread option S_j^o, fee rate c_j and the commitment fee for a single credit line with parameters chosen as in Table 9.30

Months	S_j^o	Fee rate (%)	Fee
1	10.76	0.06	229.68
2	40.60	0.09	361.92
3	88.79	0.14	508.71
4	153.08	0.20	713.17
5	230.54	0.27	930.62
6	318.07	0.35	1,158.35
7	412.87	0.44	1,393.11
8	511.88	0.56	1,673.96
9	612.61	0.69	1,956.74
10	712.44	0.82	2,196.77
11	808.00	0.97	2,475.55
12	894.58	1.11	2,664.78

9.4.8 Incremental pricing

The pricing of a credit line is strongly affected by considering it as a new contract to be included in the existing portfolio of credit lines, but not on a standalone basis, as we have done above: we call this incremental pricing. Here the correlation effect can play a role in making the portfolio more diversified so that the bank can close the contract by giving better terms to the counterparty, thus being competitive with other financial institutions without impairing the correct and sound remuneration for all the costs and risks borne.

Consider joint usage of a portfolio of credit lines with total notional L opened by the bank to m debtors, so that

$$L = \sum_{i=1}^{m} L_i, \tag{9.169}$$

where L_i is maximum usage of the i-th line. Because of the subadditivity of the quantile, the 99th percentile of the distribution $U_{99}(L_1, \ldots, L_m)$ and the 99th percentiles of each marginal distribution $U_{99,i}$ satisfy

$$U_{99}(L_1, \ldots, L_m) \leq \sum_{i=i}^{m} U_{99,i}. \tag{9.170}$$

When we consider the single lines of m separately, a buffer needs to be allocated that is higher than the one implied by the joint distribution of usage of the lines. If pricing of a new line is operated on a standalone basis, this will result in commitment fees having higher values. If the bank wants to improve the level of the fee to the borrower, it may consider what happens when inserting the new contract into the existing portfolio. Consider the following incremental quantile approach for usage of credit lines:

introducing

$$\tilde{U}_{99,i} = L_i \frac{\partial U_{99}(L_1, \ldots, L_m)}{\partial L_i}, \quad i \in \{1, \ldots, m\}, \tag{9.171}$$

the 99th percentile of the joint distribution satisfies

$$U_{99}(L_1, \ldots, L_m) = \sum_{i=1}^{m} \tilde{U}_{99,i}, \tag{9.172}$$

so that $U_{99}(L_1, \ldots, L_m)$ is additive in the incremental quantile. To determine the value of $U_{99,I}$ for a particular counterparty I, we proceed by first computing the 99th percentile of the distribution of joint usage in which the I-th debtor has maximum usage $L_I(1 + \epsilon)$, with $\epsilon \sim 10^{-4}$. We then compute the numerical derivative

$$\tilde{U}_{99,I} = \frac{U_{99}(L_1, \ldots, L_I(1 + \epsilon), \ldots, L_m) - U_{99}(L_1, \ldots, L_I, \ldots, L_m)}{\epsilon}. \tag{9.173}$$

This is the increment of the maximum level, at the 99% c.l., of total usage of all credit lines. This increment can be attributed to the new contract the bank is dealing with the counterparty. It is also the level to use in the formulae we presented above for standalone pricing, replacing the maximum usage level at the 99% c.l. derived from the distribution of the single line considered separately from the portfolio. The commitment fee is then calculated accordingly.

Example 9.4.13. *We consider the joint usage probability of two users of total credit lines of, respectively, $L_1 = 5,000,000$ and $L_2 = 7,000,000$. The parameters for usage probabilities are given in Table 9.42. We price the marginal probability distribution for the first credit line of total usage $L_1 = 5,000,000$. Table 9.43 summarizes pricing of the credit line without considering the incremental quantile of usage.*
    In Table 9.44, we reprice the credit line on an incremental basis by using the value of $\tilde{U}_{99,i}$ instead of $U_{99,j}$ with all other details of the distribution left unchanged.
    In Table 9.45, we summarize the results to ascertain the value of the unique fee rate c obtained whether we consider the spread option or not and whether or not we reprice the marginal credit line distribution with the incremental liquidity buffer.

Table 9.42. Parameters used to build the marginal joint usage distribution for two credit lines when there is high correlation $p_{high} = 0.99$ (see Example 9.4.13)

	Line 1	Line 2
L	5,000,000	7,000,000
κ	0.8	0.8
α	2500	2500
λ^C	1.00%	1.00%
λ^I_{high}	0.75%	0.75%
θ^C	1.00%	1.00%
θ^I_{high}	0.75%	0.75%
σ^C_{high}	9.95%	9.95%

Table 9.43. The values of U_{99}^{def}, $\overline{\mathbf{U}}^{\text{def}}$, the fee rate and the commitment fee for the marginal joint usage distribution using parameters from Table 9.33 and $p_{\text{high}} = 0.99$

Months	U_{99}^{def} (million)	$\overline{\mathbf{U}}^{\text{def}}$ (million)	Fee rate (w/o $\mathbf{S}^o$) (%)	Fee rate (w/ $\mathbf{S}^o$) (%)	Fee (w/o $\mathbf{S}^o$)	Fee (w/ $\mathbf{S}^o$)
1	0.4000	0.1377	0.05	0.06	218.90	229.72
2	0.7000	0.3151	0.08	0.09	321.26	361.92
3	1.0000	0.4969	0.11	0.14\	419.80	508.73
4	1.3500	0.6792	0.16	0.20	559.86	713.19
5	1.7000	0.8615	0.20	0.27	699.76	930.59
6	2.0500	1.0438	0.25	0.35	839.80	1,158.38
7	2.4000	1.2260	0.31	0.44	979.67	1,393.15
8	2.8000	1.4083	0.39	0.56	1,161.36	1,673.97
9	3.2000	1.5906	0.47	0.69	1,343.20	1,956.72
10	3.5500	1.7725	0.55	0.82	1,483.33	2,196.73
11	3.9500	1.9531	0.66	0.97	1,666.42	2,475.56
12	4.2500	2.1302	0.74	1.11	1,768.94	2,664.79

Table 9.44. The values of $\tilde{U}_{99}^{\text{def}}$, $\overline{\mathbf{U}}^{\text{def}}$, the fee rate and the commitment fee for the marginal joint usage distribution (from incremental pricing) using parameters from Table 9.33 and $p_{\text{high}} = 0.99$

Months	$\tilde{U}_{99}^{\text{def}}$ (million)	$\overline{\mathbf{U}}^{\text{def}}$ (million)	Fee rate (w/o $\mathbf{S}^o$) (%)	Fee rate (w/ $\mathbf{S}^o$) (%)	Fee (w/o $\mathbf{S}^o$)	Fee (w/ $\mathbf{S}^o$)
1	0.4000	0.1377	0.05	0.06	218.90	229.72
2	0.7000	0.3151	0.08	0.09	321.26	361.92
3	1.0000	0.4969	0.11	0.14	419.80	508.73
4	1.3000	0.6792	0.14	0.19	518.13	671.46
5	1.6000	0.8615	0.18	0.25	616.31	847.14
6	1.9500	1.0438	0.23	0.33	756.34	1,074.92
7	2.3000	1.2260	0.28	0.42	896.22	1,309.70
8	2.6500	1.4083	0.35	0.52	1,036.18	1,548.80
9	3.0000	1.5906	0.41	0.63	1,176.29	1,789.81
10	3.3500	1.7725	0.49	0.75	1,316.43	2,029.83
11	3.7500	1.9531	0.59	0.91	1,499.52	2,308.65
12	4.0500	2.1302	0.67	1.04	1,602.04	2,497.89

Table 9.45. The values of fee rate c when there is no spread option, when there is a spread option and when there is standalone (LB $= U_{99}$) and incremental (LB $= \tilde{U}_{99}$) pricing

	No spread option (%)	With spread option (%)
U_{99}	0.30	0.42
$\tilde{U}_{99}$	0.27	0.39

APPENDIX 9.A   GENERAL DECOMPOSITION OF HEDGING SWAPS

Assume at time t_0 the mortgage has the following contract terms:

- The mortgage notional is $A_0 = A$.
- The mortgagee pays on predefined scheduled times t_j, for $j \in (0, 1, \ldots, b)$, fixed rate c computed on the outstanding residual capital at the beginning of reference period $\tau_j = t_j - t_{j-1}$, denoted by A_{j-1}. The interest payment will then be $c\tau_j A_{j-1}$.
- On the same dates, besides interest, the mortgagee also pays I_j, which is a portion of the outstanding capital, according to an amortization schedule.
- Expiry is time $t_b = T$.
- The mortgagee has the option to end the contract by prepaying on payment dates t_j the remaining residual capital A_j, together with the interest and capital payments as defined above. The decision to prepay, for whatever reason, can be taken at any time, although actual prepayment occurs on scheduled payment dates.

The assumption that the interest, capital, and the prepayment dates are the same, can easily be relaxed.

The fair coupon rate c can be computed by balancing the present value of future cash flows with the notional at time t_0:

$$\sum_j [c\tau_j A_{j-1} + I_j] P^D(t_0, t_j) = A$$

which immediately leads to:

$$c = \frac{A - \sum_j I_j P^D(t_0, t_j)}{\sum_j \tau_j A_{j-1} P^D(t_0, t_j)}$$

where $P^D(t_0, t_j)$ is the discount factor at time t_0 for date t_j. It should be noted that the quantity $A - \sum_j I_j P^D(t_0, t_j)$ can be replaced by $\sum_j \tau_j A_{j-1} F_j(t_0) P^D(t_0, t_j)$,[38] where $F_j(t_0)$ is the forward at time t_0 starting at time t_j.

When projecting expected cash flows, the probability of an anticipated inflow of the residual notional at given time t_k has to be computed as follows:

$$PP_e(t_0, t_k) = 1 - SP_e(t_0, t_k) \tag{9.174}$$

where $SP_e(t, T)$ is the survival probability. Expected total cash flow (interest + capital) at time t_0 for each scheduled payment time[39] $\{t_j = t_k\}$ is given by the formula:

$$cf^e(t_0, t_j) = (I_j + c\tau_j A_{j-1})(1 - PP_e(t_0, t_j)) + A_{j-1}(PP_e(t_0, t_j) - PP_e(t_0, t_{j-1})) \tag{9.175}$$

The expected outstanding amount at each time is given by:

$$A_j^e(t_0, t_j) = A_{j-1} - [I_j(1 - PP_e(t_0, t_j)) + A_{j-1}(PP_e(t_0, t_j) - PP_e(t_0, t_{j-1}))] \tag{9.176}$$

Let us consider hedging this mortgage with a bundle of single-period swaps, starting from t_0 up to $t_b = T$:

- in t_0 we go long a swap $\text{Swp}(t_0, t_1) \times A_0$;

---

[38] This is trivially obtained by considering the pricing equation of an amortizing floating rate mortgage.
[39] Scheduled payment times are assumed to be equal to possible prepayment times.

- in t_1 we go long a swap $\mathrm{Swp}(t_1, t_2) \times A_j^e(t_0, t_1)$;
- ...
- in $t_b = T$ we go long a swap $\mathrm{Swp}(t_1, t_b) \times A_j^e(t_0, t_b)$.

It is possible to show, with some manipulation, that at time t_1 we have:

$$A_1^e(t_0, t_1) = A_0 - A_1(\mathrm{PP}_e(t_0, t_1) - \mathrm{PP}_e(t_0, t_0)) + I_1(\mathrm{PP}_e(t_0, t_1) - \mathrm{PP}_e(t_0, t_0)) - I_1\mathrm{PP}_e(t_0, t_1)$$
$$= A_1 - A_1\mathrm{PP}_e(t_0, t_1) \tag{9.177}$$

and at t_2:

$$A_2^e(t_0, t_j) = A_2 - A_2\Delta\mathrm{PP}_1 + I_2\Delta\mathrm{PP}_1 - A_2\Delta\mathrm{PP}_2 + I_2\Delta\mathrm{PP}_2 + I_2\mathrm{PP}_e(t_0, t_j)$$
$$= A_2 - A_2\Delta\mathrm{PP}_1 - A_2\Delta\mathrm{PP}_2 \tag{9.178}$$

where we have defined $\Delta\mathrm{PP}_i = \mathrm{PP}_e(t_0, t_i) - \mathrm{PP}_e(t_0, t_{i-1})$. By the same token, at time t_j we can write:

$$A_j^e(t_0, t_j) = A_j - \sum_{i=1}^{j} A_i\Delta\mathrm{PP}_i \tag{9.179}$$

Let us now define a set of swaps with variable notional equal to the contract-amortizing schedule of mortgage $\mathrm{Swp}^A(t_a, t_b)$: these swaps do not have to start at the same date as the mortgage, they can also start at later dates, in which case their notional amounts match the contract-amortizing schedule of the mortgage for residual dates only.

If we replace $A_j^e(t_0, t_j)$ in the hedging portfolio, we sum over all the forward-starting swaps, we see that the portfolio actually contains:

- a fixed rate payer swap $\mathrm{Swp}^A(t_0, t_b)$;
- a portfolio of short-payer (or long-receiver) forward-starting swaps, each ending in t_b and each rescaled to a given factor: $\sum_{i=1}^{j} \mathrm{Swp}^A(t_i, t_b)\Delta\mathrm{PP}_i$.

Each forward-starting swap can be, in turn, decomposed by means of put–call parity: $\mathrm{Swp}^A(t_i, t_b) = \mathrm{Pay}^A(t_i, t_b; c) - \mathrm{Rec}^A(t_i, t_b; c)$. The payer and the receiver are written on swaps mirroring the mortgage contract-amortizing schedule for the residual dates until the final date t_b. So, collecting all the results again, we have that hedging portfolio P is equal to

$$P = \mathrm{Swp}^A(t_0, t_b) - \sum_{i=1}^{j} \Delta\mathrm{PP}_i\mathrm{Pay}^A(t_i, t_b; c) + \sum_{i=1}^{j} \Delta\mathrm{PP}_i\mathrm{Rec}^A(t_i, t_b; c) \tag{9.180}$$

This is the result described in Section 9.2.3.

APPENDIX 9.B   ACCURACY OF MORTGAGE RATE APPROXIMATION

In this section we simulate risk-neutral distribution and assume lognormal forward rates with the purpose of getting a good approximation of counterparty risk which would otherwise be computed via the yield curve simulation of an internal model.

The cost borne when a mortgage is prepaid can be considered equal to the unwinding cost of a hedging swap that matches cash flows perfectly. Assuming there is no credit spread due to the default risk of the mortgagee, the swap rate is equal to the mortgage rate. EL can thus be measured as the expected positive exposure (EPE) of a hedging swap.

The assumption of lognormal forward rates also allows for a closed-form approximation to be used for the EPE of a swap contract (equal to EL of the mortgage on possible prepayment dates): we test the accuracy of the closed-form formula with respect to Monte Carlo calculation of the EPE.

9.B.1   Internal model simulation engine

We calibrated the zero curve to swap rates (pillars 1 to 10, 15, 20, 25 and 30) on each day from 2 September 1998 to 15 August 2009. For each day we then computed the 30 adjacent forward Libor rates with maturity 1 year. We then calculated percentage daily change for the panel including the 30 adjacent forward rates.

In Figure 9.37 we plot the 10Y swap over the entire period. In Figure 9.38 (left-hand side), we plot the historical annualized volatility of forward rates and on the right-hand side we plot the average correlation between all forward rate pairs with the same start date distance. On the right-hand side, we can clearly see a decay pattern going on: the more distant the start date of forward rates the smaller their correlation on average.

We next simulated the EPE for a 10-year 5% payer swap (pay fixed 5%, receive floater). We simulated the evolution of the risk-free curve using a multifactor Libor

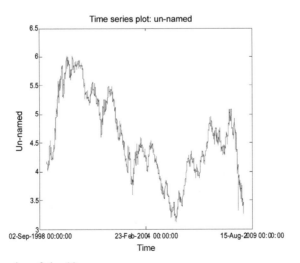

Figure 9.37. Time series of the 10-year euro swap

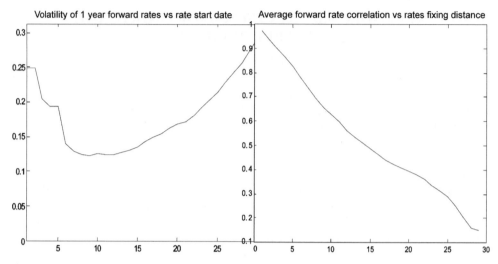

Figure 9.38. Forward rate volatilities (left-hand side) and average correlation (right-hand side)

market model where the annualized volatility of forward rates is constant for all start dates at 20% (in line with Figure 9.38, left-hand side), and the correlation between any two forward rates r_i and r_j (where t_i and t_j are the start dates of the two forward rates) is modelled as

$$\rho_{i,j} = 0.95^{|(t_i - t_j)|} \tag{9.181}$$

where the coefficient 0.95 has been calibrated to fit the decay displayed in Figure 9.38 (right-hand side).

In our simulation exercise we will model evolution of the mark-to-market of a plain vanilla swap through time. To do so we will simulate evolution of the forward rate curve given an initial forward curve, a deterministic and constant forward rate volatility term structure and a deterministic and constant correlation between forward rates as calculated in equation (9.181).

9.B.2   Results

Figures 9.39, 9.40 and 9.41 compare the analytical approximation of the EPE vs the simulated EPE for different sets of simulation scenarios in the event of a plain vanilla (non-amortizing) swap:

- Different initial shapes of the forward rate curve:
  - flat forward rate curve at the 5% level;
  - increasing the forward rate curve from 2% for the (0Y × 1Y) forward to 5% for the (9Y × 1Y) forward.
- Different initial shapes of forward rate volatility:
  - flat term structure of forward rate volatility at 20%;
  - decreasing the volatility of forward rates from 20% for the 1Y to 10% for the 20Y.
- Different correlation of future Libor rates depending on their fixing date distance:
  - high correlation, 95%, in line with Figure 9.38;

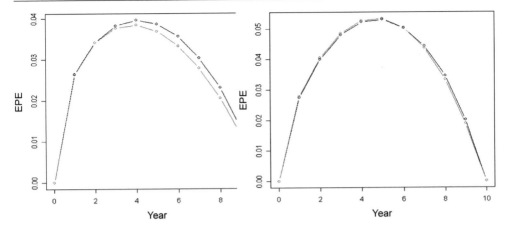

Figure 9.39. Analytic (light-grey line) and simulated EPE (black line) for a 10Y plain vanilla swap. (Left) Flat forward curve at 5% level, flat term structure of forward rate volatility at 20% and annual forward rate correlation decay equal to 99%. (Right) Forward rate curve from 2% for the $(0Y \times 1Y)$ forward to 5% for the $(9Y \times 1Y)$ forward; the term structure of forward rate volatility is flat at the 20% level and annual forward rate correlation decay equal to 99%. The number of simulations is 10,000

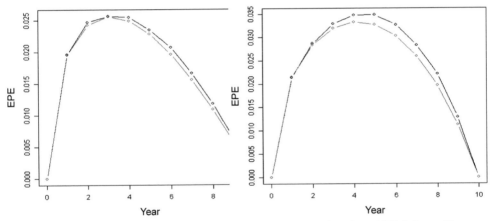

Figure 9.40. Analytic (light-grey line) and simulated EPE (black line) for a 10Y plain vanilla swap. (Left) Decreasing volatility of forward rates, from 20% for the 1Y to 10% for the 20Y; annual forward rates correlation decay equal to 99% and the forward rate curve is flat at 5%. (Right) Annual forward rate correlation decay equal to 80%, flat forward rate curve at 5% and flat volatility term strucutre of 20%. The number of simulations is 10,000

– low correlation, 80%, so as to test the approximation vs more complex forward rate term structures.

Figures 9.43, 9.44 and 9.45 are the equivalent of Figures 9.39, 9.40 and 9.41 in the event of an amortizing swap, the amortization schedule of which is depicted in Figure 9.42.

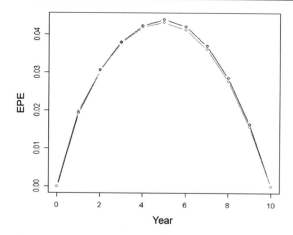

Figure 9.41. Analytic (light-grey line) and simulated EPE (black line) for a 10Y plain vanilla swap. Increasing forward rate curve, from 2% for the (0Y × 1Y) forward to 5% for the (9Y × 1Y) forward and decreasing volatility of forward rates, from 20% for the 1Y to 10% for the 20Y. The number of simulations is 10,000

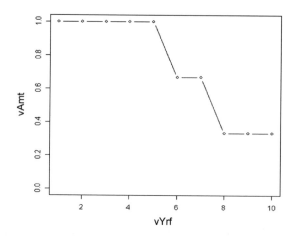

Figure 9.42. Amortization scheme for a 10Y swap

We see that the analytical approximation is satisfactory even when the initial shape of the forward rate curve, volatility term structure and forward Libor correlation are put under stress. Keeping in mind that from the regulatory standpoint the horizon of the EPE can only be up to 1 year, the analytical approximation is almost perfect.

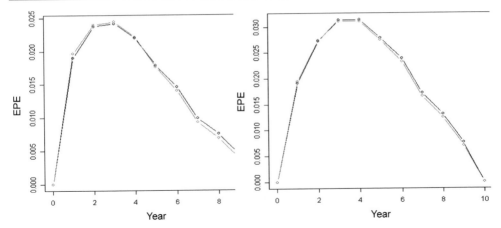

Figure 9.43. Analytic (light-grey line) and simulated EPE (black line) for a 10Y amortizing swap. (Left) Flat forward curve at 5% level, flat term structure of forward rate volatility at 20% and annual forward rate correlation decay equal to 99%. (Right) Forward rate curve from 2% for the (0Y × 1Y) forward to 5% for the (9Y × 1Y) forward; the term structure of forward rate volatility is flat at the 20% level and annual forward rate correlation decay equal to 99%. The number of simulations is 10,000

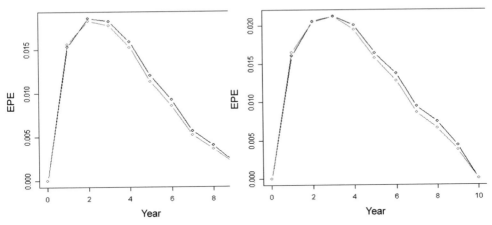

Figure 9.44. Analytic (light-grey line) and simulated EPE (black line) for a 10Y amortizing swap. (Left) Decreasing volatility of forward rates, from 20% for the 1Y to 10% for the 20Y, annual forward rate correlation decay equal to 99% and the forward rate curve is flat at 5%. (Right) Annual forward rate correlation decay equal to 80%, flat forward rate curve at 5% and flat volatility term structure of 20%. The number of simulations is 10,000

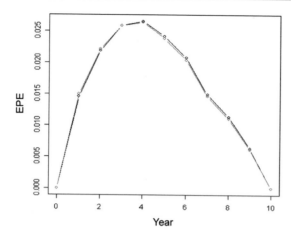

Figure 9.45. Analytic (light-grey line) and simulated EPE (black line) for a 10Y amortizing swap. Increasing forward rate curve, from 2% for the (0Y × 1Y) forward to 5% for the (9Y × 1Y) forward and decreasing volatility of forward rates, from 20% for the 1Y to 10% for the 20Y. The number of simulations is 10,000

APPENDIX 9.C   ACCURACY OF THE APPROXIMATED FORMULA FOR CORRELATED MORTGAGE RATE AND PREPAYMENT INTENSITY

As mentioned above, we use an approximation to calculate the ELoP analytically, since the assumption of a correlation between the mortgage rate and prepayment intensity does not allow for a closed-form formula and we do not want to use Monte Carlo simulation.

The approximation formula has been tested against Monte Carlo simulation to test its accuracy. In the test we used the following values for CIR intensity:

- $\theta = 0.07$
- $\lambda_0 = 0.11$
- $\kappa = 2$
- $\nu = 0.1$.

Tests were conducted assuming a generic lognormally distributed process (such as the one we chose to describe the mortgage rate) for the underlying asset and we price a call option. The volatility of the process is $\sigma = 0.2$ and the starting value of the asset is $S_0 = 100$. The test was carried out for different values of strike K, expiry T and correlation with the CIR process ρ.

Numerical results are given in Tables 9.46–9.48.

Table 9.46. In this table we summarize and list all the values computed by Monte Carlo simulation and by the theoretical approximated formula for an European call option with stochastic prepayment intensity and expiry over 1 year. We have the following parameter specification: underlying $S_0 = 100$ and volatility $\sigma = 0.2$

$K = 95$	Monte Carlo simulation	Approximated formula
$\rho = -0.8$	9.721023662	9.720309964
$\rho = -0.3$	9.673219009	9.6702378129
$\rho = 0$	9.645904229	9.640194521
$\rho = 0.3$	9.617883545	9.610151229
$\rho = 0.8$	9.561746676	9.560079077
$K = 100$		
$\rho = -0.8$	7.361434642	7.367689934
$\rho = -0.3$	7.324591341	7.325405762
$\rho = 0$	7.303152748	7.299711962
$\rho = 0.3$	7.276057017	7.274341459
$\rho = 0.8$	7.232707448	7.232057287
$K = 105$		
$\rho = -0.8$	5.465566215	5.467425472
$\rho = -0.3$	5.436503123	5.432743770
$\rho = 0$	5.414077439	5.411934749
$\rho = 0.3$	5.394966854	5.391125728
$\rho = 0.8$	5.353008293	5.356444026

Table 9.47. In this table we summarize and list all the values computed by Monte Carlo simulation and by the theoretical approximated formula for an European call option with stochastic prepayment intensity and expiry over 5 years. We have the following parameter specification: underlying $S_0 = 100$ and volatility $\sigma = 0.2$

$K = 77$	Monte Carlo simulation	Approximated formula
$\rho = -0.8$	21.049961165	21.049309899
$\rho = -0.3$	20.716536168	20.714588546
$\rho = 0$	20.516412140	20.513755734
$\rho = 0.3$	20.307963640	20.312922922
$\rho = 0.8$	19.984014866	19.978201569
$K = 100$		
$\rho = -0.8$	12.621872943	12.620335986
$\rho = -0.3$	12.374454964	12.371149878
$\rho = 0$	12.228514406	12.221638214
$\rho = 0.3$	12.072620926	12.072126549
$\rho = 0.8$	11.825045135	11.822940442
$K = 123$		
$\rho = -0.8$	7.362447945	7.362812332
$\rho = -0.3$	7.191501045	7.191129335
$\rho = 0$	7.090493312	7.088119537
$\rho = 0.3$	6.987859978	6.985109738
$\rho = 0.8$	6.811431845	6.813426741

Table 9.48. In this table we summarize and list all the values computed by Monte Carlo simulation and by the theoretical approximated formula for an European call option with stochastic prepayment intensity and expiry over 10 years. We have the following parameter specification: underlying $S_0 = 100$ and volatility $\sigma = 0.2$

$K = 68$	Monte Carlo simulation	Approximated formula
$\rho = -0.8$	20.469684436	20.494752231
$\rho = -0.3$	20.013263377	19.984333435
$\rho = 0$	19.659902243	19.678082157
$\rho = 0.3$	19.396948768	19.371830880
$\rho = 0.8$	19.834672231	18.861412083
$K = 100$		
$\rho = -0.8$	12.703904856	12.699198878
$\rho = -0.3$	12.316815432	12.312042423
$\rho = 0$	12.080911568	12.079748550
$\rho = 0.3$	11.855744828	11.847454676
$\rho = 0.8$	11.464365133	11.460298221
$K = 132$		
$\rho = -0.8$	8.007562086	7.947175508
$\rho = -0.3$	7.665304805	7.667298419
$\rho = 0$	7.507915361	7.499372165
$\rho = 0.3$	7.342696005	7.331445912
$\rho = 0.8$	7.08035348	7.051568823

APPENDIX 9.D   CHARACTERISTIC FUNCTION OF THE INTEGRAL $\Lambda_i^P(s, T) = \int_s^t \lambda_i^P(u)\, du$

Let us consider a general process: the case in Section 9.4.3 is a special case of this process. A stochastic process X on a filtrated probability space $(\Omega, F, (F)_t, \mathbb{Q})$ is said to follow CIR dynamics if it has the following form

$$dX_t = k(\theta - X_t)\, dt + \sigma\sqrt{X_t}\, dW_t + dJ_t, \tag{9.182}$$

where W_t is $\mathbb{Q}$-standard Brownian motion and J_t is an independent compound Poisson process with jump intensity l and exponentially distributed jumps with mean μ. We want to evaluate the following expectation

$$\mathbf{E}\left[\exp\left\{q\int_0^t X_s\, ds\right\}\right] = e^{\alpha(t) + \beta(t)X_0}, \tag{9.183}$$

where functions $\alpha(t)$ and $\beta(t)$ solve Riccati's equations

$$\left.\begin{aligned}
\alpha(t)' &= -k\theta\beta(t) - l\big(\phi(\beta(t)) - 1\big) \\
\beta(t)' &= k\beta(t) - \tfrac{1}{2}\sigma^2\beta(t)^2 - q,
\end{aligned}\right\} \tag{9.184}$$

with boundary condition $\alpha(0) = \beta(0) = 0$. The closed formula is given by

$$\begin{aligned}
\alpha(t) = {}&-\frac{2k\theta}{\sigma}\log\left(\frac{c_1 + d_1 e^{-\gamma t}}{c_1 + d_1}\right) + \frac{k\theta}{c_1}t \\
&+ l\left(\frac{d_1/c_1 - d_2/c_2}{-\gamma d_2}\right)\log\left(\frac{c_2 + d_2 e^{-\gamma t}}{c_2 + d_2}\right) + l\,\frac{1 - c_2}{c_2}\,t,
\end{aligned} \tag{9.185}$$

and

$$\beta(t) = \frac{1 - e^{-\gamma t}}{c_1 + d_1 e^{-\gamma t}}, \tag{9.186}$$

where

$$\left.\begin{aligned}
\gamma &= \sqrt{k^2 - 2q\sigma^2} \\
c_1 &= (k + \gamma)/(2q) \\
c_2 &= 1 - \mu/c_1 \\
d_1 &= (-k + \gamma)/(2q) \\
d_2 &= (d_1 + \mu)/c_1.
\end{aligned}\right\} \tag{9.187}$$

It is now sufficient to pose $q = u$, for $u \in \mathbb{R}$, to obtain the characteristic function of the X_t process.

Part III
Pricing liquidity risk

10

The links between credit risk and funding cost

10.1 INTRODUCTION

In this chapter we clarify the connections between funding costs and adjustments due to the compensation that a party has to pay to the counterparty for losses on a contract caused by its default (so-called debit value adjustment, hereafter DVA). We offer a robust conceptual framework so that DVA can be consistently included in the balance sheet of a financial institution.[1]

Under the perspective we present below, DVA does not manifest any counterintuitive effects, such as reduction of the current value of the liabilities of a counterparty when its creditworthiness worsens. Moreover, identifying the link between funding costs and DVA, and the contribution of the credit risk the bank bears (so-called credit value adjustment, CVA) allows us to establish a method to discount positive and negative future cash flows thoroughly. The results are quite convenient since, after taking everything into account, things surprisingly and dramatically simplify, at least from a pricing and valuation point of view.

10.2 THE AXIOM

To derive a consistent theory of the links between funding and liquidity costs and counterparty and credit risks, we need to devise an axiom that will be both sensible and widely accepted.

Axiom 10.2.1. *As in every human economic activity (by the very definition of the adjective "economic"), the stockholders of a bank aim at making profits out of their investments in business activity. As such they evaluate projects on the basis of the profits, costs and the expected profit margin to be shared at the end of the bank's activity.*

The axiom assumes that the evaluators of the bank's investments are the shareholders. In reality, it is more likely that the evaluators are the managers of the bank, but nonetheless this does not impair the statement in the axiom since, to properly evaluate the profitability of investments, managers should do so as if they were shareholders. In fact, when a project is profitable for shareholders, it will also be profitable for all other creditors of the bank with a lower priority of claim on the bank's assets, if remuneration for each component of the entire capital structure is taken into account.

The end of bank activity can be indefinite such that profits are shared periodically: this

---

[1] Connections between funding costs and DVA have been investigated (e.g., in [94]). The related issue of how to compute and consider DVA properly has been investigated by other authors (see, e.g., [75] and [32].)

is what usually happens in reality, where profits are computed and distributed on an annual basis. Alternatively, the end of bank activity can be voluntarily set at a given date.

It is worthy of note that default is not included in the definition of the voluntary end of activity, although the definition does not exclude the fact that default can be a rational option under some circumstances. In this case the decision to declare bankruptcy aims at minimizing losses and not at sharing (hopefully maximized) profits that are absent as a result of default.

Axiom 10.2.1 is sometimes referred to as a *going-concern* principle.[2]

10.3   CASH FLOW FAIR VALUES AND DISCOUNTING

We start by considering a simple loan contract (e.g., a term deposit in the interbank market). Assume there are two economic operators (e.g., two banks), B and L, the first of which would like to borrow money from the second. To keep things simple, let us assume that there exists a constant risk-free interest rate r and that each operator pays a funding spread s_X, $X \in \{B, L\}$, over the the risk-free rate when borrowing money.

The funding spread can be decomposed into two parts: (i) a premium that is required by the lender for the default probability of the borrower (indicated by π_X) and loss given default L_{GD_X} (expressed as a fraction of the lent amount), and (ii) a possible liquidity premium γ_X (we still have $X \in \{B, L\}$).

At time $t = 0$, operator B asks operator L for a loan the amount of which returned at maturity T is K. L wants to price the risks and costs born in the contract, so as to make it fair (we assume that L does not want to earn any profit margin from the entire operation) and then to determine the amount P_L that can be lent, which makes the contract fair at inception. The present value of K at time T is its discounted value at rate r if counterparty B survives, but if B goes bankrupt, it is the present value of recovery $(1 - L_{GD_X})K$; to further lighten the notation, we assume without much loss of generality that $L_{GD} = 100\%$, so that recovery is 0. We assume for the moment that $\gamma_X = 0$, so that $s_X = \pi_X$ for either parties.[3] We will relax both assumptions later on.

We have to sum the present value of the costs[4] lender L has to pay: L has to fund the amount P and the future funding cost is the difference between the amount he has to pay back $P_L e^{(r+s^L)T}$ and the same amount invested at the risk-free rate $P_L e^{rT}$.[5] Summing up these components, we get that the amount P_L that L can lend to B at time 0 can be obtained by making the value of the deal V_L at inception nil:

$$V_L = -P_L + e^{-rT}[K - KE[1 - 1_{\tau_B > T}] - P_L(e^{(r+s^L)T} - e^{rT})] = -P_L e^{s^L T} + K e^{-(r+\pi^B)T} = 0$$

$$(10.1)$$

---

[2] See [67], amongst others.
[3] The fact that, under the hypothesis that $L_{GD_X} = 100\%$, $s_X = \pi_X$, is a consequence of the reduced-form approach which we are using to model default risk. For a general treatment of the reduced-form approach to default modelling, see Chapter 8 and [61].
[4] Costs have negative values, so they can be algebraically added.
[5] Since investment in a risk-free asset is not a loss of generality, we can always adjust expected cash flows for default risk and then consider them as invested at the risk-free rate.

The fair amount lent will then be $P_L = Ke^{-(r+s^L+\pi^B)T}$, or

$$P_L = Ke^{-(r+s^L+s^B)T}$$

since we assumed the liquidity premium equal to 0.

Apparently, L has to discount the positive cash flows received at T at a discount rate that includes the risk-free rate, its own funding spread and the borrower's funding spread. Actually, this is an effective rate that can be used to determine the fair amount to lend, but it is more useful, in our opinion, to consider the discount rate as just the risk-free rate, and then use this to discount expected cash flows and costs. In fact, it is interesting to rewrite (10.1) in the following way:

$$V_L = -P_L + e^{-rT}K - \text{CVA}_B - \text{FC}_L \qquad (10.2)$$

where $\text{CVA}_B = e^{-rT}K\mathbf{E}[1 - 1_{\tau_B > T}]$ is the credit value adjustment due to the loss given default of B, in this case equal to the entire amount times the probability of default; $\text{FC}_L = e^{-rT}P_L(e^{(r+s^L)T} - e^{rT})$ is the funding cost borne by the lender. The fair amount P_L is easily recognized as the present value received at T, minus expected losses on default and minus funding costs: $e^{-rT}K - \text{CVA}_B - \text{FC}_L$.

In some works,[6] funding costs take into account the probability of default of L: when the lender goes bankrupt, she will not return the compounded amount P to the funder, so that

$$\text{FC}_L = e^{-rT}P_L(e^{(r+s^L)T} - e^{(r+s^L)T}(1 - e^{-\pi^L T}) - e^{rT})$$

Under the current assumption that $\gamma^L = 0$, funding costs would then be nil.

In our setting, given Axiom 10.2.1, it is not possible for the lender to consider her own default. Moreover, we honestly believe that it is very unlikely for the bank's management to argue in the presence of stockholders that they do not have to worry about not transferring funding costs in the pricing of their loans, because they will make up for all these extra costs when the bank goes bust. In fact, it is true that the bank will repay only a fraction (or nothing) of its debt on default, but this is a false saving of money, since not fully paying back debt obligation simply means that no equity is left to cover losses. So, saving on the repayment of the debt should more correctly be seen as a loss on shareholder equity. This will be clearer in what follows.

Let us now see how borrower B prices the loan contract. Basically, she evaluates the contract using the same principles as the lender, so that the fair amount P_B that she should receive should equal the present value of K, plus the funding costs and CVA_L for the losses suffered if the lender declares bankruptcy. In a loan contract CVA_L is zero, since the borrower has no exposure to the lender, but only an obligation. So we can write:

$$V_B = P_B - e^{-rT}[K - P_B(e^{(r+s^B)T} - e^{rT})] = -P_B e^{s^B T} + Ke^{-rT} = 0 \qquad (10.3)$$

The fair amount to B is then $P_B = Ke^{-(r+s^B)T}$, which is different from the amount fair to the lender. The latter also includes lenders' funding costs, whereas they are not considered in the valuation process by the borrower. What is more, it seems that negative cash flows should be discounted at an effective rate equal to the risk-free rate plus the borrower's spread, but this is just one way to set the fair level of the borrowed amount.

---

[6] See, for example, [94].

Actually, it is more consistent, in our view, to use just one rate, the risk-free one, to discount expected cash flows and costs. In fact, recalling that $\gamma^B = 0$, we can write (10.3) as:

$$V_B = P_B - e^{-rT}[K - P_B(e^{(r+\pi^B)T} - e^{rT})] = -P_B e^{\pi^B T} + Ke^{-rT} = 0 \qquad (10.4)$$

and hence $P_B = e^{-rT}K - DVA_B$, where $DVA_B = CVA_B = e^{-rT}K(1 - e^{-\pi^B T})$ is debit value adjustment, or the expected loss the borrower will cause the lender in the event of her default. In a loan contract, DVA_B can also be seen as FC_B, or the funding cost the borrower has to pay: we will dwell more on this later on.

It is easy to check that $P_B - P_L = FC_L$. This means that no agreement can be reached by the two counterparties in the loan contract, since the fair amount the borrower requires is higher than what the lender is willing to lend. In other words, the borrower's fair amount does not include the lender's funding costs.

While this may come as a surprise, actually it is not so far from what has really happened in the last few years, starting in 2007, when bank funding spreads dramatically increased and the ability to close loan deals with counterparties worsened. Indeed, if the borrower has easy access to the capital market and she is able to ask for funds directly from investors, intermediation of the banking system is neither required nor efficient. Investors are economic operators investing their capital without (or with small) leverage, so that they do not include funding costs in their evaluation process. In this case it is possible to have an investor fair value that clashes with the borrower fair value, since they will only consider $CVA_B = DVA_B$ in their capital allocation decisions.

An agreement can be reached between a lender who operates with funding (e.g., a bank) and a borrower only if the latter does not have direct access to the capital market, so that she will consider the lender's funding cost as unavoidable. In this case $P_L = P_B$.

The main result of this section is that the choice of discounting rate for positive and negative cash flows poses no problems even when there is a default risk premium and funding costs, when these are taken into account in a consistent manner. Actually, the discounting rate is only ever the risk-free rate. It is used to discount expected cash flows, expected losses given counterparty default and funding costs. Using effective discount rates (given by the sum of the risk-free rate, the credit spread and, where needed, the funding spread) in calculating the fair amount of a loan deal is misleading: the focus should not be on identifying the right discount rate for different cases, but on identifying expected cash flows and costs that may occur during the duration of the contract.

Following this route we totally bypass choosing the discount rate. Some people introduce a hedging argument for future cash flows and then consistently derive proper discount rates.[7] We think that the proposed argument does not take into account the fact that each cash flow is not some abstract entity in the books of a financial institution, requiring a hedging strategy whose costs entail a specific discount rate. Cash flows, instead, are always originated within a specific contract, which implies there are costs, revenues and risks. These must be accounted for to calculate the value of the contract, and cash flows related to them have to be discounted with the risk-free rate. Incidentally, note that the attribute "risk free" is quite superfluous here and it is only used since in practice (and often also in theory) effective rates are introduced that encompass many risks. For the sake of rigor, there is only one (possibly stochastic) interest rate that

---

[7] This approach was studied in [67], for example.

makes it possible to determine how much one unit of the numeraire good (i.e., money) is worth at future times.

10.4   CRITIQUE OF DEBIT VALUE ADJUSTMENT

A great debate is currently ongoing over debit value adjustment and its treatment in bank balance sheets. In this section we will endeavour to analyse what DVA really means, by looking at it from an accounting perspective as well, since we believe it adds to understanding of the issue.

We assume that borrower B is a bank with a very simplified balance sheet that is marked to the market.[8] Mark to market is operated by discounting all expected and risk-adjusted cash flows at risk free rate r, as shown in the previous section. The stockholders decide to start activity with equity E and to stop it after a period of time T; amount E is deposited in bank account D_1, which we assume risk free; moreover, they require no premium over the risk-free rate, so that it is also the hurdle rate to value investment projects. We also assume that no liquidity premium is paid by the borrower so that $s^B = \pi^B$.

10.4.1   Single-period case

Time 0

At time 0, the bank closes a loan contract with a lender (e.g., an institutional investor) which is not charging any funding cost when setting the fair amount to lend. The amount is deposited in bank account D_2, also risk-free to avoid immaterial complications at the moment. The balance sheet at time 0 looks as follows:

Assets	Liabilities
$D_1 = E$ $D_2 = Ke^{-(r+s^B)T}$	$L = Ke^{-rT}$ $-\text{DVA}_B(0) = -e^{-rT}K(1-$ $e^{-\pi^B T}) = -e^{-rT}K(1 - e^{-s^B T})$
	E

The assets and liabilities balance and $\text{DVA}_B(0)$ is deducted from the risk-free present value of the loan paying back K at T: in this way the present value of the loan matches exactly the amount of cash deposited in D_2, so that the deal generates no P&L (profits/losses) at inception.

Subtracting DVA from the current value of the risk-free present value of liabilities is generally how debit value adjustment is included in the balance sheet; this common practice brings the rather disturbing consequence that when the creditworthiness of B worsens (i.e., π^B ($= s^B$ in our case) increases), the present value of liabilities declines: something counterintuitive that has been justified by several arguments that are not

---

[8] This is not always true in reality but, at least as far as the trading book is concerned, it is a fair assumption.

particularly convincing. Some banks in the last few years benefitted from this situation given the current concept of DVA, basically seen simply as CVA which the counterparty prices in the contract, considered from the obligor's perspective. We believe instead that, given Axiom 10.2.1, DVA is something different, as we hope to completely prove in what follows.

We suggest that DVA is not a reduction in the value of liabilities due to the credit risk of the borrower, but is actually the present value of the costs (or losses, if you wish) that the borrower has to pay due to the fact that he is not a risk-free economic operator, under Axiom 10.2.1. When DVA is considered as the negative of CVA, it still keeps its notion of compensation for counterparty risk, but this notion is only valid for the lender. Looking at it from the borrower's perspective, the negative of CVA (i.e., DVA) modifies its nature from that of compensation for a risk to that of a cost. Justifying the deduction from liabilities because of the compensatory nature of DVA, in light of Axiom 10.2.1, cannot be supported since stockholders do not consider their bank's default in the investment evaluation process. If this holds true, DVA, being a cost, should appear on the balance sheet to reduce the value of net equity, rather than the risk-free present value of the debt, so that the balance sheet should read:

Assets	Liabilities
$D_1 = E$ $D_2 = Ke^{-(r+s^B)T}$	$L = Ke^{-rT}$
	E $-\mathrm{DVA}_B(0) = -Ke^{-rT}\left(1 - e^{-\pi^B T}\right)$ $= -Ke^{-rT}\left(1 - e^{-s^B T}\right)$

The assets and liabilities still balance but now we have a completely different picture of the balance sheet, since the deal produces a P&L at inception: a loss equal to DVA. We now have to prove that DVA is actually the present value of the costs borne by the borrower until the expiry of the loan and the end of borrower activity.

Time T

Let us check what happens at time T: all bank accounts earn the risk-free rate and this is also true for the risk-free value of debt; DVA(T) collapses to 0, since the debt expires. Eventually, we have:

Assets	Liabilities
$D_1 = Ee^{rT}$ $D_2 = Ke^{-s^B T}$	$L = K$
	E

The balance sheet clearly does not balance since we are missing the profits and losses realized over the period $[0, T]$. In fact, we have interest income from account D_1 (II_1) and losses (ℓ) on the funding spread given by the difference between what is the final value of D_2 and what is paid back on the loan:

$$(Ee^{rT} - E) + (Ke^{-s^B T} - K) = E(e^{rT} - 1) - K(1 - e^{-s^B T})$$
$$= II_1 - \ell$$

so that if we also add profits and losses to equity E and consider the outflow of cash to pay back the loan, the assets and liabilities balance again:

Assets	Liabilities
$D_1 = Ee^{rT}$	$L = 0$
$D_2 = Ke^{-s^B T} - K$	
	E
	$+II_1$
	$-\ell$

Lender activity is then closed and we value its profitability by also including the hurdle rate:

$$(Ee^{rT} - E) + (Ke^{-s^B T} - K) - E(e^{rT} - 1) = -K(1 - e^{-s^B T}) = -\ell$$

so that the entire activity generated a loss ℓ equal to the funding spread on amount K.

The terminal balance sheet also confirms the correctness of our suggestion to consider DVA as the value of the losses suffered at the end of the loan rather than a reduction of the risk-free present value of the loan. In fact, it is easy to check that realized losses are the compounded DVA: $\ell = DVA(0)e^{rT}$.

10.4.2 Multi-period case

Time 0

We would now like to generalize the analysis to a multi-period setting, by assuming that the bank's activity spans over the interval $[0, 2T]$ made of 2 periods T: we will strike a balance in 0, at an intermediate time T and at the end of the activity $2T$. We have the same setup as above and this time the bank asks for a loan maturing in $2T$, when it has to pay back the amount K. The balance sheet at time 0 is:

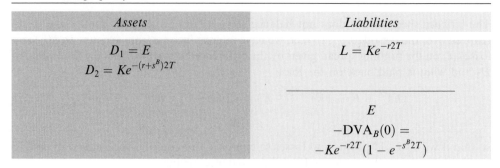

Assets	Liabilities
$D_1 = E$ $D_2 = Ke^{-(r+s^B)2T}$	$L = Ke^{-r2T}$
	E $-\mathrm{DVA}_B(0) =$ $-Ke^{-r2T}(1 - e^{-s^B 2T})$

DVA(0) is now the present value of the costs paid at $2T$. They reduce the value of the equity E, following our definition of debit value adjustment.

Time T

At time T interest accrues on the bank accounts and on the loan. The interest earned on D_1 is $II_1 = E(e^{rT} - 1)$; on D_2 the interest is $II_2 = Ke^{-s^B 2T}(e^{-rT} - e^{-r2T})$; and the loan interest is $II_L = K(e^{-(r+s^B)T} - e^{-(r+s^B)2T})$. The total is shown in the new balance sheet below, where the updated DVA is also included:

Assets	Liabilities
$D_1 = Ee^{rT}$ $D_2 = Ke^{-rT-s^B 2T}$	$L = Ke^{-rT}$
	E $II_1 = E(e^{rT} - 1)$ $-\mathrm{DVA}_B(T) = -Ke^{-rT}(1 - e^{-s^B T})$ $-\ell(0, T) = -Ke^{-rT}(e^{-s^B T} - e^{-s^B 2T})$

Equity is now incremented by interest II_1 earned on the first bank account, and it is decreased by debit value adjustment at time T, $\mathrm{DVA}_B(T)$, and by the value of the amount of losses that can be attributed to period $[0, T]$, $\ell(0, T) = II_2 - II_L$. It is very interesting to notice that:

$$-\mathrm{DVA}_B(0)e^{rT} = -\mathrm{DVA}_B(T) - \ell(0, T)$$

so that the balance sheet above can be rewritten in a totally equivalent way as:

Assets	Liabilities
$D_1 = Ee^{rT}$ $D_2 = Ke^{-rT-s^B 2T}$	$L = Ke^{-rT}$
	E $II_1 = E(e^{rT} - 1)$ $-\text{DVA}_B(0)e^{rT} = -Ke^{-rT}(1 - e^{-s^B 2T})$

This choice of bookkeeping stresses the fact that, even in a multi-period setting, the value of the loss is still the DVA of the operation computed at contract inception, compounded at each period with the risk-free rate. The first choice above, on the other hand, allows for their attribution to each period by isolating the losses. This is also true of variable (possibly stochastic) spreads and interest rates.

Time 2T

Let us see what happens at $2T$, when the loan expires and the bank (i.e., the borrower) closes the business. In this case we have once again interest accrual at T, while DVA is nil and the losses that have to be updated must also include those referring to the second period:

Assets	Liabilities
$D_1 = Ee^{2rT}$ $D_2 = Ke^{-s^B 2T} - K$	$L = 0$
	E $II_1 = E(e^{2rT} - 1)$ $-\ell(0, T) = -K(e^{-s^B T} - e^{-s^B 2T})$ $-\ell(T, 2T) = -K(1 - e^{-s^B T})$

Once more it is quite easy to check that the assets and liabilities balance. It is also interesting to notice that:

$$-\ell(0, T) - \ell(T, 2T) = -K(1 - e^{-s^B 2T}) = \text{DVA}(0)e^{r2T}$$

which confirms what we have stated above, that total losses over the contract period are the future value of DVA computed at the start of the contract and that the funding spread (and the risk-free rate) can also evolve stochastically until maturity, since eventually only the initial level of the spread is what really counts. Evolution of the funding spread matters only in the attribution of portions of the total funding costs to a given period, something that is definitely important for performance measurement purposes, under the assumption that the funding cost component has to be assigned on a mark-to-market basis.

We also calculate in this case the profitability of the bank's activity during its life, considering the hurdle rate for the invested capital, thus getting:

$$(Ee^{r2T} - E) + (Ke^{-s^B 2T} - K) - E(e^{r2T} - 1) = -K(1 - e^{-s^B 2T}) = -\ell(0, 2T)$$

so that the starting equity invested has been eroded by total funding costs.

Our analysis clearly shows that the question about whether to consider DVA or not in the balance sheet, since it apparently generates perverse effects, is actually ill posed. In reality, DVA is not a reduction of the current value of liabilities, but simply the present value of costs the counterparty has to pay to compensate other parties for the fact that it is not risk free. Given Axiom 10.2.1, the same amount is seen as a cost from the borrower's perspective, and as default risk compensation from the lender's perspective.

Viewed as the present value of cost, DVA is the reduction of the equity that can be determined from the start of the contract, although its monetary manifestation may occur only at maturity. As such, it can be included in the (marked-to-market) balance sheet in a consistent fashion as a reduction of equity, and no perverse effects manifest themselves if the creditworthiness of the borrower worsens, since the present value of costs increases and net equity is accordingly abated. From this perspective, DVA *must* be included in the balance sheet without any doubt, thus fulfilling the *sound and prudent management* principle.

10.4.3   DVA as a funding benefit

As mentioned above, several not totally satisfactory justifications for liability reduction as a result of DVA have been provided in recent works. Some authors[9] present a list of arguments on how to manage and monetize DVA, along with related pros and cons. They also warn, however, about the very delicate nature of DVA inclusion in the balance sheet.

Some other authors[10] argue that DVA should actually be viewed as a funding benefit, thus apparently fully justifying its insertion in the balance sheet as a reduction in the current value of liabilities. However, in our opinion, the argument is not justified.

Anyway, let us check if this argument somehow impairs our notion of DVA. Assume we are in a multi-period case, and we are at time T: at this moment the borrower asks for more funds from the lender, starting a new loan contract for an amount $K_2 < K$, to be paid back at time $2T$, together with the other loan K. K_2 is deposited in a (risk-free) bank account D_3. The balance sheet at time T, with the updated DVA, now reads:

---

9 See [75].
10 See [94], amongst others.

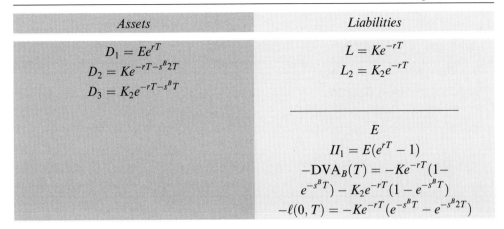

Those in favour of the "funding benefit" argument (implicitly) suggest that cash should not be deposited in a bank account (D_3 in our example), but should be used to buy back some debt, thus reducing the funding need. Nothing prevents implementation of this strategy, so that the balance sheet, after buying back a portion of the first loan, is:

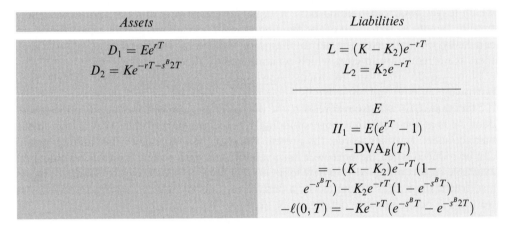

$DVA_B(T)$ is reduced consistently with the reduction of the debt whose original amount was K. The balance sheet at the end of activities $2T$ is:

Assets	Liabilities
$D_1 = Ee^{2rT}$ $D_2 = Ke^{-s^B T} + (K - K_2)e^{-s^B T}$ $-(K - K_2) - K_2$	$L = 0$

E $II_1 = E(e^{2rT} - 1)$ $-\ell(0, T) = -K(e^{-s^B T} - e^{-s^B 2T})$ $-\ell(T, 2T) = -(K - K_2)(1 -$ $e^{-s^B T}) - K_2(1 - e^{-s^B T})$

It is quite easy to check that total loss is simply:

$$-\ell(0, T) - \ell(T, 2T) = -K(1 - e^{-s^B 2T}) = \text{DVA}(0)e^{r2T}$$

or, the cost paid on the total amount borrowed $K + K_2$, considering buyback of debt K_2, which leaves total outstanding debt K equal to the staring amount. So, if we define funding benefit as reduction of the funding cost for a given amount of raised funds, we can easily see that, given the net total amount funded over the period (K in our case), there is no reduction in cost, which remains exactly the same as before.[11]

Now, we do not want to discuss how sensible the strategy of issuing debt (i.e., borrowing money) and immediately buying back issued debt is, rather we want to stress the fact that if, for whatsoever reason, the borrower has money to reduce its outstanding debt, he is at the same time correspondingly cancelling part of the DVA shown in the balance sheet. In other words, the present value of the costs due to the funding spread can be reduced when the borrower has available free cash to buy back his own debt. If available cash is obtained by a new loan, no real funding benefit can be achieved; this is also true if the cash is originated by a derivative transaction (e.g., selling an option), as we will see below in more detail.

The "funding benefit" argument does not seem to truly justify consistent insertion of DVA on the balance sheet as a reduction in the value of liabilities, even if one looks at it as a funding benefit and not from the perspective of counterparty credit risk, which we already criticized above. Actually, even in the reasoning presented above we are not referring counterparty credit risk at all, we are simply referring to costs, provided that Axiom 10.2.1 holds. Nevertheless, we need to investigate the argument further and will do so later on.

It is worthy of note that our notion of DVA does not exclude the possibility that the borrower may enjoy a reduction in his liability value: if the interest rate rises, the present value of the loan decreases. Whether this profit can actually be realized depends on the

---

[11] It is worthy of note here that we are simply confirming the ancient philosophical statement *ex nihilo nihil* (Melissus of Samos, fifth century BC): it is impossible to create something from nothing, or to get blood from a stone, as the saying goes. On the other hand, the "funding benefit" argument, in our opinion, is in striking conflict with another important principle of the Aristotelic logic: "**A** cannot be **A** and at the same time **not A**" according to πασῶν βεβαιοτάτη αρχή, the firmest of all principles (Aristotle, *Metaphysics* 1005b 15–17). In our specific case, we cannot say that borrowing money, for the borrower, is at the same time debt and not debt, as would seem to be the case if we allow for the existence of a funding benefit when debt is employed to replace other debt.

composition of the assets of the borrower, since available free cash is needed to buy back the loan.

10.5   DVA FOR DERIVATIVE CONTRACTS

CVA and DVA are concepts devised for OTC derivative contracts as measures of counterparty credit risk. As such, they are improperly used for loan contracts, but ultimately their application offers a good conceptual framework to decide how to properly include the credit risk of the debtor too in the balance sheet, and to precisely disentangle the contribution to total P&L of the several cost and income components.

When dealing with OTC derivative contracts, the main difference is that the exposure that one or both counterparties have to the other party is stochastic over time. We will investigate how DVA can be entered on the balance sheet and how to interpret it in this case.

We analyse a very simple derivative contract: a forward contract on asset S. The main setup is the same as above: we assume that the bank (which is now no longer a borrower) B strikes a deal at 0 to buy at T one unit of the asset at price X. We also assume, to simplify things, but with no loss of generality, that the counterparty of the bank is risk free, so that we do not have to consider any CVA in the analysis. The bank can only default at the end of activities at T.

The value of contract $H(0)$ can be derived according to standard techniques[12] as:

$$H(0) = e^{-rT}(\mathbf{E}[S_T] - X) + \text{DVA}_B(0) \tag{10.5}$$

where $\mathbf{E}[]$ is the expectation operator and $\text{DVA}_B(0)$ is (assuming independence between default probability, asset price and zero recovery on default):

$$\text{DVA}_B(0) = e^{-rT}\mathbf{E}[\min(H_T, 0)(1 - 1_{\tau_B > T})] = e^{-rT}\mathbf{E}[\max(X - S_T, 0)](1 - e^{-s^B T}) \tag{10.6}$$

In words, DVA is the discounted expected negative value of the contract at expiry, weighted by the probability of default of the bank. This is the loss that the counterparty may expect to suffer, given the default of the bank. The fair forward price is the level of X making nil the value of the contract at inception:

$$H(0) = e^{-rT}(\mathbf{E}[S_T] - X) + \text{DVA}_B(0) = 0$$

so that:

$$X = \mathbf{E}[S_T] + e^{rT}\text{DVA}_B(0)$$

It is manifest that the bank can close a forward contract at conditions worse than those it can get if it were risk free. In fact, B buys at expiry the underlying asset at price $X > X^{rf}$, where $X^{rf} = \mathbf{E}[S_T]$ is the fair forward price if B cannot go bankrupt, and hence $\text{DVA}_B(0)$ is zero.

Let us consider how to include a forward contract in the balance sheet (the equity is the same as in the case examined above). The value of the contract has to be computed by discounting the expected terminal value of the contract, plus expected losses due to counterparty risks (i.e., CVA, which is nil in our case by assumption) and other costs

---

[12] See [32]. Although not specified up to now, it is important to stress that we are valuing all contracts under a risk-neutral measure, and all expectations should be considered as computed with respect to this measure.

(DVA in the framework we have suggested). The value of the contract to B is:

$$H_B(0) = e^{-rT}(\mathbf{E}[S_T] - X) = -\mathrm{DVA}_B(0)$$

which is negative and a (positive) liability (although it should be noted that the value may change sign at any time until maturity, and hence become an asset). The bank has to recognize a liability due to the mark to market immediately after closing the deal, and this is equal to the DVA of the contract, as just shown. On the other hand, it also has to consider DVA as the present value of costs due to the fact that it is not default risk free. So the balance sheet reads as:

Assets	Liabilities
$D_1 = E$	$-H_B(0) = \mathrm{DVA}_B(0) =$ $e^{-rT}\mathbf{E}[\max(X - S_T, 0)](1 - e^{-s^B T})$
	E $-\mathrm{DVA}_B(0) =$ $-e^{-rT}\mathbf{E}[\max(X - S_T, 0)](1 - e^{-s^B T})$

Assets and liabilities clearly balance and we are consistently considering the value of the contract and related extra costs borne by B. In this way, closing the deal generates no further P&L.

We now have to check what happens at time T. Assume that underlying asset price S_T is equal to the expected price at the contract's inception $S_T = \mathbf{E}[S_T]$: the bank then suffers a loss calculated from the value of the forward contract as follows:

$$H_B(T) = \ell = \mathbf{E}[S_T] - X = -\mathrm{DVA}_B(0)e^{rT}$$

The balance sheet in T is then:

Assets	Liabilities
$D_1 = Ee^{rT}$	$-H_B(T) = \mathrm{DVA}_B(0)e^{rT}$
	E $II_1 = E(e^{rT} - 1)$ $-\ell = -\mathrm{DVA}_B(0)e^{rT}$

The loss has to be financed by the cash available in the bank account, where the original equity was deposited, so that the final form of the balance sheet in T is:

Assets	Liabilities
$D_1 = Ee^{rT} - \text{DVA}_B(0)e^{rT}$	
	E
	$II_1 = E(e^{rT} - 1) - \ell = -\text{DVA}_B(0)e^{rT}$

This confirms the fact that the DVA for a derivative contract is also the present value of a cost. Anyway, the definition can be slightly refined by moving one step forward. In fact, let us assume that the underlying asset's price at expiry T is some $S_T \neq \mathbf{E}[S_T]$: the value of the forward contract is then:

$$H_B(T) = S_T - X = S_T - X^{rf} - \text{DVA}_B(0)e^{rT}$$

which may result in a profit or a loss, depending on the level S_T. Anyway, when this value is compared with the corresponding value of a forward contract whose fair price was determined by assuming that B is a risk-free counterparty, it is straightforward to see that:

$$H_B(T) - H^{rf}(T) = S_T - X^{rf} - \text{DVA}_B(0)e^{rT} - S_T - X^{rf} = -\text{DVA}_B(0)e^{rT}$$

So DVA is a cost that worsens losses, or abates profits, at expiry T with respect to the same contract dealt by a risk-free counterparty: this cost is once again due to the fact that the bank is not a risk-free economic agent. If we introduce a multi-period setting we will have the same conclusion as above:[13] variability of the DVA allows allocating portions of total costs on different subperiods, but it is immaterial to determining total cost, which is still the DVA calculated at the start of the contract.

It is also worth analysing what happens with derivatives starting with a nonzero value at inception, such as options. Some authors[14] recently provided a proof on how to replicate a derivative contract including CVA, DVA and funding. Their approach relies on the bank trading in the counterparty's bonds to replicate the CVA and its own bonds to replicate the DVA: the argument hinges on the funding benefit that can be received by buying back its own bonds. The existence of issued bonds to be bought back is assumed, otherwise a replica would not be possible: if we accept this assumption, DVA inclusion in the balance sheet, as a correction of the contract's value, would be fully justified because it can actually be replicated. Let us check if this is true.

At time 0, let bank B sell call option O expiring at T to a counterparty, struck at level X. The value of this contract is its risk-free value minus DVA, with no CVA since the bank has no exposure to the counterparty.[15] The value can be written as (with the same assumptions made for the forward contract):

$$O(0) = e^{-rT}\mathbf{E}[S_T - X]^+ - \text{DVA}_B(0) \tag{10.7}$$

where the $\text{DVA}_B(0)$ is:

$$\text{DVA}_B(0) = e^{-rT}\mathbf{E}[S_T - X]^+(1 - e^{-s^B T}) \tag{10.8}$$

---

[13] This argument has to be generalized by considering loss in the period as $-\ell(0, T) = -(P_0 e^{rT}(e^{-s^B T} - e^{-s^B 2T})$ $+ (P_T - P_0)e^{rT}(1 - e^{-s^B T}))$, where $P_i = \mathbf{E}_i[\max(S_{2T} - X, 0)]$ and $\mathbf{E}_i$ is expectation at time i.
[14] See [42].
[15] DVA has negative sign in this case since the sign of the contract is negative.

We include this contract in the balance sheet, where there is also a debt. The value of the debt is equal to the value of the option and is deposited in a risk-free bank account D_2. The value of the option contract to the borrower is risk-free premium $V(0) = O(0) + \text{DVA}_B(0) = O^{rf}(0)$, and $\text{DVA}_B(0)$ is accounted for, according to our proposed notion, as a loss:

Assets	Liabilities
$D_1 = E$ $D_2 = Ke^{-(r+s^B)T} = O(0)$ $D_3 = O(0)$	$L = Ke^{-rT}$ $V(0) = O(0) + \text{DVA}_B(0)$
	E $-\text{DVA}_B^T(0) = -e^{-rT}K(1 - e^{-s^BT})$ $-e^{-rT}\mathbf{E}[S_T - X]^+(1 - e^{-s^BT})$

where $\text{DVA}_B^T(0)$ is total DVA including the option's and the debt's. Now, according to those supporting DVA replication[16] the replica generates enough cash to buy back the debt. In fact, in our example we have cash deposited in account D_3 equal to the premium received.[17] This can be used to buy back outstanding debt, whose value is equal to the premium, as assumed above to make things as simple as possible. So the balance sheet now reads:

Assets	Liabilities
$D_1 = E$ $D_2 = Ke^{-(r+s^B)T} = O(0)$	$L = 0$ $V(0) = O(0) + \text{DVA}_B(0)$
	E $-\text{DVA}_B^T(0) =$ $-e^{-rT}\mathbf{E}[S_T - X]^+(1 - e^{-s^BT})$

The debt is now nil and DVA has been updated. The funding benefit has to be verified at expiry of the option, when the option is worth $O(T)$ and its $\text{DVA}_B(T) = 0$. The P&L generated by the option is $-(O(T) - O(0)e^{rT})$ giving:

---

[16] See [42].

[17] Having got to the heart of the matter, we need to point out that we are not considering the entire replication portfolio, but we are limiting the analysis to hedging the DVA, with the strategy suggested in [42].

Assets	Liabilities
$D_1 = Ee^{rT}$ $D_2 = Ke^{-s^B T} = O(0)e^{rT}$ $D_3 = -O(T)$	$L = 0$
	E $II_1 = E(e^{rT} - 1)$ $\text{P\&L}(T) = -(O(T) - O(0)e^{rT})$

We do not appear to have suffered any loss deriving from DVA, but this is a false perception. Actually, if DVA is the extra cost the bank has to pay for not being risk free, then if we compare the final P&L with respect to the P&L of a risk-free bank we get:

$$(O(T) - O(0)e^{rT}) - (O(T) - O(0)e^{rT} + \text{DVA}_B(0)e^{rT}) = -\text{DVA}_B(0)e^{rT} = -\ell$$

So the P&L has a hidden cost that is not only equal to $\text{DVA}_B(0)e^{rT}$, but also to the compounded DVA on the outstanding debt before it was bought back. So, given the funds available to the bank over the period, which are equal to $O(0)$, the losses incurred are in every case of $\text{DVA}_B(0)$ explicitly or implicitly shown in the balance sheet. In the end, even the argument of buying back the bank's own bonds does not justify inclusion of DVA in the balance sheet to reduce liabilities, as expected after having criticized the "funding benefit" argument above.[18]

We would like to stress that we are not saying that the replication strategy is wrong because it is impossible to buy back issued bonds, or that the assumption of existing outstanding debt is weak (although no issued bonds being available is something that may actually happen). We believe we have only proved that, however you define it, abating liabilities using DVA is an accounting and financial mistake, apparently subtle but with huge practical impacts that are analysed in more depth later on in this chapter.

We are finally in a positon to propose the following definition, which encompasses all the cases we have analysed so far.

Definition 10.5.1. *Debit value adjustment (DVA) is the compensation a counterparty has to pay, when closing a contract, to the other party to remunerate the default risk that the latter bears and that is specularly measured as credit value adjustment (CVA).*

This compensation is the present value of the extra costs (given Axiom 10.2.1) that the counterparty has to pay with respect to a risk-free counterparty and as such it must *be included in a marked-to-market balance sheet as a reduction of equity.*

In a multi-period setting, the portion of the initial DVA attributed at each period may depend on the stochasticity of the probability of default of the counterparty, and of the underlying asset of the contract, but in any case the total cost over the entire duration of the contract is still the DVA calculated at the beginning of the contract.

---

[18] An easier way to look at the DVA on an option would be to consider immediately closing out the short position by buying an identical option from a risk-free counterparty. In this case the premium paid by the bank would be $V(0) = O(0) + \text{DVA}_B(0)$, and the loss, equal to $\text{DVA}_B(0)$, would be financed with other available cash and written in the balance sheet as a reduction of equity, thus confirming the new notion of DVA we have proposed.

Hopefully, the lengthy discussion contained in the present chapter will eventually give birth to a new way of looking at the problem of how to correctly strike a marked-to-the-market balance sheet.

10.6   EXTENSION TO POSITIVE RECOVERY AND LIQUIDITY RISK

In the analysis above we assumed that the loss given default of the exposure is full (i.e., $L_{GD} = 100\%$), and that the liquidity spread is nil ($\gamma = 0$). In this section we release these two assumptions and we analyse which effects are produced after that.

Let us start with the case when $L_{GD} < 100\%$ and $\gamma = 0$. It is very well known that the spread, in a reduced-form setting to model credit risk when recovery is a fraction of the market value, is:

$$s = \pi \times L_{GD} \tag{10.9}$$

This can be seen as an approximation of the formula for loss given default on an exposure of amount K: $L_{GD}K(1 - e^{-\pi T}) \approx L_{GD}\pi TK \approx K(1 - e^{-sT})$, with $s = \pi L_{GD}$. When valuing the expected value received at expiry T, one gets:

$$Ke^{-rT} - Ke^{-rT}(1 - e^{-\pi L_{GD}T}) = Ke^{-(r+s)T}$$

thus confirming equation (10.9). Given market spread s and assuming loss given default L_{GD}, we can derive the probability of default trivially as: $\pi = s/L_{GD}$.

With this information at hand, it is quite straightforward to adapt the framework above to the case when $L_{GD} < 100\%$. Actually, CVA (equal to DVA from the borrower's perspective in formula (10.2) can be written as $CVA_B = DVA_B = L_{GDB}K\mathbf{E}[1 - 1_{T_B>T}] \approx K(1 - e^{-s^B T})$. On the other hand, funding cost FC_L is computed with s^L, which is now equal to $\pi^L L_{GDL}$ instead of simply π^L, but this change will not affect our subsequent analysis at all.

We now add a liquidity premium $\gamma \neq 0$. When included in the lender's spread, we have that $s^L = \pi^L L_{GDL} + \gamma^L$, and this is the new spread to insert in quantity FC_L of equation (10.2), but no other effects are produced.

For the borrower's spread the treatment of the DVA deserves more attention.[19] Let us define the spread including the liquidity premium as $s^{B^*} = \pi^B L_{GDB} + \gamma^B$ and the spread including just the credit component as $s^B = \pi^B L_{GDB}$. Now equation (10.3) has to be modified as follows:

$$V_B = P_B - e^{-rT}[K - P_B(e^{(r+s^{B^*})T} - e^{rT})] = -P_B e^{s^{B^*}T} + Ke^{-rT} = 0 \tag{10.10}$$

and we have

$$P_B = e^{-rT}K - DVA_B - LPC_B$$

where

$$DVA_B = CVA_B = e^{-rT}K(1 - e^{-s^B T})$$

is DVA, and

$$LPC_B = e^{-rT}K(e^{-s^B T} - e^{-s^{B^*}T})$$

is the liquidity cost due to liquidity premium γ^B. Quantity LPC_B is an extra cost that is in all respects equal to DVA for the borrower and, hence, has to be included in the balance sheet as a reduction of net equity, similarly to DVA:

---

[19] Incidentally, note that FC_L is the funding cost of L, which also implies that L is actually a borrower of someone else's money. So when it comes to disentangling total funding cost FC_L from DVA and the liquidity component, what we show as applicable to the borrower B actually applies to the lender L as well.

Assets	Liabilities
$D_1 = E$ $D_2 = Ke^{-(r+s^{B^*})T}$	$L = Ke^{-rT}$
	E $-\text{DVA}_B(0) = -Ke^{-rT}(1 - e^{-s^B T})$ $-\text{LPC}_B(0) = -e^{-rT}(e^{-s^B T} - e^{-s^{B^*} T})$

The analysis then can easily be extended to consider costs related to liquidity as well.

It is worth stressing here that the sum of DVA_B and liquidity costs LPC_B is just the total funding cost FC_B for the borrower. In fact, if the borrower takes money from economic agents who do not pay any funding spread, such as investors, then it is easy to see that (from the definition of P_B):

$$\text{FC}_B = e^{-rT} P_B(e^{(r+s^B)T} - e^{rT}) = e^{-rT} K(1 - e^{-s^B T}) = \text{DVA}_B$$

If the borrower also has to pay the funding spread charged by a lender who has to fund the activity, such as a bank, then one gets:

$$\text{FC}_B = e^{-rT} P_B(e^{(r+s^L+s^B)T} - e^{(r+s^L)T}) = \text{DVA}_B + \text{IC}_B$$

where IC_B is the intermediation cost that the borrower has to pay to the lender for not having direct access to the capital market, and it is defined as:

$$\text{IC}_B = e^{-rT} P_B(e^{s^L T} - 1)(e^{(r+s^B)T} - e^{rT})$$

Although we left it unspecified, the funding cost of lender FC_L is actually the sum of his DVA_L (and intermediation costs IC_L in this case) and liquidity costs LPC_L.

We are now in a position to give a definition of the funding cost for loan and derivative contracts

Definition 10.6.1. *The funding cost FC for a loan contract is the present value of extra costs, with respect to a risk-free operator, that a counterparty has to pay for the liquidity premium, for intermediation costs for not having direct access to the capital market, and to compensate the other party for the default risk that the latter bears.*

The funding cost FC related to a derivative contract is the sum of funding costs that a counterparty has to pay on money it borrows to match negative cash flows. Given that the present (risk-free discounted) value of the sum of (expected) negative and positive cash flows is nil when the contract is fairly priced, borrowing of money is only needed when cumulated cash flows are negative during the life of the contract, before receiving counter-balancing flows. So, funding costs for a derivative contract depend on the cash flow schedule which determines whether they materialize or not.

From Definition 10.6.1 we can deduce that, assuming no liquidity premiums and intermediation costs, the funding cost and DVA are one and the same thing for a loan contract. For derivative contracts DVA is completely unrelated to funding costs, which can be seen as the sum of DVAs relating to loans needed to fund negative cumulated cash flows during the life of the contract. Evaluation of these costs has to be carried out on a case-by-case basis, depending on the type of contract and even on the position (long/short) that the counterparty is taking in it. We will examine these aspects in greater detail in Chapter 12.

10.7   DYNAMIC REPLICATION OF DVA

We now investigate more thoroughly the feasibility of dynamically replicating the DVA. If it is, then DVA is a quantity that can be fairly deducted from the liabilities of a financial institution. In this case, the argument of such works as [42], where a dynamic replication strategy is derived in great detail, could be accepted. If, on the contrary, it is not feasible, then DVA should be considered a cost and as such should be deducted from the equity of the financial institution. In this second case we confirm the results we derived above.

We will analyse the problem from a very wide perspective. We will show that dynamically replicating the DVA hides very subtle assumptions about the composition of the balance sheet of the financial institution. We will also point out the (negative) consequences for the financial institution if it organizes its derivative business so as to hedge and also replicate the DVA and we will demonstrate how the bank's franchise will be gradually eroded.

10.7.1   The gain process

We start from a very basic concept in option pricing theory. It seems that we are just repeating very well-known results, but we do so because we do not understand why these results are strangely forgotten when DVA is involved in the analysis.

Let X_t be the stochastic variable representing the price of an asset. The evolution of X_t is given by the following SDE (Ito process):[20]

$$dX_t = \mu(X,t)dt + \sigma(X,t)dZ_t \tag{10.11}$$

Define a trading strategy as an adapted process θ specifying at each state ω and time t the number $\theta_t(\omega)$ of units of the asset held by an economic operator. The gain process generated by θ is the stochastic integral:

$$\int_0^T \theta_t dX_t = \int_0^T \theta_t \mu(X,t)dt + \int_0^T \theta_t \sigma(X,t)dZ_t \tag{10.12}$$

Basically, the gain process indicates the gains (which can be both positive and negative) generated by θ_t units held at each time t given variation dX_t of the asset.

Assume we have a constant quantity $\bar{\theta}$ held between time T and T'. The gain process is simply $\bar{\theta} \int_T^{T'} dX_t = \bar{\theta}[X_{T'} - X_T]$. It is immediately apparent that the gain process is nil with probability 1 between the two times T and T' if $\bar{\theta} = 0$.

Assume now we short one unit of the asset between 0 and T and buy it back between T and T', so that $\theta_t = -1$ for $t \in \{0, T\}$ and $\theta_t = 0$ for $t \in \{T, T'\}$. The total gain process is:

$$-1 \times [X_T - X_0] + 0 \times [X_{T'} - X_T] = -1 \times [X_T - X_0]$$

---

[20] For technical details see, for example, [58].

The calculations are pretty simple and lead us to trivially state that when we do not hold any quantity of the asset for a given period we do not earn any gain.

The asset can be a stock, a commodity or a bond. When a financial institution (say, a bank) issues at time 0 a bond ($X = B$) to finance its business activity, this is the same as going short (i.e., sells without having previously bought) the same bond ($\theta_0 = -1$). Assume for simplicity, but with no loss of generality, that it is a zero-coupon bond. The bond is usually paid back at expiry T by the bank, which is in practice buying back the bond shorted ($\theta_T = 0$), and the gain process typically entails a loss for the issuer ($-1 \times [B_T - B_0]$) which is the amount of interest granted to the bondholder. The bond can be bought back even before expiry, at time $u < T$, thus producing a gain $-1 \times [B_u - B_0]$ that could be positive or negative if we are in a stochastic interest rate and default probability economy. On the other hand, if we are in a deterministic interest rate and default probability economy, buying back issued bonds always implies a loss for the bank, although lower than that suffered at expiry (i.e., the bank pays less interest, since it keeps a short position in the bond for a shorter period). It is clear that, from time u until expiry T, the gain process is nil since $\theta_t = 0$ for $t \in \{u, T\}$, unless the bank decides to issue the same bond once again.

10.7.2 Dynamic replication of a defaultable claim

Dynamic replication relies on getting the same payoff structure as a derivative contract via a trading strategy in primary securities (e.g., stocks and bonds). Assume we have a vector of N securities defined by the price process $X = (X^1, \ldots, X^N)$. We want to replicate dynamically a derivative claim whose terminal payoff at expiry T is V_T and whose initial price at time 0 is V_0.

The replication portfolio is set up at 0. We have to find a trading strategy θ such that it satisfies the following well-known conditions:[21]

1. *Self-financing condition*: No other investment is required to operate the strategy besides the initial one:

$$\theta_t \cdot X_t = \theta_0 \cdot X_0 + \int_0^t \theta_s dX_s \tag{10.13}$$

2. *Replicating condition*: At any time t the replicating portfolio's value equals the value of the contract and of the collateral account:

$$V_t = \theta_t \cdot X_t \tag{10.14}$$

for $t \in [0, T]$.

We apply replication to a defaultable derivative contract $\widehat{V}$ whose corresponding default risk-free value is denoted by V: the deal is written between bank B and counterparty C. In building the replication portfolio we strictly follow [42], to which we refer for details. $\widehat{V}$ is the value of the contract seen from counterparty C's perspective and is also the value bank B has to replicate once it closes the deal, so as to hedge the exposure it has towards C.

---

[21] For a general treatment see [58] or [92].

Since we want to investigate whether CVA and DVA can be replicated, we exclude any collateralization and/or credit risk mitigation agreement, which would reduce or eliminate these two quantities. Moreover, we do not consider agreements related to credit-rating triggers, such as the rating-based termination events analysed in Mercurio et al. [91, second part of reference]: in case there are such agreements, the results we derive below will require further adjustment.

Let $X^1 \equiv S$ be the underlying asset on which the contract's payoff is contingent, $X^2 \equiv P$ be a risk-free zero-coupon bond, $X^3 \equiv P^B$ be a default-risky zero-coupon bond issued by bank B and finally $X^4 \equiv P^C$ a default-risky zero-coupon bond issued by counterparty C. The two risky bonds depend on the respective issuer defaulting, so that they can be used to hedge exposures the derivative contract implies to party defaults. Both bonds have zero recovery if the issuer defaults.

The dynamics for S are the same as in (10.11), whereas the dynamics for the bonds are:

$$dP_t = r_t P_t dt$$

$$dP_t^B = (r_t + \lambda_t^B)P_t^B dt - dJ^B P_t^B$$

$$dP_t^C = (r_t + \lambda_t^C)P_t^C dt - dJ^B P_t^C$$

where r_t is the deterministic time-dependent instantaneous risk-free interest rate and λ^I is the yield spread of operator $I \in \{B, C\}$, which in equilibrium should also be the instantaneous default intensity.

We apply Ito's lemma to the value function $\widehat{V}(S, t, J^B, J^C)$, where J^B and J^C are two point processes that jump from 0 to 1 on default of, respectively, B and C with default intensity λ^B and λ^C. We get:

$$d\widehat{V}_t = \mathcal{L}^a \widehat{V}_t dt + \sigma(t, S)\frac{\partial V_t}{\partial S_t}dZ_t + D\widehat{V}_t^B dJ^B + D\widehat{V}_t^C dJ^C \qquad (10.15)$$

where we used the operator $\mathcal{L}^a \cdot$ defined as:

$$\mathcal{L}^a \cdot = \frac{\partial \cdot}{\partial t} + a(S, t)\frac{\partial \cdot}{\partial S_t} + \tfrac{1}{2}\sigma^2(S, t)\frac{\partial^2 \cdot}{\partial S_t^2} \qquad (10.16)$$

and we set variation of the contingent claim value on default of one of the two parties as:

$$D\widehat{V}_t^B = \widehat{V}(S, t, 1, 0) - \widehat{V}(S, t, 0, 0)$$

and

$$D\widehat{V}_t^C = \widehat{V}(S, t, 0, 1) - \widehat{V}(S, t, 0, 0)$$

On the other hand, bank B wants to build a replicating portfolio comprising quantity Δ_t of underlying assets, α_t^B of zero-coupon bonds issued by the bank itself, α_t^C of zero-coupon bonds issued by counterparty C, and finally an amount of cash β_t, so that it satisfies the two conditions stated above:

$$\widehat{V}_t = \Delta_t S_t + \alpha_t^B P_t^B + \alpha_t^C P_t^C + \beta_t \qquad (10.17)$$

and

$$d\widehat{V}_t = \Delta_t dS_t + \alpha_t^B dP_t^B + \alpha_t^C dP_t^C + d\beta_t \qquad (10.18)$$

Quantity β_t is defined as:

$$\beta_t = (\widehat{V}_t - \delta_t S_t - \alpha_t^B P_t^B - \alpha_t^C P_t^C)$$

and its evolution depends on the assumptions made on how to finance the asset and the two bonds.[22] We assume that the position in the underlying asset is financed by a repo transaction: if the repo rate is r^R and the asset grants continuous yield y, then for this part cash will evolve as:

$$\Delta_t(y_t - r_t)S_t dt$$

The position in the counterparty's bonds can be financed at repo as well, and we assume there is no haircut and a repo rate equal to the risk-free rate r, so that evolution for this component of the cash is:

$$-\alpha_t^C r_t P_t^C dt$$

Finally, the position in the bank's bonds can be financed by the amount $\widehat{V}$ that the replication strategy implies as an investment at the start of the contract; any remaining sum of cash will be invested at the risk-free rate if positive, or financed at the risk-free rate plus the bank's funding spread s^B if negative, thus yielding the dynamic for this last part of the cash:

$$r_t(\widehat{V}_t - \alpha_t^B P_t^B) + s_t^B(\widehat{V}_t - \alpha_t^B P_t^B)^-$$

Collecting the results we eventually get:

$$d\beta_t = [\Delta_t(y_t - r_t)S_t - \alpha_t^C r_t P_t^C + r_t(\widehat{V}_t - \alpha_t^B P_t^B) + s_t^B(\widehat{V}_t - \alpha_t^B P_t^B)^-]dt$$

By equating (10.18) with (10.15) we can derive the quantities of the different assets to include in the portfolio so that it perfectly replicates the derivative contract. It can be shown that they are:

$$\delta_t = \frac{\partial V_t}{\partial S_t}$$

$$\alpha_t^B = -\frac{\Delta \widehat{V}_t^B}{P_t^B} = \frac{\widehat{V}_t^B - (M^- + R^B M^+)}{P_t^B}$$

$$\alpha_t^C = -\frac{\Delta \widehat{V}_t^C}{P_t^C} = \frac{\widehat{V}_t^C - (M^+ + R^C M^-)}{P_t^C}$$

where we have defined M as the mark-to-market value of the contract upon default of one of the two parties and R^I, $I \in \{B, C\}$, as the recovery fraction of the contract paid by defaulting party I to the other party.

By rearranging terms, it can be shown that the final **PDE**, whose solution is the value of the derivative contract, is:

$$\mathcal{L}^{r-y}\widehat{V}_t = r_t\widehat{V}_t + s_t^B M^- - \lambda_t^B(M^- + R^B M^+) - \lambda_t^C(M^+ + R^C M^-) \quad (10.19)$$

If we assume that the mark-to-market value on default of one of the parties is the defaultable value of the contract, then $M = \widehat{V}$.[23] In this case the total value of the

---

[22] We accept the same assumptions as in [42]. We are not affirming that we agree on all of them, but they are immaterial to the point we want to prove, so we do not try to introduce other assumptions that we may deem more reasonable.
[23] Burgard and Kjaer [42] also examine the case when the mark to market on default is the risk-free value of contract $M = V$. Our analysis applies exactly to this second case as well. For an analysis of the closeout conventions upon default, see [36].

contract can be decomposed as $\widehat{V} = V + \widehat{U}$ (i.e., a risk-free component plus an adjustment due to credit events), which is the solution of the PDE:

$$\mathcal{L}^{r-y}\widehat{U}_t = s_t^B(V_t + \widehat{U}_t)^- + (1 - R^B)\lambda_t^B(V_t + \widehat{U}_t)^+ + (1 - R^C)\lambda_t^C(V_t + \widehat{U}_t)^-$$

where V is known and can be derived by standard techniques. Application of the Feynman–Kac theorem provides the solution to the adjustment term as:[24]

$$\widehat{U}(S,t) = -(1 - R^B)\int_t^T \lambda_s^B e^{-\int_s^T r_u du}\mathbf{E}[(V(S,s) + \widehat{U}(S,s))^+]ds$$

$$-(1 - R^C)\int_t^T \lambda_s^C e^{-\int_s^T r_u du}\mathbf{E}[(V(S,s) + \widehat{U}(S,s))^-]ds$$

$$-\int_t^T s_s^B e^{-\int_s^T r_u du}\mathbf{E}[(V(S,s) + \widehat{U}(S,s))^-]ds \tag{10.20}$$

Formula (10.20) contains two elements related to counterparty credit risk: the right-hand side of the first line shows the CVA (from C's perspective) and is the correction to the risk-free fair value V needed to remunerate the risk C bears for B's default (recall that value V is seen from C's perspective); the second line is the DVA (again, from C's perspective) and is the correction needed to remunerate the specular risk that B bears for C's default. Finally, the third line, shows the cost bank B has to bear when trying to replicate a long position in the contract, which is related to the funding spread it pays over the risk-free rate.

Since we are interested in studying the effectiveness of the replication strategy of $U(S,t)$ from bank B's perspective, and more specifically its DVA, we will focus on the DVA from this perspective (i.e., the quantity in the first line of (10.20)); in mirror-image fashion, the DVA from counterparty C's perspective (second line in (10.20)) is in fact the CVA for the bank.

Let us take a closer look at the sign of the quantities the bank has to hold in the portfolio to replicate $U(S,t)$ and hence to hedge its mirror-image position $-U(S,t)$ against counterparty C.[25] The CVA (or DVA from the counterparty's perspective; second line in (10.20)) can quite easily be replicated by selling an amount of bonds issued by counterparty C equal to $\alpha_t^C = (1 - R^C)\widehat{V}_t^-/P_t^C$: this can be achieved in a simple way by a repo agreement with a third party, or even in more heterodox ways such as buying credit protection via a CDS (with all the related caveats). The funding component of $U(S,t)$ (the third line) is also not very worrisome in terms of replicability: the bank has to issue new bonds to fundagainst any negative cash flow originated by setting up the replication portfolio. Provided there are no liquidity issues in the market, borrowing money from other operators should be a straightforward matter.

Replication of the DVA (i.e., the CVA from the counterparty's perspective; the first line in (10.20)) is trickier: it entails the bank going long a quantity of its own bonds equal to $\alpha_t^B = (1 - R^B)\widehat{V}_t^+/P_t^B$. Now, while going short its own bonds is relatively straightfor-

---

[24] A similar pricing formula, accounting for bilateral counterparty risk adjustment but not for funding rate, can be found in [32], although it is not derived by a dynamic replication argument. For a more general formula including collateralization and funding costs, see [102].

[25] The component $V(S,t)$ is dynamically replicated according to the well-known principles of the standard option pricing theory: this advocates holding a position Δ_t of the underlying asset at each time t, partially financed by shorting bonds or with a repo transaction, as is the case in the analysis we are conducting.

ward for the bank, since in the end it amounts to borrowing more money from the market, going long its own bond is not possible, although this is often overlooked in the literature. Actually, Burgard and Kjaer [42] also suggest an apparently simple way for the bank to go long its own bonds by buying back bonds issued in the past. Although in theory one cannot exclude the possibility that a bank has never issued bonds in the past, in practice the strategy is admittedly not very difficult to implement: in fact, banks regularly issue debt and there are many bonds in the market to buy back. So, is buyback a strategy to go long its own bonds for the bank? The answer is definitely not, and the reason is not because we object that is quite hard to find an issued bond in the market that exactly matches the features of bond P^B needed for the replication strategy. We claim there is a more fundamental reason the buyback strategy is not effective.

In fact, there is a difference between buying a security and being long it. We stressed that in Section 10.7.1, when we somewhat redundantly showed that buying back a short position clearly makes the net position nil for the dynamic replicator: if the replica prescribes a long position in a given security, the replicator should keep on buying until she is net long the security. But when a bank buys back its own bonds, it is simply reducing its short position or it is making it at most equal to zero, by not going long its own bonds (i.e., adding a positive amount in its portfolio). The gain process for the bonds bought back stops (since the quantity of the "bond" asset $\theta = 0$, using the notation in Section 10.7.1); from the time of the buyback on, the gain process simply sticks to the amount of profits or losses generated since the issuance of the bond and no other variation occurs. So, replication of the DVA (from the bank's perspective) simply does not happen since there is no actual contribution from the gain process of the bank's bonds. Despite the robustness of this statement, it hinges on the belief that it is not possible for the bank to go long its own bonds in any fashion. However, our statement may be subject to possible critiques that we both devise and rebut in the next section.

10.7.3   Objections to the statement "no long position in a bank's own bonds is possible"

As a first attack on the statement "No long position in a bank's own bonds is possible", we may object that despite it being true that the bank never really goes long its own bonds, if we consider the replication strategy as a closed system, then the bank is actually long the bond such that replication is effective. This objection is based on an "abstract concept of an abstract concept", as proposed by philosopher Emanuele Severino.[26] The long position of the bank in its bonds within the closed system "dynamic replication of its DVA" without considering the total net position of the bank within its balance sheet (i.e., the total of its assets and liabilities to which the "dynamic replication of its DVA" subsystem also belongs) is an abstract concept: being long in the subsystem means that a short position is opened somewhere else in the total "balance sheet" system, so as to preserve the zero position in the bank's own bonds at an aggregated level. So in the end the bank is long in the "dynamic replication of its DVA" subsystem and short somewhere else in the overall "balance sheet" system. Moreover, assuming the long position in bonds actually exists and produces effects is an abstract concept as well, since at an aggregated level the effects just offset each other.

---

[26] See [109, chapter 9].

In the end the bank cannot attain an effective long position in its own bonds, although it is possible at the subsystem level to assume this position. Nevertheless, it still has to be counterbalanced at the system level by an opposite position. This means that if replication of the DVA is formally attained in the "dynamic replication of its DVA" subsystem, in practice replication is simply paid by abating some assets or increasing some liabilities in the "balance sheet" system, so that the net total result is that the replication strategy ends up as a loss (in other words, as a cost) for the bank. This is simply due to the strength of logic consequences and with this in mind we will be better equipped to face another possible critique as well.[27]

The second, and somehow subtler, critique we may raise to the impossibility of having a long position in bonds is based on the "funding benefit" argument; that is: if the bank has money to buy back its own bonds issued in the past, then it gets a benefit in terms of the smaller funding costs it pays on outstanding debt. So, despite the critique implicitly accepting the statement that it is not possible for the bank to go long its bonds, it introduces the gains, or benefits, the bank obtains with a smaller outstanding debt. Funding benefits are also mentioned in [42] and [94], although in vague terms. To be completely honest, this argument does appear to hold water, but we have to investigate it further to ascertain its validity.

Granted, for the sake of argument, that the funding benefit really exists,[28] it is not clear how it is related to replication of the bank's DVA and how its variations actually track variations in DVA.

10.7.4 DVA replication by the funding benefit

Keeping our discussion in the previous section in mind, what is undeniable is if a bank has some cash and can buy back all or some of the bonds issued in the past, then it reduces the amount of debt. This is not precisely a funding benefit, which in our opinion should be defined as a saving of funding costs given a certain amount of debt, but can be loosely thought of as a benefit since the bank has to pay less interest, taken as an absolute value. So we loosely define funding benefit as deduction of the amount of paid interest that can be obtained by reducing total outstanding debt after buyback.

Since the replication strategy is formally self-financing, when it prescribes buying back a bank's own bonds, it is also generating the amount of cash needed to perform this. So we can be pretty sure that, as far as the DVA component is concerned, the bank has cash to buy back a quantity of its own bonds thus reducing its total outstanding debt. To investigate whether this amount of debt "missing" from the original total amount really contributes to replicating the DVA we need to to look at the entire bank's balance sheet and how assets and liabilities are originated.

Let us commence with a very basic situation: when the bank starts its activities at time 0, with an amount of capital E, deposited in an account $D_1 = E$. We observe the bank's activity at discrete time intervals of length T. At 0 the bank also issues an amount K of zero-coupon bonds P^B with unit face value and expiring at $3T$. Adopting the same notation introduced above, the amount of cash raised by the bank is $Ke^{-(r+s^B)3T}$ (recall

---

[27] In simpler and more heuristic terms, this has also been shown above. In what follows we will investigate the way in which the cost originating from DVA replication affects the bank's franchise negatively.

[28] We showed above that the funding benefit is little more than a badly posed concept since, given the amount of funding available, the bank is paying in any case its funding spread without any saving, or benefit.

that s^B is the bank's funding spread); this cash is used to buy K zero-coupon bonds P^Y, issued by a third party Y, with unit face value and expiring at $3T$. The third party has a funding spread s^Y such that the present value of the bond is $Ke^{-(r+s^Y)3T}$; if both bonds have the same funding spread, $s^B = s^Y$, then the money raised by the bank is enough to buy the bond from issuer Y.

For the moment we assume that the funding spread is due to some unspecified factors and make no attempt to link it to default risk, which in reality should be the first cause of its existence. We will very soon consider default risk explicitly in the following analysis, but for now we simply disregard it. Continuing with our assumption, we can then affirm that the bank is operating a very simple replication strategy for asset A_1, with the opposite sign used to hedge it, via issuance of its own bonds.

The marked-to–market balance sheet of the bank at time 0 looks like:[29]

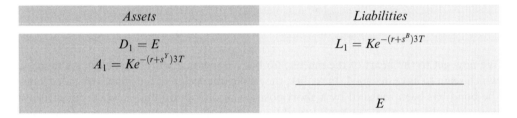

Assets	Liabilities
$D_1 = E$ $A_1 = Ke^{-(r+s^Y)3T}$	$L_1 = Ke^{-(r+s^B)3T}$
	E

Let us now assume one period T elapses and the bank closes a derivative contract. To make things more explicit and to avoid unnecessary complications (but in any case with no loss of generality), we suppose that bank B sells to counterparty C an option on some underlying S whose value to the latter is $\widehat{V} = V + \widehat{U}$ (this choice will allow us to exclude from the analysis the CVA for the bank, which is zero for short options); clearly, the option is worth the same to the bank but with the opposite sign. Since it has a negative value to bank B, the option is a liability; on the other hand, the premium paid by C increases the cash available to B and is deposited in deposits D_2. The balance sheet will then be:

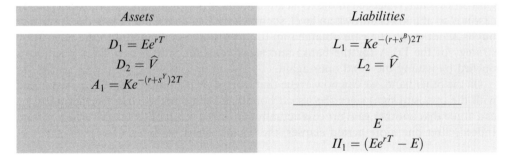

Assets	Liabilities
$D_1 = Ee^{rT}$ $D_2 = \widehat{V}$ $A_1 = Ke^{-(r+s^Y)2T}$	$L_1 = Ke^{-(r+s^B)2T}$ $L_2 = \widehat{V}$
	E $II_1 = (Ee^{rT} - E)$

Assets and liabilities accrue interest and a net profit $(Ee^{rT} - E)$ is earned between 0 and T. The bank immediately commences its dynamic replication strategy as well: for simplicity's sake we only focus on the DVA part (from the bank's perspective) of the

---

[29] We do not follow the suggestion we made above which considers the DVA of a contract as a cost to be deducted from equity, since our purpose here is to investigate whether DVA is actually a replicable quantity. Hence, we suspend our judgement on how best to consider it and each contract is written in the balance sheet at its trading price.

quantity $U(S,t)$ in (10.20) (i.e., the CVA from the counterparty's perspective), without considering the Δ-hedge with the underlying asset. We assume that quantity α^B of the bank's bond to buy back is exactly equal to K, or the amount of the bond outstanding issued at time 0. Obviously, to buy back the bond, the amount of available cash in D_2 is abated correspondingly so that the balance sheet reads as:

Assets	Liabilities
$D_1 = Ee^{rT}$	$L_1 = 0$
$D_2 = \hat{V} - Ke^{-(r+s^B)2T}$	$L_2 = \hat{V}$
$A_1 = Ke^{-(r+s^Y)2T}$	
	E
	$II_1 = (Ee^{rT} - E)$

We now get to the heart of the matter: no bond appears amongst the bank's liabilities, which seem to have declined. In reality, they have not declined, they have increased since the bond has been replaced by a short position in the option that is worth (negatively) even more. In any case, the bond issued to counterbalance asset A_1 no longer exists, and this is a fact: much as if the bank has a long position in the asset that does not need to be financed by cash, whose availability to the bank increased as is manifest by the amount in deposit D_2 that did not exist before. This can be termed "funding benefit", as suggested above; apparently, this makes it possible to have assets in the balance sheet without explicitly paying (or by paying fewer) funding costs.

We have already shown this saving is but an illusion. Anyway, we would like to check here whether this apparent saving is effective in the replication strategy. It turns out it could actually be effective if a certain set of circumstances are true. We have already stressed that when the bank buys back its own bonds, it is not really going long, but is simply making its former position nil, considering things at the balance sheet level. The gain process that is needed in the replication strategy is only abstractly produced (just in case it is so at a lower subsystem level, such as a trading desk), but in practice it stops at buyback (although the gain obtained up to this instant is immaterial to the replication strategy of the DVA for the bank) and stays constant until a new short position is opened by issuing the bond once again.

On the other hand, we can now argue that asset A_1 is no longer hedged (i.e., replicated with the opposite sign) since the issued bond has been bought back. Furthermore, we can argue that another gain process actually starts as a result of this uncovered position. Indeed, after one more period elapses, the balance sheet reads as:

Assets	Liabilities
$D_1 = Ee^{r2T}$ $D_2 = (\widehat{V} - Ke^{-(r+s^B)2T})e^{rT}$ $A_1 = Ke^{-(r+s^Y)T}$	$L_1 = 0$ $L_2 = \widehat{V}$

$$E$$
$$II_1 = (Ee^{r2T} - E)$$
$$II_2 = (\widehat{V} - Ke^{-(r+s^B)2T})(e^{rT} - 1)$$
$$P\&L = K[e^{-(r+s^Y)T} - e^{-(r+s^Y)2T}]$$

The amount of capital deposited in D_1 accrues interest II_1, so that related profits increase; interest II_2 that has accrued on deposits D_2 generates other profits $((\widehat{V} - Ke^{-(r+s^B)2T})(e^{rT} - 1))$. We further assume that the value of the option stays constant under a certain set of circumstances, so that it does not contribute to the period's P&L.[30]

The balance sheet shows we are left with a profit equal to $K[e^{-(r+s^Y)T} - e^{-(r+s^Y)2T}]$ which would not be generated if the bond issued by the bank had not been bought back. In fact, the issued bond would generate a perfectly counterbalancing loss $K[e^{-(r+s^B)T} - e^{-(r+s^B)2T}]$ (since $s^B = s^Y$) and the total effect on the balance sheet would be zero.

On the other hand, and for the same reason of equal funding spreads, the profit appearing in this case is the same as the profit that the bank would earn if it had a "true" long position in its own bonds.[31] If the replication strategy indicates a quantity $\alpha_T^B = \Delta \widehat{V}_T / P_T^B = K$, then in equation (10.18) (recalling we are working in a discrete time setting)

$$\alpha_T^B \Delta P_T^B = \alpha_T^B \Delta P_T^Y = K[e^{-(r+s^B)T} - e^{-(r+s^B)2T}] = K[e^{-(r+s^Y)T} - e^{-(r+s^Y)2T}]$$

so the gain process is in reality working (although it is generated by an asset different than the bank's bond) and the replication strategy for the DVA (from the bank's perspective) is actually operating as expected. So, is the "funding benefit" argument correct? Should we then admit that the replication strategy suggested in [42] is right and that we were wrong above when we negated its effectiveness? As we hinted above, things are subtler than they may appear. Let us analyse the hidden assumptions under which the replication strategy is working.

First, we stated earlier that the profit earned after the bank's bonds were bought back is equal to the profit that the bank would have earned had it been able to actually buy its own bonds – this was easily proved in the example above. We assumed a constant spread, though, for both bank B and issuer Y: this is the reason we can be sure that the profit generated by bond P^Y is exactly equal to that generated by bond P^B. We can relax

---

[30] We could replace "under a certain set of circumstances" by "if the option were hedged": in this case we should include in the balance sheet the underlying asset quantity dealt for hedging purposes and related cash movements. In order to simplify the balance sheet we omitted these items and assumed the option as not fully hedged.

[31] Since the option is not fully replicated, as assumed above, the replication of DVA generates a gain different from zero. We made this choice to highlight the contribution to the replica of the DVA of the long position in asset A_1, which mimics a theoretically long bank bond position.

the assumption of a constant spread by introducing for both issuers a more realistic time-dependent spread s_t^I, $I \in \{B, Y\}$. However, in this case we must make sure that, if the two spreads are commanded by a deterministic function of time, then they are commanded by the same function; alternatively, if funding spreads are stochastic processes, they have to follow the same dynamics *and* the same paths: starting from the same value, they evolve in the future precisely in the same way.

Second, we now have to explicitly consider the possibility of default by the bank and issuer Y: actually, the spread simply indicates that this probability is not zero. In an environment where there is no recovery upon default and no liquidity premium or intermediation costs, it is well known that $s^I = \lambda^I$, where λ^I is (as above) the instantaneous default intensity for issuer I. Assume now that the condition for the identity of time functions for deterministic spreads, or of the perfect correlation of stochastic spreads, is fulfilled. Then, equality $\alpha_t^B dP_t^B = \alpha_t^B dP_t^Y$ is guaranteed only if either bank B's or issuer Y's default occurs in the interval of time T. Either default, though, affects the effectiveness of the replication strategy in different ways.

In fact, if the bank goes bankrupt before issuer Y, then the replication strategy would still work, although it will be very likely stopped, as the rest of the bank's activity and the default procedure would kick in to start to pay creditors, if possible. So, in this case right up to the time of default of the bank, the replication strategy works and afterwards it no longer needs to work so that issuer Y may default at any time without material consequences (for the limited scope of the replication, of course).

If issuer Y's default occurs first, then the replication strategy fails completely and replication is not attained. Thus, when default is considered, another condition we must add to those above is that issuer Y's default has to occur after bank B's default. We can slightly relax this assumption and accept that they may happen together: in this case replication is attained up to the last instant needed by the bank and hence has no negative consequences on strategy.

Armed with these results, we can recapitulate the conditions under which the "funding benefit" argument is valid and DVA (from the bank's perspective) is effectively replicated:

1. The spread over the risk-free rate (the funding rate) of the asset and of the bank's bond must start at the same value at inception of the replication strategy and they must be driven by the same deterministic function of time or they must be commanded by two identical, perfectly matching stochastic processes.
2. The times of the default of bank B and issuer Y must be perfectly correlated so that when either defaults, so does the other.

These conditions are trivially fulfilled when issuer Y coincides with bank B, but we know that in this case it is impossible for the bank to go long its own bonds. In other cases conditions can only be imperfectly, or not at all, fulfilled and the replication strategy will not be effective.

Moreover, it should be stressed that the analysis presented refers to a very simplified situation, where the "bond" asset A_1 can be clearly isolated from other assets and its variations can be compared with those of the bank's DVA. In reality, the composition of assets is pretty complicated, such that it would be an extremely hard task identifying which bond has to be considered to measure the funding benefit for a given derivative contract.

10.7.5 DVA replication and bank's franchise

In bank management books, "franchise" is defined as the value the bank is able to create from its branch network, its systems and people and from its customer base and brand. According to the widely supported "special information hypothesis" proposed in [19], banks play a unique role in financial markets because they have private information about costumers unavailable to other, non-bank lenders (see also [22]). A different, not necessarily alternative, view is that the franchise value of banks originates in their provision of liquidity and payment services to their customers. That is, banks are special institutions not because of their privileged information with respect to other lenders but because they can grant funds more easily than other economic operators. The hypothesis is presented and tested in [113].

However originated, banks create a franchise if they are able to buy assets yielding more than required by the risks they embed or if they are able to issue liabilities at a level lower than their fair value. This can be done, for instance, by trading in assets mispriced in the market: the franchise value of the bank is increased by the skills[32] of the traders and asset managers in this case. Although it is quite rare, sometimes in fact financial markets work efficiently, as happens when liquid assets are traded. For example, let us go back to the case we have analysed in the previous section: if we assume that the spread over the risk-free rate yielded by bond P^Y is due only to default risk and that recovery is zero, so that $s^Y = \lambda^Y$ (the notation is the same as above), then if the market prices the risks correctly, the expected return over a small period dt is:

$$\mathbf{E}[dP_t^Y] = \mathbf{E}[(r_t + s_t^Y)P_t^Y dt - dJ^Y P_t^Y] = r_t P_t^Y dt$$

In this case the bank franchise does not really increase, even if the spread over the risk-free rate is positive. On the contrary, the bank is actually losing money on an expectation basis, since the funding spread on bank's liabilities has to be paid anyway, so that they instantaneously accrue interest at rate $r_t + s_t^B$ with certainty[33] and asset $A_1 = P^Y$ yields just an expected risk-free rate r_t.

Another way to create the franchise is to charge a margin over the fair rate that remunerates risks and costs and provides for a profit, when the bank lends money to clients that have weaker bargaining power: especially retail ones that do not have easy access to capital markets. Going back to the case above, let us assume that bond P^Y is issued by a very particular obligor who is default risk free and does not have access to the capital market but can borrow money from bank B. In this case the bank may apply spread m over the risk-free rate which is simply a margin and not remuneration for the default risk. This means that expected return on asset $A_1 = P^Y$ is $r + m$ on an expectation basis. So, if $m > s^B$ then the bank increases its franchise since it is able to generate profits in the future on a sound basis covering its funding costs. This is also true of a bank lending money to defaultable obligors if it is able to charge a spread $s^Y = \lambda^Y + s^B + m'$ that remunerates costs and risks (i.e., the bank's funding spread s^B and default risk λ^Y) and includes a positive margin m'.

---

[32] A large part of skills consists of luck. Actually, luck is the greatest skill a trader could be gifted with, in our opinion.
[33] As discussed above, the bank should consider itself a risk-free operator when evaluating its investments and when drawing its balance sheet.

When we considered the two conditions under which DVA (from the bank's perspective) can be effectively replicated, we mentioned that the default times of the bank and of obligor Y must be perfectly correlated. This condition is tantamount, from the bank's perspective, to assuming the possibility to buy an asset that is default risk free and yet yields more than the risk-free rate. In fact, when bank B does not default, neither does the obligor, hence when pricing the asset issued by Y and evaluating it against the costs and risks borne by the bank, the obligor's default does not need to be considered.[34]

Under these conditions, if spread $s^Y > s^B$ then the bank actually creates a franchise, notwithstanding the asset being defaultable. If $s^Y = s^B$ then the bank just covers its funding costs without any profit margin. This is a very hypothetic and hardly realistic situation, but should it happen then the bank's power to apply this rate over the risk-free rate (which could also produce a franchise) is used to replicate DVA, thus confirming what we said above when we affirmed that replication of the DVA would end up, keeping the entire balance sheet in mind, as a cost that has to be covered by a margin above the risk-free rate on some other contracts.

Since the funding spread process of obligor Y and bank B, jointly with perfect correlation between the times of default of both, are conditions very unlikely matched in reality, the obligor's bankruptcy has to be considered in the evaluation process and spread s^Y is the remuneration for Y's default risk. So this spread cannot be used for replication of DVA.

On the other hand, if the bank is able to apply a margin over the rate needed to remunerate default risk, so as to compensate funding costs s^B, this margin can be effective in replicating the DVA, although the bank should be able to update it frequently, so as to track variations of its own funding spread. In other words, assets cannot be fixed rate bonds and spreads have to be reviewed not only to reflect the obligor's default risk but also that of the bank.

Moreover, the bank is here using its ability to finance some investments to cover losses represented by DVA. So DVA is formally hedged, but the cost has been indirectly charged to other business areas and eventually, considering the total level of funding available, the bank will always bear the same total funding cost.

In the end, should the bank receive some cash on closing a derivative contract, this can be used to buy back a quantity of the bank's own bonds. In this case the balance sheet shrinks, because an asset (the cash received) is used to abate liabilities (the bank's bonds): given the reduced amount of liabilities, there is a smaller cost to pay, and this will be equal to the DVA of the derivative contract (under the stated conditions). Were the bank able to buy assets yielding more than the risk-free rate on a risk-adjusted basis, with bonds issued before closing the derivative contract, and this extra yield was enough to cover funding costs over the risk-free rate of the bank's bonds, then it would be enough to cover the cost of the DVA too. There is nothing special nor a funding benefit here, simply reduced liabilities (balancing reduced assets) produce smaller funding to compensate for increased DVA costs.

The problem of considering rather naively the DVA as a funding benefit stands out more clearly when derivative contracts do not produce positive cash flows, as when the bank deals a forward or a swap contract, for example. In these kinds of contracts, with both parties starting at the zero value, DVA can either be paid immediately to the

---

[34] This is a consequence of the fact that the bank's default does not need to be considered when it evaluates investments.

Table 10.1. Hedging of a short forward contract by a sell-and-buyback repo contract: bank position in the asset and cash of the bank at the start of the contract and at expiry

Contract		Time	
		0	T
Forward	Cash	—	$+\widehat{F}$
	Asset	—	-1
Repo	Cash	S	$-Se^{rT} = -F$
	Asset	-1	1
Spot	Cash	$-S$	—
	Asset	1	—
Net	Cash	0	$\widehat{F} - F < 0$
	Asset	0	0

counterparty, and there is no way to treat it differently than a cost, or it can be embedded in the value of the contract by modifying the fair forward or swap price so that it is worse than the risk-free equivalent for the bank.[35] In this second case the bank could include the value of the contract in the balance sheet without separating the DVA component and treating it as a cost. However, according to the funding benefit argument, it should be considered replicable by a buyback of its own bonds as explained.

The impossibility of buying back bonds and then considering the DVA as a funding benefit is easily checked in this case, and we will show why: assume the bank sold asset S forward at future time T to a risk-free counterparty and that the fair risk-free forward price is $F = Se^{rT}$. Only the default risk of the bank has to be included in the valuation, so that the new forward price making the value of the contract nil at inception, which also includes the DVA, will be some $\widehat{F} < F$.

In Table 10.1 we show how to hedge the forward contract and related positions in the underlying asset and in cash at the start and at expiry. Replication is attained with a strategy whereby the bank sells and buys back asset S by a repo transaction also expiring at T (we work under the assumption made above that the repo rate clashes with the risk-free rate). To deliver the underlying to the repo counterparty, the bank buys the asset on the spot market using the cash it receives from the repo sell leg. Then, at contract expiry the bank has to buy the underlying back from the repo counterparty: it will pay $Se^{rT} = F$ against receiving one unit of the underlying, which will be delivered to the forward counterparty receiving an amount of cash equal to the forward price $\widehat{F}$. The net result is that the bank loses an amount of money $\widehat{F} - F$ that exactly equals the DVA.[36]

A bank strictly following the dynamic strategy indicated in [42] should also buy back a quantity of its own bonds, but since in a forward contract no cash is received at

---

[35] We have already presented a simplified example of how a forward fair price would be modified when DVA is included in the value of the contract.

[36] Things are in reality more complex since the repo rate is different from the risk-free rate when trying to account for the default risk of the bank (in the sell and buyback we are considering) and the possibility that the underlying asset price is not going to fully cover the amount of cash lent by the counterparty. We disregard all this here since it is beyond the scope of the analysis.

inception by the bank, the purchase can only be financed by resorting to a loan in the market, hence generating the ineffectual situation of replacing bank debt with equivalent bank debt, which produces no result at all.

Let us clarify matters by considering the DVA of the derivative contracts and of the issued bonds (for which DVA is exactly the funding cost) as costs reducing equity. If positive cash flows are received for whatever reason by the bank, then it can shrink the balance sheet by buying back outstanding debt, thus paying less interest on remaining liabilities. In this case, assets generating an extra yield covering the funding costs of bonds can be used to cover the DVA of derivative contracts, once they are bought back. If no positive cash flow occurs from derivative transactions, the balance sheet cannot be shrunk and both the DVA and the funding costs of the outstanding debt are costs to be paid in the future.

In conclusion, if we disregard the need, hardly met in practice, to update the spread for assets continuously and keep in mind that positive cash flows are not always received at inception, a bank that does not recognize the DVA as a cost when booking its derivative contracts, based on the false idea that it can be replicated, is implicitly using the margins that it is able (if it is ever able to do so) to charge on other products (typically, the banking book) to cover costs generated by derivatives desks (trading book). Simple buyback of its own bonds is not enough to justify the "funding benefit" argument if it is unsure as to which of the assets of other contracts is covering funding costs.

So, if a financial institution comprises only an investment bank arm trading in the financial markets, the derivatives desk would rely on the profits of other desks to cover DVA, so that the bank is destroying the franchise (in the event one is created).

If the institution also operates as a retail bank, the derivatives desk would rely on the ability of desks dealing contracts in the banking book to include funding costs as margins above the risk-free rate plus credit spreads in the pricing. Moreover, if the bank's spread is volatile, these margins should be reviewed frequently to align them with the current funding spread paid by the bank. All this hardly happens in reality so it is more likely that even in this case the bank would end up either by destroying value or by just covering total funding costs.

If the bank allows traders to implement replication strategies for DVA but fails to recognise this quantity as a cost, there are two immediate negative consequences.

First, when traders implement replication strategies, the bank uses margins generated in profitable businesses to cover the losses caused by the derivatives business losing money. In some cases this loss can be compensated by shrinking the balance sheet with cash flows received. So, at best the bank's franchise is not increasing; at worst it is actually being destroyed. This could be a very long and unclear process, especially when long-dated contracts are involved (e.g., a swap book), but the "bleeding" will be inexorable.

Second, traders (and possibly salespeople) think they can hedge the DVA and do not consider it as a cost, so no attempt is made to transfer it to other clients when dealing with them. If the bank is unable to avoid paying DVA on some trades or to charge the DVA of other deals that it has to pay on these trades, then the derivatives business is a lossmaker, so it is best to close it. This is equivalent to the bank lending money when it is not able to transfer its funding spreads to clients: sooner or later, the bank ends up losing money.

10.8 RECAPITULATION OF RESULTS

In the following table we recapitulate the main quantities studied above, their nature and the relationships existing amongst them.

Quantity	Nature
CVA = −DVA	Compensation for the counterparty risk borne by a party, given the exposure, the probability of default and loss given default.
DVA	Cost paid by a party that worsens the contract's conditions for a risk-free counterparty, given the exposure, the probability of default and loss given default.
IC	Cost paid by a party for not having direct access to the capital market.
LPC	Cost paid by a party for the premium required in the market to provide liquidity.
FC = DVA + LPC + IC	Cost paid by a party over the risk-free rate to raise funds. Some components may be nil.

10.9 ACCOUNTING STANDARD AND DVA

International accounting standards (IAS and FAS) agree on the inclusion of DVA in the fair value of the liabilities of a bank.[37] In other words, revaluation of liabilities taking into account the credit risk of the issuer (or of the counterparty with negative NPV in a derivative contract) is possible.

IASC [51], the board setting IAS accounting standards, tries to justify the inclusion of DVA as a liability reduction by saying:

"However, the Board noted that because financial statements are prepared on a going concern basis, credit risk affects the value at which liabilities could be repurchased or settled. Accordingly, the fair value of a financial liability reflects the credit risk relating to that liability. Therefore, it decided to include credit risk relating to a financial liability in the fair value measurement of that liability for the following reasons:
(a) entities realize changes in fair value, including fair value attributable to the liability's credit risk, for example, by renegotiating or repurchasing liabilities or by using derivatives;
(b) changes in credit risk affect the observed market price of a financial liability and hence its fair value;
(c) it is difficult from a practical standpoint to exclude changes in credit risk from an observed market price; and
(d) the fair value of a financial liability (i.e., the price of that liability in an exchange between a knowledgeable, willing buyer and a knowledgeable, willing seller) on initial recognition reflects its credit risk.

---

[37] The expression "debit value adjustment" or its acronym DVA is never used in the documents of accounting standards but, despite being worded differently, its inclusion in the balance sheet as a reduction of the current value of the liabilities is clear.

The Board believes that it is inappropriate to include credit risk in the initial fair value measurement of financial liabilities, but not subsequently."

This is the basis for conclusion (BC89) of the IAS 39 document: needless to say we consider the entire assertion to be weak. The first part astoundingly cites the "going concern basis" as justifying (also) a reduction of liabilities due to the credit spread of the issuer: we think we have demonstrated at length why DVA inclusion should be a reduction of net equity, which also entails a reduction in the value of equity when the credit standing worsens.

Moreover, point (a) is simply false as far as credit spreads are concerned,[38] except in the part referring to "repurchasing liabilities", but in this case it is unlikely to have a widening of credit spreads (and hence a reduction of the value in liabilities) and to be cash-rich enough to buy back debt. Realizing revaluation profits "by using derivatives" means the bank selling CDS protection on its own debt, which is clearly not possible. Renegotiating debt means that that the bank is trying to update the interest it is paying on its debt, so as to get the new value of liabilities more in line with the notional value: from a financial perspective this new situation is exactly the same as the initial one.

Point (b) is a truism that does not need comment. Point (c) is probably the most sensible statement, at least it attempts to find a practical reason. Point (d) is again a truism. The last statement is frankly not even worth a comment, given its complete lack of rational sense (better, lack of comprehension of financial contract valuation).

According to [27], the board setting FASB standards:

"The reporting entity should consider the effect of its credit risk (credit standing) on the fair value of the liability in all periods in which the liability is measured at fair value because those who might hold the entity's obligations as assets would consider the effect of the entity's credit standing in determining the prices they would be willing to pay."

Revaluation of liabilities including the entity's credit spread is then supported with claims such as:

"Like all measurements at fair value, fresh start measurement of liabilities can produce unfamiliar results when compared with reporting the liabilities on an amortized basis. A change in credit standing represents a change in the relative positions of the two classes of claimants (shareholders and creditors) to an entity's assets. If the credit standing diminishes, the fair value of creditors' claims diminishes. The amount of shareholders' residual claim to the entity's assets may appear to increase, but that increase probably is offset by losses that may have occasioned the decline in credit standing. Because shareholders usually cannot be called on to pay a corporation's liabilities, the amount of their residual claims approaches, and is limited by, zero. Thus, a change in the position of borrowers necessarily alters the position of shareholders, and vice versa."

Even in this case, although there is tentative justification on a microeconomic basis, the

---

[38] As noted above, a change in market rates implying a reduction in the value of liabilities is admissible in our framework and could even be monetized by a buyback of issued debt. So, when change in the current value of liabilities is due to factors other than credit risk, it can be assumed that revaluation profit/loss can be recognized in the balance sheet as a correction of the fair value of liabilities.

very slippery ground it stands on is patently indicated by the wording "but that increase probably is offset by losses that may have occasioned the decline in credit standing". Beyond that, it is rather irrational to consider the value of liabilities from the creditors' perspective within the balance sheet, which represents the value of the company from the shareholders' perspective. To the debtor, the value of the liability is just the present value (discounted at the risk-free rate) of the notional amount (thus strictly adhering to the going concern principle). The comment "change in the position of borrowers necessarily alters the position of shareholders"[39] is true, but the balance sheet should report just the latter position and not mix both together. What is more, the correct representation of the bank's value to the shareholders is given if DVA is considered as a cost (loss) abating net equity.

DVA should be considered a cost to derivatives portfolios and as such should be deducted from equity.

In conclusion, we believe current accounting standards are not firmly grounded and they allow the accounting conduct of banks to produce very misleading information for those investors relying on balance sheet data. Hopefully, what we have shown above will contribute to better understanding of how to properly mark-to-market liabilities and how to represent costs related to the credit standing of the debtor (which are simply costs – not gains, as they appear according to existing accounting standards and practices). This is in accordance with the Basel Committee on Banking Supervision,[40] which not only explicitly forbids considering variations in DVA as P&L, but also makes clear that the DVA of derivative contracts at inception is a cost to be deducted from bank equity.

10.10   DISTINCTION BETWEEN PRICE AND VALUE

The difference between "price" and "value" has been investigated in economic theory, but economists (whether classical, neoclassical, or Marxist) typically reserve these terms for commodities. When a financial contract is not executed by simply (almost) immediately delivering an asset (in which case it can be assimilated to purchase/sale of a commodity) but, on the contrary, implies a given performance by possibly both parties for an extended duration, then price and value should be defined in a more refined way.

We define the "price" (from either party's perspective) of a derivative contract as the terms that both parties agree upon when closing the deal. These take into account the present value of expected profits and losses, while considering all the costs and losses due to counterparty credit risk, funding and liquidity premiums, for both parties. When both parties have even bargaining power, they have to acknowledge all the risks and costs the other party bears, so that the final price includes total (net) risks and costs borne by both parties.

On the other hand, we define the "production costs" (to one of the parties) of a derivative contract as the present value of the costs paid to attain the intermediate and final payoff until expiry, while considering the costs and losses due to counterparty credit risk, funding and liquidity premiums, related to that specific party. Production

---

[39] The FASB very likely meant "creditors" instead of "borrowers", otherwise the assertion makes little sense. Our interpretation is likely confirmed because the paragraph is referring to the "two classes of claimants (shareholders and creditors)". The borrower is the bank, which clearly has no claim on its own liabilities.
[40] www.bis.org/press/p120725b.htm

costs, assuming no other margin is charged, are how much the contract is worth to the party or, in other words, they are the "value" of the contract.

The price of a contract is an *objective* quantity, given by the level at which the two parties agree to trade the contract; the value of the contract is a *subjective* measure and is given by how much a contract is worth to one party. For either party the value of a contract should exactly equal the price – had it enough bargaining power – to completely transfer production costs (excluding other extra profit margins) to the counterparty, without recognizing during setting of the contract's terms the costs and risks borne by the other party. When the bargaining process involves counterparties with even bargaining power, then the value of the contract to each of them will be lower than the price as they are both yielding a share of the value to cover each other's risks and costs. The price and the value of a contract are also the same when both parties operate in a perfect and frictionless market, where there are no transaction costs and counterparty risks. In fact, in this case they will agree a production cost for the contract that is the same for both.

We have shown that DVA cannot be replicated using a dynamic strategy nor can it under very unrealistic assumptions justify the "funding benefit" argument. This does not mean that we do not have to consider bilateral counterparty risk when pricing a derivative contract. Neglecting transaction costs, which in practice further add to the final price of the contract, the bargaining process results in each party trying to include the relevant risks it bears in the price, so each party considers adjustments due to counterparty credit risk or CVA. This quantity can be replicated without any theoretical and practical hindering, since it is possible to trade short bonds issued by the other party. From the other's party perspective, the CVA is the DVA and since it cannot be replicated with a suitable dynamic strategy, it has to be considered a cost in the dealing price.

When the bank wants to compute the value of the contract, it has to consider itself a risk-free operator. The same is true for the counterparty. This does not mean that funding costs are not considered in the evaluation process, simply one's own default has to be excluded: this leads to cancelling DVA in the bilateral counterparty credit risk component from the traded price to determine the value to the party.

Let CVA^B be credit value adjustment due to the default risk of bank B, which equals DVA^B or DVA seen from the bank's perspective; analogously, let CVA^C be CVA due to the default risk of counterparty C, equal to DVA^C or DVA seen from the counterparty's perspective. Since each party considers itself default risk-free in the evaluation process, the value of the contract to C is:

$$V - \text{CVA}^B$$

On the other hand, the value of the contract to B is:

$$-(V + \text{CVA}^C)$$

Let us consider the absolute value of the price of the contract and take the absolute values of the contract to each party. Both parties may acknowledge that the other party bears counterparty risk related to its default, even if when determining the value of the contract they exclude their own default risk. In practice, each party knows that it may be forced to yield something with respect to the value of the contract.

In other words, each party will trade at a price that includes a fraction (possibly all) of the CVA charged by the counterparty or, put another way, a price including a fraction of a quantity that cannot be replicated given by its DVA. Let $0 \leq \gamma^B \leq 1$ be the fraction of $\mathrm{CVA}^B \equiv \mathrm{DVA}^B$ acknowledged to the bank by the counterparty, and γ^C the fraction of $\mathrm{CVA}^C \equiv \mathrm{DVA}^C$ acknowledged to the counterparty by the bank. The trading price p will then be:

$$V - \mathrm{CVA}^B \leq p \leq V + \mathrm{CVA}^C$$

where

$$p = V - \gamma^B \mathrm{CVA}^B + \gamma^C \mathrm{DVA}^C \equiv V + \gamma^C \mathrm{CVA}^C - \gamma^B \mathrm{DVA}^B$$

When both parties yield 100% of their respective DVA to the other party (i.e., both parties can fully charge CVA and fully accept the other party's CVA), then we have traded price p equal to the price including full bilateral counterparty risk and the pricing formula would be the same as in [32]. The pricing formula would also be the same as the one derived in [42] and shown above, if the funding costs related to implementation of the replication stretegy (third line in equation (10.20)) are ignored. This price can be defined as the fair dealing price.

Funding costs are specific to each party and come about from the same default risk as the DVA. If we also consider funding costs, then the value to each counterparty would be even farther away from the fair price at which they can deal in the market. Denoting by FC^B the present value of funding costs paid by bank B in replicating the contract and, analogously, by FC^C the present value of funding costs paid by counterparty C, we can generalize the bounds within which the price of the contract deals:

$$V - \mathrm{CVA}^B - \mathrm{FC}^C \leq p \leq V + \mathrm{CVA}^C + \mathrm{FC}^B$$

and the dealing price of the contract p is now:

$$p = V - \gamma^B \mathrm{CVA}^B + \gamma^C \mathrm{DVA}^C - \zeta^C \mathrm{FC} + \zeta^B \mathrm{FC}^B$$

$$\equiv V + \gamma^C \mathrm{CVA}^C - \gamma^B \mathrm{DVA}^B - \zeta^C \mathrm{FC} + \zeta^B \mathrm{FC}^B$$

ζ^C and ζ^B are the fraction of the present value of funding costs borne by counterparty C and bank B acknowledged by, respectively, bank B and counterparty C.

To conclude, when default risk is considered, even in the absence of transaction costs, a unique value fair to both counterparties cannot be determined. The fair dealing price, if attained during the bargaining process, would in any case be at a level different from the values to both parties. All adjustments relating to counterparty risk can be replicated by both parties, but this does not mean that any adjustment can be replicated by any party: in fact, the DVA of each party can be replicated only by the other party, for which it is the CVA.

The ultimate conclusion is that derivatives trading, amongst professionals with equal bargaining power and without credit mitigation mechanisms, is a lossmaker for banks unless they also trade with weaker parties to whom they can transfer DVA-related costs (and funding costs).

Cost of liquidity and fund transfer pricing

11.1 INTRODUCTION

In Chapter 7 we presented an approach to derive the term structure of available funding (TSFu) given the funding sources and liquidity buffer needed to cope with gap risk on rollover dates. In this chapter we design a consistent framework to build the funding (interest rate) curve of a bank, as a mix of the costs of different funding sources entering the TSFu, and we indicate a methodology on how to properly include risks related to refunding activity in the cost of funds transferred from the treasury department to business units to buy assets.

To this end, we first introduce a brief overview of fund transfer pricing (FTP) principles, then we sketch a stylized bank's balance sheet, so that in a single-period setting we can clearly disentangle the several cost and risk components entering the fair pricing of assets, such as loans. We show the single building blocks that make up the price of an asset, including market, credit and liquidity costs (along the lines sketched in Chapter 10). We focus on a theoretical framework to quantify funding costs and gauge funding risk. Finally, we show how to apply the framework in practice.

11.2 PRINCIPLES OF TRANSFER PRICING

When a bank wants to invest in a given asset, it has to calculate its value. We showed in Chapter 10 a general approach to identify funding costs as well as the profit the bank can expect to make (on a risk-adjusted basis). We now expand the analysis by considering a more complex structure of funding sources and by including unexpected costs of market and credit risk as well. We present here a simplified single-period framework to introduce the basic principles of transfer pricing.

11.2.1 Balance sheet

Assume that we are at time $t = 0$ and that the bank will end all activities in one year. The bank's balance sheet is shown in Table 11.1.

There are two assets, A_0 and A_1: A_0 is a risk-free bond B yielding $i_0 = r$ and A_1 is an investment I yielding i_1 (e.g., a loan). On the liabilities' side there is equity and another three kinds of liability L_1, L_2, L_3 (e.g., long-term and short-term debt), each one yielding, respectively, interest $l_j = r + s^j$, for $j = 1, \ldots, 3$; additionally, there is equity, indicated by L_0.

The share of equity $L_0 = E$ (capital allocation) invested in the risk-free investment $A_0 = B$, is $1 - \varepsilon$, whereas share ε is invested in the other asset A_1. The return on capital

Table 11.1. Bank's stylized balance sheet

Assets	Liabilities
$A_0 = B$	$L_1 = SD$
$A_1 = I$	$L_2 = LTD$
	$L_3 = STD$
	$L_0 = E$

required by stockholders is e: this is the rate at which the capital invested in the bank's activity is expected to be remunerated.

Considering the participation of equity in funding the investment, the following constraints hold:

$$\sum_{j=1}^{3} L_j(t_0) = L = A_1(t_0) - \varepsilon E = (1 - f)A_1(t_0) \tag{11.1}$$

where $f = \varepsilon \frac{E}{A_1(t_0)}$ is the fraction of the asset financed by capital, and

$$(1 - \varepsilon)E = A_0(t_0) = B(t_0) \tag{11.2}$$

11.2.2 Bank's profits and losses

At the end of the year the assets will be sold back and they produce total profits/losses:

$$\begin{aligned} PL_A &= rB(t_0) + i_1 A_1(t_0) + (A_1(t_1) - A_1(t_0)) + (B(t_1) - B(t_0)) \\ &= r(1 - \varepsilon)E + i_1 A_1 + (A_1(t_1) - A_1(t_0)) + (B(t_1) - B(t_0)) \end{aligned} \tag{11.3}$$

where we used the constraint in (11.2).

As for liabilities, they will be bought back (minus equity) at the end of the year and they generate total profits/losses:

$$PL_L = -\sum_{j=1}^{3}(r + s_j)L_j - eE - \sum_{j=1}^{3}(L_j(t_1) - L_j(t_0)) \tag{11.4}$$

The addend $(A_1(t_0) - A_1(t_1))$ in (11.3) can be positive or negative: losses in the investment can be due to possible default of the bank's obligor (or more generally, bank's counterparty). Assuming that PD is the probability of default of the obligor and that ℓ is the stochastic loss suffered by the bank, we have that credit losses can be written as:

$$CL = \bar{\ell}A_1 + (\ell^U - \bar{\ell})A_1 = \bar{\ell}A_1 + CVAR_{A_1} \tag{11.5}$$

where $\bar{\ell}$ is the average (expected) L_{GD} (i.e., $L_{GD} \times PD$), ℓ^U is the maximum L_{GD}, calculated at some degree of confidence according to some credit model and $CVAR_{A_1}$ is the credit VaR (i.e., unexpected loss). We can alternatively write equation

(11.5) as

$$\mathrm{CL} = \mathrm{CVA}_{A_1} + \mathrm{CVAR}_{A_1} \qquad (11.6)$$

Average credit loss $\bar{\ell}A_1$ (which is CVA in a loan)[1] is a productive risk[2] and should be compensated by spread s^{A_1}, applied to the notional A_1, determined as:

$$s^{A_1} = \mathrm{PD} \times \mathrm{L_{GD}} \qquad (11.7)$$

where $\mathrm{L_{GD}}$ is the percentage loss upon default and we assume that interest is fully recovered. Unexpected credit loss (or credit VaR) is covered by economic capital, or fraction ϕ of the equity, since typically no credit instrument is available in the market to hedge this risk.[3]

The other possible variations included in $(A_1(t_0) - A_1(t_1))$, and in the addends $(B(t_1) - B(t_0))$ (in equation (11.3)) and $\sum_{j=1}^{3}(L_j(t_1) - L_j(t_0))$ (in equation (11.4)), represent profits/losses due to changes in the market value of assets and liabilities from the start t_0 to the end of the year t_1:[4]

$$\mathrm{ML} = [(\overline{A}(t_1) - A(t_0)) + (\overline{B}(t_1) - B(t_0)) - \sum_{j=1}^{3}(\overline{L}_j(t_1) - L_j(t_0))]$$

$$+ [(A^{\alpha}(t_1) - \overline{A}(t_1)) + (B^{\alpha}(t_1) - \overline{B}(t_1)) - \sum_{j=1}^{3}(L_j^{\alpha}(t_1) - \overline{L}_j(t_1))] \qquad (11.8)$$

where $\overline{A}$, $\overline{B}$ and $\overline{L}_j$ are expected values at t_1 for the risky asset, risk-free investment and liability j, whereas $A^{\alpha}(t_1)$, $B^{\alpha}(t_1)$ and $L_j^{\alpha}(t_1)$ are the values for the same variables computed at confidence level α. Expected market loss is indicated by $\mathrm{EML} = [(\overline{A}(t_1) - A(t_0)) + (\overline{B}(t_1) - B(t_0)) - \sum_{j=1}^{3}(\overline{L}_j(t_1) - L_j(t_0))]$ and unexpected market loss (i.e., market VaR) by $\mathrm{MVAR} = [(A^{\alpha}(t_1) - \overline{A}(t_1)) + (B^{\alpha}(t_1) - \overline{B}(t_1)) - \sum_{j=1}^{3}(L_j^{\alpha}(t_1) - \overline{L}_j(t_1))]$. Equation (11.8) can be rewritten as:

$$\mathrm{ML} = \mathrm{EML} + \mathrm{MVAR} \qquad (11.9)$$

We focus on market losses (and disregard possible profits) just to stress the fact that they originate from *passive* risks that should be fully hedged, via traded market instruments such as swaps or FRAs, when possible. When this is not possible, unexpected losses have to be taken into account and included in the MVAR, which implies allocation of economic capital to cover it.

---

[1] We adopt a uniform terminology both for derivative and standard banking contracts, so we apply the term CVA to a loan as well, although it is primarily used to adjust the value of a derivative contract to account for expected credit losses.

[2] See [93] for a discussion on passive and productive risks. Very briefly, *productive* risks are those that cannot be hedged or diversified away by the bank, whereas *passive* risks can. Only productive risks related to banking activity should absorb economic capital and then generate a corresponding remuneration; passive risks, on the contrary, should be properly hedged or diversified away and no capital should be allocated to cover them, since they are not strictly inherent to the banking business: an investment does not have to produce a remuneration of economic capital for these types of risks.

[3] This is not totally true since credit derivatives are available in the market, with underlying issuers being major companies in most economic sectors. Clearly, when it is possible to hedge credit risk with such instruments, unexpected losses should not be considered since the risk can be thought of as passive – not productive. For most retail business (i.e., mortgages, loans to small corporates, etc.) the risk is generally productive.

[4] Recall that B is a risk-free asset, so no loss can result from default, liabilities cannot be evaluated by including the default of the bank (see Chapter 10 for a discussion) and from the bank's point of view they are default risk-free securities.

Market losses are due to:

- *Changes in risk-free interest rates*: Expected change is captured by the slope of the risk-free interest rate term structure; it is a passive risk that can be hedged with market instruments, so it produces no MVAR.
- *Changes in financial options embedded in the contracts* (e.g., call option on the asset bought by the bank, or caps and floors for assets paying a floating rate): Expected profit/loss can be valued by the price of these options traded in the market, which can be used to hedge this passive risk, which, as such, does not generate any MVAR.
- *Changes in the value of liquidity and behavioural options* (e.g., prepayment option bought by the mortgagee): Expected cost can be valued using statistical and financial techniques,[5] but typically a hedge with market instruments is not possible. As such, these losses are in most cases originated by productive risk and an MVAR has to be computed and taken into account when measuring the PL of an investment.
- *Changes in the level of the funding spread of the bank*: Expected and unexpected market losses related to refunding risk for the rollover of liabilities cannot be hedged (as demonstrated in Chapter 10): the risk is not passive, but productive since it is strictly inherent to banking activity and as such it should be included in valuation of an investment by considering the economic capital needed to cover the corresponding MVAR as well.

In theory, almost all market risks are passive since they can be hedged, so that unexpected losses are not included in the MVAR; expected losses are considered because they also represent the price of setting up hedges in the market. Besides the losses generated by interest rate risk, which enter in the valuation process directly through the interest flows related to assets and liabilities, all other losses due to financial options are collectively indicated by FO, whereas liquidity/behavioural options are indicated by LO.

Losses originated by productive market risks, such as refunding risk and some behavioural risks,[6] are included in the MVAR since they cannot be hedged because either it is impossible or no hedging instrument is traded in the market.

There is also another productive risk that we analysed in Chapter 7 and that relates to the rollover of liabilities: this is funding gap risk, which is covered by a suitable amount of liquidity buffer. Maintenance of the LB causes costs that the bank has to pay and since they also include its funding spread, they cannot be hedged with market instruments. Hence, for liquidity buffer costs (LBC) too, the bank needs to calculate unexpected costs, to include them in the MVAR and to post a suitable amount of economic capital to cover them.

The CVAR and the MVAR absorb a fraction ϕ of equity: this is the economic capital required to run the banking activity and to face related productive risks. We assume, in our simplified balance sheet, that equity E is exactly the amount needed to cover unexpected market and credit loss, with no extra capital available, so $\phi = 1$ and:

$$E = \text{CVAR}_{A_1} + \text{MVAR}$$

---

[5] See Chapter 9.
[6] See Chapter 9 for behavioural models and related risks.

Total profits/losses are determined simply by summing up all the terms relating to assets and liabilities in equations (11.6) and (11.8):

$$PL = i_1 A_1 + r(1 - \varepsilon)E - \sum_{j=1}^{3}(r + s^j)L_j$$

$$- CVA_{A_1} - (FO + LO) - LBC - e(MVAR + CVAR_{A_1})$$

$$= i_1 A_1 - \sum_{j=1}^{3}(r + s^j)L_j - s^{A_1}A_1 - (FO + LO) - LBC - (e - r)E - \varepsilon rE \quad (11.10)$$

We indicate by $\pi = (e - r)$ the risk premium over the risk-free rate demanded by equity holders, so that:

$$PL = i_1 A_1 - \sum_{j=1}^{3}(r + s^j)L_j - s^{A_1}A_1 - (FO + LO) - LBC - (\pi + \varepsilon r)E \quad (11.11)$$

It is now possible to determine rate i_1^* that investment A_1 has to yield to break even ($PL = 0$):

$$i_1^* A_1 = \underbrace{rL}_{ir} + \underbrace{\bar{s}L}_{fu} + \underbrace{LBC}_{cl} + \underbrace{s^{A_1}A_1}_{cs} + \underbrace{FO + LO}_{op} + \underbrace{(\pi + \varepsilon r_f)E}_{cc} \quad (11.12)$$

where $\bar{s} = \sum_{j=1}^{3} s^j \frac{L_j}{L}$ is the average funding spread paid on all liabilities. Breakeven rate i_1^* comprises the following components:

- *ir*: the risk-free rate used in the total funding cost to pay on liabilities;
- *fu*: funding costs due to spreads paid over the risk-free rate on liabilities;
- *cl*: costs relating to contingent liquidity (i.e., to the liquidity buffer that has to be kept to cope with funding gap risk);
- *cs*: credit spread or remuneration for expected losses in the event of default of the obligor of asset A_1;
- *op*: the cost of financial and liquidity/behavioural options;
- *cc*: the cost of economic capital required to cover unexpected credit and market risks.

The breakeven, or fair, rate that includes all the components above covers all the costs related to the banking activity to invest in A_1. It should be noted that in most cases, when A_1 is a typical bank contract such as a loan or a mortgage, the investment can actually be considered as a product to sell to a customer. The difference between standard goods or services and a bank product is that the latter appears on a bank's balance sheet as an asset or a liability, or off balance sheet as a commitment, after it is sold. So the breakeven rate is the amount to charge the counterparty to recoup all the production costs of a product that eventually will be included on the bank's balance sheet.

The bank may also charge a margin on top of all the components we have shown to achieve a profit. This profit is remuneration to the shareholders for the equity invested in the bank: if all the investments are properly priced, remuneration is already included in the economic capital absorbed to cover related unexpected costs. This means that remuneration for the equity is already theoretically included in the valuation process in the *cc* component, so that any profit margin would mean double counting. In practice,

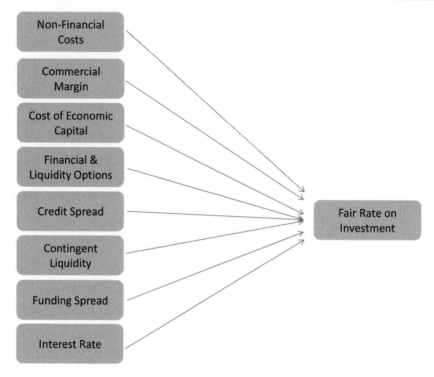

Figure 11.1. The building blocks to determine the fund transfer price of an investment

it is possible that an extra margin is added: this includes the commercial margin, which is remuneration for business units selling products to clients, and the margin to cover infrastructure and, broadly speaking, other nonfinancial costs. In Figure 11.1 we schematically recapitulate the building blocks of fund transfer pricing.

The approach we have sketched to set fund transfer prices can be defined as *full-risk* pricing and also serves the purpose of measuring the risk-adjusted return of the bank's investments. In fact, the PL can also be seen in value-added VA terms: recall that economic capital EC is, in our simplified world, equal to equity ($E = \text{EC} = \text{CVAR} + \text{MVAR}$); moreover, let us indicate by

$$\text{PL}_b = i_1 A_1 - \sum_{j=1}^{3}(r + s^j)L_j - s^{A_1}A_1 - (\text{FO} + \text{LO}) - \text{LBC}$$

the actual profits/losses brought about by business activity. We have

$$\text{VA} = \text{PL}_b - (\pi + \varepsilon r)\text{EC} \tag{11.13}$$

which is the definition of value added. The risk-adjusted return on capital RAROC is defined as:

$$\text{RAROC} = \frac{\text{PL}_b}{\text{EC}} \tag{11.14}$$

If $\text{RAROC} = (\pi + \varepsilon r)$ (i.e., exactly equal to the required remuneration for the equity capital employed to cover unexpected losses), then $\text{VA} = 0$.

Both VA and RAROC can be used as *ex ante* measures of profitability (which is basically what we have shown above) and as *ex post* measures to verify whether realized profits are satisfactory for the risks taken at inception of the contract.

In what follows we will focus on the interest rate and funding spread components of FTP. A tool that properly accounts for funding is the *funding curve*: it indicates expected and unexpected costs of the liquidity needed to fund an investment. We will first make a detour to explain the ideas underpinning the approach we propose, then we will come back to analysis of the funding curve.

11.3   FUNDING AND BANKING ACTIVITY

Funding costs and funding transfer rates have been examined in the past, and generally the analysis (often implicitly) assumed that: (i) the financial institution was able to finance its credit intermediation activity at lower rates than those earned on activities, thus generating interest margin profits (and implying the bank's creditworthiness rather than the client's); (ii) (partly) financing short-term activities with long-term maturities was not a risky activity in practice; (iii) liquidity in the market was abundant so that choice of the funding mix was determined with almost no constraints.

The turbulence in the financial markets, starting in 2007 and becoming severer in 2008 (see Chapter 1), made these assumptions either unrealistic or at least necessitous of further refinements. First, it is no longer true that financial institutions are always able to raise funds under less expensive conditions than their clients, at least in markets where bargaining power is evenly distributed between participants, such as in the capital market. Second, the volatility of banks' funding spreads over risk-free market rates dramatically increased, so that financing long-term activities with short-term debt, even partially, is riskier than in the past and the risk has to be properly taken into account. Third, as a consequence of the first two points, the funding mix is subject to constraints that abate the average funding cost and make credit intermediation activity still profitable, while keeping the liquidity gap risk under control (see Chapter 7 for a discussion on this point).

Financial institutions realized their activity would become in some cases unprofitable if they continued using past schemes. As a very simplified example, long-term loans were often priced by considering the marginal cost for the bank on the corresponding expiry as the funding cost, which had to be added to other costs so as to set a fair loan rate. On longer expiries the only available funding source is, typically, the issuance of bonds in the capital market. Currently, such an approach would reject a large, or nonnegligible in any case, part of possible investments, depending on general market and bank-specific conditions, since bonds are usually the most expensive source of funding for a bank. Additionally, it should be noted that for really long-term contracts (say, 20-year expiry) the bank has no available source for perfectly matched funding,[7] so in any case it has to make some assumptions about future evolution of the funding spread and on the rollover of liabilities.

By the very fact that banks are still doing business, they clearly have been looking at financing activity from a different perspective using new criteria along the lines we now suggest.

---

[7] Most bank bonds expire within 7 years, although longer maturities are not impossible to find in the market.

First, we suggest that funding cost has to take into account all possible funding sources available: regarding some of them, such as demand and saving deposits, the bank's bargaining power is relatively strong and funding cost can be significantly abated. Regarding others, such as wholesale funding, the bargaining power between counterparties is pretty even and the bank can expect to pay a fair funding spread.

Second, we believe funding mix has to be considered from a *dynamic* rather than *static* perspective: this makes possible the building of funding curves that account for (expected) average funding costs on short-term liabilities that will roll over on expiry, by assuming continuity of banking activity.[8]

Third, the risk inherent in liability rollover (which we term *refunding risk*) has to be consistently measured and accounted for so as to allocate an amount of economic capital and include it in investment pricing in a correct way. The risk we are dealing with here is twofold: on the one hand, the bank can face the problem of not being able to roll over maturing liabilities for the entire amount: this would produce gap risk and then generate the need for a liquidity buffer (we have extensively analysed this in Chapter 7). On the other hand, the bank may be able to roll over maturing liabilities fully, but only by paying a funding cost higher than expected: this is the *refunding risk* we have to investigate to find out how to measure and manage it. Unfortunately, this type of risk cannot be hedged, so the only way to cope with it is to set aside an adequate amount of capital in the same fashion the bank does for other productive risks.

What we propose in the following is an approach that complies with these criteria. Schematically, it can be sketched as follows:

1. A funding curve for each available source has to be built up to a given expiry, generally longer than the source's average duration, by projecting future costs based on market risk-free forward rates plus the source's specific spreads over them.
2. A weighted average funding curve is then calculated to determine the average (expected) cost borne by the bank to finance a given investment.
3. Unexpected funding costs, due to the uncertainty relating to liability rollover, are measured by a VaR-like methodology, thus identifying unexpected maximum cost at a given level of confidence for any expiry.
4. Unexpected costs imply that a given amount of economic capital has to be allocated and its remuneration has to be included in the pricing of the bank's investments.

11.4   BUILDING A FUNDING CURVE

Let us assume we have different funding sources such as demand deposits, term deposits, bonds issued in the market, etc. Let J be the number of these sources each of which entails a cost for the bank that is a function of the risk-free interest rate curve and the bank's funding spread.

Let L be, as before, the total of amount raised from different funding sources (i.e., liabilities) and define the weights $w_j = L_j/L$, for $j = 1, \ldots, J$.

---

[8] We are conscious of stating something that many operators, including some surveillance authorities, will consider opposite to best practices. Nevertheless, we strongly believe best practices inherited from the past need deep and serious revision, because either they are based on premises no longer valid in current markets or they are based on hypothetical funding activity the banks could neither operate in the past nor can they today. Although best practices from the past seemed apparently safe and sound, they hid many assumptions that must now be made explicit, analysed and taken into account in risk measurement and management.

Remark 11.4.1. *In this chapter we do not analsye how to set the weights associated with each funding source, we simply take them as given. In Chapter 7 we outlined an approach to determine the weights based on an equilibrium criterion related to funding gap risk. If the bank adopts this approach, the weights will be time dependent. In the subsequent analysis we only consider constant weights but, as will be manifest, the extension to time-dependent weights is straightforward.*

Define the discount curve $\mathcal{P}^j = \{P^j(0, t_1), \ldots, P^j(0, t_N)\}$ as the collection of discount factors that can be bootstrapped from prices of the j-th funding source. We assume that it is possible to infer discount factors up to expiry t_N equal for all funding sources via risk-free rates and the spread over these, which can reasonably be forecast or even implied from market prices. It is reasonable to assume that the OIS (or Eonia for the euro) rates are the best proxy for risk-free rates, so it is relatively easy to infer them from quoted swap rates. We also define the risk-free discount curve up to maturity t_N, derived from interbank quotes, as $\mathcal{P}^D = \{P^D(0, t_1) \ldots, P^D(0, t_N)\}$.

We do not go into details on how to bootstrap risk-free discount curves from the market prices of deposits, FRAs, swaps and OIS (or Eonia): we take them as given. More specifically, we assume they can be exactly generated by the CIR model with a given set of parameters.[9] We know that in this model the term structure of interest rates is driven by one stochastic factor, the instantaneous interest rate r_t, whose dynamics are:

$$dr_t = \kappa(\theta - r_t)dt + \sigma\sqrt{r_t}dW_t \tag{11.15}$$

The discount factors generated by the CIR model can be computed in closed form by equation (8.27).

To make things concrete, we go on to describe the theoretical framework along with a practical example.

Example 11.4.1. *Assume the bank has three funding sources: (i) the interbank deposit market (j = 1), (ii) the CD (certificate of deposit) market (j = 2) and (iii) the issuance of bonds in the capital market (j = 3). The interbank deposit market allows the bank to borrow from (but also lend to) other banks via time deposits, usually expiring up to one year. In current markets banks are considered as credit risky as any other economic operator, so a credit spread over the risk-free rate is required by the lender.[10] The CD market allows raising funds from retail customers at good levels compared with other sources, usually on average up to two years. Finally, the capital market allows medium/long-term funding (five/seven years), typically selling bonds to investors.*

In this example, following typical durations of the three funding sources, we assume a yearly refunding schedule for interbank deposits, whereas for CDs the refunding schedule is on a two-year basis and for issued bonds on a five-year basis.

We start with the simplifying assumption that it is possible to determine the cost[11] of each funding source as the risk-free rate for the relevant maturity plus a deterministic, though time-dependent, spread that is known. Since risk factors (possibly only one in the CIR model we are using) are related only to risk-free rates, it is possible at time $t = 0$ to

---

[9] See Section 8.3.3.
[10] In Chapter 10 we studied the relationship between the spread seen as credit risk compensation on one side and funding cost on the other.
[11] We may refer to the funding cost related to a given source as total interest plus possible implicit costs or optionalities. It is frequent, though, to consider funding cost just as the spread over the risk-free rate.

Table 11.2. Parameter and initial instantaneous rate values used in the CIR model to generate risk-free discount factors

r_0	0.25%
Mean reversion speed κ	0.2
Long-term average rate θ	4.50%
Volatility σ	12.00%

define the entire funding curve for each source, up to given expiry t_N, even if this source entails a refunding schedule because on average it has a much smaller duration than the total period running from 0 to t_N.

Under the deterministic spread assumption, rollover is not risky[12] since the treasury department can lock in the future cost implicit in the curves by static or dynamic strategies involving OIS (or Eonia) swaps having the same risk-free rate as the underlying, to hedge exposures on rollover dates to just a single risk factor: the risk-free interest rate. For example, CDs with an average maturity of two years have to be resold every two years, so as to keep the funded amount constant. It is possible, in the environment we are assuming, to hedge the exposures generated by reselling CDs, thus locking in the funding cost up to a maturity of, say, 20 years.

As a first step, we build the risk-free discount curve and the related term structure of zero rates. To generate such quantities we use a CIR model with values of the parameters and the starting instantaneous rate r_0 as shown in Table 11.2.

The risk-free term structures of discount factors and zero rates are shown in Table 11.3, whereas a visual representation of zero rates[13] is in Figure 11.2.

It is easy to build the term structures for the three sources by observing market prices and by forecasting reasonable expected spreads over the risk-free rate for each of them. Furthermore, we do not deal with the problem of how to bootstrap spreads from prices, but we simply take continuously compounded zero spreads over risk-free zero rates as given.

Let us start with the interbank deposit market: we build the related discount factor curve starting from zero rates for risk-free rate r_T, adding zero-spread s_T^1 and then computing discount factor $P^1(0, T) = e^{-(r_T + s_T^1)T}$. In Table 11.4 all the data for the three funding sources are shown: for example, for the interbank deposit market the zero-spread term structure is deterministic and time dependent, beginning at 0.30% for the one-year expiry and gradually increasing up to 0.90% for the 20-year expiry.

Once the term structures of discount factors for each source have been built, it is straightforward to build the bank's funding discount curve as the weighted average of the different discount curves:

$$\mathcal{P}^F = \{P^F(0, t_1), \ldots, P^F(0, t_N)\}$$

---

[12] We recall that the risk here refers only to unexpected cost of rollover (refunding risk) – not the amount to be renewed (gap risk).

[13] Worthy of a quick mention is the fact that zero-rate r_T associated with discount factor $P^D(0, T)$ for given maturity T is calculated as $r_T = -\ln(P^D(0, T))/T$.

Table 11.3. Risk-free term structure of discount factors and zero rates

Expiry	$P^D(0, T)$	Zero rates (%)
1	0.993550	0.65
2	0.980348	0.99
3	0.961979	1.29
4	0.939812	1.55
5	0.914974	1.78
6	0.888370	1.97
7	0.860706	2.14
8	0.832525	2.29
9	0.804232	2.42
10	0.776128	2.53
11	0.748429	2.63
12	0.721289	2.72
13	0.694814	2.80
14	0.669074	2.87
15	0.644112	2.93
16	0.619950	2.99
17	0.596599	3.04
18	0.574055	3.08
19	0.552310	3.12
20	0.531350	3.16

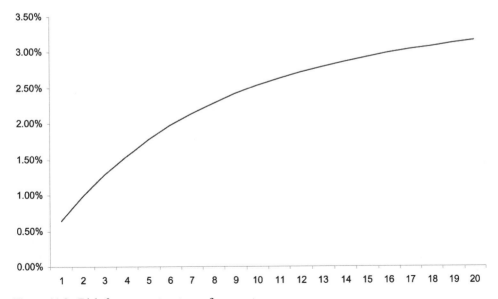

Figure 11.2. Risk-free term structure of zero rates

Table 11.4. Risk-free zero rates and interbank deposit (superscript 1), CD (superscript 2) and bond (superscript 3) market term structures of zero spreads, zero rates and discount factors

Expiry	r_T (%)	s_T^1 (%)	$r_T + s_T^1$ (%)	$P^1(0;T)$	s_T^2 (%)	$r_T + s_T^2$ (%)	$P^2(0;T)$	s_T^3 (%)	$r_T + s_T^3$ (%)	$P^3(0;T)$
1	0.65	0.30	0.95	0.990574	0.15	0.80	0.992061	0.30	0.95	0.990574
2	0.99	0.30	1.29	0.974483	0.15	1.14	0.977411	0.55	1.54	0.969623
3	1.29	0.35	1.64	0.951931	0.15	1.44	0.957660	0.80	2.09	0.939167
4	1.55	0.35	1.90	0.926746	0.15	1.70	0.934190	1.05	2.60	0.901157
5	1.78	0.40	2.18	0.896856	0.15	1.93	0.908137	1.30	3.08	0.857392
6	1.97	0.45	2.42	0.864704	0.15	2.12	0.880410	1.55	3.52	0.809477
7	2.14	0.50	2.64	0.831103	0.15	2.29	0.851716	1.80	3.94	0.758812
8	2.29	0.50	2.79	0.799882	0.15	2.44	0.822595	2.05	4.34	0.706599
9	2.42	0.55	2.97	0.765392	0.15	2.57	0.793448	2.10	4.52	0.665733
10	2.53	0.60	3.13	0.730930	0.15	2.68	0.764573	2.20	4.73	0.622857
11	2.63	0.65	3.28	0.696784	0.15	2.78	0.736181	2.30	4.93	0.581131
12	2.72	0.65	3.37	0.667167	0.15	2.87	0.708422	2.30	5.02	0.547323
13	2.80	0.70	3.50	0.634378	0.15	2.95	0.681397	2.30	5.10	0.515246
14	2.87	0.75	3.62	0.602384	0.15	3.02	0.655170	2.30	5.17	0.484877
15	2.93	0.80	3.73	0.571276	0.15	3.08	0.629781	2.30	5.23	0.456173
16	2.99	0.80	3.79	0.545465	0.15	3.14	0.605249	2.30	5.29	0.429078
17	3.04	0.85	3.89	0.516329	0.15	3.19	0.581578	2.30	5.34	0.403528
18	3.08	0.90	3.98	0.488200	0.15	3.23	0.558763	2.30	5.38	0.379451
19	3.12	0.90	4.02	0.465499	0.15	3.27	0.536791	2.30	5.42	0.356777
20	3.16	0.90	4.06	0.443821	0.15	3.31	0.515646	2.30	5.46	0.335432

where each discount factor is defined as:

$$P^F(0,t_i) = \sum_{j=1}^{J} w_j P^j(0,t_i) \tag{11.16}$$

for $i = 1, \ldots, N$.

Example 11.4.2. *From the data shown in Example 11.4.1 it is possible to build the funding discount term structure, which is shown in Table 11.5 with the weight used for each funding source as well. In Figure 11.3 the zero rates of the three funding sources and of the bank's funding curve are depicted.*

The funding curve can be used to discount the cash flows related to a loan (or to any other asset bought by the bank with a cash flow structure similar to a loan) so as to include in the pricing the average funding cost borne by the bank. In the case of deterministic spreads we have just examined, the average cost is the only cost to take into account, since it can be locked in at inception of the contract we want to price. In fact, the only risk is due to the stochasticity of market rates, which can be hedged by dealing in market instruments (such as FRAs and swaps); funding spreads, being deterministic, are not risk factors.

Clearly, the assumption of deterministic, though time-dependent, spreads is too naive and unacceptable in practice. Actually, spreads are just as stochastic as risk-free rates,

Table 11.5. Term structures of zero spreads, zero rates and discount factors for the bank's funding curve and weights for the three funding sources

Expiry	$P^F(0,T)$	Zero rate (%)	Weight of deposits (%)	Weight of CDs (%)	Weight of bonds (%)
1	0.991317	0.87	20.00	50.00	30.00
2	0.974489	1.29	20.00	50.00	30.00
3	0.950966	1.68	20.00	50.00	30.00
4	0.922791	2.01	20.00	50.00	30.00
5	0.890657	2.32	20.00	50.00	30.00
6	0.855989	2.59	20.00	50.00	30.00
7	0.819722	2.84	20.00	50.00	30.00
8	0.783253	3.05	20.00	50.00	30.00
9	0.749522	3.20	20.00	50.00	30.00
10	0.715330	3.35	20.00	50.00	30.00
11	0.681787	3.48	20.00	50.00	30.00
12	0.651841	3.57	20.00	50.00	30.00
13	0.622148	3.65	20.00	50.00	30.00
14	0.593525	3.73	20.00	50.00	30.00
15	0.565998	3.79	20.00	50.00	30.00
16	0.540441	3.85	20.00	50.00	30.00
17	0.515113	3.90	20.00	50.00	30.00
18	0.490857	3.95	20.00	50.00	30.00
19	0.468528	3.99	20.00	50.00	30.00
20	0.447217	4.02	20.00	50.00	30.00

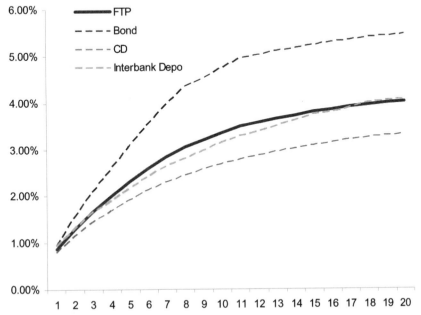

Figure 11.3. Term structures of zero rates for the bank's funding curve and the three funding sources

and they are a function of the bank's (perceived) default risk and recovery ratios on the bank's bankruptcy, which depends on the type of instrument.

When spreads are stochastic, we can no longer assume that the funding curve is determined and fixed up to expiry t_N, since the average life of the instruments underlying the different funding sources implies refunding risk, which can be defined as the greater-than-expected costs[14] to be paid when rolling over a given funding source on future expiries. In fact, we cannot simply lock in the cost implicit in the risk-free curve and the spread curves by setting up a hedging strategy for all future refunding exposures, because we have contracts traded in the market enabling the treasury department to hedge risk-free rate risk, but it is almost impossible to hedge spread risk.

For example, the spread over the risk-free rate for bonds issued by the bank could be hedged by a credit default swap written on the bank's debt, but the buyer (and the seller) of such a swap cannot be the bank itself. Statistical hedging is possible by means of proxies that mimic spread evolution but we can no longer state that the cost of funding can be locked in completely today, so that the expected funding curve cannot be considered the only cost to include in the pricing of products sold to customers.

Remark 11.4.2. *In the market it is possible not only to hedge exposures to the risk related to the risk-free (OIS/Eonia) rate, but also exposures to Libor (or Euribor for the euro) rates, since they are the underlying of FRAs and swap contracts. Libor/Euribor are not risk-free rates though, since they embed credit risk compensation for deposits used to lend to a primary bank in the interbank market. In fact, Libor/Euribor fixing quotes imply a spread over the risk-free rate which depends on the maturity of the corresponding deposit.*

The bank's funding spread can be equal to or higher than that implied by Libor/Euribor fixings, so that what matters in reality is the volatility of the spread with respect to the Libor/Euribor rate, rather than with respect to the risk-free rate. In fact, the bank can hedge spread volatility partially (or even totally if its credit grade corresponds to that of a Libor/Euribor counterparty): the model we are presenting has to be modified accordingly and in case it is possible to fully hedge spread volatility, it boils down to the hypothesis of deterministic spreads seen before, since they can be locked in at inception of an investment.

We have to follow a different line of reasoning. First, we have to introduce a stochastic model for the different spreads, describing their evolution in time; second, we have to build spread curves for the chosen model, after fitting it to current market prices; third, we have to consider these curves as average funding costs for each funding source: then, we can also build an average bank's funding curve; fourth, we have to take into account that spreads may be different from the (implied) average or possibly higher than that on rollover dates, implying a higher cost to be borne by the bank.[15] This higher cost can be considered an *unexpected funding cost* that has to be measured using a VaR-like approach and has to be covered by an amount of economic capital, in the same way as an amount of economic capital is provided to cover unexpected credit and market losses. Actually, this unexpected loss can be considered a market loss, although credit factors related to the bank contribute to it, in accordance with the analysis of Chapter 10.

In the case of bank default we choose a reduced-form approach, more specifically a doubly stochastic intensity model (see Chapter 8). Looking at this in greater detail, the

---

[14] Expected costs are those implied by the discount (or, equivalently, zero rate) curve of the funding source.
[15] Basically, we may experience future spreads higher than the forward spreads implied in the curve.

survival probability of a bank between time 0 and time T is given by:

$$SP(0, T) = \mathbf{E}\left[e^{-\int_0^T \lambda_s ds}\right]$$

where default intensity λ_t is a stochastic process that is assumed to be defined by CIR dynamics:

$$d\lambda_t = \kappa_\lambda(\theta_\lambda - \lambda_t)dt + \sigma_\lambda\sqrt{\lambda_t}dZ_t \qquad (11.17)$$

We assume that correlation between instantaneous rate r_t and default intensity λ_t is nil, although it is possible to design a model to include nonzero correlation. The probability of default is simply given by $PD(0, T) = 1 - SP(0, T)$. In this setting, $SP(0, T)$ has a closed-form solution given by (8.27).

In order to simplify calculation, for any funding source j we assume that after default a fraction $\mathcal{R}^j$ of the market value is immediately paid to the holder of the instrument issued by the bank: this is known as the recovery of market value (RMV) assumption and allows for a very convenient definition of instantaneous spread[16] $s_t^j = (1 - \mathcal{R}^j)\lambda_t$. The formula to compute the discount factor of spreads can easily be shown to be the same as for survival probability with a slight change in parameters, as indicated in formula (8.54), so that:

$$(1 - \mathcal{R}^j)\lambda_t = CIR(\kappa_\lambda, \sqrt{1 - \mathcal{R}^j}\sigma_\lambda, (1 - \mathcal{R}^j)\theta_\lambda, (1 - \mathcal{R}^j)\lambda_t, t). \qquad (11.18)$$

It is manifest that, in the setting in which we are working, what determines the actual spread of each specific source is the recovery ratio, the default intensity being the same for all of them. The recovery ratio in turn depends on the type of seniority of the funding source in the bank's balance sheet and on the ability of the bank's creditor to forecast it. We can suppose, for example, that the recovery ratio on CDs may be considered very high, either because of the seniority of the instrument, or as a result of the greater bargaining power of the bank with less sophisticated investors, or for their inabilit to attribute the correct level to it.[17]

In the following example we recompute the term structures of the discount factors and zero rates for the three sources, by removing the assumption of deterministic spreads and by using the doubly stochastic intensity model with default intensity as in (11.17).

Example 11.4.3. *In the doubly stochastic intensity model we use the values of parameters and initial level of intensity λ_0 as shown in Table 11.6.*

Table 11.6. Parameter and initial default intensity values used in the doubly stochastic default model to generate spread discount factors

λ_0	0.10%
Mean reversion speed κ_λ	0.75
Equilibrium rate θ_λ	2.00%
Volatility σ_λ	17.00%

---

[16] See Section 8.4 and [63].

[17] This is a convenient point to mention that for some funding sources, such as demand or saving deposits, the spread is much more under the bank's control and often can be modelled just as a function of short-term market (either risk-free or treasury) rates (see Chapter 7 for the fair rate to apply to non-maturing liabilities). Since this case is similar to that of deterministic spreads presented above, we do not include such sources in our setting, although they do contribute in practice to average down the total funding cost of the bank.

We are now in a position to determine the zero spreads and total discount factors for each funding source. Zero spreads are derived from spread discount factors, computed with formula (8.27) considering the dynamics in (11.18). Total zero rate is simply the sum of the risk-free instantaneous rate plus the zero spread for the same maturity; the discount factor for the funding source is then calculated in a straightforward way.

For the interbank deposit market we assume that the recovery rate is $\mathcal{R}^1 = 50\%$, for CDs $\mathcal{R}^2 = 80\%$ and, finally, for issued bonds $\mathcal{R}^3 = 40\%$. The results are given in Table 11.7 for expiries running from 1 to 20 years.

The funding curve can be calculated by means of normal weighting and is shown in Table 11.8.

The difference between the funding curve generated by means of stochastic spreads and the one produced by deterministic spreads lies in that in the second case we have a curve of funding costs for each maturity which can be locked in at any future date, whereas in the first case we have a curve of funding costs that cannot be locked in by any hedging strategy, so that at any future date the curve implies only the expected cost to raise funds. It is clear that we have somehow to take into account both expected and unexpected costs, and hence post a suitable amount of economic capital to cover them. In the setting we have just specified this can relatively easily be done.

First we have to stress the fact that a part of the total funding cost using stochastic

Table 11.7. Risk-free zero rates and interbank deposit (superscript 1), CDs (superscript 2) and bond (superscript 3) market term structures of zero spreads, zero rates and discount factors, assuming stochastic spreads. The recovery ratios for the three sources are, respectively, $\mathcal{R}^1 = 50\%$, $\mathcal{R}^2 = 80\%$ and $\mathcal{R}^3 = 40\%$

Expiry	r_T (%)	s_T^1 (%)	$r_T + s_T^1$ (%)	$P^1(0;T)$	s_T^2 (%)	$r_T + s_T^2$ (%)	$P^2(0;T)$	s_T^3 (%)	$r_T + s_T^3$ (%)	$P^3(0;T)$
1	0.65	0.33	0.98	0.990263	0.13	0.78	0.992233	0.40	1.04	0.989608
2	0.99	0.51	1.50	0.970464	0.20	1.20	0.976376	0.61	1.60	0.968505
3	1.29	0.62	1.91	0.944262	0.25	1.54	0.954835	0.74	2.04	0.940776
4	1.55	0.70	2.25	0.914040	0.28	1.83	0.929382	0.83	2.39	0.909005
5	1.78	0.75	2.52	0.881407	0.30	2.08	0.901341	0.90	2.67	0.874896
6	1.97	0.79	2.76	0.847490	0.32	2.29	0.871710	0.94	2.91	0.839615
7	2.14	0.81	2.96	0.813085	0.33	2.47	0.841235	0.97	3.12	0.803973
8	2.29	0.83	3.13	0.778759	0.34	2.63	0.810471	1.00	3.29	0.768539
9	2.42	0.85	3.27	0.744912	0.34	2.76	0.779823	1.02	3.44	0.733708
10	2.53	0.86	3.40	0.711821	0.35	2.88	0.749584	1.04	3.57	0.699753
11	2.63	0.88	3.51	0.679674	0.35	2.99	0.719963	1.05	3.68	0.666853
12	2.72	0.89	3.61	0.648592	0.36	3.08	0.691100	1.06	3.78	0.635120
13	2.80	0.89	3.69	0.618647	0.36	3.16	0.663089	1.07	3.87	0.604619
14	2.87	0.90	3.77	0.589875	0.36	3.23	0.635988	1.08	3.95	0.575379
15	2.93	0.91	3.84	0.562287	0.36	3.30	0.609829	1.08	4.02	0.547404
16	2.99	0.91	3.90	0.535878	0.37	3.35	0.584622	1.09	4.08	0.520679
17	3.04	0.92	3.95	0.510625	0.37	3.41	0.560367	1.10	4.13	0.495178
18	3.08	0.92	4.00	0.486502	0.37	3.45	0.537050	1.10	4.18	0.470868
19	3.12	0.92	4.05	0.463475	0.37	3.50	0.514655	1.11	4.23	0.447708
20	3.16	0.93	4.09	0.441504	0.37	3.53	0.493157	1.11	4.27	0.425656

Table 11.8. Term structures of zero spreads, zero rates and discount factors for the bank's funding curve and weights of the three funding sources assuming a stochastic spread over the risk-free rate

Expiry	$P^F(0, T)$	Zero rate (%)	Weight of deposits (%)	Weight of CDs (%)	Weight of bonds (%)
1	0.991052	0.90	20.00	50.00	30.00
2	0.972832	1.38	20.00	50.00	30.00
3	0.948503	1.76	20.00	50.00	30.00
4	0.920200	2.08	20.00	50.00	30.00
5	0.889421	2.34	20.00	50.00	30.00
6	0.857238	2.57	20.00	50.00	30.00
7	0.824427	2.76	20.00	50.00	30.00
8	0.791549	2.92	20.00	50.00	30.00
9	0.759006	3.06	20.00	50.00	30.00
10	0.727082	3.19	20.00	50.00	30.00
11	0.695972	3.29	20.00	50.00	30.00
12	0.665804	3.39	20.00	50.00	30.00
13	0.636660	3.47	20.00	50.00	30.00
14	0.608583	3.55	20.00	50.00	30.00
15	0.581593	3.61	20.00	50.00	30.00
16	0.555690	3.67	20.00	50.00	30.00
17	0.530862	3.73	20.00	50.00	30.00
18	0.507086	3.77	20.00	50.00	30.00
19	0.484335	3.82	20.00	50.00	30.00
20	0.462576	3.85	20.00	50.00	30.00

spreads can be locked in anyway. Actually, we can trade in hedging instruments written on the risk-free rate and that allows cancelling exposures to the risk-free component of future costs: this can be done for each source of funding. The stochastic part of the cost that cannot be hedged is only the spread and we have to compute its unexpected changes on scheduled refunding dates.

To that end it is very useful that CIR dynamics have a known terminal distribution for instantaneous default intensity, namely a non-central χ^2 distribution.[18] This allows computing, at a given date, the maximum level (with a predefined confidence level) of default intensity λ_t and hence the maximum level of the spread and of the total cost for the refunding of each funding source. Additionally, we need the expected level of the spread to be the forward spread implied by the curve referring to each source; that is, for any $t < t' < T$:

$$P^{s^J}(0, T) = P^{s^J}(0, t') \mathbf{E}^{t'}[P^{s^J}(t', T)]$$

which means that we want to compute the maximum level of the spread under a forward risk-adjusted measure.[19] We then need a forward risk-adjusted distribution of default intensity (see equation (8.36)).

---

[18] A non-central χ^2, with d degrees of freedom and non-centrality parameter c, is defined as the function $\chi^2(x; d, c)$. See Chapter 8 for more details.

[19] Superscript t' to the expectation operator $\mathbf{E}[\cdot]$ means that we are working in a t'-forward risk-adjusted measure. Technically speaking, we are calculating expectations by using bond $P^{s^J}(0, t')$ as a numeraire.

We now have all the tools to derive the unexpected funding cost associated with a given curve. Assume we still build an expected curve for each funding source up to expiry t_N with an intensity model, as in Example 11.4.3. Further assume that each funding source J has duration t^J years, so that it entails a number of refunding dates $t_N/(t^J) - 1 = n^J$. We follow the following procedure described in pseudo-code.

Procedure 11.4.1. *We first derive the maximum expected level of default intensity $\lambda_{t_i}^*$, at scheduled refunding dates, with a confidence level c.l. (e.g., 99%):*

1. **For** $i = 1, \ldots, n^J$
2. $t_i = i \cdot t^J$
3. $\lambda_{t_i}^* = \lambda_{t_i} : p_{\lambda_t}^{t_i}(\lambda_{t_i}) = cl$
4. **Next**

Having determined the maximum default intensity level, we can compute the term structure of (minimum) discount factors for zero spreads corresponding to these levels:

1. **For** $i = 1, \ldots, n^J$
2. $t_i = i \cdots t^J$
3.   **For** $k = 1, \ldots, t^J$
4. $P_{cl}^{s^J}(0, t_{i+k}) = P^{s^J}(0, t_i)P^{s^J}(t_i, t_k; \lambda_{t_i}^*, \kappa_\lambda, \theta_\lambda, \sigma_\lambda, \mathcal{R}^J)$
5.   **Next**
6. **Next**

Having the minimum discount factors for each expiry, we compute the total minimum discount factor for all expiries as:

$$P_{cl}^J(0, t_i) = P^D(0, t_i)P_{cl}^{s^J}(0, t_i) \tag{11.19}$$

for $i = 1, \ldots, N$.

In building such curves we considered the cost of funding between two refunding dates is completely determined by maximum $\lambda_{t_i}^*$ at the beginning of the period itself. In fact, we do not have any refunding risk and the curve is the same as if it had been derived using deterministic spreads.

We take up Example 11.4.3 and show a practical implementation of Procedure 11.4.1.

Example 11.4.4. *We start as before with the interbank deposit market and derive the maximum zero rates and minimum discount factors with a confidence level c.l. = 99%: they are shown in Table 11.9. In Figure 11.4 we compare the expected zero-rate term structure (from Table 11.7) with the maximum one: since the refunding schedule is yearly, the maximum term structure is smooth and similar in shape to the expected one.*

We can do the same for the other two funding sources. In Tables 11.10 and 11.11 we show maximum zero rates and minimum discount factors for, respectively, the CD market and the bond issuance market; in Figures 11.5 and 11.6 we compare the expected zero-rate term structure (again, from Table 11.7) with the related maximum one. It is clear that the distance from the expected curve is much smaller for issued bonds, since they have a refunding schedule on a five-year basis, which allows fixing of funding costs for longer periods than the two-year basis for CDs and one-year basis for interbank deposits. The shape of the maximum zero rates for bonds is the most irregular, since it changes only every five years.

Table 11.9. Maximum default intensity and zero rates, and minimum zero-spread and zero-rate discount factors for the interbank deposit market at a confidence level of 99%

Expiry	λ_T^* (%)	$P_{99\%}^{s^1}(0, T)$	$P_{99\%}^{1}(0, T)$	ZC rates 99% (%)
1	4.71	0.996692	0.990263	0.98
2	6.68	0.977456	0.958247	2.13
3	7.59	0.951981	0.915786	2.93
4	8.02	0.924191	0.868566	3.52
5	8.21	0.895874	0.819701	3.98
6	8.31	0.867824	0.770949	4.34
7	8.35	0.840383	0.723323	4.63
8	8.37	0.813688	0.677416	4.87
9	8.38	0.787787	0.633564	5.07
10	8.38	0.762686	0.591942	5.24
11	8.38	0.738374	0.552620	5.39
12	8.38	0.714831	0.515600	5.52
13	8.38	0.692038	0.480838	5.63
14	8.39	0.669970	0.448259	5.73
15	8.39	0.648605	0.417774	5.82
16	8.39	0.627922	0.389280	5.90
17	8.39	0.607898	0.362671	5.97
18	8.39	0.588512	0.337838	6.03
19	8.39	0.569745	0.314676	6.09
20	8.39	0.551576	0.293080	6.14

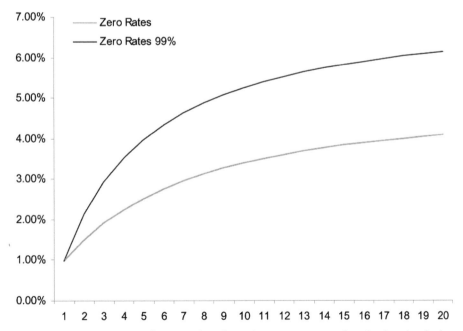

Figure 11.4. Term structures of expected and maximum zero rates for the interbank deposit market funding source

Table 11.10. Maximum default intensity and zero rates, and minimum zero-spread and zero-rate discount factors for the CD market at a confidence level of 99%

Expiry	λ_T^* (%)	$P_{99\%}^{s^2}(0, T)$	$P_{99\%}^2(0, T)$	ZC rates 99% (%)
1		0.998675	0.992233	0.78
2	6.70	0.995949	0.976376	1.20
3		0.985447	0.947979	1.78
4	8.06	0.978476	0.919583	2.10
5		0.966299	0.884138	2.46
6	8.36	0.958597	0.851588	2.68
7		0.946267	0.814458	2.93
8	8.43	0.938537	0.781356	3.08
9		0.926379	0.745024	3.27
10	8.44	0.918772	0.713085	3.38
11		0.906852	0.678714	3.52
12	8.45	0.899397	0.648725	3.61
13		0.887724	0.616803	3.72
14	8.45	0.880424	0.589069	3.78
15		0.868996	0.559731	3.87
16	8.45	0.861850	0.534304	3.92
17		0.850663	0.507505	3.99
18	8.45	0.843668	0.484312	4.03
19		0.832717	0.459918	4.09
20	0.00	0.825869	0.438825	4.12

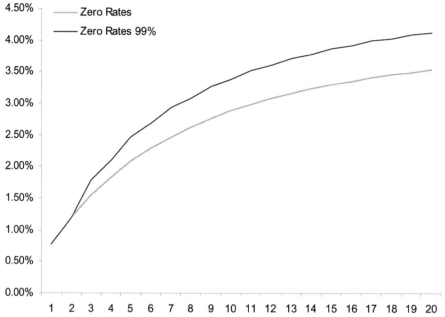

Figure 11.5. Term structures of expected and maximum zero rates for the interbank deposit market funding source

Table 11.11. Maximum default intensity and zero rates, and minimum zero-spread and zero-rate discount factors for the bond issuance market at a confidence level of 99%

Expiry	λ_T^* (%)	$P_{99\%}^{s^3}(0, T)$	$P_{99\%}^3(0, T)$	ZC rates 99% (%)
1		0.996032	0.989608	1.04
2		0.987920	0.968505	1.60
3		0.977958	0.940776	2.04
4		0.967220	0.909005	2.39
5	8.20	0.956199	0.874896	2.67
6		0.920464	0.817712	3.35
7		0.898534	0.773374	3.67
8		0.882918	0.735052	3.85
9		0.870238	0.699874	3.97
10	8.36	0.858961	0.666664	4.05
11		0.826291	0.618420	4.37
12		0.806345	0.581607	4.52
13		0.792212	0.550440	4.59
14		0.780781	0.522400	4.64
15	8.36	0.770639	0.496377	4.67
16		0.741317	0.459580	4.86
17		0.723417	0.431590	4.94
18		0.710736	0.408002	4.98
19		0.700480	0.386882	5.00
20		0.691380	0.367364	5.01

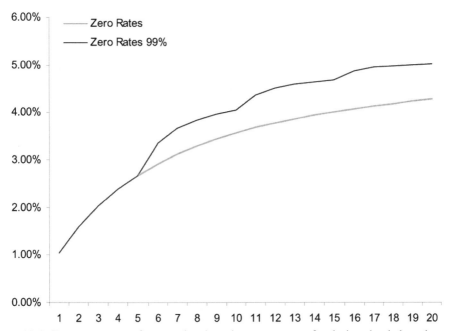

Figure 11.6. Term structures of expected and maximum zero rates for the interbank deposit market funding source

Table 11.12. Maximum zero rates and minimum discount factors for the bank's funding curve at a confidence level of 99%

Expiry	$P^F(0,T)$	Zero rate (%)	Weight of deposits (%)	Weight of CDs (%)	Weight of bonds (%)
1	0.991052	0.90	20.00	50.00	30.00
2	0.970389	1.50	20.00	50.00	30.00
3	0.939380	2.08	20.00	50.00	30.00
4	0.906206	2.46	20.00	50.00	30.00
5	0.868478	2.82	20.00	50.00	30.00
6	0.825297	3.20	20.00	50.00	30.00
7	0.783906	3.48	20.00	50.00	30.00
8	0.746677	3.65	20.00	50.00	30.00
9	0.709187	3.82	20.00	50.00	30.00
10	0.674930	3.93	20.00	50.00	30.00
11	0.635407	4.12	20.00	50.00	30.00
12	0.601965	4.23	20.00	50.00	30.00
13	0.569701	4.33	20.00	50.00	30.00
14	0.540906	4.39	20.00	50.00	30.00
15	0.512333	4.46	20.00	50.00	30.00
16	0.482882	4.55	20.00	50.00	30.00
17	0.455763	4.62	20.00	50.00	30.00
18	0.432124	4.66	20.00	50.00	30.00
19	0.408959	4.71	20.00	50.00	30.00
20	0.388238	4.73	20.00	50.00	30.00

The term structures of maximum zero rates and minimum discount factors for the funding curve can be computed as a weighted average of the corresponding term structures of the three funding sources. The results are shown in Table 11.12. Moreover, for the funding curve we compare the expected term structures (from Table 11.8) with the maximum zero rate term structure in Figure 11.7.

11.5 INCLUDING THE FUNDING COST IN LOAN PRICING

We sketched in Section 11.2 a very simplified balance sheet to stress the main factors affecting pricing of a loan. If we want to apply the expected and unexpected funding curve of Section 11.4 to the single-period setting in which we are working, formula (11.12) is still basically what we need to derive the fair interest rate to apply to the loan, but it is more convenient to express it in a slightly different way, so as to make easier its extension to a multi-period setting. In fact, after some manipulations we have:

$$PL(1) = -A_1 + (1+i_1)A_1 - (1+r+\bar{s})(1-f)A_1 + (1-f)A_1$$
$$- s^{A_1}A_1 - (FO + LO) - LBC - (\pi + \varepsilon r)E \qquad (11.20)$$

where we have used the relationships shown in (11.2) and in (11.1); by further rearranging and by discounting where needed every addend by $(1+r) = 1/P^D$, so as to

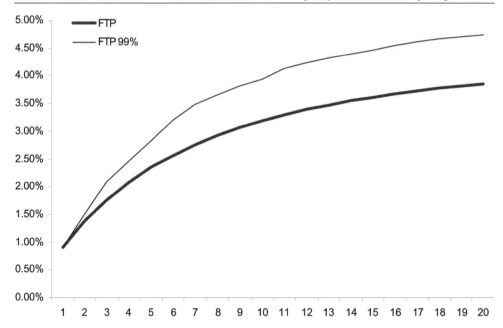

Figure 11.7. Term structures of expected and maximum zero-rates for the bank's funding curve

get the PL at time 0, we get:

$$\mathrm{PL}(1)P^D = -A_1 + (1+i_1)A_1P^D - \bar{s}(1-f)A_1P^D + (1-f)A_1P^D - (1-f)A_1$$
$$- s^{A_1}A_1P^D - (\mathrm{FO}+\mathrm{LO})P^D - \mathrm{LBC}P^D - (\pi+\varepsilon r)EP^D \qquad (11.21)$$

Equation (11.21) shows single-period profits and losses, discounted at time 0 by the risk-free curve. This way of expressing the PL allows easier calculation of fair interest rate i_1^* for the loan, properly taking into account the funding costs and all the other costs related to credit, options, contingent liquidity and refunding. If we disregard the components relating to financial and liquidity/behavioural options and to contingent liquidity, in this setting the economic capital E is:

$$E = \mathrm{CVAR} + (P^F - P_{99\%}^F)(1-f)A_1$$

This is equal to unexpected losses for credit events plus unexpected funding costs due to the difference between the expected and maximum funding curves (at the 99% c.l.).

It is worthy of note that since we are searching for fair rate i_1^* making the PL equal to zero, the curve used for discounting is actually immaterial and can be chosen so as to make calculations as convenient as possible, although the theoretically correct curve belongs to the risk-free rate (see Chapter 10).

To generalize (11.21) to a multi-period setting, let us assume we are at $t_0 = 0$ and asset A_1, which is a loan, expires at t_N and has a capital and interest payment schedule at dates $t_1, \ldots, t_N$. We define the capital payment of loan A_1 at time t_k as $C(t_k) = A_1(t_k) - A_1(t_{k-1})$, with $A_1(t_0) = A_1$, $A_1(t_N) = 0$ and $\sum_{k=1}^N C(t_k) = A_1$. Analogously, we define the liability payment schedule on the same dates as the loan and set $D(t_k) = L(t_k) - L(t_{k-1})$, with $L(t_0) = L$, $L(t_N) = 0$ and $\sum_{k=1}^N D(t_k) = L$. We can write a multi-period version of formula (11.21) as:

$$PL(t_0) = -A_1 + \sum_{k=1}^{N}(C(t_k) + i_1 A_1(t_{k-1})\delta_k)P^D(t_0, t_k)$$

$$- \sum_{k=1}^{N}(D(t_k) + (r + \bar{s})L(t_{k-1})\delta_k)P^D(t_0, t_k) + L$$

$$- \sum_{k=1}^{N}(\pi(t_k) + \varepsilon r(t_k))E(t_{k-1})\delta_k P^D(t_0, t_k) - \sum_{k=1}^{N}s^{A_1}A_1(t_{k-1})\delta_k P^D(t_0, t_k) \quad (11.22)$$

The risk-free rate for each period is derived from the risk-free discount curve ($P^D(0, t)$ is the risk-free discount factor for date t):

$$r(t_{k-1}, t_k) = r(t_k) = \left[\frac{P^D(0, t_{k-1})}{P^D(0, t_k)} - 1\right]\frac{1}{\delta_k}$$

where $\delta_k = t_k - t_{k-1}$ is the accrual period. In the same way we can derive the risk-free rate from the risk premium curve $\pi(t_k)$, if this is time dependent. The fair (fixed) funding cost $r + \bar{s}$ to pay on liabilities can be inferred from the funding curve:

$$r + \bar{s} = \frac{L - \sum_{k=1}^{N}D(t_k)P^F(0, t_k)}{\sum_{k=1}^{N}P^F(0, t_k)L(t_{k-1})\delta_k}$$

Let

$$F^D = \sum_{k=1}^{N}(D(t_k) + (r + \bar{s})L(t_{k-1})\delta_k)P^D(t_0, t_k)$$

and

$$F^F = \sum_{k=1}^{N}(D(t_k) + (r + \bar{s})L(t_{k-1})\delta_k)P^F(t_0, t_k) = L$$

We rewrite equation (11.22) as follows:

$$PL(t_0) = -A_1 + \sum_{k=1}^{N}(C(t_k) + i_1 A_1(t_{k-1})\delta_k)P^D(t_0, t_k)$$

$$- F^D - F^F + F^F + L$$

$$- \sum_{k=1}^{N}(\pi(t_k) + \varepsilon r(t_k))E(t_{k-1})\delta_k P^D(t_0, t_k) - \sum_{k=1}^{N}s^{A_1}A_1(t_{k-1})\delta_k P^D(t_0, t_k) \quad (11.23)$$

Now, $L = \sum_{k=1}^{N}(1 - f_k)A_1(t_k) = \sum_{k=1}^{N}[C(t_k) - \varepsilon E(t_k)]$, which is the total liability needed to finance asset A_1, net the fraction of equity used to cofinance the investment. Assuming perfect cash flow replicating funding, it is easy to check that

$$F^D = \sum_{k=1}^{N} -(1 - f_k)A_1 + (1 - f_k)A(C(t_k) + i_1 A_1(t_{k-1})\delta_k)P^D(t_0, t_k)$$

and that

$$F^F = \sum_{k=1}^{N} -(1-f_k)A_1 + (1-f_k)A(C(t_k) + i_1 A_1(t_{k-1})\delta_k)P^F(t_0,t_k)$$

must both hold. So equation (11.23) can be rewritten as:

$$PL(t_0) = -A_1 + \sum_{k=1}^{N}(C(t_k) + i_1 A_1(t_{k-1})\delta_k)[(1-f_k)P^F(t_0,t_k) + f_k P^D(t_0,t_k)]$$

$$- \sum_{k=1}^{N}(\pi(t_k) + \varepsilon r(t_k))E(t_{k-1})\delta_k P^D(t_0,t_k) - \sum_{k=1}^{N} s^{A_1}A_1(t_{k-1})\delta_k P^D(t_0,t_k) \quad (11.24)$$

To determine fair rate i_1^* we set $PL(t_0) = 0$. The economic capital at each time t_k is:

$$E(t_k) = CVAR_k + \sum_{m=k+1}^{N^*}(P^F(t_k,t_m) - P_{99\%}^F(t_k,t_m))(1-f_k)C(t_m)$$

$P^F(t_k,t_m) = P^F(0,t_m)/P^F(0,t_k)$ is the forward discount factor derived from the expected term structure of the funding curve and $P_{99\%}^F(t_k,t_m)$ is similarly defined. $N^* \leq N$ is the number of periods that the financial institution deems reasonable to recapitalize the firm, should unexpected economic losses occur. The safest assumption is to set $N^* = N$, so that the full economic capital needed up to expiry of the loan is taken into account. This is not what happens for other risks, though: for example, credit risk VaR is computed over one year and the posted economic capital can cover unexpected losses only for this period. Something similar could also be done for refunding risk.[20]

Refunding risk VaR at time t_0 is then:

$$RFVAR_0 = \sum_{m=1}^{N^*}(P^F(t_0,t_m) - P_{99\%}^F(t_k,t_m))(1-f_k)C(t_m)$$

which is the amount of unexpected costs generated by the contract's funding; by discounting economic capital, as in equation (11.24), we get the present value of these costs. On the other hand, the present value of expected funding costs can be derived from equation (11.24), by isolating the effects of funding. This is done in two steps:

1. Derive fair rate $\hat{i}_1$ of the contract without considering credit risk and economic capital, but still taking into account its participation in funding, by the following equation:[21]

$$PL(t_0) = -A_1 + \sum_{k=1}^{N}(C(t_k) + \hat{i}_1 A_1(t_{k-1})\delta_k)[(1-f_k)P^F(t_0,t_k) + f_k P^D(t_0,t_k)] \quad (11.25)$$

---

[20] If the bank calculates economic capital for a horizon shorter than the duration of the contract, the pricing could not be sufficient to remunerate the greater amount of capital needed if unexpected losses exceed those related to the chosen period. This is why we suggest including the full amount of economic capital in the pricing, even if it is not allocated entirely at inception of the contract.

[21] See equation (10.1) for a simplified version of the formula we are presenting here and for a discussion on funding costs.

2. Value the contract with rate $\widehat{i}_1$ by discounting all cash flows with risk-free discount factors and subtract the quantity in equation (11.25). The value obtained in this way is the present value of expected funding costs:

$$\text{EFC}(t_0) = \sum_{k=1}^{N} (C_k + \widehat{i}_1 A_1(t_{k-1})\delta_k) \left[P^D(t_0, t_k) - [(1 - f_k)P^F(t_0, t_k) + f_k P^D(t_0, t_k)] \right]$$

$$= \sum_{k=1}^{N} (C_k + \widehat{i}_1 A_1(t_{k-1})\delta_k) \left[(1 - f_k)(P^D(t_0, t_k) - P^F(t_0, t_k)) \right] \quad (11.26)$$

which is a positive number.

We will now present an example to demonstrate use of the tools developed in practice. To make things simpler we assume no credit risk, so that spread s^{A_1} and the CVAR component in economic capital are nil: our example only includes unexpected costs related to refunding activity.

11.5.1 Pricing of a fixed rate bullet loan

Assume we want to price a bullet loan expiring at time t_N with notional amount A_1, paying fixed rate i_1 at dates $t_1, \ldots, t_N$. Capital is fully repaid at maturity, so that $C(t_k) = 0$ for $k = 0, \ldots, N - 1$ and $C(t_N) = A_1$. To compute the fair rate we apply formula (11.24) and we get:

$$\text{PL}(t_0) = \sum_{k=1}^{N} i_1 \delta_k A_1 [(1 - f_k)P^F(t_0, t_k) + f_k P^D(t_0, t_k)]$$

$$- \{1 - [(1 - f_k)P^F(t_0, t_N) + f_k P^D(t_0, t_N)]\} A_1$$

$$- \sum_{k=1}^{N} (\pi(t_k) + \varepsilon r(t_k)) E(t_{k-1})\delta_k P^D(0, t_k) \quad (11.27)$$

where $\delta_j = t_j - t_{j-1}$ is the accrual period and:

$$E(t_k) = (P^F(0, t_n) - P^F_{99\%}(0, t_N))(1 - f_k)A_1$$

is the economic capital to cover refunding risk (we set $N^* = N$). The fair rate i_1^* is obtained be setting $\text{PL}(0) = 0$, so that:

$$i_1^* = \frac{(1 - P^m(t_0, t_N))A_1 + \sum_{k=1}^{N}(\pi(t_k) + \varepsilon r(t_k))E(t_{k-1})\delta_k P^D(0, t_k)}{\sum_{j=1}^{K} \delta_j A_1 P^m(t_0, t_k)} \quad (11.28)$$

where $P^m(t, T) = [(1 - f_T)P^F(t, T) + f_T P^D(t, T)]$. Given the relation between ε and f (see equation (11.1)), it seems that a circular argument is in formula (11.28). Actually, having defined percentage ε of the economic capital that the bank wishes to invest in the loan, we have that f_k is linked to it via the following formula:

$$f_k = \frac{\sum_{m=k+1}^{N^*}(P^F(t_k, t_m) - P_{99\%}^F(t_k, t_m))C(t_m)\varepsilon}{A_1(t_k) + \sum_{m=k+1}^{N^*}(P^F(t_k, t_m) - P_{99\%}^F(t_k, t_m))C(t_m)\varepsilon} \tag{11.29}$$

Example 11.5.1. *We derive the fair fixed rate of a 20-year expiry loan, assuming we have the risk-free zero curve in Table 11.3 and the funding curves in Tables 11.8 and 11.12. The notional amount is $A_1 = 100$ and it is paid back fully at expiry (bullet loan with no amortization schedule). We assume that the counterparty is not credit risky and we do not consider financial and liquidity/behavioural options and costs related to contingent liquidity.*

We value the contract by assuming different percentages of economic capital's participation (ε) in funding. The results for the economic capital needed to cover refunding risk and the value for f_k (i.e., the percentage of the asset that is funded by the capital at each period) are in Table 11.13. For example, $\varepsilon = 0$, economic capital is $E(1) = 7.434$ for the first year, gradually declining to 0.574 for the 20th year.

If there is zero capital investment in the loan ($\varepsilon = f_k = 0$) then the fair rate is $i_1^* = 4.019\%$; in this case it is also easy to compare the fair rate by including refunding risk, with the fair rate without refunding, which is $\hat{i}_1^* = 3.729\%$, so that the spread due to the economic capital for refunding risks accounts for $i_1^* - \hat{i}_1^* = 0.290\%$. The fair spread for the other levels of ε are in Table 11.14.

Table 11.13. Economic capital and values of f_k for a 20-year bullet loan for different levels of ε

	$\varepsilon = 0\%$		$\varepsilon = 20\%$		$\varepsilon = 40\%$		$\varepsilon = 60\%$		$\varepsilon = 80\%$		$\varepsilon = 100\%$	
Year	$E(t)$	f_k (%)	$E(t)$	f_k (%)	$E(t)$	f_k (%)	$E(t)$	f_k (%)	$E(t)$	f_k (%)	$E(t)$	f_k (%)
1	7.43368	0.00	7.32478	1.46	7.21903	2.89	7.11628	4.27	7.01642	5.61	6.91932	6.92
2	7.50080	0.00	7.38994	1.48	7.28231	2.91	7.17777	4.31	7.07619	5.66	6.97744	6.98
3	7.54080	0.00	7.42876	1.49	7.32001	2.93	7.21439	4.33	7.11177	5.69	7.01204	7.01
4	7.43975	0.00	7.33067	1.47	7.22475	2.89	7.12184	4.27	7.02182	5.62	6.92458	6.92
5	7.42680	0.00	7.31810	1.46	7.21254	2.89	7.10997	4.27	7.01029	5.61	6.91336	6.91
6	7.30527	0.00	7.20008	1.44	7.09787	2.84	6.99852	4.20	6.90191	5.52	6.80794	6.81
7	6.91890	0.00	6.82447	1.36	6.73257	2.69	6.64312	3.99	6.55602	5.24	6.47117	6.47
8	6.58259	0.00	6.49705	1.30	6.41371	2.57	6.33248	3.80	6.25328	5.00	6.17604	6.18
9	6.44378	0.00	6.36179	1.27	6.28187	2.51	6.20392	3.72	6.12789	4.90	6.05369	6.05
10	6.20077	0.00	6.12482	1.22	6.05070	2.42	5.97835	3.59	5.90771	4.73	5.83873	5.84
11	6.09805	0.00	6.02457	1.20	5.95284	2.38	5.88281	3.53	5.81440	4.65	5.74756	5.75
12	5.36400	0.00	5.30706	1.06	5.25133	2.10	5.19675	3.12	5.14329	4.11	5.09092	5.09
13	4.98107	0.00	4.93194	0.99	4.88377	1.95	4.83652	2.90	4.79019	3.83	4.74473	4.74
14	4.50902	0.00	4.46872	0.89	4.42913	1.77	4.39024	2.63	4.35203	3.48	4.31448	4.31
15	4.23323	0.00	4.19770	0.84	4.16275	1.67	4.12838	2.48	4.09457	3.28	4.06131	4.06
16	3.75765	0.00	3.72962	0.75	3.70201	1.48	3.67480	2.20	3.64799	2.92	3.62157	3.62
17	2.84336	0.00	2.82728	0.57	2.81138	1.12	2.79567	1.68	2.78012	2.22	2.76475	2.76
18	1.95273	0.00	1.94513	0.39	1.93760	0.78	1.93012	1.16	1.92269	1.54	1.91533	1.92
19	1.37831	0.00	1.37452	0.27	1.37075	0.55	1.36700	0.82	1.36327	1.09	1.35957	1.36
20	0.57426	0.00	0.57360	0.11	0.57294	0.23	0.57228	0.34	0.57163	0.46	0.57098	0.57

Table 11.14. Fair fixed interest rate for a 20-year bullet loan as a function of fraction ε of the economic capital invested in the loan and difference from the fair rate without refunding risk VaR $(\widehat{i}_1^* = 3.729\%)$

ε (%)	i_1* (%)	Difference (%)
0	4.019	0.290
20	4.045	0.315
40	4.070	0.340
60	4.094	0.365
80	4.118	0.388
100	4.141	0.411

11.6   MONITORING FUNDING COSTS AND RISK CONTROL OF REFUNDING RISK

The framework outlined is suitable to monitor how expected funding costs evolve along with market movements of interest rates and funding spreads. Liabilities on balance sheets have their contract rates determined, so that the cost associated with them is known (at least as far as the spread over the risk-free rate is concerned), but rollover can occur under conditions for funding spreads different than expected. Economic capital, posted when deals are dealt, should be used to cover these unexpected costs.

Expected and unexpected funding costs change because the funding spreads paid by the bank change. In any event, the bank should also consider that the funding cost of liabilities on the balance sheet is locked in until the next corresponding rollover period. Monitoring economic capital is an activity the bank should operate on a regular basis, analogously with monitoring economic capital for market and credit risks using relevant VaR metrics. For funding costs, this risk-monitoring activity is focussed on the evolution of funding spreads in the market and computation of the amount of expected and unexpected funding costs, and checking at the same time whether the quantity of economic capital posted in the past is still enough to cover unexpected costs. Hence, economic capital for unexpected funding costs not only has to be included in the pricing of new contracts, but should also be monitored for existing deals.

Monitoring expected and unexpected funding costs mitigates the impact of distressed periods on:

- *funding policies*, because the bank does not have to change them as a result of an increase in costs that may be unsustainable without a suitable amount of capital to cover them;
- *ongoing activity*, because the bank does not have to suddenly stop its investment policies under stressed conditions for funding operations;
- *profitability*, since the bank can stabilize earnings using capital reserves to offset the volatility of funding spreads.

We now provide an example.

Example 11.6.1. *We go back to the loan we priced in Example 11.5.1. Let us assume that the spreads paid by the bank over its funding sources suddenly rise. The CIR parameters fitting the new funding spreads are given in Table 11.15.*

Table 11.15. Parameters of the CIR model used to calibrate new funding spreads

λ_0	1.10%
Mean reversion speed κ_λ	0.75
Equilibrium rate θ_λ	3.00%
Volatility σ_λ	17.00%

The new funding curve will shift upward, but we still have to consider the fact that the funding has been locked for:

- *1 year on interbank deposits;*
- *2 years on CDs;*
- *5 years on bonds.*

The original and the new zero-rate funding curve are shown in Table 11.16 and in Figure 11.8. In Table 11.17 we compare the first and the updated EFC after the increase in spreads. If economic capital does not participate in funding the deal ($\varepsilon = 0$), the EFC

Table 11.16. New expected and maximum funding curves after an increase in the funding spreads

Expiry	P^F	Zero-coupon rates (%)	$P^F_{99\%}$	Zero-coupon rates 99% (%)	Weight of deposits (%)	Weight of CDs (%)	Weight of bonds (%)
1	0.991052	0.90	0.991052	0.90	20.00	50.00	30.00
2	0.972832	1.38	0.970908	1.50	20.00	50.00	30.00
3	0.948503	1.76	0.942856	2.08	20.00	50.00	30.00
4	0.920200	2.08	0.912912	2.69	20.00	50.00	30.00
5	0.889421	2.34	0.880632	3.08	20.00	50.00	30.00
6	0.857238	2.57	0.838271	3.70	20.00	50.00	30.00
7	0.824427	2.76	0.803242	3.98	20.00	50.00	30.00
8	0.791549	2.92	0.768404	4.15	20.00	50.00	30.00
9	0.759006	3.06	0.734146	4.32	20.00	50.00	30.00
10	0.727082	3.19	0.700734	4.43	20.00	50.00	30.00
11	0.695972	3.29	0.668344	4.63	20.00	50.00	30.00
12	0.665804	3.39	0.637090	4.73	20.00	50.00	30.00
13	0.636660	3.47	0.607036	4.83	20.00	50.00	30.00
14	0.608583	3.55	0.578212	4.89	20.00	50.00	30.00
15	0.581593	3.61	0.550621	4.95	20.00	50.00	30.00
16	0.555690	3.67	0.524252	5.05	20.00	50.00	30.00
17	0.530862	3.73	0.499079	5.12	20.00	50.00	30.00
18	0.507086	3.77	0.475070	5.15	20.00	50.00	30.00
19	0.484335	3.82	0.452184	5.20	20.00	50.00	30.00
20	0.462576	3.85	0.430382	5.22	20.00	50.00	30.00

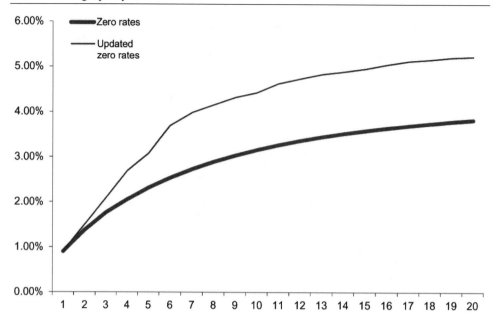

Figure 11.8. Term structures of funding zero rates with the starting and updated levels of the bank's funding spreads

equal 10.21. This is the result of computing the present value of the loan, by discounting it by the risk-free curve, when it pays an annual coupon without refunding risk (i.e., 3.729%), which yields 110.212, and subtracting from this the value of the same loan obtained by discounting it by the funding curve, which yields 100.00. The expected costs increase to 14.42 from 10.21 with the new level of spreads: these are greater-than-expected costs which, should they occur, can be covered with the economic capital posted when closing the deal (7.43385).

Table 11.17. Expected funding costs before and after change in the bank's funding spreads

	Starting	*Updated*
EFC	10.21194	14.42253

It is also possible to simulate distressed market or bank conditions entailing a different and more expensive composition of the funding mix. The liquidity buffer we analysed in Chapter 7 should be enough to prevent a change in the composition of the funding mix. Nonetheless, we have also examined suboptimal liquidity policies when funding gaps are more severe than implied by buffers. Within the framework just presented, the bank can measure any change in the funding curve to identify adverse changes in the funding mix. Example 11.6.2 deals with such a stress test exercise.

Example 11.6.2. *Let us assume the bank starts with a funding mix producing the funding curves in Tables 11.8 and 11.12. The bank tests a stressed scenario resembling an idiosyncratic crisis: starting from the fourth year, its principal resort is interbank money*

Table 11.18. Changes in the expected and maximum funding curves in a stress scenario similar to an idiosyncratic crisis

Expiry	P^F	Zero-coupon rates (%)	$P^F_{99\%}$	Zero-coupon rates 99% (%)	Weight of deposits (%)	Weight of CDs (%)	Weight of bonds (%)
1	0.991052	0.90	0.991052	0.90	20.00	50.00	30.00
2	0.972832	1.38	0.970389	1.50	20.00	50.00	30.00
3	0.948503	1.76	0.939379	2.08	20.00	50.00	30.00
4	0.921207	2.05	0.898118	2.69	40.00	50.00	10.00
5	0.890723	2.31	0.857439	3.08	40.00	50.00	10.00
6	0.858813	2.54	0.815945	3.39	40.00	50.00	10.00
7	0.826249	2.73	0.773896	3.66	40.00	50.00	10.00
8	0.793593	2.89	0.735150	3.85	40.00	50.00	10.00
9	0.761247	3.03	0.695926	4.03	40.00	50.00	10.00
10	0.729496	3.15	0.659987	4.16	40.00	50.00	10.00
11	0.698536	3.26	0.622248	4.31	40.00	50.00	10.00
12	0.668499	3.36	0.588765	4.41	40.00	50.00	10.00
13	0.639465	3.44	0.555782	4.52	40.00	50.00	10.00
14	0.611482	3.51	0.526080	4.59	40.00	50.00	10.00
15	0.584570	3.58	0.496615	4.67	40.00	50.00	10.00
16	0.558730	3.64	0.468824	4.73	40.00	50.00	10.00
17	0.533951	3.69	0.441981	4.80	40.00	50.00	10.00
18	0.510213	3.74	0.418093	4.84	40.00	50.00	10.00
19	0.487488	3.78	0.394519	4.90	40.00	50.00	10.00
20	0.465746	3.82	0.373383	4.93	40.00	50.00	10.00

market, with a weight changing from 20 to 40%; at the same time the weight for bonds experiences a sharp decline of 20%, from 30 to 10%. The resulting funding curve is shown in Table 11.18.

Table 11.19 shows the expected funding costs and economic capital at inception for the loan in Example 11.5.1 (notional = 100) and how they would be modified if the weights of each funding source alter after the fourth year under the distressed condition above. In the stressed scenario, on the one hand, expected funding costs decrease; on the other hand, economic capital to cover unexpected costs increases since the shorter maturities of interbank deposits imply more frequent rollover activity.

Table 11.19. Change in expected funding costs and required economic capital for unexpected funding costs in the stressed scenario of Table 11.18

Scenario	EFC	EC
Base	10.21194	7.43385
Stressed	9.73862	9.23631

11.7   FUNDING COSTS AND ASSET/LIABILITY MANAGEMENT

In Chapter 10 we introduced the main concepts underlying robust and consistent revaluation of the assets and liabilities on the bank's balance sheet. The main idea is to use a single, risk-free discount curve to compute the present value of future payoffs and of expected and unexpected losses and costs, thus allowing for clear decomposition of the total value of contracts and proper attribution to relevant departments. These ideas can also be applied to the framework we presented for funding costs.

Let us assume we have a marked-to-market balance sheet. At time 0, the bank closes a loan contract with a lender (e.g., an institutional investor) which is not charging any funding cost when setting the fair amount to lend. The amount is deposited in bank account D_2, also risk free to avoid immaterial complications. Equity E is held in a risk-free deposit account D_1. The balance sheet at time 0 looks as follows:

Assets	Liabilities
$D_1 = E$	$L = Ke^{-rT}$
$D_2 = Ke^{-(r+s_B)T}$	
	E
	$-\text{DVA}(0) = -\text{FC}(0)$

We now know (see Chapter 10) that DVA is not a reduction in the value of liabilities, rather it is the expected present value of funding costs the bank has to pay due to the fact that it is not a risk-free economic operator. As such, it has to be shown in the balance sheet as a reduction of the value of net equity, rather than of the risk-free present value of debt. The lending deal produces a P&L at inception of a loss equal to $\text{DVA}(0) = \text{FC}(0) = e^{-rT}K(1 - e^{-s_B T})$, assuming that the $L_{\text{GD}} = 100\%$, so that instantaneous spread s^B equals the instantaneous probability of default.

When buying asset A (e.g., lending money to a customer) the bank has to charge the FC it pays for the business activity to be profitable. Let us assume that the counterparty is default risk free, so that the bank does not have to charge any compensation for credit risk in the value of the asset. If the bank has enough bargaining power, the asset will be bought paying $Ke^{-(r+s_B)T}$. Revaluing this at the risk-free rate will produce a profit equal to FC, so that the balance sheet is:

Assets	Liabilities
$D_1 = E$	$L = Ke^{-rT}$
$A = Ke^{-rT}$	
	E
	$-\text{DVA}(0) = -\text{FC}(0)$
	$+\text{FC}(0)$

Funding costs can be split into an expected part EFC plus an unexpected part (computed at a given confidence level) covered by economic capital EC, which is absorbed from equity E. This part of equity needs to be remunerated at the risk-free rate plus a premium $(r + \pi)$, so that the bank also needs to charge this cost when buying the asset (we assume no participation of economic capital to funding of the asset). When computing the present value of the asset by discounting everything at the risk-free rate, an extra profit will result equal to $e^{-rT}\text{EC}(0)e^{(r+\pi^*)T} - \text{EC}(0)$ (with π^* chosen so that it will grant $\text{EC}(0)e^{(r+\pi^*)T} - \text{EC}(0)e^{rT} = \text{EC}(0)e^{(r+\pi)T}$ at time T), which will be used to compensate for remuneration of economic capital. The balance sheet at time 0 is then:

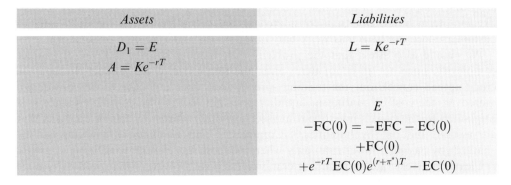

Assets	Liabilities
$D_1 = E$ $A = Ke^{-rT}$	$L = Ke^{-rT}$
	E $-\text{FC}(0) = -\text{EFC} - \text{EC}(0)$ $+\text{FC}(0)$ $+e^{-rT}\text{EC}(0)e^{(r+\pi^*)T} - \text{EC}(0)$

Economic capital $\text{EC}(0)$ will be used only if unexpected costs actually occur, so that equity E will be abated for the corresponding amount. In any case, equity should be at least enough to cover them: $E \geq \text{EC}(0)$. The bank's stockholders are properly remunerated with profit $\text{EC}(0)e^{(r+\pi)T}$ at the end of the activity.

11.8   INTERNAL FUND TRANSFER PRICING SYSTEM

In theory, the framework sketched above should be used not only as a robust method to evaluate deals, but also should serve as the sound base for an internal system of FTP. We adopted an "industrial" approach in the design of FTP (see Section 11.2.1): in practice, having identified all the building blocks to evaluate a product, the business unit tasked with selling is charged the production costs by the relevant units involved in the production process.

When products are assets or off-balance-sheet commitments of the bank, it is quite obvious how to charge and assign single components of FTP. For example, for a typical banking book asset, such as a loan, total FTP is charged to the business unit tasked with selling, which will then pass these costs on to the counterparty (the bank's customer/debtor). Then FTP is split internally amongst the units involved in the production process as follows:

- the interest rate, the funding spread and the contingent liquidity components are paid to the treasury department;
- the credit spread is paid to the credit department;
- market and liquidity/behavioural options are paid to the ALM department;
- remuneration for economic capital is paid to the shareholders as dividends;

- the commercial margin is assigned to the business unit selling the loan;
- the non-financial margin is assigned to the operation/general services, IT departments.

While it is relatively clear how to determine and charge all the components in this case, when the bank tries to do the same with a product that is a liability, things are more complex and several solutions can be adopted. Products on the liability side of the balance sheet include funding sources (such as sight or saving accounts) whose counterparties are retail customers: when dealing with them the bank has strong bargaining power and typically is a pricemaker. More generally speaking, though, the problem of assigning components of the value extends to all kinds of liabilities (i.e., funding sources like long-term bonds not fully considered or not considered at all, products sold to customers since the bank has weak bargaining power and is often a pricetaker).

We should also stress that the problem with funding sources' FTP is of simpler complexity, since not all components enter the total price of the product. In fact, the credit spread cancels out the funding spread, so it does not have to be considered; moreover, the cost of contingent liquidity does not have to be considered since it is originated by the bank's investment in assets (in other words, by selling products that are assets), and not by liabilities.[22] Commercial and nonfinancial margins can be charged (by paying a lower rate) only when the bank has enough bargaining strength.

Clearly, interest rate and funding components pose a problem that eventually boils down to whether the bank should use a single funding curve, or multiple funding curves to price all the contracts. We want to make it immediately clear that funding curves are effective rate curves that can only be used to quickly and easily incorporate funding costs in the value of typical banking book products, but they cannot be absolutely used to include funding costs in more complex (derivative) contracts[23] and/or to include other components such as financial options or credit risk compensation. So, when we speak of multiple curves we are referring just to curves with different levels of funding costs embedded within and nothing else (i.e., no optionalities or contingent liquidity). These curves only serve the purpose of allocating profits and losses to business units – not to evaluate contracts, since we believe these should be evaluated by using the risk-free discounting curve in a fashion like that outlined in Chapter 10.

Moreover, given the general ideas put forward in Section 11.3, multiple curves are not related to assets, since the cost of funding assets is computed out of the weighted average of costs of different funding sources, condensed into a single curve that also takes the dynamic nature of the funding activity into account. It is true that in our framework there is a second funding curve, related to unexpected levels of funding spreads, but in reality this is always the same curve considered under different market conditions. So, when we talk of multiple curves we are always referring to different curves to evaluate the funding component of different liabilities.

There are many other variations on the multiple curve theme: we deem them inconsistent and highly misleading in terms of incentives and signals provided to business units, so we limit our analysis to two alternative solutions which we find acceptable and then flesh out their advantages and disadvantages.

---

[22] The only case in which a buffer is not originated by assets is that of nonmaturing liabilities, but this is due to the bank offering an interest rate on them, based on a behavioural rather than a financial criterion (sight deposits should be remunerated using a zero interest rate). See Chapter 7 for more details.

[23] See Chapters 10 and 12.

11.8.1 Multiple curves

When multiple curves are used, the internal FTP system is based on:

- a curve used by the treasury department to include funding costs in the price of assets: this curve is representative of the weighted average of expected and unexpected costs over the different expiries;
- an evaluation curve for each type of contract in liabilities: these curves represent the fair rate the bank should pay for a given expiry on a specific funding source.

Let us go back to the framework presented earlier and to Example 11.4.1, where the curves used to evaluate liabilities are specific to each type of funding source (in the example there were three curves for interbank deposits, the CD market and bonds issued in the capital market). The weighted average curve to include funding costs in assets is that shown in Example 11.4.2.

When the bank designs the FTP system in such a way, the treasury department is remunerated for the total costs it pays to all funding units, which is a weighted average of the costs of single funding sources. Commercial units tasked with raising funds are remunerated for the cost they pay to the source providing funds. For example, a branch selling CDs to clients will transfer funds to the central treasury department, which will in turn pay interest to the branch (as shown in Figure 11.9 where the branch is the business unit raising funds from retail customers). Disregarding all possible margins that

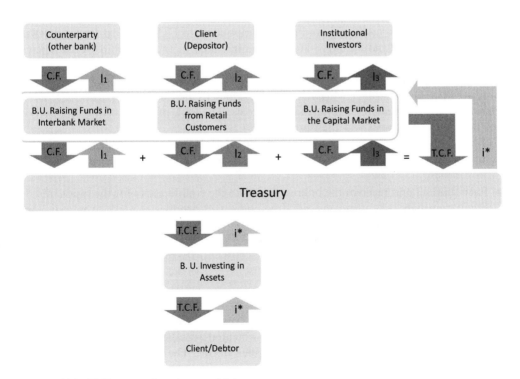

Figure 11.9. FTP system based on multiple curves

contribute to the profits of the branch, and focussing just on reconciliation of the unit's profits and losses, when the business unit transfers funds to the central treasury department (arrows labelled C.F. in the figure), it will receive sufficient interest from the latter to fulfil contract obligations with its retail customers (arrows labelled l_2). Hence the branch will eventually have P&L of zero (again, without considering any possible margin) and the cost related to funding is entirely borne by the treasury department. For other funding sources the mechanism is similar: the interest paid by the treasury department to single funding units is computed according to the curves related to each source (l_1 and l_3 in the figure).

Total cash flow (T.C.F. in the figure) passed to the treasury department is the sum of funds raised by the funding units; the treasury department pays interest to single units such that total cost is i^*.

In Chapter 10 we argued that the most correct and consistent way of evaluating all deals on the bank's balance sheet was to discount all expected cash flows, losses and costs using the risk-free rate curve . So, when revaluing liabilities using the risk-free curve, the treasury department will suffer a mark-to-market loss on each source, which was shown in Section 11.7 and in Chapter 10 to be the present value of funding costs.

The weighted average funding cost paid by the treasury department, originated by all funding sources, will then be charged to business units requiring funds for investments, such as loans. In Figure 11.9, the unit invests in its dealings with a client the money (T.C.F.) it receives from the treasury department. If the asset bought is a loan, the client will be a debtor to the bank and will pay an interest rate on the notional of the loan to the business unit, which will pass it on to the treasury department. Without considering commercial margins, credit risk and other components of FTP, the cost for liquidity is determined by the funding curve and will be included in the rate paid by the client. In Figure 11.9 it is indicated by arrows labelled i^*.

By discounting assets using the risk-free curve, a positive mark-to-market P&L is produced (see Section 11.7), which has to be assigned to the treasury department so as to compensate it for weighted average funding costs. The P&L of the investing unit and of the treasury department will then be zero.

To recapitulate, an FTP system based on multiple curves, as far as the funding component is concerned, works according to the following rules:

- Each funding unit receives the interest it pays to the counterparty for the funds raised. Evaluating liabilities using the risk-free curve will produce a mark-to-market loss equal to expected funding costs EFC.
- The treasury department pays interest for the type of source used to raise funds to each funding unit. This will offset the loss in EFC for the unit, since it is passed to the treasury department.
- The treasury department will suffer a mark-to-market loss when evaluating all the liabilities equal to weighted average EFC.
- The investment business unit asks for funds from the treasury department and will be charged an interest rate compensating for weighted average EFC, i^*, computed using the weighted average funding curve described above. The rate charged to the client will also include compensation for economic capital to cover unexpected funding costs that we have not shown in Figure 11.9.

- The investment unit will have a mark-to-market profit equal to the sum of EFC, which is passed to the treasury department, and remuneration for economic capital, which is passed to equity.
- The end result is that a P&L equal to zero is produced for the treasury department, the funding units and the investment unit.

The multiple curve approach has the following strengths: there is no distortion in investment and funding activity as a result of current market conditions since in the end no P&L is generated for any department involved. Funding sources will not be chosen by business units because of the spread they require. Incentives given to single units to increase the amount of funding from a specific source have to be given by means of external rules. These should be independent of current funding spread levels, so that the bank's management has more control in concentrating funding activity on certain sources (we will analyse this in greater detail in the next section). The weakness of the approach lies in the complexity of the mechanism and the amount of data to maintain.

11.8.2 Single curve

When a single curve is used, the internal FTP system relies on just one curve (i.e., the one used to include funding costs in the price of assets). As in the multiple-curve case, this curve is representative of weighted average expected and unexpected costs over the different expiries. Differently from the multiple-curve case, though, the same single curve is used to compute the fair rate to pay for *all* funding sources, without any reference to the actual rate paid by the funding units on the contracts they deal to raise funds.

The mechanism to allocate P&L amongst the bank's departments, when FTP based on a single curve is adopted, is shown in Figure 11.10. The main difference with respect to Figure 11.9 is in the interest paid by the treasury department to the funding units: a single rate i^*, common to all sources, is received by the units, for the simple reason that a single curve is used in any event. The treasury department will bear a cost that is equal to the total funding cost for all funding sources, as in the multiple-curve case, but in this case single units will suffer a negative or positive P&L depending on the level of the actual spread they have to pay on the source used to raise funds.

For example, assume the single curve used is the FTP curve depicted in Figure 11.3. The business unit raising funds in the CD market has to pay an interest rate that is lower than the FTP curve, so it will receive interest i^* and will pay interest $l_2 < i^*$ to the client (depositor). By evaluating CDs using the risk-free curve, the mark-to-market loss representing expected funding costs implied in the curve of the CDs (the lowest curve in Figure 11.3) will be more than compensated by the interest received from the treasury department. The final result is that the business unit will have a positive P&L when raising funds from CDs sold to retail clients.

On the other hand, when the business unit raising funds in the capital market is considered, the amount of interest l_3 paid to investors is higher than interest i^* received from the treasury department. The mark-to-market loss of the bonds evaluated by the risk-free curve will not be compensated by interest paid by the treasury department, so the funding unit will end up with a negative P&L for conducting fundraising activity in the capital market.

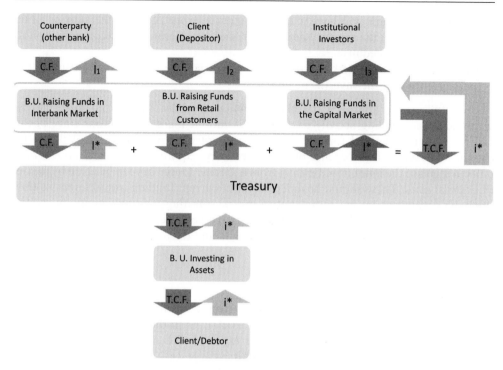

Figure 11.10. FTP system based on a single curve

The treasury department will charge the total funding cost to the investing unit, as in the multiple-curve case. This will be total expected funding cost i^*, as in the multiple-curve case, charged in the final rate passed to the client (which will also include compensation for the economic capital to cover unexpected funding costs, not shown in Figure 11.10). Hence the treasury department will be compensated for the total funding cost that it pays, on an aggregated basis, to the funding units and its final P&L will be zero. The same happens to the investment unit, which will pass the interest it receives from the client (debtor) to the treasury department and to equity .

To summarize, an FTP system based on a single curve that only analsyes the funding component and disregards all others, works according to the following rules:

- each funding unit receives an amount of interest computed on the basis of a single funding curve – not on the specific funding source curve. Evaluating each contract's liabilities with the risk-free curve will produce a mark-to-market loss equal to expected funding costs EFC, which will be more or less compensated by interest received from the treasury department depending on whether the funding source curve lies above or below the single funding curve used. So, fundraising activity generates a positive or negative P&L for the funding units depending on the type of source used;
- the treasury department pays the interest computed by the single curve to each funding unit. On an aggregated basis, the cost paid by the treasury department will always be the total funding cost for all sources, so it will suffer a mark-to-market loss when evaluating all the liabilities with the risk-free rate, equal to the weighted average EFC;

- the investment business unit asks for funds from the treasury department and it will be charged an interest rate that compensates weighted average EFC i^* computed with the weighted average funding curve we described above. The rate charged to the client will also include compensation for the economic capital to cover the unexpected funding costs that we have not shown in Figure 11.9;
- the investment unit will have a mark-to-market profit equal to the sum of EFC that is passed to the treasury department and remuneration of economic capital passed to equity;
- the final result is that a P&L equal to zero is produced for the treasury department and the investment unit; a positive and negative P&L are produced for the funding units.

The advantage of the single-curve approach is that it is simple to implement and to maintain, especially when compared with the multiple-curve approach. On the other hand, it has the disadvantage of generating distortions in funding activity due to the P&L it produces for single funding units. These distortions may not always be welcome to the management of the bank.

For example, sight deposits are one of the cheapest sources of funding for the bank, since the interest rate paid by the funding unit is typically a fraction of the risk-free rate. Hence the funding spread is not just small, most of the time it is negative, thus contributing to abating the average and total cost of funding. Every time the business units raise funds from sight deposits in their dealings with retail customers, they receive an interest rate calculated on the single curve and make a profit. Similarly, units raising funds by selling bonds to institutional investors make a loss since the interest paid is above that implied by the single funding curve.

The single-curve mechanism creates, on the one hand, an incentive for the funding units to continue raising funds by dealing with retail customers through sight deposits; on the other hand, it discourages fundraising from institutional investors. Although this might be seen at first sight as a simple way to make the cost of single funding sources approach average cost and award a fair profit to the funding units that use less expensive sources, in reality it can generate a strongly imbalanced funding mix, with too high a percentage of short-term funding with retail customers.

In our opinion the multiple-curve approach is preferable since it does not create bias in funding activity by generating P&L. Specific funding policies can be implemented by adopting external rules, as we explain in the next section.

Example 11.8.1. *In this simplified example we demonstrate how the multiple and single funding curve approaches work in practice. Let us assume that three funding units operating in the interbank, retail and capital markets raise funds for an amount of 100 each: all liabilities have a maturity of 1 year. The risk-free rate is 5% and the three sources have to be paid at a spread over it as shown below:*

	Funding spread (%)	Total funding cost (%)
Interbank	2	7
Retail	1	6
Capital market	4	9

Figure 11.11. Balance sheet of the three funding units after having raised funds in the market

So, after 1 year the three funding units must pay back 107, 106 and 109, respectively. When these sums are evaluated with the risk-free curve (i.e., by discounting them at a risk-free rate of 5%), the mark-to-market value is inserted in the liabilities of each unit as shown in Figure 11.11. If business units were separate and independent firms, they could invest sums raised at the risk-free rate in a riskless investment earning 5%, so that the present value is 100, and this is what appears on the asset side of the balance sheet of single units. In this case each unit would suffer a loss inserted in the marked-to-market balance sheet as shown in Figure 11.11.

In reality, the three funding units transfer funds to the treasury department. Let us assume that the FTP hinges on a multiple-curve system: each funding unit will receive the interest it has to pay to its creditor, so it invests in the treasury department the funds raised at the same rate it pays on liabilities. Hence, the value of assets on the balance sheet of each funding unit now equals the value of liabilities (as shown in Figure 11.12); this will clearly produce a zero P&L for all the funding units.

The treasury department collects funds from the three units and shows a liability on its balance sheet equal to the present value of the funds raised by them (i.e., 101.9047 + 100.9523 + 103.8095 = 306.6667). Were the treasury department an independent firm, it could invest total raised funds in the risk-free rate, so that the present value of its asset would be 300 (as shown in Figure 11.12). In this case the treasury department would record a loss on its marked-to-market balance sheet.

But the treasury department transfers the funds to the investment unit and charges the total funding cost it has to pay to the single funding units (i.e., (7% + 6% + 9%) × 100 or 7.33% × 300). The investment unit, in turn, will charge this cost to the counterparty, so that the present value of its assets and liabilities match, both being equal to 306.6667, thus producing zero P&L. Furthermore, the present value of the assets on the treasury department's balance sheet now equals 306.6667, so that its P&L is also zero. All this is shown in Figure 11.13, along with the aggregated balance sheet of the bank: clearly, since the bank as a whole raises 300 which it invests in an asset charging total funding costs, the present value of assets and liabilities are the same and total P&L is zero.

Let us now assume the bank structures the FTP system such that it is based on a single funding curve. The three funding units raise funds on the market and transfer them to the treasury department. Each funding unit then receives remuneration common to all funding sources, which we suppose equal to the average funding cost (i.e., (7% + 6% + 9%)/ 3 = 7.33%). The balance sheets of the single units are shown in Figure 11.14: comparing them with the balance sheets in Figure 11.13, it can clearly be seen that the FTP mechanism now generates a P&L for each funding unit. The units working in the interbank and retail markets, paying their creditors less than the average funding rate credited to them when transferring funds to the treasury department, will mark a profit in the marked-to-market

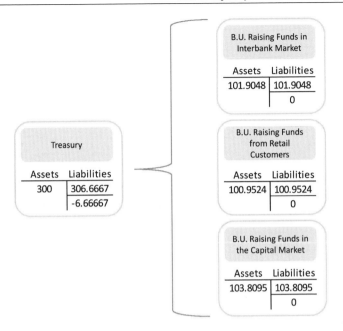

Figure 11.12. Balance sheet of the three funding units and of the treasury department after internal transfer of raised funds (FTP is based on multiple funding curves in this case).

balance sheet. The funding unit working in the capital market will suffer a loss, since the funding costs it pays are higher than the average rate credited.

The treasury department is unaffected by the single funding curve mechanism: its total cost is still the same, 7.333% × 300, so that the present value of all its liabilities is the same as when the bank adopts a multiple-curve based FTP. Moreover, the transfer of funds from the treasury department to the investment unit is unaffected by the single-curve choice, so that the balance sheet and the P&L are the same as in the multiple-curve case. At an aggregated level, the bank balance sheet is also unaffected.

This example confirms what we affirm in the main text: the choice between a single or multiple-curve FTP is important only for P&L attribution of the funding units, otherwise it is quite immaterial.

11.8.3 Implementation of funding policies

The framework described above takes as given the number of funding sources and their weight in the funding mix. We now also know how to assign the funding costs amongst funding and investment units, via the treasury department, and how finally to charge them to the client (debtor). We now examine how to implement a funding policy, with given targets in terms of composition of the funding mix and possibly of total cost paid for funding.

It is very likely that the bank has more bargaining power on some funding sources (e.g., those sold to retail customers) than others (e.g., bonds issued). This usually means the most effective way to abate the total funding cost is to act on the funding mix, by identifying less expensive costs and by incentivizing business units to sell those funding

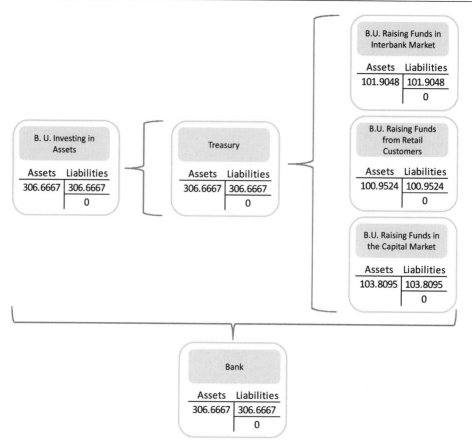

Figure 11.13. Balance sheets of the three funding units, the treasury department and the investment unit after internal transfer of raised funds (FTP is based on multiple funding curves in this case)

products whose weight in the mix is lower than targeted and not to sell those products whose weight is higher. As suggested before, the best way to do this is by using a set of rules separated from the FTP system. One possible solution, provided the bank adopts a multiple-curve approach,[24] is the following.

Assume the target average funding cost is given by the funding curve:

$$\overline{P}^F(0, t_i) = \sum_{j=1}^{J} w_j^* P^j(0, t_i) \tag{11.30}$$

where w_j^* is the targeted weight for funding source j. If the business unit, when raising funds and transferring them to the treasury department, is given back not only the interest it has to pay, but also an extra payment:

$$I_j = \max[\phi \times (w_j^* - w_j), 0] \tag{11.31}$$

---

[24] The analysis of this section can also be applied to the single-curve approach, but in a more complicated way.

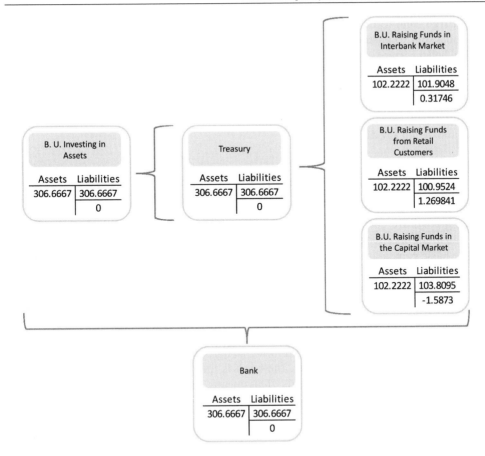

Figure 11.14. Balance sheets of the three funding units, the treasury department and the investment unit after internal transfer of raised funds (FTP based on single funding curves in this case)

then the funding units make a positive P&L which is proportional to the distance of the actual weight from its targeted value. Looking at this in greater detail:

- if the source is underweighted ($w_j^* > w_j$), then the total payment transferred from the treasury department will be higher than the interest the unit has to pay and it will earn a profit;
- when the source is overweighted ($w_j^* < w_j$), there should be no incentive so that no extra amount is paid to the unit.

This is a very simple rule and much more complex rules can be designed to help the bank reach its target.

The problem we now have is whether incentives have to be charged to the treasury department or to some other department. In theory, if the funding policy is not strictly decided by the treasury department, as usually happens in banks, but by top management, these costs are ultimately borne by the shareholder. In practice, the bank may decide to assign these implementation costs to the treasury department, which in turn will charge them to the investment units. These will finally charge costs in the pricing of products sold to customers.

We believe rules designed as above are more effective than the incentives and disincentives implied in a single-curve based FTP. It should be noted that the rule presented above creates an incentive based on the target weight – not the cheapness/expensiveness of the funding source with respect to the average funding source: we already briefly alluded above to the unintended consequences that this second type of mechanism can produce.

11.9 BEST PRACTICES AND REGULATION

We argued at the beginning of this chapter that prevailing best practices, as far as funding costs are concerned, should be considered antiquated and inadequate for the current financial environment.

The basic principle to account for funding in a new investment is so-called *marginal cost* or *matched maturity*: it is the cost paid by the bank to raise funds in the market (usually the capital market) with the same maturity as the investment. This rule, although considered by many practitioners and some surveillance authorities as sound practice, has many drawbacks.

First, this is far removed from the actual funding activity of the bank, which uses a mix of funding sources – not just bond issuance in the capital market. Second, for investments expiring after 10 years, the bank is unable to raise funds with a matched maturity, not even by issuing bonds. This means that the marginal cost in this case would be an assumption based on extrapolation of the funding costs paid by the bank on existing liabilities.

The framework presented above recognizes that the matched maturity rule is in theory the correct way to include funding costs when valuing an investment; at the same time it also improves the rule and eliminates the two drawbacks we mentioned. In fact, it considers a mix of sources that contribute aggregately to the funding of investments; additionally, it takes liability rollover activity into account, which in many cases cannot be avoided by the bank. This activity implies a refunding risk (i.e., a greater-than-expected funding cost) that is explicitly measured and included in the pricing, without pretending that the bank can always fund its assets with liabilities of equal duration. Actually, our framework hinges on the marginal cost, matched maturity principle, although it extends it to all components of the funding mix (and does not limit it to bonds) and to the dynamic nature of fundraising activity.

On the assumption current practices need to be revised, the ideas presented in this chapter and, more generally, in the entire book need to be verified as compliant with current regulation. We start with Basel regulation and the document *Principles for Sound Liquidity Risk Management and Supervision* [99]. The document does not deal in depth with FTP, but there is mention of it in Principle 4:

"A bank should incorporate liquidity costs, benefits and risks in the internal pricing, performance measurement and new product approval process for all significant business activities (both on- and off-balance sheet), thereby aligning the risk-taking incentives of individual business lines with the liquidity risk exposures their activities create for the bank as a whole."

This principle seems to confirm the general setting we have outlined above, including liquidity buffer costs too, although it is so generic that alternative approaches can also be suggested. In the comments to Principle 5, the document reads:

"A bank should consider the interactions between exposures to funding liquidity risk and market liquidity risk. A bank that obtains liquidity from capital markets should recognise that these sources may be more volatile than traditional retail deposits. For example, under conditions of stress, investors in money market instruments may demand higher compensation for risk, require roll over at considerably shorter maturities, or refuse to extend financing at all."

The interconnection between liquidity and market risks is captured in our framework by the volatility of funding spreads. The volatility of capital market sources more likely refers to the amount to roll over (and hence to funding gap risk) rather than to funding spreads, but in reality the consideration can be applied to both.

FTP is given much fuller treatment in the EBA's documentation *Guidelines on Liquidity Cost Benefit Allocation* [7], the key goals of which are:

- development of an adequate and comprehensive pricing mechanism;
- the mechanism should incorporate all relevant liquidity costs, benefits and risks; and
- the resulting mechanism should allow management to give appropriate incentives to ensure prudent management of liquidity risk.

Furthermore, [7] goes on to point out:

"The funding transfer price concept in this paper consists of two components. First, at a minimum, the costs of raising funds from an asset and liability management perspective and the interest rate curve cost component (direct costs of funding) should both be captured. Second, to calculate the correct fund transfer price, indirect liquidity costs are to be added.

Amongst these liquidity costs, one should at least distinguish between (i) the mismatch liquidity cost, for which, the liquidity tenor (not the interest rate tenor) is relevant*; (ii) the cost of contingent liquidity risk, including inter alia, the cost of holding stand-by liquidity available to cover unexpected liquidity needs (liquidity buffer) as well as the cost of roll-over risk; and (iii) other categories of liquidity risk exposure that an institution may have e.g. a country risk cost that may arise for institutions where balance sheets in non-fungible currencies are being funded."

Indirect liquidity costs include not only those related to the liquidity buffer, but also rollover risk, which is meant to be the risk related to unexpected funding costs if the phrase is but an alternative way to refer to the liquidity buffer. Additionally, the footnote is fully in line with the our proposed approach.

The EBA's Guideline 5, "The internal prices should be determined by robust methodologies, taking into account the various factors involved in liquidity risk" supports decomposition of FTP suggested in this chapter. Moreover, in the comments

---

* "For example, if a 3 year fixed rate loan is granted and is funded by 3 month commercial paper that will be rolled over each quarter, the appropriate liquidity cost is the 3 year funding cost and not the initial 3 month cost of CP issued."

by the EBA following the statement, the components of the transfer prices they present strongly resemble those listed in Section 11.2.

As far as incentives are concerned, the EBA's document seems to indirectly agree with our view, since "if management wishes to incentivise certain behaviours, this should be subject to a separate, formal approval and reporting process.". We interpret this as FTP should not implicitly or explicitly incorporate incentives on a systematic basis.

Finally, the need for complex quantitative modelling is indicated in the comments to Guideline 5:

> "Selecting an internal pricing yield curve is a critical aspect since it determines how profit contributions to net interest rate margin are measured. ... For maturities exceeding that of an institution's securities having the longest maturity, the curve may be calculated using an interest rate term structure model. When appropriate and with respect to the proportionality principle, institutions should use internal funding cost curves broken down by currencies."

In the first draft of the document (known as EBA CP36), the last comment on Guideline 5 reads as follows:

> "The internal prices used should reflect the marginal cost of funding. The price should reflect the marginal cost over a homogenous product group as an average, but it should also reflect current costs. Funding already acquired (tapped) should already be taken into account in the prices of products sold (or being sold). To achieve a reliable marginal funding cost, an institution should be able to adjust transfer prices according to current demand for new funding, mainly, when calculating the contingent liquidity cost price. As the required size of the liquidity buffer (and its cost) changes with any new product sold, as well as any new funding tapped, an institution should ideally be able to recalculate the transfer price according to its expected balance sheet term structure (Dynamic Price Setting)."

This was basically a short description of the framework we presented. The final version of the document, although not modifying opinion, is shorter and open to a different view, since it now reads:

> "The internal prices used should reflect the marginal cost of funding*. The prices should reflect the marginal cost over a homogenous product group. As the required size of the liquidity buffer (and its cost) changes with any new product sold, as well as any new funding tapped, an institution should ideally be able to recalculate the contingent liquidity cost element of the transfer price."

In conclusion, the approach we proposed above is not in contrast with any suggestion, recommendation or guideline provided by international regulators.

Amongst national regulations, in a letter sent to all institution treasurers the British FSA [11] highlighted the importance of consistent fund transfer pricing practices. In the letter, the FSA takes a clear stance against the weighted average approach:

> "Of the firms surveyed, 5 charged FTP by reference to the weighted average cost of funding either already on balance sheet or projected in an annual budget process. This

---

* "Cost of making new funding transactions in the market."

cost was expressed as a reference rate plus spread, which was then applied to business line balance sheets, irrespective of duration. This methodology in isolation lacks sufficient flexibility for the FTP framework to be used to incentivise or discourage business behaviour and appropriately charge for the duration of risk. This was demonstrated in some cases in 2007 with the buildup of large inventory positions in certain asset classes, where returns were not commensurate with risk taken, and in the onset of volatile conditions where marginal costs rose sharply and the FTP regime did not appropriately reflect market conditions to business lines."

The point to stress is that the approach "in isolation" lacks of flexibility to direct business behaviuor, but this does not mean it cannot be improved and embedded in a richer and more complex framework to properly account for all relevant risks. Moreover, we believe the same lack of flexibility is also suffered by a pure marginal cost approach, taken in isolation. We do not believe that the poor performance of the FTP systems alluded to by the FSA is due to some banks adopting a weighted average approach, but rather that it is the result of the more structural flaws of designed systems.

12

Liquidity risk and the cost of funding in derivative contracts

12.1 PRICING OF DERIVATIVE CONTRACTS UNDER COLLATERAL AGREEMENTS

The liquidity risk embedded in derivative contracts requires careful analysis because of the complex nature of payoffs and of cash flow profiles. For derivative contracts too the general principle is that the value at inception should be the present value of all future (expected) cash flows, and it should be zero in order to be defined "fair". All costs and remuneration for risks must be included in the fair value to one of the parties involved,[1] hence funding costs and remuneration for liquidity risks have to be considered as well.

Funding costs arise from the replication (i.e., dynamic hedging) strategy of derivative contracts, and in the first part of this chapter we will study how these costs are originated: we will investigate all the components related to funding of the replication strategy and of the collateral accounts in case the contract provides for it.

Currently, most contracts dealt in interbank OTC derivatives are collateralized. A collateral agreement is characterized by the following features, amongst others:

- *Initial margin* (in some contracts defined as independent amount): This is the amount of cash (or other eligible assets, possibly illiquid) that a counterparty has to post to the other in order to cover potential negative exposure of the derivative contract. It is usually related to as the VaR of the deal and theoretically should be exchanged between parties in a symmetric way.
- *Variation margin*: This is variation of the collateral subsequent to variation in the NPV of the derivative contract.
- *Maintenance margin*: This is the level of the collateral below which it is not possible to drop after variation margins are posted. If the balance drops below the level, the initial margin has to be restored.

The most widespread form of collateral agreement is represented by the CSA (i.e., a credit support annex to the ISDA Master Agreement for derivative transactions). Though a legal document, it is not mandatory (banks can in theory sign an ISDA agreement without a CSA), and regulates credit support, represented by collateral, for derivative products.

The CSA defines the asset classes of covered transactions and rules under the terms of which collateral is posted or transferred between derivative counterparties to mitigate credit risk arising from in-the-money derivative positions. If on any valuation date, the delivery amount equals or exceeds the pledgor's minimum transfer amount (MTA), the

---

[1] See Chapter 10 for the distinction between "price" and "value".

pledgor is required to transfer eligible collateral with a value at least equal to the delivery amount. The delivery amount is the amount of the CSA that exceeds the value of all posted collateral held by the secured party.

The CSA is equal to the secured party's exposure plus pledgor's independent amount (if any) minus secured party's independent amount (if any) minus the pledgor's threshold.

The collateral to post must meet the eligibility criteria in the agreement (e.g., which currencies it may be in, what types of bonds are allowed, and which haircuts are applied . Rules are defined in order to settle disputes arising over the valuation of derivative positions.

Although a standard CSA is a long way from being defined by practitioners, some market conventions are common features for many CSAs, as there is no threshold or symmetric terms between parties – only cash as eligible collateral is remunerated at the OIS rate.

It is also worthy of note that CSA agreements usually operate on an aggregated basis: the NPVs of all contracts (also for different types of underlying) included in a netting set are summed algebraically and the net amount is posted as collateral by the counterparty who has a negative total NPV. Clauses relating to minimum transfer amount and thresholds also apply. We will not dwell on netting sets, minimum transfer amounts and thresholds in what follows.

Variation and initial margins are commonly remunerated at different rates. The cash posted for variation margin is remunerated at the OIS rate defined for the reference currency, the cash posted for initial margin is typically remunerated at the OIS rate minus. Eligible assets are not remunerated at all and they are typically transferred "free of payment".

Futures contracts have features similar to CSA agreements, *but*: the initial margin (collateral) is always required by the clearing house and is determined as a small percentage of the value of future delivery (futures price times the notional of the contract), based on the VaR of the contract. Variation margins occur daily but, differently from the CSA,[2] they can be withdrawn if positive to a counterparty, provided that the maintenance margin has not be eroded. In the end they are not real variation margins, but daily liquidation of the variation in terminal value of the contract. There is remuneration for the initial margin, but no remuneration for variation margins.

In what follows we analyse the pricing of derivatives under a CSA agreement, without considering netting, minimum transfer amounts and thresholds. So, we will investigate the pricing of a contract on a "standalone" basis, although we are aware that "incremental" pricing, when netting is considered, may significantly alter the result and then it should not be overlooked if a more refined methodology needs to be applied.

Fujii and Takahashi [70] is a work closely related to the analysis below: they study the effects of imperfect collateralization and introduce a decomposition of total contract value which resembles the one we offer below, which also includes bilateral CVA. On the other hand, we extend their analysis to include the effects that funding costs have on final contract value, disregarding the residual counterparty credit risk due to imperfect collateralization.

---

[2] Some CSA agreements allow rehypothecation of collateral, so the counterparty receiving collateral can actually freely use the cash (or the assets) it receives.

Another recent work related to our analysis is [104], which studies the effects of partial collateralization on bilateral credit risk, keeping the costs due to different rates paid and received on the collateral account in mind. Although their pricing fomulae somehow encompass the formulae we give below as well, we believe we offer a different and intuitive approach to the inclusion of funding costs, with the same proviso as before of not considering credit risk. We also have to stress the fact that [104] focuses on deriving a general formula to calculate the *price* of the contract,[3] whereas we try and derive the *value* of the contract to a counterparty.

12.1.1   Pricing in a simple discrete setting

Let us assume we have an underlying asset S at time 0 that can go up to $S_u = Su$ or down to $S_d = Sd$, with $d < 1$, $u > 1$ and $u \times d = 1$ in the next period. Let V^C be the price of a contingent claim at time 0 (the "C" at the exponent stands for "collateralized"), and V_u^C and V_d^C its value when the underlying jumps to, respectively, S_u and S_d. C is the value of the collateral account to be posted to the counterparty holding a position in the contingent claim when the NPV is positive to it; the collateral account earns collateral rate c. We will assume that percentage γ of the contract's NPV is continuously collateralized, so that at any time $C = \gamma V$.[4] B is the value of a bank account earning risk-free rate r at each period. In this framework, following the classical binomial approach in [56], we build a portfolio of underlying asset S and bank account B perfectly replicating the value of the contingent claim in each of the two states of the world (i.e., possible outcomes of the underlying asset's price), jointly with the value of the collateral account. In other words, we want to replicate a long position in the collateralized contingent claim.

To do so, we have to set the following equalities in each of the two states of the world:

$$V_u^C - C(1+c) = \alpha Su + \beta B(1+r) \tag{12.1}$$

and

$$V_d^C - C(1+c) = \alpha Sd + \beta B(1+r) \tag{12.2}$$

Equation (12.1) states that the value of the contingent claim V_u^C, when the underlying jumps to S_u from the starting value S, minus the value of the collateral account, must be equal to the value of the replicating portfolio, comprised of α units of the underlying and β units of the bank account. The collateral account at the end of the period will be equal to the initial value C at time 0, plus the interest rate accrued c. The replicating portfolio has to be revalued at prices prevailing at the end of the period (i.e., S_u for the underlying asset and initial value B plus accrued interest r for the bank account). In a very similar way, equation (12.2) states that the value of the contingent claim, minus the value of the collateral account, must be equal to the value of the replicating portfolio when the underlying jumps to S_d.

---

[3] In fact, they take bilateral counterparty credit risk into account, as well as the cost of funding borne by each of the counterparties involved.

[4] When $\gamma < 100\%$ (i.e., there is not full collateralization), then residual counterparty credit risk should be priced into the contract. To isolate the effect of collateral, we do not consider counterparty credit risk still present in the event of imperfect collateralization. The inclusion of counterparty credit risk in the pricing of derivative contracts, keeping the funding costs due to collateral management in mind, has been studied in [104], where arguably the most comprehensive pricing formula is presented.

Equations (12.1) and (12.2) can be easily solved for quantities α and β, yielding:

$$\alpha = \Delta = \frac{V_u^C - V_d^C}{(u-d)S} \tag{12.3}$$

and

$$\beta = \frac{uV_d^C - dV_u^C - (1+c)C(u-d)}{(u-d)B(1+r)} \tag{12.4}$$

We indicated $\alpha = \Delta$ because it is easily seen in (12.3) that it is the numerical first derivative of the price of the contingent claim with respect to the underlying asset, as usually indicated in option pricing theory.

If the replicating portfolio is able to mimic payoff of the collateralized contingent claim, then its value at time 0 is also the arbitrage-free price of the collateralized contingent claim:

$$V^C - C = \Delta S + \beta B = \frac{V_u^C - V_d^C}{(u-d)} + \frac{uV_d^C - dV_u^C - (1+c)C(u-d)}{(u-d)(1+r)} \tag{12.5}$$

It is possible to express (12.5) in terms of discounted expected value under the risk-neutral measure and, recalling that $C = \gamma V^C$ and rearranging, we get:

$$V^C \frac{[(1+r)(1-\gamma) + (1+c)\gamma]}{1+r} = \frac{1}{1+r}[pV_u^C + (1-p)V_d^C] \tag{12.6}$$

with $p = \frac{(1+r)-d}{u-d}$. The value of the collateralized contingent claim V^C is trivially:

$$V^C = \frac{1}{[(1+r)(1-\gamma) + (1+c)\gamma]}[pV_u^C + (1-p)V_d^C] \tag{12.7}$$

which is the expected risk-neutral value multiplied by the factor $\frac{[(1+r)(1-\gamma)+(1+c)\gamma]}{1+r}$, making the final formula look like the expected value discounted by a rate that is a weighted average of the risk-free and collateral rate, instead of just the risk-free rate, despite the fact we are still in a risk-neutral world.

The right-hand side of equation (12.6) is also equal to the expression we would get when replicating a contingent claim without any collateral agreement.[5] Let V^{NC} be the value of such a claim, then we have:

$$V^C \frac{[(1+r)(1-\gamma) + (1+c)\gamma]}{1+r} = V^C - \gamma \frac{r-c}{1+r}V^C = V^{NC} \tag{12.8}$$

Equation (12.8) states that a non-collateralized contingent claim is equal to an otherwise identical collateralized claim, minus a quantity we name liquidity value adjustment (LVA) and precisely define as follows.

Definition 12.1.1. *LVA is the discounted value of the difference between the risk-free rate and the collateral rate paid (or received) on the collateral over the life of the contract. It is the gain (or loss) produced by liquidation of the NPV of the derivative contract due to the collateralization agreement.*

The fact that we are still working in a risk-neutral world is confirmed by the expected

---

[5] This can easily be verified by setting $\gamma = 0$ in equation (12.6).

return on the underlying asset:

$$pS_u + (1 - p)S_d = (1 + r)S$$

which is equal to the risk-free rate.

Note that by extending the binomial approach to a multi-period setting, thus introducing a dynamical replicating strategy whereby the contingent claim is replicated by dynamically rebalancing the underlying asset and bond portfolio, the final result of the replica is not terminal payoff of the contingent claim, but includes both the latter and the terminal value of cumulated losses/gains arising from LVA. This has some very important implications at the dealing room level which we examine in Section 13.2.

Example 12.1.1 clarifies how the replication argument works under the collateral and payoff attained at expiry.

Example 12.1.1. *Assume[6] we want to price a call option that is fully collateralized ($\gamma = 100\%$) and written on an underlying asset whose starting value is 80, which is also the strike price. The risk-free rate for one period is $r = 0.10$, whereas the collateral rate for each period is $c = 0.06$. The option expires in three periods; at the end of each period the underlying asset can jump upward or downward by a factor, respectively, of $u = 1.5$ and $d = 0.5$, so that the probability to jumping upward is $p = 0.6$. In Table 12.1 we show how the underlying asset price evolves (with the associated probability below each possible outcome).*

Table 12.1. Evolution of the underlying asset and (in italics) associated probabilities below each possible outcome

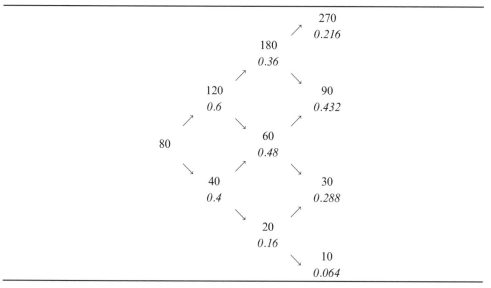

The value of the option can be computed via (12.7) backward recursion starting from the known terminal payoff. The value of the option at each point of the binomial grid is also the value of the collateral account (with the sign reversed). Table 12.2 gives the results and shows the value of the collateralized option at time 0 is $V^C = 38.0851$.

---

[6] This example is the same as an example in [56], with the exception that our example includes a collateral agreement.

Table 12.2. Value of the call option at each point of the grid and of the collateral account (same but with the sign reversed)

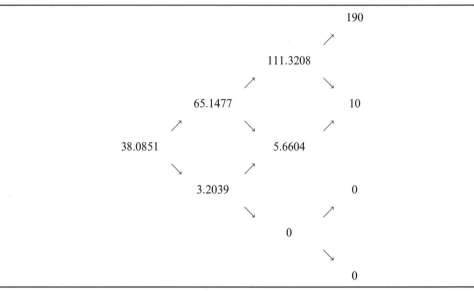

A replicating portfolio can be built be computing the Δ for the underlying asset and the quantity β of the bank account needed to finance the purchase. In Table 12.3 the Δ is shown for each node of the binomial tree along a predefined path of the underlying asset (it is arbitrary and for illustration purposes only); below each Δ we also indicate the quantity to trade in the bank account, plus the interest paid on the amount of the bank account traded in the previous period. At the end of the last period we consider both types of jumps, so as to examine what happens when the option terminates in-the-money or out-of-the-money.

Table 12.3. Amount of underlying asset to trade at each point of the predefined path. Below each Δ the amount of the bank account plus accrued interests from the previous period are shown (in italics)

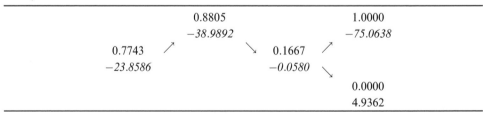

At time 0, the quantity of the underlying to hold in the portfolio to replicate one call option is 0.7743. To finance this purchase, we have to borrow money by selling a bank account for an amount of -23.8586. The difference is the amount of money we have to invest to begin the replication strategy, and it is exactly the value of the option at time 0.

At time 1, $\Delta = 0.8805$ so we have to buy more assets and increase selling the value of the bank account to borrow more money, besides paying accrued interest on the initial borrowing of 23.8586, which we still have. The value of the bank account is then -38.9892. When we arrive at the last period either with one asset in the portfolio or a bank account value of

−75.0638, when the option expires in-the-money; otherwise, we end up with no asset or a bank account value of 4.9362 when the option expires out-of-the-money.

There is an additional amount of money to be borrowed when replicating a collateralized option, and this is the amount needed to finance the collateral account value. Hence, a long position in a collateralized option entails a short position in the collateral account, since we have a cash amount of money equal to the value of the contingent claim. The total cost to replicate the collateral account is given by the difference between the risk-free and collateral rate, times the amount of the collateral account at the previous period. In Table 12.4 we show the cost associated to each point of the predefined path we have chosen for the underlying asset; the cost is nil at time 0 and has to be financed for the other periods.

Table 12.4. Cost to replicate the collateral account at each point of the predefined underlying asset's path

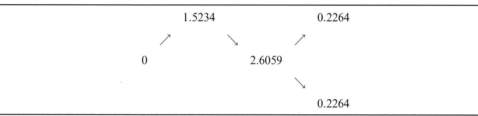

Let us now investigate the replicated value of the call option. This is shown in Table 12.5, where we revaluate at each point of the predefined path the replicating portfolio as far as the quantity of the underlying asset and bank account needed to finance its purchase are concerned. As can easily be seen, the replicating portfolio does not exactly mimic the value of the call, and at expiry the two possible payoffs (i.e., 10 when the call terminates in-the-money and 0 otherwise) do not actually match in either case.

Table 12.5. Replica of the call option with the underlying asset and bank account portfolio

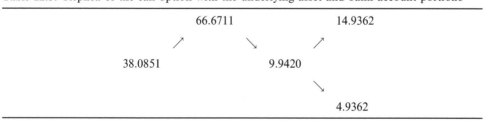

The error in the replica is exactly equal to the cost to finance the collateral account. Actually, when adding the sum of values from Table 12.4 and compounding them at each period with the risk-free rate, we get the total result in Table 12.6, which shows that at each period, including at expiry, the call option value is exactly replicated. At the first period, the total replica is 66.6711 plus the cost of the collateral account 1.5234, for a total of 65.14774, which is exactly the call value in Table 12.2. At the end of the second period, we need to compound 1.5234 at the risk-free rate (0.10) and sum it to the cost for the second period (2.6059). By adding this total cost to the replicated value of the option (9.9420) we finally get the total replication value of 5.6604, once again the same as in Table 12.2. By the same token we can also derive the total replication value at expiry for the two cases of moneyness.

Table 12.6. Call replica including the cost to finance the collateral account

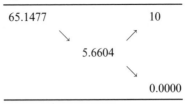

65.1477   10

5.6604

0.0000

12.1.2 The replicating portfolio in continuous time

Now we extend the binomial approach we sketched above to a continuous and more general setting. Assume the underlying asset follows dynamics of the type:

$$dS_t = (\mu_t - y_t)S_t dt + \sigma_t S_t dZ_t \tag{12.9}$$

The underlying has a continuous yield of y_t and volatility σ_t.

The dynamics of the contingent claim are derived via Ito's lemma:

$$dV_t = \mathcal{L}^\mu V_t + \sigma_t S_t \frac{\partial V_t}{\partial S_t} dZ_t \tag{12.10}$$

where we used the operator $\mathcal{L}^a$· defined as:

$$\mathcal{L}^a \cdot = \frac{\partial \cdot}{\partial t} + a_t S_t \frac{\partial \cdot}{\partial S_t} + \tfrac{1}{2}\sigma_t^2 S_t^2 \frac{\partial^2 \cdot}{\partial S_t^2} \tag{12.11}$$

Moreover, we will also set $\Delta_t = \frac{\partial V_t}{\partial S_t}$ in what follows. The dynamics of the cash collateral account are defined as

$$dC_t = \gamma dV_t + c_t C_t dt \tag{12.12}$$

where the first part on the left-hand side is variation of collateral $dC_t = \gamma dV_t$, equal to fraction γ of variation of the NPV of the contract (the initial value of the collateral account is equal to the collateral $C_0 = C = \gamma V_0$); the second part on the left-hand side is the amount of interest produced by the collateral during period dt, given the collateral rate c_t. We denote the funding/investment rate by r_t. The collateral account can be seen as a bank account (actually, it is a bank account), so that receiving cash collateral means being short the collateral account (such as when shorting a bond and receiving cash). At the end the collateral account (i.e., collateral plus interest) is returned to the transferor (at the same time the final payoff of the contingent claim is received by the transferee).

Remark 12.1.1. *It is worth stressing the difference between "collateral" and "collateral account". Collateral is posted by the party for whom the contract has a negative value, to protect the other party against the risk of default. The collateral account is the sum of collateral received by the party for whom the contract has a positive value, plus the interest it generates, which the receiving party has to pay to the other side.*

Evolution of the cash account of a bank is deterministic and equal to:

$$dB_t = r_t B_t dt \tag{12.13}$$

where, as was the case with the cash collateral account, being short B means receiving cash.

At time 0, the replication portfolio in a long position in derivatives V that is cash-collateralized is set up. It comprises a given quantity of the underlying asset and of the bank account such that their value equals the starting value of the contract and of the collateral:

$$V_0 - C_0 = \alpha_0 S_0 + \beta_0 B_0 \tag{12.14}$$

We have to find a trading strategy $\{\alpha_t, \beta_t\}$ such that it satisfies the following well-known conditions:

1. *Self-financing condition*: No other investment is required to operate the strategy besides the initial one:

$$\alpha_t S_t + \beta_t B_t = \alpha_0 S_0 + \beta_0 B_0 + \int_0^t \alpha_u (\mu_u - y_u) S_u du + \int_0^t \alpha_u \sigma_u S_u dZ_u$$

$$+ \int_0^t \beta_u dB_u + \int_0^t \alpha_u y_u S_u du \tag{12.15}$$

2. *Replicating condition*: At any time t the replicating portfolio's value equals the value of the contract and of the collateral:

$$V_t - C_t = \alpha_t S_t + \beta_t B_t \tag{12.16}$$

for $t \in [0, T]$.

The way in which the replicating portfolio evolves can be written as:

$$\alpha_t dS_t + \beta_t dB_t = \alpha_t (\mu_t - y_t) S_t dt + \alpha_t \sigma_t S_t dZ_t + \beta_t r_t B_t dt + \alpha_t y_t S_t dt \tag{12.17}$$

On the other hand:

$$dV_t - dC_t - c_t C_t dt = \mathcal{L}^{\mu - y} V_t dt + \sigma_t S_t \Delta_u dZ_t - \gamma dV_t - c_t C_t dt \tag{12.18}$$

Remark 12.1.2. *Although evolution of the collateral is equal to fraction γ of the value of contract V_t (i.e., $dC_t = \gamma dV_t$), the collateral account C_t also generates an additional cash flow equal to collateral rate c_t times collateral amount C_t (i.e., $c_t C_t dt$). We added these interest amounts when computing variation of the contract value and of the collateral on the left-hand side of (12.18). We are interested in variation of the collateral account – not simply the collateral – since the strategy needs to replicate the former and not just the latter.*

Equating (12.17) and (12.18) and imposing self-financing and replicating conditions, we get:

$$\mathcal{L}^{\mu - y} V_t dt + \sigma_t S_t \Delta_u dZ_t - \gamma dV_t - c_t C_t dt$$
$$= \alpha_t (\mu_t - y_t) S_t dt + \alpha_t \sigma_t S_t dZ_t + \beta_t r_t B_t dt + \alpha_t y_t S_t dt \tag{12.19}$$

We can determine α and β such that the stochastic part in (12.19) is cancelled out:

$$\alpha_t = \Delta_t \tag{12.20}$$

$$\beta_t = \frac{V_t - C_t - \Delta_t S_t}{B_t} \tag{12.21}$$

Substituting in (12.19):

$$\mathcal{L}^{r - y} V_t dt = r_t V_t dt + \gamma dV_t - (r_t - c_t) C_t dt \tag{12.22}$$

Let us split (12.22) in two parts. The first is a standard PDE under the risk-neutral argument:

$$\mathcal{L}^{(r-y)} V_t = r_t V_t \tag{12.23}$$

The second part is more unusual:

$$\gamma \left(\mathcal{L}^u V_t dt + \sigma_u S_u \Delta_u dZ_u \right) + c_t C_t dt = r_t C_t dt \tag{12.24}$$

It shows how a collateral account evolves under a *real* world measure by equating the cost of the bank account used to finance it.

Equation (12.22) has a solution that can be found by means of the Feynman–Kac theorem:

$$V_0^C = -C_0 + \mathbf{E}^Q \left[e^{-\int_0^T r_u du} V_T + \int_0^T e^{-\int_0^u r_v dv} (r_u - c_u) C_u du - \int_0^T e^{-\int_0^u r_v dv} \gamma dV_u \right] \tag{12.25}$$

Keeping in mind the fact that the collateral at expiry will be paid back to the counterparty who posted it, $C_T = 0$, we have:

$$\mathbf{E}^Q \left[\int_0^T e^{-\int_0^u r_v dv} \gamma dV_u \right] = \mathbf{E}^Q \left[\int_0^{T^-} e^{-\int_0^u r_v dv} \gamma dV_u - e^{-\int_0^T r_v dv} \gamma V_T \right] = -\gamma V_0 = -C_0$$

so that equation (12.25) can be written as:

$$V_0^C = \mathbf{E}^Q \left[e^{-\int_0^T r_u du} V_T \right] + \mathbf{E}^Q \left[\int_0^T e^{-\int_0^u r_v dv} (r_u - c_u) C_u du \right] \tag{12.26}$$

Equation (12.26) states the same result derived in a binomial setting above: a collateralized claim is equal to the value of an otherwise identical non-collateralized claim, plus the present value of the cost incurred to finance the collateral, or LVA:

$$V_0^C = V_0^{NC} + \mathrm{LVA}$$

Note that we have not introduced any credit risk until now, so LVA cannot be confused with any adjustment due to the risk of default. On the other hand, it is still possible to derive an arbitrage-free price when the risk-free rate and collateral rate are different, something counterintuitive at first sight.

Recalling that $C_t = \gamma V_t$, equation (12.22) can be equivalently decomposed as:

$$\mathcal{L}^{(r-y)} V_t dt = [r_t(1 - \gamma) + c_t \gamma] V_t dt + \gamma dV_t \tag{12.27}$$

The solution to (12.27) as a result of applying the Feynman–Kac theorem is:

$$V_0^C = \mathbf{E}^Q \left[e^{-\int_0^T [r_u(1-\gamma)+c_u\gamma]du} V_T \right] - C_0 - \mathbf{E}^Q \left[\int_0^T e^{-\int_0^u [r_u(1-\gamma)+c_u\gamma]dv} dV_u \right] \tag{12.28}$$

The second part on the right-hand side is nil, since as before:

$$\mathbf{E}^Q \left[\int_0^T e^{-\int_0^u [r_u(1-\gamma)+c_u\gamma]dv} \gamma dV_u \right]$$

$$= \mathbf{E}^Q \left[\int_0^{T^-} e^{-\int_0^u [r_u(1-\gamma)+c_u\gamma]dv} \gamma dV_u - e^{-\int_0^T [r_u(1-\gamma)+c_u\gamma]dv} \gamma V_T \right] = -\gamma V_0 = -C_0$$

So:

$$V_0^C = \mathbf{E}^Q \left[e^{-\int_0^T [r_u(1-\gamma)+c_u\gamma]du} V_T(S^{r-y}) \right] \tag{12.29}$$

We have added the dependency of the value of the claim on the underlying price, whose drift is indicated as superscript characters. Thus, we have perfect analogy with the discrete case examined above.

When the deal is fully collateralized (i.e., $\gamma = 100\%$), the discount rate in equation (12.29) collapses to collateral rate c_t, which is a well-known result (see, amongst others, [69], [89] and [105]). We think equation (12.26) offers more insight. Actually, discounting by means of the collateral rate is a good way of using an effective rate to reproduce the effects of risk-free discounting and LVA. Should we want to disentangle the effects, however, then we should resort to (12.29). For example, in a dealing room correct evaluation of the LVA allows liquidity costs related to collateralization on relevant desks to be correctly allocated. If a collateral desk exists, LVA can be the compensation it receives for managing a given deal, whereas the trading desk closing the deal will be left to manage just the risk-free value of the contract.

12.1.3 Pricing with a funding rate different from the investment rate

Let us assume the operator of the replication strategy is a bank. The difference between the investment and funding rate is due mainly to credit factors (barring the trivial bid/ask factor and liquidity premiums), so that when considering rates actually paid or received by the bank, we should also model default. Nevertheless, this is not necessary since we are assuming that pricing is operated from the bank's perspective.

Actually, the funding rate r^F that a bank has to pay, when financing its activity, should just be considered a cost from its own perspective, on the basis of *the going concern principle*. On the other hand, from the lender's perspective, the spread over the risk-free rate paid by the bank, is the remuneration for bearing the risk of default of the borrowing bank.[7]

When the bank sells a bank account, it will pay interest r^F on received funds until maturity; conversely, when the bank buys a bank account, we assume there is a default risk-free borrower paying risk-free rate r. Evolution of the bank account in (12.13) becomes:

$$dB_t = \tilde{r}_t B_t dt \tag{12.30}$$

where $\tilde{r}_t = r_t 1_{\{\beta>0\}} + r_t^F 1_{\{\beta<0\}}$ and $1_{\{\}}$ is an indicator function equal to 1 when the condition at the subscript is verified. If quantity β of the bank account is negative (i.e., the bank borrows money) then the bank account grows at funding rate r_t^F; when quantity β is positive (i.e., the bank lends money) the bank account grows at risk-free rate r_t.

If a risk-free borrower does not exist such that we actually have to buy bank accounts issued by other defaultable banks, then we can invest at rate $r^B > r$, and the difference between the two rates is remuneration for credit risk. The expected return earned on the investment will be in any case risk-free rate r. Default of the counterparty, to whom the bank lends money, will affect the performance of the replication strategy of the

---

[7] See Chapter 10 for a detailed discussion on this. For an alternative view, see [95].

contingent claim in any event, so that counterparty credit risk should be eliminated or mitigated whenever possible. We will come back to this issue later.

Assuming that the funding rate is the risk-free rate plus spread s_t^F, we can write the rate at which bank account interest accrues as:

$$\tilde{r}_t = r_t + s_t^F 1_{\{\beta<0\}} \tag{12.31}$$

Replacing the risk-free rate r_t with $\tilde{r}_t$ in equation (12.22), we get:

$$\mathcal{L}^{r-y} V_t dt = \tilde{r}_t V_t dt + \gamma dV_t - (\tilde{r}_t - c_t) C_t dt \tag{12.32}$$

From (12.32) we can easily derive two ways to express the value of the contingent claim at time 0 equivalent to formulae (12.26) and (12.29), respectively, as:

$$V_0^C = \mathbf{E}^Q \left[e^{-\int_0^T \tilde{r}_u du} V_T \right] + \mathbf{E}^Q \left[\int_0^T e^{-\int_0^u \tilde{r}_v dv} (\tilde{r}_u - c_u) C_u du \right] \tag{12.33}$$

and

$$V_0^C = \mathbf{E}^Q \left[e^{-\int_0^T [\tilde{r}_u(1-\gamma)+c_u\gamma] du} V_T \right] \tag{12.34}$$

Equation (12.33) breaks the value of the collateralized contract down as the sum of an otherwise identical non-collateralized deal and of LVA.

To get even more insight and allow for further decomposition useful when allocating revenues and costs within a dealing room, we rewrite equation (12.32) as:

$$\mathcal{L}^{r-y} V_t dt = r_t V_t dt + \gamma dV_t - (r_t - c_t) C_t dt + s_t^F 1_{\{\beta<0\}} (V_t - C_t - \Delta_t S_t) dt \tag{12.35}$$

The solution to (12.35) is:

$$V_0^C = V^{NC} + LVA + FVA \tag{12.36}$$

where V^{NC} is the price of a non-collateralized contract assuming no funding spread and LVA is liquidity value adjustment originated by the difference between the collateral and risk-free rate:

$$LVA = \mathbf{E}^Q \left[\int_0^T e^{-\int_0^u r_v dv} (r_u - c_u) C_u du \right] \tag{12.37}$$

and finally FVA is funding value adjustment due to the funding spread and paid to replicate the contract and the collateral account:

$$FVA = \mathbf{E}^Q \left[-\int_0^T e^{-\int_0^u r_v dv} s_u^F 1_{\{\beta<0\}} (V_u - C_u - \Delta_u S_u) du \right] \tag{12.38}$$

where β has been defined above and FVA is a correction to the risk-free value of the non-collateralized contract, which has to be (algebraically) added to the LVA correction. We define it as:

Definition 12..2. *FVA is the discounted value of the spread paid by the bank over the risk-free interest rate to finance the net amount of cash needed for the collateral account and the underlying asset position in the dynamic replication strategy.*

It is interesting to break total FVA down into its components: this decomposition is not essential as far as pricing is concerned, but it is very useful within a dealing room to charge the desks involved in trading (we will dwell more on this later). Let us now isolate the initial part of total FVA due to the funding cost of the replication strategy of the premium and the collateral:

$$\text{FVA}^\text{P} = \mathbf{E}^Q\left[-\int_0^T e^{-\int_0^u r_v dv} s_u^F 1_{\{\beta<0\}}(V_u - C_u)du\right] \tag{12.39}$$

and the second part relating to the funding cost borne to carry the position of the underlying asset in the replication strategy:

$$\text{FVA}^\text{U} = \mathbf{E}^Q\left[\int_0^T e^{-\int_0^u r_v dv} s_u^F 1_{\{\beta<0\}}\Delta_u S_u du\right] \tag{12.40}$$

Hence, total funding value adjustment is $\text{FVA} = \text{FVA}^\text{P} + \text{FVA}^\text{U}$. Since the indicator function $1_{\{\beta<0\}}$ appears in both components, the FVA of individual components takes the net funding need into account at the financial institution level. Thus, single trading desks also enjoy funding benefit at an aggregated level.

For example, consider the FVA for the cost borne to fund the underlying asset's position: the derivatives desk should pay the funding costs when it has a positive position, but this cost is paid only if the net amount of the bank account is negative ($\beta < 0$). When the underlying asset's position is positive but the net amount in the bank account is positive ($\beta > 0$), the derivatives desk will not be charged for any funding cost, although it actually requires funds to buy the asset.

We are now in a position to analyse five different cases:

1. Let us assume we have to replicate a contingent claim that has a constant positive-sign NPV (e.g., a long European call option) with a constant positive-sign Δ_t. Since $V_t - C_t - \Delta S_t$ is always negative (implying borrowing), the total amount of bank account β is always negative, implying that we always have to borrow money in the replica at rate r^F. The pricing equation (12.35) then reads:

    $$\mathcal{L}^{r-y}V_t dt = r_t V_t dt + \gamma dV_t - (r_t - c_t)C_t dt + s_t^F(V_t - C_t - \Delta_t S_t)dt \tag{12.41}$$

    Although the decomposition in (12.36) still applies, pricing can be performed very simply by means of an effective discount rate:

    $$V_0^C = \mathbf{E}^Q\left[e^{-\int_0^T [r_u^F(1-\gamma)+c_u\gamma]du} V_T(S^{r^F-y})\right] \tag{12.42}$$

    So we can simply replace the risk-free rate with the funding rate paid by the bank and perform the same pricing as when lending and borrowing rates are equal. Equation (12.42) is a very convenient way of computing the price at 0 of the contracts, but is of little use in allocating its components to the different desks of the bank.

2. When the same (as in point 1) contingent claim (constant positive-sign NPV and Δ) is short, the underlying asset has to be sold in the replication strategy as well, which implies that $\beta > 0$ and that the bank always has to invest at the risk-free rate. The pricing formula will be as in formula (12.26) (with reversed signs since we are selling the contract). In this case FVA will be nil. An example of this claim is a short European call option.

3. Let us now assume that the contingent claim has a constant positive-sign NPV, but its replication implies a negative position in the underlying asset (e.g., a long

European put option), then once again we have $\beta > 0$ at any time. The pricing formula is (12.26) in this case too (i.e., the same as in the case with no funding spread).

4. If the NPV has a constant negative sign and the replica entails a long position in the underlying (e.g., short European put option), then the total amount of bank account β is always negative, implying that we always have to borrow money in the replica at rate r^F. The pricing formula is (12.42) (as in point 1).

5. Finally, if the NPV has a constant positive or negative sign and the Δ can flip from one sign to the other, then it is not possible to determine the sign of amount β of the bank account throughout the entire life of the contract. In this case the pricing formula (12.35) cannot be reduced to a convenient representation as in the cases above, and very likely has to be computed numerically. Examples of contracts with non-constant sign Δ are exotic options, such as reverse knockouts.

From the analysis above it is also clear that when the contract is fully collateralized, the effective discount rate is just the collateral rate, whereas the drift rate of the asset can be either the risk-free rate or the funding rate depending on whether the bank account always preserves, respectively, a positive or negative sign until expiry.

Example 12.1.2. *We now show a simple example of how these ideas can be put into practice for a European call option on an underlying asset that could be an equity, an FX spot rate or a commodity. Typically, the model used to price options in these cases is the standard Black and Scholes one:*

$$C(S, K, T, \sigma, r, y, d) = e^{-rT}[FN(d_1) - KN(d_2)] \qquad (12.43)$$

where $N()$ is the normal cumulated distribution function, $F = Se^{(r-y)T}$ is the forward price and:

$$d_1 = \frac{\ln\frac{F}{K} + 0.5\sigma^2 T}{\sigma\sqrt{T}}, \quad d_2 = d_1 - \sigma\sqrt{T}$$

Equation (12.43) valuates a call expiring at T, struck at K, when the underlying spot price is S.

Assume we want to price the call option with the input data in Table 12.7. Since a European call option is a contract of the type shown in point 1 of our list, decomposition of the total value into the several components can be done withtut computing the integral in the definition of LVA and FVA.

Actually, the risk-free non-collateralized value of the call (with risk-free rate drift to set

Table 12.7. Input data for a European call option

S	100		σ	20%
K	100		r	2%
T	1		y	1%
c	2.5%		r^F	3%

the forward price) can immediately be computed as:

$$V^{NC} = V^{NC-RF-RD} = \mathbf{C}(S, K, T, \sigma, r, y, r)$$

The total adjustment of a collateralized option, keeping in mind funding costs both in the discounting and in the drift of the asset to set the forward price, is:

$$\text{TA} = V^{C-FU-FD} - V^{NC-RF-RD}$$

$$= \mathbf{C}(S, K, T, \sigma, r^F, y, (r^F(1 - \gamma) + c\gamma)) - \mathbf{C}(S, K, T, \sigma, r, y, r)$$

Superscript C/NC stands for collateralized/non-collateralized, RF/FU for risk-free/ funding rate discounting and RD/FD for risk-free/funding rate drift.
    The quantity TA can be decomposed as follows:

$$\text{TA} = V^{C-FU-FD} - V^{C-FU-RD}$$

$$+ V^{C-FU-RD} - V^{C-RF-RD}$$

$$+ V^{C-RF-RD} - V^{NC-RF-RD} \tag{TA}$$

Now, LVA is represented by the third line of equation (TA) and can be computed by the Black and Scholes formula:

$$\text{LVA} = V^{C-RF-RD} - V^{NC-RF-RD}$$

$$= \mathbf{C}(S, K, T, \sigma, r, y, (r(1 - \gamma) + c\gamma)) - \mathbf{C}(S, K, T, \sigma, r, y, r)$$

Total FVA is represented by the first two lines of equation (TA); namely, the difference between the collateralized option, discounted by the funding rate and drift equal to the funding rate, and the non-collateralized option, discounted by the risk-free rate and drift equal to the risk-free rate:

$$\text{FVA} = V^{C-FU-FD} - V^{C-RF-RD}$$

We can break total FVA down by recognizing that FVA^U (i.e., FVA due to the underlying asset) is the difference in the first line of equation (TA):

$$\text{FVA}^U = V^{C-FU-FD} - V^{C-FU-RD}$$

$$= \mathbf{C}(S, K, T, \sigma, r^F, y, (r^F(1 - \gamma) + c\gamma)) - \mathbf{C}(S, K, T, \sigma, r, y, (r^F(1 - \gamma) + c\gamma))$$

FVA due to the premium and collateral is:

$$\text{FVA}^P = V^{C-FU-RD} - V^{C-RF-RD}$$

$$= \mathbf{C}(S, K, T, \sigma, r, y, (r^F(1 - \gamma) + c\gamma)) - \mathbf{C}(S, K, T, \sigma, r, y, (r(1 - \gamma) + c\gamma))$$

In Table 12.8 we show decomposition of the total option value into the components examined for different percentages γ of collateralization of the contract's NPV. It is quite obvious that for the non-collateralized contract ($\gamma = 0\%$) LVA is nil. Note also that the total values can be computed straightforwardly via formula (12.42), clearly obtaining the same result. Nevertheless, with this slightly longer procedure we are able to exactly disentangle the different cost contributions.

Table 12.8. Decomposition of the call option value into the risk-free, LVA and FVA components

	γ					
	100%		50%		0%	
V^{NC}	8.34941		8.34941		8.34941	
LVA	−0.04164		−0.02085		0.00000	
FVA	0.56381		0.52086		0.47792	
FVA^P		0.00000		−0.04154		−0.08308
FVA^U		0.56381		0.56240		0.56099
Total	8.87157		8.84942		8.82732	

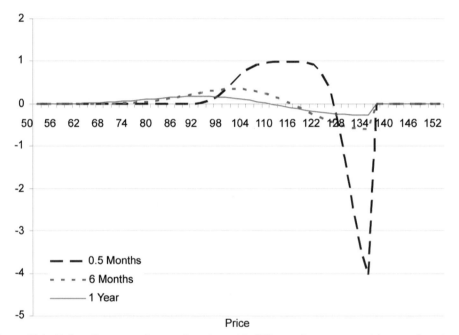

Figure 12.1. Delta of an up-and-out call option with different times to maturities as a function of the price of the underlying asset. The barrier is at 135 and all other data are as in Example 12.1.2

Example 12.1.3. *Let us now assume we have the same data as in Example 12.1.2 and that the European call is no more plain vanilla, but has a barrier set above the strike level at 135. The option is an up-and-out call and can be priced in a closed-form formula in a Black and Scholes economy (see [44] for a thorough discussion of barrier options and for pricing formulae, with a focus on the FX market).*

In this case it is not possible to use the decomposition used in Example 12.1.2 because the Δ of the up-and-out call can flip from one sign to the other, depending on the level of the underlying asset. We are now in the fifth case of the above list. In Figure 12.1 we depict the Δ as a function of the price of the underlying asset, for three different times to maturity, progressively approaching the contract's expiry: the plots simply confirm what

Table 12.9. Decomposition of the value of an up-and-out call option in its non-collateralized risk-free value, LVA and FVA

V^{NC}	4.04127
LVA	−0.02215
FVA	0.21679
Total	4.23502

we have written. In this case we resort to a numerical integration of formulae (12.37) and (12.38).[8]

Decomposition of the price is given in Table 12.9 only for the case when the contract if *fully collateralized (γ = 100%). This means that FVA contains only the component related to financing of the underlying asset. The lower amount of both LVA and FVA with respect to the corresponding European plain vanilla call just examined is easily justified.*

12.1.4 Funding rate different from investment rate and repo rate

We now introduce the possibility of lending and borrowing money (or, alternatively, the underlying asset) via a repo transaction. This is actually the way traders finance and buy the underlying asset (typically in the stock market), by borrowing money and lending the asset as collateral until expiry of the contract.

A repo transaction can be seen as a collateralized loan and the rate paid is lower than the unsecured funding rate of the bank, since in case of default of the borrower, the asset can be sold to guarantee the (possibly only partial) recovery of the lent sum. The difference between repo rate r^E and the risk-free rate is due to the fact that the underlying asset can be worth less than the lent amount when default occurs: so volatility of the asset and probability of default both affect the repo rate.

We assume that the repo rate is the same when borrowing money or lending money against the underlying asset (repo and reverse repo). This means that we are assuming that the two banks involved in the transaction have the same probability of default with the same recovery rate in the event of default. We will investigate replication costs and the pricing formulae for four of the five possible cases in the list above.

A repo transaction is the proper way to finance buying the underlying asset in the replication strategy. On the other hand, if we really want to consider the actual alternatives that are available to a trader to invest received sums in a less credit-risky way, reverse repo seems an effective option in most cases. So, as far as the buying and selling of the underlying asset are concerned, we go back to the case when there is no asymmetry between investment (lending) and the funding rate, although the risk-free rate is replaced by the repo rate. The amount to be lent/borrowed via the bank account is now:

$$\beta_t = \frac{V_t - C_t}{B_t} \tag{12.44}$$

---

[8] We used 45 time steps within the contract's duration of 1 year and a 50-point Gauss–Legendre quadrature scheme for each time step.

whereas the quantity $\alpha_t = \Delta_t$ of the underlying asset is repoed/reverse-repoed, thus paying/receiving interest $r_t^E \Delta_t S_t$. Replacing these quantities in equation (12.22), we get:

$$\mathcal{L}^{r^E - y} V_t dt = \tilde{r}_t V_t dt + \gamma dV_t - (\tilde{r}_t - c_t) C_t dt \tag{12.45}$$

The solution to (12.45) is:

$$V_0^C = V^{NC} + \text{LVA} + \text{FVA} \tag{12.46}$$

where, as usual, V^{NC} is the price of the non-collateralized contract assuming no funding spread and repo, LVA is liquidity value adjustment due to the collateral agreement:

$$\text{LVA} = \mathbf{E}^Q \left[\int_0^T e^{-\int_0^u r_v dv} (r_u - c_u) C_u du \right]$$

and FVA is funding value adjustment:

$$\text{FVA} = \mathbf{E}^Q \left[-\int_0^T e^{-\int_0^u r_v dv} [s_u^F \mathbf{1}_{\{\beta < 0\}} (V_u - C_u) - s_t^E \Delta_u S_u] du \right] \tag{12.47}$$

FVA in this case is split into the funding cost needed to finance the collateral $(s_u^F \mathbf{1}_{\{\beta < 0\}} (V_u - C_u))$ and the spread of the repo rate over the risk-free rate $(s_t^E = r_t^E - r_t)$ paid on the position of amount Δ_t of the underlying asset.

To better understand how total FVA is built, we split formula (12.47) into two components: the first is FVA^P, the cost borne to fund the premium and the collateral (it is the same as in (12.39)). The second part refers to the repo cost to buy or sell the underlying asset to replicate the payoff:

$$\text{FVA}^R = \mathbf{E}^Q \left[\int_0^T e^{-\int_0^u r_v dv} s_t^E \Delta_u S_u du \right] \tag{12.48}$$

Furthermore, it is possible in this case to rewrite (12.46) in a more convenient fashion for computational purposes:

$$V_0^C = \mathbf{E}^Q \left[e^{-\int_0^T [\tilde{r}_u(1-\gamma) + c_u \gamma] du} V_T(S^{r^E - y}) \right] \tag{12.49}$$

Formula (12.49) applies to the five cases analysed in the previous section: the discount factor depends on the sign of the bank account needed to fund the collateral account, whereas the drift of the underlying asset is always the repo rate r^E.

Example 12.1.4. *We revert to Example 12.1.2 for the pricing of a European call option, but we now assume that the bank can buy or sell the underlying asset via repo transactions. We ascertain how the components of total value change in this case. We still use the same inputs as in Table 12.7, but we add to them the repo rate set at $r^E = 2.25\%$, which is lower than the unsecured funding rate $r^F = 3\%$, but higher than the risk-free rate $r = 2\%$ to account for volatility of the collateral (the underlying asset) and the possibility of a smaller collateral value on default of the borrower (the bank).*

Let us exploit once again the fact that a European option is a type of contract that falls in the first case analysed above and keep the same considerations we made in Section 12.1.2.

Table 12.10. Decomposition of the value of the call option into the risk-free, LVA and FVA components when the underlying asset is traded via repo contracts

	γ					
	100%		50%		0%	
V^{NC}	8.34941		8.34941		8.34941	
LVA	−0.04164		−0.02085		0.00000	
FVA	0.13860		0.13860		0.13895	
FVA^P		0.00000		0.00000		0.00000
FVA^R		0.13860		0.13895		0.13930
Total	8.44636		8.46751		8.48870	

We define LVA as above:

$$\text{LVA} = V^{C-RF-RD} - V^{NC-RF-RD}$$

$$= \mathbf{C}(S, K, T, \sigma, r, y, (r(1-\gamma) + c\gamma)) - \mathbf{C}(S, K, T, \sigma, r, y, r)$$

and the two components of FVA as:

$$\text{FVA}^R = V^{C-FU-FD} - V^{C-FU-RD}$$

$$= \mathbf{C}(S, K, T, \sigma, r^E, y, (r(1-\gamma) + c\gamma)) - \mathbf{C}(S, K, T, \sigma, r, y, (r(1-\gamma) + c\gamma))$$

Decomposition of total option value into the different components for different percentages of collateralization is given in Table 12.10.

12.1.5 Interest rate derivatives

As far as the pricing of interest rate derivatives is concerned, we have to consider the credit issue as being critically important. Despite analysing replication of a contingent contract with repo transactions, which virtually eliminates credit risk, or at least makes it negligible, unfortunately, it is not possible to replicate interest rate derivatives with such a low level of credit risk, since the replication strategy involves unsecured lending (besides the borrowing) as part of the underlying itself. For example, without credit risk, a FRA can be replicated by selling/buying a shorter maturity bond and buying/selling a longer maturity bond. With credit risk this strategy is clearly flawed since the counterparty to whom we lent money can default before expiry of the bond.

This means that in practice basic interest rate derivatives are no longer real derivatives, but primary securities that cannot be replicated by means of other primary securities (e.g., bonds). The derivative contract can be made credit risk-free by a collateral agreement, but we can no longer set up a strategy to replicate the payoff and evolution of the collateral account, as we have done above for derivatives on different assets. The implications of being unable to implement a replication strategy become apparent by analysing a couple of contracts: a forward rate agreement (FRA) and an interest rate swap (IRS).

Forward rate agreement

Let us introduce a setup to price interest rate derivatives under collateral agreements.[9] Let us consider times t, T_{i-1} and T_i, $t \leq T_{i-1} < T_i$. The time t forward rate is defined as the rate to be exchanged at time T_i for the Libor rate $L_i(T_{i-1}) = L(T_{i-1}, T_i)$ fixed at time T_{i-1}, in a $\text{FRA}(t; T_{i-1}, T_i)$ contract, so that the contract has zero value at time t.

In the absence of credit risk (i.e., in a single-curve environment), the forward rate can be determined via a portfolio of long and short zero-coupon bonds. The absence of arbitrage also implies the existence of a single, risk-free, discounting curve. Let us assume we have a discount curve denoted by D; we then have:

$$L^D(t; T_{i-1}, T_i) = \frac{1}{T_i - T_{i-1}} \left[\frac{P^D(t, T_{i-1})}{P^D(t, T_i)} - 1 \right] \tag{12.50}$$

The FRA fair forward rate can be set according to definition of the contract:

$$\text{FRA}(T_1; T_1, T_2) = \frac{T_i - T_{i-1}}{1 + L_i(T_{i-1})(T_i - T_{i-1})} \left[L_i(T_{i-1}) - K \right] \tag{12.51}$$

Let us now assume we are in a credit-risky economy. Selling and buying bonds does not allow replicating the FRA payoff since it is always possible that the counterparty to whom we lent money defaults. The forward that is being traded in the market in this case should be simply considered as the expected value of Libor at the fixing time. If we accept that market quotes refer to trades between counterparties with a collateral agreement, then we can quite safely assume that the expected value is taken under a risk-free bond numeraire. The pricing formula is similar to the one presented above for contracts on other underlying assets, although in this case it is not derived from a replication argument, rather it is an assertion:

$$\text{FRA}(t; T_{i-1}, T_i) = P^D(t, T_i) \tau_i E^{T_i} [L_i(T_{i-1}) - K] + \text{LVA}_{\text{FRA}(t;T_{i-1},T_i)} \tag{12.52}$$

that is, the expected Libor rate under the T_i forward measure of the value of the contract at expiry T_{i-1} plus LVA. In (12.52) $\tau_i = T_i - T_{i-1}$.

The LVA in this case is the present value of the difference between the risk-free rate $L_j^D(t)$ and the collateral rate $O_j(t)$, fixed at date t_{j-1} and valid until date t_j, applied to fraction γ of the value of contract $\text{FRA}(t_j; T_{i-1}, T_2)$ for a total of N days between t and the forward settlement T_1, so that $t_N = T_1$:

$$\text{LVA}_{\text{FRA}(t;T_{i-1},T_i)} = \sum_{j=1}^{N} P^D(t, t_j) E^{t_j} \left[\tau_j^C [L_j^D(t) - O_j(t)] \gamma \text{FRA}(t_j; T_{i-1}, T_i) \right] \tag{12.53}$$

where $\tau_j^C = t_j - t_{j-1}$ is the difference in the fraction into which the year is split between two rebalancing times of the collateral: one day in our case. Formula (12.52), given the definition of LVA in (12.53), is recursive. We assume that market quotes for FRAs refer to the case when LVA is nil. This means that the collateral rate is supposed to be risk-free rate $L^D(t; t_{j-1}, t_j) = O(t; t_{j-1}, t_j)$, for all j, which is not unreasonable since standard

---

[9] Both the setup and the notation are the same as in [89].

CSA agreements between banks provide for remuneration of the collateral account at the OIS (or equivalent for other currencies) rate. The OIS rate can also be considered as a virtually risk-free rate or at least as embedding a negligible spread for default risk. If this holds true, then equation (12.52) reads as:

$$\text{FRA}(t; T_{i-1}, T_i) = P^D(t, T_i)\tau_i \mathbf{E}^{T_i}[L_i(T_{i-1}) - K] \tag{12.54}$$

so that we retrieve the standard result, as in [89], that the FRA fair rate is the expected value of Libor at the settlement date of the contract under the T_i forward risk measure at expiry:

$$K = L_i(t) = \mathbf{E}^{T_i}[L_i(T_{i-1})] \tag{12.55}$$

Despite assuming that the market FRA settles at T_i, according to market conventions it actually settles the present value of the T_i payoff at T_{i-1}. The market FRA fair rate is then different from the "theoretical" rate in (12.55), since the latter should be corrected by means of convexity adjustment as discussed in [91]. The adjustment is nevertheless quite small (fraction of a basis point) and can be neglected under typical market conditions, so we will not consider it.

When the collateral agreement provides for remuneration of the collateral that is different from the OIS rate, then we have LVA $\neq 0$, and the FRA fair rate has to be valued recursively. Let $Q_i(t) = L_i^D(t) - O_i(t)$ be the spread between the daily risk-free rate and the collateral rate and assume it is a stochastic process independent of the value of the FRA; we can rewrite equation (12.53) as:

$$\text{LVA}_{\text{FRA}(t; T_{i-1}, T_i)} = \sum_{j=1}^{N} P^D(t, t_j) \mathbf{E}^{t_j}[\tau_j^C Q_j(t)] \mathbf{E}^{t_j}[\gamma \text{FRA}(t_j; T_{i-1}, T_i)] \tag{12.56}$$

The second expectation in (12.56) is $P^D(t, T_i)\tau_i \mathbf{E}_D^{T_i}[\gamma(L_i(T_{i-1}) - K)]/P^D(t, t_j)$, so that we finally get:

$$\text{LVA}_{\text{FRA}(t; T_{i-1}, T_i)} = \sum_{j=1}^{N} P^D(t, t_j) \left[\mathbf{E}^{t_j}[\tau_j^C Q_j(t)] \frac{P^D(t, T_i)\tau_i \mathbf{E}_D^{T_i}[\gamma(L_i(T_{i-1}) - K)]}{P^D(t, t_j)} \right] \tag{12.57}$$

In much the same way, we can derive the FVA for an FRA: let $L^F(t; t_{i-1}, t_i) = L_i^F(t)$ be the funding rate paid by the bank (same notation as above). When financing the collateral (i.e., when the NPV of the contract is negative to the bank), it has to pay this rate to fund the collateral it has to post. In the opposite situation (i.e., when the NPV is positive), the bank invests the collateral received at the risk-free rate, paying the collateral rate.

Let $U(t; t_{i-1}, t_j) = U_j(t) = L_j^F(t) - L_j^D(t)$ be the funding spread over the risk-free rate and assume it is not correlated with the NPV of the FRA. FVA is then:

$$\text{FVA}_{\text{FRA}(t; T_{i-1}, T_i)} = \sum_{j=1}^{N} P^D(t, t_j) \left[\mathbf{E}^{t_j}[\tau_j^C U_j(t)] \frac{P^D(t, T_i)\tau_i \mathbf{E}^{T_i}[\gamma(L_i(T_{i-1}) - K)^-]}{P^D(t, t_j)} \right] \tag{12.58}$$

where $\mathbf{E}[X^-] = \mathbf{E}[\min(X, 0)]$. It is easy to check that:

$$\frac{P^D(t, T_i)\tau_i \mathbf{E}^{T_i}[\gamma(L_i(T_{i-1}) - K)^-]}{P^D(t, t_j)} = -\frac{[\gamma\tau_i\text{Floorlet}(t_j; T_{i-1}, T_i, K)]}{P^D(t, t_j)}$$

where Floorlet$(t_j; T_{i-1}, T_i, K)$ is the price of a floorlet at time t_j, expiry at T_{i-1}, settlement at T_i, with strike K. If the bank has a short position in the FRA, then FVA is

$$\frac{P^D(t, T_i)\tau_i \mathbf{E}^{T_i}[\gamma(K - L_i(T_{i-1}))^-]}{P^D(t, t_j)} = -\frac{[\gamma\tau_i \text{Caplet}(t_j; T_{i-1}, T_i, K)]}{P^D(t, t_j)}$$

where Caplet$(t_i; T_{i-1}, T_i, K)$ is the price of a caplet and the arguments of the function are the same as for the floorlet.

The total value of the FRA is:

$$\text{FRA}(t; T_{i-1}, T_i) = P^D(t, T_i)\tau_i \mathbf{E}^{T_i}[L_i(T_{i-1}) - K] + \text{LVA}_{\text{FRA}(t;T_{i-1},T_i)} + \text{FVA}_{\text{FRA}(t;T_{i-1},T_i)}$$
(12.59)

In any case, the fair rate making the value of the contract at inception zero, has to be computed recursively.

Interest rate swap

Let us now consider an IRS whose fixed leg pays a rate denoted by K on dates $T_c^S, \ldots, T_d^S$ ($\tau_k^S = T_i^S - T_{i-1}^S$). The present value of these payments is obtained by discounting them with discount curve D. The floating leg receives Libor fixings on dates $T_a, \ldots, T_b$ and the present value is also obtained by discounting with discount curve D. We assume that the set of floating rate dates includes the set of fixed rate dates. The value at time t of the IRS is:

$$\text{IRS}(t, K; T_a, \ldots, T_b, T_c^S, \ldots, T_c^S) = \left[\sum_{k=a}^{b} P^D(t, T_k)\tau_k L_k(t) - \sum_{j=c}^{d} P^D(t, T_j)\tau_j^S K\right]$$
$$+ \text{LVA}_{\text{IRS}(t;T_a,T_b)}$$
(12.60)

where LVA is defined as:

$$\text{LVA}_{\text{IRS}(t;T_a,T_b)} = \sum_{j=1}^{N} P^D(t, t_j)\mathbf{E}^{t_j}\left[\tau_j^C[L_j^D(t) - O_j(t)]\gamma \text{IRS}(t_j; T_a, T_b)\right] \quad (12.61)$$

where $\text{IRS}(t; T_a, T_b) = \text{IRS}(t, K; T_a, \ldots, T_b, T_c^S, \ldots, T_c^S)$. LVA in this case is once again the difference between the risk-free rate and the collateral rate applied to fraction γ of the NPV, for a total of N days occurring between valuation date t and the end of the contract $t_N = T_b$.

As far as swaps are concerned, we make the assumption that market quotes refer to the situation when LVA $= 0$, implying that the risk-free and collateral rates are the same. The market swap rate is then the level making the value of the contract at inception T_a zero:

$$K = S_{a,b}(t) = \frac{\sum_{k=a}^{b} P^D(t, T_k)\tau_k L_k(t)}{\sum_{j=c}^{d} P^D(t, T_j)\tau_j^S}$$
(12.62)

When the risk-free and collateral rates are different, LVA can be evaluated in much the same was as the FRA. We then have:

$$\mathrm{LVA}_{\mathrm{IRS}(t;T_a,T_b)} = \sum_{j=1}^{N} P^D(t,t_j)\mathbf{E}^{t_j}[\tau_j^C Q_j(t)]\mathbf{E}^{t_j}[\gamma\mathrm{IRS}(t_j;T_a,T_b)] \qquad (12.63)$$

The second expectation in (12.63) is $C_D^{a,b}(t)\mathbf{E}^{a,b}[\gamma(S_{a,b}(t)-K)]/P^D(t,t_j)$, where $\mathbf{E}^{a,b}$ is the expectation taken under the swap measure, with the numeraire equal to annuity $C_D^{a,b}(t) = \sum_{j=a+1}^{b} P^D(t,T_j)\tau_j^S$. So we can finally write:

$$\mathrm{LVA}_{\mathrm{IRS}(t;T_a,T_b)} = \sum_{j=1}^{N} P^D(t,t_j)\left[\mathbf{E}^{t_j}[\tau_j^C Q_j(t)]\frac{C_D^{a,b}(t)\mathbf{E}^{a,b}[\gamma(S_{a,b}(t)-K)]}{P^D(t,t_j)}\right] \qquad (12.64)$$

FVA can also be defined analogously with the FRA case and, using the same notation as above, we have:

$$\mathrm{FVA}_{\mathrm{IRS}(t;T_a,T_b)} = \sum_{j=1}^{N} P^D(t,t_j)\left[\mathbf{E}^{t_j}[\tau_j^C U_j(t)]\frac{C_D^{a,b}(t)\mathbf{E}^{a,b}[\gamma(S_{a,b}(t)-K)^-]}{P^D(t,t_j)}\right] \qquad (12.65)$$

We can make use of the option on swaps to express the second expectation in (12.65) as:

$$\frac{C_D^{a,b}(t)\mathbf{E}^{a,b}[\gamma(S_{a,b}(t)-K)^-]}{P^D(t,t_j)} = -\frac{c[\gamma\mathrm{Rec}(t_j;T_a,T_b)]}{P^D(t,t_j)}$$

where $\mathrm{Rec}(t;T_a,T_b)$ is the price of a receiver swaption priced at time t_j, expiry at T_a, on a swap starting at T_a and maturing at T_b, with strike K. If the bank has a short position in the IRS (i.e., it is a fixed rate receiver), then FVA is

$$\frac{C_D^{a,b}(t)\mathbf{E}^{a,b}[\gamma(K-S_{a,b}(t))^-]}{P^D(t,t_j)} = -\frac{[\gamma\mathrm{Pay}(t_j;T_a,T_b)]}{P^D(t,t_j)}$$

where $\mathrm{Pay}(t;T_a,T_b)$ is the price of a payer swaption and the arguments of the function are the same as for the receiver.

Finally, the total value of IRS is:

$$\mathrm{IRS}(t,K;T_a,\ldots,T_b,T_c^S,\ldots,T_c^S) = \left[\sum_{k=a}^{b} P^D(t,T_k)\tau_k L_k(t) - \sum_{j=c}^{d} P^D(t,T_j)\tau_j^S K\right]$$

$$+ \mathrm{LVA}_{\mathrm{IRS}(t;T_a,T_b)}$$

$$+ \mathrm{FVA}_{\mathrm{IRS}(t;T_a,T_b)} \qquad (12.66)$$

At inception, the swap rate $K = S_{a,b}(t)$ is the level that makes the value of the contract zero, which can be computed recursively from (12.66).[10]

Example 12.1.5. *Let us consider an IRS, assuming the risk-free rate is equal to the Eonia rate and Euribor forward fixings are at spreads over the Eonia rate. Yearly Eonia forward rates, spreads and Euribor forward rates are shown in Table 12.11.*

---

[10] We present an analysis of how funding costs should be included in a non-collateralized swap later on; the analysis here applies to the non-collateralized fraction of the contract (i.e., $100\% - \gamma$).

Table 12.11. Yearly OIS forward rates and spreads over them for forward Euribor fixings

Time	Eonia forward (%)	Spread (%)	Forward Euribor (%)
0	0.75	0.65	1.40
0.5	0.75	0.64	1.39
1	1.75	0.64	2.39
1.5	2.00	0.63	2.63
2	2.25	0.63	2.88
2.5	2.37	0.62	2.99
3	2.50	0.61	3.11
3.5	2.65	0.61	3.26
4	2.75	0.60	3.35
4.5	2.87	0.60	3.47
5	3.00	0.59	3.59
5.5	3.10	0.59	3.69
6	3.20	0.58	3.78
6.5	3.30	0.58	3.88
7	3.40	0.57	3.97
7.5	3.50	0.57	4.07
8	3.60	0.56	4.16
8.5	3.67	0.56	4.23
9	3.75	0.55	4.30
9.5	3.82	0.55	4.37
10	3.90	0.54	4.44

We price, under a CSA agreement with full collateralization ($\gamma = 100\%$), a receiver swap whereby the bank pays the Euribor fixing semiannually (set at the previous payment date) and receives the fixed rate annually. Keeping market data in mind, the fair rate can easily be calculated by formula (12.62) and found to be equal to 3.3020. We also assume that the bank has to pay a funding spread of $U_j(t) = \overline{U} = 15\,bps$ over the Eonia curve. Finally, we assume that collateral is remunerated at the Eonia rate.

Under these assumptions, the LVA of the swap is nil, as is clear from its definition in (12.64). FVA is different from zero, since there is a funding spread. To compute the FVA in (12.65), we have to compute a portfolio of payer swaptions. To this end we make a simplifying assumption that the NPV of swaptions is constant between two Euribor fixing dates (i.e., it is constant over periods of six months). Swaptions can be computed by means of volatilities in Table 12.12 using a standard Black formula. It is then possible to plot the profile of the NPVs of swaptions, which is actually the (approximated) expected negative exposure (ENE) of the receiver swap (the profile is plotted in Figure 12.2).

The results are given in Table 12.13. FVA is quite small for a swap starting at-the-money, accounting for about half a basis point: an almost negligible impact on the fair swap rate including the funding costs. This rate should be set by a numerical search and is the rate making the value of the swap zero, given by the risk-free component plus FVA at inception.

A more conservative FVA can be based on potential future exposure (PFE) rather than expected exposure as we did with ENE. PFE is computed in much the same way as ENE,

Table 12.12. Implied volatilities for the portfolio of swaptions used to replicate the ENE of the receiver swap

Swaptions		
Expiry	Tenor	Volatility (%)
0.5	9.5	27.95
1	9	28.00
1.5	8.5	27.69
2	8	27.09
2.5	7.5	26.61
3	7	26.32
3.5	6.5	26.16
4	6	26.02
4.5	5.5	25.90
5	5	25.79
5.5	4.5	25.68
6	4	25.57
6.5	3.5	25.46
7	3	25.37
7.5	2.5	25.28
8	2	25.22
8.5	1.5	25.21
9	1	25.34
9.5	0.5	25.50
10	0	

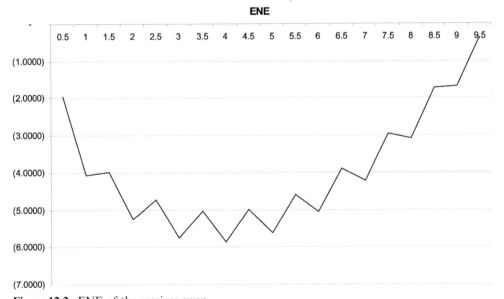

Figure 12.2. ENE of the receiver swap

Table 12.13. Fair swap rate, FVA and FVA-adjusted fair swap rate

FVA	−0.0512%
Fair swap rate	3.3020%
Swap rate including FVA	3.3079%
Difference	0.0059%

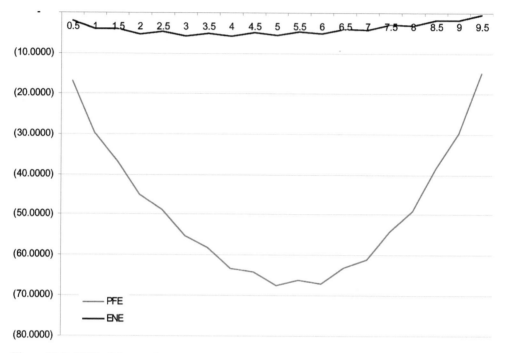

Figure 12.3. PFE of the receiver swap

Table 12.14. Fair swap rate, FVA and FVA-adjusted fair swap rate using PFE

FVA	−0.6265%
Fair swap rate	3.3020%
Swap rate + collateral fund	3.3728%
Difference	0.0708%

but considering the level of the future swap rate set at a given confidence level instead of the forward level. We choose 99% as the confidence level.[11] PFE is plotted in Figure 12.3 and the results are shown in Table 12.14. In this case, FVA is larger as a percentage of the notional and accounts for about 7 bps when included in the fair rate.

---

[11] At a given confidence level *c.l.*, we used the equation $S_{a,b}(T) = S_{a,b}(t)\exp[-\frac{\sigma^2}{2}(T-t) + \sigma\sqrt{T-t}\alpha]$ (where α is a point of the normal standard distribution returning probability *c.l.*) to determine the corresponding swap rate value at time T. In the example, *c.l.* = 99% implies that $\alpha \approx 2.326$.

FVA is rather small when the swap starts and is at-the-money. It can become bigger and bigger as the NPV of the swaps evolves and becomes more negative, or it can become completely negligible as NPV increases.

12.2 PRICING OF COLLATERALIZED DERIVATIVE CONTRACTS WHEN MORE THAN ONE CURRENCY IS INVOLVED

In this section we complete the analysis conducted in Section 12.1 by investigating the valuation of collateralized derivative contracts when more than one currency is involved. This can happen for three reasons:

1. The contract payoff is denominated in some currency YYY but collateral is posted in another currency XXX.
2. The contract is written on an FX rate.
3. The contract payoff depends on assets or market variables denominated in different currencies (e.g., a cross-currency interest rate swap).

In theory, many currencies could be involved, but in what follows we restrict our analysis to when only two currencies have to be considered. We analyse all the cases enumerated above and define liquidity value adjustments and funding value adjustments for collateralized contracts.

12.2.1 Contracts collateralized in a currency other than the payoff currency

Let us assume we have to value a contract whose underlying asset follows dynamics of type:

$$dS_t = (\mu_t - y_t)S_t dt + \sigma_t S_t dZ_t$$

The underlying has a continuous yield of y_t and volatility σ_t and is denominated in a currency that we name "domestic" and refer to as YYY. There is also a foreign currency XXX and an exchange rate $\mathcal{X} = $ XXXYYY[12] following the dynamics:

$$d\mathcal{X}_t = \eta_t \mathcal{X}_t dt + \nu_t \mathcal{X}_t dW_t$$

with $dW_t dZ_t = \rho dt$.

We want to replicate a derivative contract V written on S, which is collateralized continuously in XXX instead of YYY; the latter would normally be the case. Following the same approach outlined in Section 12.1, we build a portfolio replicating both the underlying and the collateral account.

The dynamics of the contingent claim are derived via Ito's lemma:

$$dV_t = \mathcal{L}^\mu V_t dt + \sigma_t S_t \frac{\partial V_t}{\partial S_t} dZ_t$$

---

[12] Units of domestic per foreign currency, so that XXX is the base and YYY is the numeraire currency.

where we used operator $\mathcal{L}^a$. defined as:

$$\mathcal{L}^a. = \frac{\partial.}{\partial t} + a_t S_t \frac{\partial.}{\partial S_t} + \frac{1}{2}\sigma_t^2 S_t^2 \frac{\partial^2.}{\partial S_t^2}$$

Moreover, we will set $\Delta_t = \frac{\partial V_t}{\partial S_t}$ in what follows. The dynamics of the cash collateral account are defined as

$$dC_t = \gamma d\left(\frac{V_t}{X_t}\right) + \mathrm{cf}_t \mathrm{Cf}_t dt$$

The account is denominated in XXX as long as it earns the collateral rate cf_t; rf_t is the funding/investment rate in YYY. For the collateral account it is also true that:

$$\mathrm{Cf}_0 = \gamma(V_0/X_0)$$

$$\mathrm{Cf}_{T^-} = \mathbf{E}^Q\left[\int_0^{T^-} e^{-\int_u^{T^-} \mathrm{cf}_v dv} \gamma d(V_u/X_u)\right]$$

$$\mathrm{Cf}_T = 0$$

Evolution of the YYY bank cash account is deterministic and equal to:

$$dB_t = r_t B_t dt \tag{12.67}$$

and evolution of the XXX bank cash account is:

$$d\mathrm{Bf}_t = \mathrm{rf}_t \mathrm{Bf}_t dt \tag{12.68}$$

At time 0, the replication portfolio in a long position in derivative V, YYY cash-collateralized, is set up with a given quantity of the underlying asset and of XXX and YYY bank accounts such that their value equals the starting value of the contract and of the collateral account:

$$V_0 - \mathrm{Cf}_0 = \alpha_0 S_0 + \beta_0 B_0 + \theta_0 \mathrm{Bf}_0 \tag{12.69}$$

As usual, we impose self-financing and replicating conditions to find quantities $\{\alpha_t, \beta_t, \theta\}$. We can write the way in which the replicating portfolio evolves as:

$$(\alpha_t dS_t + \beta_t dB_t)\mathrm{YYY} + \theta_t d\mathrm{Bf}_t \mathrm{XXX}$$
$$= (\alpha_t(\mu_t - y_t)S_t dt + \alpha_t \sigma_t S_t dZ_t + \beta_t r_t B_t dt + \alpha_t y_t S_t dt)\mathrm{YYY} + \theta_t \mathrm{rf}_t \mathrm{Bf}_t dt \mathrm{XXX} \tag{12.70}$$

On the other hand:

$$dV_t \mathrm{YYY} - d\mathrm{Cf}_t \mathrm{XXX} = \left(\mathcal{L}^{\mu-y} V_t dt + \sigma_t S_t \Delta_u dZ_t\right)\mathrm{YYY} - \left[\gamma d\left(\frac{V_t}{X_t}\right) + \mathrm{cf}_t \mathrm{Cf}_t dt\right]\mathrm{XXX} \tag{12.71}$$

Equating (12.70) and (12.71) we get:

$$\left(\mathcal{L}^{\mu-y} V_t dt + \sigma_t S_t \Delta_u dZ_t\right)\mathrm{YYY} - \left[\gamma d\left(\frac{V_t}{X_t}\right) + \mathrm{cf}_t \mathrm{Cf}_t dt\right]\mathrm{XXX}$$
$$= (\alpha_t(\mu_t - y_t)S_t dt + \alpha_t \sigma_t S_t dZ_t + \beta_t r_t B_t dt + \alpha_t y_t S_t dt)\mathrm{YYY} + \theta_t \mathrm{rf}_t \mathrm{Bf}_t dt \mathrm{XXX} \tag{12.72}$$

We can determine α and β such that the stochastic part in (12.72) is cancelled out:

$$\left.\begin{array}{c} \alpha_t = \Delta_t \\[2mm] \beta_t = \dfrac{V_t - \Delta_t S_t}{B_t} \\[3mm] \theta_t = -\dfrac{\mathrm{Cf}_t}{\mathrm{Bf}_t} \end{array}\right\} \tag{12.73}$$

Substituting in (12.72):

$$(\mathcal{L}^{r-y} V_t dt - r_t V_t dt)\mathbf{YYY} = [\gamma d(V_t/\mathcal{X}_t) - (\mathrm{rf}_t - \mathrm{cf}_t)\mathrm{Cf}_t dt]\mathbf{XXX} \tag{12.74}$$

We can express equation (12.74) in terms of **YYY** only by multiplying the second term by FX rate $\mathcal{X}_t$ and then we have:

$$\mathcal{L}^{r-y} V_t dt = r_t V_t dt + \gamma dV_t - (\mathrm{rf}_t - \mathrm{cf}_t)C_t dt \tag{12.75}$$

where C is the collateral account converted in **YYY** units (we suppressed indication of the currency to lighten the notation).

It can be shown (see Section 12.1) that the solution to equation (12.75) is:

$$V_0^{\mathrm{Cf}} = \mathbf{E}^Q\left[e^{-\int_0^T r_u du} V_T\right] + \mathbf{E}^Q\left[\int_0^T e^{-\int_0^u r_v dv}(\mathrm{rf}_u - \mathrm{cf}_u)C_u du\right] \tag{12.76}$$

which is the same result as when the collateral is posted in **YYY**, with the only difference that the amount of the collateral account in **YYY** is multiplied by the difference between the risk-free rate and the collateral rate applied to the collateral amount in **XXX** units.

We can also denote the second part of the formula as the LVA, which is the present value of the cost incurred to finance the collateral in **XXX** units:

$$V_0^{\mathrm{Cf}} = V_0^{NC} + \mathrm{LVA}$$

Recalling that $\mathrm{Cf}_t = \gamma(V_t/\mathcal{X}_t)\mathbf{XXX}$, or $C_t = \gamma V_t \mathbf{YYY}$, equation (12.75) has another solution:

$$V_0^{\mathrm{Cf}} = \mathbf{E}^Q\left[e^{-\int_0^T [r_u - (\mathrm{rf}_u - \mathrm{cf}_u)\gamma]du} V_T(S^{r-y})\right] \tag{12.77}$$

In this equation we added the dependency of the value of the claim on the underlying price, whose drift is indicated by superscripts. In practice, we can use standard valuation formulae derived, for example, in a Black and Scholes economy by simply changing the discount rate: this will no longer be the only domestic **YYY** risk-free rate, there will also be a correction depending on collateralization percentage γ and on the foreign **XXX** risk-free and collateral rates.[13]

Remark 12.2.1. *The value of a contract, collateralized in a currency different from the one in which the payoff is denominated, does not depend on the FX rate $\mathcal{X}$, but on the risk-free and collateral rates of currency XXX, in addition to the risk-free rate of currency YYY.*

---

[13] A similar formula was derived in [69].

Pricing with funding rate different from investment rate

Let us assume that the replication strategy is operated by an agent (say, a bank), for which the investment and funding rates are different, due mainly to credit factors. The bank pays funding rate r^F when financing its activity in the domestic YYY currency; analogously, rf^F is the rate that it pays when financing its activity in the foreign YYY currency. Evolution of the domestic bank account in (12.67) is:

$$dB_t = \widetilde{r}_t B_t dt \tag{12.78}$$

where $\widetilde{r}_t = r_t 1_{\{\beta>0\}} + r_t^F 1_{\{\beta<0\}}$ and $1_{\{\}}$ is the indicator function equal to 1 when the condition at the subscript is fulfilled. The XXX bank account evolves as follows:

$$d\text{Bf}_t = \widetilde{\text{rf}}_t B_t dt \tag{12.79}$$

The funding rate can be written as the risk-free rate plus a spread:

$$\widetilde{r}_t = r_t + s_t^F 1_{\{\beta<0\}} \tag{12.80}$$

and similarly for the foreign rate

$$\widetilde{\text{rf}}_t = \text{rf}_t + \text{sf}_t^F 1_{\{\theta<0\}} \tag{12.81}$$

Replacing risk-free rates r_t and rf_t with $\widetilde{r}_t$ and $\widetilde{\text{rf}}_t$ in equation (12.75), we get:

$$\mathcal{L}^{\widetilde{r}-y} V_t dt = \widetilde{r}_t V_t dt + \gamma dV_t - (\widetilde{\text{rf}}_t - \text{cf}_t) C_t dt \tag{12.82}$$

From (12.82) we can easily derive the two ways of expressing the value of the contingent claim at time 0 equivalent to formulae (12.76) and (12.77), respectively, as:

$$V_0^{\text{Cf}} = \mathbf{E}^Q \left[e^{-\int_0^T \widetilde{r}_u du} V_T \right] + \mathbf{E}^Q \left[\int_0^T e^{-\int_0^u \widetilde{r}_v dv} (\widetilde{\text{rf}}_u - \text{cf}_u) C_u du \right] \tag{12.83}$$

and

$$V_0^{\text{Cf}} = \mathbf{E}^Q \left[e^{-\int_0^T [\widetilde{r}_u - (\widetilde{\text{rf}}_u - \text{cf}_u)\gamma] du} V_T (S^{\widetilde{r}-y}) \right] \tag{12.84}$$

In equation (12.83) decomposition of the collateralized contract value is given as the sum of the otherwise identical non-collateralized deal and of LVA.

We would also like to isolate the effect due to the funding spread, so we introduce a further decomposition by rewriting equation (12.82) as:

$$\mathcal{L}^{r-y} V_t dt = r_t V_t dt + \gamma dV_t - (\text{rf}_t - \text{cf}_t) C_t dt + s_t^F 1_{\{\beta<0\}} (V_t - \Delta_t S_t) dt - \text{sf}_t^F 1_{\{\theta<0\}} C_t dt \tag{12.85}$$

The solution to (12.85) is:

$$V_0^{\text{Cf}} = V^{NC} + \text{LVA} + \text{FVA} \tag{12.86}$$

where V^{NC} is the price of the non-collateralized contract assuming no funding spread, LVA is the liquidity value adjustment originated by the difference between the collateral and risk-free rate:

$$\text{LVA} = \mathbf{E}^Q \left[\int_0^T e^{-\int_0^u r_v dv} (\text{rf}_u - \text{cf}_u) C_u du \right] \tag{12.87}$$

and, finally, FVA is the funding value adjustment due to the funding spread, which is paid to replicate the contract and the collateral account:

$$\text{FVA} = \mathbf{E}^Q\left[-\int_0^T e^{-\int_0^u r_v dv}[s_u^F 1_{\{\beta<0\}}(V_u - \Delta_u S_u) - \text{sf}_u^F 1_{\{\theta<0\}}C_u]du\right] \quad (12.88)$$

where β is defined as above. FVA is the correction to the risk-free value of the non-collateralized contract that has to be (algebraically) added to the LVA correction. For a definition of LVA and FVA see [45].

We are now in a position to analyse five different cases:

1. Let us assume a contingent claim with a constant positive-sign NPV (e.g., a long European call option) with a constant positive-sign Δ_t has to be replicated. In this case $\beta_t = V_t - \Delta S_t < 0$ and $\theta_t = -C_t < 0$ always (implying borrowing always takes place in both currencies). The pricing equation (12.85) then reads:

$$\mathcal{L}^{r-y}V_t dt = r_t V_t dt + \gamma dV_t - (\text{rf}_t - \text{cf}_t)C_t dt + s_t^F(V_t - \Delta_t S_t)dt - \text{sf}_t^F C_t dt \quad (12.89)$$

Although the decomposition in (12.86) still applies, pricing can be performed very simply by means of an effective discount rate:

$$V_0^{\text{Cf}} = \mathbf{E}^Q\left[e^{-\int_0^T [r_u^F - (\text{rf}_u^F - \text{cf}_u)\gamma]du}V_T(S^{r^F-y})\right] \quad (12.90)$$

So we can simply replace the risk-free rate with the funding rate paid by the bank and perform the same pricing as when lending and borrowing rates are the same.

2. When the same contingent claim (constant positive-sign NPV and Δ) as in point 1 is sold, the underlying asset has also to be sold in the replication strategy, which implies that $\beta_t > 0$ and that the bank always has to invest at the risk-free rate in YYY; the bank account in XXX, $\theta_t = -C_t$, will always be positive as well. The pricing formula will be the same as in formula (12.77) (with reversed signs since we are selling the contract). In this case FVA will be nil. An example of this claim is a short European call option.

3. Let us now assume that the contingent claim has a constant positive-sign NPV, but its replication implies a negative position in the underlying asset (e.g., a long European put option). So, once again we not only always have $\beta_t = V_t - \Delta S_t 0 > 0$, but also $\theta_t = -C_t < 0$, implying that the bank has to borrow money in XXX. PDE (12.85) now reads:

$$\mathcal{L}^{r-y}V_t dt = r_t V_t dt + \gamma dV_t - (\text{rf}_t^F - \text{cf}_t)C_t dt - \text{sf}_t^F C_t dt \quad (12.91)$$

Pricing can be performed via the compact formula:

$$V_0^{\text{Cf}} = \mathbf{E}^Q\left[e^{-\int_0^T [r_u - (\text{rf}_u^F - \text{cf}_u)\gamma]du}V_T(S^{r-y})\right] \quad (12.92)$$

In this case we replace the risk-free rate with the funding rate paid by the bank for XXX.

4. If the NPV has a constant negative sign and the replica entails a long position in the underlying (e.g., short European put option), then the total amount of bank account $\beta_t = V_t - \Delta S_t < 0$ is always negative, implying that the bank always has to borrow money in the replica at rate r^F in YYY; since $\theta_t = -C_t > 0$ always, the bank will

invest the collateral at the risk-free rate rf. The pricing formula is derived similarly to (12.92) and is:

$$V_0^{\mathrm{Cf}} = \mathbf{E}^Q \left[e^{-\int_0^T [r_u^F - (\mathrm{rf}_u - \mathrm{cf}_u)\gamma] du} V_T(S^{r^F - y}) \right] \tag{12.93}$$

5. Finally, if the NPV has a constant positive or negative sign and the Δ can flip from one sign to the other, then it is not possible to determine the sign of amount β_t of the bank account throughout the entire life of the contract, although it is always possible to determine whether θ_t is always positive or negative. In this case pricing formula (12.85) cannot be reduced to a convenient representation as in the cases above and has to be done so numerically.

Funding rate different from investment rate and repo rate

We mentioned in Section 12.1 that the proper way to finance buying of the underlying asset in the replication strategy is through a repo transaction. On the other hand, if we really want to consider the actual alternatives available to a trader to invest received sums in a less credit-risky way, reverse repo seems an effective option in most cases. The amount to be lent/borrowed via domestic and foreign bank accounts is now:

$$\beta_t = \frac{V_t}{B_t}$$

$$\theta_t = -\frac{\mathrm{Cf}_t}{\mathrm{Bf}_t}$$

where quantity $\alpha_t = \Delta_t$ of the underlying asset is repoed/reverse-repoed, thus paying/receiving interest $r_t^E \Delta_t S_t$. Replacing these quantities in equation (12.75), we get:

$$\mathcal{L}^{r^E - y} V_t dt = \tilde{r}_t V_t dt + \gamma dV_t - (\mathrm{rf}_t - \mathrm{cf}_t) C_t dt + s_t^F 1_{\{\beta < 0\}} V_t dt - \mathrm{sf}_t^F 1_{\{\theta < 0\}} C_t dt \tag{12.94}$$

The solution to (12.94) is:

$$V_0^{\mathrm{Cf}} = V^{NC} + \mathrm{LVA} + \mathrm{FVA} \tag{12.95}$$

where, as usual, V^{NC} is the price of the non-collateralized contract assuming no funding spread or repo, LVA is the liquidity value adjustment due to the collateral agreement:

$$\mathrm{LVA} = \mathbf{E}^Q \left[\int_0^T e^{-\int_0^u r_v dv} (\mathrm{rf}_u - \mathrm{cf}_u) C_u du \right]$$

and FVA is the funding value adjustment:

$$\mathrm{FVA} = \mathbf{E}^Q \left[-\int_0^T e^{-\int_0^u r_v dv} [s_u^F 1_{\{\beta < 0\}} V_u - \mathrm{sf}_u^F 1_{\{\theta < 0\}} C_u - s_t^E \Delta_u S_u] du \right] \tag{12.96}$$

FVA is split into the funding cost needed to finance collateral ($s_u^F 1_{\{\beta < 0\}} V_u - \mathrm{sf}_u^F 1_{\{\theta < 0\}} C_u$) and the spread of the repo rate over the risk-free rate ($s_t^E = r_t^E - r_t$) paid on the position of amount Δ_t of the underlying asset in this case.

To better understand how total FVA is built, we split formula (12.96) into two components: the first is $\mathrm{FVA}^{\mathbf{P}}$, the cost borne to fund the premium and the collateral, and is the same as in (12.88). The second part refers to the repo cost to buy or sell the underlying asset to replicate the payoff:

$$FVA^R = E^Q\left[\int_0^T e^{-\int_0^u r_v dv} s_t^E \Delta_u S_u du\right] \tag{12.97}$$

Furthermore, in this case it is possible to rewrite (12.95) in a more convenient fashion for computational purposes:

$$V_0^{Cf} = E^Q\left[e^{-\int_0^T [\widetilde{r}_u - (\widetilde{rf}_u - cf_u)\gamma] du} V_T(S^{r^E - y})\right] \tag{12.98}$$

Formula (12.98) is applicable to the five cases analysed in the previous section: the discount factor depends on the sign of the bank account needed to fund the collateral account, whereas the drift of the underlying asset is always repo rate r^E.

12.2.2 FX derivatives

We now want to compute the value to the bank of an FX derivative contract: it is a function of FX rate $\mathcal{X}$ and of time $V(\mathcal{X}_t, t)$. We start with a simple forward contract, named *outright* in the FX market.

Collateral posted in numeraire currency

When collateral is posted in numeraire currency YYY, the case examined in Section 12.1 for a general derivative contract is applicable, although here we need to replace the underlining asset with the exchange rate. We focus only on the more realistic case of different borrowing/lending rates and apply the replication argument as before.

The difference between FX trades and trades in other securities (say, equities) is that, in the case of FX, we are actually buying money in some currency by paying a price in another currency, and money received can be invested in a bank account that we assume to be default risk free.[14] So by buying, for example, foreign currency XXX (which we assumed to be the base), the bank can invest this amount in a XXX-denominated bank account. On the other hand, when the bank needs to short the base currency to buy numeraire currency, it has to borrow money in XXX.

The evolution of contract $V(\mathcal{X}_t, t) = V_t$, according to Ito's lemma, is:

$$dV_t = \mathcal{M}^\mu V_t + \sigma_t \mathcal{X}_t \frac{\partial V_t}{\partial \mathcal{X}_t} dW_t \tag{12.99}$$

where

$$\mathcal{M}^a\cdot = \frac{\partial\cdot}{\partial t} + a_t \mathcal{X}_t \frac{\partial\cdot}{\partial \mathcal{X}_t} + \tfrac{1}{2} v_t^2 \mathcal{X}_t^2 \frac{\partial^2\cdot}{\partial \mathcal{X}_t^2} \tag{12.100}$$

The replicating portfolio comprises at time t a given amount α_t of the base currency XXX worth $\mathcal{X}_t$ and a given amount of cash β_t borrowed or invested in YYY. The

---

[14] In practice, the bank will never be able to find a completely risk-free counterparty, but if the interest yielded by the bank account issued by the latter is fair, it should include remuneration for expected default losses, so that on a risk-adjusted basis net yield is still the risk-free rate.

portfolio must equal the value of the FX derivative at time 0:

$$V_0 - C_0 = \alpha_0 \mathcal{X}_0 + \beta_0 B_0 \tag{12.101}$$

Considering that α units of XXX are either invested in or borrowed from a bank account depending on the sign of α, evolution of the replicating portfolio is:

$$(\alpha_t d\mathcal{X}_t + \beta_t dB_t)\text{YYY} + \alpha_t d\text{Bf}_t\text{XXX} = (\alpha_t d\mathcal{X}_t + \beta_t dB_t + \alpha_t \mathcal{X}_t d\text{Bf}_t)\text{YYY}$$

$$= \alpha_t \eta_t \mathcal{X}_t dt + \alpha_t v_t \mathcal{X}_t dZ_t + \beta_t \tilde{r}_t B_t dt + \alpha_t \widetilde{\text{rf}}_t \mathcal{X}_t dt \tag{12.102}$$

where $\widetilde{\text{rf}}_t = \text{rf}_t + \text{sf}_t^F 1_{\{\alpha<0\}}$ and denomination in YYY has been omitted in the last line. Setting $\alpha_t = \Delta_t = \frac{\partial V_t}{\partial \mathcal{X}_t}$ and $\beta_t = (V_t - C_t - \Delta_t \mathcal{X}_t)/B_t$, and following the same mathematical passages as in Section 12.1, we come up with the PDE:

$$\mathcal{L}^{\tilde{r}-\widetilde{\text{rf}}} V_t dt = \tilde{r}_t V_t dt + \gamma dV_t - (\tilde{r}_t - c_t) C_t dt \tag{12.103}$$

From (12.103) we can easily derive the two ways of expressing the value of the contingent claim at time 0:

$$V_0^C = \mathbf{E}^Q \left[e^{-\int_0^T \tilde{r}_u du} V_T(\mathcal{X}^{\tilde{r}-\widetilde{\text{rf}}}) \right] + \mathbf{E}^Q \left[\int_0^T e^{-\int_0^u \tilde{r}_v dv} (\tilde{r}_u - c_u) C_u du \right] \tag{12.104}$$

and

$$V_0^C = \mathbf{E}^Q \left[e^{-\int_0^T [\tilde{r}_u(1-\gamma)+c_u\gamma] du} V_T(\mathcal{X}^{\tilde{r}-\widetilde{\text{rf}}}) \right] \tag{12.105}$$

We have explicitly indicated the drift that the FX rate must have under the bank's replication measure. In equation (12.104) decomposition of the value of the collateralized contract is given as the sum of the otherwise identical non-collateralized deal and of LVA.

We introduce a further decomposition that can be used to allocate revenues and costs within a dealing room. We rewrite equation (12.103) as:

$$\mathcal{L}^{r-\text{rfs}} V_t dt = r_t V_t dt + \gamma dV_t - (r_t - c_t) C_t dt + s_t^F 1_{\{\beta<0\}} (V_t - C_t - \Delta_t \mathcal{X}_t) dt$$

$$+ \text{sf}_t^F 1_{\{\alpha<0\}} \Delta_t \mathcal{X}_t dt \tag{12.106}$$

The solution to (12.106) is:

$$V_0^C = V^{NC} + \text{LVA} + \text{FVA} \tag{12.107}$$

where V^{NC} is the price of the non-collateralized contract assuming no funding spread, LVA is the liquidity value adjustment originated by the difference between the collateral and risk-free rates:

$$\text{LVA} = \mathbf{E}^Q \left[\int_0^T e^{-\int_0^u r_v dv} (r_u - c_u) C_u du \right] \tag{12.108}$$

and, finally, FVA is the funding value adjustment due to the funding spread and paid to replicate the contract and the collateral account:

$$\text{FVA} = \mathbf{E}^Q \left[-\int_0^T e^{-\int_0^u r_v dv} [s_t^F 1_{\{\beta<0\}} (V_t - C_t - \Delta_t \mathcal{X}_t) + \text{sf}_u^F 1_{\{\alpha<0\}} \Delta_u \mathcal{X}_u du] \right] \tag{12.109}$$

FVA can be decomposed according to the spread paid in YYY:

$$\text{FVA}^{\text{YYY}} = \mathbf{E}^Q\left[-\int_0^T e^{-\int_0^u r_v dv} s_t^F 1_{\{\beta<0\}}(V_t - C_t - \Delta_t\mathcal{X}_t)du\right] \qquad (12.110)$$

and the funding adjustment due to the spread paid in XXX:

$$\text{FVA}^{\text{XXX}} = \mathbf{E}^Q\left[-\int_0^T e^{-\int_0^u r_v dv} \text{sf}_u^F 1_{\{\alpha<0\}}\Delta_u\mathcal{X}_u du\right] \qquad (12.111)$$

Collateral posted in base currency

When collateral is posted in base currency XXX, we can apply the results derived above for a general derivative contract to an FX derivative contract. The replicating portfolio is built as follows

$$V_0 - C_0 = \alpha_0\mathcal{X}_0 + \beta_0 B_0 + \theta_0\text{Bf} \qquad (12.112)$$

and its evolution is:

$$\alpha_t\eta_t\mathcal{X}_t dt + \alpha_t\nu_t\mathcal{X}_t dZ_t + \beta_t\tilde{r}_t B_t dt + \theta\widetilde{\text{rf}}_t\text{Bf}_t dt + \alpha_t\widetilde{\text{rf}}_t\mathcal{X}_t dt \qquad (12.113)$$

Choosing $\beta_t = (V_t - \Delta_t\mathcal{X}_t)/B_t$ and $\theta = -(\text{Cf}_t - \Delta_t)/\text{Bf}_t\text{XXX} = -(C_t - \Delta_t\mathcal{X}_t)/\text{Bf}_t$ YYY, we derive the following PDE:

$$\mathcal{L}^{r-\text{rf}}V_t dt = r_t V_t dt + \gamma dV_t - (\text{rf}_t - \text{cf}_t)C_t dt + s_t^F 1_{\{\beta<0\}}$$
$$\times (V_t - \Delta_t\mathcal{X}_t)dt - \text{sf}_t^F 1_{\{\theta<0\}}(C_t - \Delta_t\mathcal{X}_t)dt \qquad (12.114)$$

The solution is

$$V_0^{\text{Cf}} = \mathbf{E}^Q\left[e^{-\int_0^T [\tilde{r}_u-(\text{rf}_u-\text{cf}_u)\gamma]du}V_T(\mathcal{X}^{\widetilde{r-\text{rf}}})\right] \qquad (12.115)$$

Another solution to (12.114) is:

$$V_0^{\text{Cf}} = V^{\text{NC}} + \text{LVA} + \text{FVA} \qquad (12.116)$$

where V^{NC} is the price of the non-collateralized contract assuming no funding spread, LVA is the liquidity value adjustment originated by the difference between the collateral and risk-free rates:

$$\text{LVA} = \mathbf{E}^Q\left[\int_0^T e^{-\int_0^u r_v dv}(\text{rf}_u - \text{cf}_u)C_u du\right] \qquad (12.117)$$

and, finally, FVA is the funding value adjustment due to the funding spread, which is paid to replicate the contract and the collateral account:

$$\text{FVA} = \mathbf{E}^Q\left[-\int_0^T e^{-\int_0^u r_v dv}[s_u^F 1_{\{\beta<0\}}(V_u - \Delta_u\mathcal{X}_u) - \text{sf}_u^F 1_{\{\theta<0\}}(C_u - \Delta_u\mathcal{X}_u)]du\right] \qquad (12.118)$$

Value of an FX forward (outright) contract

Let us assume collateral is posted in YYY. A (long) FX forward contract, or outright, struck at level X has a terminal value:

$$V_T = \mathcal{X}_T - X \qquad (12.119)$$

so that applying the compact formula (12.105)

$$V_0^C = \mathbf{E}^Q\left[e^{-\int_0^T [\tilde{r}_u(1-\gamma)+c_u\gamma]du}(\mathcal{X}_T - X)\right] \qquad (12.120)$$

The value at inception of the contract is nil: if we disregard for the moment all the adjustments due to the default risk of the bank and its counterparty, we can price the contract and find level $X = X^C(t, T)$ that makes the value at the beginning of the contract zero with formula (12.104). If the bank needs to replicate a long position in the outright contract, then the outright price can easily be shown to be:

$$X^C(t, T) = \mathcal{X}_0 e^{\int_0^T (r_u + s_u^F - \text{rf}_u)du} \qquad (12.121)$$

On the other hand, when the bank wants to replicate a short position, the outright price is:

$$X^C(t, T) = \mathcal{X}_0 e^{\int_0^T (r_u - \text{rf}_u - \text{sf}_u^F)du} \qquad (12.122)$$

Remark 12.2.2. *In both cases, collateralization and, hence, the collateral rate do not affect the fair level of the outright contract, although LVA contributes to the value of the contract when the outright is seasoned and no longer at-the-money as at inception. On the contrary, funding spreads paid on either currency (YYY or XXX) enter into the formula and are crucial to defining both the replication value of the contract to the bank and the fair level.*

Remark 12.2.3. *Equation (12.106) makes it abundantly clear that we are still within a risk-neutral framework, where everything is discounted using the risk-free rate, and the drift of the FX rate process $\mathcal{X}_t$ is the difference between the numeraire and base currency: a standard result. Using PDE (12.103) leads to more convenient valuation formulae, but in our opinion makes it less clear how the value is composed or why it can be different to different parties, despite still working in a dynamic replication setting that produces a risk-neutral value.[15]*

If collateral is posted in XXX, then the forward price is the level making the contract value at inception zero computed via PDE (12.114) whose solution can be written as the compact formula (12.115), so that

$$V_0^{Cf} = \mathbf{E}^Q\left[e^{-\int_0^T [\tilde{r}_u - (\widetilde{\text{rf}}_u - \text{cf}_u)\gamma]du}(\mathcal{X}_T - X)\right] \qquad (12.123)$$

It is quite easy to check that both the long and short outright fair price level is the same as in formulae (12.121) and (12.122), so that $X^C(t, T) = X^{Cf}(t, T)$, with X^{Cf} the outright fair price at time t for maturity T when the collateral is posted in the base currency.

Remark 12.2.4. *Although the fair level of the outright (FX forward) price is independent of the currency in which the collateral is posted, the value of the contract does depend on it. The values of two contracts one collateralised in the numeraire and the other in the base currency differ during their life, being equal (i.e., zero) only at inception and at expiry.*

---

[15] Just the value – *not* the price – is risk-neutral. This means that an economic agent bearing the same costs to replicate the contract agrees on the value of the contract independently of its risk aversion. Replication, in the presence of funding and collateral costs, depends on the long or short position we wish to reproduce.

Replication with FX swap

The funding spread in both currencies can be strongly abated if the bank uses collateralized instead of unsecured lending. In the FX this can easily be achieved via an FX swap, which is in all respects equal to a repo traded in other markets. The FX swap is the sum of a spot contract plus an outright, but it can also be seen as the borrowing/lending of an XXX amount against collateral represented by the YYY amount.[16]

FX swaps for given expiry T are quoted in the market in points over the spot rate $\mathcal{X}$, so that the level at which the outright is traded is defined as $\mathcal{F}(t, T) = \mathcal{X}_t + p(t, T)$, where $p(t, T)$ are the swap points prevailing at time t for an FX swap expiring at time T.[17] The outright level also defines the FX swap implied rate, which mainly depends on the differential between the numeraire and the base currency, but there are other factors (even beyond credit risk) that determine the generally defined cross-currency basis. The implied FX swap (continuous) rate is defined as:

$$ r_t^{\mathcal{X}} = -\frac{\partial \ln \frac{\mathcal{F}(t,T)}{\mathcal{X}_t}}{\partial t} \tag{12.124} $$

Using an FX swap to replicate the FX derivative contract and assuming for the moment that it is CSA-collateralized in YYY, formula (12.102) is modified as follows:

$$ \alpha_t \eta_t \mathcal{X}_t dt + \alpha_t \nu_t \mathcal{X}_t dZ_t + \beta_t \tilde{r}_t B_t dt - \alpha_t r_t^{\mathcal{X}} \mathcal{X}_t dt \tag{12.125} $$

Setting $\alpha_t = \Delta_t = \frac{\partial V_t}{\partial \mathcal{X}_t}$ and $\beta_t = (V_t - C_t)$, the evaluation PDE becomes:

$$ \mathcal{L}^{r^{\mathcal{X}}} V_t dt = \tilde{r}_t V_t dt + \gamma dV_t - (\tilde{r}_t - c_t) C_t dt \tag{12.126} $$

The solution to (12.126) is:

$$ V_0^C = V^{NC} + \text{LVA} + \text{FVA} \tag{12.127} $$

where, again, V^{NC} is the price of the non-collateralized contract on exchange rate $\mathcal{X}$, assuming no funding spread and repo rate; LVA is the liquidity value adjustment due to the collateral agreement:

$$ \text{LVA} = \mathbf{E}^Q \left[\int_0^T e^{-\int_0^u r_v dv} (r_u - c_u) C_u du \right] $$

and FVA is the funding value adjustment:

$$ \text{FVA} = \mathbf{E}^Q \left[-\int_0^T e^{-\int_0^u r_v dv} [s_u^F 1_{\{\beta<0\}} (V_u - C_u) - s_t^{\mathcal{X}} \Delta_u \mathcal{X}_u] du \right] \tag{12.128} $$

where FVA is split into two parts: the funding cost needed to finance collateral $(s_u^F 1_{\{\beta<0\}} V_u - \text{sf}_u^F 1_{\{\theta<0\}} C_u)$ and the spread of the repo rate over the risk-free rate $(s_t^{\mathcal{X}} = r_t^{\mathcal{X}} - r_t)$ paid on the position of amount Δ_t of the underlying asset.

---

[16] Note that the borrowing is collateralized in static fashion at the start of the contract (i.e., the amount of the currency one party pays against receiving an amount of the other currency). This static collateral is not readjusted daily as happens with a CSA agreement, so there is still the risk that, on counterparty default, the market value is unable to fully cover the loss suffered by the surviving party.

[17] See [44] for details on FX market conventions.

It is possible to rewrite (12.127) in a more convenient fashion for computational purposes:

$$V_0^C = \mathbf{E}^Q \left[e^{-\int_0^T [\tilde{r}_u(1-\gamma) + c_u \gamma] du} V_T(\mathcal{X}^{r^{\mathcal{X}}}) \right] \tag{12.129}$$

The FX swap can be used to replicate the outright contract shown above: in the end the FX swap is just the replication strategy of an outright operated with a single counterparty, thus minimizing loss given defaults and hence the spread paid. Keeping in mind that the FX swap, being a derivative contract itself, is CSA-collateralized, we also get the same cash flow profile for both the outright and the FX swap, so that funding spreads should not be considered in the evaluation process. The replica of the contract is then independent of the creditworthiness of the replicator bank. This means that, in practice, they are the same contract when a CSA agreement is in operation and that the outright fair price is just the FX swap price:

$$\mathcal{X}^C = \mathcal{F}(t, T) = \mathcal{X}_0 e^{\int_0^T r_u^{\mathcal{X}} du} \tag{12.130}$$

The dynamics for the FX rate, when replication is operated via the FX swap, are:

$$d\mathcal{X}_t = r_t^{\mathcal{X}} \mathcal{X}_t dt + v_t \mathcal{X}_t dW_t \tag{12.131}$$

Let us now see what happens if replication is performed using a repo contract and the collateral is posted in the base currency (XXX). Equation (12.113) modifies as follows:

$$\alpha_t \eta_t \mathcal{X}_t dt + \alpha_t v_t \mathcal{X}_t dZ_t + \beta_t \tilde{r}_t B_t dt + \theta \mathrm{rf}_t \mathrm{Bf}_t dt + \alpha_t r_t^{\mathcal{X}} \mathcal{X}_t dt \tag{12.132}$$

Setting $\beta_t = V_t / B_t$ and $\theta = -\mathrm{Cf}_t / \mathrm{Bf}_t \mathrm{XXX} = -C_t / \mathrm{Bf}_t \mathrm{YYY}$, we derive the following PDE:

$$\mathcal{L}^{r^{\mathcal{X}}} V_t dt = \tilde{r}_t V_t dt + \gamma dV_t - (\widetilde{\mathrm{rf}}_t - \mathrm{cf}_t) C_t dt \tag{12.133}$$

where $\widetilde{\mathrm{rf}}_t = \mathrm{rf}_t + \mathrm{sf}_t^F 1_{\{\theta < 0\}}$. The solution to (12.133) is:

$$V_0^{\mathrm{Cf}} = V^{NC} + \mathrm{LVA} + \mathrm{FVA} \tag{12.134}$$

where, as usual, V^{NC} is the price of the non-collateralized contract on the exchange rate $\mathcal{X}$, assuming no funding spread and repo rate, LVA is the liquidity value adjustment due to the collateral agreement:

$$\mathrm{LVA} = \mathbf{E}^Q \left[\int_0^T e^{-\int_0^u r_v dv} (\mathrm{rf}_u - \mathrm{cf}_u) C_u du \right]$$

and FVA is the funding value adjustment:

$$\mathrm{FVA} = \mathbf{E}^Q \left[-\int_0^T e^{-\int_0^u r_v dv} [s_u^F 1_{\{\beta < 0\}} V_u - \mathrm{sf}_u^F 1_{\{\theta < 0\}} C_u - s_t^{\mathcal{X}} \Delta_u \mathcal{X}_u] du \right] \tag{12.135}$$

with $s_t^{\mathcal{X}} = r_t^{\mathcal{X}} - r_t$ as above. A compact solution in this case is:

$$V_0^{\mathrm{Cf}} = \mathbf{E}^Q \left[e^{-\int_0^T [\tilde{r}_u - (\widetilde{\mathrm{rf}}_u - \mathrm{cf}_u)\gamma] du} V_T(\mathcal{X}^{r^{\mathcal{X}}}) \right] \tag{12.136}$$

It is clear that the currency of the collateral is immaterial when a FX swap is used to replicate a forward contract, since from (12.136) we can derive the fair outright level

when collateral is posted in the base currency, which is the same as in (12.130), so that:
$X^{Cf} = X^C$.

12.2.3 Interest rate derivatives

We argued above that interest rate derivatives should be considered as primary securities, so that pricing formula cannot be derived by a true replication argument, but they are simply market pricing formulae. We illustrate how to evaluate two basic contracts of the interest rate derivative market: a forward rate agreement (FRA) and an interest rate swap (IRS).

Forward rate agreement

Assume we have the risk-free discount curve in both currencies denoted by D and D^f, respectively, for YYY and XXX. The pricing formula for a FRA written on Libor rate $L_i(T_{i-1})$ in YYY, but with collateral posted in XXX can be written in much the same way as that presented above for contracts on other underlying assets and derived from a replication argument:

$$\text{FRA}^{Cf}(t; T_{i-1}, T_i) = P^D(t, T_i)\tau_i \mathbf{E}^{T_i}[L_i(T_{i-1}) - K] + \text{LVA}_{\text{FRA}^{Cf}(t;T_{i-1},T_i)} \quad (12.137)$$

that is, the expected Libor rate under the T_i forward measure of the value of the contract at expiry T_{i-1} plus the LVA. We used $\tau_i = T_i - T_{i-1}$ in equation (12.137).

LVA is the present value of the difference between the risk-free rate $L_j^{D^f}(t)$ and the collateral rate $O_j^f(t)$, fixed at date t_{j-1} and valid until date t_j, both for currency XXX, applied to fraction γ of the value of contract $\text{FRA}(t_j; T_{i-1}, T_2)$ for a total of N days between t and the forward settlement T_1, so that $t_N = T_1$:

$$\text{LVA}_{\text{FRA}^{Cf}(t;T_{i-1},T_i)} = \sum_{j=1}^{N} P^D(t, t_j)\mathbf{E}^{t_j}\left[\tau_j^C[L_j^{D^f}(t) - O_j^f(t)]\gamma\text{FRA}^{Cf}(t_j; T_{i-1}, T_i)\right] \quad (12.138)$$

where $\tau_j^C = t_j - t_{j-1}$ is the difference in the fraction into which the year is split between two rebalancing times of the collateral (typically, one day). Let us assume that market quotes for FRAs refer to when LVA is nil, implying that the collateral rate is supposed to be risk-free rate $L^{D^f}(t; t_{j-1}, t_j) = O^f(t; t_{j-1}, t_j)$ for all j: this is not unreasonable given that the standard CSA between banks provides for remuneration of the collateral account at the OIS rate and the latter can be considered a very good proxy for the risk-free rate. Equation (12.137) will then be:

$$\text{FRA}^{Cf}(t; T_{i-1}, T_i) = P^D(t, T_i)\tau_i \mathbf{E}^{T_i}[L_i(T_{i-1}) - K] \quad (12.139)$$

which is exactly the same result as given in Section 12.1 and of the current pricing theory based on a multi-curve setup.[18] The FRA fair rate is the expected value of Libor at the settlement date of the contract, under the expiry T_i forward risk measure:

$$K^{Cf} = L_i(t) = \mathbf{E}^{T_i}[L_i(T_{i-1})] \quad (12.140)$$

According to market conventions, the contract actually settles the present value of payoff T_i at T_{i-1} using the FRA fair rate in (12.140), since the latter is corrected by

---

[18] See, for example, [89].

a convexity adjustment as discussed in [91]. The adjustment is nevertheless quite small (a fraction of a basis point).

Let us now assume the collateral agreement provides for remuneration of collateral different from the OIS rate: setting $Q_i^f(t) = L_i^{D^f}(t) - O_i^f(t)$ equal to the spread between the daily risk-free rate and collateral rate in XXX, and assuming it is a stochastic process independent of the value of the FRA, we can rewrite equation (12.138) as:

$$\mathrm{LVA}_{\mathrm{FRA}^{\mathrm{Cf}}(t;T_{i-1},T_i)} = \sum_{j=1}^{N} P^D(t,t_j)\mathbf{E}^{t_j}[\tau_j^C Q_j^f(t)]\mathbf{E}^{t_j}[\gamma \mathrm{FRA}^{\mathrm{Cf}}(t_j; T_{i-1}, T_i)] \quad (12.141)$$

The second expectation in (12.141) is $\tau_i P^D(t, T_i)\mathbf{E}_D^{T_i}[\gamma(L_i(T_{i-1}) - K)]/P^D(t, t_j)$, so that we finally get:

$$\mathrm{LVA}_{\mathrm{FRA}(t;T_{i-1},T_i)}^{\mathrm{Cf}} = \sum_{j=1}^{N} P^D(t,t_j)\left[\mathbf{E}^{t_j}[\tau_j^C Q_j^f(t)]\frac{\tau_i P^D(t, T_i)\mathbf{E}_D^{T_i}[\gamma(L_i(T_{i-1}) - K)]}{P^D(t, t_j)}\right] \quad (12.142)$$

Apart from a slight change of notation, the results are the same as in [45] and this is also the case when we consider FVA. To this end, define $L^{F^f}(t; t_{i-1}, t_i) = L_i^{F^f}(t)$ as the funding rate paid by the bank in XXX. When financing the collateral (i.e., when the NPV of the contract is negative) the bank has to pay this rate and receive the collateral rate, whereas in the opposite situation (i.e., positive NPV), then it invests the collateral received at the risk-free rate, paying the collateral rate. Let the funding spread over the risk-free rate be $U^f(t; t_{j-1}, t_j) = U_j^f(t) = L_j^{F^f}(t) - L_j^{D^f}(t)$: we further assume that it is not correlated with the NPV of the FRA. FVA is:

$$\mathrm{FVA}_{\mathrm{FRA}^{\mathrm{Cf}}(t;T_{i-1},T_i)}(t; T_{i-1}, T_i)$$

$$= \sum_{j=1}^{N} P^D(t,t_j)\left[\mathbf{E}^{t_j}[\tau_j^C U_j^f(t)]\frac{\tau_i P^D(t, T_i)\mathbf{E}^{T_i}[\gamma(L_i(T_{i-1}) - K)^-]}{P^D(t, t_j)}\right] \quad (12.143)$$

where $\mathbf{E}[X^-] = \mathbf{E}[\min(X, 0)]$. It is straightforward to show that:

$$\frac{\tau_i P^D(t, T_i)\mathbf{E}^{T_i}[\gamma(L_i(T_{i-1}) - K)^-]}{P^D(t, t_j)} = -\frac{[\gamma\tau_i \mathrm{Floorlet}(t_j; T_{i-1}, T_i, K)]}{P^D(t, t_j)}$$

where $\mathrm{Floorlet}(t_j; T_{i-1}, T_i, K)$ is the price of a floorlet priced at time t_j, expiry at T_{i-1}, settlement at T_i, with strike K. If the bank has a short position in the FRA, then FVA is

$$\frac{\tau_i P^D(t, T_i)\mathbf{E}^{T_i}[\gamma(K - L_i(T_{i-1}))^-]}{P^D(t, t_j)} = -\frac{[\gamma\tau_i \mathrm{Caplet}(t_j; T_{i-1}, T_i, K)]}{P^D(t, t_j)}$$

where $\mathrm{Caplet}(t_j; T_{i-1}, T_i, K)$ is the price of a caplet and the arguments of the function are the same as for the floorlet. The total value of the FRA is:

$$\mathrm{FRA}^{\mathrm{Cf}}(t; T_{i-1}, T_i)$$

$$= P^D(t, T_i)\tau_i\mathbf{E}^{T_i}[L_i(T_{i-1}) - K] + \mathrm{LVA}_{\mathrm{FRA}^{\mathrm{Cf}}(t;T_{i-1},T_i)} + \mathrm{FVA}_{\mathrm{FRA}^{\mathrm{Cf}}(t;T_{i-1},T_i)} \quad (12.144)$$

The fair rate making the value of the contract at inception zero has to be computed recursively.

Remark 12.2.5. *Formula (12.139) shows that the FRA fair rate is independent of the currency in which the collateral is posted: this is the same as the result derived above for derivatives with different underlying assets that can be replicated by a dynamic strategy. The difference between FRA fair rates relating to contracts collateralized in two different currencies can be caused by more difficult access to the money market in XXX for banks operating in the domestic country (where YYY is the currency used). This will produce generalized and higher funding costs borne by domestic banks when posting collateral in the foreign currency, so that an average FVA, typically paid by all banks, is added to the XXX-collateralized FRA. In this case the FRA fair rate will be dependent on the currency chosen to post the collateral.*

Interest rate swap

We will not devote much space to the results for an IRS since they are derived in much the same way as those for a FRA and are in any event the same as in Section 12.1 (to which we refer the reader for more details).

Consider an IRS whose fixed leg pays rate K on dates $T_c^S, \ldots, T_d^S$ ($\tau_k^S = T_i^S - T_{i-1}^S$); the floating leg receives Libor fixings on dates $T_a, \ldots, T_b$. We assume that the set of floating rate dates includes the set of fixed rate dates. For both legs the present value of these payments is obtained by discounting them using the YYY discount curve D. If collateral is posted in XXX, the value at time t of the IRS is:

$$\text{IRS}^{\text{Cf}}(t, K; T_a, \ldots, T_b, T_c^S, \ldots, T_c^S)$$
$$= \left[\sum_{k=a}^{b} P^D(t, T_k)\tau_k L_k(t) - \sum_{j=c}^{d} P^D(t, T_j)\tau_j^S K \right] + \text{LVA}_{\text{IRS}^{\text{Cf}}(t;T_a,T_b)} \quad (12.145)$$

with:

$$\text{LVA}_{\text{IRS}^{\text{Cf}}(t;T_a,T_b)} = \sum_{j=1}^{N} P^D(t, t_j)\mathbf{E}^{t_j}\left[\tau_j^C[L_j^{D^f}(t) - O_j^f(t)]\gamma \text{IRS}^{\text{Cf}}(t_j; T_a, T_b) \right] \quad (12.146)$$

where $\text{IRS}^{\text{Cf}}(t; T_a, T_b) = \text{IRS}^{\text{Cf}}(t, K; T_a, \ldots, T_b, T_c^S, \ldots, T_c^S)$. LVA is as usual the difference between the XXX currency's risk-free rate and the collateral rate applied to fraction γ of the NPV, for a total of N days occurring between valuation date t and the end of the contract $t_N = T_b$. As far as swaps are concerned, we can also make the assumption that market quotes refer to the situation when LVA $= 0$, implying that the XXX currency's risk-free and collateral rates are the same. When the two rates are different, LVA is:

$$\text{LVA}_{\text{IRS}^{\text{Cf}}(t;T_a,T_b)} = \sum_{j=1}^{N} P^D(t, t_j)\mathbf{E}^{t_j}[\tau_j^C Q_j^f(t)]\mathbf{E}^{t_j}[\gamma \text{IRS}^{\text{Cf}}(t_j; T_a, T_b)] \quad (12.147)$$

The second expectation in (12.141) is $C_D^{a,b}(t)\mathbf{E}^{a,b}[\gamma(S_{a,b}(t) - K)]/P^D(t, t_j)$, where $\mathbf{E}^{a,b}$ is the expectation taken under the swap measure, with the numeraire equal to annuity $C_D^{a,b}(t) = \sum_{j=a+1}^{b} P^D(t, T_j)\tau_j^S$. So, we can write:

$$\text{LVA}_{\text{IRS}^{\text{Cf}}(t;T_a,T_b)} = \sum_{j=1}^{N} P^D(t, t_j)\left[\mathbf{E}^{t_j}[\tau_j^C Q_j^f(t)] \frac{C_D^{a,b}(t)\mathbf{E}^{a,b}[\gamma(S_{a,b}(t) - K)]}{P^D(t, t_j)} \right] \quad (12.148)$$

FVA is defined analogously to the FRA case:

$$\text{FVA}_{\text{IRS}^{\text{Cf}}(t;T_a,T_b)} = \sum_{j=1}^{N} P^D(t,t_j) \left[\mathbf{E}^{t_j}[\tau_j^C U_j^f(t)] \frac{C_D^{a,b}(t)\mathbf{E}^{a,b}[\gamma(S_{a,b}(t)-K)^-]}{P^D(t,t_j)} \right] \quad (12.149)$$

Introducing options on swaps, the second expectation in (12.149) is:

$$\frac{C_D^{a,b}(t)\mathbf{E}^{a,b}[\gamma(S_{a,b}(t)-K)^-]}{P^D(t,t_j)} = -\frac{[\gamma\text{Rec}(t_j;T_a,T_b)]}{P^D(t,t_j)}$$

where $\text{Rec}(t;T_a,T_b)$ is the price of a receiver swaption priced at time t_j, expiry at T_a, on a swap starting at T_a and maturing at T_b, with strike K. If the bank has a short position in the IRS (i.e., it is a fixed rate receiver), then FVA is

$$\frac{C_D^{a,b}(t)\mathbf{E}^{a,b}[\gamma(K-S_{a,b}(t))^-]}{P^D(t,t_j)} = -\frac{[\gamma\text{Pay}(t_j;T_a,T_b)]}{P^D(t,t_j)}$$

where $\text{Pay}(t;T_a,T_b)$ is the price of a payer swaption. So, the total value of the IRS can be written as:

$$\text{IRS}^{\text{Cf}}(t,K;T_a,\ldots,T_b,T_c^S,\ldots,T_c^S) = \left[\sum_{k=a}^{b} P^D(t,T_k)\tau_k L_k(t) - \sum_{j=c}^{d} P^D(t,T_j)\tau_j^S K \right]$$

$$+ \text{LVA}_{\text{IRS}^{\text{Cf}}(t;T_a,T_b)}$$

$$+ \text{FVA}_{\text{IRS}^{\text{Cf}}(t;T_a,T_b)} \quad (12.150)$$

It is worthy of note that fair market swap rates are also independent of the currency used to post collateral, although the same considerations as those in Remark 12.2.5 apply.

12.2.4   Cross-currency swaps

Cross-currency swaps (CCS) involve at least two currencies since they are the periodic exchange of Libor rates in one currency against the Libor rates of another currency, usually with a basis spread paid over one of them. Most CCS are against US dollars, and the basis spread quoted in the market is paid over the Libor of the other currency of the deal. We now learn how to price a CCS when collateral is posted in US dollars, which we name "major currency" in what follows and which can be thought of as XXX introduced above.[19] The other currency is named "minor currency" and is YYY as before. To avoid any confusion, we will add superscript X or Y to refer to the relative currency whenever needed.

Let T_b be the expiry of a swap starting at T_a with fixed rate $S_{a,b}(t)$. Let $L_k^X(t)$ be the forward Libor rate corresponding to the payment frequency of the floating leg (e.g., 6-month Libor for semiannual payments) for the period between T_{k-1} and T_k, computed at time t, with $T_k \geq T_a$ and $T_a \leq t < T_k$. The notation is the same as above. $P^{D^X}(t,v)$ is

---

[19] This seems to be the standard when swaps are cleared via the LCH, since the collateral is always posted in USD. Although the collateralization process involves multilateral netting in this case, its mechanics are the same as in the bilateral CSA agreement and, hence, valuation of the contract can be operated in the same way.

the US risk-free discount factor for the period t to v. If $S^X_{a,b}(t)$ is the fair market rate of the swap, the IRS can be computed under the assumption of nil LVA, so that:

$$\text{IRS}^X(t, S_{a,b}; T_a, \ldots, T_b, T^S_c, \ldots, T^S_c)$$

$$= \left[\sum_{k=a}^{b} P^{D^X}(t, T_k)\tau_k L^X_k(t) - \sum_{j=c}^{d} P^{D^X}(t, T_j)\tau^S_j S^X_{a,b}(t) \right] \quad (12.151)$$

The swap is collateralized in **XXX**. The first term in the sum on the right-hand side is the present value of the stream of floating rate cash flows, whereas the second is the present value of fixed leg payments. The sum is nil for par swaps. We indicate the present value of the floating leg by $\text{Float}^X(t, T_a, T_b) = \sum_{k=a}^{b} P^{D^X}(t, T_k)\tau_k L^X_k(t)$, such indication will be found convenient in what follows. We can define in much the same way an IRS in minor currency, collateralized in major currency, with fair swap rate $S^Y_{a,b}(t)$.

Let $\text{CCS}^X(t, b^{ccs}_{a,b}; T_a, \ldots, T_b)$ be a cross-currency swap against the US dollar, with the same start T_a, maturity T_b and frequency as the standard IRS in (12.151) for both floating legs denominated in the two currencies; $b^{ccs}_{a,b}$ is the basis paid over Libor L^Y of the minor currency leg. Collateral is posted in US dollars (or **XXX**). The value of the YYY-receiver CCS, keeping LVA and FVA in mind, is:

$$\text{CCS}^X(t, b^{ccs}_{a,b}; T_a, \ldots, T_b) = \left[\mathcal{X}_t \left(\sum_{k=a}^{b} P^{D^Y}(t, T_k)\tau^Y_k \left(\mathbf{E}^{T_k}_{D^Y}[L^Y_k(T_{k-1})] + b^{ccs}_{a,b} \right) \right. \right.$$

$$\left. + P^{D^Y}(t, T_a) - P^{D^Y}(t, T_b) \right)$$

$$\left. - \sum_{k=a}^{b} P^{D^X}(t, T_k)\tau^X_k \mathbf{E}^{T_i}_{D^X}[L^X_k(T_{k-1})] + P^{D^X}(t, T_a) - P^{D^X}(t, T_b) \right]$$

$$+ \text{LVA}_{\text{CCS}^X} + \text{FVA}_{\text{CCS}^X} \quad (12.152)$$

Let us focus on the first three lines of (12.152) (i.e., the part in square brackets) and postpone for the moment our analysis of the LVA_{CCS}. To price a CCS, it is convenient to adopt the vantage point of an agent operating in the major (USD) currency economy. Therefore, we need to know how to evaluate a Libor payment in the minor currency when seen from the major-currency economy.

To this end, assume we have at time $t = 0$ (i) discount factors $P^{D^X}(0, T)$ for the major currency, (ii) a minor-currency par swap rate paying $S^Y_{0,b}$ with the swap collateralized in the major currency and cross-currency basis swap spreads $b^{ccs}_{0,b}$ and (iii) the spot exchange rate $\mathcal{X}$ (i.e., the number of minor-currency units equal to 1 unit of the major currency). For simplicity we consider the same schedule for all legs. We can establish the following relationship.

Proposition 12.2.1. *When collateral is in a major currency, the following equation holds:*

$$(S^Y_{0,b} + b^{ccs}_{0,b}) \sum_{k=0}^{b} \tau^Y_k P^{D^X}(0, T_i) \frac{\mathcal{X}_0}{\mathcal{F}(t, T_i)} + P^{D^X}(0, T_b) \frac{\mathcal{X}_0}{\mathcal{F}(0, T_i)}$$

$$= (\text{Float}^X(0, 0, T_b) + P^{D^X}(0, T_b)) \quad (12.153)$$

Proof. Let us consider the following portfolio, which contains a set of transactions and its associated cash flows, disregarding the effects of collateral, for a swap starting at time $t = 0$, and with all $\tau = 1$ to lighten the notation:

Transaction	Cash flow today	Interim cash flow	Terminal cash flow
Receive fixed on foreign swap	0	$S_{0,b}^Y - L_t^X$	0
Cross-currency basis foreign flows	-1	$L_t^Y + b_{0,b}^{ccs}$	$+1$
Cross-currency basis dollar flows	$1/\mathcal{X}_0$	$-L_t^X/\mathcal{X}_0$	$-1/\mathcal{X}_0$
Spot FX foreign	1	0	0
Spot FX USD	$-1/\mathcal{X}_0$	0	0
Forward sale foreign	0	$-(S_{0,b}^Y + b_{0,b}^{ccs})$	-1
Forward buy USD	0	$(S_{0,b}^Y + b_{0,b}^{ccs})/\mathcal{F}(0,t)$	$1/\mathcal{F}(0,T_b)$
Subtotal float	0	$-L_t^X/\mathcal{X}_0$	$-1/\mathcal{X}_0$
Subtotal fixed	0	$(S_{0,b}^Y + b_{0,b}^{ccs})/\mathcal{F}(0,T_b)$	$1/\mathcal{F}(0,T_b)$

Since collateral from all contracts is posted in the major currency, the collateral of net cash flows is by assumption posted in the major currency as well. These net cash flows resemble those of a swap of major-currency Libor against a schedule of fixed payments. Therefore, from the results derived above for an IRS, net stated cash flows can be valued by discounting them at the major-currency risk-free rate.

The present value of paying Libor on notional $1/\mathcal{X}_0$ and a terminal payment of $1/\mathcal{X}_0$ is obviously $-\frac{1}{\mathcal{X}_0}\left(\text{Float}^X(t,0,T_b) + P^{D^X}(t,T_b)\right)$. Since there are no net cash flows at time $t = 0$, total present value of the two subtotal cash flows must equal 0. Therefore:

$$(S_{0,b}^Y + b_{0,b}^{ccs}) \sum_{k=0}^{b} \tau_k^Y P^{D^X}(t,T_k) \frac{1}{\mathcal{F}(0,T_k)} + P^{D^X}(0,T_b) \frac{1}{\mathcal{F}(0,T_b)}$$

$$-\frac{1}{\mathcal{X}_0}\left(\text{Float}(0,0,T_b) + P^{D^X}(0,T_b)\right) = 0 \quad (12.154)$$

Multiplying all terms by $\mathcal{X}_0$, to express everything in minor-currency units, and rearranging yields the desired result. $\qquad\square$

Remark 12.2.6. *From the analysis conducted above for standard IRSs collateralized in some other currency, the fair swap rate $S_{a,b}^Y$ can be considered as independent of the choice of collateral currency, since LVA is unaffected. We already stressed in Remark 12.2.5 that it may be possible for the fair FRA and IRS rates to differ according to the choice of currency used to post collateral. So, if different IRSs are quoted in the market for the different possible currencies in which the collateral is posted, we can use these quotes for $S_{0,b}^Y$ in equation (12.153). Otherwise, we can quite safely assume that swap rates for IRSs collateralized in a minor currency are the same for any other collateral currency.*

It is straightforward to derive the present value of receiving Libor rates in a minor currency from a major-currency perspective: since foreign par swaps are fair the value of fixed cash flows must equal the value of floating cash flows. The value of fixed cash flows, from (12.153), is $S_{0,b}^Y \sum_{k=0}^b \tau_k^Y P^{D^X}(t,T_k)\frac{\mathcal{X}_0}{\mathcal{F}(0,T_k)}$, so that:

$$\text{Float}^Y(t,0,T_b) = S_{0,b}^Y \sum_{k=0}^b \tau_k^Y P^{D^X}(t,T_k)\frac{\mathcal{X}_0}{\mathcal{F}(0,T_k)}$$

$$= \text{Float}^X(t,0,T_b) + P^{D^X}(0,T_b) - b_{0,b}^{ccs}\sum_{k=0}^b \tau_k^Y P^{D^X}(t,T_k)\frac{\mathcal{X}_0}{\mathcal{F}(0,T_k)}$$

$$- P^{D^X}(0,T_b)\frac{\mathcal{X}_0}{\mathcal{F}(0,T_b)}$$

$$= \sum_{k=0}^b \frac{P^{D^X}(t,T_i)\mathcal{X}_0}{\mathcal{F}(0,T_i)}\tau_k^Y \mathbf{E}_{D^X}^{T_k}[L_k^Y(T_{k-1})] \qquad (12.155)$$

So, we are able to switch to a major-currency T_k forward measure for each minor-currency Libor rate. This allows us to price a CCS collateralized in the major currency, since we can insert equation (12.155) into (12.152), setting $t = T_a = 0$:

$$\text{CCS}^X(t,b_{a,b}^{ccs};0,\dots,T_b) = \left[\mathcal{X}_0\left(\sum_{k=0}^b P^{D^Y}(0,T_k)\text{Float}^Y(0,0,T_b) + b_{0,b}^{ccs} +1 - P^{D^Y}(0,T_b)\right)\right.$$

$$\left. - \text{Float}^X(0,0,T_b) + 1 - P^D(t,T_b)\right]$$

$$+ \text{LVA}_{\text{CCS}_{(0;0;T_b)}^X} + \text{FVA}_{\text{CCS}_{(0;0;T_b)}^X} \qquad (12.156)$$

LVA is defined as:

$$\text{LVA}_{\text{CCS}_{(0;0;T_b)}^X} = \sum_{j=1}^N P^D(t,t_j)\left[\mathbf{E}_{D^X}^{t_j}[\tau_j^C Q_j^X(t)]\mathbf{E}_{D^X}^{t_j}\left[\gamma\text{CCS}(t_j;0,T_b)\right]\right] \qquad (12.157)$$

where the notation is the same as above. FVA is defined similarly as:

$$\text{FVA}_{\text{CCS}^X(0;0,T_b)} = \sum_{j=1}^N P^{D^X}(0,t_j)\left[\mathbf{E}_{D^X}^{t_j}[\tau_j^C U_j^X(t)]\mathbf{E}_{D^X}^{t_j}\left[\gamma\min(\text{CCS}(t_j;0,T_b),0)\right]\right] \qquad (12.158)$$

Remark 12.2.7. *The setup outlined above allows consistent valuation of IRSs in different currencies and of CCSs. From (12.153) we can derive the term structure of implied FX swap levels. These are then used in (12.155) to bootstrap YYY Libors seen from the XXX economy perspective: they guarantee that CCSs are repriced correctly. So, in this approach we do not build a basis-adjusted discount curve to match CCS prices, a method usually adopted in practice in many banks. We prefer to build, in our opinion more consistently, adjusted Libor projection curves and leave discount curves unchanged. By definition, IRSs in the two currencies are correctly repriced as long as proper discount and projection curves are used.*

12.3 VALUATION OF NON-COLLATERALIZED INTEREST RATE SWAPS INCLUDING FUNDING COSTS

In Chapter 10 we correctly defined the debit value adjustment (DVA) of a derivative contract and put forward a definition that declares the DVA worsens contract conditions for a counterparty because it has to compensate the other party for the possibility of its own default. DVA is very strictly linked to funding costs (FCs) when the contract is a loan, a bond or more generally some kind of borrowing. The link is much less tight (maybe even nonexistent) for some derivative contracts such as swaps. The funding costs for a derivative contract is actually the DVA (plus liquidity premium and intermediation cost, if priced in market quotes) that a counterparty has to pay on the loan contracts it has to close to fund, if needed, negative cumulated cash flows until maturity.

In what follows we study how to include funding costs in the valuation of interest rate swaps (IRSs) and show how they affect the value of the swap via funding value adjustment (FVA), in analogy to credit value adjustment (CVA) and DVA. We consider valuation of IRS contracts in the absence of collateral agreement or any other form of credit risk mitigation.

IRS valuation effectively demonstrates how the inclusion of funding costs makes even relatively simple contracts very complex especially when all the relevant risks are considered.

12.3.1 The basic setup

Let us assume that, at time t, we want to price a very general (nonstandard) swap, such as an amortizing or zero-coupon swap, with possibly different amounts for the fixed and floating rates, and accompanied, possibly, by a time-varying fixed rate.

Let us introduce the meta-swap, which is a swap with unit notional and a time-varying fixed rate that is equivalent to the contract fixed rate times the notional amount for each date N_{i-1}^K (i.e., the one at the start of the calculation period). The start date of the swap is T_a and the end date is T_b.

Let us assume that the swap's floating leg pays at times $T_{a+1}, \ldots, T_b$, where T_{a+1} is the first fixing time (dates are equally spaced acording to floating leg payment frequency); $F_i(t)$ are the forward rates, as at time t, paid at time T_i and fixed at T_{i-1}, for $a + 1 \leq i \leq b$; the swap's fixed leg pays at times $T_{c_1}, \ldots, T_{c_J}$, where $c_1 \geq a$ and $c_J = b$. Fixed leg times are assumed to be included in the set of floating leg times and this is usually the case for standard swaps quoted in the OTC market, for which floating flows are paid semiannually or quarterly, whereas fixed flows are paid annually.

The fixed rate payment at each payment date T_{c_j} is:

$$R_j = \beta_j K \tag{12.159}$$

where

$$\beta_j = N_{j-1}^K \delta_j^K \tag{12.160}$$

and δ_j^K denotes the fraction into which the year is divided (or year fraction) between payment dates for the fixed leg.

The floating leg will exchange future Libor fixing times α_i, which is the year fraction times the notional N^L_{i-1} at the beginning of the calculation period:

$$\alpha_i = N^L_{i-1} \delta^L_i \qquad (12.161)$$

Note that despite the fact that the meta-swap has unit notional, both the total fixed rate and the year fraction contain the notional of the swap.

Define

$$\bar{C}_{a,b}(t) = \sum_{j=1}^{J} \beta_j P(t, T_{c_j}) \qquad (12.162)$$

as the annuity, or DV01 in market lore, of the meta-swap. We assume $\bar{C}_{a,b}(t) > 0$. Discount factors (or discount bonds) $P(t, T)$ are taken from a risk-free curve; in the current market environment, the best approximation to the risk-free rate is given by overnight rates. An entire curve based on these rates can be bootstrapped from OIS swaps. Define also:

$$w_i(t) = \frac{\alpha_i P(t, T_i)}{\bar{C}_{a,b}(t)} \qquad (12.163)$$

We then have:

$$S_{a,b}(t) = \sum_{i=a+1}^{b} w_i(t) F_i(t) \qquad (12.164)$$

which is the swap rate $\mathrm{Swp}_{a,b}(t) = 0$ that makes the value of the meta-swap at t equal zero ($\mathrm{Swp}_{a,b}(t)$ is the value at time t of a swap starting at T_a and terminating at T_b). In a standard swap the fair rate is the average forward Libor rate F_i weighted as a function of discount factors. In the case of the meta-swap the average forward Libor rate is weighted as a function of the notionals and discount factors. It is easily checked that this is the rate making the present value of the floating leg equal to that of the fixed leg. Note that the risk-free rates used to derive discount factors are not the same as those used to determine Libor forward rates F_i.[20]

Some points are worth stressing here. First, pricing is correct if both counterparties involved are risk free; second, since at least one of the two counterparties is usually a bank, the fact that Libor rates are above risk-free rates is in conflict with the first point, Libor being rates applied to unsecured lending to an ideal bank with a good credit rating, but not risk free in any case; third, as a consequence of the second point, full risk pricing should also include credit adjustments (CVA and DVA) as compensation for default risk relating to either party.

To isolate the funding component of the value of a swap, we consider an abstraction and disregard adjustments due to counterparty credit risk. We will include counterparty credit risk later on. To help us analyse the problem linked to the cost of funding, we first introduce a hedging strategy for the swap and then analyse the cash flows implied by it.

12.3.2 Hedging swap exposures and cash flows

Assume a bank takes a position in a swap starting at T_a and ending at T_b that can be described by the general formulae given above: the fair swap rate is $\bar{S}_{a,b} = S_{a,b}(t)$. The

---

[20] For more details on the new pricing formulae that have been developed in the wake of the financial crisis of 2007 see [21] and [89].

swap can either be a fixed rate payer or fixed rate receiver, in which case the fixed leg has a negative (positive) sign. The bank wants to hedge exposures to interest rates, but at the same time wants to come up with a well-defined, possibly deterministic schedule of cash flows so as to plan its funding and/or investment. To lock in future cash flows, we suggest the following strategy:

- take stock of all dates $T_{c_1}, \ldots, T_{c_J}$ when fixed leg payments occur;
- close (forward) starting swaps $\mathrm{Swp}(T_{c_{i-1}}, T_{c_i})$, for $i = 1, \ldots, J$ using fixed rate payments opposite to those of the swap the bank wants to hedge (the fair rate for each swap is $\bar{S}_{c_{i-1},c_i} = S_{c_{i-1},c_i}(t)$).

Let $\mathrm{cf}(T_k)$ be the amount of cash to receive or pay at time T_k, generated by the hedged portfolio above. The floating leg of each hedging swap balances the floating leg of the meta-swap for the corresponding period so that at each time T_i, with $a + 1 \leq i \leq b$ we have $\mathrm{cf}(T_i) = 0$. On the dates T_{c_j}, for $1 \leq j \leq J$, when the fixed legs of the total portfolio (comprising the meta-swap and hedging swaps) are paid, the net cash flows are:

$$\mathrm{cf}(T_{c_j}) = [(1_{\{R\}} - 1_{\{P\}})\bar{S}_{a,b} - (1_{\{R\}} - 1_{\{P\}})\bar{S}_{c_{j-1},c_j}]\delta_j^K$$

where $1_{\{R\}}$ (respectively, $1_{\{P\}}$) is the indicator function equal to 1 if the swap is receiver (respectively, payer).

Furthermore, let $\mathrm{CF}(T_a, T_{c_j})$ be the compounded cumulated cash flows from the start time T_a up to time T_{c_j} via the recurrent equation:

$$\mathrm{CF}(T_a, T_{c_j}) = \mathrm{CF}(T_a, T_{c_{j-1}}) \frac{P^D(t, T_{c_{j-1}})}{P^D(t, T_{c_j})} + \mathrm{cf}(T_{c_j}) \tag{12.165}$$

with the starting value $\mathrm{CF}(T_a, T_a) = 0$.

Cash flows are assumed to be reinvested at the risk-free rate: this is possible if the cumulated cash flows start at zero, increase and do not become negative. We indicate by $\mathrm{cf}^{\pm}(c_k)$ a positive/negative cash flow, whereas we indicate by $\overline{\mathrm{CF}}(a, b)$ the maximum number of cumulated cash flows between start date T_a and end date T_b:

$$\overline{\mathrm{CF}}(T_a, T_b) = \max[\mathrm{CF}(T_a, T_{c_1}), \mathrm{CF}(T_a, T_{c_2}), \ldots, \mathrm{CF}(T_a, T_{c_J})] \tag{12.166}$$

Analogously, we denote by $\underline{\mathrm{CF}}(T_a, T_b)$ the minimum number of cumulated cash flows:

$$\underline{\mathrm{CF}}(T_a, T_b) = \min[\mathrm{CF}(T_a, T_{c_1}), \mathrm{CF}(T_a, T_{c_2}), \ldots, \mathrm{CF}(T_a, T_{c_J})] \tag{12.167}$$

For standard market swaps, we generally have two possible patterns of cumulated cash flows, depending on the side of the swap (fixed rate payer/receiver) and on the shape of the term structure of interest rates: the first pattern is always negative, while the second is always positive. This means that $\overline{\mathrm{CF}}(T_a, T_b)$ is zero and $\underline{\mathrm{CF}}(T_a, T_b)$ is a negative number in the first case; in the second case $\underline{\mathrm{CF}}(a, b)$ is zero and $\overline{\mathrm{CF}}(a, b)$ is a positive number. For funding costs to be included in the pricing, we need only focus on the first case, whereas the second case poses no problems. In fact, in the second case, the cash flows generated internally within the deal, including their reinvestment in a risk-free asset, imply no need to resort to additional funding. This is not true in the first case.

Negative cash flows need to be funded and related costs should be included in the pricing. As mentioned above, we disregard the effect of the defaults of either parties on funding costs for the moment: we will consider this later.

Now, given the market term structure of forward Libor rates, a swap usually implies for a counterparty a string of negative cash flows compensated by a subsequent string of positive cash flows. The present (or, equivalently, the future at expiry) value of negative cash flows is equal to the present (or future) value of positive cash flows, provided there is no default by either counterparty and that each counterparty is able to lend and borrow money at the risk-free rate.

If we assume that it is possible for the counterparties to lend money at the risk-free rate, but that they have to pay a funding spread over the risk-free rate to borrow money, then the problem of how to correctly consider this cost arises. We suggest two strategies to fund negative cash flows, the second one has two variants. We examine them separately from the perspective of one of the two parties (say, the bank), whereas the other party is assumed to be a client that is unable to transfer his funding costs to the pricing.

12.3.3   Funding spread modelling

To keep things simple, let us assume that the funding spread is due only to credit factors and that there are no liquidity premiums. More specifically, the bank has to pay a spread that originates from its default probability and loss given default. If we assume that after default a fraction $\mathcal{R}$ of the market value of the contract is immediately paid to the counterparty – recovery of market value (RMV) assumption – then we have a very convenient definition of the instantaneous spread[21] as $s_t = (1 - \mathcal{R})\lambda_t$, where λ is default intensity (i.e., the jump intensity of a Poisson process, default being the first jump). We choose a doubly stochastic intensity model so that the survival probability between time 0 and time T is given by (see Chapter 8):

$$SP(0, T) = e^{-\int_0^T \lambda_u du}$$

where default intensity λ_t is a stochastic process that is assumed to be defined by CIR-type dynamics as in equation (8.140). In this setting, $SP(0, T)$ has the closed-form solution given in equation (8.141).

The formula to compute spread discount factors is readily shown to be the same as for survival probability with a slight change in parameters:

$$P^s(0, T; \lambda_0, \kappa_\lambda, \theta_\lambda, \sigma_\lambda, \mathcal{R}) = SP\left(0, (1 - \mathcal{R})T; \lambda_0, \frac{\kappa_\lambda}{1 - \mathcal{R}}, \theta_\lambda, \frac{\sigma_\lambda}{\sqrt{1 - \mathcal{R}}}\right) \quad (12.168)$$

where we used properties inherent in the CIR process.[22]

Let $P^D(0, T)$ be the price at 0 of a default risk-free zero-coupon bond (bootstrapped from the OIS swap curve, for example) maturing at T; the price of a correspondent zero-coupon bond issued by the bank is $P^B(0, T) = P^D(0, T)P^s(0, T)$ (where we have omitted some parameters of function $P^s(0, T)$ to lighten the notation), assuming default intensity as given by the dynamics in (8.140) and a recovery rate $\mathcal{R}$. This is also the discount factor used to compute the present value of money borrowed by the bank and should be considered effective at embedding funding costs.[23]

---

[21] See [63].
[22] See Chapter 8.
[23] See Chapter 10 for a discussion on this point.

12.3.4 Strategy 1: Funding all cash flows at inception

The first strategy is based on the idea of funding all negative cash flows from the very inception of the swap. To this end, we compute the minimum cumulated amount $\underline{CF}(a, b)$ over the entire duration of the swap $[T_a, T_b]$. Assuming that $\underline{CF}(a, b) < 0$, this implies a certain amount of cash that needs to be entirely funded at inception. The idea is to borrow money and then use the cash flows generated by the hedged swap portfolio to repay it, possibly according to a predefined amortization schedule determined by the cash flow pattern. We need to consider some relevant practical matters too:

- The total sum entirely funded at inception can be invested in a risk-free asset (a zero-coupon bond issued by a risk-free counterparty,[24] for example). The amounts needed when negative cash flows occur can be obtained by selling back a fraction of the investment. The interest earned has to be included in the pricing.
- The funding for long maturities can be done with a loan that the bank trades with another counterparty; this usually implies periodic payment of interest on the outstanding amount. Periodic paid interest also needs to be included in the evaluation process.

To formalize all this, let us consider the bank pays annual interest on the outstanding of the borrowed amount on an annual basis, according to a fixed rate calculated at the start keeping the probability of default in mind. We assume that the bank pays a fraction of the market value of the loan should it default.

Let $t = 0$ and A be the initial amount of a loan that expires at T_b (equal to expiry of the swap) and has a capital and interest payment schedule at dates $[T_{d_1}, \ldots, T_{d_M}]$: we assume that this set also contains the set of payment dates for the fixed leg of the swaps. We define capital payment of loan A at time T_k as $K(T_{d_k}) = A(T_{d_k}) - A(T_{d_{k-1}})$, with $A(t) = A$, $A(T_b) = 0$ and $\sum_{k=1}^M K(T_{d_k}) = A$. Note that the loan starts at the inception of contract t, which could even be before the start of swap T_a; moreover, interest payments can also occur before T_a. Let $\bar{i}$ be the fixed rate that the bank has to pay on this loan: it can be derived from the following relationship

$$A = \sum_{k=1}^M (K(T_{d_k}) + \bar{i} A(T_{d_{k-1}}) \delta_{d_k}) P^B(0, T_{d_k}) \tag{12.169}$$

where $\delta_{d_k} = T_k - T_{k-1}$ is the accrual period. Discounting is carried out by means of discount factors $P^B(T_0, T_k)$ such that the losses the lender suffers on the bank's default can also be taken into account. From the bank's perspective the spread paid over the risk-free rate is a funding cost, whereas it is compensation for the default risk borne from the lender's perspective.[25] The loan's fair fixed rate $\bar{i}$ is:

$$\bar{i} = \frac{A - \sum_{k=1}^M K(T_{d_k}) P^B(0, T_{d_k})}{\sum_{k=1}^M A(T_{d_{k-1}}) \delta_k P^B(0, T_{d_k})} \tag{12.170}$$

As mentioned above, once the amount of loan A is received by the bank at time 0, it can

---

[24] As far as defaultable issuers are concerned, their debt should be remunerated by a spread over the risk-free rate to compensate for the risk of default so that, ultimately, expected return is still the risk-free rate.
[25] See Chapter 10 for a more detailed discussion.

be reinvested at the risk-free rate and partially reduced to cover future outflows of cash when they occur. Let us define available liquidity at time T_{d_k} via the recurrent equation:

$$\text{AVL}(T_{d_k}) = \text{AVL}(T_{d_{k-1}}) \frac{P^D(t, T_{d_{k-1}})}{P^D(t, T_{d_k})} + \text{cf}(T_{d_k}) - K(T_{d_k}) - \bar{i}A(T_{d_{k-1}}) \quad (12.171)$$

with $\text{AVL}(0) = A$. Equation (12.171) states that liquidity available to the bank at time T_{d_k} is liquidity available at the previous time $T_{d_{k-1}}$ invested at the forward risk-free rate over the period $[T_{d_{k-1}}, T_{d_k}]$, plus the cash flow occurring at time T_{d_k}, minus the sum of instalment and interest rate payments. Cash flows can either be positive or negative. When positive cash flow $\text{cf}(T_{d_k}) > 0$ occurs, it is used to abate the outstanding amount of the loan; on the other hand, when negative cash flow $\text{cf}(T_{d_k}) < 0$ occurs, then there is no capital instalment and $K(T_{d_k}) = 0$. Since it is possible to lock in future cash flows at contract inception via the suggested hedging portfolio, the amortization plan for the loan, however irregular it may be, can be established at time $t = 0$. The amortization plan can then be defined as:

$$A(T_{d_k}) = A(T_{d_{k-1}}) - \text{cf}^+(T_{d_k})$$

The amount of the loan the bank has to borrow will be a function of the term structure of Libor interest rates and of bank funding spreads, the fixed leg notional schedule of the swap and the fixed rate of the swap:

$$A = f(F_1(0), \dots, F_b(0), s_1(t), \dots, s_b(t), N_1^K, \dots, N_J^K, \bar{S}_{a,b})$$

where $s_k(t)$ is the funding spread for period $[T_{k-1}, T_k]$. Amount A has to be determined so as to satisfy two constraints:

1. Available liquidity $\text{AVL}(T_{d_k})$ at each time T_{d_k} must always be positive, so that no other funding is required until the end of the swap. This constraint is satisfied if $A = \sum_{j=1}^{J} \text{cf}^-(T_j)$ (i.e., if it is at least equal to the sum of negative cash flows occurring in the future).
2. At the maturity of swap T_b available liquidity should be entirely used to finance all negative cash flows, so that $\text{AVL}(T_b) = 0$, thus minimizing funding costs (assuming no unnecessary funding at inception has been requested by the bank).

Amount A can be determined very quickly numerically. Given a positive funding spread, the positive cash flows originated by the hedged portfolio will not be sufficient to cover the loan's amortization plan, so that on the last capital instalment date extra cash must be provided by the bank to pay back its debt in its entirety; ultimately, this represents a cost that has to be included in the pricing of the swap. Let FC be the present value of this cost. It can then be added to the fair swap rate as follows:

$$S_{a,b}^{\text{FC}}(0) = \sum_{i=a+1}^{b} w_i(0) F_i(0) + (1_{\{R\}} - 1_{\{P\}}) \frac{\text{FC}}{\bar{C}_{a,b}(0)} \quad (12.172)$$

where annuity $\bar{C}_{a,b}(0)$ and weights $w_i(0)$ are defined as in (12.162) and (12.163). Equation (12.172) increases (decreases) the fair swap rate if the bank is a fixed rate receiver (payer) in the contract, thus compensating the extra costs due to funding costs.

Since the amount of loan A is a function of swap rate $S_{a,b}(0)$, which in turn is affected by funding cost FC that depends of A, a numerical search is needed to determine the final fair swap rate $\bar{S}_{a,b}^{FC}$, which makes both the available liquidity and the FC equal to zero. Convergence is typically achieved in a few steps.

The value of the swap, when the rate is $\bar{S}_{a,b}^{FC}$, is:

$$\text{Swp}^{FC}(T_a, T_b) = \bar{C}_{a,b}(0)\left[(1_{\{R\}} - 1_{\{P\}})[\bar{S}_{a,b}^{FC}\bar{C}_{a,b}(0) - \sum_{i=a+1}^{b} w_i(0)F_i(0)]\right] = -\text{FVA}$$

(12.173)

since for payer (receiver) swap $\bar{S}_{a,b}^{FC} < \bar{S}_{a,b}$ ($\bar{S}_{a,b}^{FC} > \bar{S}_{a,b}$), the swap has a positive value that equates the reverse sign FVA, which is the quantity that makes the swap value nil at inception when funding costs are included in the pricing.

12.3.5 Strategy 2: Funding negative cash flows when they occur

The second strategy we propose involves matching negative cash flows when they occur by resorting to new debt, given that cumulated cash flows are not positive and/or insufficient. The debt is carried on by rolling it over and paying a periodic interest rate plus a funding spread; moreover, it can be increased when new negative cash flows occur and decreased when positive cash flows are received. Interest rates and funding spreads paid are those prevailing in the market at the time of rollover, so that they are not fixed at inception of the contract.

The advantage this strategy has over the first is that the bank borrows money only when necessary and does not have to pay any interest and funding spread for the time preceding cumulated cash flows becoming negative. On the other hand, the bank is exposed to liquidity shortage risks and to uncertain funding costs that cannot be locked in at the start of the contract. The latter statement will become clearer in what follows.

Let us assume that the hedged swap portfolio generates at given time T_k a negative cash flow $\text{cf}^-(T_k)$ and that cumulated cash flows are negative: the bank funds the outflow by borrowing money in the interbank market. We assume that the debt is rolled over in the future and that the bank pays interest plus a funding spread over period $[T_k, T_{k+1}]$; the borrowed amount varies depending on the cash flow available at time T_{k+1}. Hence, the debt evolves according to the following recurrent equation:

$$\text{FDB}(T_{d_{k+1}}) = \text{FDB}(T_k)\frac{P^B(t, T_{d_k})}{P^B(t, T_{d_{k+1}})} - \text{cf}(T_{d_{k+1}})$$

(12.174)

Note we are using defaultable discount factors to include interest payments over period $[T_{d_k}, T_{d_{k+1}}]$. This means we are forecasting the future total interest paid by the bank as forward rates implicit in the Libor rates and funding spreads at time $t = 0$. If the credit spread of the bank is positive, the positive cash flows generated by the hedged portfolio will not be enough to cover payback of the debt and related funding costs in their entirety. The terminal amount left is, as in the first strategy, a cost that the bank has to pay as it is strictly related to its credit spread. Ultimately, this is a funding cost to include in the pricing of the swap.

The Libor component of the total interest rate paid can be hedged by market instruments (e.g., OIS swaps) such that implicit forward rates can be locked in. There is another component, though, that has to be considered: the forward funding spread implicit in defaultable bond prices cannot be locked in easily at the start of the swap contract: this would entail the bank trading credit derivatives on its own debt, which is either impossible (in the case of CDSs) or difficult (in the case of spread options). The unexpected funding cost, due to volatility of the credit spread of the bank, has to be measured in any event and should also be included in the pricing. We suggest two possible approaches to measure unexpected future funding costs.

Measuring unexpected funding costs via spread options

The first approach is the measurement of unexpected funding costs via spread options. Let us assume rollover of debt is operated at dates $[T_{d_1}, \ldots, T_{d_M}]$, a set that also contains the set of payment dates of the fixed leg of the swaps. The forward rate, computed at t, paid on the outstanding debt at given date T_{d_k} is:

$$F_{d_k}^B(t) = \left(\frac{P^B(t, T_{d_{k-1}})}{P^B(t, T_{d_k})} - 1 \right) \frac{1}{\delta_{d_k}} = \left(\frac{1}{P_t^B(T_{d_{k-1}}, T_{d_k})} - 1 \right) \frac{1}{\delta_{d_k}}$$

where $P_t^B(T_{d_{k-1}}, T_{d_k})$ is the forward price of a defaultable bond calculated at t. Expected debt rollover at time T_{d_k} is:

$$\text{EFD}(T_{d_k}) = \text{EFD}(T_{d_{k-1}})[1 + F_{d_k}^B(t)\delta_{d_k}]$$

$$= \text{EFD}(T_{d_{k-1}}) \frac{1}{P_t^B(T_{d_{k-1}}, T_{d_k})}$$

$$= \text{EFD}(T_{d_{k-1}}) \frac{1}{P_t^D(T_{d_{k-1}}, T_{d_k})} \frac{1}{P_t^s(T_{d_{k-1}}, T_{d_k})} \quad (12.175)$$

with $\text{EFD}(T_{d_k-1}) = \text{FDB}(T_{d_k-1})$.

Let $s_{d_k}(t)$ be the forward funding spread, linked to the spread discount factor as follows:

$$1 + s_{d_k}(t)\delta_{d_k} = \frac{1}{P_t^s(T_{d_{k-1}}, T_{d_k})} \quad (12.176)$$

so that

$$\text{EFD}(T_{d_k}) = \text{EFD}(T_{d_{k-1}}) \frac{1}{P_t^D(T_{d_{k-1}}, T_{d_k})} [1 + s_{d_k}(t)\delta_{d_k}] \quad (12.177)$$

As pointed out above, this is simply expected rollover running parallel with expected funding spread (under the forward risk survival measure[26]). The rollover of debt carried out by compounding it at an unexpected funding spread level has to be considered; it can be written as:

$$\text{UFD}(T_{d_k}) = \text{FDB}(T_{d_k-1}) \frac{1}{P_t(T_{d_{k-1}}, T_{d_k})} \max[s_{d_k}(T_{d_k})\delta_{d_k} - s_{d_k}(t)\delta_{d_k}; 0] \quad (12.178)$$

Equation (12.178) expresses the unexpected funding cost to apply to roll over outstanding debt as a call spread option, with strike equal to the forward spread calculated at time t. Clearly, we are interested in cases when the spread is above the expected forward level: if it is actually lower, then the bank will pay less than expected,

---

[26] The forward risk survival measure uses the defaultable discount bond as a numeraire. For more details see [110]. We would like to stress that we are measuring funding costs under a *going concern principle*, which frees the bank from considering its own default in the evaluation process.

but we do not consider this potential benefit here. It is possible, with a little algebra, to rewrite the equation in terms of an option on a discount bond:

$$\mathrm{UFD}(T_{d_k}) = \mathrm{FDB}(T_{d_{k-1}}) \frac{1}{P_t(T_{d_{k-1}}, T_{d_k})} (1 + s_{d_k}(t)\delta_{d_k}) \mathrm{ZCP}(1/(1 + s_{d_k}(t)\delta_{d_k}), t, T_{d_{k-1}}, T_{d_k})$$

$$(12.179)$$

where ZCP is the future value computed at t of a put option with expiry $T_{d_{k-1}}$ on a zero-coupon bond maturing at T_{d_k}, struck at $1/(1 + s_{d_k}(t)\delta_{d_k})$. The option is computed under the assumption that default intensity is a mean-reverting square root process, as described above. The solution for the present value of a put option expiring at T, written on a bond expiring at S, is provided in equation (8.40). If recovery rate $\mathcal{R}$ is different from 0, then the formula's parameters have to be adjusted as follows:

$$\kappa_\lambda \rightarrow \frac{\kappa_\lambda}{1-\mathcal{R}}, \quad \sigma_\lambda \rightarrow \frac{\sigma_\lambda}{1-\mathcal{R}}, \quad t \rightarrow t(1-\mathcal{R}), \quad T \rightarrow T(1-\mathcal{R}), \quad S \rightarrow S(1-\mathcal{R})$$

The future value of the put option on the spread's zero-coupon bond is:

$$\mathrm{ZCP}(1/(1 + s_{d_k}(t)\delta_{d_k}), t, T_{d_{k-1}}, T_{d_k}) = \frac{1}{P_t^s(t, T_{d_{k-1}})} \mathrm{Put}_{\mathrm{CIR}}(t, T_{d_{k-1}}, T_{d_k}, 1/(1 + s_{d_k}(t)\delta_{d_k}))$$

which inserted in (12.179) yields:

$$\mathrm{UFD}(T_{d_k}) = \mathrm{FDB}(T_{d_{k-1}}) \frac{1}{P_t(T_{d_{k-1}}, T_{d_k})} \frac{1}{P_t^s(t, T_{d_k})} \mathrm{Put}_{\mathrm{CIR}}(t, T_{d_{k-1}}, T_{d_k}, 1/(1 + s_{d_k}(t)\delta_{d_k}))$$

$$(12.180)$$

Total funding cost is the present value of the amount of the debt left at expiry of the swap (according to expected rollover) that has to be covered by the bank and hence is a cost, plus the present value of the spread options needed to hedge unexpected funding costs for each period:

$$\mathrm{FC} = P(t, T_b)\mathrm{EFD}(T_b) + \sum_{k=1}^{M} P(t, T_{d_{k-1}})\mathrm{UFD}(T_{d_k})$$

$$(12.181)$$

This quantity is then used to determine the fair swap rate, via a numerical search as in equation (12.172): this is the rate making the present value of the funding cost $\mathrm{FC} = 0$.

Measuring unexpected funding costs with a confidence level

The second approach to measuring unexpected funding costs is justified by the bank's difficulty to buy options on its own credit spread. This is the reason we suggest considering unexpected cost as a loss that cannot be hedged and that has to be covered by economic capital, similarly to VaR methodology.

Expected funding cost is still the same as in formula (12.175). Unexpected cost is computed by

$$\mathrm{UFD}(T_{d_k}) = \mathrm{FDB}(T_{d_{k-1}}) \frac{1}{P_t(T_{d_{k-1}}, T_{d_k})} [s_{d_k}^*(T_{d_k})\delta_{d_k} - s_{d_k}(t)\delta_{d_k}]$$

$$(12.182)$$

or, equivalently,

$$\text{UFD}(T_{d_k}) = \text{FDB}(T_{d_{k-1}}) \frac{1}{P_t(T_{d_{k-1}}, T_{d_k})} \left[\frac{P^{s^*}(t, T_{d_{k-1}})}{P^{s^*}(t, T_{d_k})} - \frac{P^s(t, T_{d_{k-1}})}{P^s(t, T_{d_k})} \right] \quad (12.183)$$

The price of the spread discount bond $P^{s^*}(t, T_{d_{k-1}})$ is computed at a given confidence level (say, 99%). Since the probability of default follows a sqare root mean-reverting process at time t, the distribution at future time t' of different levels of default intensity λ_t is known to be a non-central χ^2 distribution.[27] This allows us to compute, at a given date, the maximum level (with a predefined confidence level) of default intensity λ_t and hence the maximum level of the spread and total cost of refunding each funding source. Moreover, we want the expected level of the spread to be the forward spread implied by the curve related to spread discount bonds; that is, for any $t < t' < T$:

$$P^s(0, T) = P^s(0, t') \mathbf{E}^{t'}[P^s(t', T)]$$

which means that we want to compute the maximum level of the spread under a forward risk-adjusted measure.[28]

The forward risk distribution for a CIR process has been given in equation (8.36). We can build a term structure of stressed spread discount bonds up to expiry T_b. Let us assume that rollover of the debt occurs every J years, hence entailing a number of refunding dates $\frac{(T_b - T_a)}{J-1} = n$. We give the following procedure as a pseudocode.

Procedure 12.3.1. *We first derive the maximum expected levels of default intensity $\lambda_{t_i}^*$, at the scheduled refunding dates, with a confidence level c.l. (e.g., 99%):*

1.   **For** $i = 1, \ldots, n$
2. $T_i = i \cdot J$
3. $\lambda_{T_i}^* = \lambda_{T_i} : p_{\lambda_t}^{T_i}(\lambda_{T_i}) = cl$
4.   **Next**

Having determined the levels of maximum default intensity, we can compute the term structure of (minimum) discount factors for the zero-spreads corresponding to those levels:

1.   **For** $i = 1, \ldots, n$
2. $T_i = i \cdots J$
3.   **For** $k = 1, \ldots, J$
4. $P^{s^*}(0, T_{i+k}) = P_{cl}^s(0, T_{i+k}) = P^s(0, T_i) P^s(T_i, T_k; \lambda_{T_i}^*, \kappa_\lambda, \theta_\lambda, \sigma_\lambda, \mathcal{R}^J)$
5.   **Next**
6.   **Next**

Armed with the minimum discount factors for each expiry, we can compute the total minimum discount factor for all expiries as:

$$P_{cl}^D(0, T_i) = P^D(0, T_i) P_{cl}^s(0, T_i) = P^D(0, T_i) P^{s^*}(0, T_i) \quad (12.184)$$

for $i = 1, \ldots, N$.

---

[27] A non-central χ^2 with d degrees of freedom and non-centrality parameter c is defined as function $\chi^2(x; d, c)$.
[28] The superscript t' to the expectation operator $\mathbf{E}[\cdot]$ means that we are working in the t' forward risk-adjusted measure. Technically speaking, we are calculating expectations by using the bond $P^s(0, t')$ as a numeraire.

In building such curves we considered the cost of funding between two refunding dates as completely determined by the maximum $\lambda_{T_i}^*$ at the beginning of the same period. In fact, there is no refunding risk and the curve is no different from that of deterministic spreads.

The unexpected funding cost in (12.183), at a given confidence level, can now be readily computed for each period. To cover these unexpected costs the bank posts economic capital. At time T_{d_k} the posted capital is:

$$E(T_{d_k}) = \sum_{m=k+1}^{b^*-k-1} \text{UFD}(T_{d_m}) \tag{12.185}$$

where $b^* \leq b$ is the number of periods that the financial institution deems necessary to recapitalize the firm, should unexpected economic losses occur. The safest assumption is to set $b^* = b$, so that the full economic capital needed up to expiry of the swap is taken into account. It is also true that market VaR is typically computed for a period of 1 year in banks, so that different choices can be adopted.

Assuming that the required economic capital is invested in risk-free assets, the annual premium rate π over the risk-free rate to remunerate it[29] is a cost that the bank has to bear to cover unexpected funding costs. For simplicity's sake, without too great a loss of generality, let π be a constant; we thus have total funding cost given by the amount of debt left unpaid at the end of the swap, plus the present value of the annual premium paid on the economic capital for each period:

$$\text{FC} = P(t, T_b)\text{EFD}(T_b) + \sum_{k=1}^{M} P^D(t, T_{d_{k-1}})\pi E(T_{d_{k-1}})\delta_{d_k} \tag{12.186}$$

As above, FC is plugged into (12.172) to derive the fair swap rate, via a numerical search. The rate is once again the level making the present value of the funding cost $\text{FC} = 0$.

12.3.6   Including counterparty credit risk

Counterparty credit risk is a component of valuation that has not been considered up to this point. What is more, should the counterparty go bankrupt, then CVA should be included in the valuation.[30]

Let us assume that counterparty credit risk is nil for hedging swaps. This is not an unrealistic assumption as portfolio of hedging swaps is dealt with other banks, and they are provided with a CSA agreement that practically reduces expected losses to zero upon counterparty default.[31] So we focus only on the effects that default of the main swap counterparty may produce on funding costs.

Let τ be the time the counterparty of the swap defaults: if it occurs when the NPV of the swap is positive to the bank, then the latter will suffer a loss equal to NPV minus the recovery. This loss can be seen as the replacement cost the bank has to pay to re-enter a swap with the same contract terms as the one closed after the counterparty's default. The

---

[29] Basically, the ROE minus the risk-free rate.
[30] Bilateral counterparty risk implies that DVA should also be included in the pricing during the bargaining process. Once the deal has been struck, DVA is simply a cost that the bank has to bear. On the differences between price and value and on the notion of DVA as a cost see Chapter 10.
[31] The funding costs due to the collateralization of swap contracts can be included in the analysis using this approach.

expected present value of this loss is simply the CVA, so the very fact of including it in the valuation at inception means the bank is basically receiving compensation for it. CVA can either be collected as a reserve or considered as a premium of an option and then hedged with market instruments, when available. In any case, the bank does not have to pay other costs when the counterparty goes bankrupt and the NPV is positive, since CVA covers their expected amount.

Let us now consider the case when the NPV of the swap is negative on counterparty default: the contract is closed out and its value has to be paid by the bank to the defaulting party. The amount needed for this payment can in theory be funded by reopening the same contract with another counterparty, under the hypothesis that the NPV paid to the defaulting party is the risk-free value of the contract and that the new contract is dealt with a default risk-free counterparty.[32] In this case an upfront fee is paid to the bank by the new counterparty so as to compensate for the negative NPV and thus make the deal fair at inception. Nevertheless, it is easier for the bank to deal in par swaps quoted in the market and to fund with new debt the negative NPV to pay to the defaulting party.

Let us assume that counterparty default is the first jump of a Poisson process (with intensity λ_C) that can also be time dependent. We also assume it follows a CIR process such as bank default intensity. The probability of default between t and T is defined as:

$$\mathrm{PD}_C(t, T) = 1 - \mathbf{E}^Q \left[\exp \left(- \int_0^T \lambda_{C,u} du \right) \right] \tag{12.187}$$

Let T_τ be the first fixed leg payment date of the closed swap after default. Expected exposure at a certain time τ is given by the expected negative value of the swap's NPV:

$$\mathrm{ENE}(t, \tau) = \bar{C}_{T_\tau,b}(t) \mathbf{E}^{\tau,b} [((1_{\{R\}} - 1_{\{P\}}) \bar{S}_{a,b} - (1_{\{R\}} - 1_{\{P\}}) S_{\tau,b}(t))^-] \tag{12.188}$$

which is the difference between the original swap and the new par swap dealt in the market at T_τ and expiring at T_b. Let $\mathrm{cf}(T_\tau) = \mathrm{ENE}(t, \tau)$: this is a negative cash flow and has to be funded by the bank for payment of the NPV to the defaulting party: the funded amount is repaid using additional cash flows produced by the original portfolio of hedging swaps and the new swap struck at $S_{\tau,b}$. At time T_{c_j}, given the default at time $\tau \leq T_{c_j}$, the cash flow is:

$$\mathrm{cf}^*(T_{c_j}) = [(1_{\{R\}} - 1_{\{P\}}) \bar{S}_{a,b} - (1_{\{R\}} - 1_{\{P\}}) S_{c_{i-1},c_i}] \delta_j^K$$

$$- \mathbf{E}^{\tau,b} [((1_{\{R\}} - 1_{\{P\}}) \bar{S}_{a,b} - (1_{\{R\}} - 1_{\{P\}}) S_{\tau,b}(t))^-] \delta_j^K \tag{12.189}$$

The first line in (12.189) is the same as when there is no default, whereas the second line is an additional cash flow, increasing (decreasing) the positive (negative) cash flows fixed before default, which can be used to repay the capital instalments of the debt. We define $\mathrm{cf}^\tau(T_{c_j})$ as the additional cash flow such that the total new cash flow after default can be written as:

$$\mathrm{cf}^*(T_{c_j}) = \mathrm{cf}(T_{c_j}) + \mathrm{cf}^\tau(T_{c_j}) \tag{12.190}$$

We are now in a position to generalize the two strategies explained above and determine the funding cost that includes the effects of counterparty risk.

---

[32] For an analysis of the different closeout clauses see [36].

More on Strategy 1: Funding all cash flows at inception

Let us assume we are computing funding costs implied by Strategy 1 in Section 12.3.4. For a default at τ we need to find the additional amount of loan A^τ, with fixed interest rate $\bar{i}^\tau$ and amortization schedule defined similarly to (12.169) (we use the same notation as above):

$$A^\tau = \sum_{k=T_{\tau+1}}^{M} (K^\tau(T_{d_k}) + \bar{i}^\tau A^\tau(T_{d_{k-1}})\delta_{d_k}) P^B(T_\tau, T_{d_k}) \tag{12.191}$$

Available liquidity is defined as in (12.171) for given τ, keeping in mind that it is created only if counterparty default occurs in the interval $[T_{\tau-1}, T_\tau]$. So, we weight it by the probability of default:

$$\mathrm{AVL}^\tau(T_{d_k}) = \left[\mathrm{AVL}^\tau(T_{d_{k-1}}) \frac{P^D(t, T_{d_{k-1}})}{P^D(t, T_{d_k})} \right.$$

$$\left. + \mathrm{cf}^\tau(T_{d_k}) - K^\tau(T_{d_k}) - \bar{i} A^\tau(T_{d_{k-1}}) \right] (\mathrm{PD}_C(t, T_\tau) - \mathrm{PD}_C(t, T_{\tau-1})) \tag{12.192}$$

for $T_{d_{k-1}} > T_\tau$, with $\mathrm{AVL}^\tau(T_\tau) = A^\tau \geq \mathrm{cf}(T_\tau)$ and $K(T_{d_k}) = \mathrm{cf}^\tau(T_{d_k})$.

Let us now consider the M possible defaults that may occur in the interval $[T_{d_{k-1}}, T_{d_k}]$, at times τ_m, with $M \in \{1, 2, \ldots, M\}$. Total available liquidity is:

$$\mathrm{TAVL}(T_{d_k}) = \mathrm{AVL}(T_{d_k}) + \sum_{m=1}^{M} \mathrm{AVL}^{\tau_m}(T_{d_k}) \tag{12.193}$$

Total available liquidity must satisfy the same two conditions as when there is no counterparty risk. Funding cost FC is defined in exactly the same way as when there is no credit risk: it is the present value at time t of the amount the bank needs to add to the final instalment, not generated by the cash flow structure of the hedged deal, that allows it to fully repay the debt, keeping in mind the funding of the NPV that has to be paid to the defaulting party.

More on Strategy 2: First approach to compute unexpected funding costs

If Strategy 2 (Section 12.3.5) is adopted to compute funding costs, then we have to consider that at each possible default time an additional outflow has to be added to the rollover of the debt issued by the bank to finance negative cumulated cash flows, followed by additional inflows as defined in (12.189).

Let $\mathrm{FDB}^\tau(T_{k+1})$ be the amount of debt needed to fund the cash flows produced by default at τ. Its expected evolution is given by:

$$\mathrm{FDB}^\tau(T_{k+1}) = \left[\mathrm{FDB}^\tau(T_{d_k}) \frac{P^B(t, T_{d_k})}{P^B(t, T_{d_{k+1}})} - \mathrm{cf}(T_{d_{k+1}}) - \mathrm{cf}^\tau(T_{d_{k+1}}) \right]$$

$$\times (\mathrm{PD}_C(t, T_\tau) - \mathrm{PD}_C(t, T_{\tau-1})) \tag{12.194}$$

for $T_{d_{k-1}} > T_\tau$, and $\mathrm{FDB}^\tau(T_\tau) = (T_\tau)$.

The total debt rolled over is then:

$$\text{TFDB}(T_{d_k}) = \text{FDB}(T_{d_k}) + \sum_{m=1}^{M} \text{FDB}^{T_m}(T_{d_k}) \qquad (12.195)$$

where we use the same notation as above. The unexpected funding cost may be computed by either of the approaches sketched when there is no counterparty risk. Total funding cost is given by (12.181) or (12.186), with $\text{EFD}(T_{d_k}) = \text{TFDB}(T_{d_k})$.

Funding costs including counterparty default can be added to CVA to get:

$$S_{a,b}(0) = \sum_{i=a+1}^{b} w_i(0)F_i(0) + (1_{\{R\}} - 1_{\{P\}})\frac{\text{FC}^D + \text{CVA}}{\bar{C}_{a,b}(0)} \qquad (12.196)$$

A numerical search has to be operated in this case too so that fair swap rate $S_{a,b}(0)$ can be retrieved.

12.3.7 Practical examples

We now show how the strategies described above can be practically implemented. We will price a market standard 10-year swap, with the fixed leg paying annually and the floating rate paying semiannually: both legs have a fixed notional amount equal to 100. To value the fair rate of this swap, without including any other adjustment due to counterparty risk and funding costs, we need the term structure of OIS and 6M Libor, from which we also derive the discount factors. We adopt the market practice of considering the OIS the best proxy for the risk-free rate in the interbank market. Table 12.15 shows these data.

The funding costs that the bank has to pay depend on the probability of default modelled in a reduced-form setting with a stochastic intensity whose parameters are shown in Table 12.16. The resulting spread discount bonds and total discount factors are given in Table 12.17, as are the forward funding spreads as defined in (12.176).

Given these market data, the fair swap rate can easily be derived; it is $S_{0,10}(0) = 3.3020\%$. Future cash flows of this swap can be hedged, as suggested above, using a portfolio of 1-year forward starting swaps (except the first one which is a 1-year spot starting swap); these swaps have to be market standard, in the sense that the fixed leg pays annually whereas the floating leg pays semiannually, in much the same way as the 10-year swap. In Table 12.18 we show the fair swap rate for each hedging swap for the year when the corresponding fixed leg pays. The floating leg of each hedging swap matches a portion on the floating leg of the 10-year swap. Assuming that the bank is a fixed rate receiver of the 10-year swap, net cash flows for the hedged position are shown in Table 12.18. In Figure 12.4 we show cumulated cash flows whose value, compounded at the risk-free rate, can be summed algebraically to zero.

From Table 12.18 we can check that the receiver swap, once hedged, does not imply any negative cumulated cash flow, so that the bank does not have to resort to any additional external funding. The fair swap rate for the bank is the same as above and no adjustments for funding costs need to be included. This does not mean that the CVA for counterparty credit risk and the DVA for its own default risk can be disregarded, despite doing so in the current analysis: this example demonstrates that DVA is not the funding cost for a derivative contract, in accordance with what we stated in Chapter 10.

Table 12.15. Term structures of OIS and 6M Libor forward rates and of the corresponding discount factors for both

Year	OIS forward (%)	6M forward Libor (%)	OIS $DF^D P(0, T)$	Libor DF
0	0.75	1.40	1.00000	1.00000
0.5	0.75	1.39	0.99626	0.99305
1	1.75	2.39	0.99254	0.98618
1.5	2.00	2.63	0.98393	0.97454
2	2.25	2.88	0.97419	0.96189
2.5	2.37	2.99	0.96335	0.94826
3	2.50	3.11	0.95207	0.93430
3.5	2.65	3.26	0.94032	0.91998
4	2.75	3.35	0.92802	0.90523
4.5	2.87	3.47	0.91543	0.89031
5	3.00	3.59	0.90248	0.87514
5.5	3.10	3.69	0.88915	0.85971
6	3.20	3.78	0.87557	0.84415
6.5	3.30	3.88	0.86179	0.82849
7	3.40	3.97	0.84780	0.81274
7.5	3.50	4.07	0.83363	0.79692
8	3.60	4.16	0.81929	0.78105
8.5	3.67	4.23	0.80480	0.76513
9	3.75	4.30	0.79030	0.74930
9.5	3.82	4.37	0.77575	0.73353
10	3.90	4.44	0.76121	0.71786

Table 12.16. Parameters of default intensity

λ_0	0.50%
κ_λ	1.00
θ_λ	1.95%
σ_λ	20.00%
$\mathcal{R}$	0%

Let us now assume that the bank has a payer position in a 10-year swap: all cash flows with a positive (negative) sign in Table 12.18 should now be considered as paid (received), so that the compounded cumulated cash flow is always negative and nil at expiry. This is true if the bank is able to borrow money at the risk-free rate; since the bank can actually default with a positive probability, it pays a funding spread to borrow money. We analyse both strategies suggested above to cope with funding needs origin-ated by negative cumulated cash flows and verify how the fair swap rate is modified.

Let us start with Strategy 1, which involves funding all negative cash flows at inception. Numerical search for the starting amount of the debt, subject to the constraints stated above, and for the fair swap rate that makes the present value of the funding cost FC zero are shown in Table 12.19. The fixed interest rate paid annually

Table 12.17. Forward funding spreads and the term structures of spreads and total discount factors

Year	$P^s(0, T)$	$P^B(0, T)$	Forward funding spread (%)
0	1.00000	1.00000	
0.5	0.99597	0.99225	0.81
1	0.98975	0.98237	1.26
1.5	0.98226	0.96647	1.53
2	0.97405	0.94891	1.69
2.5	0.96545	0.93007	1.78
3	0.95666	0.91081	1.84
3.5	0.94779	0.89122	1.87
4	0.93891	0.87132	1.89
4.5	0.93005	0.85140	1.90
5	0.92125	0.83141	1.91
5.5	0.91251	0.81135	1.92
6	0.90384	0.79138	1.92
6.5	0.89525	0.77151	1.92
7	0.88674	0.75177	1.92
7.5	0.87830	0.73217	1.92
8	0.86994	0.71273	1.92
8.5	0.86167	0.69347	1.92
9	0.85347	0.67449	1.92
9.5	0.84534	0.65578	1.92
10	0.83730	0.63736	1.92

by the bank on the debt is 4.2761% and is obtained via (12.170). This rate applied to the debt oustanding at the beginning of the period yields the interest paid. Starting amount A that the bank has to borrow is 4.1746 and the amortization plan shown guarantees that it is fully repaid and that no available liquidity is left at expiry of the contract. The final fair swap rate is $S_{0,10}^{FC}(0) = 3.2403\%$, a correction of around 6 bps.

Let us now examine how Strategy 2 can be implemented: the bank borrows money when negative cash flows occur, if cumulated cash flows are negative, or the debt is rolled over in the future. The unexpected funding cost is measured in the first of the two approaches (i.e., by means of spread options). The results are shown in Table 12.20. Terminal outstanding debt is negative (i.e., there is cash inflow) and its present value compensates the sum of the present value of unexpected funding costs (last column), $\sum_{k=1}^{M} P(t, T_{d_{k-1}}) \text{UFD}(T_{d_k}) = 0.0857$; the final fair swap rate is $S_{0,10}^{FC}(0) = 3.2495\%$.

In Table 12.21 we present the results that would apply if the second approach were adopted to measure unexpected funding costs. Spread discount factors at a confidence level of 99% are computed using the procedure outlined above (they are shown in the last column). We assume a constant premium over the risk-free rate for the economic capital equal to $\pi = 5\%$. Capital is posted to cover all future losses at any time until expiry of the contract, so that $b^* = b$ in formula (12.185). The fair swap rate $(S_{0,10}(0) = 3.2089\%)$ is once again computed so that the total funding cost is nil. The

Table 12.18. Swap rates of hedging swaps and net single, cumulated and compounded cumulated cash flows for a hedged 10-year receiver swap

Year	Hedge swaps (%)	Cash flows	Cumulated cash flows	Compounded cumulated cash flows
0				
0.5				
1	1.40	1.902593	1.9026	1.9026
1.5				
2	2.52	0.780902	2.6835	2.7193
2.5				
3	2.95	0.352942	3.0364	3.1355
3.5				
4	3.21	0.096033	3.1325	3.3127
4.5				
5	3.43	−0.13114	3.0013	3.2753
5.5				
6	3.67	−0.36408	2.6373	3.0119
6.5				
7	3.86	−0.55698	2.0803	2.5536
7.5				
8	4.05	−0.75044	1.3298	1.8921
8.5				
9	4.23	−0.92912	0.4007	1.0323
9.5				
10	4.37	−1.07261	-0.6719	0.0000

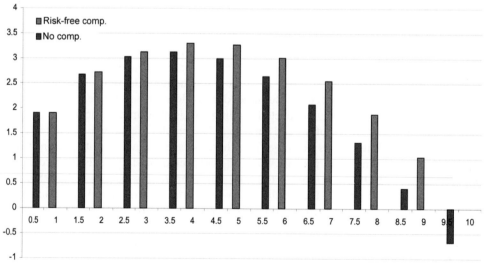

Figure 12.4. Compounded and non-compounded cumulated cash flows for a 10-year receiver swap

Table 12.19. Amount of outstanding debt, interest paid and available liquidity. Final values may be slightly different from zero due to the degree of approximation chosen in the numerical search (Strategy 1).

Year	Outstanding debt $A(T_{d_k})$	Interest paid	Available liquidity $AVL(T_{d_k})$
0	4.1746		
0.5	4.1746		
1	4.1746	0.1785	2.1866
1.5	4.1746	2.2057	
2	4.1746	0.1785	1.3300
2.5	4.1746	1.3450	
3	4.1746	0.1785	0.8912
3.5	4.1746	0.9023	
4	4.1746	0.1785	0.7014
4.5	4.1746	0.7111	
5	3.9817	0.1785	0.5428
5.5	3.9817	0.5509	
6	3.5560	0.1703	0.3892
6.5	3.5560	0.3954	
7	2.9373	0.1521	0.2499
7.5	2.9373	0.2541	
8	2.1252	0.1256	0.1330
8.5	2.1252	0.1354	
9	1.1343	0.0909	0.0470
9.5	1.1343	0.0479	
10	0.0000	0.0485	0.0000

terminal outstanding amount of the debt is negative, meaning that the bank has an inflow: the present value of a positive cash flow even in this case compensates the cost of the economic capital posted to cover unexpected funding losses, $\sum_{k=1}^{M} P^D(t, T_{d_{k-1}}) \pi E(T_{d_{k-1}}) \delta_{d_k} = 0.47889$.

Finally, in Table 12.22 we summarize results to allow easy comparison amongst the different ways to include funding costs in the pricing of a swap. Given the term structure of interest rates and the probability of default, Strategy 1 (funding everything at inception) and Strategy 2 (unexpected finding costs measured with spread options) produce very similar results: the fair rate of a payer swap is abated by about 6 bps in both cases. Strategy 2, with unexpected costs measured at a given confidence level and covered by economic capital, is more expensive and the fair swap rate decreases by around 10 bps.

It is worthy of note that this relationship amongst the three adjustments may not hold in every case. It may well be for forward starting swaps (say, a 10Y5Y) that the first approach of Strategy 2 turns out to be more convenient than Strategy 1. In any case, the only hedging scheme that fully protects the bank is Strategy 1, since it also avoids exposure to future liquidity shortages. So, this risk should always be kept in mind despite it being very difficult to measure.

Table 12.20. Single and cumulated cash flows, debt rollover and present value of unexpected funding costs for each period measured using spread options. Final values may be slightly different from zero due to the degree of approximation chosen in the numerical search (Strategy 2, first approach).

Year	Cash flows paid	Cumulated cash flows	Compounded cash flows	Debt rollover $\mathrm{FDB}(T_k)$	Unexpected FC $P(t, T_{d_{k-1}})(T_{d_k})$
0					
0.5					
1	1.8498	1.8498	1.8498	1.8498	0.0061
1.5					
2	0.7282	2.5780	2.6128	2.6432	0.0104
2.5					
3	0.3002	2.8782	2.9737	3.0540	0.0125
3.5					
4	0.0433	2.9215	3.0941	3.2357	0.0132
4.5					
5	−0.1839	2.7376	2.9978	3.2071	0.0128
5.5					
6	−0.4168	2.3208	2.6731	2.9525	0.0114
6.5					
7	−0.6097	1.7110	2.1509	2.4983	0.0094
7.5					
8	−0.8032	0.9079	1.4226	1.8320	0.0066
8.5					
9	−0.9819	−0.0740	0.4929	0.9540	0.0033
9.5					
10	−1.1254	−1.1994	−0.6136	−0.1158	

Table 12.21. Single and cumulated cash flows, debt rollover and present value of unexpected funding costs for each period, measured at a confidence level of 99%. Final values may be slightly different from zero due to the degree of approximation chosen in the numerical search (Strategy 2, second approach).

Year	Cash flows paid	Debt rollover $\mathrm{FDB}(T_{d_k})$	Unexpected cost (T_{d_k})	Posted EC $E(T_{d_k})$	EC remunerated $P^D(t, T_{d_{k-1}})\pi E(T_{d_{k-1}})\delta_{d_k}$	99% c.l. $P^{s^*}(T_{d_k})$
0					1.3983	1.00000
0.5						0.99118
1	1.8498	1.8095	1.8095	0.0000	1.3983	0.98237
1.5						0.96129
2	0.7282	2.5611	2.5785	0.0173	1.3809	0.94021
2.5						0.91692
3	0.3002	2.9281	2.9728	0.0446	1.3363	0.89362
3.5						0.86991
4	0.0433	3.0638	3.1424	0.0786	1.2578	0.84619
4.5						0.82264
5	−0.1839	2.9867	3.1033	0.1167	1.1411	0.79910
5.5						0.77591
6	−0.4168	2.6806	2.8373	0.1568	0.9843	0.75273
6.5						0.73018
7	−0.6097	2.1718	2.3681	0.1964	0.7879	0.70763
7.5						0.68577
8	−0.8032	1.4472	1.6806	0.2334	0.5546	0.66391
8.5						0.64283
9	−0.9819	0.5070	0.7723	0.2653	0.2893	0.62175
9.5						0.60158
10	−1.1254	−0.6291	−0.3398	0.2893		0.58142

Table 12.22. Effects on the fair swap rate of including funding costs according to the different methods proposed

	Fair swap rate (%)	FVA
Pure rate	3.3020	
With FC Strategy 1	3.2403	0.5463
With FC Strategy 2		
First approach UFD	3.2495	0.4649
Second approach UFD	3.2089	0.8240

13

A sort of conclusion: towards a new treasury?

13.1 INTRODUCTION

What are the likely future developments in the liquidity risk area? Obviously, answering such a question is very challenging because, even for the few topics treated in the previous chapters, state-of-the-art practices and metrics still have to be fully explored and some are a long way from being consolidated among practitioners and supervisors.

When analysing liquidity risk, the main thing to keep in mind is the specificity of each financial institution. Every bank is different from all other financial firms: it represents therefore a single case of study, with its peculiar balance sheet mix and dependence on funding sources, specific business models and processes. Understanding the bank, its customers' behaviour, its competitive environment, the characteristics of its assets and liabilities is a prerequisite not only to define sound risk management practices, but also to find a solution that best fits from the organization's point of view.

There is little value in writing pages about organization of the treasury or ALM functions let alone their missions: the best we could do would be to define a hypothetical organization that would not fit the actual structure of a real bank. Every financial firm is tasked with finding its own solutions based on its specific features. Nevertheless, there are some topics deserving further analysis because they represent the more likely "open issues" for some time to come and may affect the interaction between the treasury's function and other functions of the bank, or the core activity of the treasury itself.

13.2 ORGANIZATION OF THE TREASURY AND THE DEALING ROOM

Let us start by considering the bank's activity in derivative products. In the daily manufacture of derivative contracts in banks' dealing rooms, positions are typically hedged so that an offsetting payoff is synthetically replicated. This happens on an aggregated portfolio level, thus allowing for natural compensation of exposures originated by the dealing activity.

As shown in Chapter 12, if the relevant desks operate a replication strategy that considers a formula encompassing, for example, the LVA (or equivalently, using an effective discount rate accounting for the collateral rate), the final payoff attained is not equal to the contract's payoff, as is manifest from Example 12.1.1. This difference is due to the LVA and should be assigned to the collateral desk, if one exists in the dealing room, to compensate the costs it bears (or the gains it earns) in managing the collateral account. As a consequence the derivatives desk should try and replicate only the risk-free component of the contract, disregarding the LVA and leaving it to the collateral

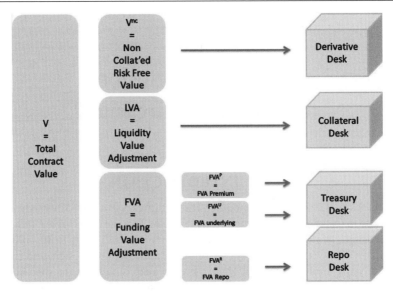

Figure 13.1. Attribution of the components of a derivative contract's value to the relevant desks of a dealing room

desk. When trading the contract, the risk-free component of the premium is assigned to the derivatives desk, while the LVA is left to the collateral desk.

By the same token, the FVA should be assigned to the treasury desk, and the repo component of the FVA, if present, to the repo desk.[1] The FVA is the premium that the derivative desk pays to (or receives from) the other desks involved in dealing room activity, to be ensured of execution of the dynamic replication at a cost equal to what it would pay in a virtual default risk-free, perfectly efficient market, where no collateral and funding effects are operating. In this way, the derivative desk's performance is measured on a proper basis, without including contributions other than the correct hedging of the contract's payoff and the margin that the desk is able to create and preserve.

On the other hand, the collateral desk is remunerated (or charged) with the LVA to run its specific activity, which is the management of collateral cash flows on which it receives or pays the collateral rate, and conversely pays or receives the risk-free rate by investing or funding them.

The treasury desk lends money to and borrows money from the other desks at the risk-free rate. In the money market the treasury desk pays the funding rate of the bank and may invest in risk-free assets receiving the risk-free rate. For this activity it is paid the FVA.

The repo desk buys and sells the quantity of the underlying asset needed for the dynamic replica. The asset is sold to or bought from the derivative desk as if it were financed at the risk-free rate. The repo component of the FVA is attributed to the repo desk to account for the difference between the repo rate and the risk-free rate.

Figure 13.1 shows the breakdown of the total premium into different components and their attribution to the relevant desks.

---

[1] See Chapter 12 for details on these quantities.

Table 13.1. Amount of underlying asset, risk-free bonds and bank's own bonds held by each desk to dynamically replicate the derivative contract

	Underlying asset	Risk-free bond	Bank bond	Collateral account
Derivative desk	$\dfrac{\partial V^{NC}}{\partial S}$	0	0	0
Collateral desk	$\dfrac{\partial \text{LVA}}{\partial S}$	0	0	C
Treasury desk	$\dfrac{\partial \text{FVA}}{\partial S}$	$(V - C - \Delta S)1_{\beta>0}$	$(V - C - \Delta S)1_{\beta<0}$	0
Total bank	$\dfrac{\partial V^{C}}{\partial S}$	$(V - C - \Delta S)1_{\beta>0}$	$(V - C - \Delta S)1_{\beta<0}$	C

Table 13.2. Amount of underlying asset, risk-free bonds and bank's own bonds held by each desk to dynamically replicate the derivative contract

	Underlying asset	Risk-free bond	Bank bond	Collateral account	Repo
Derivative desk	$\dfrac{\partial V^{NC}}{\partial S}$	0	0	0	
Collateral desk	$\dfrac{\partial \text{LVA}}{\partial S}$	0	0	C	
Treasury desk	$\dfrac{\partial \text{FVA}^{P}}{\partial S}$	$(V - C)1_{\beta>0}$	$(V - C)1_{\beta<0}$	0	
Repo desk	$\dfrac{\partial \text{FVA}^{R}}{\partial S}$			0	$-\Delta S$
Total bank	$\dfrac{\partial V^{C}}{\partial S}$	$(V - C)1_{\beta>0}$	$(V - C)1_{\beta<0}$	C	$-\Delta S$

In Table 13.1 we show the amount of cash and underlying asset held by each desk in the replication strategy process. Table 13.2 shows the same when the underlying asset is bought or sold via repo transactions, so that the repo desk is involved as well.

Understandably, this has profound implications for the organization of a dealing room. In fact, until recently desks such as treasury and repo were strongly specialized on linear contracts (deposits, FRAs, repo, reverse repo and so on) and their skills were only marginally involved in the trading and risk management of nonlinear derivative contracts, such as options. Nowadays, the importance of funding costs forces these desks to grow their skills so as to encompass nonlinear contract risk management as well. The same logic applies to the collateral desk, which should be considered more than a manager of cash flows originating from CSA agreements.

Organizing things in this way can be achieved in two ways, either by training money market and repo traders or by creating treasury, repo and collateral desks with very diffuse competences and hiring traders with money market-making and derivative market-making experience. The second option in our view is easier, quicker and more effective to adopt.

13.3   BANKING VS TRADING BOOK

In our opinion, the distinction between the trading and banking book will fade away in the near future for a number of reasons, which we briefly list below.

13.3.1   Collateralization

As already abundantly stated, the components that make up funding currently affect the price and management of a derivative portfolio. Such a portfolio basically depends on, first, the increased cost of funding of the bank sector, which is no longer able to fund itself to the risk-free rate or close to the rate used for collateral remuneration;[2] second, the fact that many hedgers in derivative markets (mainly sovereigns, supranational entities and corporate firms) do not have (or will not have in the near future) to collateralize their exposures through central clearing counterparties or under bilateral symmetric CSA agreements, thus producing strong asymmetries in terms of cash flows, although market risk is fully hedged.

So, many banks are tasked with handling a structural mismatch within their derivative portfolio, between their uncollateralized and collateralized derivative transactions. They actually have to manage two different derivative portfolios, each with their own specific dynamics and risk factors. As already explained in Chapter 12, for uncollateralized derivative transactions it is necessary to calculate the FVA whenever the cash flow profile of a new derivative transaction is not balanced over the life of the contract; for collateralized derivative transactions changes in the derivative portfolio's expected exposure to market risk (interest rate, credit, equity, forex) and in the term structure of the funding spread require dynamic hedging at the portfolio level through derivative products in order to offset negative economic effects, which will be recorded by the P&L statement only on an accrual basis.

As far as central clearing of derivative transactions is concerned, liquidity impacts may be magnified by initial margin-posting requirements, which have to be funded over time. This is an open issue not dealt with in this book, but the preliminary studies we are conducting show that it has a big impact in terms of liquidity requirements and costs borne to satisfy them.

As a result of the steady and seemingly unrelenting trend towards full collateralization of derivative contracts, it is worth stressing that even traditional banking activity is subject to relevant changes in the management of liquidity needs when it operates in the derivative transactions only for hedging purpose (i.e., to reduce the interest rate risk of the mortgage portfolio or, more generally, of the assets). The abovementioned asymmetry of cash flows produced by collateralized transactions hedging non-collateralized contracts will likely become a typical feature of the future liquidity management of the banking book, even more so than that of the trading book.

Dynamic hedging of the FVA and LVA components of the derivative portfolio (even when included in the banking book to hedge market risks) aims at offsetting over time the difference between the interest paid to fund initial and variation margins and the interest received on collateral posted, if the collateral rate is lower than the funding rate of the bank, or if it is required to fund margins on tenors longer than overnight. The

---

[2] See Chapter 6.

dichotomy between hedged items evaluated on an accrual basis (say, loans) and hedging items subject to mark-to-market evaluation (say, a swap), at the portfolio level, could even be exacerbated if the offsetting of some components of the FVA related to the derivative portfolio require some modifications to actual or expected outstanding liabilities, in terms of changes in the liquidity funding plan.

Different accounting rules for derivatives and funding-related items (i.e., liabilities) currently prevent the financial industry from finding a consistent solution to this problem, which will likely become one of the most important open issues in the coming years: it appears increasingly evident that banking and trading books can no longer be considered two separate silos or building blocks.

Supervisors are therefore faced with carrying out a comprehensive evaluation of all accounting and prudential rules in order to properly address increasingly frequent interrelations between trading and banking books. The banking book is doomed to become a natural hedge of some funding risks embedded in the trading book.

13.3.2 Links Amongst Risks

The close interconnection between the trading book and the banking book requires unavoidable rethinking of the traditional separation between treasury (focused on the short term) and ALM (focused on the medium and long term). The web of risks examined in Chapter 5 makes clear that it is not possible to disregard the links amongst the different types of risks. However, even limiting the analysis to market and liquidity risks, it is manifest that the ALM is already, and will be more in the future, subject to risks traditionally managed by treasurers and traders, such as basis risk between different indexes (Eonia, Euribor on different tenors, Libor and so on) and the bank's own funding spread volatility, which may affect economic results over time in a significant way.[3]

The challenges facing supervisors and practitioners have been put on the table: in this environment, traditional risk measures used to monitor the banking book, such as the duration gap or interest rate sensitivity of the interest margin, need to be integrated using more detailed analytical tools, in order to capture and monitor the different risks affecting the most stable part of the balance sheet: it is up to supervisors to accept for the banking book new metrics closer to trading book standards, in line with models and practices in some cases already adopted by the industry. In Chapters 8 and 9 we introduced new models to monitor the liquidity risks of specific contracts and to adapt approaches usually adopted in the trading book to liquidity risk.

On the asset side, it would be of little use to have more advanced tools to monitor risks without appropriate trading skills: diffuse market competences are therefore required not only for treasurers but also for ALM operators in order to manage the increased complexity of their business. This is probably one of the most delicate problemsthat need to be dealt with, because managing the banking book was relatively easy in the past environment and asset–liability managers were not skilled enough to cope with more turbulent and complex market environments. We are quite sure, from our personal

---

[3] In Chapter 11 we presented an approach to monitor and price the volatility of the bank's own funding spread.

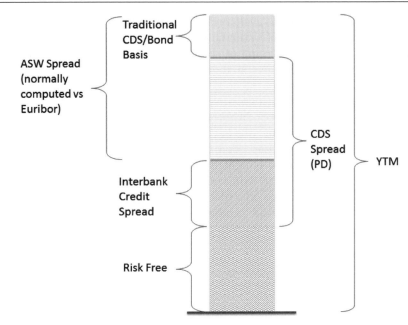

Figure 13.2. Components of the yield to maturity for a generic tenor

experience, that the learning-by-doing process is proceeding quickly in most cases, but it requires time and, more importantly, losses to be suffered by the banks.[4]

On the liability side, the volatility of funding costs deeply impacts management strategies and, more generally, bank profitability. Consider Figure 13.2, which shows the components of the bank's total cost of funding (yield to maturity for a generic tenor) in terms of its spread over Eonia (or the OIS) rate, currently taken in practice as a proxy for the risk-free rate and assigned to the desks (derivative, treasury or ALM) as a risk factor to hedge.

By summing the interbank credit spread (i.e., the spread between Euribor and Eonia, or Libor and OIS) and the asset–swap spread (normally computed vs Euribor or Libor) we arrive at the all-in spread over OIS rate to be used to compute the funding cost for traditional banking contracts or the FVA for derivative contracts. The actual owner of the funding cost or the FVA will be the treasury desk or the ALM desk according to the average weighted life of the portfolio.

Therefore, the treasury desk and/or the ALM desk have to manage three different risk factors:

1. The Euribor/Eonia (Libor/OIS) basis.
2. The residual CDS spread on its own name (i.e., the CDS spread minus the interbank credit spread).
3. The CDS/bond basis.

The basis at point 1 can be hedged on the interbank market through derivative products,

---

[4] It is a firm belief, at least for one of the authors (who proposed this in another book), that the only way a trader learns is by losing money in much the same way as does the man in the street.

the spreads in the other two points require some cross-hedges by using proxies, because it is not possible to buy/sell protection on its own name, as implied by the strategy based on replication of asset–swap spreads in Chapters 10 and 12.[5] Because of the impossibility of perfect replication of the components in 2 and 3 it is of the utmost importance for the treasury desk and/or the ALM desk to have the expertise on credit dynamics necessary to manage properly sensitivities to the volatility of its own funding spread at the portfolio level.

13.3.3 Production costs

We have already argued in Chapter 11, when discussing the FTP, that an industrial approach is needed to price banking book contracts: this means that all the components that make up costs have to be properly measured and priced into contracts when sold to clients. This process, in the financial industry, means that sophisticated analytical tools need to be designed and employed to properly appreciate the impact of any possible risk on the value of a contract.

The industrial approach is quite common on the trading book: the discussion in Chapter 12 is an extension to new risks, related to liquidity and funding, of existing frameworks commonly adopted for derivative contracts. The industrial approach is fully supportive of best practices in pricing on the banking book: this is due to the easier, more stable and less risky market environment, to the simpler structure of risks and to the irrelevance of problems related to liquidity and the cost of funding.

Under current market conditions, with business margins squeezed due to the increased volatility of both assets and liabilities, the precise measurement and management of risks is crucial to ensuring profitable survival of the bank. This means that trading book practices need take little more than a gradual approach to the banking book, although we do not mean by this that the trading book does not need to improve its risk management policies nor design new analytical tools: we are sure there is still much to do, yet a firm and robust *modus operandi* on the trading book is a good starting point toward progressing in the right direction.

We have presented some possible solutions for typical banking book risks, such as prepayment of mortgages or withdrawal of credit lines, and we have shown how analytical tools developed to value derivative contracts can be effectively adapted and used to value traditional banking contracts. Clearly, once these risks are included in the pricing, they also have to be managed and hedged whenever possible: more sophisticated applications and more skilled treasurers and asset/liability managers will be required.

All these developments are moving in the same direction: in the near future the treasury and ALM desks are destined to manage increasingly complex business risks and have increased recourse to nonlinear products in order to hedge the risks embedded in banking book activities in a more accurate way. For this challenging task flexible and open-minded operators will themselves be crucial resources and even more important than any analytic tool or metric like those presented in this book or those that are still to be developed.

---

[5] See the discussion on the impossibility of hedging own name DVA in Chapter 10, which also applies to the FVA according to Definitions 10.6.1 and 12.1.2.

References

[1] T. Adrian and H. S. Shin. *Liquidity and Leverage* (FED of New York Staff Report). Available at *http://www.papers.ssrn.com*

[2] T. Adrian and H. S. Shin. *Liquidity, Monetary Policy, and Financial Cycles* (FED of New York Staff Report). Available at *http://www.newyorkfed.org/research*

[3] G. A. Akerlof. The market for lemons: Quality uncertainty and the market mechanism. *The Quarterly Journal of Economics*, **84**(3): 488–500, 1970. Available at *http://www.jstor.org*

[4] A. Alfonsi. On the discretization schemes for the cir (and bessel squared) processes. *Monte Carlo Methods and Applications*, **11**(4): 355–467.

[5] Y. Altunbas, L. Gambacorta, and D. Marqués. Securitisation and the bank lending channel. *ECB Working Paper Series*, **838**: 1–37, 2007. Available at *http://www.ecb.int*

[6] European Banking Authority. *Guidelines on Liquidity Buffers and Survival Periods.* Available at *http://www.eba.europa.eu*, 2009.

[7] European Banking Authority. *Guidelines on Liquidity Cost Benefit Allocation.* Available at *http://www.eba.europa.eu*, 2010.

[8] Financial Services Authority. *Stage 3 – Liquidity Training.* Available at *http://www.fsa.gov.uk*, pp. 1–115.

[9] Financial Services Authority. *Bipru 12 Liquidity Standards.* Available at *http://www.fsa-handbook.info*, 2009.

[10] Financial Services Authority. *Final Notice to Barclays.* Available at *http://www.fsa.gov.uk*, p. 1–44, 2012.

[11] Financial Services Authorityy. *Dear Treasurer: Funds Transfer Pricing.* Available at *http://www.fsa.gov.uk*, 2010.

[12] P. Bag and M. J. Jacobs. Parsimonious exposure-at-default modeling for unfunded loan commitments. *The Journal of Risk Finance*, **13**(1): 77–94, 2012.

[13] W. Bagehot. *Lombard Street: A Description of the Money Market.* Henry S. King, 1873.

[14] European Central Bank. *Financial Stability Review: December 2007.* Available at *http://www.ecb.int*, 2007.

[15] European Central Bank. *Financial Stability Review: December 2008.* Available at *http://www.ecb.int*, 2008.

[16] European Central Bank. *Financial Stability Review: December 2011.* Available at *http://www.ecb.int*, 2011.

[17] European Central Bank. *Guidelines of the European Central Bank of 20 September 2011 on Monetary Policy Instruments and Procedures of the Eurosystem.* Available at *http://www.ecb.int*, 2011.

[18] European Central Bank. *Euro Money Market Survey* (ECB survey). Available at *http://www.ecb.int*, September 2012.

[19] B. S. Bernanke. Nonmonetary effects of the financial crisis in the propagation of the Great Depression. *American Economic Review*, June: 257–276, 1983.

[20] B. S. Bernanke. *Economic Outlook before the Joint Economic Committee, U.S. Congress.* Board of Governors of the Federal Reserve System. Available at *http://www.federalreserve. gov*, September 24, 2008.

[21] B. Bianchetti. Two curves, one price: Pricing and hedging interest rate derivatives decoupling forwarding and discounting yield curves. Available at *http://papers.ssrn.com*, 2008.

[22] F. Black. Bank fund management in an efficient market. *Journal of Financial Economics*, **2**: 323–339, 1975.

[23] F. Black. The pricing of commodity contracts. *Journal of Financial Economics*, **3**: 167–179, 1976.

[24] F. Black and J. Cox. Valuing corporate securities: Some effects of bond indenture provisions. *The Journal of Finance*, **31**: 351–367, 1976.

[25] F. Black and M. Scholes. The pricing of options and corporate liabilities. *Journal of Political Economy*, **81**: 637–654, 1973.

[26] A. Blochlinger. Management framework for non-maturity accounts: From the marketing to the hedging strategy. *Zurcher Kantonalbank*, 2011.

[27] Financial Accounting Standards Board. *Statement of Financial Accounting Standards No. 157: Fair Value Measurement*, 2008.

[28] Financial Stability Board. *Effective Resolution of Systemically Important Financial Institutions Recommendations and Timelines* (consultative document). Available at *http:// www. financialstabilityboard.org*, July: 1–74, 2011.

[29] Financial Stability Board. *Key Attributes of Effective Resolution Regimes for Financial Institutions*. Available at *http://www.financialstabilityboard.org*, October: 1–45, 2011.

[30] Financial Stability Board. *Policy Measures to Address Systemically Important Financial Institutions*. Available at *http://www.financialstabilityboard.org*, November 4: 1–4, 2011.

[31] A. Brace, D. Gatarek and M. Musiela. The market model of interest rate dynamics. *Mathematical Finance*, **7**(2): 127–154, 1997.

[32] D. Brigo and A. Capponi. Bilateral counterparty risk valuation with stochastic dynamical models and applications to credit default swap. *Risk*, March, 85–90, 2010.

[33] D. Brigo and N. El-Bachir. *Credit Derivatives Pricing with a Smile-extended Jump SSRJD Stochastic Intensity Model* (ICMA Centre Discussion Papers in Finance, 13), 2006.

[34] D. Brigo and F. Mercurio. A deterministic-shift extension of analytically tractable and time-homogeneous short rate models. *Finance and Stochastics*, **5**: 369–388, 2001.

[35] D. Brigo and F. Mercurio. *Interest Rate Models: Theory and Practice*, Second Edition. Springer Finance, Heidelberg, 2001.

[36] D. Brigo and M. Morini. *Dangers of Bilateral Counterparty Risk: The Fundamental Impact of Closeout Conventions* (working paper). Available at *http://arxiv.org*, 2010.

[37] V. Brousseau, A. Chailloux and A. Durré. *Interbank Offered Rate: Effects of the Financial Crisis on the Information Content of the Fixing* (Document de travail du Lille Economie & Management). Available at *http://www.ideas.repec.org*, December 4: 1–37, 2009.

[38] M. K. Brunnermeier. Deciphering the liquidity and credit crunch 2007–2008. *Journal of Economic Perspectives*, **1**: 77–100, 2009. Available at *http://www.papers.ssrn.com*

[39] M. K. Brunnermeier. *Thoughts on a New Financial Architecture*. Available at *http:// www.princeton.edu*, pp. 1–29, 2010.

[40] M. K. Brunnermeier. *Financial Crises: Mechanisms, Prevention, and Management* (discussion by Ronald W Anderson, LSE). Available at *http://www2.lse.ac.uk*, 2009.

[41] M. K. Brunnermeier and L. H. Pedersen. Market liquidity and funding liquidity. *The Review of Financial Studies*, **0**: 1–38, 2008. Available at *http://www.papers.ssrn.com*

[42] C. Burgard and M. Kjaer. *PDE Representations of Options with Bilateral Counterparty Risk and funding costs*. Available at *http://papers.ssrn.com*, 2010.

[43] L. Carver. What Libor reform will change and what it won't. *Risk*, November: 38–41, 2012. Available at *http://www.risk.net*

[44] A. Castagna. *FX Options and Smile Risk*. John Wiley & Sons, 2010.

[45] A. Castagna. *Pricing of Derivatives Contracts under Collateral Agreements: Liquidity and Funding Value Adjustments* (Iason research paper). Available at *http://iasonltd.com/resources.php*, 2012.

[46] A. Castagna and F. Mercurio. *A Methodology for Extracting Default Probability from CDS Prices* (Iason research paper), 2009.

[47] A. Castagna and F. Mercurio. *Valuation, hedging and liquidity management of prepayment options* (Iason research paper), 2010.

[48] A. Castagna and F. Mercurio. *Analytical Credit VaR Stress Tests* (Iason research paper), 2010.

[49] A. Castagna, F. Mercurio and R. Torresetti. *Analytic Calculation of EPE for Interest Rate Swaps* (Iason research paper), 2009.

[50] S. Chava and R. Jarrow. Modeling loan commitments. *Finance Research Letters*, **5**: 11–20, 2008.

[51] International Accounting Standards Committee. *International Accounting Standard 39: Financial Instruments: Recognition and Measurement*, 2008.

[52] C. Covacev. *Pricing an Option with Stochastic Interest Rates and a Zero Drift Underlying Asset* (Iason research paper), 2010.

[53] J. C. Cox, J. E. Ingersoll and S. A. Ross. The relationship between forward prices and future prices. *Journal of Financial Economics*, **9**: 321–346, 1981.

[54] J. C. Cox, J. E. Ingersoll and S. A. Ross. A theory of the term structure of interest rates. *Econometrica*, **53**: 385–467, 1985.

[55] J. C. Cox, J. E. Ingersoll and S. A. Ross. A theory of the term structure of interest rates. *Econometrica*, **53**: 385–467, 1985.

[56] J. C. Cox, S. A. Ross, and M. Rubinstein. Option pricing: A simplified approach. *Journal of Financial Economics*, **7**: 229–263, 1979.

[57] H. Dewachter, M. Lyrio and K. Maes. *A Multi-factor Model for the Valuation and Risk Management of Demand Deposits* (National Bank of Belgium Working Paper, 83), 2006.

[58] D. Duffie. *Dynamic Asset Pricing Theory*. Princeton University Press, Third Edition, 2001.

[59] D. Duffie and N. Garleanu. Risk and valuation of collateralized debt obligations. *Financial Analysts Journal*, **57**: 41, 2001.

[60] D. Duffie and J. Pan. Analytical value at risk with jumps and credit risk. *Finance and Stochastics*, **5**: 155–180, 2001.

[61] D. Duffie, M. Schroder and C. Skiadas. Recursive valuation of defaultable securities and the timing of the resolution of uncertainty. *Annals of Applied Probability*, **51**: 1075–1090, 1996.

[62] D. Duffie and K. Singleton. Modeling term structures of defaultable bonds. *Review of Financial Studies*, **12**: 687–720, 1999.

[63] D. Duffie and M. Singleton. Modeling term structure of defaultable bonds. *Review of Financial Studies*, **12**: 687–720, 1999.

[64] A. Eckner. Computational techniques for basic affine models of portfolio credit risk. *Journal of Computational Finance*, **12**: 63–97, 2009.

[65] European Central Bank Eurosystem. *EU Banks Liquidity Stress Testing and Contingency Funding Plans*. Available at *http://www.ecb.int*, 1–58, November 2008.

[66] X. Freixas, B. M. Parigi and J-C. Rochet. The lender of last resort: A 21st century approach. *ECB Working Paper Series*, **298**: 1–39, 2003. Available at *http://www.ecb.int*

[67] C. Fries. *Discounting Revisited. Valuation under Funding, Counterparty Risk and Collateralization*. Available at *http://papers.ssrn.com*, 2010.

[68] M. Fujii, Y. Shimada and A. Takahashi. *Market Model of Interest Rates with Dynamic Basis Spreads in the Presence of Collateral and Multiple Currencies* (working paper), University of Tokyo and Shinsei Bank, 2009.

[69] M. Fujii, Y. Shimada, and A. Takahashi. *Modeling of Interest Rate Term Structures under Collateralization and Its Implications* (CIRJE discussion paper). Available at *http:// www.e.u-tokyo.ac.jp/cirje/research/03research02dp.html, 2010.*

[70] M. Fujii and A. Takahashi. *Derivative Pricing under Asymmetric and Imperfect Collateralization and CVA*. Available at: *http://ssrn.com/abstract = 1731763*, February 2011.

[71] E. Gatev and P. E. Strahan. Banks advantage in hedging liquidity risk: Theory and evidence from the commercial paper market. *Journal of Finance*, **61**(2): 867–892, 2006. Available at *http://www.fic.wharton.upenn.edu*

[72] J. Gil-Pelaez. Note on the inversion theorem. *Biometrika*, **38**: 481–482, 1951.

[73] J. Goldstein. Bernanke, Paulson face tough audience. *The New York Sun*, September 2008.

[74] M. Goodfriend and R. A. King. Financial deregulation, monetary policy and central banking. *Federal Reserve Bank of Richmonds Economic Review*, **74**(3): 3–22, 1988. Available at *http://www.richmondfed.org*

[75] J. Gregory. Being two-faced over counterparty credit risk. *Risk*, February, 86–90, 2009.

[76] J. Gyntelberg and P. Wooldridge. Interbank rate fixings during the recent turmoil. *BIS Quarterly Review*, March: 59–72, 2008. Available at *http://www.bis.org*

[77] M. J. Jacobs. An empirical study of exposure at default. *Journal of Advanced Studies in Finance*, **1**(1), 2010.

[78] R. A. Jarrow and D. van Deventer. The arbitrage-free valuation and hedging of demand deposits and credit card loans. *Journal of Banking & Finance*, **22**: 249–272, 1998.

[79] R. A. Jones and Y. W. Wu. *Credit Exposure and Valuation of Revolving Credit Lines* (working paper), Bank of Canada, 2009.

[80] M. Kalkbrener and J. Willing. Risk management of non-maturing liabilities. *Journal of Banking & Finance*, **28**: 1547–1568, 2004.

[81] Y. J. Kim and N. Kumitomo. *Pricing Options under Stochastic Interest Rates: A New Approach*. University of Tokyo, 1998.

[82] D. Lando. *Credit Risk Modeling*. Princeton University Press, 2004.

[83] Scott Lanman. *Bernanke Says He Wasn't Straightforward on Lehman*. Bloomberg, 2010.

[84] High Level Expert Group. *High Level Expert Group on Reforming the Structure of the EU Banking Sector*. Available at *http://www.ec.europa.eu*, October 12: 1–137, 2012.

[85] M. Lore and L. Borodovsky. *The Professionals Handbook of Financial Risk Management*. Butterworth-Heinemann, 2000.

[86] N. Masschelein. *Liquidity Risk Course* (Euromoney page slides), 2011.

[87] L. Matz and N. Peter (Eds). *Liquidity Risk Measurement and Management: A Practitioner's Guide to Global Best Practices*. John Wiley & Sons, 2001.

[88] L. G. McDonald and P. Robinson. *A Colossal Failure of Common Sense: The Inside Story of the Collapse of Lehman Brothers*. Three Rivers Press, New York, 2010.

[89] F. Mercurio. *Interest Rates and the Credit Crunch: New Formulas and Market Models*. Available at *http://papers.ssrn.com*, 2010.

[90] F. Mercurio. *A Libor Market Model with Stochastic Basis* (Bloomberg Education and Quantitative Research Paper, 5), 2010.

[91] F. Mercurio. *LIBOR Market Models with Stochastic Basis*. Available at *http://papers.ssrn. com*, 2010. F. Mercurio, R. Caccia and M. Cutuli. Downgrade termination costs. *Risk*, February: 70–5, 2012.

[92] R. C. Merton. On the pricing of corporate debt: The risk structure of interest rates. *The Journal of Finance*, **29**: 449–470, 1974.

[93] R. C. Merton. *Continuous-Time Finance*. Basil Blackwell, 1990.

[94] R. C. Merton. You have more capital than you think. *Harvard Business Review*, **94**(11): 84–94, November 2005.

[95] M. Morini and A. Prampolini. Risky funding with counterparty and liquidity charges. *Risk*, March, 70–75, 2011.

[96] T. Newton. Libor 2.0: the runners and riders. *Risk*, November, 42–43, 2012. Available at *http://www.risk.net*

[97] K. Nikolau. Liquidity (risk) concepts definitions and interactions. *ECB Working Paper Series*, **1008**: 1–72, 2009. Available at *http://www.ecb.int*

[98] K. Nystrom. On deposit volumes and the valuation of non-maturing liabilities. *Journal of Economic Dynamics & Control*, **32**: 709–756, 2008.

[99] Committee of European Banking Supervisors. *Liquidity Identity Card*. Available at *http://www.eba.europa.eu*, pp. 1–31, 2009.

[100] Basel Committee on Banking Supervision. *Principles for Sound Liquidity Risk Management and Supervision*. Available at *http://www.bis.org*, 2008.

[101] Basel Committee on Banking Supervision. *Basel III: International Framework for Liquidity Risk Measurement, Standards and Monitoring*. Available at *http://www.bis.org*, 2010.

[102] Basel Committee on Banking Supervision. *Monitoring Indicators for Intraday Liquidity Management*. Available at *http://www.bis.org*, July 2012.

[103] Basel Committee on Banking Supervision. *Basel III: The Liquidity Coverage Ratio and Liquidity Risk Monitoring Tools*. Available at *http://www.bis.org*, January 2013.

[104] A. Pallavicini, D. Perini and D. Brigo. *Funding Valuation Adjustment: A Consistent Framework Including CVA, DVA, Collateral, Netting Rules and Rehypothecation*. Available at *http://defaultrisk.com*, December 2011.

[105] V. Piterbarg. Funding beyond disocunting. *Risk*, February, 97–102, 2010.

[106] A. Resti. Liquidity ratios and Volcker rule: Operative and strategic impacts. *Intervento al XVII Congresso AIAF ASSIOM FOREX* (page slides), 2011.

[107] S. F. Richard and R. Roll. Prepayments on fixed-rate mortgage-backed securities. *The Journal of Portfolio Management*, **15**(3): 73–82, 1989.

[108] J. C. Rochet and X. Vives. Coordination failures and the lender of last resort: Was Bagehot right after all? *Journal of the European Economic Association*, **2**(6): 1116–1147, 2004. Available at *http://www.idei.fr/doc/wp/2004*

[109] C. Schmaltz. *A Quantitative Liquidity Model for Banks*. Gabler Verlag, 2011.

[110] P. J. Schonbucher. *A Libor Market Model with Default Risk* (working paper). Available at *http://papers.ssrn.com*, 2000.

[111] E. Severino. *La Struttura Originaria*. Adelphi Edizioni, 1981 [in Italian].

[112] D. K. Tarullo. Regulating systemically important financial firms. Speech at the Peter G. Peterson Institute for International Economics. Available at *http://www.bis.org*, June 3, 2011.

[113] O. Vasicek. An equilibrium characterisation of the term structure. *Journal of Financial Economics*, **5**(2): 177–188, 1977.

[114] G. A. Vento and P. La Ganga. Bank liquidity risk management and supervision: Which lessons from recent market turmoil? *Journal of Money, Investment and Banking*, **10**: 1–125, 2009. Available at *http://www.eurojournals.com*

[115] S. R. Wiesbrod, H. Lee and L. Rojas-Suarez. *Bank Risk and the Declining Franchise Value of the Banking Systems in the United States and Japan* (IMF Working Paper, 92/45), 1992.

[116] S. D. Williamson. Liquidity constraints. *The New Palgrave Dictionary of Economics*, Palgrave Macmillan, 2008.

[117] J. Y. Zhao, D. W. Dwyer and J. Zhang. *Usage and Exposures at Default of Corporate Credit Lines: An Empirical Study*. Moody's Analytics, 2011.

Index